혼자서도 할 수 있는

신新토익
모의고사만으로
700점 넘기

신新토익, 모의고사만으로 700점 넘기

지은이 Michael A. Putlack, Stephen Poirier, Tony Covello,
다락원 토익 연구소
펴낸이 정규도
펴낸곳 (주)다락원

초판 1쇄 발행 2016년 6월 3일
초판 4쇄 발행 2020년 4월 1일

편집 조상익, 홍인표
디자인 구수정, 박선영

다락원 경기도 파주시 문발로 211
내용 문의 (02)736-2031 내선 550~551
구입 문의 (02)736-2031 내선 250~252
Fax (02)732-2037
출판 등록 1977년 9월 16일 제406-2008-000007호

Copyright © 2015 (주)다락원

저자 및 출판사의 허락 없이 이 책의 일부 또는 전부를 무단 복제·전재·발췌할 수 없습니다. 구입 후 철회는 회사 내규에 부합하는 경우에 가능하므로 구입 문의처에 문의하시기 바랍니다. 분실·파손 등에 따른 소비자 피해에 대해서는 공정거래위원회에서 고시한 소비자 분쟁 해결 기준에 따라 보상 가능합니다. 잘못된 책은 바꿔 드립니다.

값 15,200원 (본책+해설집+MP3 파일 무료 다운로드)
ISBN 978-89-277-0917-6 13740

http://www.darakwon.co.kr
다락원 홈페이지를 방문하시면 상세한 출판 정보와 함께 MP3 자료 등의 다양한 어학 정보를 얻으실 수 있습니다.

혼자서도 할 수 있는

신新토익
모의고사만으로
700점 넘기

다락원

Introduction

전 세계적으로 다양한 공인 영어 시험들이 시행되고 있지만, 그중 최고 순위를 차지하고 있는 것은 토익이다. 토익에서 높은 점수를 받은 사람은 자신의 미래를 크게 변화시킬 수 있다. 고등 교육 기관에 입학할 수도 있고 사회적으로 존경받는 기업에 취업할 수도 있다.

하지만 토익에서 고득점을 받기 위해서는, 철저한 대비가 되어 있어야 한다. 어떤 유형의 문제가 나오는지 알고 있어야 하며, 출제되는 지문의 유형에 대해서도 잘 알고 있어야 한다. 이것은 「신토익 모의고사만으로 700점 넘기」가 도움을 줄 수 있는 부분이다. 특히 이 책에 수록된 모의고사들은 내용, 스타일, 그리고 난이도 면에서 실제 토익과 비슷하다. 따라서 「신토익 모의고사만으로 700점 넘기」로 토익을 준비한다면, 수험생들은 고득점에 이를 수 있을 것이다.

토익은 다양한 변화를 겪어 왔다. 각 파트의 문항수, 지문의 유형 및 길이, 문제 유형, 그리고 난이도 등은 바뀔 수 있는 부분이다. 토익의 가장 최근의 변화는 이 책에 모두 반영되어 있다. 따라서 수험생들이 「신토익 모의고사로 700점 넘기」로 준비를 한다면, 2016년 5월부터 시행되는 신토익에 전혀 당황하지 않고, 실전에서 자신의 실력을 발휘할 수 있을 것이다.

우리는 학생들과 교사 모두 「신토익 모의고사만으로 700점 넘기」를 최대한 활용하기를 바라며, 특히 수험생들이 이 책을 통해 본인 최고의 토익 점수를 얻기를 기원한다.

Michael A. Putlack

Table of Contents

About This Book

About the TOEIC

1부 **파트별 소개** ··· p.9

2부 **실전 모의고사**

    Actual Test 01 ·· p.29

    Actual Test 02 ·· p.75

    Actual Test 03 ·· p.123

    Actual Test 04 ·· p.171

별책 **정답 및 해설**

About This Book

개요 및 유형 설명

파트에 따른 전형적인 문제, 대화 및 담화, 그리고 지문 유형 등을 정확하고 간략하게 설명하고 있다. 또한 신토익에서 새롭게 선보이는 문제 및 지문 유형들도 한 눈에 알아볼 수 있도록 정리해 두었다.

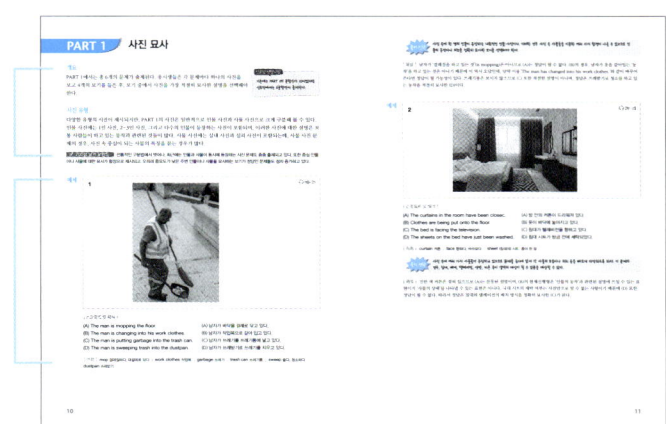

예제 및 해설

각 파트를 대표할 수 있는 유형의 문제들을 예제로 제시하여 수험생들의 빠른 이해를 돕고 있다. 또한 고득점 획득에 필수적인 다양한 팁도 소개되어 있다.

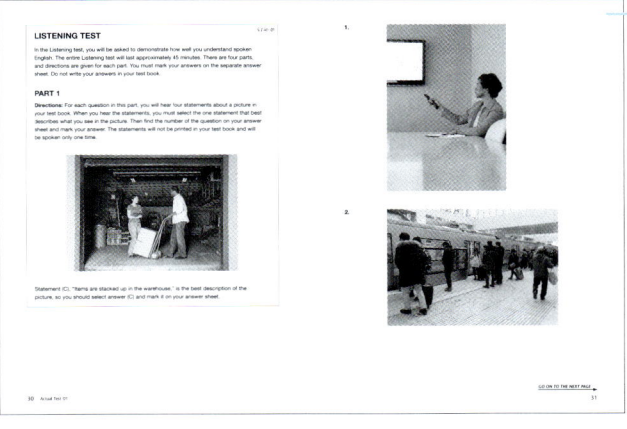

실전 모의고사

실전 모의고사 4회분을 통해 신토익에 대한 적응력을 기르고 자신의 실력을 가늠해 볼 수 있다.

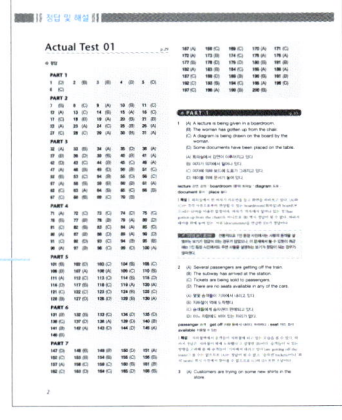

정답 및 해설

모든 문제마다 스크립트, 해석, 어휘, 그리고 해설을 제공함으로써 어떤 문제라도 모르고 지나칠 수 없도록 하였다. 또한 700점 이상의 점수를 얻기 위해 반드시 알아야 하는 사항들도 틈틈이 수록되어 있다.

About the TOEIC

토익(TOEIC)이란?

TOEIC은 Test of English for International Communication의 약자로서, 영어를 모국어로 사용하지 않는 사람이 국제 환경에서 생활을 하거나 업무를 수행할 때 필요한 실용 영어 능력을 평가하는 시험이다. 현재 한국과 일본은 물론 전 세계 약 60개 국가에서 연간 4백만 명 이상의 수험생들이 토익에 응시하고 있으며, 수험 결과는 채용 및 승진, 해외 파견 근무자 선발 등 다양한 목적으로 활용되고 있다.

시험의 구성

구성	PART	내용		문항수	시간	배점
Listening Comprehension	1	사진 묘사		6	45분	495점
	2	질의 응답		25		
	3	짧은 대화		39		
	4	짧은 담화		30		
Reading Comprehension	5	단문 공란 채우기		30	75분	495점
	6	장문 공란 채우기		16		
	7	독해	단일 지문	29		
			복수 지문	25		
TOTAL				200	120분	990점

출제 분야

토익의 목적은 일상 생활과 업무 수행에 필요한 영어 능력을 평가하는 것이기 때문에 출제 범위도 이를 벗어나지 않는다. 비즈니스와 관련된 주제를 다루는 경우라도 전문적인 지식을 요구하지는 않으며, 아울러 특정 국가나 문화에 대한 이해도 요구하지 않는다. 구체적인 출제 범위는 아래와 같다.

일반적인 비즈니스 (General Business)	계약, 협상, 마케팅, 영업, 기획, 콘퍼런스 관련
사무 (Office)	회의, 편지, 회람, 전화, 팩스 및 이메일, 사무 기기 및 사무 가구 관련
인사 (Personnel)	구직, 채용, 승진, 퇴직, 급여, 포상 관련
재무 (Finance and Budgeting)	투자, 세금, 회계, 은행 업무 관련
생산 (Manufacturing)	제조, 플랜트 운영, 품질 관리 관련
개발 (Corporate Development)	연구 조사, 실험, 신제품 개발 관련
구매 (Purchasing)	쇼핑, 주문, 선적, 결제 관련
외식 (Dining Out)	오찬, 만찬, 회식, 리셉션 관련
건강 (Health)	병원, 진찰, 의료 보험 관련
여행 (Travel)	교통 수단, 숙박 시설, 터미널 및 공항에서의 안내 사항, 예약 및 취소 관련
엔터테인먼트 (Entertainment)	영화, 연극, 음악, 미술, 전시 관련
주택 / 법인 재산 (Housing / Corporate Property)	건설, 부동산 매매 및 임대, 전기 및 가스 서비스 관련

1부

파트별 소개

PART 1
PART 2
PART 3
PART 4
PART 5
PART 6
PART 7

PART 1 사진 묘사

개요

PART 1에서는 총 6개의 문제가 출제된다. 응시생들은 각 문제마다 하나의 사진을 보고 4개의 보기를 들은 후, 보기 중에서 사진을 가장 적절히 묘사한 설명을 선택해야 한다.

> **신토익 변경사항**
> 기존에는 PART 1의 문항수가 10이었지만 신토익에서는 6문항만이 출제된다.

사진 유형

다양한 유형의 사진이 제시되지만, PART 1의 사진은 일반적으로 인물 사진과 사물 사진으로 크게 구분해 볼 수 있다. 인물 사진에는 1인 사진, 2-3인 사진, 그리고 다수의 인물이 등장하는 사진이 포함되며, 이러한 사진에 대한 설명은 보통 사람들이 하고 있는 동작과 관련된 것들이 많다. 사물 사진에는 실내 사진과 실외 사진이 포함되는데, 사물 사진 문제의 경우, 사진 속 중심이 되는 사물의 특징을 묻는 경우가 많다.

☑ **700점 넘기 포인트** 전통적인 구분법에서 벗어나, 최근에는 인물과 사물이 동시에 등장하는 사진 문제도 종종 출제되고 있다. 또한 중심 인물이나 사물에 대한 묘사가 함정으로 제시되고, 오히려 중요도가 낮은 주변 인물이나 사물을 묘사하는 보기가 정답인 문제들도 점차 증가하고 있다.

예제

1 🎧 00-01

| 스크립트 및 해석 |

(A) The man is mopping the floor.
(B) The man is changing into his work clothes.
(C) The man is putting garbage into the trash can.
(D) The man is sweeping trash into the dustpan.

(A) 남자가 바닥을 걸레로 닦고 있다.
(B) 남자가 작업복으로 갈아 입고 있다.
(C) 남자가 쓰레기를 쓰레기통에 넣고 있다.
(D) 남자가 쓰레받기로 쓰레기를 치우고 있다.

| 어휘 | mop 걸레질하다, 대걸레로 닦다 | work clothes 작업복 | garbage 쓰레기 | trash can 쓰레기통 | sweep 쓸다, 청소하다 | dustpan 쓰레받기

 사진 속에 한 명의 인물이 등장하는 대표적인 인물 사진이다. 이러한 경우 사진 속 사물들을 이용한 여러 가지 함정이 나올 수 있으므로 인물의 동작이나 외모를 정확히 묘사한 보기를 선택해야 한다.

| 해설 | 남자가 '걸레질을 하고 있는 것'(is mopping)은 아니므로 (A)는 정답이 될 수 없다. (B)의 경우, 남자가 옷을 갈아입는 '동작'을 하고 있는 것은 아니기 때문에 이 역시 오답인데, 만약 이를 'The man has changed into his work clothes.'와 같이 바꾸어 쓴다면 정답이 될 가능성이 있다. 쓰레기통은 보이지 않으므로 (C) 또한 적절한 설명이 아니며, 정답은 쓰레받기로 청소를 하고 있는 동작을 적절히 묘사한 (D)이다.

예제 2

| 스크립트 및 해석 |

(A) The curtains in the room have been closed.
(B) Clothes are being put onto the floor.
(C) The bed is facing the television.
(D) The sheets on the bed have just been washed.

(A) 방 안의 커튼이 드리워져 있다.
(B) 옷이 바닥에 놓아지고 있다.
(C) 침대가 텔레비전을 향하고 있다.
(D) 침대 시트가 방금 전에 세탁되었다.

| 어휘 | curtain 커튼 | face 향하다, 바라보다 | sheet (침대의) 시트; 종이 한 장

 사진 속에 여러 가지 사물들이 등장하고 있으므로 문제를 듣기에 앞서 각 사물의 모습이나 위치 등을 빠르게 파악하도록 하자. 이 문제의 경우, 침대, 베개, 텔레비전, 선반, 커튼 등이 설명의 대상이 될 수 있음을 예상할 수 있다.

| 해설 | 진한 색 커튼은 젖혀 있으므로 (A)는 잘못된 설명이며, (B)의 현재진행형은 '인물의 동작'과 관련된 설명에 쓰일 수 있는 표현이지 '사물의 상태'를 나타낼 수 있는 표현은 아니다. 침대 시트의 세탁 여부는 사진만으로 알 수 없는 사항이기 때문에 (D) 또한 정답이 될 수 없다. 따라서 정답은 침대와 텔레비전의 배치 방식을 정확히 묘사한 (C)가 된다.

PART 2 질의 응답

개요
PART 2에서는 총 25문항이 출제된다. 응시생들은 문제당 하나의 질문이나 진술을 듣고, 그와 가장 자연스럽게 어울릴 수 있는 대답이나 반응을 선택해야 한다. 다른 파트에서와 달리, 각 문제에 대한 보기는 3개만 제시된다.

> **신토익 변경사항**
> 기존에는 PART 2의 문항수가 30이었지만 신토익에서는 25문항만이 출제된다. 또한 PART 2의 디렉션 부분에서 예제가 사라졌다.

질문 및 진술 유형
일반적으로 질문은 질문의 형태에 따라 의문사로 시작하는 의문문, 일반 의문문, 부가 의문문, 부정 의문문, 선택 의문문 등으로 구분할 수 있다. 진술은 평서문의 형태를 지니고 있는 문장들로 이루어지며, 제안, 추천, 혹은 충고 등 다양한 의미를 전달할 수 있다.

> ☑ **700점 넘기 포인트** 전형적이지 않은 문제 및 보기에 주의해야 한다. 질문의 경우, '모르겠다' 혹은 '생각해 보겠다'와 같이 즉답을 회피하는 보기들이 증가하고 있는 추세이므로 모든 보기들을 끝까지 잘 들어야 한다. 한편 진술이 제시되는 경우에는 사실상 정해져 있는 답이 없으므로, 진술의 뉘앙스가 무엇인지를 정확히 파악하고 논리적으로 그에 가장 자연스럽게 어울릴 수 있는 보기를 정답으로 선택하도록 한다.

예제

1 Mark your answer on your answer sheet. 🎧 00-03

| 스크립트 및 해석 |

1 Why did the telephone suddenly get disconnected?
  (A) Sorry, but we have a bad connection.
  (B) Let me give you a call then.
  (C) The storm probably did it.

전화가 왜 갑자기 끊겼나요?
(A) 죄송하지만, 연결 상태가 좋지 않아요.
(B) 그러면 제가 전화를 드릴게요.
(C) 아마도 폭풍으로 끊겼을 거예요.

| 어휘 | disconnect 연락을 끊다 | have a bad connection 통화 상태가 좋지 않다 | storm 폭풍

| 해설 | 전화가 끊겼던 이유를 묻고 있다. 따라서 그 이유를 '폭풍'으로 돌리고 있는 (C)가 가장 자연스러운 답변이다. (A)와 (B)는 전화 통화상 상대방의 말이 잘 들리지 않을 경우에 할 수 있는 말로서, 주어진 질문과는 전혀 관계가 없는 문장들이다.

2 Mark your answer on your answer sheet. 🎧 00-04

| 스크립트 및 해석 |

2 I think we should consider Mr. Tanner's proposal.
  (A) You're being considered for it.
  (B) What makes you say that?
  (C) No, I didn't propose that.

Tanner 씨의 제안을 고려해 보아야 한다고 생각해요.
(A) 그에 대해 당신이 고려되고 있어요.
(B) 왜 그렇게 말하는 거죠?
(C) 아니오, 저는 그것을 제안하지 않았어요.

| 어휘 | consider 고려하다 | proposal 제안, 제의 | propose 제안하다

 평서문에 대한 적절한 답변을 묻는 문제이다. I think, I guess, I believe 등으로 시작되고 that절 안에 조동사 should가 사용되면 의견이나 주장을 나타내고 있는 문장으로 볼 수 있다. 따라서 이에 대한 동의 및 반대의 의미를 담고 있는 보기들을 주의 깊게 살피도록 하자.

| 해설 | Tanner 씨의 제안에 대한 화자의 의견을 밝히고 있는 평서문이다. 따라서 왜 그런 의견을 갖게 되었는지 되물은 (B)가 가장 적절한 답변이다. (A)는 진술에서 사용된 consider를 중복 사용한 함정이고, (C)는 proposal의 동사형인 propose를 이용해 혼동을 유발하고 있는 오답이다.

PART 3   짧은 대화

개요

PART 3에서는 길이 및 형태가 다양한 13개의 대화가 제시되며 각 대화마다 3개의 문제를 풀어야 한다. 대부분의 대화는 두 사람간의 대화이나, 세 사람간에 이루어지는 대화도 등장한다. 또한 마지막 두 개의 대화에는 시각 자료가 포함되어 있기 때문에, 응시생들은 각 시각 자료를 보고 하나의 문제를 풀어야 한다.

> **신토익 변경사항**
> 기존에는 PART 3의 문항수가 30이었지만 신토익에서는 39문항이 출제된다. 또한 대화의 길이가 보다 다양해지고 3인간에 이루어지는 대화도 새롭게 등장했다. 아울러 시각 정보를 이용하여 풀 수 있는 문제도 추가되었다.

대화 유형

먼저 주제에 따라 대화를 구분해 보면 주로 비즈니스와 관련된 사무 공간에서 이루어지는 대화가 가장 많은 비중을 차지한다. 그 외에 일상적인 주제의 대화, 즉 공공 장소나 상점 및 식당, 그리고 가정에서 이루어지는 대화도 제시될 수 있다. 한편 대화에는 구어체 문장들도 사용될 수 있고, 완전한 문장이 아닌, 절이나 구로 이루어진 표현들로 대화가 이어질 수도 있다. 길이에 따라 대화를 구분하는 경우, 3개 혹은 4개의 턴으로 이루어지는 짧은 대화와 7개에서 12개의 턴으로 이루어지는 긴 대화로 구분이 가능하다.

☑ 700점 넘기 포인트   턴이 많은 대화에서는 상대적으로 각 문장의 길이가 짧기 때문에 전체적인 대화의 길이는 크게 늘어나지 않는다. 이러한 경우에는 단편적인 내용보다 대화의 전체적인 흐름을 파악하는 것이 문제를 푸는데 더 도움이 될 수 있다.

문제 유형

대화의 전반적인 사항을 이해해야 풀 수 있는 문제로, 주제를 묻는 문제, 대화 장소를 묻는 문제, 화자의 신원을 묻는 문제 등이 출제된다. 대화의 세부적인 사항을 이해해야 풀 수 있는 문제로는 이유를 묻는 문제, 요청 사항을 묻는 문제, 혹은 화자들이 대화 이후에 할 일 등을 묻는 문제가 출제된다.

> **신토익 신유형문제**
>
> **화자의 의도를 묻는 문제**
> - What does the man imply when he says, "I don't think so"?
> - Why does the woman say, "Go ahead"?
>
> **시각 자료 문제**
> - Look at the graphic. What is the reason that the sales figure increased?
> - Look at the graphic. Who will be replaced with Dr. Smith?

🎧 00-05

예제

1 What are the speakers mainly discussing?
(A) The results of a survey
(B) A company they worked with
(C) Some comments that customers made
(D) The coming price increase

2 What does the man say about the company's prices?
(A) They have gone up recently.
(B) They are too high.
(C) They are lower than at other places.
(D) They ought to remain the same.

3 What will the woman probably do next?
(A) Read the survey results again
(B) Meet with some customers
(C) Find out about some comments
(D) Make a few purchases

| 스크립트 및 해석 |

Questions 1-3 refer to the following conversation.

M   Karen, have you seen the results of the customer satisfaction survey from March? The numbers look pretty positive, don't they?

W   Yes, but I'm a bit alarmed by how many people thought our prices are too high. That was rather shocking.
M   Yeah, I wonder why they feel that way. I was under the impression that we have some of the lowest prices in the industry.
W   That's exactly why I'm concerned. I'm going to contact the company that conducted the survey and find out if any customers left comments about our prices. That might make things clearer.

M   Karen, 3월 고객 만족도 조사의 결과를 보았나요? 수치가 꽤 긍정적으로 보이는군요, 그렇지 않나요?
W   그렇기는 하지만, 많은 사람들이 가격이 너무 높다고 생각한다는 점에서 저는 약간 놀랐어요. 상당히 놀라운 점이었어요.
M   예, 그들이 왜 그렇게 느끼는지 궁금해요. 저는 우리가 업계에서 가장 낮은 가격을 제시하고 있다고 생각했거든요.
W   그것이 바로 우려스러운 부분이에요. 저는 설문을 실시했던 업체에 연락을 해서 가격에 대해 의견을 남긴 고객이 있는지 알아볼 거예요. 그러면 상황이 보다 명확해지겠죠.

| 어휘 | customer satisfaction survey 고객 만족도 설문 조사 | positive 긍정적인 | alarm 불안하게 만들다; 경고, 주의 | shocking 놀라운, 충격적인 | under the impression that ~라고 생각하는 | conduct 실시하다 | comment 의견, 논평

1   화자들은 주로 무엇을 논의하고 있는가?
(A) 설문 결과
(B) 그들과 일한 업체
(C) 고객들이 남긴 의견
(D) 곧 있을 가격 인상

| 해설 | 대화의 주제를 묻고 있다. 화자들은 고객 만족도 설문 조사의 결과 중 이해가 가지 않는 부분에 대해 이야기하고 있으므로 정답은 (A)이다.

2   남자는 회사의 가격에 대해 무엇을 말하는가?
(A) 최근에 인상되었다.
(B) 너무 높다.
(C) 다른 곳보다 낮다.
(D) 동일하게 유지되어야 한다.

| 해설 | 'I was under the impression that we have some of the lowest prices in the industry.'라는 남자의 말에서 회사의 가격에 대해 그가 생각하는 바를 알 수 있다. 업계에서 가장 낮은 수준이라고 생각하기 때문에 가격에 대한 남자의 의견은 (C)로 볼 수 있다.

3   여자는 아마도 이다음에 무엇을 할 것인가?
(A) 설문 결과를 다시 읽는다
(B) 몇 명의 고객과 만난다
(C) 의견들을 찾아 본다
(D) 구매를 한다

| 해설 | 대화의 마지막 부분에서 여자는 '설문조사 업체에게 연락을 해서'(I'm going to contact the company that conducted the survey) 가격에 관해 의견을 남긴 고객이 있는지 묻겠다고 말한다. 따라서 여자가 할 일은 (C)이다.

풀이 전략   대화 이후의 상황을 묻는 문제가 등장하면 항상 대화의 마지막 부분을 집중해서 듣도록 한다.

🎧 00-06

4   Where most likely are the speakers?
(A) At a supermarket
(B) At a restaurant
(C) At a bakery
(D) At a department store

5   What does the woman mean when she says, "What a relief"?
(A) She is pleased that some customers are leaving soon.
(B) She would like to go home for the day.
(C) She is happy that she has not been very busy.
(D) She is glad that her work shift is about to end.

6   What is going to happen at 8:30?
(A) The manager will meet with the speakers.
(B) The speakers will finish working.
(C) A small room is going to be cleaned.
(D) A large group is going to arrive.

| 스크립트 및 해석 |

Questions 4-6 refer to the following conversation with three speakers.

Man A It looks like the last customer just left.
Man B Not yet. There's still a small group of people sitting at a table in the back corner. They should be departing in about ten minutes though.
Woman What a relief. We haven't had a break since 11:00 in the morning.
Man B I know, but we've got to get ready for the evening crowd soon.
Woman Do we have any big groups coming tonight?
Man A Yes, there's a party of 15 booked for 8:30. We're putting them in the small room beside the kitchen.
Woman Will they be ordering from the menu?
Man B Mr. Harrison told me they've already placed their orders, so we won't have to worry about that.
Woman Sounds good. Looks like we're in for another busy night.

Man A 방금 전에 마지막 고객이 떠난 것 같군요.
Man B 아직 아니에요. 뒤쪽 코너의 테이블에 소규모 무리의 사람들이 아직 앉아 있어요. 하지만 약 10분 후에는 떠날 거예요.
Woman 다행이군요. 우리는 아침 11시부터 한 번도 쉬지를 못했어요.
Man B 저도 알고는 있지만, 우리는 저녁에 올 사람들을 위해 곧 준비를 해야 해요.
Woman 오늘 밤에 많은 사람들이 오기로 되어 있나요?
Man A 네, 8시 30분에 15명 자리가 예약되어 있어요. 주방 옆의 작은 방으로 모실 거예요.
Woman 그들이 메뉴를 주문할 건가요?
Man B Harrison 씨께서 이미 주문을 해 두셔서, 그 점에 대해서는 걱정할 필요가 없을 거예요.
Woman 잘 되었군요. 오늘 밤에도 바쁠 것으로 보이네요.

| 어휘 | depart 출발하다, 떠나다 | relief 안도, 안심 | have a break 쉬다 | crowd 군중 | party 파티; 단체 | in for ~을 겪게 될

4 화자들은 어디에 있는 것 같은가?
  (A) 수퍼마켓에
  (B) 식당에
  (C) 빵집에
  (D) 백화점에

| 해설 | a party of 15 booked for 8:30(8시 30분 예약 손님 15명), the small room beside the kitchen(주방 옆 작은 방), 그리고 ordering from the menu(메뉴를 주문하다) 등과 같은 어구를 통해 화자들이 있는 곳은 (B)의 '식당'이라고 짐작할 수 있다.

5 여자가 "What a relief"라고 말할 때 여자는 무엇을 의미하는가?
  (A) 그녀는 고객들이 곧 떠날 것이어서 기뻐한다.
  (B) 그녀는 퇴근을 하고 싶어 한다.
  (C) 그녀는 그다지 바쁘지 않아서 기쁘다.
  (D) 그녀는 근무 시간이 곧 끝날 것이기 때문에 기뻐한다.

| 해설 | 주어진 문장은 'They should be departing in about ten minutes though.'라는 문장에 대한 답변으로, '다행이다' 혹은 '안심이다'라는 뜻을 나타낸다. 따라서 그녀가 의미한 바는 (A)로 볼 수 있다. 문맥상 그녀가 원하는 것은 '퇴근'이 아니라 '휴식'이기 때문에 (B)나 (D)를 정답으로 선택해서는 안 된다.

6 8시 30분에는 어떤 일이 일어날 것인가?
  (A) 매니저와 화자들이 만날 것이다.
  (B) 화자들이 일을 마칠 것이다.
  (C) 작은 방이 청소될 것이다.
  (D) 많은 사람들이 도착할 것이다.

| 해설 | '8시 30분'은 there's a party of 15 booked for 8:30라는 말에서 들을 수 있다. 따라서 이때 일어날 일은 15명의 사람들이 식당에 오는 것이므로 정답은 (D)이다.

PART 4 짧은 담화

개요
PART 4에서는 10개의 담화가 제시되며 각 담화마다 3개의 문제를 풀어야 한다. PART 3에서와 마찬가지로, 마지막 두 개의 담화에는 시각 자료가 포함되어 있기 때문에, 응시생들은 각각의 시각 자료를 보고 하나의 문제를 풀어야 한다.

담화 유형
다양한 종류의 담화가 등장할 수 있는데, 형태로 구분해 보면, 안내, 전화 메시지, 발표, 소개, 라디오 방송, 그리고 광고 등으로 나눌 수 있다.

질문 유형
PART 3의 경우와 마찬가지로, 담화의 전반적인 사항을 이해해야 풀 수 있는 문제로, 주제를 묻는 문제, 담화 장소를 묻는 문제, 화자의 신원을 묻는 문제 등이 출제된다. 세부적인 사항을 이해해야 풀 수 있는 문제로는 이유를 묻는 문제, 요청 사항을 묻는 문제, 화자가 담화 이후에 할 일 등을 묻는 문제가 출제된다.

> **신토익 신유형 문제**
>
> **화자의 의도를 묻는 문제**
> - What does the speaker mean when she says, "We will do it later"?
> - Why does the man say, "It couldn't be better"?
>
> **시각 자료 문제**
> - Look at the graphic. How much money will be paid?
> - Look at the graphic. Which item was the best seller?

🎧 00-07

예제

1. Where most likely is the speaker?
   (A) At a check-in counter
   (B) At the arrival area
   (C) At immigration
   (D) At a baggage claim area

2. According to the speaker, what will happen at 3:00?
   (A) Mr. Spitz's plane will arrive.
   (B) Mr. Winston will attend a meeting.
   (C) Mr. Spitz will check in at his hotel.
   (D) Mr. Winston will negotiate with a client.

3. Why does the speaker say, "But according to the arrival boards, his plane has been delayed"?
   (A) To request that the listener hurry to the airport
   (B) To state that he will be late for his meeting
   (C) To complain about his late departure
   (D) To indicate that his plans have changed

| 스크립트 및 해석 |

Questions 1-3 refer to the following telephone message.

M Hello, Mr. Winston. This is Derrick Sanderson calling from the airport. I'm waiting for Mr. Spitz to arrive so that I can drive him to the office. But according to the arrival board, his plane has been delayed. It was originally scheduled to arrive at 11:45; however, it's not going to land until 12:20. I know you have an appointment at 3:00, so I'll try to take Mr. Spitz to the office before then. Let me give you a call after he comes out of the baggage claim area. By then, I'll be able to estimate when we'll arrive.

M 안녕하세요, Winston 씨. 저는 Derrick Sanderson으로, 공항에서 전화를 드리고 있습니다. 저는 Spitz 씨를 차에 태워서 사무실로 가기 위해 Spitz 씨를 기다리고 있는 중입니다. 하지만 도착 상황판에 따르면, 그의 비행기가 연착되었습니다. 원래 11시 45분에 도착할 예정이었으나, 12시 20분 이후에야 착륙을 할 것입니다. 저는 당신에게 3시 약속이 있다고 알고 있기 때문에, Spitz 씨를 그 시간 전까지 사무실로 데려가기 위해 노력할 것입니다. 그가 수화물 찾는 곳에서 나온 후에 제가 전화를 드리겠습니다. 그때쯤에는, 우리가 도착하게 될 시간을 제가 예측해 볼 수 있을 것입니다.

| 어휘 | **so that ~ can** ~하기 위하여 | **arrival board** 도착 상황판 | **originally** 원래, 본래 | **land** 착륙하다, 상륙하다 | **take A to B** A를 B로 데리고 가다 | **baggage claim area** 수화물 찾는 곳 | **estimate** 어림잡아 계산하다, 추산하다

1 화자는 어디에 있는 것 같은가?
   (A) 탑승 수속대에
   (B) 도착 구역에
   (C) 출입국 관리소에
   (D) 수화물 찾는 곳에

   | 해설 | 화자는 자신이 공항에서 전화를 하고 있다는 사실을 밝힌 후, Spitz 씨라는 사람을 기다리고 있다고 말한다. 보기 중 도착 승객을 기다릴 수 있는 곳은 (B)의 '도착 구역' 밖에 없으므로 (B)가 정답이다. 또한 arrival board(도착 상황 게시판)라는 어구를 통해서도 정답이 (B)임을 다시 한 번 확인할 수 있다.

2 화자에 의하면, 3시에 어떤 일이 일어날 것인가?
   (A) Spitz 씨의 비행기가 도착할 것이다.
   (B) Winston 씨가 회의에 참석할 것이다.
   (C) Spitz 씨가 호텔에서 체크인을 할 것이다.
   (D) Winston 씨가 고객과 협상을 할 것이다.

   | 해설 | 'I know you have an appointment at 3:00, so I'll try to take Mr. Spitz to the office before then.'이라는 말에서 3시에 Spitz 씨와 Winston 씨가 만나기로 약속되어 있다는 점을 알 수 있다. 보기 중 이러한 의미에 부합되는 것은 (B)이다.

이와 같이 문제에 구체적인 시각이 들어 있는 경우, 해당 시간이 언급되는 부분을 집중해서 듣도록 하자. 대화를 듣기 전에 문제를 눈으로 훑어보는 습관을 기르면, 이러한 문제들을 놓치지 않을 것이다.

3 화자는 왜 "But according to the arrival board, his plane has been delayed"라고 말하는가?
   (A) 청자에게 서둘러 공항에 오라고 요청하기 위해
   (B) 자신이 회의에 늦을 것이라는 점을 말하기 위해
   (C) 자신의 출발 지연에 불만을 표시하기 위해
   (D) 그의 계획이 변경되었다는 점을 알리기 위해

   | 해설 | 화자는 주어진 문장을 통해 비행기가 연착되고 있음을 알리고 있다. 이는 Spitz 씨를 데리고 가려는 자신의 계획이 시간상 차질을 빚고 있다는 의미와 상통하므로 정답은 (D)로 볼 수 있다.

🎧 00-08

Speaker	Topic
Hanna Richards	Movie Making
Greg Dean	Watching the Night Sky
Edna Birch	How to Write Fiction
Joseph Watcher	The Art of Oil Painting

4 Who is Hiroki Ito?
   (A) An astronomer
   (B) An economist
   (C) A movie director
   (D) An artist

5 Look at the graphic. Which person won an award?
   (A) Greg Dean
   (B) Joseph Watcher
   (C) Hanna Richards
   (D) Edna Birch

6 What does the speaker say about tickets?
   (A) They can be bought online.
   (B) They are available only on the day of the event.
   (C) They are being given away for free.
   (D) They can be used for all events in May.

| 스크립트 및 해석 |

Questions 4-6 refer to the following announcement and schedule.

M Welcome to the first special lecture in the month of May. Before we start today's event with noted economist Hiroki Ito, let me tell you a bit about this month's other lectures. There are four more scheduled for May. We've got an artist, a movie director, an award-winning writer, and an astronomer set to give talks on their professions. I think you'll enjoy listening to what each has to say. Tickets, as always, are complimentary and may be picked up at the front desk. Now, with no further ado, please welcome Mr. Hiroki Ito, the author of the bestselling economics book *Economics Made Simple*.

M 5월의 첫 번째 특별 강연에 오신 것을 환영합니다. 저명한 경제학자인 Hiroki Ito와의 오늘 행사를 시작하기에 앞서, 이번 달의 다른 강연에 대해 잠시 말씀을 드리도록 하겠습니다. 5월에 4개의 강연이 더 예정되어 있습니다. 화가, 영화 감독, 수상 경력이 있는 작가, 그리고 천문학자가 자신의 분야에 관해 강연을 할 예정입니다. 저는 여러분들께서 각 연사들이 말하는 내용을 재미있게 들으실 것이라고 생각합니다. 티켓은, 항상 그렇듯이, 무료이며 프런트 데스크에서 가져가실 수 있습니다. 이제, 군말할 필요 없이, 베스트셀러인 경제 서적, *간단한 경제학*의 저자인 Hiroki Ito를 환영해 주십시오.

| 어휘 | lecture 강연 | noted 저명한 | economist 경제학자 | movie director 영화 감독 | award-winning 수상 경력이 있는 | astronomer 천문학자 | profession 직업, 직종 | complimentary 무료의 | with no further ado 군말할 필요 없이

4 Hiroki Ito는 누구인가?
(A) 천문학자
(B) 경제학자
(C) 영화 감독
(D) 화가

| 해설 | 담화 초반부에 화자는 Hiroki Ito를 noted economist라고 소개하고 있다. 이를 놓쳤어도 담화 후반부에 bestselling economics book(베스트셀러 경제 서적)이라는 표현에 유의하면 정답은 (B)의 '경제학자'라는 점을 알 수 있다.

5 도표를 보아라. 어떤 사람이 수상을 했는가?
(A) Greg Dean
(B) Joseph Watcher
(C) Hanna Richards
(D) Edna Birch

| 해설 | 담화 중반부에서 연사들을 소개하는 문장, 즉 'We've got an artist, a movie director, an award-winning writer, and an astronomer set to give talks on their professions.'가 정답의 단서이다. 여기서 수상 이력은 '작가'(writer)에게 있다고 나와 있으므로, 도표에서 글쓰기와 관련된 주제를 찾아 보면 How to Write Fiction(소설 쓰는 법)이라는 강연이 있다. 따라서 How to Write Fiction에 대해 강연을 할 (D)의 Edna Birch가 수상 경력을 가지고 있을 것이다.

6 화자는 티켓에 대해 무엇을 말하는가?
(A) 온라인으로 구입할 수 있다.
(B) 행사가 진행되는 날에만 구입이 가능하다.
(C) 무료로 배포된다.
(D) 5월의 모든 행사에서 사용이 가능하다.

| 해설 | 티켓에 관한 내용은 담화 후반부의 'Tickets, as always, are complimentary and may be picked up at the front desk.'에서 찾을 수 있다. 여기서 티켓은 '무료'라고 했으므로 정답은 (C)이다.

PART 5 단문 공란 채우기

개요

PART 5에서는 총 30개의 문제가 출제된다. 응시생들은 공란이 들어 있는 짧은 문장을 읽고 4개의 보기 중에서 공란에 들어가기에 가장 적절한 단어를 선택해야 한다.

> **신토익 변경사항**
> 기존에는 PART 5의 문항수가 40이었지만 신토익에서는 30문항만이 출제된다.

문제 유형

PART 2의 문제는 크게 어휘 문제와 문법 문제로 구분될 수 있다. 즉, 응시생들은 보기 중에서 주어진 문장의 의미를 가장 자연스럽게 만들 수 있는 어휘를 고르거나, 어법에 부합되는 형태의 단어를 선택해야 한다. 어휘 문제에는 관용 표현에 대해 묻는 문제가 포함되며, 문법 문제에는 문장의 구조, 품사, 시제, 특수 구문 등과 관련된 사항을 묻는 문제들이 포함된다.

예제

1 According to the latest reports, exports to Europe ------- by more than 10% during the first quarter of the year.
  (A) increased
  (B) transported
  (C) resulted
  (D) approached

| 해석 |
최근 보고서에 따르면, 올해 1분기 동안 유럽으로의 수출량이 10% 이상 증가했다.
(A) 증가했다   (B) 수송했다   (C) 발생했다   (D) 접근했다

| 어휘 | latest 최근의 | export 수출 | transport 수송하다, 이동하다 | approach 접근하다

| 해설 | 보기가 서로 다른 동사들로 이루어져 있으므로, 빈칸에 들어갈 알맞은 동사를 묻는 어휘 문제이다. by more than 10%라는 어구와 어울릴 수 있기 위해서는 '증감'의 의미를 나타내는 동사가 정답이 되어야 한다. 보기 중에서 그러한 의미를 나타낼 수 있는 것은 (A)의 increased(증가하다)뿐이므로 (A)가 정답이다.

2 Mr. Taylor expects every member of the staff ------- the meeting regarding the merger discussions with Utica Metals.
  (A) attending
  (B) has attended
  (C) to attend
  (D) be attending

| 해석 |
Taylor 씨는 전 직원들이 Utica 금속과의 합병 협상과 관련된 회의에 참석할 것으로 기대한다.
(A) 참석하는   (B) 참석했다   (C) 참석할 것으로   (D) 참석 중인

| 어휘 | regarding ~와 관련된 | merger 합병

| 해설 | attend의 알맞은 형태를 묻는 전형적인 문법 문제이다. 동사 expect는 to부정사를 목적보어로 취하는 동사이므로 정답은 (C)의 to attend이다. 참고로 want, encourage, persuade, enable, allow, urge 등도 to부정사를 목적보어로 취한다.

PART 6 장문 공란 채우기

개요

PART 6에서는 총 16문항이 출제되며 응시생들은 4개의 긴 지문을 읽고 각 지문당 4개의 문제를 풀어야 한다. 문제는 어휘 문제와 문법 문제, 그리고 빈칸에 들어갈 알맞은 문장을 묻는 문제로 구성된다. 한편 지문은 편지, 공지 사항, 광고, 회람, 기사 등 다양한 형태로 제시될 수 있다.

> **신토익 변경사항**
> 기존에는 PART 6의 문항수가 12였지만 신토익에서는 16문항이 출제된다. 또한 지문당 빈칸에 들어갈 문장을 고르는 문제가 하나씩 추가되었다.

질문 유형

PART 5에서와 마찬가지로 어휘 문제와 문법 문제가 출제되며, 특정 위치에 들어갈, 전체적인 문맥과 부합되는 문장을 묻는 문제도 출제된다. PART 5에서와 다른 점은, 단순히 각각의 문장의 의미를 파악하는 것에 그치지 않고, 지문의 전체적인 흐름을 이해해야 정답을 고를 수 있는 경우가 많다는 것이다.

예제

Questions 1-4 refer to the following memo.

To: All Employees
From: Harrison Clark
Subject: Summer Picnic
Date: June 14

The date for the annual summer picnic has finally been determined. It will take place on Saturday, July 15, from 10 in the morning until 7 in the evening. Like last year's event, the picnic ---1.--- in Forest Park in the southeastern part of the city. We're going to barbecue all kinds of foods, including hamburgers, hotdogs, and chicken. ---2.--- We will be playing games and doing various activities all throughout the day. Be sure to bring your swimsuit if you plan to swim ---3.--- the lake. Please be aware that fishing is no longer allowed in the lake as of this year. Your spouses and children are all invited to the ---4.---. Let Peggy Hamilton (extension 568) know if you plan to attend no later than July 1.

1. (A) was held
   (B) is holding
   (C) will be held
   (D) can hold

2. (A) Thanks for volunteering to help set up everything for the picnic.
   (B) We hope that all of you enjoyed the food that we served this year.
   (C) No decisions have yet been made regarding what we will do at the picnic.
   (D) There will also be various meatless dishes for those of you who are vegetarians.

3. (A) by
   (B) in
   (C) on
   (D) at

4. (A) event
   (B) ceremony
   (C) concert
   (D) game

| 해석 |

받는 사람: 전 직원
보낸 사람: Harrison Clark
제목: 여름 야유회
날짜: 6월 14일

마침내 여름 야유회 날짜가 확정되었습니다. 야유회는 7월 15일 토요일 오전 10시부터 저녁 7시까지 진행될 것입니다. 작년 행사와 마찬가지로, 야유회는 시의 동남쪽에 있는 Forest 공원에서 열릴 것입니다. 햄버거, 핫도그, 그리고 치킨 등 온갖 종류의 음식들로 바비큐 파티를 열 것입니다. 또한 여러분 중 채식주의자이신 분들을 위해 육류가 배제된 음식들도 다양하게 나올 것입니다. 우리는 하루 동안 게임도 하고 다양한 활동도 하게 될 것입니다. 호수에서 수영할 계획이 있으시다면 잊지 말고 수영복도 가지고 오십시오. 올해부터는 호수에서 더 이상 낚시가 허용되지 않는다는 점을 알려 드립니다. 배우자나 아이들 모두 행사에 초대합니다. 늦어도 7월 1일까지 참석 여부를 Peggy Hamilton에게(내선 번호 568) 알려 주십시오.

| 어휘 | **determine** 결심하다, 결정하다 | **take place** 일어나다, 발생하다 | **barbecue** 숯불로 굽다, 바비큐 파티를 하다 | **various** 다양한 | **meatless** 고기가 없는 | **vegetarian** 채식주의자 | **swimsuit** 수영복 | **as of** ~일자로 | **spouse** 배우자 | **extension** 확장; 내선 번호 | **no later than** 늦어도 ~까지

1 (A) 열렸다
  (B) 열고 있다
  (C) 열릴 것이다
  (D) 열 수 있다

  | 해설 | 동사 hold(개최하다)의 알맞은 형태를 묻고 있다. 주어가 사물인 picnic이고 문맥상 시제는 미래여야 한다. 따라서 수동태와 미래시제가 함께 쓰인 (C)의 will be held가 정답이다.

2 (A) 야유회 준비에 자발적으로 도움을 주셔서 감사합니다.
  (B) 여러분 모두가 올해 제공된 음식들을 맛있게 드셨기를 바랍니다.
  (C) 야유회에서 무엇을 할 것인가에 관해서는 아직 아무런 결정이 이루어지지 않았습니다.
  (D) 또한 여러분 중 채식주의자이신 분들을 위해 육류가 배제된 음식들도 다양하게 나올 것입니다.

  | 해설 | 빈칸 바로 앞에서 음식에 관한 이야기를 하고 있으므로 이와 가장 자연스럽게 연결될 수 있는 문장을 고르도록 한다. 정답은 채식주의자들을 위한 음식도 마련될 것이라는 의미를 전달하고 있는 (D)이다.

적정한 문장을 고르는 문제가 출제되면, 전체적인 문맥을 이해하는 것도 중요하지만 빈칸 앞뒤의 문장들을 주의 깊게 살펴보아야 한다. 특히, 이 문제에서와 같이, 빈칸 앞 문장에서 정답의 단서가 드러나는 경우가 가장 일반적이라고 할 수 있다.

3 (A) ~ 곁에서
  (B) ~ 안에서
  (C) ~ 위에서
  (D) ~에서

  | 해설 | swim(수영하다)과 lake(호수)의 관계를 생각해 보면 정답을 쉽게 찾을 수 있다. 호수 '안에서' 수영을 하는 것이기 때문에 정답은 (B)의 in이 되어야 한다.

4 (A) 행사
  (B) 의식
  (C) 공연
  (D) 게임

  | 해설 | 문맥상 빈칸에는 summer picnic을 대신할 수 있는 단어가 들어가야 한다. 보기 중에서 그러한 역할을 할 수 있는 단어는 (A)의 '행사'이다

PART 7 독해

개요

PART 7에서는 길이 및 형태가 다양한 지문이 제시되며 각 지문마다 2개에서 5개의 문제를 풀어야 한다. 지문은 하나가 주어질 수도 있고, 두 개 혹은 세 개가 한 묶음으로 주어질 수도 있다.

신토익 변경사항
기존에는 PART 7의 문항수가 48이었지만 신토익에서는 54문항이 출제된다. 또한 3중 지문 문제도 새롭게 등장했다. 아울러 문자 메시지나 온라인 채팅과 같은 새로운 형태의 지문과 화자의 의도 및 문장의 위치를 묻는 문제들도 추가되었다.

지문 유형

형태에 따라 지문을 구분해 보면 편지, 이메일, 공지, 안내, 광고, 회람, 기사 형태의 지문이 가장 전형적인 지문에 속한다. 인터넷 시대에 부응하여 문자 메시지나 온라인 채팅의 형식을 갖춘 지문들도 등장할 수 있다. 지문의 개수에 따라 단일 지문, 2중 지문, 그리고 3중 지문으로도 구분이 가능한데, 대부분의 복수 지문에는 하나 이상의 이메일이 포함된다.

문제 유형

전반적인 사항을 이해해야 풀 수 있는 문제로, 글의 주제나 목적을 묻는 문제, 글을 읽는 대상을 묻는 문제, 그리고 문장 삽입 문제 등이 출제된다. 세부적인 사항을 이해해야 풀 수 있는 문제로는 언급된 내용을 묻는 문제, 요청 사항을 묻는 문제, 혹은 화자의 의도 등을 묻는 문제가 출제된다. 그리고 PART 7에서만 볼 수 있는 단어의 의미를 묻는 문제도 등장할 수 있다.

신토익 신유형 문제

화자의 의도를 묻는 문제
- At 11:00 A.M., what does Mr. Smith mean when he writes, "I'll take care of it"?
- At 2:35 P.M. why does Ms. Carter write, "This is the worst that I've ever seen"?

문장 삽입 문제
- In which of the positions marked [1], [2], [3], and [4] does the following sentence best belong?

예제
Questions 1-3 refer to the following notice.

Proper Attire at Work

This is a reminder that all employees are expected to wear the proper attire while at work. Recently, there have been several violations of the basic dress code, and two happened to be commented upon by important clients. Please remember that you are all representatives of the company and that our clients judge the company as a whole by how our employees dress. Clothing that is too casual reflects poorly upon everyone. To make sure that there are no misunderstandings, the following items are not permitted to be worn at any time: jeans, sneakers, T-shirts, shorts, caps, and sandals. Khakis and polo shirts are acceptable but must not be wrinkled. Suits and ties are optional for men, and there is no casual Friday. Questions regarding the dress code may be directed to Laura Porter in the HR Department.

---

1 Why was the notice written?
(A) To answer some common questions about the dress code
(B) To remind employees to wear appropriate clothing
(C) To announce that the company's dress code has changed
(D) To tell employees to dress more casually at work

3 What is NOT mentioned about the company dress code?
(A) Sandals and sneakers may not be worn by employees.
(B) Employees may not wear casual clothes on Friday.
(C) The clothes employees wear ought to be pressed.
(D) Men are supposed to wear suits and ties to work.

2 What is suggested about some of the company's clients?
(A) They complained about how employees were dressed.
(B) They canceled their contracts with the company.
(C) They attended meetings while wearing casual clothes.
(D) They decided to do business with other firms.

| 해석 |

적절한 근무 복장

모든 직원들은 근무 시 적절한 복장을 갖추고 있어야 한다는 점을 다시 한 번 알려 드립니다. 최근, 기본적인 복장 규정을 위반한 사례들이 몇 건 있었는데, 두 건은 중요한 고객들에 의해 지적이 되었습니다. 여러분들은 회사의 대표라는 점과, 고객들은 우리 직원들의 옷 입는 방식으로 회사를 전체적으로 평가한다는 점을 기억해 주십시오. 지나치게 캐주얼한 차림은 모든 사람들에게 부정적으로 비춰집니다. 오해가 없도록 하기 위해, 다음 아이템들은 언제라도 착용이 허용되지 않습니다: 청바지, 운동화, 티셔츠, 반바지, 모자, 그리고 샌들입니다. 카키 바지와 폴로 셔츠는 허용되지만 주름이 있어서는 안 됩니다. 정장과 넥타이는 남성의 경우 선택 사항이며, 캐주얼 프라이데이는 없습니다. 복장 규정과 관련된 질문은 인사부의 Laura Porter에게 하실 수 있습니다.

| 어휘 | proper 적절한 | attire 복장 | reminder 상기시키는 것 | at work 근무 중에, 직장에서 | recently 최근에 | violation 위반, 침해 | dress code 복장 규정 | comment 논평하다; (잘못을) 지적하다 | representative 대표 | judge 판단하다 | as a whole 전체적으로 | misunderstanding 오해 | wrinkle 주름지게 하다 | optional 선택적인 | casual Friday 캐주얼 프라이데이 (평상복 차림을 허용하는 금요일)

1 공지는 왜 작성되었는가?
(A) 복장 규정에 관한 흔한 질문에 대해 답하기 위해
(B) 직원들에게 적절한 복장을 갖추어야 한다는 점을 상기시키기 위해
(C) 회사의 복장 규정이 변경되었다는 점을 알리기 위해
(D) 직원들에게 근무 시간 중 보다 캐주얼하게 옷을 입으라고 말하기 위해

| 해설 | 글의 제목과 첫 문장인 'This is a reminder that all employees are expected to wear the proper attire while at work.'를 통해 이 글이 적절한 복장을 갖출 것을 독려하기 위해 작성된 것임을 알 수 있다. 정답은 (B)이다.

2 회사의 고객에 대해 무엇이 암시되어 있는가?
(A) 직원들이 옷 입는 방식에 대해 불만을 제기했다.
(B) 회사와의 계약을 취소했다.
(C) 캐주얼한 복장을 입고 회의에 참여했다.
(D) 다른 회사와 거래를 하기로 결정했다.

| 해설 | 지문 초반에서 복장 규정 위반 사례가 몇 건 있었다는 점과 '두 건은 중요 고객에 의해 지적되었다'(two happened to be commented upon by important clients)는 점이 소개되고 있다. 따라서 일부 고객들이 직원들의 복장 상태를 비판했다고 생각할 수 있으므로 정답은 (A)가 된다.

3 회사의 복장 규정에 대해 언급되지 않은 것은 무엇인가?
(A) 샌들과 운동화는 직원들이 착용할 수 없다.
(B) 직원들은 금요일에 캐주얼한 복장을 입을 수 없다.
(C) 직원들이 입는 옷은 다림질이 되어야 한다.
(D) 남성들은 정장에 넥타이를 착용하고 일을 해야 한다.

| 해설 | 착용 금지 아이템을 설명하고 있는 부분에서 (A)의 내용을, 캐주얼 프라이데이는 없다는 공지에서 (B)의 내용을, 카키 바지와 폴로 티셔츠에는 '구김이 있어서는 안 된다'(must not be wrinkled)는 언급에서 (C)의 내용을 확인할 수 있다. 반면 정장에 넥타이 차림은 '선택 사항'(optional)이라고 했으므로 (D)는 사실과 다른 내용이다.

Questions 4-8 refer to the following advertisement and e-mails.

 Summer Sale at Crosstown Clothes

Get ready for summer by visiting Crosstown Clothes starting this weekend. From May 9 to June 1, you can get all kinds of brand-new summer apparel for low, low prices. We've got the top names in blue jeans for 30% off, brand-name T-shirts and blouses for 20% off, and swimsuits for half price. And don't forget about accessories such as sunglasses and ball caps. You can get them for 40% off. Of course, at prices this low, supplies won't last, so be sure to come here as soon as possible. And while you're here, sign up for a Crosstown Clothes membership and get access to all kinds of special deals. We're located on the second floor of the Greenbrier Shopping Center in Newton, and we're open every day of the week from 9 A.M. to 8 P.M. on weekdays and from 10 A.M. to 7 P.M. on Saturday and Sunday.

To: customerservice@crosstownclothes.com
From: mhardaway@privatemail.com
Date: May 15
Subject: Membership

To Whom It May Concern,

My name is Melissa Hardaway. On May 12, I visited your store in Newton to take advantage of the summer sale. I had never been to a Crosstown Clothes store, but I definitely plan on going there again. I was impressed not only by the wide variety of brand-name items for sale but also by the low prices. Then, to top things off, the items were being sold at such great discounts. I got a couple of bathing suits at great prices. I can't wait to go to the beach in them. I decided to sign up to become a member of the store. However, I'm not sure what the actual benefits are. Would you mind telling me what I can get by being a member?

Sincerely,

Melissa Hardaway

To: mhardaway@privatemail.com
From: customerservice@crosstownclothes.com
Date: May 15
Subject: Re: Membership

Dear Ms. Hardaway,

Thank you for shopping at Crosstown Clothes. We are pleased you were impressed with the selection of items and the prices we charge for them. We at Crosstown Clothes take great pride in providing quality items at affordable prices.

As for your question, I have attached a brochure that fully explains the benefits you can take advantage of by being a member. One of the most popular benefits is that you'll find out in advance what clothes we're going to be getting in the near future. For instance, you specifically mentioned a couple of the items you purchased. You'll be happy to know that we're receiving some other ones made by the famous brand Lionel James. Since you're a member, you can purchase these and other items from our online store up to 10 days before they are available to regular shoppers. Isn't that a great deal?

Sincerely,

Ferdinand Iglesias
Customer Service Representative
Crosstown Clothes

4. According to the advertisement, what is true about Crosstown Clothes?
    (A) It just opened a new store in Newton.
    (B) It has the same hours every day of the week.
    (C) It is having a sale for less than a month.
    (D) It is trying to sell clothes that are out of season.

5. Why did Ms. Hardaway write the e-mail?
    (A) To complain about how she was treated
    (B) To ask about some store benefits
    (C) To describe her interest in becoming a member
    (D) To praise the quality of the womenswear at the store

6. How much of a discount did Ms. Hardaway get on the items she bought?
    (A) 20%
    (B) 30%
    (C) 40%
    (D) 50%

7. What did Mr. Iglesias send to Ms. Hardaway?
    (A) A refund
    (B) A pamphlet
    (C) A coupon
    (D) An application

8. What is suggested about Lionel James?
    (A) It sells clothes only at Crosstown Clothes.
    (B) It offers its items at low prices.
    (C) It is a maker of swimming wear.
    (D) It competes with Crosstown Clothes.

| 해석 |

Crosstown Clothes의 여름 맞이 세일

이번 주말부터 Crosstown Clothes를 방문하셔서 여름을 준비하십시오. 5월 9일부터 6월 1일까지, 모든 종류의 여름 의류 신상품들을 저렴하고 저렴한 가격으로 구입하실 수 있습니다. 일류 청바지 제품들은 30% 할인된 가격에, 브랜드 제품의 티셔츠와 블라우스는 20% 할인 가격에, 그리고 수영복은 절반 가격에 준비해 놓았습니다. 그리고 선글라스와 야구 모자와 같은 액세서리에 관해서도 잊지 마십시오. 이들은 40% 할인된 가격에 구입하실 수 있습니다. 물론, 이처럼 낮은 가격으로는, 물량이 오래 남아 있지 못할 것이기 때문에, 잊지 마시고 가능한 빨리 이곳으로 오십시오. 그리고 이곳에 오시면, Crosstown Clothes의 회원으로 가입하셔서 온갖 종류의 특별 세일을 누리십시오. 저희는 뉴턴의 Greenbrier 쇼핑 센터 2층에 위치해 있으며, 주중에는 매일 오전 9시부터 오후 8시까지, 그리고 토요일과 일요일에는 오전 10시부터 오후 7시까지 영업합니다.

| 어휘 | from A to B A에서 B까지 | brand-new 신제품의 | apparel 의류 | brand-name 브랜드 제품의 | ball cap 야구 모자 | get access to ~에 접근하다, ~을 이용하다

받는 사람: customerservice@crosstownclothes.com
보낸 사람: mhardaway@privatemail.com
날짜: 5월 15일
제목: 회원 가입

담당자님께,

제 이름은 Melissa Hardaway입니다. 5월 12일, 저는 뉴턴에 있는 귀하의 매장을 방문하여 여름 맞이 세일을 이용했습니다. 저는 Crosstown Clothes 매장에 가 본 적이 없었지만, 반드시 그곳에 다시 갈 계획을 가지고 있습니다. 저는 세일 중인 다양한 브랜드 제품뿐만 아니라 낮은 가격에도 큰 감명을 받았습니다. 그리고, 가장 좋았던 것은, 제품들이 그처럼 큰 폭으로 할인되어 판매되고 있었다는 점입니다. 저는 놀라운 가격으로 수영복을 두어 벌 샀습니다. 빨리 수영복을 입고 해변에 가고 싶습니다. 저는 매장의 회원이 되기 위해 가입을 하기로 결심했습니다. 하지만, 실질적인 혜택이 무엇인지 잘 모르겠습니다. 제가 회원이 되면 무엇을 얻을 수 있는지 말씀해 주시겠습니까?

Melissa Hardaway 드림

| 어휘 | take advantage of ~을 이용하다 | definitely 분명, 확실히 | to top things off 가장 좋은 점을 말하면 | bathing suit 수영복 | benefit 혜택

| 해석 |

받는 사람: mhardaway@privatemail.com
보낸 사람: customerservice@crosstownclothes.com
날짜: 5월 15일
제목: 회신: 회원 가입

친애하는 Hardaway 씨께,

Crosstown Clothes에서 쇼핑해 주셔서 감사합니다. 귀하께서 제품들과 제품에 부과된 가격에 깊은 인상을 받으셨다니 기쁩니다. 저희 Crosstown Clothes는 적정한 가격으로 우수한 품질의 제품을 제공해 드리고 있다는 점에 큰 자부심을 느끼고 있습니다. 질문에 관해 말씀을 드리면, 귀하께서 회원이 되실 경우 받으실 수 있는 혜택을 모두 설명해 주는 브로셔를 첨부해 놓았습니다. 가장 인기가 높은 혜택 중 하나는 저희가 가까운 미래에 어떤 의류를 들여올 것인지에 대해 미리 아실 수 있다는 점입니다. 예를 들어, 귀하께서는 구입하신 두어 벌의 제품에 대해 특별히 언급을 하셨습니다. 저희가 유명 브랜드인 Lionel James에서 생산한 또 다른 제품을 들여올 것이라는 점을 아시게 된다면 귀하께서는 기뻐하실 것입니다. 귀하께서 회원이시므로, 일반 쇼핑객들에게 판매되기 열흘 전에 귀하께서는 온라인 매장에서 이러한 그리고 기타 제품들을 구입하실 수 있습니다. 놀라운 기회이지 않습니까?

Ferdinand Iglesias 드림
고객 서비스 담당
Crosstown Clothes

| 어휘 | be impressed with ~에 감명을 받다 | charge 부과하다 | take pride in ~에 대해 자부심을 갖다, ~을 자랑스럽게 생각하다 | affordable 입수 가능한, 가격이 적정한 | take advantage of ~을 이용하다 | in advance 미리 | specifically 분명히, 특별히 | mention 언급하다 | regular 보통의, 정규의 | deal 거래

4 광고에 의하면, Crosstown Clothes에 대해 사실인 것은 무엇인가?
   (A) 얼마 전에 뉴튼에서 매장을 열었다.
   (B) 일주일 동안 매일 영업 시간이 같다.
   (C) 한 달 미만 동안 세일을 할 것이다.
   (D) 철이 지난 의류를 판매하려고 한다.

   | 해설 | 광고의 초반부에서 세일이 '5월 9일부터 6월 1일까지' 진행될 것이라고 안내하고 있으므로 (C)가 사실이다. (A)는 언급된 바 없는 사항이고, 주중과 주말 영업 시간이 다르다고 했으므로 (B)는 잘못된 내용이다. 5월부터 여름맞이 세일을 실시할 것이라는 점에서 (D) 역시 광고와 반대되는 내용이다.

5 Hardaway 씨는 왜 이메일을 작성했는가?
   (A) 그녀가 받은 대우에 불만을 표시하기 위해
   (B) 매장에서 받을 수 있는 혜택에 관해 문의하기 위해
   (C) 회원 가입에 관한 그녀의 관심을 설명하기 위해
   (D) 매장 내 여성복의 품질을 칭찬하기 위해

   | 해설 | 이메일의 마지막 문장, 'Would you mind telling me what I can get by being a member?'에서 그녀가 이메일을 작성한 이유는 (B)로 볼 수 있다. '회원 가입에 대한 관심'도 이메일에서 찾아볼 수 있는 내용이기는 하지만, '회원에 가입하고 싶다'는 요청을 하고 있는 것은 아니므로 (C)를 정답으로 선택해서는 안 된다.

6 Hardaway 씨는 구입한 제품에 대해 얼마의 할인을 받았는가?
   (A) 20%
   (B) 30%
   (C) 40%
   (D) 50%

   | 해설 | 두 번째 이메일에서 Hardaway 씨는 '두어 벌의 수영복'(a couple of bathing suits)을 구입했다고 적었는데, 첫 번째 이메일에서 수영복은 '반값'(for half price)에 구입이 가능하다고 안내되어 있다. 따라서 그녀가 받은 할인은 (D)의 50%이다.

7 Iglesias 씨는 Hardaway 씨에게 무엇을 보냈는가?
   (A) 환불
   (B) 팜플렛
   (C) 쿠폰
   (D) 신청서

   | 해설 | 마지막 지문인 이메일의 두 번째 단락에서 Iglesias 씨는 자신이 '회원이 될 경우 받을 수 있는 혜택을 설명해 주는 브로셔'(a brochure that fully explains the benefits you can take advantage of by being a member)를 첨부했다고 밝히고 있다. 따라서 그가 보낸 것은 (B)의 '팜플렛'이다.

8 Lionel James에 관해 암시되어 있는 것은 무엇인가?
   (A) Crosstown Clothes에서만 의류를 판매한다.
   (B) 낮은 가격으로 제품을 판매한다.
   (C) 수영복을 만드는 회사이다.
   (D) Crosstown Clothes와 경쟁한다.

   | 해설 | 마지막 지문에서 Iglesias 씨는 회원 가입의 혜택을 예를 들어 설명하기 위해 Hardaway 씨가 구입한 수영복을 언급한 후, 'Lionel James라는 유명 브랜드의 또 다른 옷이 들어올 것을 안다면 기뻐할 것'(You'll be happy to know that we're receiving some other ones made by the famous brand Lionel James.)이라고 말한다. 이를 통해 Lionel James라는 회사는 수영복을 만드는 회사라는 점을 추측할 수 있으므로 정답은 (C)가 된다.

2부

실전 모의고사

Actual Test 01
Actual Test 02
Actual Test 03
Actual Test 04

Actual Test
01

LISTENING TEST

In the Listening test, you will be asked to demonstrate how well you understand spoken English. The entire Listening test will last approximately 45 minutes. There are four parts, and directions are given for each part. You must mark your answers on the separate answer sheet. Do not write your answers in your test book.

PART 1

Directions: For each question in this part, you will hear four statements about a picture in your test book. When you hear the statements, you must select the one statement that best describes what you see in the picture. Then find the number of the question on your answer sheet and mark your answer. The statements will not be printed in your test book and will be spoken only one time.

Statement (C), "Items are stacked up in the warehouse," is the best description of the picture, so you should select answer (C) and mark it on your answer sheet.

1.

2.

GO ON TO THE NEXT PAGE

3.

4.

5.

6.

PART 2

🎧 01-02

Directions: You will hear a question or statement and three responses spoken in English. They will not be printed in your test book and will be spoken only one time. Select the best response to the question or statement and mark the letter (A), (B), or (C) on your answer sheet.

7. Mark your answer on your answer sheet.
8. Mark your answer on your answer sheet.
9. Mark your answer on your answer sheet.
10. Mark your answer on your answer sheet.
11. Mark your answer on your answer sheet.
12. Mark your answer on your answer sheet.
13. Mark your answer on your answer sheet.
14. Mark your answer on your answer sheet.
15. Mark your answer on your answer sheet.
16. Mark your answer on your answer sheet.
17. Mark your answer on your answer sheet.
18. Mark your answer on your answer sheet.
19. Mark your answer on your answer sheet.
20. Mark your answer on your answer sheet.
21. Mark your answer on your answer sheet.
22. Mark your answer on your answer sheet.
23. Mark your answer on your answer sheet.
24. Mark your answer on your answer sheet.
25. Mark your answer on your answer sheet.
26. Mark your answer on your answer sheet.
27. Mark your answer on your answer sheet.
28. Mark your answer on your answer sheet.
29. Mark your answer on your answer sheet.
30. Mark your answer on your answer sheet.
31. Mark your answer on your answer sheet.

PART 3

🎧 01-03

Directions: You will hear some conversations between two or more people. You will be asked to answer three questions about what the speakers say in each conversation. Select the best response to each question and mark the letter (A), (B), (C), or (D) on your answer sheet. The conversations will not be printed in your test book and will be spoken only one time.

32. Who most likely is the man?
    (A) A real estate agent
    (B) A tour guide
    (C) A travel agent
    (D) An airline employee

33. What does the woman want to do?
    (A) Sign a contract
    (B) Look at a home
    (C) Furnish her office
    (D) Make an order

34. When are the speakers going to meet?
    (A) At 2:00
    (B) At 3:30
    (C) At 4:00
    (D) At 5:20

35. What are the speakers discussing?
    (A) The company's new interns
    (B) Their feelings about their new boss
    (C) The performance of another employee
    (D) The results of some interviews

36. What does the woman say about last year's activities?
    (A) They took less time to finish.
    (B) They had better applicants.
    (C) They required two days to complete.
    (D) They were difficult to conduct.

37. What is the man's opinion of Sarah Carpenter?
    (A) She should be hired immediately.
    (B) She is worth being interviewed again.
    (C) She performed better than he had expected.
    (D) She was the best of all the job candidates.

GO ON TO THE NEXT PAGE

38. What are the speakers mainly discussing?

(A) The results of a test
(B) A design the man finished
(C) A report the woman wrote
(D) The due date for a project

39. Where most likely do the speakers work?

(A) At a construction company
(B) At an architectural firm
(C) At a home decorating firm
(D) At a computer design company

40. What does the woman mention about her work?

(A) She needs someone else to help her with it.
(B) She is unable to finish it by tomorrow.
(C) She wants to speak to the client about it.
(D) She requires a larger budget to complete it.

---

41. What is being discussed?

(A) The promotion of a colleague
(B) The opening of another branch
(C) A special offer at a store
(D) How to request a transfer

42. What do the speakers say about Alice Milton?

(A) She is the company's new CEO.
(B) She recently transferred from another branch.
(C) She was fired from her previous job.
(D) She is going to be their supervisor.

43. How does the man feel?

(A) He is worried about his job.
(B) He is nervous about what is happening.
(C) He is displeased about the news.
(D) He is satisfied with the results.

44. Where does the conversation take place?

(A) In a library
(B) At a bank
(C) At a school
(D) At a driver's license testing center

45. What kind of identification does the woman suggest?

(A) A passport
(B) A driver's license
(C) A library card
(D) A student ID card

46. What does the man give the woman?

(A) A utilities bill
(B) A registration form
(C) A copy of his lease
(D) A canceled check

47. Why does the man say, "You can say that again"?
    (A) To express his agreement with the woman
    (B) To confirm that a person made a mistake
    (C) To ask the woman to repeat her previous comment
    (D) To express his desire to have attended the ceremony

48. Why are the speakers surprised?
    (A) A company event was canceled on short notice.
    (B) Someone they did not expect won an award.
    (C) The company failed to land a new contract.
    (D) A person in the IT Department made a mistake.

49. What does the woman say about Andrew Simmons?
    (A) He resigned to work at a rival firm.
    (B) He won a million dollars in the lottery.
    (C) He announced that he just signed a big contract.
    (D) He was the winner of an award at the company.

50. Why is the man asking for assistance?
    (A) He would like to get his money back.
    (B) He is interested in exchanging something.
    (C) He wants to buy a present for a friend.
    (D) He cannot find a shirt that he is looking for.

51. Why does the man dislike the item?
    (A) It does not fit him well.
    (B) The sleeves are too short.
    (C) The style does not suit him.
    (D) It is too formal.

52. What will the speakers probably do next?
    (A) Process a refund
    (B) Look at some clothes
    (C) Open the plastic wrapping
    (D) Search for the receipt

53. What are the speakers mainly discussing?
    (A) Their work performance
    (B) A recent lunch meeting
    (C) An incoming supervisor
    (D) The restructuring of a department

54. What does the woman mean when she says, "It's hard to tell"?
    (A) She does not want to answer the question.
    (B) She is not sure what Mr. Thompson will be like.
    (C) She is not allowed to tell the men anything.
    (D) She is not sure when she will meet Mr. Thompson.

55. What are the speakers concerned about?
    (A) The employees may have their salaries reduced.
    (B) They are in danger of getting demoted.
    (C) None of the employees will receive bonuses.
    (D) Some of them might lose their jobs soon.

56. Why does the man call the woman?
    (A) To cancel his order
    (B) To complain about a missing delivery
    (C) To renew his subscription
    (D) To find out how to pay a bill

57. Why does the woman say the man's address?
    (A) To confirm his identity
    (B) To find out where to send his order
    (C) To make sure she knows his new address
    (D) To ask where to mail a bill

58. What does the woman tell the man about?
    (A) A free magazine
    (B) A discounted price
    (C) An online service
    (D) A complimentary gift

59. What is the problem?

(A) Some parts that were delivered were poorly made.
(B) A shipment was sent late due to the weather.
(C) A snowstorm kept employees from getting to work.
(D) The assembly line was shut down for three days.

60. Why does the woman say, "That's a relief"?

(A) To request that the man double-check the results
(B) To show that she is pleased with the man's comment
(C) To express her disappointment with some news
(D) To state that there is nothing she can do about a problem

61. What does the woman request that the man do?

(A) Get in touch with a supplier
(B) Renegotiate a contract
(C) Contact the post office
(D) Speak to the assembly line workers

62. What is being discussed?

(A) How to attract more customers
(B) Which individuals gave good interviews
(C) Which company should be selected
(D) What should be said in a proposal

63. What does the man say about the Powell Corporation?

(A) It provides good support to its customers.
(B) He has worked with the company in the past.
(C) The prices it offers are lower than its competitors'.
(D) The company is having financial difficulties.

64. What will happen at 5:00 P.M.?

(A) A presentation will be given.
(B) A decision will be made.
(C) An interview will be scheduled.
(D) A contract will be signed.

GO ON TO THE NEXT PAGE

Money Spent	Discount
$1-$50	5%
$51-$100	10%
$101-$200	15%
$201 or more	20%

Topic	Room
New Medical Procedures	404
Using Lasers in Surgery	210
Advances in Robotics	106
Vaccinations	309

65. What does the woman indicate about the blender by Nelson Electronics?

(A) It is the store's bestselling model.
(B) It costs less than other blenders.
(C) It is useful for professional chefs.
(D) It comes with a money-back guarantee.

66. How often will the man use his blender?

(A) Every day
(B) Two or three times a week
(C) Once or twice a month
(D) Only on special occasions

67. Look at the graphic. How much will the man spend on the item?

(A) $1-$50
(B) $51-$100
(C) $101-$200
(D) $201 or more

68. Where most likely are the speakers?

(A) At a hospital
(B) At a medical conference
(C) At a medical school
(D) At a healthcare clinic

69. Look at the graphic. Which room will the woman be in?

(A) Room 106
(B) Room 210
(C) Room 309
(D) Room 404

70. What does the man suggest about Dr. Probst?

(A) He works as a doctor at the local hospital.
(B) The two of them are personally acquainted.
(C) He retired from his teaching duties recently.
(D) A new medical procedure was made by him.

PART 4

🎧 01-04

Directions: You will hear some talks given by a single speaker. You will be asked to answer three questions about what the speaker says in each talk. Select the best response to each question and mark the letter (A), (B), (C), or (D) on your answer sheet. The talks will not be printed in your test book and will be spoken only one time.

71. Where most likely does the talk take place?

(A) In an office
(B) In a laboratory
(C) In a store
(D) In a factory

72. What does the speaker say about the Dayton facility?

(A) An explosion was reported there.
(B) Several people have been hired there.
(C) People have been sent to look at it.
(D) It is going to close in the near future.

73. What does the speaker tell the listeners to do?

(A) Start finishing their work more quickly
(B) Work more closely with their supervisors
(C) Report problems when they see them
(D) Show up for work earlier than normal

74. What does the speaker ask Mr. Russell to do?

(A) Make a payment
(B) Call her back
(C) Give some feedback
(D) Visit the store

75. What time will Winston's open tomorrow?

(A) At 8:00 A.M.
(B) At 8:30 A.M.
(C) At 9:00 A.M.
(D) At 9:30 A.M.

76. According to the speaker, how was the problem solved?

(A) By installing a new speaker
(B) By putting some software back onto the computer
(C) By cleaning the computer thoroughly
(D) By replacing the computer's hard drive

GO ON TO THE NEXT PAGE

77. What is the restaurant celebrating?
   (A) The opening of a new branch
   (B) The finishing of some renovations
   (C) The completion of its first year in business
   (D) The serving of more than 5,000 customers

78. When is the restaurant having a sale?
   (A) From Monday to Friday
   (B) On the weekend
   (C) All next week
   (D) During the entire month

79. What can customers get during the sale period?
   (A) Free meals
   (B) Gift certificates
   (C) Special prizes
   (D) Coupons for free drinks

80. What caused the delay?
   (A) A mechanical problem
   (B) Ice on the wings
   (C) A missing passenger
   (D) Snow on the runway

81. What does the speaker ask the passengers to do?
   (A) Put their seats in the upright position
   (B) Listen carefully to the flight attendants
   (C) Fasten their seatbelts
   (D) Turn off their electric devices

82. What does the speaker mean when he says, "After that, I expect to make up for lost time"?
   (A) The plane is going to take off on time.
   (B) The flight will be quicker than usual.
   (C) The pilot will take a faster route.
   (D) The flight should arrive in a few hours.

83. What happened to the bridge?
   (A) A part of it fell into the river.
   (B) It just opened to all motorists.
   (C) It developed some cracks.
   (D) Two vehicles collided on it.

84. What does the speaker indicate about traffic?
   (A) It is moving slowly.
   (B) It is improving.
   (C) It is normal.
   (D) It is better than usual.

85. What will listeners hear next?
   (A) A commercial
   (B) A breaking news update
   (C) Local news
   (D) Sports news

86. What is the main purpose of the talk?
   (A) To congratulate the listeners for the performance
   (B) To encourage the listeners to work hard
   (C) To criticize the listeners for not working hard enough
   (D) To warn the listeners about some complaints

87. What did the attendees mention about the event?
   (A) They wanted it to be a bit longer.
   (B) They learned a great deal at it.
   (C) They thought the price was worth it.
   (D) They wanted more feedback from the lecturers.

88. What will the speaker most likely do next?
   (A) Have the listeners fill out some forms
   (B) Pass out some handouts
   (C) Present some awards to the listeners
   (D) Talk about an upcoming seminar

89. What is the speaker mainly discussing?

    (A) How some new stores are doing
    (B) The company's future plans
    (C) Where the company is expanding
    (D) The company's most recent profits

90. What does the speaker mean when she says, "They're performing according to our expectations"?

    (A) The new products are popular with customers.
    (B) The Asian branches are doing well.
    (C) The products are selling well everywhere.
    (D) The stores in Europe have many customers.

91. What did the company do this week?

    (A) It announced its plans for next year.
    (B) It released some commercials.
    (C) It employed an ad agency.
    (D) It canceled a contract with its marketer.

Room	Room Rate
Single	$110/night
Double	$130/night
Junior Suite	$170/night
Suite	$220/night

92. Why did the speaker call Mr. Jackson?

    (A) To cancel a reservation
    (B) To provide an upgrade
    (C) To offer an apology
    (D) To make a suggestion

93. Look at the graphic. How much more for a room must Mr. Jackson pay?

    (A) $20
    (B) $30
    (C) $40
    (D) $50

94. Why does the speaker tell Mr. Jackson to call her back?

    (A) The special offer is going to end today.
    (B) The hotel will have no space left soon.
    (C) He did not complete his reservation form properly.
    (D) He forgot to indicate when he is arriving.

GO ON TO THE NEXT PAGE

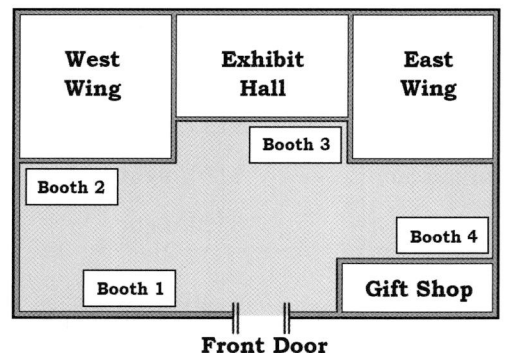

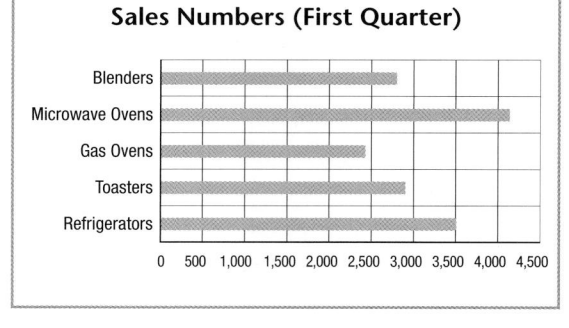

95. What is the man's job?

    (A) Ticket seller
    (B) Guide
    (C) Curator
    (D) Translator

96. Look at the graphic. Where can visitors buy tickets to the special exhibit?

    (A) Booth 1
    (B) Booth 2
    (C) Booth 3
    (D) Booth 4

97. What will the speaker do next?

    (A) Provide the listeners with tickets
    (B) Talk about a display
    (C) Hand out some pamphlets
    (D) Visit an exhibit on colonial times

98. Look at the graphic. What product will the speaker talk about first?

    (A) Microwave ovens
    (B) Blenders
    (C) Gas ovens
    (D) Toasters

99. Who is Sheila Roberts?

    (A) An intern
    (B) A salesperson
    (C) The company CEO
    (D) A new employee

100. What will probably happen next?

    (A) A person will greet the others at the meeting.
    (B) The contents of the graph will be discussed.
    (C) Suggestions on improving sales will be made.
    (D) An interview with a job candidate will be conducted.

This is the end of the Listening test. Turn to Part 5 in your test book.

NO TEST MATERIAL ON THIS PAGE

READING TEST

In the Reading test, you will read a variety of texts and answer several different types of reading comprehension questions. The entire Reading test will last 75 minutes. There are three parts, and directions are given for each part. You are encouraged to answer as many questions as possible within the time allowed.

You must mark your answers on the separate answer sheet. Do not write your answers in your test book.

PART 5

Directions: A word or phrase is missing in each of the sentences below. Four answer choices are given below each sentence. Select the best answer to complete the sentence. Then mark the letter (A), (B), (C), or (D) on your answer sheet.

101. The plant is running at full ------- now that the machinery on the assembly lines has been repaired.

    (A) availability
    (B) capacity
    (C) appearance
    (D) resemblance

102. ------- guarantee the timely delivery of the product, it should be paid for at the time it is purchased.

    (A) With respect to
    (B) In tune with
    (C) Regarding
    (D) In order to

103. Wilson Florists extended its operating hours during February for the purpose of ------- the increase in customers.

    (A) accommodate
    (B) accommodation
    (C) accommodating
    (D) accommodatingly

104. Ms. Wellman, one of the members of the board of directors, ------- given an update regarding progress on the newest line of products.

    (A) has
    (B) was
    (C) be
    (D) have

105. George Thacker applied for a job with Ellison Construction but was ------- due to a lack of experience.

    (A) hired
    (B) considered
    (C) rejected
    (D) interviewed

106. The passengers ------- offered to assist the bus driver in changing the deflated tire.

    (A) they
    (B) themselves
    (C) their
    (D) them

107. ------- at the meat plant fined the owner on account of the unsanitary conditions inside the facility.

(A) Inspectors
(B) Reporters
(C) Assemblers
(D) Politicians

108. Mr. Hamilton was supposed to attend the conference in Boise but was unable to make it there due to a scheduling -------.

(A) conflict
(B) confliction
(C) conflicted
(D) conflictive

109. Of all the customers who were polled, only a ------- of them thought the prices at Shop Right were too high.

(A) proportion
(B) variable
(C) fraction
(D) piece

110. Many diners had to wait to be seated for more than an hour ------- the establishment was so busy on its opening night.

(A) therefore
(B) since
(C) where
(D) if

111. It appears as though the machine suffered a major ------- and cannot be repaired at all.

(A) malfunction
(B) malfunctioned
(C) malfunctions
(D) malfunctioning

112. The customer ------- for more than an hour before someone at the store offered to assist her.

(A) will wait
(B) are waiting
(C) had been waiting
(D) have waited

113. Although she ------- her application in July, Erica still has not heard anything back from the firm.

(A) received
(B) approved
(C) submitted
(D) responded

114. Library ------- are permitted to borrow up to six books at a time for no longer than two weeks.

(A) donors
(B) patrons
(C) shoppers
(D) diners

115. ------- complaints by customers is one of the duties that the new intern was given.

(A) Handle
(B) Handled
(C) Handles
(D) Handling

116. When the deliveryman arrived with the package, there was nobody in the office able to ------- for it.

(A) pack
(B) open
(C) receive
(D) sign

GO ON TO THE NEXT PAGE

117. At the awards ceremony, Ms. Trellis thanked her entire staff for the assistance they had provided -------.
(A) she
(B) her
(C) they
(D) them

118. It appears that the negotiations between the two sides ------- their completion.
(A) are neared
(B) will have neared
(C) are nearing
(D) nears

119. ------- the weather starts to clear up in the next few hours, the company's annual outing will be moved indoors.
(A) Unless
(B) Despite
(C) Although
(D) Consequently

120. Taking the vehicle for a ------- drive is a common action for a person looking to purchase a new car.
(A) test
(B) testing
(C) tester
(D) tested

121. There was a water leak on the top floor that caused a great amount of ------- to the electronic items in one office.
(A) injury
(B) wound
(C) damage
(D) impairment

122. The exhibition of modern art at the Leo Gallery is going to ------- from August 2 to September 14.
(A) hold
(B) holding
(C) be held
(D) have been holding

123. As a result of the rainy weather, the summer fruit harvest in the area is expected to be ------- poorer than usual.
(A) some
(B) very
(C) much
(D) so

124. The museum is going to host an ------- of relics from ancient China starting in September.
(A) exhibits
(B) exhibition
(C) exhibiting
(D) exhibited

125. The owners of the building made it more handicapped ------- by adding ramps and other facilities on each floor.
(A) approachable
(B) apparent
(C) accessible
(D) available

126. All qualified individuals are encouraged to apply for the position ------- of their age, gender, or race.
(A) regarding
(B) regardless
(C) regarded
(D) regards

127. Because there were so many problems with the project, a new manager was ------- to run everything.

(A) revealed
(B) conceived
(C) invested
(D) appointed

128. Even though the country was suffering -------, sales at Vertigo, Inc. had never been better.

(A) economics
(B) economical
(C) economists
(D) economically

129. The outdoor performance by the Centerville Orchestra has been postponed ------- next week due to the rain.

(A) by
(B) until
(C) for
(D) still

130. The city council intends to vote on whether or not to ------- the company to build some apartments downtown.

(A) permit
(B) grant
(C) consent
(D) agree

PART 6

Directions: Read the texts that follow. A word, phrase, or sentence is missing in parts of each text. Four answer choices for each question are given below the text. Select the best answer to complete the text. Then mark the letter (A), (B), (C), or (D) on your answer sheet.

Questions 131-134 refer to the following announcement.

The Delmont Paper Mill has been in business since 1878. During that time, we have made all kinds of paper products that have been sold around the country. We are in the process of -------- **131.** our facilities so that we can increase our production of paper approximately 25% by the end of the year. When the process is complete, we will require more raw materials, especially wood pulp, for our mill. We are now accepting bids from suppliers. For a list of the materials that we need as well as the required amounts, please visit our Web site at www.delmontpaper.com/supplies. -------- **132.** Those interested in bidding to become a supplier can then contact Mr. Peter Hopkins at 850-3043. All bids must be submitted no later than October 1. -------- **133.** parties will be contacted on or around October 10. Those companies selected to become new suppliers -------- **134.** providing shipments of supplies by the middle of December.

131. (A) designing
    (B) expanding
    (C) planning
    (D) financing

132. (A) Please do not contact us by phone to get more information.
    (B) All the information that is necessary to know may be found there.
    (C) Suppliers can learn about the needed materials by calling us.
    (D) The bidding process will be closed in the month of November.

133. (A) Win
    (B) Winner
    (C) Winning
    (D) Winners

134. (A) began
    (B) have begun
    (C) are beginning
    (D) must begin

Questions 135-138 refer to the following letter.

December 10

Dear Mr. Thompson,

Thank you for opening a checking account at Savers' Bank. We have been providing our customers with high-quality services for more than 35 years, and we --------- to do the same thing for you.
                                                                                                    135.

We are currently printing your checks. You should receive them no later --------- December 15.
                                                                                136.
Please note that most places in the city require you to present a form of picture ID when paying for goods or services with a check. --------- In addition, we charge a $40 fee if you write a check on an overdrawn account.
                                            137.

You may feel free to contact one of our customer service representatives at 808-4243 at any time should you have any questions or comments regarding your account. We look forward to having a long and mutually --------- relationship with you.
                              138.

Sincerely,

Carla Hampton

Vice President

Savers' Bank

135. (A) respect
(B) require
(C) await
(D) intend

136. (A) from
(B) within
(C) than
(D) by

137. (A) For instance, an electricity bill with your name on it is acceptable.
(B) To make payments to these businesses, simply call us for more information.
(C) In order to get paid, be sure that you have the proper identification on you.
(D) In most cases, a driver's license is considered acceptable by vendors.

138. (A) beneficial
(B) apparent
(C) respective
(D) suspicious

Questions 139-142 refer to the following advertisement.

Volunteers Needed

The Greenbrier Community Center is looking for volunteers to work during the summer months. We require people to teach some of the classes we hope to offer, and we could also use people to work at the information desk. --------- with the time and ability to teach classes on painting, arts
                                                                                                139.
and crafts, needlepoint, and sewing are highly desired. --------- Please call Mary Ashford at 382-
                                                                                  140.
8594 for more information.

While volunteers at the Greenbrier Community Center will not receive any --------- compensation
                                                                                                          141.
for their time, they will be rewarded in other ways. Anyone volunteering up to ten hours a week will receive 50% off the price of a yearly membership. And anyone who volunteers 20 hours or more each week will receive a free annual membership.

Become a volunteer at the Greenbrier Community Center. Help the residents of our community --------- their lives by giving a bit of time from yours.
  142.

---

139. (A) They
(B) Them
(C) These
(D) Those

140. (A) You will be paid well for the time that you spend with us.
(B) So are people who would like to coach sports teams or act as referees.
(C) We would also like someone to replace Ms. Ashford, who recently resigned.
(D) There will not be any arts and crafts classes taught this summer.

141. (A) finance
(B) financial
(C) financing
(D) financier

142. (A) improve
(B) donate
(C) dedicate
(D) approach

Questions 143-146 refer to the following memo.

To: All Staff Members, Accounting Department

From: Darren Smith, Director, Accounting Department

Subject: Restructuring

Date: November 4

In the past two weeks, three of the employees in the Accounting Department have --------- their **143.** positions to work at other companies. Unfortunately, HR has decided that only one of those positions --------- with a new worker. As a result, all of us are going to take on additional duties to **144.** do the work that Jeb Marconi and Jenna Wilkins used to do.

We're going to have a staff meeting to discuss this matter on Friday, November 6. It's going to start at 9 in the morning and will end when we cover everything. --------- Attendance at the **145.** meeting is mandatory, so please cancel all other plans or appointments you may have scheduled for that time. If you have any suggestions regarding this matter, please feel free to mention them at the meeting. I am interested in hearing everyone's ideas on how we can assume extra duties without making our --------- too heavy. **146.**

143. (A) transferred
 (B) altered
 (C) suspended
 (D) resigned

144. (A) is filling
 (B) will fill
 (C) has been filled
 (D) will be filled

145. (A) I anticipate that it will last for at least 2 hours.
 (B) The agenda for the meeting has not yet been set.
 (C) Please try to make it to the meeting if you have the time.
 (D) I will be the only one who will be speaking at the meeting.

146. (A) schedules
 (B) workloads
 (C) appointments
 (D) jobs

PART 7

Directions: In this part your will read a selection of texts, such as magazine and newspaper articles, e-mails, and instant messages. Each text or set of texts is followed by several questions. Select the best answer for each question and mark the letter (A), (B), (C), or (D) on your answer sheet.

Questions 147-148 refer to the following advertisement.

Aloha from Hawaii!

Ono, the best Hawaiian restaurant in the city, is having a celebration. Our new head chef, Mr. Hanale Akoni, has revised our entire menu and will soon be preparing some of the finest delicacies in the entire Pacific Ocean. To share our brand-new menu with you, we're offering a remarkable deal. Start your meal with a delicious appetizer of taro chips and Hawaiian salsa made with tomatoes, onions, peppers, coconuts, and sea salt. Then enjoy an entrée of barbecued blue marlin or Kalua pig with a side of long rice. Finish off your meal with a dessert of malasada, a Hawaiian donut coated with sugar. This meal is being offered at the low price of only $22. But hurry as this sale only lasts until the end of the month.

147. Why is the restaurant having a special offer?

(A) It is having its grand opening.
(B) The restaurant has a brand-new owner.
(C) It is celebrating its tenth anniversary.
(D) The food being offered has just changed.

148. What is NOT mentioned as a part of the meal being offered?

(A) An entrée
(B) A salad
(C) An appetizer
(D) A dessert

Questions 149-150 refer to the following text message chain.

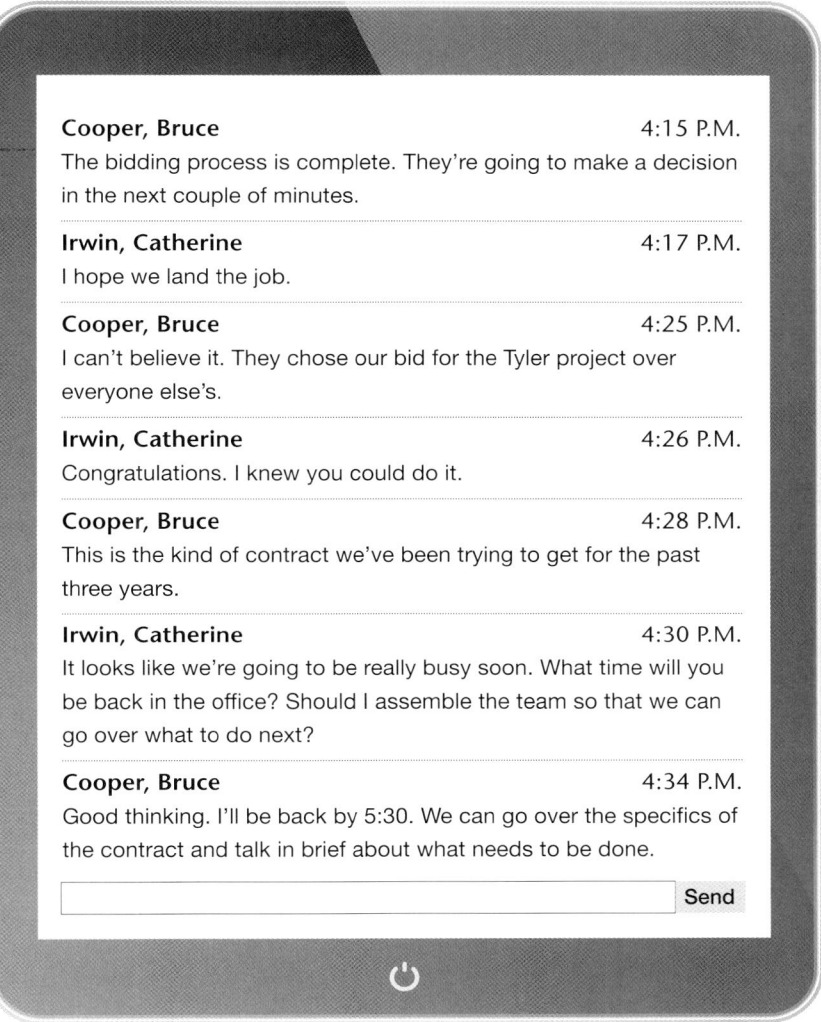

149. At 4:28 P.M., why does Mr. Cooper write, "This is the kind of contract we've been trying to get for the past three years"?

    (A) To congratulate Ms. Irwin for her work on the project
    (B) To express his happiness at being awarded the deal
    (C) To state that the company will turn a profit soon
    (D) To mention how hard the last three years have been

150. What is going to happen around 5:30?

    (A) A contract will be signed.
    (B) A bid will be made.
    (C) Assignments will be given.
    (D) A meeting will be held.

Questions 151-152 refer to the following memo.

MEMO

To: All employees
From: Melissa Jenkins
Date: April 10
Re: Restructuring

Please be aware that the company is going to undergo a major restructuring involving the Sales, Marketing, and Accounting departments. —[1]—.
The Sales and Marketing departments will be combined into a single department to be called the Commerce Department. George Jenkins, who is currently the manager of the Sales Department, will take over as the head of this department. —[2]—. In addition, the Accounting Department will be downsized by 25%. Employees in all three of these departments will be notified of their future status here this Friday morning. —[3]—. All changes will go into effect on May 1. We are implementing these changes to streamline company operations and to ensure future profitability. We hope that everyone will pull together during this difficult time so that we can emerge from the current recession as a leaner, but more profitable, firm. —[4]—.

151. According to the memo, what is going to happen?
(A) A new department is going to be formed.
(B) George Jenkins will become the CEO.
(C) All employees in a department will be fired.
(D) The company will lay off 25% of its workforce.

152. In which of the positions marked [1], [2], [3], and [4] does the following sentence best belong?
"Some of you will be laid off while others will receive promotions or transfers."
(A) [1]
(B) [2]
(C) [3]
(D) [4]

Questions 153-155 refer to the following itinerary.

Falcon Air
Itinerary

Passenger Name: Ms. Naomi Strauss   Reservation Code: ERE6095

From	Flight Number	Cabin	Departure Time	To	Arrival Time
Zurich	FA394	Economy	2:15 P.M.	Barcelona	4:05 P.M.
Barcelona	FA211	Economy	10:30 A.M.	Paris	12:25 P.M.
Paris	FA95	Business	4:20 P.M.	Copenhagen	6:10 P.M.
Copenhagen	FA575	Economy	7:10 P.M.	Zurich	8:50 P.M.

Please print this document and present it at the check-in counter. You may check in 2 bags weighing up to a total of 20 kilograms. For each additional bag you check in, you will be charged 50 euros. If you exceed the weight allowance, you must pay an additional 7 euros per kilogram.

This ticket may only be used by the passenger whose name is on it. It may not be transferred. This is a nonrefundable ticket, but it may be changed 1 time with no financial penalty.

153. Which flight departs in the morning?

(A) FA95
(B) FA211
(C) FA394
(D) FA576

154. How many kilograms of luggage may a passenger check in for free?

(A) 7 kilograms
(B) 20 kilograms
(C) 40 kilograms
(D) 50 kilograms

155. According to the ticket, which statement is correct?

(A) The passenger will sit in the same cabin on every flight.
(B) The passenger is traveling with another person.
(C) The passenger may change a flight on the ticket.
(D) The passenger can get a full refund on the ticket.

GO ON TO THE NEXT PAGE

Questions 156-158 refer to the following instructions.

Thank you for purchasing a Safety Pro Car Seat from the Whitman Corporation. Car seats can only protect your children when they are installed properly, so please carefully read and then follow the instructions below.

- ✓ Do not install this car seat in the front seat of your vehicle. It is meant only to be installed in the back seat.
- ✓ If your child weighs fewer than 10 kilograms or is 18 months of age or younger, the car seat should be positioned facing the rear. Children who are both 18 months of age or older and who weigh 10 kilograms or more may sit in seats facing forward.
- ✓ Pull the seatbelt through the belt path while ensuring that there are no twists. Then, lock the seatbelt in place.
- ✓ Pull the seatbelt tightly so that the car seat fits securely. Side-to-side movement decreases the effectiveness of the car seat.
- ✓ Place your child in the car seat and then adjust the straps to guarantee that the child fits snugly within the seat. Your child should not wear a jacket while riding in the car seat.

For more information, including a video with step-by-step instructions, please visit our Web site at www.safetyprocarseat.com. You may also call us toll free at 1-888-555-4938 if you have any questions regarding the Safety Pro Car Seat.

156. Where most likely would these instructions be found?

(A) On a Web site
(B) In an instruction manual
(C) In a newspaper
(D) In a letter

157. What is NOT true according to the instructions?

(A) A child should be able to move from side to side in the seat.
(B) It is unacceptable for a child in the seat to have a jacket on.
(C) A child weighing 7 kilograms should sit facing the rear.
(D) There should not be any twists in the seatbelt when it is fastened.

158. What should a person do to get access to a video of the car seat being installed?

(A) Call a telephone number
(B) Watch a videotape
(C) Visit a Web site
(D) Send a text message

Questions 159-161 refer to the following e-mail.

TO James Walker <jwalker@ssuncorp.com>
FROM Helen Trent <htrent@westing.com>
RE Repair Work
DATE July 16

Dear Mr. Walker,

I am writing to you with regard to the repair work that a team from your firm did on the main office air conditioning system last week. Since the work was completed on Thursday, I have received several complaints from employees with regard to the excessive noise that the air conditioning system is making. The problem only arose after your repairmen departed, so I assume that the noise has something to do with the work that they did on the system. As I am sure that you can understand, the high level of noise is making it hard for everyone to concentrate on their work, so we have had to turn the system off. Naturally, we are all very hot due to the ongoing heatwave, so we are in need of a functioning air conditioning system. As per our contract, your company guarantees all the work it does, so I request that your repairmen return to my firm as soon as possible. Would you please be kind enough to inform me when this will be possible? I look forward to hearing from you soon.

Sincerely,

Helen Trent
Westing Corporation

159. Why did Ms. Trent write to Mr. Walker?

(A) To praise him for some work done
(B) To ask him to send a bill to her
(C) To inform him about a problem
(D) To complain about the weather

160. The word "concentrate" in line 7 is closest in meaning to

(A) decide
(B) focus
(C) practice
(D) stress

161. What does Ms. Trent request Mr. Walker do?

(A) Replace an air conditioning unit
(B) Send a team to deal with the noise
(C) Tell her how to solve a problem
(D) Call her to set up an appointment

Questions 162-164 refer to the following announcement.

Escape to the Bendburg Ski Resort

The snow has started falling, which means that it's time to go skiing. The Bendburg Ski Resort has just opened for the winter and is taking reservations. Don't miss out on the excellent new facilities at the finest ski resort in the state. During the summer, a slope called the Green Mountain Run, was added. The Green Mountain Run is our longest and most challenging slope. You can also take advantage of our newly renovated ski lifts to maximize your time on the mountains. And don't forget to stop by Ricardo's, our new café, for some hot chocolate, an espresso, or a snack and for the best view of the surrounding area once you're done skiing. New to skiing? Bendburg has four instructors able to help novices and veteran skiers alike. Get the lowest prices for lessons when you book in advance. Located 30 minutes south of Milton on Highway 152, the Bendburg Ski Resort offers a daily shuttle service to downtown Milton. Call 953-8201 for more information or to make a booking.

162. What is the purpose of the announcement?

(A) To describe some renovations in detail
(B) To discuss how to get to a resort
(C) To advertise a place of business
(D) To compare a resort with other places

163. What is mentioned about the Green Mountain Run?

(A) Beginners should ski on it.
(B) Ricardo's is at the bottom of it.
(C) The new ski lift leads to it.
(D) It was built recently.

164. What can visitors do at the Bendburg Ski Resort?

(A) Rent rooms with a mountain view
(B) Go on hiking tours of the region
(C) Take lessons to improve their skiing abilities
(D) Reserve rooms on the resort's Web site

Questions 165-167 refer to the following letter.

Dear Kristin,

I opened my most recent copy of *Business Today* this morning, and imagine my surprise when I saw a picture of you. Congratulations on being featured in an article in the magazine. And well done on being promoted to vice president at Pinewood, Inc. I remember back when we were colleagues at Ceti Heavy Industries. Everyone there knew that you were destined for great things. And it appears as though you are reaching your potential.

According to the article, you're going to be transferred to Omaha soon. As luck would have it, that is where I happen to work now. It would be great to have a chance to get together with you and to get caught up with each other. Why don't you e-mail me at daveb@tristan.com whenever you get a chance, and we can set up a mutually convenient time to meet? In addition, if you need to know anything about the city or need help finding a place to live, feel free to use me as a reference. I've been here for the past 6 years, so I'm quite familiar with the area.

Talk to you soon.

Yours,

Dave Babson

165. What does Mr. Babson mention about *Business Today*?

(A) It has an article written by Kristin.
(B) He reads the magazine every week.
(C) He has an annual subscription to it.
(D) There is an article about Kristin in it.

166. Where does Kristin currently work?

(A) At Ceti Heavy Industries
(B) At Pinewood, Inc.
(C) At *Business Today*
(D) At the Tristan Corporation

167. What is indicated about Mr. Babson?

(A) He currently resides in Omaha.
(B) He used to work at Pinewood, Inc.
(C) He works at a real estate agency.
(D) He recently met Kristin.

GO ON TO THE NEXT PAGE

Questions 168-171 refer to the following online message chain.

	Cash, Leona [1:30 P.M.]	The group from Toronto is landing at the airport in a couple of hours. Is everything ready for the inspection of the facility they're going on tomorrow?
	Bergeron, Neil [1:33 P.M.]	I've done everything you asked of me.
	Alderson, John [1:35 P.M.]	Same here. I'll also be ready to show them around the factory tomorrow morning.
	Cash, Leona [1:38 P.M.]	That's good news. Which one of you two is planning to pick them up at the airport and take them to their hotel?
	Alderson, John [1:39 P.M.]	I wasn't aware you wanted us to do that.
	Bergeron, Neil [1:40 P.M.]	Me neither. I thought you told us last week that you and Harold were going to do that.
	Cash, Leona [1:42 P.M.]	Oh . . . I guess I forgot to tell you about the change in plans. I've got to meet with the VP of sales this afternoon, and Harold left for Costa Rica this morning. Are either of you available?
	Bergeron, Neil [1:45 P.M.]	I'm scheduled to meet Irene Chang at 4:00. But I suppose I could ask her to come here another day.
	Alderson, John [1:48 P.M.]	Don't do that, Neil. I can go there and meet them. I've spoken with Claude Messier several times, so it will be nice to get a chance to see him in person. Can you send me their flight info, Leona?
	Cash, Leona [1:50 P.M.]	Check your e-mail in two minutes. Thanks, John. I owe you one.

168. What is the online message chain mainly about?

(A) A plane trip that will be taken soon
(B) The schedule for the next day's events
(C) Preparations for the arrival of some visitors
(D) The meetings each person will attend

169. At 1:35 P.M., what does Mr. Alderson mean when he writes, "Same here"?

(A) He agrees with Mr. Bergeron's opinion.
(B) He is looking forward to meeting the clients.
(C) He did everything he was supposed to.
(D) He is presently with Mr. Bergeron.

170. What is suggested about Mr. Messier?

(A) He is coming in from Toronto.
(B) He is good friends with Mr. Alderson.
(C) He is going to Costa Rica soon.
(D) He is meeting Ms. Cash tomorrow morning.

171. What will Mr. Alderson probably do next?

(A) Inspect a factory
(B) Go to the airport
(C) Check his e-mail
(D) Talk to Mr. Bergeron

Questions 172-175 refer to the following article.

Literacy Awareness Month to Conclude Soon

Literacy Awareness Month is about to come to a close. Before it reaches its end, we would like to salute all of the members of the community who are making a difference to our children. We at the Reading Club of Kent (RCK) have been battling illiteracy among impoverished children by hosting daily events that encourage both children and their parents to read every day. This year's program has been a big success thanks to the hard work of our volunteers. —[1]—.

Knowing that reading is the key to education and that education is fundamental to staying out of poverty, the RCK has been hosting reading sessions at the Kent Public Library. —[2]—. Elementary schoolchildren throughout the city have been coming to read and to listen to local athletes, singers, actors, and other celebrities read their favorite stories aloud. A combined total of more than 2,500 children have attended these events. —[3]—.

The RCK was established by Joseph Stack and his family. The Stack family resettled in Kent in 1892 and was disturbed by the number of children who were unable to read. They therefore vowed to fight illiteracy in Kent and the surrounding area. —[4]—. Since then, the RCK has donated more than 20,000 books to children living in poverty and has held special events such as this one an annual basis.

172. Where does the article most likely appear?

(A) In a weekly newsletter
(B) In a history book
(C) In a national newspaper
(D) In a recruiting pamphlet

173. What has been happening during Literacy Awareness Month?

(A) Free books have been given to poor individuals.
(B) Famous people have read books to children.
(C) Reading classes for adults have been held.
(D) Fundraisers have been held to help buy books.

174. Who is Joseph Stack?

(A) The founder of the city of Kent
(B) A Literacy Awareness Month volunteer
(C) An original member of the RCK
(D) A worker that Kent Public Library

175. In which of the positions marked [1], [2], [3], and [4] does the following sentence best belong?

"More than 220 people have donated their time and effort to helping others learn to read this month."

(A) [1]
(B) [2]
(C) [3]
(D) [4]

GO ON TO THE NEXT PAGE

Questions 176-180 refer to the following invoice and e-mail.

Outdoorsman
384 E. Atlantic Street, Bangor, Maine
(804) 434-8594

Order Date: September 30
Order Number: 505954
Customer Name: Thomas Heckbert
Delivery Address: 34 Lansing Avenue, Trenton, New Jersey

Item Number	Item Description	Quantity	Price
606-544	Men's Black Cashmere Sweater (L)	1	$125.00
204-994	Men's Blue Jeans (L)	2	$45.00
766-121	Women's Green Blouse (S)	1	$80.00
653-476	Men's Red Windbreaker (L)	1	$22.00

Subtotal	$272
Outdoorsman Silver Club Discount	- $27.20
Tax	$14.69
Delivery Fee*	$15.00
Total	$274.49

* You selected express shipping. Your order will arrive within 2 business days.

Thank you for shopping at Outdoorsman. If you have any questions, please call us or e-mail us at customerservice@outdoorsman.com.

To: customerservice@outdoorsman.com
From: theckbert@marketmail.com
Subject: Order Number 505954
Date: October 21
Attachment: Pic

To Whom It May Concern,

My name is Thomas Heckbert. I am a long-time shopper at Outdoorsman. My Silver Club membership number is 49A0433. I'm writing to you with regard to an order I made last month. As always, the items arrived in perfect condition, and my wife and I are both pleased with how they fit. The quality of the items sold by Outdoorsman is the main reason I buy something from your Web site practically once a month.

The problem, however, concerns the amount of money I was charged for the items I bought. While the invoice I received with the items noted that I was given a 10% discount, when I received my credit card bill, I noticed that the discount had actually not been applied. I was therefore charged too much for my purchase. I have attached a picture of the invoice so that you can see how much of a discount I should have received. Would you be kind enough to refund the money, please? You can simply give me store credit as I am planning to make another order this Thursday or Friday. If there are any questions, please feel free to write me back.

I look forward to hearing a positive response soon.

Regards,
Thomas Heckbert

176. What is NOT mentioned on the invoice?

(A) The method of payment
(B) The receiver's address
(C) The number of each item bought
(D) The phone number of the company

177. Which item did Mr. Heckbert pay the most money for?

(A) 204-994
(B) 606-544
(C) 653-476
(D) 766-121

178. What does Mr. Heckbert suggest about one of the items he ordered?

(A) He was overcharged for it.
(B) He cannot fit in it.
(C) He bought it on sale.
(D) He purchased it for his wife.

179. How much money would Mr. Heckbert like back?

(A) $15.00
(B) $14.69
(C) $22.00
(D) $27.20

180. What does Mr. Heckbert send with his e-mail?

(A) A new clothing order
(B) A copy of his bill
(C) A picture of the faulty merchandise
(D) A file containing his credit card bill

GO ON TO THE NEXT PAGE

Questions 181-185 refer to the following notice and memo.

Templeton Manufacturing

will be holding its annual end-of-the-year dinner on

Friday, December 29
from 6:30 P.M. to 10:00 P.M.
in the Rose Ballroom
at the Garden Hotel

The following events will take place:
6:30 P.M. – the year in review by CEO James Lambert
7:00 P.M. – five-course dinner
8:30 P.M. – awards ceremony
9:00 P.M. – live entertainment

All Templeton Manufacturing employees and their spouses or significant others are welcome.
Please contact Ms. Virginia Snyder at vsnyder@templetonmanu.com
to confirm your attendance.

To: Elisa Standish
From: Percy Wilson
Re: December 29 Event
Date: December 20

It looks like everything is about ready for the big event next week. I spoke with Kevin Crawford at the Garden Hotel, and he has assured me that all of the food we requested for the event will be available. He invited me to drop by the hotel to sample the dishes this Friday, December 22. If you'd like to accompany me, let me know. I'll be leaving here around 2:30 so that I can make it back to the office for a 5:00 meeting. There's one change in the schedule though. Connie Parker wants to present the awards right after Mr. Lambert gives his talk. So we need to contact the printer to make sure the schedules that get printed have the correct order of events. You're the contact person for the printer, so would you mind doing that? Let me know as soon as you're done so that I can inform Connie. This is the first awards ceremony she's responsible for, and she's really eager to avoid any mistakes. You remember how things went last year with Todd Seager in charge, don't you? We don't want a repeat of that.

181. What is the purpose of the notice?

(A) To mention a change in a schedule
(B) To invite company employees to an event
(C) To provide the contact information of some employees
(D) To announce the winners of some awards

182. The word "confirm" in line 15 of the notice is closest in meaning to

(A) certify
(B) refute
(C) purchase
(D) admit

183. According to the memo, when will the awards be given?

(A) At 6:30
(B) At 7:00
(C) At 8:30
(D) At 9:00

184. What does Mr. Wilson ask Ms. Standish to do?

(A) Go to the Garden Hotel in his place
(B) Send an e-mail to Ms. Snyder
(C) Arrange for a schedule to be changed
(D) Coordinate with Ms. Parker

185. What is suggested about Todd Seager?

(A) He performed his duties poorly last year.
(B) He is one of this year's award winners.
(C) He is employed at the Garden Hotel.
(D) He works closely with Ms. Parker.

GO ON TO THE NEXT PAGE

Questions 186-190 refer to the following advertisement, invoice, and letter.

Come to Al's Electronics for a Special Offer

You often hear the phrase, "Out with the old and in with the new." At Al's Electronics, we believe in keeping the old along with the new. This weekend only, bring your old, broken radios, CD players, toasters, and any other electronics in to the store. If you bring it, we'll fix it at absolutely no cost to you. We can repair TVs, laptops, and heaters as well. Each shopper can receive up to $50 worth of free repairs. All you need to do is make a nonrefundable purchase of $100 or more. So pay a visit to your garage, attic, or toolshed and search for that item you've been meaning to get repaired. Visit Al's Electronics at 549 Vernon Avenue this Saturday or Sunday, May 7 and 8, and we'll have it working for you in no time. Call 675-9303 for more information.

Al's Electronics
549 Vernon Avenue
Pittsburgh, PA
675-9303

Date: May 8
Customer Name: Eric Simpson
Phone Number: 509-4485

Item Number	Description	Quantity	Price
685-5542	64GB Thumb Drive	2	$12.00
054-1022	Sidewinder Toaster (Model RT40)	1	$52.00
966-6854	Pampas DVD Player (Model 600TE)	1	$65.00
N/A	Repair Work (Video Game Console)	1	$0.00
		Subtotal	$129.00
		Tax	$6.45
		Total	$135.45

NOTES: Repair work done by Jason Hampton

Thank you for shopping at Al's Electronics. We hope you come again soon.

May 10

To Whom It May Concern,

My name is Eric Simpson. On the eighth of May, I visited your store and made a couple of purchases. I took advantage of the chance to have my old video game console repaired while I was there. I must say that the person who fixed the machine did an outstanding job. The machine hadn't worked for more than a decade, but it runs perfectly now. My younger brother and I have been having a great time playing video games from the 1990s for the past couple of days. Please be sure to thank the person who did the repair work. I can't recall his name, but I know he is one of the managers there. I've got an old tape recorder that's in pretty poor shape. I'm probably going to visit in the next week to have it fixed. I realize that will cost money, but I would like to listen to some of my old tapes, so I don't mind paying a fee.

Sincerely,
Eric Simpson

186. What kind of offer is being advertised?

(A) An opportunity to get a free service
(B) A discount on selected items
(C) A chance to exchange old items for new ones
(D) A free consultation regarding purchases

187. What is mentioned about the offer?

(A) It is not applied to some types of items.
(B) It will last for the entire month of May.
(C) It requires shoppers to make a purchase.
(D) It is only being offered to members.

188. What is suggested on the invoice?

(A) Mr. Simpson can exchange the items that he bought.
(B) The toaster was purchased at a discounted price.
(C) A shipping fee was charged to deliver the items.
(D) The repairs on the video game were worth less than $50.

189. Why did Mr. Simpson write the letter?

(A) To ask about getting an item he owns repaired
(B) To express his pleasure with the service he received
(C) To find out how his video game machine was fixed
(D) To complain about the quality of some repairs

190. What does Mr. Simpson indicate about Al's Electronics?

(A) It will have another special sale soon.
(B) It employs Jason Hampton as a manager.
(C) It was unable to repair his tape recorder.
(D) It overcharged him for an item that he bought.

GO ON TO THE NEXT PAGE

Questions 191-195 refer to the following announcement, memo, and e-mail.

VP to Retire Soon

Chamberlain Savings Bank wishes to announce the retirement of Sebastian Brown, our vice president, on Friday, November 28. Mr. Brown has been an employee here for the past 43 years. Starting as a bank teller straight out of college, he swiftly showed his value and was promoted to manager. He was appointed to three other positions here until being named vice president 14 years ago. During Mr. Brown's tenure as vice president, Chamberlain Savings Bank has transitioned from a small local bank to one of the largest privately owned banks in the Midwest, with 34 branches in 7 states. Mr. Brown is a beloved employee, noted philanthropist, and loving father, and his presence will be missed. There will be a retirement ceremony for him at 3 P.M. on his final day of work. It will be held at the Chamberlain Savings Bank branch in St. Louis at 56 Cutler Street.

To: All Employees, Chamberlain Savings Bank
From: Kelly Rudolph, Director, 56 Cutler Street Branch
Re: Retirement Party
Date: November 7

You are invited to attend the retirement party being held for Sebastian Brown. Please note that due to the Thanksgiving holiday, which takes place one day prior to Mr. Brown's retirement date, the party for Mr. Brown has been moved up by one week. It will therefore take place the Friday before Thanksgiving. The time and location of the event, however, have not changed.

While David Chamberlain, our bank's owner, intends to give Mr. Brown a present, some employees think we should give him something ourselves. So we're taking up a collection for him. Since Mr. Brown loves golfing, we're hoping to buy him a new set of clubs. You can give your donations to me or your manager, who will make sure that I get them. All of the donated funds will be used for Mr. Brown's gift. I'm going to order the clubs on the 16th, so if you're planning to donate, please do so by then.

> **TO** Kelly Rudolph <krudolph@chamberlainsavings.com>
> **FROM** Susan Walters <susan_walters@redbirdsportinggoods.com>
> **DATE** November 17
> **SUBJECT** Order #204-KL-505

Dear Ms. Rudolph,

We received the order you placed on our Web site yesterday. We are pleased to have you as a new customer and hope you continue to buy from us in the future.

I would like to let you know that the Delmar's Deluxe Golf Club set (item number 59505594) that you ordered is being prepared for shipping. Unfortunately, the Delmar's Black Golf Bag (item number 68586965) that you ordered is not currently in stock and will not arrive for 7 more days. You requested express shipping, so we assume you need your order in a hurry. May I suggest that you substitute the missing item by getting either item number 69658494 or 23420534? Simply click on each number to see a description of the item. While they are slightly more expensive, we will not charge you the extra cost, so the price of your order will remain $3,500.

Sincerely,

Susan Walters, Redbird Sporting Goods

191. For whom is the announcement most likely intended?
   (A) Residents of St. Louis
   (B) Bank employees
   (C) Bank customers
   (D) Mr. Brown's family

192. What is NOT mentioned about Mr. Brown?
   (A) The employees at the bank like him.
   (B) He has worked at the bank for four decades.
   (C) He founded the branch in St. Louis.
   (D) The bank has done well since he has worked there.

193. According to the memo, when will the retirement party be held?
   (A) On November 7
   (B) On November 21
   (C) On November 27
   (D) On November 28

194. Why did Ms. Walters write the e-mail?
   (A) To suggest using express shipping
   (B) To offer a discount on an ordered item
   (C) To discuss a problem with an item
   (D) To note that some items have been shipped

195. What is suggested about the employees at the bank?
   (A) They donated $3,500 for Mr. Brown's gift.
   (B) They will all attend Mr. Brown's retirement party.
   (C) They suggested what to buy to Ms. Rudolph.
   (D) They are eager to meet their new vice president.

Questions 196-200 refer to the following information and e-mails.

The Sussex Salad-Mixing Bowl

Thank you for purchasing a Sussex Salad-Mixing Bowl. We expect you to enjoy many healthy and nutritious meals mixed with it. Before using your new appliance, please read the following instructions carefully.

* Wash the bowl and make sure it is completely dry before adding anything to it.
* Make sure you only use fresh vegetables that have been cut into small pieces. Large pieces will block the mixing mechanism and could result in a mechanical failure.
* Place the cover over the bowl and grasp the handle of the mixing mechanism. Then, gently turn the handle counterclockwise up to ten times.
* Lift the cover and inspect the salad. If it requires more mixing, repeat the process.
* When your meal is complete, clean the bowl, lid, and mixing mechanism with hot water and dishwashing detergent. Do not place the bowl in a dishwasher.

For questions, please contact information@sussex.com. Not following the instructions voids all warranties.

TO: information@sussex.com
FROM: trussell@sunmail.com
DATE: June 12
RE: Sussex Salad-Mixing Bowl

Dear Sir/Madam,

One week ago, I purchased a Sussex Salad-Mixing Bowl from my local department store. A salesclerk there convinced me that it would be great for all the summer salads I intend to make. I paid $45 and left the store with one. When I arrived home that night, I decided to make a delicious salad for my family. So I added some lettuce, carrots, peppers, and tomatoes to the bowl and poured some dressing on it. Then, I tried mixing everything together. Imagine my surprise when not only did the bowl fail to mix the vegetables, but it also did not cut them. To top it off, the bowl won't even work anymore. I'm very disappointed with my purchase and would like my money back. Since the department store does not offer refunds, I believe you should return my money. I have attached a copy of the receipt so that you can verify my purchase.

Regards,

Tina Russell

TO: trussell@sunmail.com
FROM: mmartin@sussex.com
DATE: June 13
RE: RE: Sussex Salad-Mixing Bowl

Dear Ms. Russell,

We at Sussex received the e-mail that you wrote regarding your Sussex Salad-Mixing Bowl. According to the description of how you used the bowl, you failed to follow the instructions that should have been included in the bowl. As a result, we are unable either to refund your money or to repair the bowl at no cost.

However, we at Sussex take pride in helping our customers, and we don't want you to be disappointed with one of our products. So I am including a downloadable coupon for $30. You can use it to purchase anything we sell on our Web site. Just go to www.sussexinc.com, and you can see all of the items that we have for sale.

Please feel free to contact me again if you have any questions. I would be glad to be of assistance to you.

Sincerely,

Matthew Martin
Customer Service Representative
Sussex, Inc.

196. What is the purpose of the instructions?

(A) To describe how to repair a product
(B) To show how to assemble the product
(C) To demonstrate how to take apart a product
(D) To explain how to use a product

197. According to the first e-mail, how did Ms. Russell use the bowl improperly?

(A) She turned the handle the wrong way.
(B) She washed the bowl in her dishwasher.
(C) She added vegetables that were not cut.
(D) She failed to clean the bowl properly.

198. What does Ms. Russell send along with her e-mail?

(A) A copy of a receipt
(B) A picture of the bowl
(C) A completed customer survey
(D) A copy of the instruction manual

199. Why does Mr. Martin refuse to refund Ms. Russell's money?

(A) She did not buy the item from Sussex's Web site.
(B) Her use of the bowl voided the warranty.
(C) Sussex has a policy banning giving refunds.
(D) She bought the item more than one month ago.

200. What does Mr. Martin suggest that Ms. Russell do?

(A) Call him if she has any future problems
(B) Use a coupon to purchase another item
(C) Visit the store and request a refund
(D) Attempt to repair the bowl herself

Stop! This is the end of the test. If you finish before time is called, you may go back to Parts 5, 6, and 7 and check your work.

1.

2.

3.

4.

5.

6.

PART 2

🎧 02-02

Directions: You will hear a question or statement and three responses spoken in English. They will not be printed in your test book and will be spoken only one time. Select the best response to the question or statement and mark the letter (A), (B), or (C) on your answer sheet.

7. Mark your answer on your answer sheet.
8. Mark your answer on your answer sheet.
9. Mark your answer on your answer sheet.
10. Mark your answer on your answer sheet.
11. Mark your answer on your answer sheet.
12. Mark your answer on your answer sheet.
13. Mark your answer on your answer sheet.
14. Mark your answer on your answer sheet.
15. Mark your answer on your answer sheet.
16. Mark your answer on your answer sheet.
17. Mark your answer on your answer sheet.
18. Mark your answer on your answer sheet.
19. Mark your answer on your answer sheet.
20. Mark your answer on your answer sheet.
21. Mark your answer on your answer sheet.
22. Mark your answer on your answer sheet.
23. Mark your answer on your answer sheet.
24. Mark your answer on your answer sheet.
25. Mark your answer on your answer sheet.
26. Mark your answer on your answer sheet.
27. Mark your answer on your answer sheet.
28. Mark your answer on your answer sheet.
29. Mark your answer on your answer sheet.
30. Mark your answer on your answer sheet.
31. Mark your answer on your answer sheet.

PART 3

🎧 02-03

Directions: You will hear some conversations between two or more people. You will be asked to answer three questions about what the speakers say in each conversation. Select the best response to each question and mark the letter (A), (B), (C), or (D) on your answer sheet. The conversations will not be printed in your test book and will be spoken only one time.

32. What is the man's job?

    (A) Museum curator
    (B) Bus driver
    (C) Tour guide
    (D) Artist

33. What does the woman ask about?

    (A) The availability of pamphlets
    (B) The price of tickets
    (C) The history of the building
    (D) The life of John Cumberland

34. What will happen at 11:30?

    (A) A museum will be visited.
    (B) The bus will leave.
    (C) The visitors will enter an art gallery.
    (D) A history lecture will be heard.

35. What is the purpose of the woman's call?

    (A) To ask the man to provide some assistance
    (B) To schedule a job interview
    (C) To offer to work for free
    (D) To learn about an upcoming event

36. What is scheduled for Saturday?

    (A) A beach party
    (B) A charity event
    (C) A special dinner
    (D) A book reading

37. What does the man request that the woman do?

    (A) Visit his organization's Web page
    (B) Meet him in his office
    (C) Call him tomorrow afternoon
    (D) Send her donation by bank transfer

GO ON TO THE NEXT PAGE

38. Where does the conversation take place?

    (A) On a subway
    (B) In a bus terminal
    (C) In an airport
    (D) At a train station

39. What is the woman's problem?

    (A) She bought the wrong ticket.
    (B) She does not have enough money.
    (C) She arrived at her destination late.
    (D) She forgot where she had to go.

40. What will the woman probably do next?

    (A) Get some food
    (B) Purchase a ticket
    (C) Request a refund
    (D) Do some shopping

---

41. Where most likely are the speakers?

    (A) At a law firm
    (B) In a computer laboratory
    (C) In an office
    (D) In a meeting room

42. Why does the man praise the woman?

    (A) She negotiated a contract with a company.
    (B) She found a solution to a problem.
    (C) She saved the company some money.
    (D) She rescheduled a staff meeting.

43. What does the woman say about Info Solutions?

    (A) It has lawyers working at it.
    (B) It charges low prices.
    (C) It has the best maintenance staff.
    (D) It provides effective services.

44. What is the purpose of the man's call?

    (A) To cancel his registration
    (B) To ask to speak to a teacher
    (C) To inquire about a class
    (D) To learn when a class will be held

45. What is suggested about Ms. Pollard?

    (A) She has sold many paintings.
    (B) She works full time at the community center.
    (C) She teaches classes on oil painting.
    (D) She is a popular teacher.

46. What does the man mean when he says, "This must be my lucky day"?

    (A) He is fortunate that there is room in the class.
    (B) He is lucky that he has enough money to pay for the class.
    (C) He is happy that he has met Ms. Pollard before.
    (D) He is pleased that he has free time during the winter.

47. Why is the woman upset?
    (A) Her carpet was not vacuumed.
    (B) Her office was not cleaned.
    (C) The bathrooms are a mess.
    (D) The trashcans were not emptied.

48. What does the man suggest about B&G, Inc.?
    (A) It is going to go out of business soon.
    (B) It does not hire people who do good work.
    (C) It charges more than the current cleaning service.
    (D) It was not selected for a job due to poor performance.

49. What will the woman most likely do next?
    (A) Arrange a meeting
    (B) Make a phone call
    (C) Send an e-mail
    (D) Visit a vendor

50. What is the problem?
    (A) A computer has stopped working.
    (B) The electricity keeps going out.
    (C) The Internet cannot be accessed.
    (D) Some software has problems.

51. What does the man want to do?
    (A) Request the services of a repairperson
    (B) File a report with his supervisor
    (C) Ask his boss to purchase new equipment
    (D) Try to log onto the Internet again

52. What does the woman tell the man to do?
    (A) Visit the Maintenance Department
    (B) Speak with the receptionist
    (C) Look up the correct extension
    (D) Stop trying to repair the problem

53. What are the speakers discussing?
    (A) Their new schedules
    (B) Training some employees
    (C) The company's incoming workers
    (D) Their vacation plans

54. According to the woman, what is the problem?
    (A) Her travel plans have been delayed.
    (B) She does not get along well with her sister.
    (C) There are too many inexperienced people on her shift.
    (D) She cannot work at a time she is scheduled to.

55. Why is the woman pleased?
    (A) She has not seen her sister for many years.
    (B) Dean can work on Wednesday evening.
    (C) Brad is going to help her train the workers.
    (D) She is going to travel to Sydney soon.

GO ON TO THE NEXT PAGE

56. When is the negotiating team going to go to Madrid?
    (A) After work
    (B) Tomorrow
    (C) The day after tomorrow
    (D) This weekend

57. Why does the man say, "That's sufficient"?
    (A) To express his satisfaction with the woman's statement
    (B) To encourage the woman to provide more information
    (C) To reject the suggestion that the woman makes
    (D) To point out a problem with the woman's solution

58. What does the man suggest that the woman do?
    (A) Leave the office soon
    (B) Call Diana Matthews
    (C) Start studying Spanish
    (D) Update her passport

59. Where most likely does the conversation take place?
    (A) At an immigration desk
    (B) At a baggage claim area
    (C) At a check-in counter
    (D) At a boarding gate

60. What does the man suggest?
    (A) Carrying his bags on board
    (B) Filing a claim for a lost bag
    (C) Taking some items out of his bag
    (D) Having his bag X-rayed

61. What does the woman request that the man do?
    (A) Pay an extra fee
    (B) Keep his boarding pass
    (C) Write his name on his bag
    (D) Lock his luggage

62. What is suggested about the speakers?
  (A) They work for the same company.
  (B) They are giving a joint presentation.
  (C) They are employed as engineers.
  (D) They helped design the DV5000.

63. What does the woman mean when she says, "That's a distinct possibility"?
  (A) The engineers may want to redesign the DV5000.
  (B) The DV5000 will probably sell very well.
  (C) There could be problems marketing the DV5000.
  (D) Some people who use the DV5000 may get injured.

64. What is mentioned about the DV5000?
  (A) It is the most expensive iron on the market.
  (B) It has a 98% satisfaction rate.
  (C) Most of its buyers will be able to use it properly.
  (D) The company will market it to young adults.

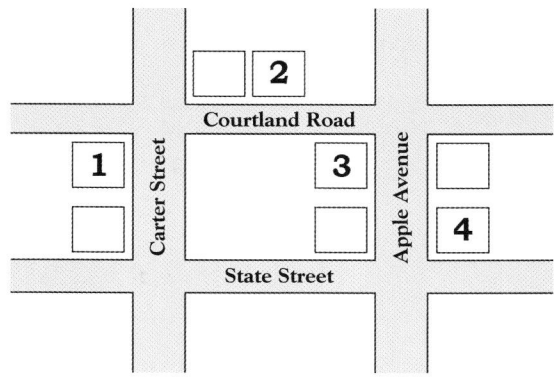

65. Where most likely are the speakers?
  (A) At a bank
  (B) On a street
  (C) In an office
  (D) At a bus stop

66. What does the man say about the bank?
  (A) It has changed locations.
  (B) He keeps his money there.
  (C) The woman should take the bus there.
  (D) It is going to close soon.

67. Look at the graphic. Where is the woman's final destination?
  (A) 1
  (B) 2
  (C) 3
  (D) 4

GO ON TO THE NEXT PAGE

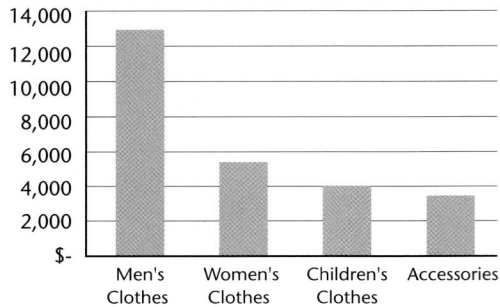

68. What are the speakers mainly discussing?

    (A) The need to sell more clothes
    (B) The poor sales of men's clothes
    (C) The style of clothes being sold
    (D) The store's weekly performance

69. What is suggested about the store?

    (A) It hired some new salespeople.
    (B) It is located in a shopping center.
    (C) It opened a few months ago.
    (D) It sells brand-name items.

70. Look at the graphic. What was the value of the men's clothes sold last week?

    (A) $3,500
    (B) $4,000
    (C) $5,500
    (D) $13,000

PART 4

🎧 02-04

Directions: You will hear some talks given by a single speaker. You will be asked to answer three questions about what the speaker says in each talk. Select the best response to each question and mark the letter (A), (B), (C), or (D) on your answer sheet. The talks will not be printed in your test book and will be spoken only one time.

71. Who most likely is the speaker?
    (A) A radio host
    (B) A music producer
    (C) A music critic
    (D) A singer

72. What happened to Jeff Gonzalez last year?
    (A) He got married.
    (B) He signed a contract.
    (C) He took singing lessons.
    (D) He released his second album.

73. What will the listeners hear next?
    (A) A live performance
    (B) Some commercials
    (C) A traffic update
    (D) Some recorded music

74. What is the purpose of the talk?
    (A) To praise the attendees for their work
    (B) To talk about the release of a new product
    (C) To discuss the results of a survey
    (D) To mention the company's new Web site

75. What does the woman mean when she says, "So we don't need to make any adjustments there"?
    (A) The company will not change its prices.
    (B) No more employees will be hired.
    (C) The Web site does not need to be updated.
    (D) Staff members do not require more training.

76. What does the speaker suggest doing?
    (A) Talking about the critical remarks that were made
    (B) Better educating the company's staff
    (C) Hiring a firm to improve the company's Web site
    (D) Conducting another survey the following month

GO ON TO THE NEXT PAGE

77. Why is the speaker calling?
    (A) To confirm an order
    (B) To describe a special offer
    (C) To advertise a new position
    (D) To request payment of a bill

78. What can Mr. Marino get for $40?
    (A) Cable TV installation
    (B) Triple the number of movie channels
    (C) Cable TV for three months
    (D) Double the number of sports channels

79. What does the caller request that Mr. Marino do?
    (A) Fill out an online form
    (B) Visit his workplace
    (C) Return his phone call
    (D) Complete a survey

80. What is the purpose of the talk?
    (A) To go over some rules
    (B) To ask for assistance
    (C) To give an explanation
    (D) To request an apology

81. What must the listeners do before installing software on their computers?
    (A) Make sure it is compatible with the computer
    (B) Purchase it properly
    (C) Receive permission
    (D) Prove its importance to their work

82. What does the speaker indicate about the computers?
    (A) They must be turned off every night.
    (B) They are the most recently released models.
    (C) They should be scanned for viruses daily.
    (D) They must only be used for work.

83. Why is the train delayed?
    (A) It collided with a vehicle on the tracks.
    (B) There is an object on the tracks.
    (C) The train suffered a mechanical problem.
    (D) Bad weather is making it go slowly.

84. When is the train expected to arrive?
    (A) In thirty minutes
    (B) In one hour
    (C) In one and a half hours
    (D) In two hours

85. What can listeners receive in the departure lounge?
    (A) Refunds
    (B) Free upgrades
    (C) Complimentary snacks
    (D) New tickets

86. What is the speaker's problem?
    (A) She forgot about her appointment.
    (B) She has to cancel her daughter's appointment.
    (C) She will be late for her appointment.
    (D) She cannot make it to her appointment.

87. When does the speaker have time?
    (A) On Wednesday morning
    (B) On Wednesday afternoon
    (C) On Thursday morning
    (D) On Thursday afternoon

88. How does the speaker want to change her appointment?
    (A) By getting only a haircut
    (B) By getting her hair dyed
    (C) By getting a perm
    (D) By getting her hair straightened

89. Where mostly likely are the listeners?

    (A) At a meeting
    (B) At an awards ceremony
    (C) At a retirement party
    (D) At an orientation session

90. What does the speaker mean when he says, "We had an eventful year full of ups and downs"?

    (A) The company made more money than it spent.
    (B) More negative events than positive events occurred.
    (C) There were both good and bad events that happened.
    (D) The future is going to be more positive than negative.

91. What is going to happen next?

    (A) A speech will be given.
    (B) Music will be performed.
    (C) Dinner will be served.
    (D) An award will be presented.

Dessert	Quantity
Cupcakes	45
Brownies	70
Cheesecake (Slices)	35
Muffins	50

92. Why is there a problem?

    (A) Some people are vegetarians.
    (B) Some people cannot eat certain types of food.
    (C) Some people dislike sugary foods.
    (D) Some people do not like to eat chocolate.

93. Look at the graphic. How many items must be replaced?

    (A) 35
    (B) 45
    (C) 50
    (D) 70

94. What will the listeners most likely do next?

    (A) Contact the caterer
    (B) Look at a menu
    (C) Sample some food
    (D) Visit a bakery

GO ON TO THE NEXT PAGE

State	Number of Restaurants
Indiana	27
Ohio	14
Oklahoma	17
Tennessee	10

Day	Doctor
Monday	Dr. Brandt
Tuesday	Dr. Murphy
Wednesday	Dr. Fuji
Thursday	Dr. DeLorean

95. What does the speaker indicate about the restaurants in Alabama?

    (A) They are closing down.
    (B) They are expanding.
    (C) They are making money.
    (D) They are losing money.

96. What does the speaker say must be done?

    (A) New franchise owners must be chosen.
    (B) New menu items must be selected.
    (C) New locations must be decided upon.
    (D) New prices must be established.

97. Look at the graphic. How many restaurants are performing well?

    (A) 17
    (B) 31
    (C) 37
    (D) 51

98. Why will Dr. Russell be away from the office?

    (A) He is going on vacation with his family.
    (B) He has become too ill to work.
    (C) He is attending an educational event.
    (D) He will work at another hospital.

99. Look at the graphic. Who will Ms. Kimball's replacement doctor be?

    (A) Dr. Fuji
    (B) Dr. DeLorean
    (C) Dr. Brandt
    (D) Dr. Murphy

100. What does the speaker request that Ms. Kimball do?

    (A) Send her an e-mail
    (B) Complete an online form
    (C) Make a phone call
    (D) Visit another clinic

This is the end of the Listening test. Turn to Part 5 in your test book.

NO TEST MATERIAL ON THIS PAGE

READING TEST

In the Reading test, you will read a variety of texts and answer several different types of reading comprehension questions. The entire Reading test will last 75 minutes. There are three parts, and directions are given for each part. You are encouraged to answer as many questions as possible within the time allowed.

You must mark your answers on the separate answer sheet. Do not write your answers in your test book.

PART 5

Directions: A word or phrase is missing in each of the sentences below. Four answer choices are given below each sentence. Select the best answer to complete the sentence. Then mark the letter (A), (B), (C), or (D) on your answer sheet.

101. Part of the ------- of the new café is that its outdoor seating overlooks the nearby lake.

(A) appeal
(B) consent
(C) standard
(D) model

102. Ms. Blaire has been working tirelessly to improve the ------- environment in the office.

(A) worked
(B) worker
(C) working
(D) works

103. ------- remains to be determined is how much money will be allocated to the department's budget.

(A) That
(B) How
(C) What
(D) Which

104. Mr. Thompson's secretary told him to call the vice president as soon as he ------- back from lunch.

(A) returned
(B) called
(C) stayed
(D) arrived

105. Ms. Hampton decided to take her vacation in the first week of August ------- on a trip abroad with her family.

(A) go
(B) going
(C) to go
(D) will go

106. Reserving tickets in advance is recommended for those who want to be ------- close to the stage.

(A) seats
(B) seating
(C) seated
(D) seater

107. ------- all of the promotions have been confirmed, the names and positions will be posted on the company Web page.

(A) Once
(B) Therefore
(C) In spite of
(D) With regard to

108. In order to gain a ------- advantage over their rivals, the company supervisors decided to pursue graduate studies.

(A) compete
(B) competitive
(C) competition
(D) competing

109. Ms. Jameson of Eager Travel called the office to provide the ------- for Mr. Smith's upcoming business trip.

(A) itinerary
(B) roster
(C) ticket
(D) lease

110. The computer system was malfunctioning and would not ------- any users to log on to the Internet.

(A) allow
(B) report
(C) enter
(D) submit

111. Mr. McGregor ------- machines for Ernst Welding for more than two decades.

(A) is repairing
(B) has been repairing
(C) was repaired
(D) had been repaired

112. Unless Mr. Murray's train arrives ------- the next ten minutes, he is going to be late for the meeting.

(A) by
(B) for
(C) within
(D) about

113. The captain announced that the plane was being sent to another airport due to the poor ------- in the Chicago area.

(A) vision
(B) visible
(C) visibility
(D) visibly

114. Driving without lights at night is hazardous not only to other drivers ------- to pedestrians.

(A) and so
(B) but also
(C) nor
(D) as with

115. Many of the employees expressed their ------- at being obligated to work overtime on the weekend.

(A) frustrate
(B) frustrating
(C) frustrated
(D) frustration

116. All those ------- pass the first stage in the application process will be invited to have an interview at the company's headquarters.

(A) which
(B) who
(C) where
(D) whom

GO ON TO THE NEXT PAGE

117. Mr. Wilkins encourages his employees to ------- with one another to help them improve their teamwork.

(A) interact
(B) discuss
(C) combine
(D) reveal

118. The CEO is scheduled to take a tour of the new manufacturing facility the day before it ------- opens.

(A) officiate
(B) official
(C) office
(D) officially

119. Customers at Davis Consulting are encouraged to provide ------- of either a positive or negative nature.

(A) response
(B) promotion
(C) feedback
(D) reaction

120. The mechanic indicated that the car had suffered serious engine problems and ------- a week to be repaired.

(A) will be taking
(B) would take
(C) has been taken
(D) was taken

121. ------- ten people rejected the manager's request to work overtime on the holiday weekend.

(A) As much as
(B) No fewer than
(C) At around
(D) With about

122. Tickets for the musical may be ------- online or by calling the box office at 509-5430.

(A) purchased
(B) demanded
(C) reviewed
(D) donated

123. Katmandu Travel ------- in guided tours of some of the most fascinating places in Southeast Asia.

(A) specializing
(B) has been specialized
(C) specializes
(D) was specialized

124. Only ------- personnel are permitted to walk through the lower levels of the research facility without an escort.

(A) authority
(B) authorized
(C) authorities
(D) authorizing

125. ------- the two employees have some differences, they also share quite a large number of similarities.

(A) Because
(B) Therefore
(C) If
(D) While

126. While Rabbit Logistics charges high prices, it guarantees ------- the packages it delivers will arrive on time.

(A) what
(B) that
(C) which
(D) when

127. Although the marketing campaign was widely hailed as a success, ------- at J. Gilman, Inc. actually declined in the last quarter.

(A) revenue
(B) sale
(C) product
(D) quantity

128. The first step ------- sales is to make solid connections with one's client base.

(A) improves
(B) being improved
(C) to improving
(D) have been improving

129. Ervin Textiles sells high-quality products made domestically at ------- prices anyone can afford.

(A) reasoning
(B) reason
(C) reasonable
(D) reasonably

130. The firm is going to bring in several outside experts to ------- what the cause of all the problems is.

(A) determine
(B) approach
(C) regulate
(D) discuss

GO ON TO THE NEXT PAGE

PART 6

Directions: Read the texts that follow. A word, phrase, or sentence is missing in parts of each text. Four answer choices for each question are given below the text. Select the best answer to complete the text. Then mark the letter (A), (B), (C), or (D) on your answer sheet.

Questions 131-134 refer to the following advertisement.

Darby's Printing Services

--------- Darby's Printing Services has just opened for business. We are located at 67 Washburn Avenue and are right across the street from the Whitman Steakhouse. --------- we may be a new business, our employees are old hands at the printing industry. Clarence Darby, the owner, has more than five decades of experience in the industry, and his employees have been working for more than two decades each.

To celebrate the opening of our store, --------- service we provide will be available at a 40% discount during our first week of business. So come here and have your company reports printed. Or request new business cards. We can print signs, advertisements, and posters as well. If it has anything to do with printing, we are the ---------. Call us at 701-7649 or visit our Web site at www.darbysprinting.com to learn more about us and to see how much we charge for our services. We hope to see you soon.

131. (A) Darby's Printing Services is reopening its doors.
(B) There's a new store in town, and we want to serve you.
(C) Thanks for making our first week in business a success.
(D) Darby's Printing Services is celebrating its tenth year of doing business.

132. (A) While
(B) However
(C) Since
(D) If

133. (A) some
(B) which
(C) every
(D) that

134. (A) sellers
(B) designers
(C) architects
(D) experts

Questions 135-138 refer to the following article.

Odessa Spring Festival Comes to an End

Odessa (May 10) – After five days, the Odessa Spring Festival came to its -------- **135.** yesterday. The festival finished with a fireworks show above Big Bass Lake that lasted until late at night.

-------- **136.** This was the first time since 2011 that the festival received five straight days of sunny weather. The temperature was also unseasonably high, which made for a more pleasant -------- **137.** for most of the attendees. Festival organizer Diane Armstrong said, "I can't think of a single thing that went wrong this year. I'm pleased that we had a great festival and that so many people from the local community came here to support us."

On the last day of the festival, the annual fishing contest was held. The winner was Pete Wellman, who caught six fish -------- **138.** a combined total of 11.4 kilograms. He is a three-time winner of the contest, having won it last year as well as six years ago.

135. (A) conclusion
 (B) final
 (C) stop
 (D) over

136. (A) The festival's organizers hope the sunny skies will attract many people.
 (B) Not as many people as expected visited the festival due to the heavy rain.
 (C) There were a number of problems at the festival, especially the weather.
 (D) This year's festival was widely considered the most successful in recent years.

137. (A) attempt
 (B) experience
 (C) visualization
 (D) appearance

138. (A) weigh
 (B) weighted
 (C) weighing
 (D) weighs

GO ON TO THE NEXT PAGE

Questions 139-142 refer to the following e-mail.

To: Wilma Arlington <wilma_a@trr.com>

From: Chad Silva <csilva@trr.com>

Re: Orientation

Date: August 24

Wilma,

As you are aware, the orientation session for new employees is scheduled for next Monday, August 31. Unfortunately, there's a slight problem. Matt Powell was supposed --------- the session. However, he just submitted his resignation this morning, so the CEO doesn't want him running the ---------. Mr. Jenkins instead suggested that you be responsible for everything. I know you've never done this before, but it's a fairly straightforward --------- I can get you up to speed on everything you need to do and let you know what must be done before next Monday as well. --------- Why don't we get together today? I'm going to be out of the office until around 2 in the afternoon. But I'm available any time after then until 6 in the evening. How about leaving a text message for me on my cell phone since I can't check my e-mail while I'm out of the office? My number is (205) 365-8434.

I will wait for your response.

Sincerely,

Chad Silva

139. (A) leading
(B) led
(C) to lead
(D) have led

140. (A) negotiation
(B) program
(C) ceremony
(D) workplace

141. (A) process
(B) procession
(C) processed
(D) processing

142. (A) It would be ideal for us to meet in person soon.
(B) Let's talk on the phone to cover all the details.
(C) I'm going to be away from the office until tomorrow.
(D) We don't want there to be mistakes like the last time.

Questions 143-146 refer to the following memo.

To: All Employees

From: Rachel Hunter, HR Department

Subject: Internal Transfers

Date: October 2

--------- **143.** The forms for transfer can be picked up in the HR Department or may be downloaded from the company Web site at www.jacksons.com/transfers. They must be completed in full, signed by your direct supervisor, and submitted no later than October 10. Any other paperwork that is required should be turned in --------- **144.** your application. Be sure to state which department or branch you are applying to and why you would like to work there.

Please note that we have opened several new branches in foreign countries this year. We now have branches in Brazil, South Africa, Singapore, China, and Australia. If you are interested in transferring to one of these branches, you must be --------- **145.** in the primary language spoken in that particular country. Contact me anytime at extension 33 if you have any questions or concerns --------- **146.** transferring.

143. (A) We have just hired several new employees here.
(B) It is time to start considering employees for promotions.
(C) HR is currently accepting applications for internal transfers.
(D) You need to prepare for your annual employee evaluations.

144. (A) in lieu of
(B) regardless of
(C) along with
(D) with respect to

145. (A) fluent
(B) talkative
(C) aware
(D) prepared

146. (A) regards
(B) regardless
(C) regarding
(D) regarded

GO ON TO THE NEXT PAGE

PART 7

Directions: In this part your will read a selection of texts, such as magazine and newspaper articles, e-mails, and instant messages. Each text or set of texts is followed by several questions. Select the best answer for each question and mark the letter (A), (B), (C), or (D) on your answer sheet.

Questions 147-148 refer to the following e-mail.

TO Joan Jackson <jjackson1@gumpers.com>
FROM Marvin White <mwhite@gumpers.com>
SUBJECT Reimbursement
DATE February 16

Dear Ms. Jackson,

It has come to my attention that your request for reimbursement for your latest sales trip is incomplete. You failed to submit several receipts along with your reimbursement claim form. For one, you wrote that you stayed at the Old Country Inn in Davenport for three nights, but you turned in a receipt for a two-night stay. You are also missing receipts for several meal claims at restaurants and for a visit to a gas station you said you made. The company's policy regarding reimbursements is clear. All receipts must be included in the request. You must give me the missing receipts by the end of the week in order to receive the full amount you are requesting. Please drop by my office (room 509) anytime if you have any questions regarding this matter.

Sincerely,

Marvin White
Senior Accountant
Gumpers, Inc.

147. What is indicated about Ms. Jackson?

(A) She will turn in a form this Friday.
(B) She is moving to Davenport soon.
(C) She went on a sales trip recently.
(D) She rented a car while on a trip.

148. How can Ms. Jackson solve her problem?

(A) By submitting some missing receipts
(B) By filling out a form correctly
(C) By adjusting the claims that she is making
(D) By providing her bank account information

Questions 149-150 refer to the following instructions.

Grasshopper 350 Laptop Computer Warranty

The warranty for this item is valid for two years after the date of purchase on your receipt. Please read the instructions on this warranty carefully. Failure to follow any of the instructions will instantly invalidate the warranty.

* Do not open the computer's casing at any time.
* Do not attempt to repair this machine or to replace any part of it by yourself.
* Do not connect the computer with a power cable made by any company other than Grasshopper.
* Do not immerse the product in water or other liquids.
* Do not place the computer near sources of high heat, such as an oven, or extreme cold, such as a refrigerator.
* Do not use software that has been illegally downloaded.

For questions regarding this warranty, visit www.grasshopper.com/350laptopwarranty or contact the nearest Grasshopper dealer.

149. Who are these instructions for?

(A) Computer designers
(B) Computer dealers
(C) Computer owners
(D) Computer repair people

150. What is NOT mentioned in the instructions?

(A) The computer should not be put near places with low temperatures.
(B) Only software made by Grasshopper should be used on the computer.
(C) More information about the warranty can be found at a Web site.
(D) There should be no attempt to fix any problems with the computer.

Questions 151-152 refer to the following text message chain.

Treadway, Peter   1:24 P.M.

Thanks for accepting our offer. We at the Trueheart Clinic are looking forward to you working with us.

Grant, Marcus   1:26 P.M.

I'm glad we're going to be colleagues soon.

Treadway, Peter   1:29 P.M.

So do you have any questions about your compensation package? The salary and benefits are fine, right?

Grant, Marcus   1:31 P.M.

Correct. I'm pleased with everything you offered me at today's meeting. Do I need to sign a contract or something?

Treadway, Peter   1:32 P.M.

Yes. I'll e-mail it to you sometime later in the day.

Grant, Marcus   1:35 P.M.

Sounds good. You know, you mentioned that you wanted me to start working on April 28, but I can start anytime beginning on April 20 if you need me to.

Treadway, Peter   1:38 P.M.

I'll have to get back to you on that. But I'll let Dr. Hearst know what you just told me.

---

151. What is mainly being discussed?

(A) A contract negotiation
(B) The terms of a new job
(C) An upcoming promotion
(D) A transfer to a new branch

152. At 1:38 P.M., why does Mr. Treadway write, "I'll have to get back to you on that"?

(A) He is unable to tell Mr. Grant when to start working.
(B) He does not want to give Mr. Grant a negative response.
(C) He cannot offer Mr. Grant a higher salary or more benefits.
(D) He is going to provide a date for the meeting later.

Questions 153-155 refer to the following advertisement.

Good Times Studio

Good Times Studio is a family-owned photography studio specializing in capturing the monumental moments of people's lives. Our photographers understand the minute details of outdoor photography, so they can record precious moments at events such as birthdays, graduations, weddings, and anniversaries. The pictures they take will provide you with memories that will last a lifetime. Our hard work starts even before the event begins. Good Times specialists will provide advice on where to stage your events to ensure that the sun, weather, and background will contribute to taking the best shots possible. Our objective is for everyone to see you at your best. For those individuals who come to our studio for photographs, we can provide you with everything you need, from photographs for passports and identification cards to family portraits. While walks-in are accepted at the studio, we typically require a week's notice for special events. Earlier booking, however, is recommended. Call 737-3921 for more reservations and pricing information.

153. Who most likely would need the services of Good Times Studio?

(A) A family that wants their picture painted
(B) A photographer who is looking for a job
(C) A student who needs to make an ID card
(D) Newlyweds that are going on their honeymoon

154. According to the advertisement, what do the specialists at Good Times Studio do?

(A) Choose the locations of events
(B) Decide what time events will be held
(C) Discuss weather conditions with clients
(D) Tell people what to wear to events

155. What is NOT indicated about Good Times Studio?

(A) It accepts reservations over the telephone.
(B) It takes pictures in the studio and in other places.
(C) It requires some events to be reserved in advance.
(D) It charges extra for pictures taken outside the studio.

GO ON TO THE NEXT PAGE

Questions 156-158 refer to the following notice.

Transfer Applications

Due to the high number of overseas transfer requests made in recent months, the Human Resources (HR) Department has decided to implement some rules regarding future requests that are effective immediately. First, all requests must be submitted on the proper form. It can be found on the HR Department intranet site. From now on, informal requests submitted by e-mail will no longer be accepted and will simply be disregarded. Second, the transfer request form must be properly filled out in its entirety, or it will be rejected. —[1]—. Third, a decision has been made to limit the number of transfers made by employees in each department. In any six-month period, no more than two employees from the same department may transfer abroad. —[2]—. The final rule is only being implemented for the remainder of the calendar year. No more employees may transfer to Mexico or Italy as both places are fully staffed. However, the branches in Sweden, Poland, and Germany are still undermanned and could use some assistance. —[3]—. Please note that facility in the language spoken in the country you are applying to be transferred to will greatly improve your chances of being selected for a position. As always, please remember that the head of your department and the company president must give their final approval for your transfer request for it to go into effect. —[4]—.

156. How can employees apply for a transfer?

(A) By submitting an e-mailed request
(B) By speaking with their department head
(C) By visiting the Human Resources Department
(D) By downloading a form on their computers

157. Which rule is in effect for a limited amount of time?

(A) Employees cannot apply to transfer to certain company offices.
(B) The head of a department must approve an employee transfer.
(C) Only two employees may transfer from a department every two months.
(D) Employees transferring must be able to speak a foreign language.

158. In which of the positions marked [1], [2], [3], and [4] does the following sentence best belong?

"If any part of the form happens to be left blank or is filled in improperly, it will be discarded."

(A) [1]
(B) [2]
(C) [3]
(D) [4]

Questions 159-161 refer to the following schedule.

Columbus Weekly Newsletter

The following events are scheduled in Columbus for the week beginning on June 15.

Monday, June 16

The Columbus Public Swimming Pool will offer swimming lessons between the hours of 8 A.M. and 10 A.M. Children ages four to thirteen are eligible for the lessons, which are free of charge. Those families wishing to become members of the pool will receive 30% discounts on an annual membership if they sign up on that day.

Thursday, June 19

A book reading will be held at the West Street Library at 1:00 P.M. Noted children's author Dee Matthews will read from her latest book, *My Pet Dragon*. Both children and their parents are welcome to attend. The reading will take place in the children's section on the first floor. Some light refreshments will be served.

Saturday, June 21

The annual 10-kilometer summer road race will start at city hall at 9 A.M. The course will take runners through historic downtown Columbus and will end at Broadway Park. Call 495-3939 for more information or to register to run in the race. At 11:00 A.M., the first annual summer picnic will be held in Broadway Park. There will be games, live music, and other entertainment. Hamburgers, hotdogs, and chicken, as well as numerous side dishes, will be served. Adults must pay $5 and children $3 for lunch.

159. For whom is the schedule most likely intended?

(A) Local high school students
(B) Residents of Columbus
(C) Shopkeepers in Columbus
(D) Students on summer vacation

160. What will participants at the June 19 event do?

(A) Ask an author questions
(B) Listen to a writer read a book
(C) Get a person's autograph
(D) Learn how to write a book

161. According to the schedule, what will attendees at the June 21 event NOT be able to do?

(A) Attend a baseball game
(B) Listen to music being performed
(C) Participate in a running race
(D) Purchase some food

Questions 162-164 refer to the following memo.

TO: Stan Erickson, Accounting Department
FROM: Mika Oh, Sales Department
RE: Training
DATE: March 14

The Sales Department officially requests extra funding to be able to train some of our sales staff. To be specific, we would like funds so that three individuals can attend the special event being hosted by Walter Perkins in Los Angeles on April 5 and 6. I have attached a brochure for the two-day seminar for you to examine. Mr. Perkins is an expert in sales strategies and on the art of closing deals. Those individuals who have attended his seminars in the past have attested to the value of the information they acquired. We believe that by sending three members of our sales team (Jodie Welch, Alana Monroe, and Jeff Stevens), they will personally benefit. In addition, those three members, who are among the top people in the department, have agreed to provide training based on what they learn about Mr. Perkins's methods to the other staff members. The cost for all three people, including transportation, accommodations, food, and registration fees, should not exceed $5,000. We require a response no later than March 22 since it is the last day that registration for the event is possible. Please call me at extension 798 if you need more information.

162. Why did Ms. Oh write the memo?

(A) To describe the benefits of an upcoming seminar
(B) To encourage employees to register for an event
(C) To give permission to some employees to go to a seminar
(D) To request money for people to attend an event

163. Who is Alana Monroe?

(A) A special lecturer
(B) A member of the Sales Department
(C) An accountant
(D) A trainer in sales methods personally

164. What is NOT indicated about the seminar?

(A) A brochure describing it has been published.
(B) It will be held in Los Angeles for two days.
(C) Discounts are given to those registering in groups.
(D) There is a deadline for signing up for it.

Questions 165-167 refer to the following article.

Economy Showing Signs of Life

Lakeland Hills (October 25) — All across the country, countless cities and states are raising the minimum wage in an effort to improve their struggling economies. However, here in Lakeland Hills, Mayor Rush Nelson and the city council have been attempting another strategy, and it appears to be paying off as the city is showing signs of emerging from the lengthy recession that began when Mark Sanders was mayor.

Mr. Nelson encouraged the city council to slash local taxes, including both the city's sales tax and property tax, around half a year ago. While some council members and local residents protested the decision, it appears as though Mr. Nelson's move was the right one. Not only have several local companies started hiring new employees, but a few businesses in nearby places have also shuttered their doors and moved to the business-friendly confines of Lakeland Hills. The owners of these companies specifically mentioned the city's low tax rate as the primary reason for moving.

In the past four months, unemployment has dropped steadily and now stands at only 4.2%. That is much better than the 7.4% rate for the entire state. Thanks to the city's booming economy, tax revenues have gone up despite the decrease in tax rates. This is enabling the city to pay for improvements in infrastructure that have long been needed. Among these projects are the repaving of parts of Main Street and Oak Avenue and the construction of another bridge across the Golden River.

165. What happened when Mr. Sanders was the mayor?

(A) The unemployment rate in Lakeland Hills improved.
(B) The economy of Lakeland Hills got worse.
(C) Many residents of Lakeland Hills moved away.
(D) Taxes were raised higher than normal.

166. What did Mr. Nelson do six months ago?

(A) Requested that taxes in the city be lowered
(B) Won an election against Mr. Sanders
(C) Opened his own business in Lakeland Hills
(D) Decided to stop collecting property taxes

167. What is stated about Lakeland Hills's current economic situation?

(A) Businesses are departing the region for nearby cities.
(B) The unemployment rate in the local area is 7.4%.
(C) It is good enough to pay to improve some streets.
(D) Less tax revenue than normal is being collected.

Questions 168-171 refer to the following e-mail.

To: Emily Williams <ewilliams@tayloraccounting.com>
From: Gwen Scott <gwen_s@tayloraccounting.com>
Subject: Thanks
Date: April 28

Emily,

I really appreciate your agreeing to handle my clients while I'm away on my honeymoon in Hawaii. It's such a comforting feeling knowing that everyone will be in your capable hands.

To make the process go as smoothly as possible, I thought I should provide you with a few notes regarding some clients you'll be handling. First off, the file examination for the Westside Bakery tax report hasn't been done yet because Mr. Thompson hasn't submitted all of his information to us. He said he'll do that by May 1. The examination was set to take place on May 3 but has been bumped back by two days. It will still occur at the same place and time though. Second, the Douglas Bank file can wait a while, so I'm going to work on it when I return. If anyone from the bank calls, remind them that I spoke with Alicia Franks and confirmed my plans with her. Last, and most importantly, the Baker Construction account needs to be reexamined from top to bottom. City inspectors are investigating the construction of Lincoln Stadium, which Baker is working on, so you need to read everything in the file to make sure there's nothing unusual. Sorry for dumping that one on you, but I only found out about it this morning.

That's everything you need to know. I'll be leaving the day after tomorrow and will return in ten days. If anything comes up, you know how to reach me. Thanks again. I owe you big time.

Best,

Gwen

168. Why was the e-mail written?

(A) To request that some meetings be scheduled
(B) To provide some work instructions
(C) To thank a person for the work she did
(D) To apologize for a heavy workload

169. What is suggested about Ms. Scott?

(A) She runs the Accounting Department.
(B) She will visit Douglas Bank today.
(C) She needs to meet Alicia Franks.
(D) She is getting married soon.

170. Why has the work for Westside Bakery been delayed?

(A) The owner only wants to work with Ms. Scott.
(B) Some information is missing.
(C) A payment has not been made yet.
(D) The client is not available.

171. What does Ms. Scott mention about Baker Construction?

(A) It is one of her newest clients.
(B) It just signed a contract to build a stadium.
(C) It is in danger of going out of business.
(D) It is being investigated by the government.

GO ON TO THE NEXT PAGE

Questions 172-175 refer to the following online message chain.

Ortega, Pedro [2:12 P.M.]		Great news, everyone. Mr. Butler just informed me that our team has been selected to work on the Madison account.
Atwell, Gary [2:15 P.M.]		Seriously? That's awesome news. I was expecting it to be given to Samantha's team.
Struthers, Lucy [2:16 P.M.]		So was I. How did we manage to get it?
Ortega, Pedro [2:19 P.M.]		I had a long chat with Mr. Butler and informed him that we're up to the task. So don't let me down. The company has high expectations for this account.
Struthers, Lucy [2:21 P.M.]		We'll do our best. Oh . . . do we need to get together for a meeting sometime soon?
Ortega, Pedro [2:23 P.M.]		Yes, that's one of the reasons I'm writing to both of you. I won't be back at the office until 4:30, so how about getting together at 5:00 to discuss what needs to be done this week?
Atwell, Gary [2:24 P.M.]		Sure. I can do that. How about you, Lucy?
Struthers, Lucy [2:24 P.M.]		That works for me as well.
Atwell, Gary [2:25 P.M.]		Shall I talk to Denise and have her reserve the small conference room on the third floor? That will give us a quiet place to meet.
Ortega, Pedro [2:27 P.M.]		I'd appreciate that, Gary. Lucy, could you go into my office and print three copies of the report sitting on my desk, please? It's in a yellow folder labeled "Madison." You can't miss it.
Struthers, Lucy [2:30 P.M.]		Consider it done. See you in a couple of hours, Pedro.

172. What is mostly being discussed?

(A) The work that has been done on a new project
(B) The competition against Samantha's team
(C) The requirements for the Madison account
(D) Preparations for a meeting on a new account

173. How did Mr. Ortega get the Madison account?

(A) By meeting the CEO of Madison, Inc. in person
(B) By convincing Mr. Butler to give him the project
(C) By working harder than Samantha's team
(D) By performing better than the company's other teams

174. What will Mr. Atwell probably do next?

(A) Visit Mr. Ortega's office
(B) Read a file on the Madison account
(C) Make arrangements to book a room
(D) Get together with Ms. Struthers

175. At 2:30 P.M., what does Ms. Struthers mean when she writes, "Consider it done"?

(A) She has already complied with Mr. Ortega's request.
(B) She is going to do her best on the Madison account.
(C) She will copy the files that Mr. Ortega asked about.
(D) She is looking forward to discussing the new assignment.

Questions 176-180 refer to the following memo and survey.

To: All Staff, Fairview Convention Center
From: Helga Matzner
Subject: Upcoming Conference
Date: October 12

We're only three days away from the start of the annual National Geologists' Conference that's set to take place from October 15 to 17. We need to make sure everything is prepared since the attendees are going to begin arriving to check out the premises tomorrow. Please remember that most of the attendees will be staying at the Emporium Hotel or the Marconi Hotel. Since the Marconi Hotel is right across the street from the convention center, those individuals can get here with no problem. But we'll be running a complimentary shuttle bus to the Emporium every 30 minutes from 8 A.M. to 10 P.M. on all three days of the conference. It takes roughly 25 minutes to get here from the hotel, so we'll have a couple of buses running nonstop. Those of you who are responsible for the electronics need to double-check everything to make sure we don't have any glitches. And we need to confirm with the caterers that the snacks, sandwiches, and drinks are going to arrive exactly when they need to be here. Let's do our best to make this a successful conference.

Fairview Convention Center
Survey Card

Thank you for attending an event at the Fairview Convention Center. In order to improve the quality of the service we provide, please take a few moments to fill out this card and to answer the questions in full.

Name: *Rupert Helmond*
Event: *National Geologists' Conference*
Date(s) Attended: *October 15-17*
E-Mail: *rupert@gemstones.org*
Telephone Number: *(604) 455-5847*

How did you feel about the following:

	Conference Organization	Professionalism of the Staff	Shuttle Bus	Overall Quality of the Conference
Outstanding		✓	✓	
Good	✓			✓
Poor				
Terrible				

Comments: *This was the first event I ever attended at your convention center. However, I have attended numerous conferences at other similar centers. Your staff members compare very favorably to those individuals working at those places. Anytime I had a problem, a staff member was able to assist me almost immediately. The shuttle bus was impressive as well. I took it several times, and not once was it late. There were a couple of problems with the electronics malfunctioning during speeches though. For example, a microphone stopped working for around ten minutes during one individual's speech. But the conference went quite well overall.*

176. Why did Ms. Matzner write the memo?

(A) To review how well a conference went
(B) To discuss some final preparations
(C) To provide an overview of the day's events
(D) To mention some changes in plans

177. According to the memo, what is true about the attendees at the conference?

(A) Most of them have never visited Fairview before.
(B) They are all staying at the Marconi Hotel.
(C) A few of them have not registered yet.
(D) Some of them will arrive on October 13.

178. What does the memo NOT mention about the conference?

(A) People interested in geology will be attending it.
(B) The shuttle bus for passengers will be free of charge.
(C) It is going to last for three days.
(D) Attendees must pay for the catered food.

179. How does Mr. Helmond feel about the staff at the Fairview Convention Center?

(A) They were not very knowledgeable.
(B) They provided him with lots of help.
(C) They acted rudely to attendees at times.
(D) They made the conference a success.

180. What is suggested about Mr. Helmond?

(A) He stayed at the Emporium Hotel.
(B) He is a professor of geology.
(C) He is a resident of Fairview.
(D) He has an interest in electronics.

GO ON TO THE NEXT PAGE

Questions 181-185 refer to the following advertisement and letter.

Morrell Bank Seeks New Employee

Morrell Bank, one of the oldest banks in the state of Texas, is looking for a qualified individual to manage its branch on Gila Street in Waco.

Responsibilities: The manager will be responsible for the daily operations of the bank. He or she will be in charge of looking after the financial stability of the bank and will give final approval for all loan applications. The manager will also make sure the employees at the branch are providing quality service and are sufficiently representing the values of Morrell Bank.

Qualifications: The manager should have the following qualifications:
- Have a minimum of five years of experience in a supervisory position at a bank
- Be outgoing and get along well with others
- Have a thorough knowledge of the banking industry, finance, and economics
- Be a good organizer

How to Apply: Qualified applicants should send a résumé, a cover letter, and the names of and contact information for three professional references to Urania Desmond, HR Director, Morrell Bank, 46 Alamo Drive, Dallas, TX. Ms. Desmond may be contacted with any questions at udesmond@morrellbank.com.

Morrell Bank is an equal opportunity employer and does not discriminate on the basis of an individual's age, gender, or ethnicity.

Urania Desmond
HR Director
Morrell Bank
46 Alamo Drive
Dallas, Texas

August 2

Harry Astley
302 Rio Grande Boulevard
Waco, TX

Dear Mr. Astley,

Thank you for submitting your application for branch manager at the Morrell Bank in Waco. In normal situations, I would not be contacting you since you have only managed Freedom Bank for the past couple of years. However, I am aware of how well your bank is doing, so I took the liberty of speaking with two of the references you provided. Both of them spoke about you in glowing terms. They stressed that you not only possess a keen financial mind but that you also are good with people and that your employees all like you.

You sound like the kind of individual who would excel at Morrell Bank. As such, I would like to invite you to interview for the position. While the job is in Waco, the first interview will be held at our headquarters in Dallas. We have scheduled you for an interview on Saturday, August 16, at 10 A.M. If you can interview then, a first-class round-trip plane ticket from Waco to Dallas will be reserved for you, and we will also book you a room at the Emerson Hotel. Please note that should you do well, we will conduct a second interview at the Waco branch where you would be working. That interview would take place on August 30.

Please call me at (382) 634-6468 to confirm that you will be interviewing with us.

Sincerely,
Urania Desmond
HR Director
Morrell Bank

181. What is the bank manager expected to do?

(A) Interview individuals requesting loans
(B) Organize training sessions for employees
(C) Oversee all matters related to personnel
(D) Confirm that employees are doing their duties

182. How can people apply for the position?

(A) By filling out an application on a Web page
(B) By submitting their applications by e-mail
(C) By sending their applications in the mail
(D) By turning in their applications in person

183. According to Ms. Desmond, why is Mr. Astley NOT qualified for the position?

(A) He has poor organizational skills.
(B) He does not have a degree in economics.
(C) He has fewer than five years of experience.
(D) He has never worked at a bank before.

184. In the letter, the word "keen" in paragraph 1, line 5 is closest in meaning to

(A) sharp
(B) curious
(C) adequate
(D) precise

185. What is Mr. Astley asked to do?

(A) Reserve a plane ticket to Dallas
(B) Confirm he can interview on August 16
(C) Send an e-mail to Ms. Desmond
(D) Visit Waco for an interview on August 30

Questions 186-190 refer to the following advertisement and e-mails.

Harper Realtor
86 Peachtree Boulevard
Atlanta, GA
Tel: 731-4932   Fax: 731-4931

Let Harper Realtor find the ideal business or commercial space for you. Tell us what you're looking for, and our staff will locate exactly the place you need at just the right price. Here are a few of the properties we have for sale or rent:

498 Main Street – 1,200 square meters of commercial space in 12-story building; on the second floor; perfect for a clothing store or similar place; rent only; $4,500/month

84 16th Avenue – 800 square meters; on the first floor of a 20-story building; restaurant facility; for purchase or rent; $250,000 or $2,000/month

590 7th Avenue – 5-story building; for purchase only; call for price

15 Pine Street – entire third floor of 10-story building; ideal for small or medium-sized company; for rent only; $10,500/month

Call or e-mail us (information@harperrealtor.com) to inquire about the available properties or to schedule a tour of one. All prices are negotiable. We hope to do business with you.

To: Greg Turner <gturner@hamilton.com>
From: Marcie Aybar <marcie@harperrealtor.com>
Subject: Visit
Date: April 16

Dear Mr. Turner,

Thank you for sending us an e-mail regarding the property you saw on our Web site. I would like to let you know that it is still available. According to what you told me, it appears to be the ideal location for your diner. I'm very familiar with the building it is in. It has a large number of office workers. In addition, the neighborhood has a high amount of pedestrian traffic, so you should have no problem attracting customers.

Why don't I show you the property? I'm available anytime this week. If you are familiar with the Atlanta area, I can meet you right in front of the property. If you're not sure where it is, how about telling me where to meet you, and then I can pick you up and drive you there? Let me know which option you prefer.

Sincerely,

Marcie Aybar
Harper Realtor

To: Marcie Aybar <marcie@harperrealtor.com>
From: Greg Turner <gturner@hamilton.com>
Subject: Offer
Date: April 20

Dear Ms. Aybar,

I appreciate your taking the time to meet me yesterday. The property you showed me looks to be perfect for the business that I intend to open. I'm very interested in renting the property and would like to sign a 2-year agreement at the soonest possible time.

There is one thing though. I noticed that the facilities in the property are a bit old. My guess is that it will require around $4,000 to $5,000 to upgrade everything. Normally, that would be the responsibility of the owner. In this case though, I'm willing to pay for all of the upgrades myself if I can get a reduction in the monthly rent I would be paying. If I can pay $500 less per month, I will visit your office tomorrow to sign a contract. I wonder if this is possible.

Sincerely,

Greg Turner

186. What is NOT mentioned about Harper Realtor?

(A) It has places that are for sale.
(B) It helps customers get bank loans.
(C) It is willing to negotiate on prices.
(D) It deals with commercial properties.

187. In the advertisement, the word "ideal" in line 9 is closest in meaning to

(A) interesting
(B) unique
(C) perfect
(D) possible

188. Which property is Mr. Turner interested in?

(A) 15 Pine Street
(B) 498 Main Street
(C) 590 7th Avenue
(D) 84 16th Avenue

189. What does Ms. Aybar suggest that Mr. Turner do?

(A) Visit her office to sign a contract
(B) Look at a property with her
(C) Make a counteroffer to the owner
(D) Pick her up to go to the property

190. How much would Mr. Turner like to pay in rent?

(A) $500 a month
(B) $1,500 a month
(C) $4,000 a month
(D) $4,500 a month

Questions 191-195 refer to the following article, announcement, and letter.

Surprise Merger Announced

Richmond (October 3) – This morning, the CEO of Pennington's, Amy Emery, spoke at a press conference and said that her company and Rosebud, Inc. had agreed to merge. Both businesses are among the most popular grocery stores in the states of California, Nevada, and Arizona. Pennington's has 186 stores in those three states while Rosebud has 109. When the companies merge, the Rosebud name will be dropped, and all of the stores will be renamed Pennington's.

Rosebud was founded only 3 years ago but has seen its popularity dramatically increase due to the high quality of the food it sells at low prices. Ms. Emery stated that Pennington's will be adopting many of the business practices at Rosebud. She also mentioned that some stores will be closed to avoid redundancy in certain areas where two stores are located close to each other. The merger is expected to be complete by November 1.

Rosebud Store to Close

On October 31, the Rosebud Grocery Store located at 494 Sedona Avenue in Phoenix, Arizona, is going to close its doors for the last time at midnight. This is related to the merger between Rosebud, Inc. and Pennington's and has nothing to do with the financial performance of the store, which is quite strong. We urge all Rosebud customers to shop at Pennington's, where they can expect the same fantastic quality and low prices they currently get at Rosebud.

Since the store will be closing, everything in it must go. On October 30 and 31, we will be having a special sale. Everything we sell will be available at half off its regular price. We're also going to remain open all day and night for those two days to make sure that our customers can maximize their shopping experience.

November 1

Dear Rosebud Gold Card Member,

While Rosebud, Inc. no longer exists as a corporation, you can still have the same shopping experience you were used to getting there. Just visit your nearest Pennington's Supermarket. We understand it may take a while to get used to shopping at a new grocery store, so we'd like to make the transition easier for you.

First, visit your local Pennington's and trade your Rosebud Gold Card for a Pennington's Gold Card. You will get all the benefits you had at Rosebud and more. From now until November 15, you qualify for a 20% discount off every purchase you make. In addition, check out the coupons we included with this letter. They offer discounts on the most popular items Rosebud used to sell.

We'd like to make Pennington's your new home for grocery shopping. If there is anything we can do for you, don't hesitate to ask. Call 1-888-559-5768 with any questions or comments.

Sincerely,

Amy Emery
CEO, Pennington's

191. Why was the article written?

(A) To suggest a solution to a problem
(B) To advertise a sale
(C) To describe a business deal
(D) To announce the hiring of a new CEO

192. What is suggested about the Rosebud at 494 Sedona Avenue?

(A) It was the first Rosebud ever to open.
(B) The company's headquarters is there.
(C) A Pennington's is located near it.
(D) The store is not attracting customers.

193. What is going to happen on October 30?

(A) A supermarket is not going to close.
(B) Some new employees will be hired.
(C) A store is going to go out of business.
(D) All items will be sold at 25% discounts.

194. What will Rosebud Gold Card members NOT receive?

(A) A discount
(B) A new card
(C) A free item
(D) Coupons

195. What does Ms. Emery encourage Rosebud Gold Card members to do?

(A) Call her directly with questions
(B) Begin shopping at Pennington's
(C) Sign up on her firm's Web site
(D) Complete a customer survey card

GO ON TO THE NEXT PAGE

Questions 196-200 refer to the following e-mails and memo.

To: Ryan Crisp <ryancrisp@privatemail.com>
From: Jessica Peabody <j_peabody@ytp.com>
Subject: Managerial Position
Date: September 9

Dear Mr. Crisp,

After careful consideration, the board of directors would like to offer you the position of manager of the IT Department at the YTP Corporation. We want you to start as soon as possible but no later than October 1.

Your starting salary will be $74,000 a year, and you will be paid twice a month. You will receive a comprehensive benefits package (please download the attachment to see what you qualify for) as well as 2 weeks' paid vacation, 6 sick days, and 3 personal days a year.

In your position, you will be responsible for the daily operations of the IT Department. This includes, but is not limited to, the hiring and firing of employees and the managing of the departmental budget.

We request that you respond to this offer within 2 days. Please let me know if you accept our offer or not.

Sincerely,

Jessica Peabody
Manager, HR Department
YTP, Co.

To: Jessica Peabody <j_peabody@ytp.com>
From: Ryan Crisp <ryancrisp@privatemail.com>
Subject: Re: Managerial Position
Date: September 10

Dear Ms. Peabody,

Thank you for your offer of employment. I reviewed the benefits and am pleased with them, but the salary you are offering is too low. At the second interview I attended, I was assured that I would receive a salary no lower than $85,000 a year. Accepting the job at YTP means that I will have to move my family to a state with a higher cost of living than the one I currently reside in. Since I make $70,000 a year now, there is no incentive for me to accept the position unless my salary demands are met. Therefore, I conditionally accept the offer. If you raise my pay to the above-mentioned number, I can begin the moving process and start work on September 24. If you cannot match that number, then I am afraid I must reject your offer.

Sincerely,

Ryan Crisp

To: All Employees, IT Department
From: Helga Martinez, Assistant Manager, IT Department
Subject: Ryan Crisp
Date: September 21

It is my pleasure to announce that we finally have a new head of the IT Department. Ryan Crisp has accepted the job and will begin his first day of work next Monday. Mr. Crisp attended the University of Texas, where he double-majored in physics and economics. After graduating, he worked at Fairmount Manufacturing for three years and then Haverford, Inc. for four years. His last place of employment was the Landers Company, where he worked for three years.

On Monday at 10 A.M., we are going to have a reception for him. Everyone in the department should attend. We will also have lunch together at Benson's at noon. Please don't bother Mr. Crisp with your problems on the first day of work. He's going to be meeting with each of you individually on Wednesday and Thursday, so you can discuss any issues or projects you'd like to work on with him then.

196. What does the position of IT Department manager require a person to do?

(A) Handle financial matters
(B) Conduct scientific research
(C) Promote employees
(D) Assist with transfers

197. What does Ms. Peabody send to Mr. Crisp?

(A) A contract to sign
(B) A résumé to look at
(C) A file to read
(D) A budget to examine

198. What does Mr. Crisp need before he accepts the position?

(A) Financial compensation for moving
(B) $11,000 more for his annual salary
(C) One more week of paid vacation
(D) Assistance setting after moving

199. According to the memo, what is NOT going to happen on September 24?

(A) Employees will have a meal together.
(B) A new employee will begin working.
(C) A special reception will be held.
(D) Individual meetings will take place.

200. What is suggested about Mr. Crisp?

(A) He has already met all of his colleagues.
(B) He will go on a business trip in October.
(C) He will receive an annual salary of $85,000.
(D) He has several projects he wants to work on.

Stop! This is the end of the test. If you finish before time is called, you may go back to Parts 5, 6, and 7 and check your work.

Actual Test

03

LISTENING TEST

In the Listening test, you will be asked to demonstrate how well you understand spoken English. The entire Listening test will last approximately 45 minutes. There are four parts, and directions are given for each part. You must mark your answers on the separate answer sheet. Do not write your answers in your test book.

PART 1

Directions: For each question in this part, you will hear four statements about a picture in your test book. When you hear the statements, you must select the one statement that best describes what you see in the picture. Then find the number of the question on your answer sheet and mark your answer. The statements will not be printed in your test book and will be spoken only one time.

Statement (C), "Items are stacked up in the warehouse," is the best description of the picture, so you should select answer (C) and mark it on your answer sheet.

1.

2.

3.

4.

5.

6.

PART 2

🎧 03-02

Directions: You will hear a question or statement and three responses spoken in English. They will not be printed in your test book and will be spoken only one time. Select the best response to the question or statement and mark the letter (A), (B), or (C) on your answer sheet.

7. Mark your answer on your answer sheet.
8. Mark your answer on your answer sheet.
9. Mark your answer on your answer sheet.
10. Mark your answer on your answer sheet.
11. Mark your answer on your answer sheet.
12. Mark your answer on your answer sheet.
13. Mark your answer on your answer sheet.
14. Mark your answer on your answer sheet.
15. Mark your answer on your answer sheet.
16. Mark your answer on your answer sheet.
17. Mark your answer on your answer sheet.
18. Mark your answer on your answer sheet.
19. Mark your answer on your answer sheet.
20. Mark your answer on your answer sheet.
21. Mark your answer on your answer sheet.
22. Mark your answer on your answer sheet.
23. Mark your answer on your answer sheet.
24. Mark your answer on your answer sheet.
25. Mark your answer on your answer sheet.
26. Mark your answer on your answer sheet.
27. Mark your answer on your answer sheet.
28. Mark your answer on your answer sheet.
29. Mark your answer on your answer sheet.
30. Mark your answer on your answer sheet.
31. Mark your answer on your answer sheet.

PART 3

🎧 03-03

Directions: You will hear some conversations between two or more people. You will be asked to answer three questions about what the speakers say in each conversation. Select the best response to each question and mark the letter (A), (B), (C), or (D) on your answer sheet. The conversations will not be printed in your test book and will be spoken only one time.

32. What are the speakers mainly discussing?
    (A) The new arrangement of the office
    (B) What the interns will be doing
    (C) Some office equipment that they need
    (D) Their plans for the summer

33. What will the woman do with the area by the window?
    (A) Move her desk there
    (B) Install some computers in it
    (C) Set up the copier there
    (D) Put some cubicles in it

34. According to the man, what happened to the interns last year?
    (A) They interfered with other employees.
    (B) They all had their own desks.
    (C) They performed their duties well.
    (D) They were used to make copies.

35. What does the man ask the woman to do?
    (A) Sign a contract
    (B) Work on a presentation
    (C) Deliver some documents
    (D) Speak with a client

36. Who is Mr. Murphy?
    (A) A deliveryman
    (B) A lawyer
    (C) A client
    (D) A presenter

37. What does the woman suggest?
    (A) Requesting an extension
    (B) Using a delivery company
    (C) Renegotiating with a client
    (D) Sending some items by fax

GO ON TO THE NEXT PAGE

38. What are the man and woman talking about?
    (A) When the company's products will be released
    (B) The results of a survey taken of some workers
    (C) The prices of items that were recently bought
    (D) Some products purchased from another company

39. What does the man tell the woman to do?
    (A) Make a deal with a supplier
    (B) Speak with some assembly line workers
    (C) Write a letter to Lewis Manufacturing
    (D) Visit a client's factory

40. What does the woman indicate about Jeff Lambert?
    (A) She is acquainted with him.
    (B) He is in upper management.
    (C) He has a degree in engineering.
    (D) She enjoys collaborating with him.

41. Where does the woman mostly likely work?
    (A) At a restaurant
    (B) At a hotel
    (C) At a caterer
    (D) At a supermarket

42. What problem does the man mention?
    (A) He was overcharged for a meal.
    (B) Some food he ordered never arrived.
    (C) His food was prepared improperly.
    (D) The food he bought was spoiled.

43. What will the woman probably do next?
    (A) Make a telephone call
    (B) Speak with a chef
    (C) Prepare a new bill for the man
    (D) Refund the man's money

44. Where does the conversation take place?
    (A) On the telephone
    (B) At a box office
    (C) On a stage
    (D) At a concession stand

45. What does the man want to watch?
    (A) A musical
    (B) A concert
    (C) A play
    (D) A movie

46. What time is the man going to watch the event?
    (A) At 4:00
    (B) At 5:30
    (C) At 7:00
    (D) At 9:15

47. What does the man mean when he says, "I'm afraid not"?

(A) He cannot change the amount of the estimate.
(B) His crew is unable to work on the woman's home.
(C) His team cannot start working until next week.
(D) He will not be able to do the repairs the woman wants.

48. According to the man, what is the problem with the woman's house?

(A) The wiring was done badly.
(B) It has leaky pipes.
(C) It is very old.
(D) The floors need replacing.

49. What does the woman tell the man she will do?

(A) Send him a check tomorrow
(B) Speak with another contractor
(C) Pay the amount he stated
(D) Make a decision later

50. Who most likely is the man?

(A) An architect
(B) A customer
(C) A telephone operator
(D) A hardware store employee

51. What does the man ask about?

(A) Some missing items
(B) An upcoming sale
(C) A special discount
(D) A bill he received

52. What does the woman say will happen this afternoon?

(A) The store will receive some products.
(B) The Web site will be updated.
(C) The sale at the store will end.
(D) The man's order will be sent out.

GO ON TO THE NEXT PAGE

53. What is the man going to do tomorrow?
    (A) Go sightseeing in L.A.
    (B) Visit a colleague
    (C) Interview for a position
    (D) Meet a potential client

54. What is mentioned about James Hooper?
    (A) He was injured in an accident.
    (B) He is going to accompany the man.
    (C) He is at an event in Toronto.
    (D) He and the man are not on friendly terms.

55. Why does the man say, "It looks like we just might be shorthanded"?
    (A) To state that the company will not hire any new employees
    (B) To indicate that there might not be a replacement worker
    (C) To mention that one of his team members resigned his position
    (D) To argue that his team can handle the duties by themselves

56. Where does the woman most likely work?
    (A) At a dry cleaner's
    (B) At a pharmacy
    (C) At a grocery store
    (D) At a printing shop

57. What is the problem?
    (A) One of the man's coupons is no good.
    (B) The store does not have an item the man wants.
    (C) The man does not have enough money.
    (D) A sale ended the previous day.

58. What does the man give the woman?
    (A) A check
    (B) His driver's license
    (C) A bank card
    (D) A gift certificate

59. What does the woman want to do?

(A) Go to lunch now
(B) Download a computer program
(C) Finish the work she is doing
(D) Take a short break

60. What does the woman mean when she says, "Actually, I haven't the slightest idea"?

(A) She does not know where a restaurant is located.
(B) She is not sure what the problem with the computer is.
(C) She is unaware that the man forgot to eat breakfast.
(D) She cannot remember what she and the man spoke about.

61. Why is the man surprised?

(A) His computer has stopped working properly.
(B) The woman has not eaten at Papa Gino's before.
(C) He thought that the program had already been written.
(D) The woman intends to move to a new neighborhood.

62. What is the woman's job?

(A) Chef
(B) Waitress
(C) Dishwasher
(D) Cashier

63. What will the woman bring to the men?

(A) Some coffee
(B) Dessert
(C) Some menus
(D) The bill

64. What will the woman probably do next?

(A) Prepare some food
(B) Go to the kitchen
(C) Pour a drink
(D) Deliver some food

GO ON TO THE NEXT PAGE

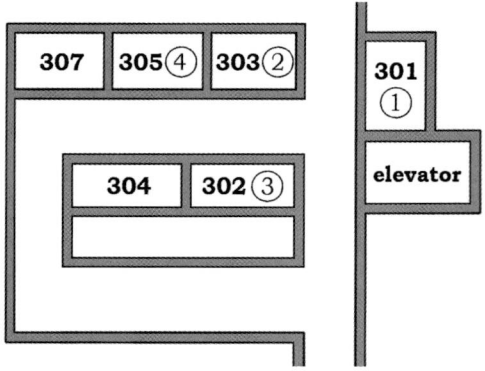

Date	Activities
October 10-12	Attend conference in Paris
October 13-16	Meet with Mr. Lindsay in Amsterdam
October 17-20	Visit museums in London
October 21-22	Negotiate with Harstadt Motors in Oslo

65. What does the man ask about?

(A) The meeting with the staff
(B) The rearranging of his department
(C) The arrival of some new employees
(D) The renovating of the office

66. Look at the graphic. Where is the man's new office?

(A) 1
(B) 2
(C) 3
(D) 4

67. Why is the man pleased?

(A) He has been given some extra time off.
(B) His meeting with a buyer went well.
(C) He does not have to move anywhere.
(D) He is going to get a larger office.

68. Where does the man most likely work?

(A) At an airline
(B) At a train station
(C) At a travel agency
(D) At a rental car agency

69. Look at the graphic. On which day does the woman need to change her travel plans?

(A) October 12
(B) October 16
(C) October 20
(D) October 22

70. What does the man offer to do?

(A) Call an airline
(B) Send the woman a new itinerary
(C) Recalculate a bill
(D) Upgrade the woman to first class

PART 4

🎧 03-04

Directions: You will hear some talks given by a single speaker. You will be asked to answer three questions about what the speaker says in each talk. Select the best response to each question and mark the letter (A), (B), (C), or (D) on your answer sheet. The talks will not be printed in your test book and will be spoken only one time.

71. What is the purpose of the call?
    (A) To cancel plans to meet
    (B) To request a later due date
    (C) To ask for some help on a report
    (D) To go over an ongoing project

72. Where most likely does Tina Westerly work?
    (A) In the Sales Department
    (B) In the Marketing Department
    (C) In the Accounting Department
    (D) In the Shipping Department

73. What does the speaker say he needs to do?
    (A) Transfer to another department
    (B) Attend a meeting with his boss
    (C) Work faster on his own assignment
    (D) Assist a colleague with a project

74. What does the speaker say about the mechanics at West Side Auto Repairs?
    (A) They receive special training every year.
    (B) They are only qualified to work on cars and trucks.
    (C) They have been in the business a long time.
    (D) They work in pairs on every vehicle they look at.

75. What will the mechanics do before working on a vehicle?
    (A) Ask the customer to sign a contract
    (B) Explain why the work needs to be done
    (C) Give the customer some repair options
    (D) Mention the price of the work they will do

76. What is indicated about West Side Auto Repairs?
    (A) It is located in the suburbs.
    (B) It has space for five vehicles.
    (C) It specializes in motorcycles.
    (D) It is open all year round.

GO ON TO THE NEXT PAGE

135

77. What is the speaker mainly discussing?
    (A) The performance of some employees
    (B) The need to hire more workers
    (C) A training session that will be held
    (D) How to reduce complaints from customers

78. What does the speaker mean when she says, "I'd appreciate it if you would do that for me"?
    (A) She wants the listeners to work harder at their jobs.
    (B) She wants the listeners to assist some other employees.
    (C) She wants the listeners to be politer to customers.
    (D) She wants the listeners to do their duties much better.

79. What does the speaker suggest may happen?
    (A) Some stores may be closed.
    (B) The prices of services may increase.
    (C) The orientation session may be canceled.
    (D) Some individuals may lose their jobs.

80. Where most likely does this talk take place?
    (A) In a parking lot
    (B) In an office
    (C) At a park
    (D) In a store

81. What is the problem?
    (A) A car is in the wrong place.
    (B) No parking spots are available.
    (C) The front doors are locked.
    (D) People cannot get out of the building.

82. What does the speaker request?
    (A) That a fee be paid
    (B) That a door be opened
    (C) That a vehicle be moved
    (D) That a person be quiet

83. What does the speaker mention about the company's recent performance?
    (A) It earned half a million dollars.
    (B) It released six new products.
    (C) It had lower revenues than before.
    (D) It had its best month in years.

84. How do customers feel about the new product line?
    (A) They believe it costs too much.
    (B) They think it is easy to use.
    (C) They have responded positively.
    (D) They consider it poorly made.

85. What does the speaker ask the listeners to do?
    (A) Try to sell more new items
    (B) Think of some solutions
    (C) Suggest alternative products
    (D) Speak with some customers

86. What is going to happen at 6:30?

    (A) A staff meeting will be held.
    (B) A dinner event will begin.
    (C) People will leave on a company trip.
    (D) An awards ceremony will be catered.

87. Why does the speaker say, "I'm not sure how that happened"?

    (A) To provide an excuse for Amy not being invited
    (B) To explain why Amy did not get directions
    (C) To apologize since Amy did not receive an award
    (D) To state that he does not know why the event changed

88. What does the speaker suggest that Amy do?

    (A) Download directions from a Web site
    (B) Send him an e-mail before work ends
    (C) Get a ride with one of her coworkers
    (D) Confirm that she wants to transfer

89. Where most likely does this talk take place?

    (A) In a library
    (B) At a bookstore
    (C) At a school
    (D) At a publishing company

90. What will Mr. Hooper do first?

    (A) Answer questions
    (B) Give a speech
    (C) Read from a book
    (D) Sign copies of his book

91. What does the speaker say about Mr. Hooper's books?

    (A) They are for sale.
    (B) They are all checked out.
    (C) They are nonfiction works.
    (D) They are available to check out.

GO ON TO THE NEXT PAGE

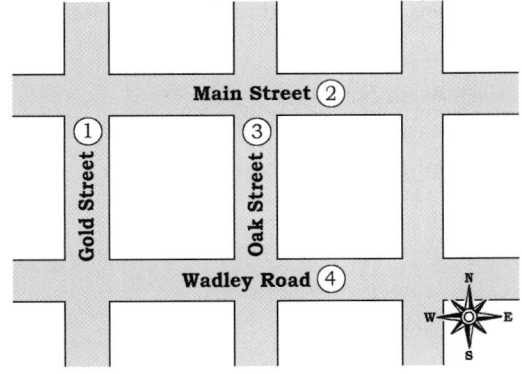

Item	Number Ordered
soup bowl	10
dinner plate	20
wine glass	16
coffee cup	22

92. Where is Ms. Wallace?
    (A) In a news van
    (B) In a studio
    (C) At a radio station
    (D) In a helicopter

93. Look at the graphic. Which part of the city had a traffic accident?
    (A) Number 1
    (B) Number 2
    (C) Number 3
    (D) Number 4

94. When will Ms. Wallace make another traffic report?
    (A) In 5 minutes
    (B) In a quarter of an hour
    (C) In half an hour
    (D) In an hour

95. What does the speaker indicate about the delivery?
    (A) It was very fast.
    (B) It cost too much.
    (C) It was slower than normal.
    (D) It was faster than usual.

96. Look at the graphic. How many new items does Mr. Tenaglia need?
    (A) 8
    (B) 10
    (C) 12
    (D) 14

97. What does the speaker want?
    (A) The address of a local store that he can visit
    (B) Information on how to get the missing items
    (C) A full refund for the broken items
    (D) A way to return the incorrect items to the company

Time	Talk/Speaker
10:30 – 11:15	Making Outlines for Essays by Ronald Devers
11:15 – 12:00	Imagining Creative Plots by Lisa Delacruz
1:00 – 2:00	Improving Dialogue by Linus McDowell
2:00 – 3:00	Building New Worlds by Mark Haverford

98. What is the purpose of the talk?

(A) To request full participation by the audience
(B) To introduce the keynote speaker
(C) To encourage people to sign up
(D) To welcome guests to an event

99. Who is Mary Lattimore?

(A) A novelist
(B) A creative writing professor
(C) A poet
(D) The host

100. Look at the graphic. What time is Lisa Delacruz going to speak?

(A) At 10:30
(B) At 11:15
(C) At 1:00
(D) At 2:00

This is the end of the Listening test. Turn to Part 5 in your test book.

READING TEST

In the Reading test, you will read a variety of texts and answer several different types of reading comprehension questions. The entire Reading test will last 75 minutes. There are three parts, and directions are given for each part. You are encouraged to answer as many questions as possible within the time allowed.

You must mark your answers on the separate answer sheet. Do not write your answers in your test book.

PART 5

Directions: A word or phrase is missing in each of the sentences below. Four answer choices are given below each sentence. Select the best answer to complete the sentence. Then mark the letter (A), (B), (C), or (D) on your answer sheet.

101. Unless funds are added to the -------, the project will be unable to be completed on time.
    (A) laboratory
    (B) budget
    (C) election
    (D) proposal

102. The decision to produce the new line of vehicles must be made soon ------- next year's marketing campaign.
    (A) prepares
    (B) preparing
    (C) will prepare
    (D) to prepare

103. ------- on the city's newest hotel is taking longer than expected and will be finished behind schedule.
    (A) Construct
    (B) Constructive
    (C) Construction
    (D) Constructing

104. Ms. Hall suggested that the tourists find a hotel closer to the airport ------- one out in the countryside.
    (A) in opposition to
    (B) according to
    (C) rather than
    (D) as a result of

105. Applications for ------- to overseas branches must be received no later than the third Friday in November.
    (A) transfer
    (B) transferred
    (C) transferable
    (D) transference

106. Either the director of the Sales Department ------- Karen Wolf, the vice president, will attend the staff meeting.
    (A) and
    (B) or
    (C) also
    (D) so

107. The appeal of the product to people in all age groups resulted in sales that were higher than -------.

(A) approved
(B) regarded
(C) anticipated
(D) resolved

108. All first-time customers ------- 15% off their orders when shopping at the online store.

(A) receive
(B) await
(C) purchase
(D) exchange

109. It is highly suggested that guests ------- their reservations with the hotel during the peak season.

(A) confirm
(B) confirming
(C) have been confirmed
(D) to confirm

110. The renovations on the Dynasty Hotel should be completed no later ------- the start of the summer season.

(A) than
(B) which
(C) when
(D) such

111. According to the schedule, Ms. Harper is going to give the ------- speech at the conference in Boise.

(A) opens
(B) opening
(C) opener
(D) opened

112. As soon as the merger between the two firms was complete, several employees were ------- that they were being laid off.

(A) approached
(B) reported
(C) notified
(D) expected

113. Numerous souvenir shops are located in the part of the city ------- tourists commonly visit.

(A) when
(B) which
(C) how
(D) then

114. Once the ------- have been signed by Ms. Murrell, they will be taken to the Legal Department.

(A) documents
(B) documentary
(C) documented
(D) documenting

115. Numerous passengers were ------- at the airport overnight when bad weather caused their flights to be canceled.

(A) boarded
(B) waited
(C) transferred
(D) stranded

116. Ms. Lakewood ------- with the house the realtor showed her and decided to buy the property on the spot.

(A) impressed
(B) will be impressed
(C) was impressed
(D) has impressed

GO ON TO THE NEXT PAGE

117. The store manager promised to have the furniture delivered to the office ------- the end of the day.
    (A) until
    (B) for
    (C) on
    (D) by

118. Those who ------- in the study will be given gift certificates that may be redeemed at local establishments.
    (A) participant
    (B) participatory
    (C) participative
    (D) participate

119. Each spring, Westside Construction ------- individuals for new positions at its various worksites.
    (A) fires
    (B) transfers
    (C) recruits
    (D) offers

120. Should it be necessary to receive an extension on the deadline, please ------- us as soon as possible.
    (A) inform
    (B) to inform
    (C) are informing
    (D) be informed

121. Mr. Worthy has given no indication of ------- when the employment contract is going to be signed.
    (A) know
    (B) knowledge
    (C) knowing
    (D) knowable

122. An announcement was made that Travis Bean had been ------- the company's newest head of Accounting.
    (A) hired
    (B) named
    (C) proposed
    (D) agreed

123. ------- of the attendees was aware that Judy Garcia, the keynote speaker, had failed to arrive yet.
    (A) Nobody
    (B) None
    (C) Many
    (D) Much

124. Limnos, Inc. ------- its latest line of appliances at the sales exhibition in New Orleans next week.
    (A) introduced
    (B) has introduced
    (C) is introducing
    (D) will be introduced

125. Dirk Powers, the head of the labor union, was arrested on suspicion of making ------- to politicians.
    (A) bribe
    (B) bribes
    (C) bribed
    (D) bribery

126. The surprise inspection ------- that many of the factory workers were not adhering to safety standards.
    (A) alerted
    (B) revealed
    (C) suspected
    (D) completed

127. Mr. Dawson tried to ------- his colleagues to support him in his attempt to become a member of the board of directors.

(A) elect
(B) regard
(C) approach
(D) persuade

128. ------- being offered a promotion and a sizable raise, Ms. Lansing resigned and took a job at another firm.

(A) Despite
(B) In fact
(C) Nevertheless
(D) Regarding

129. Several engineers were replaced when large numbers of customers ------- complaints about the designs of the products at Weber, Inc.

(A) are filing
(B) have filed
(C) filed
(D) had been filed

130. The store manager changed the ------- of the store to place men's clothing right by the front door.

(A) layout
(B) budget
(C) advertisement
(D) schedule

GO ON TO THE NEXT PAGE

PART 6

Directions: Read the texts that follow. A word, phrase, or sentence is missing in parts of each text. Four answer choices for each question are given below the text. Select the best answer to complete the text. Then mark the letter (A), (B), (C), or (D) on your answer sheet.

Questions 131-134 refer to the following announcement.

New Terminal to Open at Airport

Springfield International Airport is proud to announce that its newest terminal is going to open soon. After thirty months of construction, Terminal 2 is ready to start sending passengers to destinations --------- the world. The new terminal has twenty-five gates that will be used by nine
       131.
different airlines. Local budget airline Ace Airways will be the --------- occupant of the terminal
                                                                    132.
as it will have control over ten of the gates. Terminal 2 will be able to process several thousand passengers each day. It will also have all kinds of facilities, including duty-free shops and a number of franchise restaurants. --------- Its gates will be able to handle the largest passenger
                                 133.
airliners in the world, too. The terminal is set to open on Thursday, April 10. There will be a small ceremony at 7 A.M., and then passengers will be --------- so that they can start going to their
                                                         134.
gates to catch their flights.

131. (A) over
     (B) in
     (C) around
     (D) within

132. (A) primate
     (B) primary
     (C) primed
     (D) priming

133. (A) Passengers have already complimented the quality of items sold in the stores.
     (B) In addition, the gates are specifically designed for small commuter planes.
     (C) It is anticipated that they will bring in millions of dollars in revenue annually.
     (D) There is not yet anywhere for passengers to eat or to go shopping though.

134. (A) charged
     (B) admitted
     (C) dispatched
     (D) booked

Questions 135-138 refer to the following notice.

To: All Tenants, Bluebird Tower

From: Cliff Samuels, Building Manager

Re: Rent Increase

Date: August 2

Please be aware that as of September 1, all rents in the building will increase by 10%. This increase applies both to individuals renting apartments --------- those people who are renting office or commercial spaces. --------- I will be sending new contracts to all tenants within the next five business days. You need to sign them and return them to me at my office on the first floor no later than August 15. Those of you who do not wish to pay the higher rent must --------- the premises by August 31. Your security deposit --------- as soon as we in the management office confirm that your space has not suffered any damage. You may feel free to speak with me about the rent increase or anything else that is on your mind. Just call me at 856-4584 during regular business hours.

135. (A) and
(B) so
(C) or
(D) that

136. (A) There are unfortunately no more places available for rent at the moment.
(B) There is no need for any of you to sign a new lease if you do not wish to do so.
(C) All tenants must renegotiate the amount of rent that they pay sometime this week.
(D) The rents are being increased to account for the recent rise in utilities prices.

137. (A) remove
(B) sell
(C) repair
(D) vacate

138. (A) have been returned
(B) returned
(C) will be returned
(D) was returned

Questions 139-142 refer to the following letter.

March 15

Dear Member of the Association of Auto Mechanics,

The Association of Auto Mechanics (AAM) is going to hold its annual conference on September 14 and 15. The event is going to be held in Memphis, Tennessee. This is the same location as last year's event. Due to the tremendous --------- of the conference last year, it was unanimously decided by the members of the executive staff at the AAM to have it in Memphis once again.
139.

This year's conference will have a large number of events, including talks, workshops, and a sales fair. The keynote speaker will be --------- mechanic Robert McGuffin, an expert in the art
140.
of repairing antique vehicles. As a member of the AAM, you are --------- to pay the discounted
141.
registration rate of $75. That will get you access to every event that is being held at the conference. Some airlines and hotels are offering discounts to our members. Please call (405) 326-8695 for more information regarding that. ---------
142.

Sincerely,

Tim Matterhorn

President, Association of Auto Mechanics

139. (A) succeed
(B) sucess
(C) sucession
(D) succeeding

140. (A) famed
(B) imitation
(C) novice
(D) incompetent

141. (A) excepted
(B) avoided
(C) entitled
(D) reported

142. (A) Thanks for attending the event.
(B) A great time was had by everyone.
(C) We hope to see you in September.
(D) Calls regarding this matter will be ignored.

Questions 143-146 refer to the following article.

Pearl Resident of the Year Named

Pearl (December 28) – In a ceremony held at city hall last night, Jason O'Brien was ---------- the
143.
resident of the year by Mayor Anna Harper. Mr. O'Brien, who has lived in Pearl for more than forty years since moving to the city as a child, has been in the news a lot this year. First, when a tornado swept through the city in the spring, Mr. O'Brien helped organize groups of residents to rescue those needing assistance. ---------- He also ---------- a large amount of money to relief
144. **145.**
efforts in the city. He came to the rescue once again when the Red River flooded its banks in summer and left half the city under two feet of water. Finally, Mr. O'Brien provided $2 million for the building of a local community center, where residents will be able to go for various leisure activities once construction on it is complete 14 months from now. According to Mayor Harper, ---------- else was even considered for the award.
146.

143. (A) nominated
 (B) reported
 (C) named
 (D) stated

144. (A) He was on a team that stopped the flooding from affecting the entire city.
 (B) His efforts resulted in 20 people being saved from inside collapsed homes.
 (C) Those groups warned local residents about the tornado and led them to safety.
 (D) The money that he provided helped repair people's homes that burned in fires.

145. (A) donated
 (B) deposited
 (C) invested
 (D) contracted

146. (A) everybody
 (B) anybody
 (C) somebody
 (D) nobody

PART 7

Directions: In this part your will read a selection of texts, such as magazine and newspaper articles, e-mails, and instant messages. Each text or set of texts is followed by several questions. Select the best answer for each question and mark the letter (A), (B), (C), or (D) on your answer sheet.

Questions 147-148 refer to the following e-mail.

TO customerservice@perseusmart.com
FROM amcclain@personalmail.com
SUBJECT Freeport Store
DATE July 11

To Whom It May Concern,

My name is Alice McClain. Yesterday, my husband and I visited the Perseus Mart in Freeport, where we had an unpleasant experience involving an employee there. We were shopping for a humidifier and requested assistance from Tim Nelson. We just moved from an area which is not dry during the winter months, so we had a number of questions about the basic functions of the machine and how to operate it. Not only was Tim unable to answer our questions, but he contradicted himself with some responses. When my husband pointed this out, Tim became rude and insinuated that we, not him, were at fault for not knowing about the product. We immediately left the store and went across the street to Electromart, where we were treated pleasantly and our questions were answered. We had expected to become loyal customers of Perseus Mart like we were in Albany, but it appears that won't be the case.

Regards,

Alice McClain

147. Why did Ms. McClain write the e-mail?

(A) To complain about some service she received
(B) To inquire about a product sold at Perseus Mart
(C) To get the location of the Freeport Perseus Mart
(D) To praise an employee for the way he acted

148. What is indicated in the e-mail?

(A) Ms. McClain intends to visit Perseus Mart again.
(B) Electromart has lower prices than Perseus Mart.
(C) Ms. McClain moved to Freeport from Albany.
(D) Tim Nelson is the manager at Perseus Mart.

Questions 149-150 refer to the following advertisement.

Harvey's Home Appliances Is Having a Sale!

This Saturday, September 24, Harvey's Home Appliances is going to be opening our doors for the first time. We are located in the Grandview Shopping Mall next to the Wellman Theater on the second floor. Visit us to check out the latest in home appliances, including refrigerators, microwaves, ovens, dishwashers, toasters, and coffeemakers. To celebrate our grand opening, the first 20 customers who make a purchase of $150 or more will get a 30% discount. On top of that, we will be holding a drawing for a brand-new Jenkins refrigerator at 6:30 P.M. All customers who make a purchase will be automatically entered. We'll open at 9:00 A.M. and close at 7:30 P.M. Be sure not to miss this special event.

149. What is the purpose of the sale?

(A) The store is going out of business.
(B) An anniversary is being celebrated.
(C) Last year's items need to be sold.
(D) The store is having its grand opening.

150. What will all customers who make a purchase on September 24 receive?

(A) A discount
(B) A chance to win a prize
(C) A gift certificate
(D) A coupon

GO ON TO THE NEXT PAGE

Questions 151-152 refer to the following text message chain.

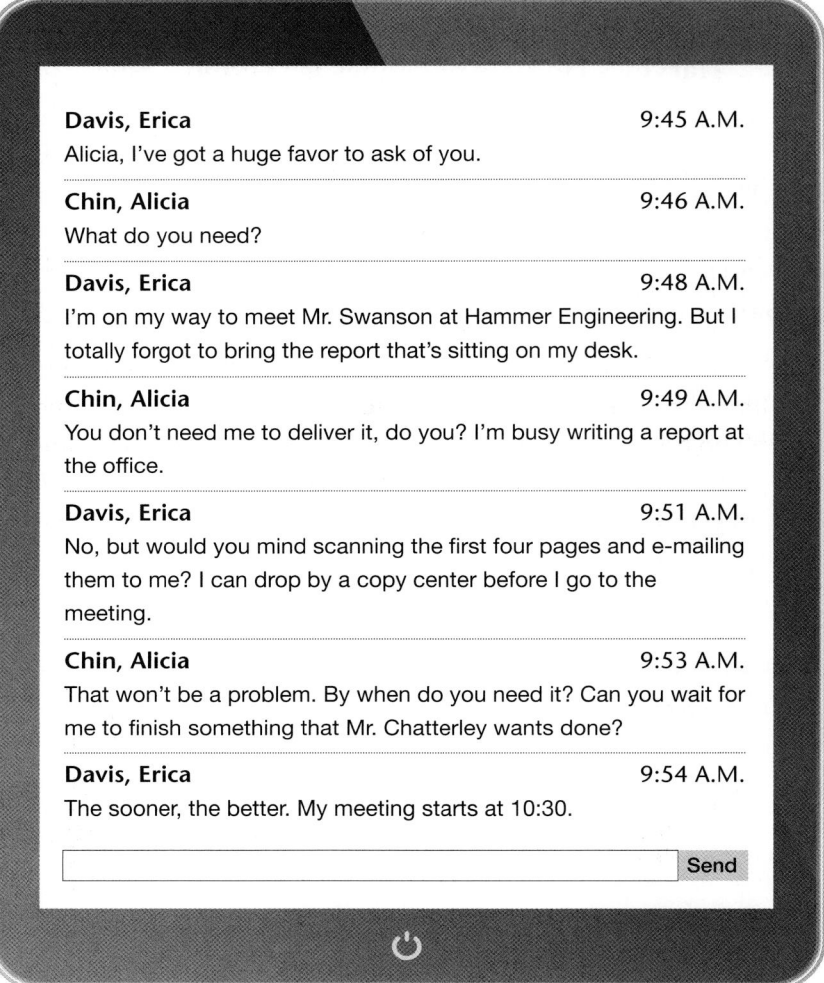

151. At 9:49 A.M., why does Ms. Chin write, "You don't need me to deliver it, do you?"

(A) To indicate she does not have time to visit Ms. Davis
(B) To turn down a request to deliver some items
(C) To point out that delivering items is not in her job description
(D) To ask Ms. Davis where she should meet with her

152. What will Ms. Chin probably do next?

(A) Check her e-mail
(B) Visit Mr. Chatterley
(C) Scan a document
(D) Attend a meeting

Questions 153-155 refer to the following notice.

City Gas to Conduct Inspections

There will be routine inspections of the gas meters of some Greenwood residents on July 10 and 11 between the hours of 7 A.M. and 9 P.M. —[1]—. The inspections, which take place biannually, will be conducted at homes located between Elm Avenue and Pike Road and which are east of 12th Street and west of 28th Street. —[2]—. Residents of homes being inspected should cooperate by creating a clear and safe path from the sidewalk to the gas meter, which is affixed on the side of the home. All obstacles should be removed, dogs and other animals should be chained, and fences should be kept unlocked or opened. —[3]—. City Gas officials will arrive without notice. According to city regulations, gas company employees are allowed to walk onto private property for the purpose of inspections. —[4]—. However, they may not enter a residence at any time. Call 849-1042 for more information.

153. How often do the inspections probably occur?

(A) Every month
(B) Every four months
(C) Every six months
(D) Every year

154. What are residents asked to do?

(A) Report any problems with their meters to City Gas
(B) Make it easy for officials to inspect their meters
(C) Record their gas usage beneath their gas meters
(D) Put up signs indicating they have pets in their yards

155. In which of the positions marked [1], [2], [3], and [4] does the following sentence best belong?

"Residents who fail to comply and therefore prevent City Gas officials from doing their work will be fined."

(A) [1]
(B) [2]
(C) [3]
(D) [4]

Questions 156-158 refer to the following letter.

Robert Shaver
491 Magnolia Boulevard
Rome, GA

August 3

Dear Robert Shaver,

Congratulations! You have been named the employee of the month at Knight's Home Repair Warehouse for the month of July. This award is determined by a vote of store managers. You were unanimously selected for the prize. In addition, during our most recent customer satisfaction survey, your name was at the top of the list as our friendliest and most helpful employee. We at Knight's Home Repair Warehouse are proud of your hard work and determination. As a reward, you may use the parking space at the front of the store for the entire month of August, and you may take Friday, August 10, off as a paid holiday. You will also be given the item of your choice (worth no more than $100). You may select it from all the items we sell. We would like to hang your picture by the front door, so please see Betty Smith as soon as possible. You need to wear your company shirt when you take the photo. Again, congratulations, and thank you for being such an outstanding employee. We'll be expecting even greater things from you in the future.

Sincerely,

David Knight
Owner, Knight's Home Repair Warehouse

156. According to the letter, what is true about Mr. Shaver?

(A) He has worked at Knight's Home Repair Warehouse for two years.
(B) He is employed in a management position.
(C) He received everyone's vote for the July award.
(D) He helped conduct the recent customer satisfaction survey.

157. What does Mr. Shaver NOT receive for winning the award?

(A) A cash prize
(B) A free gift
(C) A parking spot
(D) A day of vacation

158. What is suggested about Ms. Smith?

(A) She will take Mr. Shaver's picture.
(B) She works in the Public Relations Department.
(C) She is a previous award winner.
(D) She works closely with Mr. Knight.

Questions 159-161 refer to the following advertisement.

Pandemonium Real Estate Agency
409 Dobson Street
Mesa, AZ 85204
(805) 281-5632

Pandemonium Real Estate Agency has some of the best deals in Mesa. Check out these homes that went on sale this week:

32 Guadalupe Drive – 4 bedrooms; 3 bathrooms; recently refurbished kitchen; large backyard w/swimming pool; several orange and lemon trees in yard; 5-minutes' walk from local elementary and high schools; $320,000

483 Desert Avenue – 2 bedrooms, 1 bathroom; fenced-in yard; quiet neighborhood near golf course; great for retirees looking to downsize; $205,000

904 Erickson Street – 3 bedrooms, 2 bathrooms; large kitchen; all electricity provided by solar panels; swimming pool & hot tub in backyard; lots of privacy; near shopping district; $380,000

1954 Hidalgo Road – 4 bedrooms; 2 bathrooms; huge front yard and backyard; next to Superstition Freeway; close to business district; $428,000

For more listings, visit www.pandemoniumrealestate.com. Our agents are ready to help you find your dream house. They'll assist you through the entire process. Moving from out of state? Don't worry. We can help you get settled. We've done it with hundreds of others.

159. Where would this advertisement most likely be found?

(A) In a local newspaper
(B) In an economics magazine
(C) In a national journal
(D) In a community center's newsletter

160. Which home would a family with young children be the most interested in?

(A) 904 Erickson Street
(B) 1954 Hidalgo Road
(C) 32 Guadalupe Drive
(D) 483 Desert Avenue

161. How are people recommended to learn about other homes available for sale?

(A) By calling a telephone number
(B) By visiting the agency in person
(C) By writing a letter
(D) By going to a Web site

Questions 162-164 refer to the following e-mail.

To: Peter Carter <pcarter@worldmail.com>
From: William Folsom <willfolsom345@viscount.com>
Subject: Application
Date: September 28

Dear Mr. Carter,

I received your application for the position of assistant editor here at Viscount Publishing. Unfortunately, I regret to inform you that the position was filled by an internal hire this morning.

I did, however, look over your entire application, and I must admit that I was impressed with both your résumé and the reference letters that were submitted in your application packet. You have a great deal of experience editing children's books, and I am quite familiar with three of the books that you have worked on while at Milton, Inc.

It just so happens that Viscount is in the process of opening a children's division, and we are currently looking for new staff members. While I realize you applied for a position editing young adult fiction, your experience makes you a top candidate for a job in the new department. If you are interested, I will gladly pass your résumé on to Ms. Mary Farnsworth.

However, I should point out that the children's division will be in Boston, not New York, and that you need to give me a response no later than tomorrow afternoon since a decision on who to interview will be made soon. Time is of the essence, so please respond to me quickly.

Sincerely,

William Folsom
Viscount Publishing

162. Why did Mr. Folsom write the e-mail to Mr. Carter?

(A) To suggest applying for a different position
(B) To offer him a job at Viscount Publishing
(C) To reject his proposal for a children's book
(D) To compliment a work that he authored

163. What is mentioned about Mr. Carter?

(A) He is an author of children's books.
(B) He currently works on young adult fiction.
(C) He works as an editor at Milton, Inc.
(D) He is colleagues with Mary Farnsworth.

164. What does Mr. Carter need to do by September 29?

(A) Provide a response to the job offer he was given
(B) Set up a time and date to be interviewed
(C) Submit his résumé to someone at Milton, Inc.
(D) Decide if he wants to be considered for a position

Questions 165-167 refer to the following letter.

December 3

Clive Robertson
Walker Resources
495 11th Avenue
Birmingham, AL

Dear Mr. Robertson,

Thank you for taking the time to visit my company and to give a presentation on your firm's products. Your talk was lively and enjoyable, and it provided us with insight regarding your company's newest line of products.

We at RX Products are especially interested in the container sealing machine you spoke about in brief as we feel that it might be exactly what we need. We are opening a factory in Brazil together with Ramos Manufacturing, and we are worried about the humidity there. As you know, high humidity levels makes it difficult to seal containers properly. We currently use sealers manufactured by Robinson, Inc., but the product was discontinued by the company a few months ago. Your sealer is not only new but also appears to use the latest technology, which we anticipate will improve its efficiency.

I would like to enter into talks with you regarding the purchase of your company's sealing machines. At present, however, the machine's price is too high. Perhaps your company can be flexible on pricing if we order a significant number of machines. I realize that you just returned to Birmingham, but would you mind coming back to Pensacola next week? We are in a hurry to make a deal as our factory is set to open on January 10.

Sincerely,

James Matters
Vice President of Procurements, RX Products

165. Why does Mr. Matters want to purchase a product from Walker Resources?

(A) The price of the item is lower than that of others on the market.
(B) His company has worked with Walker Resources in the past.
(C) He is unable to buy a similar product from any other firm.
(D) The item will be an upgrade from what his company uses now.

166. What is mentioned about Ramos Manufacturing?

(A) It is located in Birmingham.
(B) It is involved in a joint venture with RX Products.
(C) It quit making a machine recently.
(D) It is having trouble building its newest factory.

167. What does Mr. Matters request?

(A) A pamphlet
(B) A bulk discount
(C) A free sample
(D) A product demonstration

Questions 168-171 refer to the following online message chain.

	McCartney, Laurie [10:49 A.M.]	That was an interesting demonstration by Ms. Sanders just now. How about providing me with your immediate thoughts, both good and bad?
	Patrick, Rebecca [10: 52 A.M.]	I don't think her firm can help ours.
	Daniels, George [10:53 A.M.]	I liked what she had to say.
	McCartney, Laurie [10:54 A.M.]	Fascinating. You two arrived at opposing conclusions. Can I get some more details? George, you go first.
	Daniels, George [10:56 A.M.]	Whitewater Consulting has assisted lots of startups in getting their products into foreign markets. So they've sold huge numbers of products and increased their revenues. It's that simple.
	Patrick, Rebecca [10: 57 A.M.]	But the point is that Whitewater helps firms in foreign markets, not domestic ones.
	McCartney, Laurie [10:59 A.M.]	I think I see where you're going with this.
	Patrick, Rebecca [11:02 A.M.]	We're not trying to break into any foreign markets. That's something we'll consider a few years from now. We need to get our goods onto the domestic market.
	Daniels, George [11:04 A.M.]	But didn't Ms. Sanders say her company has done work here? I know she focused on European markets, but she talked about her firm's work in the U.S. at the beginning, too.
	Patrick, Rebecca [11: 07 A.M.]	Yes, she did. But her lack of focus on the U.S. shows she either didn't want to discuss Whitewater's performance here or she hadn't prepared properly. Neither choice is appealing.
	McCartney, Laurie [11:10 A.M.]	Both of you are making legitimate points. Let's meet for lunch at noon, and then we can discuss the matter in person.

Send

168. What is mostly being discussed?

(A) Working with Whitewater Consulting
(B) How to improve the company's performance
(C) Opinions regarding a presentation
(D) The importance of foreign and domestic markets

169. How does Mr. Daniels feel about the presentation?

(A) It proved his company can break into foreign markets.
(B) It convinced him that Whitewater Consulting should be hired.
(C) It explained the problems of selling goods domestically.
(D) It showed how Whitewater Consulting can help his firm.

170. At 10:59 A.M., what does Ms. McCartney mean when she writes, "I think I see where you're going with this"?

(A) She has to go to a meeting with Ms. Patrick.
(B) She knows what Ms. Patrick will write next.
(C) She is going to attend a presentation soon.
(D) She wants Ms. Patrick to provide more details.

171. What does Ms. Patrick suggest about Ms. Sanders?

(A) Ms. Sanders made a mistake by ignoring the U.S. market.
(B) Ms. Sanders's presentation brought up some valid points.
(C) Ms. Sanders's company should be able to help hers.
(D) Ms. Sanders needs to clarify some arguments she made.

GO ON TO THE NEXT PAGE

Questions 172-175 refer to the following letter.

July 28

Dear Ms. Rice,

On behalf of my colleagues at Evercrest Shipping, it is my great pleasure to offer you the position of head price analyst. We are all looking forward to working with you, and I believe you will find working here to be both rewarding and challenging. —[1]—. Evercrest Shipping is a company that truly values its employees and strives to work with the local community to have a positive influence not only in the world of business but also in the city of San Fernando.

Should you accept our offer, your first day of work will be on August 31. You will work directly under the deputy director of pricing, Rob Hamilton. —[2]—. You will receive a salary of $55,000 per year, a yearly raise of 4%, and an annual performance bonus. Since you will be moving from another state, we will contribute $7,500 for your moving costs. —[3]—. Like all other employees, you will receive 10 paid sick days a year, half of which may be rolled over to the following year. During your first year of employment, you will get 10 days of paid vacation. Beginning in the second year, that will increase to 20 days each year.

Please look at the contract I have included with this letter. It contains all of the above terms. —[4]—. If the terms are amenable, please sign and date the contract, and return it to me within 10 days. This offer is nonnegotiable and cannot be changed in any way.

Sincerely,

Shirley Gathers
HR Department
Evercrest Shipping

172. Why did Ms. Gathers write the letter?

   (A) To invite Ms. Rice to apply for a job
   (B) To extend an offer of employment
   (C) To promote her company to a job candidate
   (D) To list Ms. Rice's job duties

173. Which of the following is NOT a part of Ms. Rice's compensation package?

   (A) Enrollment in a benefits plan
   (B) A raise given each year
   (C) Paid vacation and sick leave
   (D) A bonus for doing well

174. What is stated in the letter?

   (A) Evercrest Shipping is active in politics in San Fernando.
   (B) Ms. Rice interviewed for the position two times.
   (C) The terms of the contract may not be changed.
   (D) Ms. Gathers is in charge of all hiring decisions.

175. In which of the positions marked [1], [2], [3], and [4] does the following sentence best belong?

"You can contact Vince Hoover at 950-1434 for more details regarding your transition here."

   (A) [1]
   (B) [2]
   (C) [3]
   (D) [4]

GO ON TO THE NEXT PAGE

Questions 176-180 refer to the following e-mails.

FROM: Laurel Flanagan <laurel_f@privatemail.com>
TO: Customer Service <customerservice@broadwayelectronics.com>
RE: Order 65059697
DATE: May 6

Dear Sir/Madam,

I'm writing with regard to an order (order number 65059697) I made on April 20. I spent more than $1,100, but there were still problems with my order. To begin with, the items arrived more than two weeks after being purchased. In addition, I bought some ink for my printer. I ordered two packs of TR440 black ink but was sent two packs of TR687 black ink. I checked which printers that ink is compatible with, and mine isn't one. The other problem concerns the Montague P2000 digital camera I purchased. While the camera arrived in fine condition, the user's manual was not included. I therefore have no idea how to operate my new camera.

I want the missing items sent immediately and further request to know how to return the ink to you. Please do this as soon as possible since I am traveling abroad in five days and would like to take my camera with me. This is the third shipping mistake made by your company in the past seven months. While I enjoy shopping at your online store due to the low prices, I am tired of receiving incorrect items and incomplete orders. If something similar happens again, I will no longer frequent your store.

Regards,
Laurel Flanagan

FROM: Customer Service <customerservice@broadwayelectronics.com>
TO: Laurel Flanagan <laurel_f@privatemail.com>
RE: RE: Order 65059697
DATE: May 6

Dear Ms. Flanagan,

On behalf of everyone in the Shipping Department at Broadway Electronics, I wholeheartedly apologize for the mistakes we made. I assure you that we will do our utmost to ensure that your orders no longer have any problems. In fact, I will personally pack and ship your orders from now on so that you can be sure to receive every item you buy. Your orders will also be sent by premium express mail at absolutely no cost to you. And the next time you purchase some items from us, please use coupon code BIGSAVINGS to receive 50% off any order of $1,000 or less. I hope these actions will convince you to continue using our services for many years to come.

As for the missing items, the ink has been shipped by courier and will arrive before noon tomorrow. The other item is not in stock at the moment, so I ordered it from the manufacturer. It should get here tomorrow, and we will then send it straight to you. You should therefore receive it before you go on your trip.

If you experience any more problems in the future, please call me directly at (403) 679-5495, and I shall do my best to assist you.

Sincerely,
Carmen Diego
Director, Shipping Department
Broadway Electronics

176. What is the purpose of the first e-mail?

(A) To ask why prices have been rising lately
(B) To acknowledge the receipt of some products
(C) To mention the poor quality of a purchased product
(D) To complain about some missing items

177. What does Ms. Flanagan indicate she might do in the future?

(A) Tell her friends about the bad service
(B) Stop shopping with Broadway Electronics
(C) Request a refund on some of her purchases
(D) Visit a Broadway Electronics offline store

178. In the second e-mail, the word "ensure" in paragraph 1, line 2 is closest in meaning to

(A) guarantee
(B) predict
(C) admit
(D) confirm

179. Which item did Ms. Diego order from a manufacturer?

(A) TR440 black ink
(B) TR687 black ink
(C) Montague P2000 digital camera
(D) Montague P2000 digital camera user's manual

180. Which issue that Ms. Flanagan wrote about does Ms. Diego NOT respond to in her e-mail?

(A) How to stop receiving incorrect items
(B) How to return an item to the company
(C) How to receive the items that were ordered
(D) How to get items more quickly

GO ON TO THE NEXT PAGE

Questions 181-185 refer to the following itinerary and letter.

Carter Manufacturing
Itinerary for Reggie Simmons

Date	Time	Event	Accommodations
Monday, September 14	4:15 P.M.	Arrive at Chicago O'Hare Airport Pick up car at Davis Rentals Check into hotel	Lakeside Hotel, Chicago
Tuesday, September 15	9:00 A.M. – 3:00 P.M.	Meeting at Turner, Inc. Tour new facility	Paradise Hotel, Peoria
Wednesday, September 16	1:00 P.M. – 4:00 P.M.	Product demonstration at MTR, Inc.	Traveler's Inn, Springfield
Thursday, September 17	1:30 P.M. – 6:00 P.M.	Negotiation at Riverside Tractors	Royal Inn, Ames
Friday, September 18	2:45 P.M.	Return car to Davis Rentals Check in at Western Air counter Depart from Chicago O'Hare Airport	N/A

Ted Lyons
Jade Travel Agency
465 Mountain Drive
Salt Lake City, UT

September 1

Reggie Simmons
Cater Manufacturing
309 12th Avenue
Salt Lake City, UT

Dear Mr. Simmons,

I made the travel arrangements you requested for your upcoming trip to the Midwest. I sent a copy of your itinerary to you by e-mail but have included a paper copy along with this letter. If you require any modifications, inform me, and I shall make the necessary arrangements.

Upon arriving in Chicago, please head to the Davis Rentals counter at Terminal 3 to pick up your vehicle. I was able to upgrade you to a luxury sedan for the same price that you normally pay for a midsized vehicle. You need to return the vehicle with a full tank of gas on September 18 to avoid paying any excessive fees.

As for your hotels, you have stayed in all but one of them before. There's a hotel that recently opened in Springfield, and I've heard other clients make complimentary remarks about it. It's newer and cheaper than your normal accommodations at the Welcome Inn, so I thought I would reserve you a room there. If you prefer the Welcome Inn though, I will be glad to make a booking for you there.

I'll send the bill for the airfare, car, and hotels to Ms. Thompson in Accounting like I always do. Have a wonderful trip.

Sincerely,

Ted Lyons
Travel Agent
Jade Travel Agency

181. What is Mr. Simmons NOT scheduled to do on his trip?

(A) Attend a conference
(B) Negotiate with a company
(C) Go on a tour
(D) Demonstrate how to use a product

182. Where will Mr. Simmons stay on September 17?

(A) In Ames
(B) In Chicago
(C) In Springfield
(D) In Peoria

183. What does Mr. Lyons send to Mr. Simmons along with the letter?

(A) A bill
(B) A plane ticket
(C) A confirmation code
(D) An itinerary

184. What does Mr. Lyons mention about Mr. Simmons's rental car?

(A) It comes with a full tank of gas.
(B) It costs the same as usual.
(C) It is smaller than normal.
(D) It can be picked up in Peoria.

185. What is indicated about the Welcome Inn?

(A) It is the newest hotel in Ames.
(B) Its owner also runs the Paradise Hotel.
(C) It is currently fully booked.
(D) It costs more than the Traveler's Inn.

GO ON TO THE NEXT PAGE

Questions 186-190 refer to the following advertisement and e-mails.

Celebrate the Grand Opening of the Seaside Resort with Us

The Seaside Resort in Fort Lauderdale, Florida, is opening on May 1, and everyone is invited. Every room has an ocean view, and we provide a daily complimentary breakfast buffet on the beach for our guests. Enjoy free Wi-Fi and discounted prices at our five-star restaurant as well if you stay with us.

Single Room: one queen-sized bed; $129.99/night
Double Room: two queen-sized beds or one king-sized bed; $159.99/night
Junior Suite: two rooms; two king-sized beds; $209.99/night
Luxury Suite: three rooms; three king-sized beds; $259.99/night

Visit www.seasideresort.com to see pictures of our rooms as well as the facilities. We have a private beach, an outdoor swimming pool, a fitness center, and tennis courts. We also arrange scuba diving trips, fishing trips, and cruises on the Atlantic Ocean.

Reserve a room from now until April 30, and you'll get 50% off the regular price. Don't pass up a deal like this. Contact us at reservations@seasideresort.com now.

From: hwalker@homemail.com
To: reservations@seasideresort.com
Re: Reservation Request
Date: May 2

Dear Sir/Madam,

I saw your resort advertised in my local newspaper, and I knew instantly that it's the place where I want to take my family for our annual summer trip. There are four of us (my wife and two daughters), so we'd like to stay in a junior suite. We'll be arriving on May 28 and departing on June 5. We will receive the discounted rate, won't we?

My wife and I are avid scuba divers, so we'd like to arrange a couple of trips while we're there. We'd love to have the opportunity to dive on some shipwrecks or coral reefs. My daughters don't dive, so are there any activities they can do while we are on the ocean? In addition, where do the cruises go? Finally, do you allow dogs on the premises? We'd like to bring our golden retriever Rusty if that's possible.

Sincerely,

Henry Walker

From: reservations@seasideresort.com
To: hwalker@homemail.com
Re: Welcome to the Seaside Resort
Date: May 2

Dear Mr. Walker,

Thank you for reserving a room at the Seaside Resort. You are confirmed for the following:

1 junior suite – May 28 to June 5 (nine days)

Check-in is at 2 P.M. If you require early check-in, please inform us as soon as possible so that we can make the proper arrangements. A small fee may be required.

Our diving instructor is Cliff Swan. He can answer your questions about scuba diving in the Fort Lauderdale area. He conducts both group and private dives. You can reach him at cliffswan@seasideresort.com.

We regret to inform you that pets are not permitted at the resort. In addition, you need to pay full price for the room as the special offer is no longer being offered. As for your children, they can go swimming, visit the beach, or go fishing with one of our employees for a small fee.

Please feel free to contact us should you have any questions. We look forward to serving you and your family in a few weeks.

Sincerely,

Christie McDougal
Seaside Resort

186. Which of the following is mentioned about the Seaside Resort?

(A) It provides free lunch buffets for guests.
(B) It offers many types of entertainment.
(C) Guests can get cheaper rates by staying for a week.
(D) Its facilities were awarded five stars.

187. Why will Mr. Walker be traveling to Fort Lauderdale?

(A) To conduct business
(B) To take a vacation
(C) To visit relatives
(D) To attend a conference

188. How much will Mr. Walker pay?

(A) $129.99 a night
(B) $159.99 a night
(C) $209.99 a night
(D) $259.99 a night

189. Why would Mr. Walker most likely contact Mr. Swan?

(A) To set up tennis lessons
(B) To learn how to swim
(C) To go on a cruise
(D) To arrange a diving session

190. Which question by Mr. Walker does Ms. McDougal NOT respond to?

(A) What activities there are for children
(B) Whether a cheaper price will be offered
(C) Whether animals can be brought with guests
(D) Which places passengers can visit on boat trips

Questions 191-195 refer to the following online review, announcement, and letter.

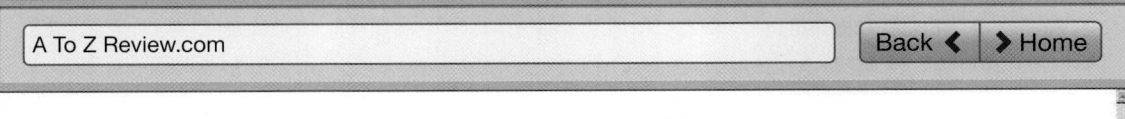

Self-Improvement: A Guide

A Review by Art Mooney

Self-help guru Sabrina Lattimore has done it again with her latest book, *Self-Improvement: A Guide*. This work, published in hardback by Nelson Publishers, is her eighth and, in my opinion, best book. It provides a step-by-step method for improving every aspect of a person's life. Of course, the writing is filled with witty comments and fascinating personal anecdotes, making the book even more interesting. I've already found myself adopting some of the steps Ms. Lattimore suggests for improving myself, and I've personally recommended this book to several friends and family members, something I almost never do. The only real drawback to this book is the lack of an index, so it was sometimes difficult to go back to find something I was looking for. Nevertheless, that's hardly anything to get upset about. I wholeheartedly recommend this book and believe the $19.99 it is retailing for is quite a bargain. Go out and buy it at once.

Sabrina Lattimore to Speak on Friday

This Friday, August 11, Sabrina Lattimore is going to give a talk in the auditorium at 3:00 P.M. Ms. Lattimore is a well-known motivational speaker who has given countless talks around the country. We at Murray Consulting are pleased that she has agreed to speak to us. The speech will last for two hours and will cover the material she wrote in her book *How to Become a Leader*. At the conclusion of her talk, Ms. Lattimore will answer questions, and then there will be a short reception afterward. All Murray Consulting employees are welcome to attend. You may also invite one guest. This may be a family member, friend, or client. Please inform Julie Richardson (extension 564) if you will be attending as well as the name of your guest no later than Wednesday, August 9.

August 14

Dear Ms. Lattimore,

On behalf of everyone at Murray Consulting, thank you for the speech you gave on Friday afternoon. I learned a great deal, and you inspired me to find a bookstore so that I could purchase your newest work as soon as I left the office in the evening. I spoke with several of my colleagues, and they were impressed with the advice you provided in your speech. They also appreciated your accepting their invitation to go out for dinner afterward and your being so gracious in taking the time to answer everyone's questions. I wonder if you would be interested in returning around six months from now and speaking about another topic. I know you have given many talks in the past, so perhaps you could suggest a new subject to discuss. When you have the opportunity, please let me know.

Sincerely,

Charles Murray
Owner, Murray Consulting

191. What does Mr. Mooney indicate in his review?

(A) *Self-Improvement: A Guide* is available as a paperback.
(B) The stories in *Self-Improvement: A Guide* are the best part.
(C) He gave copies of *Self-Improvement: A Guide* to his friends.
(D) He did not like every aspect of *Self-Improvement: A Guide*.

192. In the review, the word "witty" in line 4 is closest in meaning to

(A) obvious
(B) helpful
(C) clever
(D) thoughtful

193. What is suggested about *How to Become a Leader*?

(A) It was published before *Self-Improvement: A Guide*.
(B) It has sold more copies than any of Ms. Lattimore's other books.
(C) It was the first book Ms. Lattimore ever wrote.
(D) It has been read by all Murray Consulting employees.

194. According to the letter, what did Mr. Murray do on Friday evening?

(A) Had dinner with his colleagues
(B) Purchased *Self-Improvement: A Guide*
(C) Hosted a special event at work
(D) Asked Ms. Lattimore some questions

195. What does Mr. Murray ask Ms. Lattimore to do?

(A) Give another speech in the future
(B) Autograph some copies of her book
(C) Provide some advice on a book he is writing
(D) Respond to some questions by e-mail

GO ON TO THE NEXT PAGE

Questions 196-200 refer to the following survey, memo, and article.

Best Value

Customer Satisfaction Survey

Thank you for shopping at Best Value. We appreciate your patronage. We always strive to improve the quality of the items we sell and the service we provide. So we request that you take a few moments to complete this form. Please answer all the questions and leave any comments you have. Then, present this survey to any store employee and receive a coupon for 10% off on your next visit here.

How do you feel about the following at Best Value?

	Poor	Bad	Good	Excellent
Prices				X
Selection		X		
Hours				X
Employees	X			

Comments: *Many of the employees here don't seem to care about the customers. When I ask them questions, they don't know or give me incorrect answers. Just a moment ago, I tried getting the attention of one employee, and she totally ignored me. Please do something to improve the quality of the service here.*

Name: *Thaddeus Toole*

TO: All Managers, Best Value
FROM: Marcus Dupree, VP, Best Value
SUBJECT: Recent Survey
DATE: November 10

The company that we hired to conduct last month's survey for us just submitted the data along with the comments that people left. We scored very high marks on our prices and the selection of items. Most shoppers like our hours, but a few wish that we would stay open 24 hours a day. However, more than 50% of all respondents rated our employees as either bad or poor. The comments were incredibly harsh. We apparently have an employee problem, and we need to do something about it. Several customers commented that they no longer intend to shop here since our employees ignore them or can't answer their questions. We must do something about this quickly. The holiday season is fast approaching, and we have to make sure sales don't suffer. We get most of our revenue then, so losing customers could cause us to miss our objective for the year.

A New Program at Old Store

Trenton (December 5) – One of the oldest stores in the city is starting one of the newest programs. Best Value, which has been in business since 1852, realized it had a problem when it received the results of a survey conducted more than a month ago. "Our customers weren't happy," said owner Travis Butler. "So we instituted a new program, and it appears to be successful." All Best Value employees now receive ten hours of training. They learn about customer relations, and they also learn about everything the store sells. "When I started here, I couldn't answer any questions, but now I know how to use all the items here," said Kimberly Charles, who works at the store. "I love helping customers now, and I even like staying here after my shift is over to practice using some gadgets," she added.

196. What can customers receive for completing a survey?

(A) A free gift
(B) A discount coupon
(C) A beverage
(D) A gift certificate

197. What does Mr. Toole mention about Best Value employees?

(A) They need to be trained better.
(B) They do not perform their duties well.
(C) They are able to answer his questions.
(D) They speak rudely to him at times.

198. In which category does Mr. Toole's evaluation differ from the majority of the respondents?

(A) Prices
(B) Selection
(C) Hours
(D) Employees

199. What does Mr. Dupree suggest doing?

(A) Starting a new program
(B) Offering items at discounts
(C) Firing some employees
(D) Keeping sales from falling

200. Who is Kimberly Charles?

(A) A Best Value manager
(B) A Best Value customer
(C) A Best Value employee
(D) The CEO of Best Value

Stop! This is the end of the test. If you finish before time is called, you may go back to Parts 5, 6, and 7 and check your work.

Actual Test

04

LISTENING TEST

In the Listening test, you will be asked to demonstrate how well you understand spoken English. The entire Listening test will last approximately 45 minutes. There are four parts, and directions are given for each part. You must mark your answers on the separate answer sheet. Do not write your answers in your test book.

PART 1

Directions: For each question in this part, you will hear four statements about a picture in your test book. When you hear the statements, you must select the one statement that best describes what you see in the picture. Then find the number of the question on your answer sheet and mark your answer. The statements will not be printed in your test book and will be spoken only one time.

Statement (C), "Items are stacked up in the warehouse," is the best description of the picture, so you should select answer (C) and mark it on your answer sheet.

1.

2.

3.

4.

5.

6.

GO ON TO THE NEXT PAGE

PART 2

Directions: You will hear a question or statement and three responses spoken in English. They will not be printed in your test book and will be spoken only one time. Select the best response to the question or statement and mark the letter (A), (B), or (C) on your answer sheet.

7. Mark your answer on your answer sheet.
8. Mark your answer on your answer sheet.
9. Mark your answer on your answer sheet.
10. Mark your answer on your answer sheet.
11. Mark your answer on your answer sheet.
12. Mark your answer on your answer sheet.
13. Mark your answer on your answer sheet.
14. Mark your answer on your answer sheet.
15. Mark your answer on your answer sheet.
16. Mark your answer on your answer sheet.
17. Mark your answer on your answer sheet.
18. Mark your answer on your answer sheet.
19. Mark your answer on your answer sheet.
20. Mark your answer on your answer sheet.
21. Mark your answer on your answer sheet.
22. Mark your answer on your answer sheet.
23. Mark your answer on your answer sheet.
24. Mark your answer on your answer sheet.
25. Mark your answer on your answer sheet.
26. Mark your answer on your answer sheet.
27. Mark your answer on your answer sheet.
28. Mark your answer on your answer sheet.
29. Mark your answer on your answer sheet.
30. Mark your answer on your answer sheet.
31. Mark your answer on your answer sheet.

PART 3

🎧 04-03

Directions: You will hear some conversations between two or more people. You will be asked to answer three questions about what the speakers say in each conversation. Select the best response to each question and mark the letter (A), (B), (C), or (D) on your answer sheet. The conversations will not be printed in your test book and will be spoken only one time.

32. What are the speakers mainly discussing?
   (A) Their relationship with Mark Kenmore
   (B) The topic of an upcoming talk
   (C) A seminar that they attended
   (D) Their plans for later in the day

33. What does the woman mention?
   (A) She plans to use the knowledge she learned in the future.
   (B) She hopes to meet Mark Kenmore in person later.
   (C) She took notes on what Mark Kenmore said in his talk.
   (D) She is trying to market some products in other countries.

34. What is going to happen on Monday?
   (A) The woman will give a presentation.
   (B) The man will speak with his colleagues.
   (C) The man will attend a special event.
   (D) The woman will meet with her supervisor.

35. Why is the woman pleased?
   (A) The man fixed her problems.
   (B) She does not need to repair anything.
   (C) The man is visiting her apartment.
   (D) She solved the problems by herself.

36. What is the problem in the kitchen?
   (A) There is a gas leak.
   (B) The refrigerator has stopped working.
   (C) A pipe is dripping water.
   (D) A light is turning on and off.

37. What will the man probably do next?
   (A) Fix the problem in the bathroom
   (B) Replace a light bulb
   (C) Clean up the water on the floor
   (D) Leave a voicemail message

GO ON TO THE NEXT PAGE

38. How did the woman order the items?

(A) By making a telephone call
(B) By visiting the store in person
(C) By mailing in an order form
(D) By going to a Web site

39. What will the store send to the woman first?

(A) A sofa
(B) A table
(C) A bed
(D) A dresser

40. What does the woman say about her home?

(A) It was recently renovated.
(B) It is located near the warehouse.
(C) It has no furnishings in it.
(D) It is currently for sale.

---

41. What does the woman suggest?

(A) Getting together tomorrow afternoon
(B) Contacting one of the factory foremen
(C) Having another employee assist her
(D) Making some slides for a presentation

42. What are the speakers planning to do?

(A) Interview some job candidates
(B) Fill out some forms
(C) Visit a factory
(D) Have a meeting

43. What does the woman imply?

(A) She is in favor of replacing some machinery.
(B) She has not visited the factory for several weeks.
(C) She hopes that the equipment does not break down soon.
(D) She plans to submit some order forms this afternoon.

44. What is the man's problem?

(A) He was charged too much for something.
(B) An item he bought is not working properly.
(C) The store manager refused to give him a receipt.
(D) His radio suddenly stopped working yesterday.

45. What does the woman mean when she says, "But I'll make an exception in this case"?

(A) The man can exchange his item without a receipt.
(B) The man may cancel the order that he just made.
(C) The man does not have to fill out any more forms.
(D) The man will be allowed to get his money back.

46. What will the speakers probably do next?

(A) Call the store manager
(B) Fix the broken item
(C) Go to another department
(D) Look for a replacement part

47. What are the speakers discussing?

(A) A presentation they will attend
(B) The results of an interview
(C) Their work on some projects
(D) The man's transfer application

48. Who is Eric Harrison?

(A) A college professor
(B) A pharmacist
(C) A manager
(D) A job candidate

49. What does the man tell the woman to do?

(A) Look at the résumés of some other individuals
(B) Do more research on the pharmaceutical industry
(C) Learn how to be less nervous at work
(D) Schedule another interview with a person

---

50. What is the purpose of the man's call?

(A) To confirm a meeting
(B) To receive directions
(C) To schedule a visit
(D) To request more time

51. What will the speakers do later in the day?

(A) Attend a presentation
(B) Eat lunch together
(C) Check out a property
(D) Visit a client

52. Where is the man going to meet the woman?

(A) At his office
(B) At a restaurant
(C) On Hampton Road
(D) At her office

53. What are the speakers talking about?

(A) The gifts that they purchased
(B) The hiring of a new supervisor
(C) The bonuses they were given
(D) The resignation of a coworker

54. What is scheduled to happen next Friday?

(A) An awards ceremony
(B) A birthday party
(C) A farewell party
(D) A company picnic

55. What does the man imply about Mary Burns?

(A) She used to work with the speakers.
(B) She is an executive at the company.
(C) She will ask the speakers for donations.
(D) She was recently hired as a receptionist.

GO ON TO THE NEXT PAGE

56. What are the speakers mainly discussing?
   (A) The possibility of moving to another company
   (B) The desire of the man to transfer
   (C) The condition of the Marketing Department
   (D) The intentions of the man to retire

57. Why does the man want to live in St. Louis?
   (A) To be near his family
   (B) To attend school there
   (C) To work with his old boss
   (D) To help start a new branch there

58. Why does the man say, "I can handle that"?
   (A) To prove he is capable of going on a business trip
   (B) To indicate he is willing to accept a lower salary
   (C) To state that he can work in the Market Department
   (D) To show his willingness to be promoted

59. What does the woman plan to do tomorrow?
   (A) Go to a conference
   (B) Visit a lab facility
   (C) Travel to Framingham
   (D) Meet a consultant

60. When will the speakers have their meeting?
   (A) On Tuesday
   (B) On Wednesday
   (C) On Thursday
   (D) On Friday

61. Why does the man say, "That works for me"?
   (A) To ask the woman to repeat the comment she just made
   (B) To request that the woman work harder on the problem
   (C) To express his agreement with the woman's suggestion
   (D) To suggest an alternative time to meet with the woman

62. What does the man mean when he says, "There isn't enough money in the budget for that"?

(A) The company will not purchase any new computers.
(B) No employees will receive pay raises this year.
(C) All orders of new office supplies will be canceled.
(D) Staff members may no longer attend conferences.

63. What did the women have problems doing?

(A) Arranging a time to see their boss
(B) Installing a computer program
(C) Getting financing for a project
(D) Attending a staff meeting

64. What does the man say he will do?

(A) Replace the old equipment
(B) Download a program
(C) Speak with an expert
(D) Request some money

Size	Quantity
S	10
M	26
L	20
XL	14

65. Why does the woman need T-shirts?

(A) For a company picnic
(B) For a conference
(C) For a field trip
(D) For a sporting event

66. Look at the graphic. Which size shirt does the woman order more of?

(A) Small
(B) Medium
(C) Large
(D) Extra large

67. When will the company mail the shirts?

(A) On Tuesday
(B) On Wednesday
(C) On Thursday
(D) On Friday

GO ON TO THE NEXT PAGE

Floor	Shops
5	Westwood Theater
4	Dan's Deli, Modern Fashions
3	Toys for Tots, Wilson's Bookstore
2	Jackson Pharmacy, Food Court

68. What does the man want to purchase?

    (A) Books
    (B) Electronics
    (C) Clothes
    (D) Kitchen items

69. Why is the man asking for assistance?

    (A) He has never visited the mall before.
    (B) A store closed earlier than expected.
    (C) A store is not listed on a map.
    (D) He forgot the name of a store.

70. Look at the graphic. Which floor should the man go to?

    (A) 2
    (B) 3
    (C) 4
    (D) 5

PART 4

Directions: You will hear some talks given by a single speaker. You will be asked to answer three questions about what the speaker says in each talk. Select the best response to each question and mark the letter (A), (B), (C), or (D) on your answer sheet. The talks will not be printed in your test book and will be spoken only one time.

71. What is the problem?
    (A) The speaker forgot about an appointment.
    (B) The speaker's son suffered an injury.
    (C) The speaker is going to be late for school.
    (D) The speaker's boss made her miss a meeting.

72. When does the speaker want to meet Craig?
    (A) This afternoon
    (B) This evening
    (C) Tomorrow morning
    (D) Tomorrow evening

73. What does the speaker ask Craig to do?
    (A) Invite another person to the meeting
    (B) Contact her regarding his availability
    (C) Send her a contact number by text message
    (D) Fax her the report that she requests

74. How has the weather in December been?
    (A) Normal
    (B) Warmer than usual
    (C) Cold
    (D) Very cold

75. What does the speaker mean when he says, "And that's not the worst part"?
    (A) The weather is going to become bad.
    (B) He heard some bad news just now.
    (C) It will not stop raining for several days.
    (D) The cold weather is going to continue.

76. What will the weather be like on the day after tomorrow?
    (A) Warm and cloudy
    (B) Cool and windy
    (C) Cold and snowy
    (D) Cool and rainy

GO ON TO THE NEXT PAGE

77. What is the purpose of the announcement?
   (A) To explain how to get a rebate
   (B) To mention a deadline for an event
   (C) To remind listeners about a sale
   (D) To describe a special offer

78. Who qualifies for discounts on swimming lessons?
   (A) Children of employees
   (B) Only full-time employees
   (C) Only part-time employees
   (D) All employees

79. What should listeners do to get more information?
   (A) Send an e-mail
   (B) Call the swimming pool
   (C) Speak with another employee
   (D) Read a pamphlet

---

80. Who most likely is the announcement for?
   (A) Musicians
   (B) Audience members
   (C) Conductors
   (D) Music instructors

81. What is mentioned about the event?
   (A) It is going to last for two days.
   (B) Individuals must play three pieces of music.
   (C) Attendees must be able to play two instruments.
   (D) Only violinists are encouraged to try out.

82. What are orchestra members given?
   (A) Salaries
   (B) CDs of their performances
   (C) Instruments
   (D) Concert tickets

83. Who is the speaker talking to?
   (A) Telephone operators
   (B) Shipping Department employees
   (C) Delivery personnel
   (D) Office receptionists

84. What problem does the speaker mention?
   (A) Some money was stolen.
   (B) Some boxes were lost.
   (C) Some items were broken.
   (D) Some orders were never received.

85. What does the speaker suggest may happen?
   (A) Individuals may lose their jobs.
   (B) Individuals may be suspended.
   (C) Individuals may be given more training.
   (D) Individuals may be transferred.

86. What is mainly being discussed?
    (A) The qualifications of some job candidates
    (B) The interviews that will be conducted
    (C) A job search that is currently going on
    (D) A position that needs to be filled soon

87. What does the speaker indicate about herself?
    (A) She knows which person she prefers for a job.
    (B) She has already made her final decision.
    (C) She has meet with Vladimir Sobieski twice.
    (D) She wants to conduct some more interviews.

88. Why does the speaker say, "Jeff, let's start with you"?
    (A) To say that he needs to speak to one of the candidates
    (B) To request that he state the individual he supports
    (C) To tell him that he needs to give his presentation now
    (D) To ask him to provide the results of his interview

89. What job did Jay Carpenter accept?
    (A) Human Resources employee
    (B) Computer programmer
    (C) Manager
    (D) Software designer

90. Why was the offer to Delilah Cohen withdrawn?
    (A) She wanted a higher salary.
    (B) She demanded more benefits.
    (C) She did not want to start in two weeks.
    (D) She insisted on a bonus.

91. What can the woman do for Lucy van Horton?
    (A) Offer her health insurance
    (B) Pay for her to move
    (C) Help her find housing
    (D) Increase her starting salary

Day	Lecture
Monday	Solving Workplace Problems
Tuesday	Getting along with Subordinates
Wednesday	Foreign Currency Exchange
Thursday	Methods for Increasing Sales

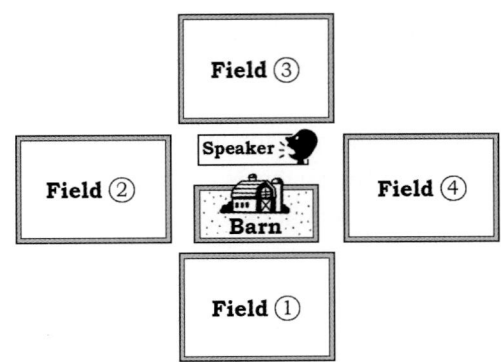

92. Who is Ms. Jenkins?

(A) A lecturer
(B) A consultant
(C) A conference participant
(D) A banker

93. Look at the graphic. When is Ms. Richardson going to give her lecture?

(A) On Monday
(B) On Tuesday
(C) On Wednesday
(D) On Thursday

94. What did Brian Andropov do?

(A) Paid to attend a conference
(B) Organized a conference
(C) Agreed to speak at a conference
(D) Ended his role in a conference

95. Who is the speaker?

(A) A tour guide
(B) A teacher
(C) A farmer
(D) A horse trainer

96. What does the speaker indicate about the corn?

(A) It is growing poorly.
(B) It will be picked soon.
(C) It has been harvested.
(D) It was recently planted.

97. Look at the graphic. In which field can people ride horses?

(A) Number 1
(B) Number 2
(C) Number 3
(D) Number 4

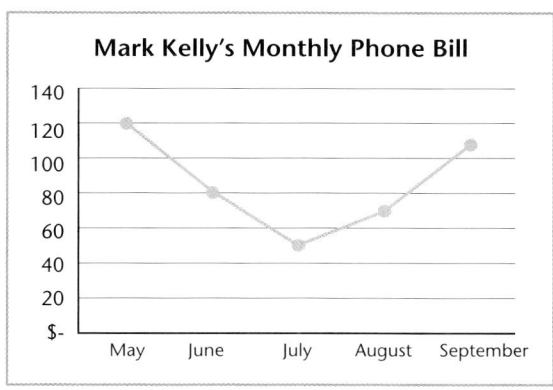

98. What is the purpose of the speaker's call?
    (A) To cancel a service
    (B) To file a complaint
    (C) To pay his phone bill
    (D) To request a new service

99. What does the speaker say that he did?
    (A) Took his phone on vacation with him
    (B) Canceled his service a few months ago
    (C) Traveled abroad for a couple of months
    (D) Called foreign countries with his phone

100. Look at the graphic. In which month does the speaker believe he was charged too much?
    (A) In May
    (B) In June
    (C) In July
    (D) In August

This is the end of the Listening test. Turn to Part 5 in your test book.

READING TEST

In the Reading test, you will read a variety of texts and answer several different types of reading comprehension questions. The entire Reading test will last 75 minutes. There are three parts, and directions are given for each part. You are encouraged to answer as many questions as possible within the time allowed.

You must mark your answers on the separate answer sheet. Do not write your answers in your test book.

PART 5

Directions: A word or phrase is missing in each of the sentences below. Four answer choices are given below each sentence. Select the best answer to complete the sentence. Then mark the letter (A), (B), (C), or (D) on your answer sheet.

101. The mechanic is replacing the ------- part and will require around an hour to fix the engine.

    (A) defection
    (B) defecting
    (C) defective
    (D) defect

102. All the invitations to the company's annual ball have been sent to ------- associated with the firm.

    (A) everyone
    (B) each one
    (C) someone
    (D) anyone

103. It is widely expected that Mr. Durant will ------- the decision to sell the Davenport facility to Kenmore Technology.

    (A) approve
    (B) prompt
    (C) withdraw
    (D) portray

104. Mr. McDaniel plans ------- advertisements for his studio in all of the local papers and magazines.

    (A) placing
    (B) will place
    (C) to place
    (D) having placed

105. Every shipment is ------- to arrive within 48 hours, or Gateway Logistics will refund the sender's payment.

    (A) promised
    (B) assumed
    (C) conditioned
    (D) guaranteed

106. ------- expenses enabled Wilson Electronics to become profitable during the second quarter of the year.

    (A) Abandoning
    (B) Declining
    (C) Reducing
    (D) Supporting

107. Customers may opt to receive their invoices either ------- the mail or by fax.
(A) within
(B) on
(C) through
(D) around

108. Because the machinery has been in ------- use, it needs to be inspected sometime next week.
(A) continue
(B) continual
(C) continuity
(D) continuing

109. On account of the poor harvest, many people in the agricultural sector had to declare -------.
(A) bankrupt
(B) bankrupted
(C) bankruptcy
(D) bankrupting

110. Dr. Beale is internationally ------- for his work in the fields of robotics and medicine.
(A) renowned
(B) approved
(C) revealed
(D) anticipated

111. The special discount ------- offered to all members does not apply for purchases of $1,000 or more.
(A) was
(B) is
(C) will be
(D) being

112. The latest version of Robin Electronics' laptop is twice ------- the earlier version of the model.
(A) faster
(B) as fast as
(C) fastest
(D) faster than

113. Thousands of individuals in search of gainful ------- appeared at the job fair in Peoria over the weekend.
(A) employee
(B) employer
(C) employment
(D) employable

114. Ms. Rogers had to pay an extra fee because her suitcase ------- more than 3 kilograms above the permitted amount.
(A) weighed
(B) appeared
(C) measured
(D) evaluated

115. Two days after the jobs ------- on the Web site, more than 200 applications arrived in the company's mailbox.
(A) posted
(B) will be posted
(C) are posting
(D) were posted

116. The new software by Poko, Inc. is not just inexpensive but is also more efficient than anything ------- on the market.
(A) other
(B) then
(C) else
(D) which

GO ON TO THE NEXT PAGE

117. The staff members unanimously agreed to accept the offer of a bonus and pay ------- from management.
   (A) rose
   (B) raise
   (C) raising
   (D) raised

118. Jefferson Lee has a ------- in the local business community for being a dependable and honest man.
   (A) standard
   (B) status
   (C) condition
   (D) reputation

119. Only ------- applicants who have graduated with a degree in engineering will be considered for the positions at World Tech, Inc.
   (A) qualifies
   (B) qualified
   (C) qualification
   (D) qualitied

120. In an effort to get rid of its unwanted winter clothing, New Style Fashions had a sale in ------- it offered discounts of up to 70%.
   (A) that
   (B) when
   (C) where
   (D) which

121. The only people who are permitted into the boarding area are those individuals with ------- tickets.
   (A) dignified
   (B) valid
   (C) verbal
   (D) legal

122. When the survey -------, the data must be compiled in a form that can be properly analyzed.
   (A) is completed
   (B) completes
   (C) will complete
   (D) is being completed

123. According to the terms of the agreement, payment must be made no later than the fifth day of ------- month for the next two years.
   (A) each
   (B) some
   (C) any
   (D) no

124. WTRT, the local radio station, is offering discounted rates on advertisements to its primary -------.
   (A) sponsorships
   (B) sponsoring
   (C) sponsors
   (D) sponsored

125. The store manager at David's always calls customers to ------- if they file complaints about service.
   (A) ask around
   (B) follow up
   (C) advise
   (D) feedback

126. Henry's Fish and Chips, a ------- chain restaurant, is going to expand to more than 25 countries by this time next year.
   (A) growth
   (B) growing
   (C) grow
   (D) grower

127. Mr. Scott, Ms. Chandler's lawyer, ------- to permit the release of any of her personnel files last night.

(A) refuses
(B) is refusing
(C) has refused
(D) refused

128. Several items on the ------- had not been covered at the meeting by the time it adjourned.

(A) degree
(B) agenda
(C) transcript
(D) staff

129. ------- additional information on its products, people can visit the company's Web site to download a pamphlet.

(A) For
(B) With
(C) By
(D) Through

130. There is some ------- beneficial research on pharmaceuticals being done in the laboratories at the Nelson Corporation.

(A) energetically
(B) potentially
(C) carefully
(D) patiently

GO ON TO THE NEXT PAGE

PART 6

Directions: Read the texts that follow. A word, phrase, or sentence is missing in parts of each text. Four answer choices for each question are given below the text. Select the best answer to complete the text. Then mark the letter (A), (B), (C), or (D) on your answer sheet.

Questions 131-134 refer to the following e-mail.

To: Samantha Wallace, Edward Kershaw

From: Ted Winters

Subject: Changes

Date: June 10

I've been giving some thought to an idea, and I'd like to find out what -------- of you think about it. Since the Sales and Marketing departments collaborate so much, I'm considering putting
                                                                            131.

the two offices in the same room. So Sales would no longer be on the first floor, -------- would
                                                                                  132.

Marketing be on the third floor. Instead, they'll be on the second floor in a large, open area.

There will be no individual offices except for those of the director and assistant director of each

department.

I believe this would foster a sense of teamwork between the members of both departments. By

-------- what the salespeople are doing, the marketing people could create better advertisements
133.

and devise more ways to induce shoppers to buy our products. And by learning how the

marketers think, the sales staff could come up with more effective ways to pitch our products.

What do you two think of this proposal? --------
                                        134.

131. (A) each
 (B) some
 (C) either
 (D) both

132. (A) and
 (B) nor
 (C) thus
 (D) which

133. (A) knowledge
 (B) knowing
 (C) knowable
 (D) will know

134. (A) Wouldn't you agree that everything I did worked out well?
 (B) Don't you think that everyone approves of the changes we made?
 (C) How about providing feedback on this idea when you have some time?
 (D) When will you two have some time to start moving the desks around?

Questions 135-138 refer to the following notice.

Electricity to Be Disconnected

--------- The area that is going to be covered by the blackout will be on Carter Street between
135.
Eastern Avenue and Kenmore Road. Work crews from Alameda Power are going to be working on

some high-powered lines on Carter Street, so electricity there must be turned off to let them do

their jobs ---------. Electricity will be disconnected at 9 A.M. and should be turned back on around
         136.
11:30 A.M. Residents who will be --------- ought to take precautions so that they will be prepared
                                    137.
during this time. If the work is not complete by 11:30, the electricity will remain off. City employees

will make --------- by loudspeaker in the area so that residents can be updated on the work crews'
          138.
progress. Please visit the Alameda Power Web site at www.alamedapower.com/carterstreet to

learn more about which areas will be covered by the blackout. Questions or complaints can be

e-mailed to info@alamedapower.com and will be responded to within 4 hours of being received

---

135. (A) Work crews are going to be repairing the street this Friday, October 10.
(B) On Wednesday, July 25, a water pipe is going to be repaired on Carter Street.
(C) Some parts of the city will not have electricity on Thursday, September 14.
(D) This Saturday, August 11, the gas will be shut off in the Freemont neighborhood.

136. (A) safer
(B) the safest
(C) safely
(D) safety

137. (A) affected
(B) upset
(C) absent
(D) reported

138. (A) decisions
(B) announcements
(C) repairs
(D) upgrades

GO ON TO THE NEXT PAGE

Questions 139-142 refer to the following e-mail.

TO: Mary Lewis <m_lewis@dmmt.com>
FROM: Eloise Purcell <eloisep@dmmt.com>
RE: Meeting
DATE: October 3

Mary,

I know we are supposed to meet today right after lunch, but I'm afraid I'm not going to be able to get together with you then. Mr. Colter, my supervisor, requested that I give a presentation for the delegation from Spain --------- arrived last night. I need to discuss the benefits of our latest line
139.
of software with them at 2:30 this afternoon. --------- I therefore need to spend every minute until
140.
then working on what I intend to say.

How does your schedule look tomorrow morning? I've got --------- time between 9 and noon, so
141.
I can meet you then. If that doesn't work for you, I'm also available between the hours of 4 and 6. Why don't you let me know what the best time for you to meet is? I apologize for canceling our meeting on such --------- notice, but this is a matter that is out of my control. I hope you
142.
understand.

Regards,

Eloise

139. (A) what
(B) when
(C) where
(D) that

140. (A) However, I haven't prepared any of my remarks yet.
(B) In case you don't know, I was the lead designer on the software.
(C) Unfortunately, the software still has some big problems.
(D) Consequently, I'll be leaving for Spain as soon as possible.

141. (A) a variety of
(B) very little
(C) no type of
(D) plenty of

142. (A) apparent
(B) short
(C) surprising
(D) tight

Questions 143-146 refer to the following article.

Bixby Bank to Open New Branch Downtown

Hampton City (January 17) – Yesterday, a spokeswoman for Bixby Bank announced that the bank -------- a new branch in the downtown part of Hampton City. The office will be located on the
143.
second floor of the Silverwood Shopping Center. -------- Headquartered in Montgomery, the
144.
bank has been opening branch offices at a swift pace during the past two years. This year, it plans to open more than 30 branch offices across the entire state. The office in the mall will be Hampton City's fourth Bixby Bank. The bank has been growing so much thanks to its -------- on customer
145.
relations and quality service. In a recent survey, Bixby Bank ranked much higher than all of its competitors regarding how well it -------- its customers and which services it provides for them.
146.
Bixby Bank recorded more than $25 million in profits last year, and analysts believe it will more than double that number this year.

143. (A) opened
(B) has opened
(C) is opening
(D) to open

144. (A) The shopping center recently closed due to poor sales.
(B) Experts believe Bixby Bank must improve its services.
(C) Bixby Bank is the state's fastest growing bank.
(D) This will be the first branch that the bank has opened.

145. (A) emphasis
(B) impression
(C) consideration
(D) dedication

146. (A) considers
(B) treats
(C) appoints
(D) behaves

GO ON TO THE NEXT PAGE

PART 7

Directions: In this part your will read a selection of texts, such as magazine and newspaper articles, e-mails, and instant messages. Each text or set of texts is followed by several questions. Select the best answer for each question and mark the letter (A), (B), (C), or (D) on your answer sheet.

Questions 147-148 refer to the following invoice.

Petunia Stationery
We have everything your office could possibly need.
999 Main Street, Des Moines, Iowa
Tel: 293-2394   Fax: 293-2395

Customer: Harold Marley
Address: 41 Brighton St., Des Moines, IO
Telephone: 954-4502

Order Placed: Tuesday, March 23
Order Sent: Tuesday, March 23

Order Number: 454-5055

Item Description	Item Number	Amount Ordered	Cost/Unit	Total Cost
Staples (Box of 1,000)	565595	3	$2.00	$6.00
Copy Paper (Box of 5,000)	965686	2	$22.00	$44.00
Number 2 Pencils (Box of 10)	103434	10	$5.50	$55.00
Black Ballpoint Pens (Box of 20)	249558	4	$9.00	$36.00
Blue Ballpoint Pens (Box of 20)	249560	3	$9.00	$27.00

Subtotal: $168.00
Shipping Fee: $12.00
Total: $180.00

Thank you for your order. Your order has been billed to the credit card ending in 5205. For questions regarding this shipment, please contact Matt Stone at matt@petuniastationery.com.

---

147. How many pencils were ordered?

(A) 10
(B) 60
(C) 80
(D) 100

148. What is the order number of the least expensive item?

(A) 103434
(B) 249558
(C) 565595
(D) 249560

Questions 149-150 refer to the following text message chain.

Walker, Harriet — 9:12 A.M.
Good morning, Mr. Davis. My name is Harriet Walker. I'm with Sandpiper Logistics. We have a package we'd like to deliver to you today.

Davis, Sam — 9:15 A.M.
That's great. When are you planning to come here?

Walker, Harriet — 9:17 A.M.
The deliveryman is scheduled to arrive at your home between 10:00 and 10:30. Will you be home then?

Davis, Sam — 9:18 A.M.
I'm afraid not. What about noon?

Walker, Harriet — 9:21 A.M.
Our delivery personnel have a mandatory lunch break between 12:00 and 1:00. Is there some time during the afternoon you'll be at your residence?

Davis, Sam — 9:22 A.M.
2:30 would be fine with me. Just have the deliveryman call me before he arrives, please.

Walker, Harriet — 9:25 A.M.
He can make it there then. I'll inform him to call you 10 minutes before he visits your house. Thank you.

---

149. At 9:18 A.M., what does Mr. Davis mean when he writes, "I'm afraid not"?

(A) He will not be home at a certain time.
(B) He does not recall receiving a package.
(C) He cannot wait for the deliveryman to arrive.
(D) He is unable to visit Sandpiper Logistics.

150. What time will the deliveryman call Mr. Davis?

(A) At 2:00 P.M.
(B) At 2:10 P.M.
(C) At 2:20 P.M.
(D) At 2:30 P.M.

Questions 151-152 refer to the following memo.

MEMO

To: All Dayton City Employees
From: Frieda Thompson, City Hall
Date: May 26
Subject: Volunteering

Summer is just around the corner, and that's the busiest time of the year for our city's parks and recreation facilities. Due to budget cuts, we had to lay off a few groundskeepers. There are only 6 full-time employees to work at the city's 7 parks, some of which are quite extensive. —[1]—.

We are therefore going to have a cleanup day this Saturday, May 29. This is purely a volunteer event, but we hope as many of you as possible will contribute to the effort. —[2]—. We're going to do all kinds of cleanup work at our parks, including painting, picking up trash, cutting grass, and making minor repairs. You won't get paid, but anyone who works a full day will receive a paid day of vacation in either June or July. —[3]—.

If you're interested in helping out, contact Debby Reynolds at extension 4032. We're going to meet in the city hall parking lot at 8:30 in the morning on May 29. —[4]—. You'll then be driven to your work assignment. A free T-shirt and lunch will be provided to everyone who volunteers.

151. According to the memo, why are volunteers needed?

(A) The city's parks are in poor condition.
(B) The winter weather caused a lot of damage.
(C) There are not enough paid employees to do all the work.
(D) The city hopes to save money to use on other projects.

152. In which of the positions marked [1], [2], [3], and [4] does the following sentence best belong?

"So we need all of the helping hands that we can possibly get."

(A) [1]
(B) [2]
(C) [3]
(D) [4]

Questions 153-155 refer to the following letter.

September 18

Dear Mr. Hansen,

This letter is being written with regard to your cable television bill, which is presently overdue by two months. At the current time, the amount you owe is $134.65. This must be paid in full no later than September 29. You may pay the bill in cash at any local bank or send us a check made out to Ace Cable Systems. If you opt to pay by check, please be sure to post it early enough so that it will reach our office by the due date. Failure to pay the bill in full by the required date will result in the immediate termination of your cable television service. Your service can then be reestablished once you have paid the bill in full. There will also be an additional charge of $50 to reconnect the service. Should you fail to make this month's payment, your bill will be turned over to a collection agency, which may have a harmful effect on your credit rating.

Sincerely,

Silvia Patterson
Ace Cable Systems

153. What will happen on September 29?

(A) A service may be ended.
(B) A check will be cashed.
(C) A bill will be mailed.
(D) A customer may be contacted.

154. What is Mr. Hansen instructed to do?

(A) Open an account at a bank
(B) Send a check after September 29
(C) Make a payment immediately
(D) Contact a collection agency

155. What is suggested about Ace Cable Systems?

(A) It will stop communicating with Mr. Hansen after September 29.
(B) It will send a person to Mr. Hansen's home soon.
(C) It will provide Mr. Hansen with an upgrade for $50.
(D) It will sue Mr. Hansen for the money that he currently owes.

Questions 156-158 refer to the following information.

Welcome to the Sunrise Campground

Thank you for staying at the Sunrise Campground at Mount Rainier. Please remember to be courteous to your fellow campers and to do your best not to disturb them. During your stay here, you must obey all three of the following rules:

1) Do not waste water in the bathrooms, which are located in the northeast and southeast corners of the campground. Take short showers and do not let the water in the faucet run continually.

2) Make sure that all fires are extinguished and that burning fires are never left unattended. Remember to pour, stir, and pour. First, pour water on the fire, and then stir the coal and ashes. After that, pour more water on the fire. Firewood can be acquired in lot #1 for a minimal fee.

3) Do not leave any garbage at the campground. Keep the site clean both to prevent pollution and to keep wild animals way from the site. Anyone who is caught littering will be fined $100.

Remember the Golden Rule of camping: The only thing you should leave at your campground is your footprints.

Call 805-4395 to speak with the manager of the campground or dial 595-4943 to get in touch with a park ranger.

156. Who are the instructions for?

(A) Park rangers
(B) Day visitors
(C) Hikers
(D) People staying overnight

157. What can be purchased at the campground?

(A) Bottled water
(B) Wood
(C) Snacks
(D) Tents

158. What action can cause a person to pay a fine?

(A) Littering
(B) Making noise
(C) Feeding wild animals
(D) Wasting water

Questions 159-161 refer to the following article.

A New Shop Downtown

New Haven (June 15) – Visitors downtown can easily get lost on account of the plethora of small businesses and the vibrant atmosphere they create. Those who find themselves at the corner of Third Street and Eli Road should be sure to have a look inside Watson's Arts and Crafts. While it's a new store, it's also home to a small bit of history and passion in New Haven.

Owner Rachel Watson opened the store this May. "My father loved art and believed that art is the heart of every society. I decided to honor him by opening a store to provide supplies for artists while simultaneously displaying some of the artwork he created throughout the store," she said. All of the numerous paintings and drawings adorning the walls of the store were made by her late father, Marcus Watson.

Mr. Watson was a well-known artist in the local community who passed away last year.

Customers at Watson's Arts and Crafts therefore get not only great service but also the opportunity to admire outstanding works of art. Tony Brown, a frequent customer at the store, commented, "Ms. Watson understands art and sells her wares for low prices, but she's also doing the community a service by opening what's essentially a gallery. There are times that I come here just to admire the works instead of to buy something." Customers don't need to worry that the artwork will disappear anytime soon. Despite some hefty offers, Ms. Watson is thus far refusing to sell any of her father's works.

---

159. Where is artwork by Mr. Watson displayed?

(A) At Ms. Watson's home
(B) In a local gallery
(C) At Watson's Arts and Crafts
(D) Alongside Eli Road

160. What is suggested about Mr. Brown?

(A) He creates art.
(B) He knew Mr. Watson.
(C) He is friends with Ms. Watson.
(D) He works at Watson's Arts and Crafts.

161. The word "hefty" in paragraph 3, line 14 is closest in meaning to

(A) persistent
(B) heavy
(C) considerable
(D) unique

GO ON TO THE NEXT PAGE

Questions 162-164 refer to the following announcement.

Denton Merchants Association to Hold Annual Meeting

The Denton Merchants Association will hold its annual meeting three months from now from Friday, June 20, to Sunday, June 22. The event will take place in the Carlyle Convention Center. All members of the association are eligible to take part in the event, and guests are also permitted to attend. Registration for the meeting is currently open. Online applications may be submitted at www.dentonmerchants.org/annualmeeting, or places may be reserved by calling 509-2395. Registration closes after June 10, and tickets may not be purchased at the door either. The cost of attending all three days of the meeting is $75 for members and $100 for guests. This fee provides access to every event except for the banquet held on the last night of the meeting. Attending it costs $50 for members and nonmembers alike. A list of the activities and speakers at the meeting may be accessed on the association's Web site. There will be several lectures by guest speakers, including talks on legal issues facing merchants, recent changes in tax laws, and how to advertise effectively on the Internet.

162. For whom is the announcement most likely intended?

(A) Store owners
(B) Tax attorneys
(C) Local residents
(D) Caterers

163. According to the announcement, what is NOT true?

(A) Members pay less to attend the event than guests.
(B) The meeting is scheduled to last for three days.
(C) Registration for the meeting can only be done online.
(D) Tickets will not be sold on the days the meeting is held.

164. How much must a nonmember pay to attend the meeting and banquet?

(A) $75
(B) $100
(C) $125
(D) $150

Questions 165-167 refer to the following memo.

TO: All Employees
FROM: Ernest Jenson, Tech Support Department
RE: This Friday
DATE: Tuesday, April 9

All employees are hereby notified that the company's main computer servers will be shut down on Friday, April 12, from 3 P.M. to 9 P.M. This shutdown is necessary because the system needs to be upgraded, which will enable the computer system to operate at a higher speed and with greater effectiveness. At the same time, several new timesaving programs, which will improve overall employee output, will be installed. The new programs will be thoroughly explained by the Tech Support Department on an interoffice video that will be uploaded onto the company's Web site at 8 A.M. on Monday, April 15.

During the six-hour period starting at 3, employees will be unable to use the computer system. Therefore, before the shutdown period begins, employees should save anything currently being worked on. We strongly advise saving the work both on the company's computer system and on a personal flash drive. Furthermore, the Tech Support Department will not be responsible for any files lost during the upgrade. So it is highly advisable that individuals with sensitive or valuable files copy them to an external source. We appreciate your support and hope the shutdown does not cause too much inconvenience.

165. Why is the computer system being shut down?

(A) To upgrade the company's accounting software
(B) To remove some viruses from the system
(C) To install some newly purchased computers
(D) To make the computers more efficient

166. What will happen on April 15?

(A) The upgrade will be complete.
(B) A video will be available for viewing.
(C) Lost files will be recovered.
(D) The computer system will shut down.

167. What are employees advised to do?

(A) Turn off their computers before the shutdown
(B) Bring their laptops from home on Friday
(C) Transfer important files to keep them safe
(D) Contact the Tech Support Department with questions

Questions 168-171 refer to the following online message chain.

	Wright, Bruce [3:34 P.M.]	I just received the list of people HR wants us to interview for the open position.
	Bannister, William [3:35 P.M.]	Who are they?
	Wright, Bruce [3:36 P.M.]	There are four people on the list: Melissa Abercrombie, Shen Wu, Patrick Kennedy, and Molly Toole.
	Houston, Jennifer [3:38 P.M.]	If I remember correctly, the second one on the list is the most qualified. I can't recall much about the other three though.
	Bannister, William [3:40 P.M.]	I went to school with Patrick Kennedy six years ago. I remember him as a hardworking person, but I haven't kept up with him at all.
	Wright, Bruce [3:43 P.M.]	Well, we need to contact everybody today and inform them that we need to interview them for the position. Uh, if they're still interested in it, of course.
	Houston, Jennifer [3:45 P.M.]	I'll do that if you want. I just finished a report and have some free time. What should I tell them if they have a problem with the interview date?
	Wright, Bruce [3:47 P.M.]	That's a good question. We're supposed to interview them on either January 10 or 11. I'll contact HR and ask them if any other dates are acceptable.
	Houston, Jennifer [3:50 P.M.]	While you're doing that, find out if we'll pay for their travel expenses if they're going to be coming from out of town, too, please.
	Wright, Bruce [3:52 P.M.]	Sure. I'll get back to you in a bit. But check your e-mail now. I just sent the contact information for each person.

168. What is mainly being discussed?

(A) The need to interview candidates at once
(B) A job that is going to be filled
(C) Questions to ask the HR Department
(D) Some applicants to be interviewed

169. What does Ms. Houston indicate about the applicants?

(A) They all submitted excellent résumés.
(B) She has already interviewed a couple of them.
(C) None of them is very qualified for the job.
(D) One person has better credentials than the others.

170. At 3:40 P.M., what does Mr. Bannister mean when he writes, "I haven't kept up with him at all"?

(A) He does not remember Mr. Kennedy well.
(B) He believes Mr. Kennedy is not qualified.
(C) He has not spoken with Mr. Kennedy since school.
(D) He never worked well with Mr. Kennedy.

171. What does Mr. Wright tell Ms. Houston to do?

(A) Contact the HR Department
(B) Read her e-mail
(C) Make some phone calls
(D) Look at some résumés

Questions 172-175 refer to the following e-mail.

FROM Fred Stallings <fred_stallings@wprinters.com>
TO Wanda Lancaster <wandal@familymail.com>
SUBJECT Order 5AR-5594
DATE November 12

Dear Ms. Lancaster,

We received the order you placed for a Wellington All-in-One 460 Printer this morning. Unfortunately, we no longer have that printer in stock, and my company has ceased the manufacture of them. I apologize for this inconvenience.

If you wish to cancel your order, please let me know, and I can process a refund on your credit card. But if you still wish to purchase a printer from my company, let me recommend the Wellington All-in-One 470 Printer. It belongs to the same line of printers you attempted to order. In fact, it is the same as the 460 except for the fact that it comes with a few extras. It is a printer, scanner, fax machine, and photocopier just like the 460. But it also has the ability to send scanned documents as e-mail attachments straight from the printer. On top of that, the ink cartridges used for it last longer since they are slightly larger than those used in the 460.

I have attached a file to this e-mail. It contains a brochure describing the specifications of the 470 model. While the 470 costs slightly more than the 460, I have been authorized to sell one to you for the same price you paid for the 460. So simply respond to me that you would like the 470, and I can have it sent to you at once.

Sincerely,

Fred Stallings

Customer Service Representative

Wellington Printers

172. Why was the e-mail written?

(A) To suggest an alternative item
(B) To apologize for a mistake
(C) To promote a company's new product
(D) To deal with a customer's complaint

173. According to the e-mail, how is the 470 model different from the 460 model?

(A) It uses less electricity.
(B) It can e-mail documents directly.
(C) It prints pictures at high speeds.
(D) It includes a fax machine.

174. What does Mr. Stallings send to Ms. Lancaster with the e-mail?

(A) Some information
(B) An invoice
(C) An order form
(D) A picture

175. What does Ms. Lancaster need to do to get the 470 model?

(A) Pay some more money
(B) Fill out an order form
(C) Put her name on a waiting list
(D) Send a response e-mail

Questions 176-180 refer to the following article and e-mail.

Carney Shipbuilding Hires New Sales Director

Norfolk (June 16) Carney Shipbuilding, one of the country's largest ship manufacturers, just announced it has hired Jerod Morris to serve as the company's director of the Sales Department. Mr. Morris will assume his new position on July 1. The move was widely praised by experts in the industry, who cite Mr. Morris's record of success at his previous three places of employment. At his most recent position, which was at Gregory Manufacturing, Mr. Morris helped the company transform from being a multimillion-dollar loser to earning a profit of more than $50 million in a mere three years. He is expected to do the same for Carney, which has seen its revenues decline lately.

Darren Jackson, the CEO of Carney Shipbuilding, commented, "We're extremely pleased to have Mr. Morris on board. We're confident that with his contacts in the industry and his outstanding business mind, we'll be able to increase our sales and once again become the country's number-one shipbuilder." Carney had revenues of $775 million last year and is projecting a slight increase in the coming year.

To: Jerod Morris <jmorris@carneyships.com>
From: Cindy Roman <cindyr@carneyships.com>
Subject: Meeting
Date: July 1

Dear Mr. Morris,

I hope you've finished your meetings with HR and CEO Jackson. All of us in the Sales Department are looking forward to meeting you and to working with you. I'd like you to know that you have a busy afternoon scheduled for today. As soon as lunch ends, you're going to be meeting with Rajiv Merhra and Scott Pulaski, both of whom are senior salesmen here. They need to speak to you about a potential deal with the firm you just departed. Since you were there for five years, they hope you can provide some invaluable insight as to how they should approach the negotiations.

Then, at 2:00, you're scheduled to have a meeting regarding deals we signed with the Wellman Corporation and CGR, Inc. in June. That should take an hour and a half to complete. At 4:00, you'll conduct your final meeting of the day. It's with Karen Chu and Dansby Burgess. This is mostly a chance for them to meet you and to get to know your management style. However, expect them to bring up the Sybax Corporation. There's a folder on your desk with the relevant information.

If you need anything from me, just respond to this e-mail or call me at extension 21.

Regards,

Cindy Roman

176. Where would the article most likely be found?

(A) In a quarterly report
(B) In a leisure magazine
(C) In a business journal
(D) On a travel Web site

177. What is mentioned about Carney Shipbuilding?

(A) It earned a profit of $50 million last year.
(B) It recently hired Darren Jackson as its CEO.
(C) It is expected to take in more revenue than last year.
(D) It signed a multimillion-dollar deal last month.

178. Why did Ms. Roman write the e-mail?

(A) To provide information about meetings
(B) To ask about the Sybax Corporation
(C) To congratulate a person on his hiring
(D) To request that Mr. Morris see her in person

179. Where does Ms. Roman work?

(A) At the Sybax Corporation
(B) At Gregory Manufacturing
(C) At Carney Shipbuilding
(D) At CGR, Inc.

180. What will Mr. Morris do right after lunch?

(A) Sign a contract with the Sybax Corporation
(B) Talk about the Wellman Corporation
(C) Have a discussion about Gregory Manufacturing
(D) Meet with representatives from CGR, Inc.

GO ON TO THE NEXT PAGE

Questions 181-185 refer to the following letter and sales chart.

August 3

Dear Mr. Jacoby,

We at Fifth Avenue Fashions are pleased to inform you that we have opted to hire your marketing firm to provide advertisements and commercials for us. While we considered several qualified companies for the contract, yours stood head and shoulders above the rest.

We have a new line of men's casual clothing coming out at the end of October, so we're eager to begin promoting it. In addition, sales for both men's and women's formal clothing have been lower than we had expected this year. We hope that Freeman, Inc. can come up with some ways to make those clothes more appealing to our customers in the last quarter of the year. Finally, we're also considering exporting our clothes to foreign markets, particularly Russia, Japan, and Sweden. We will be asking you to create ad campaigns for those countries.

Would it be possible for your representatives to meet with us next Monday, August 11? We would like to sign a contract with your firm to confirm our relationship. And we would additionally like to discuss the approach to the ads and commercials we would like your team to take. Please contact me at 852-5743 at the earliest convenient time.

Sincerely,

Kendrick Carpenter
Vice President of Marketing
Fifth Avenue Fashions

Fifth Avenue Fashions
Annual Sales Figures

The following are the sales figures by quarter for men's and women's clothes.

	First Quarter	Second Quarter	Third Quarter	Fourth Quarter
Men's Casual Clothes	$16,494	$18,549	$21,392	$19,594
Men's Formal Clothes	$11,899	$9,856	$8,435	$14,770
Women's Casual Clothes	$26,667	$30,321	$33,568	$37,948
Women's Formal Clothes	$15,695	$14,890	$14,857	$14,098

181. Which profession most likely is Mr. Jacoby involved in?

(A) Sales
(B) Marketing
(C) Accounting
(D) Shipping

182. In the letter, the word "appealing" in paragraph 2, line 4 is closest in meaning to

(A) attractive
(B) apparent
(C) affordable
(D) accessible

183. According to the letter, what is NOT stated about Fifth Avenue Fashions?

(A) It wants to sell its clothes in other countries.
(B) It is hiring Freeman, Inc. to do work for it.
(C) It will be selling some new clothes in October.
(D) It recorded a minor loss in the second quarter.

184. Which type of clothing had the lowest overall sales in the second quarter?

(A) Women's casual clothes
(B) Women's formal clothes
(C) Men's casual clothes
(D) Men's formal clothes

185. What is suggested about Freeman, Inc.?

(A) It has worked closely with Fifth Avenue Fashions for years.
(B) It is responsible for the increase in sales of women's casual clothes.
(C) It created a successful ad campaign for men's formal clothes.
(D) It will receive a percentage of the increased revenues from clothing sales.

GO ON TO THE NEXT PAGE

Questions 186-190 refer to the following announcement, article, and memo.

The Portland Job Fair

The eleventh annual Portland Job Fair will take place on Friday, April 10, and Saturday, April 11. This year's fair promises to be bigger and better than ever. The event will be held in the Portland Civic Center and will begin at 8 in the morning and conclude at 7 in the evening on each day. Representatives from 450 local, national, and international businesses have pledged to attend. These companies represent some of the biggest names in the aerospace, financial, manufacturing, robotics, and shipping industries. In addition, local airplane manufacturer Plautus will be in attendance and hopes to hire 100 individuals at the fair. Attendees are advised to wear formal clothes as some of them will be given interviews on the spot. They should also arrive with résumés, portfolios, and other documents. Attendance is free, and there is no need to make reservations.

Portland Job Fair Ends in Success

Portland (April 12) – The Portland Job Fair ended yesterday, and organizers are calling it the most successful event in the history of the fair. More than 15,000 jobseekers are estimated to have visited the Portland Civic Center in an attempt to land jobs. The most popular booth by far was the Plautus one as the company had publicly announced its intentions to hire attendees at the fair. Plautus did not disappoint. Company spokesman Rod Merchant said, "The high quality of the attendees convinced us to hire double the number of individuals that we had initially planned. We're very pleased with the results of this year's fair." Other multinational firms, such as Orion, Walker Research, and PT Systems, claim to have hired several individuals at the fair as well. Orion representative Wilma O'Neil stated, "This is one of the best job fairs in the country. We know we'll be getting attendees who are well educated and ambitious when we come here."

TO: All Employees, R&D Department
FROM: David Murphy, HR
SUBJECT: New Employees
DATE: April 21

Please be aware that there will be 38 new workers starting in the R&D Department here at Plautus. The individuals will all begin on Monday, May 1. All of them were hired at the Portland Job Fair, where many of you also found employment here. Since we've never hired this many new workers at the same time, we need to be sure that the orientation process goes smoothly. After consulting with Samir Punjab, the head of your department, I decided to set up a mentoring program. Some of you will be assigned to act as mentors to new employees. You will be responsible for teaching your mentee everything he or she needs to know about his or her new position. I'd prefer that everyone involved be a volunteer. So if you think you'd be a good mentor, please contact either me (extension 549) or Mr. Punjab no later than April 25.

186. What is NOT stated about the Portland Job Fair?

(A) Around 450 companies will be represented there.
(B) It has been held on multiple occasions.
(C) Companies conduct interviews at it.
(D) A firm must pay a fee to get a booth.

187. In the announcement, the word "pledged" in line 5 is closest in meaning to

(A) promised
(B) decided
(C) registered
(D) paid

188. What is suggested about Plautus?

(A) It hired 200 people at the Portland Job Fair.
(B) It is the country's largest airplane manufacturer.
(C) It recently merged with Walker Research.
(D) It is one of the founders of the Portland Job Fair.

189. Why did Mr. Murphy write the memo?

(A) To invite people to apply for new positions
(B) To request volunteers for a program
(C) To introduce some new employees
(D) To announce a new orientation session

190. Where does Mr. Punjab work?

(A) In the HR Department
(B) In the Manufacturing Department
(C) In the R&D Department
(D) In the Accounting Department

Questions 191-195 refer to the following schedule, letter, and e-mail.

Winston Academy
Providing the finest writing instruction in the city

How about taking a class at the Winston Academy? The summer semester is about to start, and we have some exciting classes on offer. In addition to our regular classes, here are four that we're hosting for the first time:

Class Name	Class Number	Instructor	Time
Creative Writing	11	May Carpenter	Mon, Tues 9 A.M. – 11 A.M.
Poetry	42	Josh Herald	Wed 1 P.M. – 4 P.M.
Essay Writing	38	Stan Morris	Mon, Fri 1 P.M. – 3 P.M.
Nonfiction Writing	23	Alicia Woodruff	Thurs, Fri 10 A.M. – 12 P.M.

The semester begins on June 1 and ends on August 20. All of our instructors are professors at universities around the country, and they are published authors as well. Many students who have taken our classes have gone on to become published writers themselves. All classes cost $800 for the session. Call 485-5837 for more information.

May 16

Dear Mr. Lincoln,

I regret to inform you that I will not be able to fulfill my duties as an instructor at the Winston Academy this summer. While I had intended to be here in Knoxville for the entire summer so that I could teach class and complete my book, I have been instructed by the dean at my university that my services are required on campus. Apparently, one of the summer school instructors at my college suddenly fell ill and will be hospitalized for three months. He was scheduled to teach two summer school classes. The English Department has been unable to find a replacement instructor in the local area, so my dean has insisted that I return to Charlotte to teach in his place. I truly feel bad as I was looking forward to having my first class at the Winston Academy. I apologize for the inconvenience and hope you have enough time to find a suitable replacement.

Sincerely,

Stan Morris

To: Christine Solo <csolo@personalmail.com>
From: Susan Lincoln <slincoln@winstonacademy.com>
Subject: Summer Schedule
Date: May 20

Dear Ms. Solo,

You recently inquired if David Powell was going to be an instructor at the academy this year, and I responded that he would not. However, there has been a sudden change in the schedule as one of our instructors will not be able to teach a class this summer. As a result, Mr. Powell is going to be an instructor at the Winston Academy this summer. He will be teaching a class on how to write a proper essay. I believe you expressed an interest in learning about that, so this would be the perfect opportunity to do so. There are currently 5 seats available for the class, so I suggest that you hurry to enroll as Mr. Powell is popular with many students here. They may rush to register for the class once they find out he is teaching it.

Sincerely,

Susan Lincoln
Winston Academy

191. What is suggested about Mr. Herald?

(A) He has worked at the Winston Academy before.
(B) He is popular with many students.
(C) He studied at the Winston Academy.
(D) He teaches poetry to college students.

192. Which class does the Winston Academy need to find a new instructor for?

(A) Essay Writing
(B) Poetry
(C) Creative Writing
(D) Nonfiction Writing

193. Why is Mr. Morris unable to work at the Winston Academy?

(A) The compensation is not sufficient.
(B) He has to be in another city during the summer.
(C) He suffered an illness and has been hospitalized.
(D) He needs to complete his book by the end of August.

194. When is Mr. Powell scheduled to have class?

(A) On Monday and Tuesday
(B) On Monday and Friday
(C) On Wednesday
(D) On Thursday and Friday

195. What does Ms. Lincoln recommend that Ms. Solo do?

(A) Pay her course fee soon
(B) Register for a class
(C) Speak with Mr. Powell
(D) Learn about poetry

GO ON TO THE NEXT PAGE

Questions 196-200 refer to the following notice and e-mails.

Silver Lake Apartments Open House

This Saturday and Sunday, August 1-2, Silver Lake Apartments is having an open house. After two years of construction, Silver Lake Apartments is almost complete. So people will be able to move in at the beginning of October. There are still more than 250 units available for purchase or rent. These include apartments with two, three, and four bedrooms. There are both furnished and unfurnished apartments available. All furnished apartments are only available to rent though. The facilities at Silver Lake Apartments are top notch, and the complex is located near outstanding schools and the main shopping district in Knoxville. Anyone is welcome to attend the open house. Tours of the available apartments will be given, and visitors will be shown around the entire complex as well. Call 984-5859 for more information and to get directions to the complex.

To: inquiries@desmondrealty.com
From: patsanders@homemail.com
Subject: Silver Lake Apartment
Date: August 6

To Whom It May Concern,

Last Sunday, my wife and I attended the open house that took place at Silver Lake Apartments. We were extremely impressed with what we saw there, and we have decided that we would like to live there. We are planning to move to Knoxville in November, and we intend to live in the city for the next three years. After that, I expect to be transferred to my company's headquarters in Denver. As a result, we are not interested in buying an apartment but would instead prefer to rent one. We would like to have a three-bedroom apartment so that each of my sons can have his own room. I'm currently in Miami, but I can arrange to fly to Knoxville whenever you need me to sign a contract. Is the monthly rent on the unit I want still $2,200?

Sincerely,

Patrick Sanders

To: patsanders@homemail.com
From: rdesmond@desmondrealty.com
Subject: Silver Lake Apartments
Date: August 8

Dear Mr. Sanders,

Thank you for inquiring about Silver Lake Apartments. Like you, many people are very pleased with how the apartments look, so it's one of the most popular properties in the entire city. Due to that fact, there are no longer any three-bedroom units available. In addition, the last two-bedroom apartment was just sold this morning. There are currently only a few four-bedroom apartments available to rent left. Of course, the rent for these apartments is a bit higher. It costs $600 a month more to rent a four-bedroom unit than it does to rent a three-bedroom unit. If you are still interested, please inform me immediately, and, once I receive a nonrefundable payment of $2,500, I can reserve a unit for you until you are able to fly here to sign a contract. If you are no longer interested in Silver Lake Apartments, I can introduce you to several other properties in the same neighborhood that I'm sure you would approve of.

Regards,

Richard Desmond
Desmond Realty

---

196. What is mentioned about Silver Lake Apartments?
 (A) It is in a suburb of Knoxville.
 (B) It is across from a school.
 (C) It is still being built.
 (D) It is 20 stories high.

197. What will happen at the open house?
 (A) Construction will be halted.
 (B) Contracts will be signed.
 (C) Visitors will be given tours.
 (D) A presentation will be made.

198. When did Mr. Sanders visit Silver Lake Apartments?
 (A) On August 1
 (B) On August 2
 (C) On August 6
 (D) On August 8

199. How much does it cost to rent a four-bedroom unit at Silver Lake Apartments?
 (A) $2,000 a month
 (B) $2,200 a month
 (C) $2,500 a month
 (D) $2,800 a month

200. What does Mr. Desmond suggest that Mr. Sanders do?
 (A) Pay a fee to guarantee he gets an apartment
 (B) Fly to Knoxville this coming weekend
 (C) Consider buying an apartment instead of renting one
 (D) Get a smaller apartment for a lower price

Stop! This is the end of the test. If you finish before time is called, you may go back to Parts 5, 6, and 7 and check your work.

ANSWER SHEET

TOEIC 실전 테스트

성명 / 한글 / 영문

LISTENING (Part I-IV)

No.	ANSWER	No.	ANSWER	No.	ANSWER	No.	ANSWER
1	Ⓐ Ⓑ Ⓒ Ⓓ	21	Ⓐ Ⓑ Ⓒ	41	Ⓐ Ⓑ Ⓒ Ⓓ	61	Ⓐ Ⓑ Ⓒ Ⓓ	81	Ⓐ Ⓑ Ⓒ Ⓓ
2	Ⓐ Ⓑ Ⓒ Ⓓ	22	Ⓐ Ⓑ Ⓒ	42	Ⓐ Ⓑ Ⓒ Ⓓ	62	Ⓐ Ⓑ Ⓒ Ⓓ	82	Ⓐ Ⓑ Ⓒ Ⓓ
3	Ⓐ Ⓑ Ⓒ Ⓓ	23	Ⓐ Ⓑ Ⓒ	43	Ⓐ Ⓑ Ⓒ Ⓓ	63	Ⓐ Ⓑ Ⓒ Ⓓ	83	Ⓐ Ⓑ Ⓒ Ⓓ
4	Ⓐ Ⓑ Ⓒ Ⓓ	24	Ⓐ Ⓑ Ⓒ	44	Ⓐ Ⓑ Ⓒ Ⓓ	64	Ⓐ Ⓑ Ⓒ Ⓓ	84	Ⓐ Ⓑ Ⓒ Ⓓ
5	Ⓐ Ⓑ Ⓒ Ⓓ	25	Ⓐ Ⓑ Ⓒ	45	Ⓐ Ⓑ Ⓒ Ⓓ	65	Ⓐ Ⓑ Ⓒ Ⓓ	85	Ⓐ Ⓑ Ⓒ Ⓓ
6	Ⓐ Ⓑ Ⓒ Ⓓ	26	Ⓐ Ⓑ Ⓒ	46	Ⓐ Ⓑ Ⓒ Ⓓ	66	Ⓐ Ⓑ Ⓒ Ⓓ	86	Ⓐ Ⓑ Ⓒ Ⓓ
7	Ⓐ Ⓑ Ⓒ	27	Ⓐ Ⓑ Ⓒ	47	Ⓐ Ⓑ Ⓒ Ⓓ	67	Ⓐ Ⓑ Ⓒ Ⓓ	87	Ⓐ Ⓑ Ⓒ Ⓓ
8	Ⓐ Ⓑ Ⓒ	28	Ⓐ Ⓑ Ⓒ	48	Ⓐ Ⓑ Ⓒ Ⓓ	68	Ⓐ Ⓑ Ⓒ Ⓓ	88	Ⓐ Ⓑ Ⓒ Ⓓ
9	Ⓐ Ⓑ Ⓒ	29	Ⓐ Ⓑ Ⓒ	49	Ⓐ Ⓑ Ⓒ Ⓓ	69	Ⓐ Ⓑ Ⓒ Ⓓ	89	Ⓐ Ⓑ Ⓒ Ⓓ
10	Ⓐ Ⓑ Ⓒ	30	Ⓐ Ⓑ Ⓒ	50	Ⓐ Ⓑ Ⓒ Ⓓ	70	Ⓐ Ⓑ Ⓒ Ⓓ	90	Ⓐ Ⓑ Ⓒ Ⓓ
11	Ⓐ Ⓑ Ⓒ	31	Ⓐ Ⓑ Ⓒ	51	Ⓐ Ⓑ Ⓒ Ⓓ	71	Ⓐ Ⓑ Ⓒ Ⓓ	91	Ⓐ Ⓑ Ⓒ Ⓓ
12	Ⓐ Ⓑ Ⓒ	32	Ⓐ Ⓑ Ⓒ	52	Ⓐ Ⓑ Ⓒ Ⓓ	72	Ⓐ Ⓑ Ⓒ Ⓓ	92	Ⓐ Ⓑ Ⓒ Ⓓ
13	Ⓐ Ⓑ Ⓒ	33	Ⓐ Ⓑ Ⓒ	53	Ⓐ Ⓑ Ⓒ Ⓓ	73	Ⓐ Ⓑ Ⓒ Ⓓ	93	Ⓐ Ⓑ Ⓒ Ⓓ
14	Ⓐ Ⓑ Ⓒ	34	Ⓐ Ⓑ Ⓒ	54	Ⓐ Ⓑ Ⓒ Ⓓ	74	Ⓐ Ⓑ Ⓒ Ⓓ	94	Ⓐ Ⓑ Ⓒ Ⓓ
15	Ⓐ Ⓑ Ⓒ	35	Ⓐ Ⓑ Ⓒ	55	Ⓐ Ⓑ Ⓒ Ⓓ	75	Ⓐ Ⓑ Ⓒ Ⓓ	95	Ⓐ Ⓑ Ⓒ Ⓓ
16	Ⓐ Ⓑ Ⓒ	36	Ⓐ Ⓑ Ⓒ	56	Ⓐ Ⓑ Ⓒ Ⓓ	76	Ⓐ Ⓑ Ⓒ Ⓓ	96	Ⓐ Ⓑ Ⓒ Ⓓ
17	Ⓐ Ⓑ Ⓒ	37	Ⓐ Ⓑ Ⓒ	57	Ⓐ Ⓑ Ⓒ Ⓓ	77	Ⓐ Ⓑ Ⓒ Ⓓ	97	Ⓐ Ⓑ Ⓒ Ⓓ
18	Ⓐ Ⓑ Ⓒ	38	Ⓐ Ⓑ Ⓒ	58	Ⓐ Ⓑ Ⓒ Ⓓ	78	Ⓐ Ⓑ Ⓒ Ⓓ	98	Ⓐ Ⓑ Ⓒ Ⓓ
19	Ⓐ Ⓑ Ⓒ	39	Ⓐ Ⓑ Ⓒ	59	Ⓐ Ⓑ Ⓒ Ⓓ	79	Ⓐ Ⓑ Ⓒ Ⓓ	99	Ⓐ Ⓑ Ⓒ Ⓓ
20	Ⓐ Ⓑ Ⓒ	40	Ⓐ Ⓑ Ⓒ	60	Ⓐ Ⓑ Ⓒ Ⓓ	80	Ⓐ Ⓑ Ⓒ Ⓓ	100	Ⓐ Ⓑ Ⓒ Ⓓ

READING (Part V~VII)

No.	ANSWER	No.	ANSWER	No.	ANSWER	No.	ANSWER	No.	ANSWER
101	Ⓐ Ⓑ Ⓒ Ⓓ	121	Ⓐ Ⓑ Ⓒ Ⓓ	141	Ⓐ Ⓑ Ⓒ Ⓓ	161	Ⓐ Ⓑ Ⓒ Ⓓ	181	Ⓐ Ⓑ Ⓒ Ⓓ
102	Ⓐ Ⓑ Ⓒ Ⓓ	122	Ⓐ Ⓑ Ⓒ Ⓓ	142	Ⓐ Ⓑ Ⓒ Ⓓ	162	Ⓐ Ⓑ Ⓒ Ⓓ	182	Ⓐ Ⓑ Ⓒ Ⓓ
103	Ⓐ Ⓑ Ⓒ Ⓓ	123	Ⓐ Ⓑ Ⓒ Ⓓ	143	Ⓐ Ⓑ Ⓒ Ⓓ	163	Ⓐ Ⓑ Ⓒ Ⓓ	183	Ⓐ Ⓑ Ⓒ Ⓓ
104	Ⓐ Ⓑ Ⓒ Ⓓ	124	Ⓐ Ⓑ Ⓒ Ⓓ	144	Ⓐ Ⓑ Ⓒ Ⓓ	164	Ⓐ Ⓑ Ⓒ Ⓓ	184	Ⓐ Ⓑ Ⓒ Ⓓ
105	Ⓐ Ⓑ Ⓒ Ⓓ	125	Ⓐ Ⓑ Ⓒ Ⓓ	145	Ⓐ Ⓑ Ⓒ Ⓓ	165	Ⓐ Ⓑ Ⓒ Ⓓ	185	Ⓐ Ⓑ Ⓒ Ⓓ
106	Ⓐ Ⓑ Ⓒ Ⓓ	126	Ⓐ Ⓑ Ⓒ Ⓓ	146	Ⓐ Ⓑ Ⓒ Ⓓ	166	Ⓐ Ⓑ Ⓒ Ⓓ	186	Ⓐ Ⓑ Ⓒ Ⓓ
107	Ⓐ Ⓑ Ⓒ Ⓓ	127	Ⓐ Ⓑ Ⓒ Ⓓ	147	Ⓐ Ⓑ Ⓒ Ⓓ	167	Ⓐ Ⓑ Ⓒ Ⓓ	187	Ⓐ Ⓑ Ⓒ Ⓓ
108	Ⓐ Ⓑ Ⓒ Ⓓ	128	Ⓐ Ⓑ Ⓒ Ⓓ	148	Ⓐ Ⓑ Ⓒ Ⓓ	168	Ⓐ Ⓑ Ⓒ Ⓓ	188	Ⓐ Ⓑ Ⓒ Ⓓ
109	Ⓐ Ⓑ Ⓒ Ⓓ	129	Ⓐ Ⓑ Ⓒ Ⓓ	149	Ⓐ Ⓑ Ⓒ Ⓓ	169	Ⓐ Ⓑ Ⓒ Ⓓ	189	Ⓐ Ⓑ Ⓒ Ⓓ
110	Ⓐ Ⓑ Ⓒ Ⓓ	130	Ⓐ Ⓑ Ⓒ Ⓓ	150	Ⓐ Ⓑ Ⓒ Ⓓ	170	Ⓐ Ⓑ Ⓒ Ⓓ	190	Ⓐ Ⓑ Ⓒ Ⓓ
111	Ⓐ Ⓑ Ⓒ Ⓓ	131	Ⓐ Ⓑ Ⓒ Ⓓ	151	Ⓐ Ⓑ Ⓒ Ⓓ	171	Ⓐ Ⓑ Ⓒ Ⓓ	191	Ⓐ Ⓑ Ⓒ Ⓓ
112	Ⓐ Ⓑ Ⓒ Ⓓ	132	Ⓐ Ⓑ Ⓒ Ⓓ	152	Ⓐ Ⓑ Ⓒ Ⓓ	172	Ⓐ Ⓑ Ⓒ Ⓓ	192	Ⓐ Ⓑ Ⓒ Ⓓ
113	Ⓐ Ⓑ Ⓒ Ⓓ	133	Ⓐ Ⓑ Ⓒ Ⓓ	153	Ⓐ Ⓑ Ⓒ Ⓓ	173	Ⓐ Ⓑ Ⓒ Ⓓ	193	Ⓐ Ⓑ Ⓒ Ⓓ
114	Ⓐ Ⓑ Ⓒ Ⓓ	134	Ⓐ Ⓑ Ⓒ Ⓓ	154	Ⓐ Ⓑ Ⓒ Ⓓ	174	Ⓐ Ⓑ Ⓒ Ⓓ	194	Ⓐ Ⓑ Ⓒ Ⓓ
115	Ⓐ Ⓑ Ⓒ Ⓓ	135	Ⓐ Ⓑ Ⓒ Ⓓ	155	Ⓐ Ⓑ Ⓒ Ⓓ	175	Ⓐ Ⓑ Ⓒ Ⓓ	195	Ⓐ Ⓑ Ⓒ Ⓓ
116	Ⓐ Ⓑ Ⓒ Ⓓ	136	Ⓐ Ⓑ Ⓒ Ⓓ	156	Ⓐ Ⓑ Ⓒ Ⓓ	176	Ⓐ Ⓑ Ⓒ Ⓓ	196	Ⓐ Ⓑ Ⓒ Ⓓ
117	Ⓐ Ⓑ Ⓒ Ⓓ	137	Ⓐ Ⓑ Ⓒ Ⓓ	157	Ⓐ Ⓑ Ⓒ Ⓓ	177	Ⓐ Ⓑ Ⓒ Ⓓ	197	Ⓐ Ⓑ Ⓒ Ⓓ
118	Ⓐ Ⓑ Ⓒ Ⓓ	138	Ⓐ Ⓑ Ⓒ Ⓓ	158	Ⓐ Ⓑ Ⓒ Ⓓ	178	Ⓐ Ⓑ Ⓒ Ⓓ	198	Ⓐ Ⓑ Ⓒ Ⓓ
119	Ⓐ Ⓑ Ⓒ Ⓓ	139	Ⓐ Ⓑ Ⓒ Ⓓ	159	Ⓐ Ⓑ Ⓒ Ⓓ	179	Ⓐ Ⓑ Ⓒ Ⓓ	199	Ⓐ Ⓑ Ⓒ Ⓓ
120	Ⓐ Ⓑ Ⓒ Ⓓ	140	Ⓐ Ⓑ Ⓒ Ⓓ	160	Ⓐ Ⓑ Ⓒ Ⓓ	180	Ⓐ Ⓑ Ⓒ Ⓓ	200	Ⓐ Ⓑ Ⓒ Ⓓ

ANSWER SHEET

TOEIC 실전 테스트

성명
수험번호

LISTENING (Part I~IV)

No.	ANSWER	No.	ANSWER	No.	ANSWER	No.	ANSWER	No.	ANSWER
1	Ⓐ Ⓑ Ⓒ Ⓓ	21	Ⓐ Ⓑ Ⓒ Ⓓ	41	Ⓐ Ⓑ Ⓒ Ⓓ	61	Ⓐ Ⓑ Ⓒ Ⓓ	81	Ⓐ Ⓑ Ⓒ Ⓓ
2	Ⓐ Ⓑ Ⓒ Ⓓ	22	Ⓐ Ⓑ Ⓒ Ⓓ	42	Ⓐ Ⓑ Ⓒ Ⓓ	62	Ⓐ Ⓑ Ⓒ Ⓓ	82	Ⓐ Ⓑ Ⓒ Ⓓ
3	Ⓐ Ⓑ Ⓒ Ⓓ	23	Ⓐ Ⓑ Ⓒ Ⓓ	43	Ⓐ Ⓑ Ⓒ Ⓓ	63	Ⓐ Ⓑ Ⓒ Ⓓ	83	Ⓐ Ⓑ Ⓒ Ⓓ
4	Ⓐ Ⓑ Ⓒ Ⓓ	24	Ⓐ Ⓑ Ⓒ Ⓓ	44	Ⓐ Ⓑ Ⓒ Ⓓ	64	Ⓐ Ⓑ Ⓒ Ⓓ	84	Ⓐ Ⓑ Ⓒ Ⓓ
5	Ⓐ Ⓑ Ⓒ Ⓓ	25	Ⓐ Ⓑ Ⓒ Ⓓ	45	Ⓐ Ⓑ Ⓒ Ⓓ	65	Ⓐ Ⓑ Ⓒ Ⓓ	85	Ⓐ Ⓑ Ⓒ Ⓓ
6	Ⓐ Ⓑ Ⓒ Ⓓ	26	Ⓐ Ⓑ Ⓒ Ⓓ	46	Ⓐ Ⓑ Ⓒ Ⓓ	66	Ⓐ Ⓑ Ⓒ Ⓓ	86	Ⓐ Ⓑ Ⓒ Ⓓ
7	Ⓐ Ⓑ Ⓒ Ⓓ	27	Ⓐ Ⓑ Ⓒ Ⓓ	47	Ⓐ Ⓑ Ⓒ Ⓓ	67	Ⓐ Ⓑ Ⓒ Ⓓ	87	Ⓐ Ⓑ Ⓒ Ⓓ
8	Ⓐ Ⓑ Ⓒ Ⓓ	28	Ⓐ Ⓑ Ⓒ Ⓓ	48	Ⓐ Ⓑ Ⓒ Ⓓ	68	Ⓐ Ⓑ Ⓒ Ⓓ	88	Ⓐ Ⓑ Ⓒ Ⓓ
9	Ⓐ Ⓑ Ⓒ Ⓓ	29	Ⓐ Ⓑ Ⓒ Ⓓ	49	Ⓐ Ⓑ Ⓒ Ⓓ	69	Ⓐ Ⓑ Ⓒ Ⓓ	89	Ⓐ Ⓑ Ⓒ Ⓓ
10	Ⓐ Ⓑ Ⓒ Ⓓ	30	Ⓐ Ⓑ Ⓒ Ⓓ	50	Ⓐ Ⓑ Ⓒ Ⓓ	70	Ⓐ Ⓑ Ⓒ Ⓓ	90	Ⓐ Ⓑ Ⓒ Ⓓ
11	Ⓐ Ⓑ Ⓒ Ⓓ	31	Ⓐ Ⓑ Ⓒ Ⓓ	51	Ⓐ Ⓑ Ⓒ Ⓓ	71	Ⓐ Ⓑ Ⓒ Ⓓ	91	Ⓐ Ⓑ Ⓒ Ⓓ
12	Ⓐ Ⓑ Ⓒ Ⓓ	32	Ⓐ Ⓑ Ⓒ Ⓓ	52	Ⓐ Ⓑ Ⓒ Ⓓ	72	Ⓐ Ⓑ Ⓒ Ⓓ	92	Ⓐ Ⓑ Ⓒ Ⓓ
13	Ⓐ Ⓑ Ⓒ Ⓓ	33	Ⓐ Ⓑ Ⓒ Ⓓ	53	Ⓐ Ⓑ Ⓒ Ⓓ	73	Ⓐ Ⓑ Ⓒ Ⓓ	93	Ⓐ Ⓑ Ⓒ Ⓓ
14	Ⓐ Ⓑ Ⓒ Ⓓ	34	Ⓐ Ⓑ Ⓒ Ⓓ	54	Ⓐ Ⓑ Ⓒ Ⓓ	74	Ⓐ Ⓑ Ⓒ Ⓓ	94	Ⓐ Ⓑ Ⓒ Ⓓ
15	Ⓐ Ⓑ Ⓒ Ⓓ	35	Ⓐ Ⓑ Ⓒ Ⓓ	55	Ⓐ Ⓑ Ⓒ Ⓓ	75	Ⓐ Ⓑ Ⓒ Ⓓ	95	Ⓐ Ⓑ Ⓒ Ⓓ
16	Ⓐ Ⓑ Ⓒ Ⓓ	36	Ⓐ Ⓑ Ⓒ Ⓓ	56	Ⓐ Ⓑ Ⓒ Ⓓ	76	Ⓐ Ⓑ Ⓒ Ⓓ	96	Ⓐ Ⓑ Ⓒ Ⓓ
17	Ⓐ Ⓑ Ⓒ Ⓓ	37	Ⓐ Ⓑ Ⓒ Ⓓ	57	Ⓐ Ⓑ Ⓒ Ⓓ	77	Ⓐ Ⓑ Ⓒ Ⓓ	97	Ⓐ Ⓑ Ⓒ Ⓓ
18	Ⓐ Ⓑ Ⓒ Ⓓ	38	Ⓐ Ⓑ Ⓒ Ⓓ	58	Ⓐ Ⓑ Ⓒ Ⓓ	78	Ⓐ Ⓑ Ⓒ Ⓓ	98	Ⓐ Ⓑ Ⓒ Ⓓ
19	Ⓐ Ⓑ Ⓒ Ⓓ	39	Ⓐ Ⓑ Ⓒ Ⓓ	59	Ⓐ Ⓑ Ⓒ Ⓓ	79	Ⓐ Ⓑ Ⓒ Ⓓ	99	Ⓐ Ⓑ Ⓒ Ⓓ
20	Ⓐ Ⓑ Ⓒ Ⓓ	40	Ⓐ Ⓑ Ⓒ Ⓓ	60	Ⓐ Ⓑ Ⓒ Ⓓ	80	Ⓐ Ⓑ Ⓒ Ⓓ	100	Ⓐ Ⓑ Ⓒ Ⓓ

READING (Part V~VII)

No.	ANSWER	No.	ANSWER	No.	ANSWER	No.	ANSWER	No.	ANSWER
101	Ⓐ Ⓑ Ⓒ Ⓓ	121	Ⓐ Ⓑ Ⓒ Ⓓ	141	Ⓐ Ⓑ Ⓒ Ⓓ	161	Ⓐ Ⓑ Ⓒ Ⓓ	181	Ⓐ Ⓑ Ⓒ Ⓓ
102	Ⓐ Ⓑ Ⓒ Ⓓ	122	Ⓐ Ⓑ Ⓒ Ⓓ	142	Ⓐ Ⓑ Ⓒ Ⓓ	162	Ⓐ Ⓑ Ⓒ Ⓓ	182	Ⓐ Ⓑ Ⓒ Ⓓ
103	Ⓐ Ⓑ Ⓒ Ⓓ	123	Ⓐ Ⓑ Ⓒ Ⓓ	143	Ⓐ Ⓑ Ⓒ Ⓓ	163	Ⓐ Ⓑ Ⓒ Ⓓ	183	Ⓐ Ⓑ Ⓒ Ⓓ
104	Ⓐ Ⓑ Ⓒ Ⓓ	124	Ⓐ Ⓑ Ⓒ Ⓓ	144	Ⓐ Ⓑ Ⓒ Ⓓ	164	Ⓐ Ⓑ Ⓒ Ⓓ	184	Ⓐ Ⓑ Ⓒ Ⓓ
105	Ⓐ Ⓑ Ⓒ Ⓓ	125	Ⓐ Ⓑ Ⓒ Ⓓ	145	Ⓐ Ⓑ Ⓒ Ⓓ	165	Ⓐ Ⓑ Ⓒ Ⓓ	185	Ⓐ Ⓑ Ⓒ Ⓓ
106	Ⓐ Ⓑ Ⓒ Ⓓ	126	Ⓐ Ⓑ Ⓒ Ⓓ	146	Ⓐ Ⓑ Ⓒ Ⓓ	166	Ⓐ Ⓑ Ⓒ Ⓓ	186	Ⓐ Ⓑ Ⓒ Ⓓ
107	Ⓐ Ⓑ Ⓒ Ⓓ	127	Ⓐ Ⓑ Ⓒ Ⓓ	147	Ⓐ Ⓑ Ⓒ Ⓓ	167	Ⓐ Ⓑ Ⓒ Ⓓ	187	Ⓐ Ⓑ Ⓒ Ⓓ
108	Ⓐ Ⓑ Ⓒ Ⓓ	128	Ⓐ Ⓑ Ⓒ Ⓓ	148	Ⓐ Ⓑ Ⓒ Ⓓ	168	Ⓐ Ⓑ Ⓒ Ⓓ	188	Ⓐ Ⓑ Ⓒ Ⓓ
109	Ⓐ Ⓑ Ⓒ Ⓓ	129	Ⓐ Ⓑ Ⓒ Ⓓ	149	Ⓐ Ⓑ Ⓒ Ⓓ	169	Ⓐ Ⓑ Ⓒ Ⓓ	189	Ⓐ Ⓑ Ⓒ Ⓓ
110	Ⓐ Ⓑ Ⓒ Ⓓ	130	Ⓐ Ⓑ Ⓒ Ⓓ	150	Ⓐ Ⓑ Ⓒ Ⓓ	170	Ⓐ Ⓑ Ⓒ Ⓓ	190	Ⓐ Ⓑ Ⓒ Ⓓ
111	Ⓐ Ⓑ Ⓒ Ⓓ	131	Ⓐ Ⓑ Ⓒ Ⓓ	151	Ⓐ Ⓑ Ⓒ Ⓓ	171	Ⓐ Ⓑ Ⓒ Ⓓ	191	Ⓐ Ⓑ Ⓒ Ⓓ
112	Ⓐ Ⓑ Ⓒ Ⓓ	132	Ⓐ Ⓑ Ⓒ Ⓓ	152	Ⓐ Ⓑ Ⓒ Ⓓ	172	Ⓐ Ⓑ Ⓒ Ⓓ	192	Ⓐ Ⓑ Ⓒ Ⓓ
113	Ⓐ Ⓑ Ⓒ Ⓓ	133	Ⓐ Ⓑ Ⓒ Ⓓ	153	Ⓐ Ⓑ Ⓒ Ⓓ	173	Ⓐ Ⓑ Ⓒ Ⓓ	193	Ⓐ Ⓑ Ⓒ Ⓓ
114	Ⓐ Ⓑ Ⓒ Ⓓ	134	Ⓐ Ⓑ Ⓒ Ⓓ	154	Ⓐ Ⓑ Ⓒ Ⓓ	174	Ⓐ Ⓑ Ⓒ Ⓓ	194	Ⓐ Ⓑ Ⓒ Ⓓ
115	Ⓐ Ⓑ Ⓒ Ⓓ	135	Ⓐ Ⓑ Ⓒ Ⓓ	155	Ⓐ Ⓑ Ⓒ Ⓓ	175	Ⓐ Ⓑ Ⓒ Ⓓ	195	Ⓐ Ⓑ Ⓒ Ⓓ
116	Ⓐ Ⓑ Ⓒ Ⓓ	136	Ⓐ Ⓑ Ⓒ Ⓓ	156	Ⓐ Ⓑ Ⓒ Ⓓ	176	Ⓐ Ⓑ Ⓒ Ⓓ	196	Ⓐ Ⓑ Ⓒ Ⓓ
117	Ⓐ Ⓑ Ⓒ Ⓓ	137	Ⓐ Ⓑ Ⓒ Ⓓ	157	Ⓐ Ⓑ Ⓒ Ⓓ	177	Ⓐ Ⓑ Ⓒ Ⓓ	197	Ⓐ Ⓑ Ⓒ Ⓓ
118	Ⓐ Ⓑ Ⓒ Ⓓ	138	Ⓐ Ⓑ Ⓒ Ⓓ	158	Ⓐ Ⓑ Ⓒ Ⓓ	178	Ⓐ Ⓑ Ⓒ Ⓓ	198	Ⓐ Ⓑ Ⓒ Ⓓ
119	Ⓐ Ⓑ Ⓒ Ⓓ	139	Ⓐ Ⓑ Ⓒ Ⓓ	159	Ⓐ Ⓑ Ⓒ Ⓓ	179	Ⓐ Ⓑ Ⓒ Ⓓ	199	Ⓐ Ⓑ Ⓒ Ⓓ
120	Ⓐ Ⓑ Ⓒ Ⓓ	140	Ⓐ Ⓑ Ⓒ Ⓓ	160	Ⓐ Ⓑ Ⓒ Ⓓ	180	Ⓐ Ⓑ Ⓒ Ⓓ	200	Ⓐ Ⓑ Ⓒ Ⓓ

ANSWER SHEET

TOEIC 실전 테스트

성명
한글
영문

LISTENING (Part I-IV)

No.	ANSWER	No.	ANSWER	No.	ANSWER	No.	ANSWER
1	Ⓐ Ⓑ Ⓒ Ⓓ	21	Ⓐ Ⓑ Ⓒ	41	Ⓐ Ⓑ Ⓒ Ⓓ	61	Ⓐ Ⓑ Ⓒ Ⓓ	81	Ⓐ Ⓑ Ⓒ Ⓓ
2	Ⓐ Ⓑ Ⓒ Ⓓ	22	Ⓐ Ⓑ Ⓒ	42	Ⓐ Ⓑ Ⓒ Ⓓ	62	Ⓐ Ⓑ Ⓒ Ⓓ	82	Ⓐ Ⓑ Ⓒ Ⓓ
3	Ⓐ Ⓑ Ⓒ Ⓓ	23	Ⓐ Ⓑ Ⓒ	43	Ⓐ Ⓑ Ⓒ Ⓓ	63	Ⓐ Ⓑ Ⓒ Ⓓ	83	Ⓐ Ⓑ Ⓒ Ⓓ
4	Ⓐ Ⓑ Ⓒ Ⓓ	24	Ⓐ Ⓑ Ⓒ	44	Ⓐ Ⓑ Ⓒ Ⓓ	64	Ⓐ Ⓑ Ⓒ Ⓓ	84	Ⓐ Ⓑ Ⓒ Ⓓ
5	Ⓐ Ⓑ Ⓒ Ⓓ	25	Ⓐ Ⓑ Ⓒ	45	Ⓐ Ⓑ Ⓒ Ⓓ	65	Ⓐ Ⓑ Ⓒ Ⓓ	85	Ⓐ Ⓑ Ⓒ Ⓓ
6	Ⓐ Ⓑ Ⓒ Ⓓ	26	Ⓐ Ⓑ Ⓒ	46	Ⓐ Ⓑ Ⓒ Ⓓ	66	Ⓐ Ⓑ Ⓒ Ⓓ	86	Ⓐ Ⓑ Ⓒ Ⓓ
7	Ⓐ Ⓑ Ⓒ	27	Ⓐ Ⓑ Ⓒ	47	Ⓐ Ⓑ Ⓒ Ⓓ	67	Ⓐ Ⓑ Ⓒ Ⓓ	87	Ⓐ Ⓑ Ⓒ Ⓓ
8	Ⓐ Ⓑ Ⓒ	28	Ⓐ Ⓑ Ⓒ	48	Ⓐ Ⓑ Ⓒ Ⓓ	68	Ⓐ Ⓑ Ⓒ Ⓓ	88	Ⓐ Ⓑ Ⓒ Ⓓ
9	Ⓐ Ⓑ Ⓒ	29	Ⓐ Ⓑ Ⓒ	49	Ⓐ Ⓑ Ⓒ Ⓓ	69	Ⓐ Ⓑ Ⓒ Ⓓ	89	Ⓐ Ⓑ Ⓒ Ⓓ
10	Ⓐ Ⓑ Ⓒ	30	Ⓐ Ⓑ Ⓒ	50	Ⓐ Ⓑ Ⓒ Ⓓ	70	Ⓐ Ⓑ Ⓒ Ⓓ	90	Ⓐ Ⓑ Ⓒ Ⓓ
11	Ⓐ Ⓑ Ⓒ	31	Ⓐ Ⓑ Ⓒ	51	Ⓐ Ⓑ Ⓒ Ⓓ	71	Ⓐ Ⓑ Ⓒ Ⓓ	91	Ⓐ Ⓑ Ⓒ Ⓓ
12	Ⓐ Ⓑ Ⓒ	32	Ⓐ Ⓑ Ⓒ Ⓓ	52	Ⓐ Ⓑ Ⓒ Ⓓ	72	Ⓐ Ⓑ Ⓒ Ⓓ	92	Ⓐ Ⓑ Ⓒ Ⓓ
13	Ⓐ Ⓑ Ⓒ	33	Ⓐ Ⓑ Ⓒ Ⓓ	53	Ⓐ Ⓑ Ⓒ Ⓓ	73	Ⓐ Ⓑ Ⓒ Ⓓ	93	Ⓐ Ⓑ Ⓒ Ⓓ
14	Ⓐ Ⓑ Ⓒ	34	Ⓐ Ⓑ Ⓒ Ⓓ	54	Ⓐ Ⓑ Ⓒ Ⓓ	74	Ⓐ Ⓑ Ⓒ Ⓓ	94	Ⓐ Ⓑ Ⓒ Ⓓ
15	Ⓐ Ⓑ Ⓒ	35	Ⓐ Ⓑ Ⓒ Ⓓ	55	Ⓐ Ⓑ Ⓒ Ⓓ	75	Ⓐ Ⓑ Ⓒ Ⓓ	95	Ⓐ Ⓑ Ⓒ Ⓓ
16	Ⓐ Ⓑ Ⓒ	36	Ⓐ Ⓑ Ⓒ Ⓓ	56	Ⓐ Ⓑ Ⓒ Ⓓ	76	Ⓐ Ⓑ Ⓒ Ⓓ	96	Ⓐ Ⓑ Ⓒ Ⓓ
17	Ⓐ Ⓑ Ⓒ	37	Ⓐ Ⓑ Ⓒ Ⓓ	57	Ⓐ Ⓑ Ⓒ Ⓓ	77	Ⓐ Ⓑ Ⓒ Ⓓ	97	Ⓐ Ⓑ Ⓒ Ⓓ
18	Ⓐ Ⓑ Ⓒ	38	Ⓐ Ⓑ Ⓒ Ⓓ	58	Ⓐ Ⓑ Ⓒ Ⓓ	78	Ⓐ Ⓑ Ⓒ Ⓓ	98	Ⓐ Ⓑ Ⓒ Ⓓ
19	Ⓐ Ⓑ Ⓒ	39	Ⓐ Ⓑ Ⓒ Ⓓ	59	Ⓐ Ⓑ Ⓒ Ⓓ	79	Ⓐ Ⓑ Ⓒ Ⓓ	99	Ⓐ Ⓑ Ⓒ Ⓓ
20	Ⓐ Ⓑ Ⓒ	40	Ⓐ Ⓑ Ⓒ Ⓓ	60	Ⓐ Ⓑ Ⓒ Ⓓ	80	Ⓐ Ⓑ Ⓒ Ⓓ	100	Ⓐ Ⓑ Ⓒ Ⓓ

READING (Part V~VII)

No.	ANSWER	No.	ANSWER	No.	ANSWER	No.	ANSWER	No.	ANSWER
101	Ⓐ Ⓑ Ⓒ Ⓓ	121	Ⓐ Ⓑ Ⓒ Ⓓ	141	Ⓐ Ⓑ Ⓒ Ⓓ	161	Ⓐ Ⓑ Ⓒ Ⓓ	181	Ⓐ Ⓑ Ⓒ Ⓓ
102	Ⓐ Ⓑ Ⓒ Ⓓ	122	Ⓐ Ⓑ Ⓒ Ⓓ	142	Ⓐ Ⓑ Ⓒ Ⓓ	162	Ⓐ Ⓑ Ⓒ Ⓓ	182	Ⓐ Ⓑ Ⓒ Ⓓ
103	Ⓐ Ⓑ Ⓒ Ⓓ	123	Ⓐ Ⓑ Ⓒ Ⓓ	143	Ⓐ Ⓑ Ⓒ Ⓓ	163	Ⓐ Ⓑ Ⓒ Ⓓ	183	Ⓐ Ⓑ Ⓒ Ⓓ
104	Ⓐ Ⓑ Ⓒ Ⓓ	124	Ⓐ Ⓑ Ⓒ Ⓓ	144	Ⓐ Ⓑ Ⓒ Ⓓ	164	Ⓐ Ⓑ Ⓒ Ⓓ	184	Ⓐ Ⓑ Ⓒ Ⓓ
105	Ⓐ Ⓑ Ⓒ Ⓓ	125	Ⓐ Ⓑ Ⓒ Ⓓ	145	Ⓐ Ⓑ Ⓒ Ⓓ	165	Ⓐ Ⓑ Ⓒ Ⓓ	185	Ⓐ Ⓑ Ⓒ Ⓓ
106	Ⓐ Ⓑ Ⓒ Ⓓ	126	Ⓐ Ⓑ Ⓒ Ⓓ	146	Ⓐ Ⓑ Ⓒ Ⓓ	166	Ⓐ Ⓑ Ⓒ Ⓓ	186	Ⓐ Ⓑ Ⓒ Ⓓ
107	Ⓐ Ⓑ Ⓒ Ⓓ	127	Ⓐ Ⓑ Ⓒ Ⓓ	147	Ⓐ Ⓑ Ⓒ Ⓓ	167	Ⓐ Ⓑ Ⓒ Ⓓ	187	Ⓐ Ⓑ Ⓒ Ⓓ
108	Ⓐ Ⓑ Ⓒ Ⓓ	128	Ⓐ Ⓑ Ⓒ Ⓓ	148	Ⓐ Ⓑ Ⓒ Ⓓ	168	Ⓐ Ⓑ Ⓒ Ⓓ	188	Ⓐ Ⓑ Ⓒ Ⓓ
109	Ⓐ Ⓑ Ⓒ Ⓓ	129	Ⓐ Ⓑ Ⓒ Ⓓ	149	Ⓐ Ⓑ Ⓒ Ⓓ	169	Ⓐ Ⓑ Ⓒ Ⓓ	189	Ⓐ Ⓑ Ⓒ Ⓓ
110	Ⓐ Ⓑ Ⓒ Ⓓ	130	Ⓐ Ⓑ Ⓒ Ⓓ	150	Ⓐ Ⓑ Ⓒ Ⓓ	170	Ⓐ Ⓑ Ⓒ Ⓓ	190	Ⓐ Ⓑ Ⓒ Ⓓ
111	Ⓐ Ⓑ Ⓒ Ⓓ	131	Ⓐ Ⓑ Ⓒ Ⓓ	151	Ⓐ Ⓑ Ⓒ Ⓓ	171	Ⓐ Ⓑ Ⓒ Ⓓ	191	Ⓐ Ⓑ Ⓒ Ⓓ
112	Ⓐ Ⓑ Ⓒ Ⓓ	132	Ⓐ Ⓑ Ⓒ Ⓓ	152	Ⓐ Ⓑ Ⓒ Ⓓ	172	Ⓐ Ⓑ Ⓒ Ⓓ	192	Ⓐ Ⓑ Ⓒ Ⓓ
113	Ⓐ Ⓑ Ⓒ Ⓓ	133	Ⓐ Ⓑ Ⓒ Ⓓ	153	Ⓐ Ⓑ Ⓒ Ⓓ	173	Ⓐ Ⓑ Ⓒ Ⓓ	193	Ⓐ Ⓑ Ⓒ Ⓓ
114	Ⓐ Ⓑ Ⓒ Ⓓ	134	Ⓐ Ⓑ Ⓒ Ⓓ	154	Ⓐ Ⓑ Ⓒ Ⓓ	174	Ⓐ Ⓑ Ⓒ Ⓓ	194	Ⓐ Ⓑ Ⓒ Ⓓ
115	Ⓐ Ⓑ Ⓒ Ⓓ	135	Ⓐ Ⓑ Ⓒ Ⓓ	155	Ⓐ Ⓑ Ⓒ Ⓓ	175	Ⓐ Ⓑ Ⓒ Ⓓ	195	Ⓐ Ⓑ Ⓒ Ⓓ
116	Ⓐ Ⓑ Ⓒ Ⓓ	136	Ⓐ Ⓑ Ⓒ Ⓓ	156	Ⓐ Ⓑ Ⓒ Ⓓ	176	Ⓐ Ⓑ Ⓒ Ⓓ	196	Ⓐ Ⓑ Ⓒ Ⓓ
117	Ⓐ Ⓑ Ⓒ Ⓓ	137	Ⓐ Ⓑ Ⓒ Ⓓ	157	Ⓐ Ⓑ Ⓒ Ⓓ	177	Ⓐ Ⓑ Ⓒ Ⓓ	197	Ⓐ Ⓑ Ⓒ Ⓓ
118	Ⓐ Ⓑ Ⓒ Ⓓ	138	Ⓐ Ⓑ Ⓒ Ⓓ	158	Ⓐ Ⓑ Ⓒ Ⓓ	178	Ⓐ Ⓑ Ⓒ Ⓓ	198	Ⓐ Ⓑ Ⓒ Ⓓ
119	Ⓐ Ⓑ Ⓒ Ⓓ	139	Ⓐ Ⓑ Ⓒ Ⓓ	159	Ⓐ Ⓑ Ⓒ Ⓓ	179	Ⓐ Ⓑ Ⓒ Ⓓ	199	Ⓐ Ⓑ Ⓒ Ⓓ
120	Ⓐ Ⓑ Ⓒ Ⓓ	140	Ⓐ Ⓑ Ⓒ Ⓓ	160	Ⓐ Ⓑ Ⓒ Ⓓ	180	Ⓐ Ⓑ Ⓒ Ⓓ	200	Ⓐ Ⓑ Ⓒ Ⓓ

ANSWER SHEET

TOEIC 실전 테스트

LISTENING (Part I~IV)

READING (Part V~VII)

ANSWER SHEET

TOEIC 실전 테스트

성명
학급
영문

LISTENING (Part I~IV)

No.	ANSWER	No.	ANSWER	No.	ANSWER	No.	ANSWER	No.	ANSWER
1	Ⓐ Ⓑ Ⓒ	21	Ⓐ Ⓑ Ⓒ	41	Ⓐ Ⓑ Ⓒ Ⓓ	61	Ⓐ Ⓑ Ⓒ Ⓓ	81	Ⓐ Ⓑ Ⓒ Ⓓ
2	Ⓐ Ⓑ Ⓒ Ⓓ	22	Ⓐ Ⓑ Ⓒ	42	Ⓐ Ⓑ Ⓒ Ⓓ	62	Ⓐ Ⓑ Ⓒ Ⓓ	82	Ⓐ Ⓑ Ⓒ Ⓓ
3	Ⓐ Ⓑ Ⓒ Ⓓ	23	Ⓐ Ⓑ Ⓒ	43	Ⓐ Ⓑ Ⓒ Ⓓ	63	Ⓐ Ⓑ Ⓒ Ⓓ	83	Ⓐ Ⓑ Ⓒ Ⓓ
4	Ⓐ Ⓑ Ⓒ Ⓓ	24	Ⓐ Ⓑ Ⓒ	44	Ⓐ Ⓑ Ⓒ Ⓓ	64	Ⓐ Ⓑ Ⓒ Ⓓ	84	Ⓐ Ⓑ Ⓒ Ⓓ
5	Ⓐ Ⓑ Ⓒ Ⓓ	25	Ⓐ Ⓑ Ⓒ	45	Ⓐ Ⓑ Ⓒ Ⓓ	65	Ⓐ Ⓑ Ⓒ Ⓓ	85	Ⓐ Ⓑ Ⓒ Ⓓ
6	Ⓐ Ⓑ Ⓒ	26	Ⓐ Ⓑ Ⓒ	46	Ⓐ Ⓑ Ⓒ Ⓓ	66	Ⓐ Ⓑ Ⓒ Ⓓ	86	Ⓐ Ⓑ Ⓒ Ⓓ
7	Ⓐ Ⓑ Ⓒ	27	Ⓐ Ⓑ Ⓒ	47	Ⓐ Ⓑ Ⓒ Ⓓ	67	Ⓐ Ⓑ Ⓒ Ⓓ	87	Ⓐ Ⓑ Ⓒ Ⓓ
8	Ⓐ Ⓑ Ⓒ	28	Ⓐ Ⓑ Ⓒ Ⓓ	48	Ⓐ Ⓑ Ⓒ Ⓓ	68	Ⓐ Ⓑ Ⓒ Ⓓ	88	Ⓐ Ⓑ Ⓒ Ⓓ
9	Ⓐ Ⓑ Ⓒ	29	Ⓐ Ⓑ Ⓒ Ⓓ	49	Ⓐ Ⓑ Ⓒ Ⓓ	69	Ⓐ Ⓑ Ⓒ Ⓓ	89	Ⓐ Ⓑ Ⓒ Ⓓ
10	Ⓐ Ⓑ Ⓒ	30	Ⓐ Ⓑ Ⓒ Ⓓ	50	Ⓐ Ⓑ Ⓒ Ⓓ	70	Ⓐ Ⓑ Ⓒ Ⓓ	90	Ⓐ Ⓑ Ⓒ Ⓓ
11	Ⓐ Ⓑ Ⓒ	31	Ⓐ Ⓑ Ⓒ Ⓓ	51	Ⓐ Ⓑ Ⓒ Ⓓ	71	Ⓐ Ⓑ Ⓒ Ⓓ	91	Ⓐ Ⓑ Ⓒ Ⓓ
12	Ⓐ Ⓑ Ⓒ	32	Ⓐ Ⓑ Ⓒ Ⓓ	52	Ⓐ Ⓑ Ⓒ Ⓓ	72	Ⓐ Ⓑ Ⓒ Ⓓ	92	Ⓐ Ⓑ Ⓒ Ⓓ
13	Ⓐ Ⓑ Ⓒ	33	Ⓐ Ⓑ Ⓒ Ⓓ	53	Ⓐ Ⓑ Ⓒ Ⓓ	73	Ⓐ Ⓑ Ⓒ Ⓓ	93	Ⓐ Ⓑ Ⓒ Ⓓ
14	Ⓐ Ⓑ Ⓒ	34	Ⓐ Ⓑ Ⓒ Ⓓ	54	Ⓐ Ⓑ Ⓒ Ⓓ	74	Ⓐ Ⓑ Ⓒ Ⓓ	94	Ⓐ Ⓑ Ⓒ Ⓓ
15	Ⓐ Ⓑ Ⓒ	35	Ⓐ Ⓑ Ⓒ Ⓓ	55	Ⓐ Ⓑ Ⓒ Ⓓ	75	Ⓐ Ⓑ Ⓒ Ⓓ	95	Ⓐ Ⓑ Ⓒ Ⓓ
16	Ⓐ Ⓑ Ⓒ	36	Ⓐ Ⓑ Ⓒ Ⓓ	56	Ⓐ Ⓑ Ⓒ Ⓓ	76	Ⓐ Ⓑ Ⓒ Ⓓ	96	Ⓐ Ⓑ Ⓒ Ⓓ
17	Ⓐ Ⓑ Ⓒ	37	Ⓐ Ⓑ Ⓒ Ⓓ	57	Ⓐ Ⓑ Ⓒ Ⓓ	77	Ⓐ Ⓑ Ⓒ Ⓓ	97	Ⓐ Ⓑ Ⓒ Ⓓ
18	Ⓐ Ⓑ Ⓒ	38	Ⓐ Ⓑ Ⓒ Ⓓ	58	Ⓐ Ⓑ Ⓒ Ⓓ	78	Ⓐ Ⓑ Ⓒ Ⓓ	98	Ⓐ Ⓑ Ⓒ Ⓓ
19	Ⓐ Ⓑ Ⓒ	39	Ⓐ Ⓑ Ⓒ Ⓓ	59	Ⓐ Ⓑ Ⓒ Ⓓ	79	Ⓐ Ⓑ Ⓒ Ⓓ	99	Ⓐ Ⓑ Ⓒ Ⓓ
20	Ⓐ Ⓑ Ⓒ	40	Ⓐ Ⓑ Ⓒ Ⓓ	60	Ⓐ Ⓑ Ⓒ Ⓓ	80	Ⓐ Ⓑ Ⓒ Ⓓ	100	Ⓐ Ⓑ Ⓒ Ⓓ

READING (Part V~VII)

No.	ANSWER	No.	ANSWER	No.	ANSWER	No.	ANSWER	No.	ANSWER
101	Ⓐ Ⓑ Ⓒ Ⓓ	121	Ⓐ Ⓑ Ⓒ Ⓓ	141	Ⓐ Ⓑ Ⓒ Ⓓ	161	Ⓐ Ⓑ Ⓒ Ⓓ	181	Ⓐ Ⓑ Ⓒ Ⓓ
102	Ⓐ Ⓑ Ⓒ Ⓓ	122	Ⓐ Ⓑ Ⓒ Ⓓ	142	Ⓐ Ⓑ Ⓒ Ⓓ	162	Ⓐ Ⓑ Ⓒ Ⓓ	182	Ⓐ Ⓑ Ⓒ Ⓓ
103	Ⓐ Ⓑ Ⓒ Ⓓ	123	Ⓐ Ⓑ Ⓒ Ⓓ	143	Ⓐ Ⓑ Ⓒ Ⓓ	163	Ⓐ Ⓑ Ⓒ Ⓓ	183	Ⓐ Ⓑ Ⓒ Ⓓ
104	Ⓐ Ⓑ Ⓒ Ⓓ	124	Ⓐ Ⓑ Ⓒ Ⓓ	144	Ⓐ Ⓑ Ⓒ Ⓓ	164	Ⓐ Ⓑ Ⓒ Ⓓ	184	Ⓐ Ⓑ Ⓒ Ⓓ
105	Ⓐ Ⓑ Ⓒ Ⓓ	125	Ⓐ Ⓑ Ⓒ Ⓓ	145	Ⓐ Ⓑ Ⓒ Ⓓ	165	Ⓐ Ⓑ Ⓒ Ⓓ	185	Ⓐ Ⓑ Ⓒ Ⓓ
106	Ⓐ Ⓑ Ⓒ Ⓓ	126	Ⓐ Ⓑ Ⓒ Ⓓ	146	Ⓐ Ⓑ Ⓒ Ⓓ	166	Ⓐ Ⓑ Ⓒ Ⓓ	186	Ⓐ Ⓑ Ⓒ Ⓓ
107	Ⓐ Ⓑ Ⓒ Ⓓ	127	Ⓐ Ⓑ Ⓒ Ⓓ	147	Ⓐ Ⓑ Ⓒ Ⓓ	167	Ⓐ Ⓑ Ⓒ Ⓓ	187	Ⓐ Ⓑ Ⓒ Ⓓ
108	Ⓐ Ⓑ Ⓒ Ⓓ	128	Ⓐ Ⓑ Ⓒ Ⓓ	148	Ⓐ Ⓑ Ⓒ Ⓓ	168	Ⓐ Ⓑ Ⓒ Ⓓ	188	Ⓐ Ⓑ Ⓒ Ⓓ
109	Ⓐ Ⓑ Ⓒ Ⓓ	129	Ⓐ Ⓑ Ⓒ Ⓓ	149	Ⓐ Ⓑ Ⓒ Ⓓ	169	Ⓐ Ⓑ Ⓒ Ⓓ	189	Ⓐ Ⓑ Ⓒ Ⓓ
110	Ⓐ Ⓑ Ⓒ Ⓓ	130	Ⓐ Ⓑ Ⓒ Ⓓ	150	Ⓐ Ⓑ Ⓒ Ⓓ	170	Ⓐ Ⓑ Ⓒ Ⓓ	190	Ⓐ Ⓑ Ⓒ Ⓓ
111	Ⓐ Ⓑ Ⓒ Ⓓ	131	Ⓐ Ⓑ Ⓒ Ⓓ	151	Ⓐ Ⓑ Ⓒ Ⓓ	171	Ⓐ Ⓑ Ⓒ Ⓓ	191	Ⓐ Ⓑ Ⓒ Ⓓ
112	Ⓐ Ⓑ Ⓒ Ⓓ	132	Ⓐ Ⓑ Ⓒ Ⓓ	152	Ⓐ Ⓑ Ⓒ Ⓓ	172	Ⓐ Ⓑ Ⓒ Ⓓ	192	Ⓐ Ⓑ Ⓒ Ⓓ
113	Ⓐ Ⓑ Ⓒ Ⓓ	133	Ⓐ Ⓑ Ⓒ Ⓓ	153	Ⓐ Ⓑ Ⓒ Ⓓ	173	Ⓐ Ⓑ Ⓒ Ⓓ	193	Ⓐ Ⓑ Ⓒ Ⓓ
114	Ⓐ Ⓑ Ⓒ Ⓓ	134	Ⓐ Ⓑ Ⓒ Ⓓ	154	Ⓐ Ⓑ Ⓒ Ⓓ	174	Ⓐ Ⓑ Ⓒ Ⓓ	194	Ⓐ Ⓑ Ⓒ Ⓓ
115	Ⓐ Ⓑ Ⓒ Ⓓ	135	Ⓐ Ⓑ Ⓒ Ⓓ	155	Ⓐ Ⓑ Ⓒ Ⓓ	175	Ⓐ Ⓑ Ⓒ Ⓓ	195	Ⓐ Ⓑ Ⓒ Ⓓ
116	Ⓐ Ⓑ Ⓒ Ⓓ	136	Ⓐ Ⓑ Ⓒ Ⓓ	156	Ⓐ Ⓑ Ⓒ Ⓓ	176	Ⓐ Ⓑ Ⓒ Ⓓ	196	Ⓐ Ⓑ Ⓒ Ⓓ
117	Ⓐ Ⓑ Ⓒ Ⓓ	137	Ⓐ Ⓑ Ⓒ Ⓓ	157	Ⓐ Ⓑ Ⓒ Ⓓ	177	Ⓐ Ⓑ Ⓒ Ⓓ	197	Ⓐ Ⓑ Ⓒ Ⓓ
118	Ⓐ Ⓑ Ⓒ Ⓓ	138	Ⓐ Ⓑ Ⓒ Ⓓ	158	Ⓐ Ⓑ Ⓒ Ⓓ	178	Ⓐ Ⓑ Ⓒ Ⓓ	198	Ⓐ Ⓑ Ⓒ Ⓓ
119	Ⓐ Ⓑ Ⓒ Ⓓ	139	Ⓐ Ⓑ Ⓒ Ⓓ	159	Ⓐ Ⓑ Ⓒ Ⓓ	179	Ⓐ Ⓑ Ⓒ Ⓓ	199	Ⓐ Ⓑ Ⓒ Ⓓ
120	Ⓐ Ⓑ Ⓒ Ⓓ	140	Ⓐ Ⓑ Ⓒ Ⓓ	160	Ⓐ Ⓑ Ⓒ Ⓓ	180	Ⓐ Ⓑ Ⓒ Ⓓ	200	Ⓐ Ⓑ Ⓒ Ⓓ

ANSWER SHEET

TOEIC 실전 테스트

LISTENING (Part I~IV)

No.	ANSWER	No.	ANSWER	No.	ANSWER	No.	ANSWER	No.	ANSWER
1	Ⓐ Ⓑ Ⓒ Ⓓ	21	Ⓐ Ⓑ Ⓒ Ⓓ	41	Ⓐ Ⓑ Ⓒ Ⓓ	61	Ⓐ Ⓑ Ⓒ Ⓓ	81	Ⓐ Ⓑ Ⓒ Ⓓ
2	Ⓐ Ⓑ Ⓒ Ⓓ	22	Ⓐ Ⓑ Ⓒ Ⓓ	42	Ⓐ Ⓑ Ⓒ Ⓓ	62	Ⓐ Ⓑ Ⓒ Ⓓ	82	Ⓐ Ⓑ Ⓒ Ⓓ
3	Ⓐ Ⓑ Ⓒ Ⓓ	23	Ⓐ Ⓑ Ⓒ Ⓓ	43	Ⓐ Ⓑ Ⓒ Ⓓ	63	Ⓐ Ⓑ Ⓒ Ⓓ	83	Ⓐ Ⓑ Ⓒ Ⓓ
4	Ⓐ Ⓑ Ⓒ Ⓓ	24	Ⓐ Ⓑ Ⓒ Ⓓ	44	Ⓐ Ⓑ Ⓒ Ⓓ	64	Ⓐ Ⓑ Ⓒ Ⓓ	84	Ⓐ Ⓑ Ⓒ Ⓓ
5	Ⓐ Ⓑ Ⓒ Ⓓ	25	Ⓐ Ⓑ Ⓒ Ⓓ	45	Ⓐ Ⓑ Ⓒ Ⓓ	65	Ⓐ Ⓑ Ⓒ Ⓓ	85	Ⓐ Ⓑ Ⓒ Ⓓ
6	Ⓐ Ⓑ Ⓒ Ⓓ	26	Ⓐ Ⓑ Ⓒ Ⓓ	46	Ⓐ Ⓑ Ⓒ Ⓓ	66	Ⓐ Ⓑ Ⓒ Ⓓ	86	Ⓐ Ⓑ Ⓒ Ⓓ
7	Ⓐ Ⓑ Ⓒ Ⓓ	27	Ⓐ Ⓑ Ⓒ Ⓓ	47	Ⓐ Ⓑ Ⓒ Ⓓ	67	Ⓐ Ⓑ Ⓒ Ⓓ	87	Ⓐ Ⓑ Ⓒ Ⓓ
8	Ⓐ Ⓑ Ⓒ Ⓓ	28	Ⓐ Ⓑ Ⓒ Ⓓ	48	Ⓐ Ⓑ Ⓒ Ⓓ	68	Ⓐ Ⓑ Ⓒ Ⓓ	88	Ⓐ Ⓑ Ⓒ Ⓓ
9	Ⓐ Ⓑ Ⓒ Ⓓ	29	Ⓐ Ⓑ Ⓒ Ⓓ	49	Ⓐ Ⓑ Ⓒ Ⓓ	69	Ⓐ Ⓑ Ⓒ Ⓓ	89	Ⓐ Ⓑ Ⓒ Ⓓ
10	Ⓐ Ⓑ Ⓒ Ⓓ	30	Ⓐ Ⓑ Ⓒ Ⓓ	50	Ⓐ Ⓑ Ⓒ Ⓓ	70	Ⓐ Ⓑ Ⓒ Ⓓ	90	Ⓐ Ⓑ Ⓒ Ⓓ
11	Ⓐ Ⓑ Ⓒ Ⓓ	31	Ⓐ Ⓑ Ⓒ Ⓓ	51	Ⓐ Ⓑ Ⓒ Ⓓ	71	Ⓐ Ⓑ Ⓒ Ⓓ	91	Ⓐ Ⓑ Ⓒ Ⓓ
12	Ⓐ Ⓑ Ⓒ Ⓓ	32	Ⓐ Ⓑ Ⓒ Ⓓ	52	Ⓐ Ⓑ Ⓒ Ⓓ	72	Ⓐ Ⓑ Ⓒ Ⓓ	92	Ⓐ Ⓑ Ⓒ Ⓓ
13	Ⓐ Ⓑ Ⓒ Ⓓ	33	Ⓐ Ⓑ Ⓒ Ⓓ	53	Ⓐ Ⓑ Ⓒ Ⓓ	73	Ⓐ Ⓑ Ⓒ Ⓓ	93	Ⓐ Ⓑ Ⓒ Ⓓ
14	Ⓐ Ⓑ Ⓒ Ⓓ	34	Ⓐ Ⓑ Ⓒ Ⓓ	54	Ⓐ Ⓑ Ⓒ Ⓓ	74	Ⓐ Ⓑ Ⓒ Ⓓ	94	Ⓐ Ⓑ Ⓒ Ⓓ
15	Ⓐ Ⓑ Ⓒ Ⓓ	35	Ⓐ Ⓑ Ⓒ Ⓓ	55	Ⓐ Ⓑ Ⓒ Ⓓ	75	Ⓐ Ⓑ Ⓒ Ⓓ	95	Ⓐ Ⓑ Ⓒ Ⓓ
16	Ⓐ Ⓑ Ⓒ Ⓓ	36	Ⓐ Ⓑ Ⓒ Ⓓ	56	Ⓐ Ⓑ Ⓒ Ⓓ	76	Ⓐ Ⓑ Ⓒ Ⓓ	96	Ⓐ Ⓑ Ⓒ Ⓓ
17	Ⓐ Ⓑ Ⓒ Ⓓ	37	Ⓐ Ⓑ Ⓒ Ⓓ	57	Ⓐ Ⓑ Ⓒ Ⓓ	77	Ⓐ Ⓑ Ⓒ Ⓓ	97	Ⓐ Ⓑ Ⓒ Ⓓ
18	Ⓐ Ⓑ Ⓒ Ⓓ	38	Ⓐ Ⓑ Ⓒ Ⓓ	58	Ⓐ Ⓑ Ⓒ Ⓓ	78	Ⓐ Ⓑ Ⓒ Ⓓ	98	Ⓐ Ⓑ Ⓒ Ⓓ
19	Ⓐ Ⓑ Ⓒ Ⓓ	39	Ⓐ Ⓑ Ⓒ Ⓓ	59	Ⓐ Ⓑ Ⓒ Ⓓ	79	Ⓐ Ⓑ Ⓒ Ⓓ	99	Ⓐ Ⓑ Ⓒ Ⓓ
20	Ⓐ Ⓑ Ⓒ Ⓓ	40	Ⓐ Ⓑ Ⓒ Ⓓ	60	Ⓐ Ⓑ Ⓒ Ⓓ	80	Ⓐ Ⓑ Ⓒ Ⓓ	100	Ⓐ Ⓑ Ⓒ Ⓓ

READING (Part V~VII)

No.	ANSWER	No.	ANSWER	No.	ANSWER	No.	ANSWER	No.	ANSWER
101	Ⓐ Ⓑ Ⓒ Ⓓ	121	Ⓐ Ⓑ Ⓒ Ⓓ	141	Ⓐ Ⓑ Ⓒ Ⓓ	161	Ⓐ Ⓑ Ⓒ Ⓓ	181	Ⓐ Ⓑ Ⓒ Ⓓ
102	Ⓐ Ⓑ Ⓒ Ⓓ	122	Ⓐ Ⓑ Ⓒ Ⓓ	142	Ⓐ Ⓑ Ⓒ Ⓓ	162	Ⓐ Ⓑ Ⓒ Ⓓ	182	Ⓐ Ⓑ Ⓒ Ⓓ
103	Ⓐ Ⓑ Ⓒ Ⓓ	123	Ⓐ Ⓑ Ⓒ Ⓓ	143	Ⓐ Ⓑ Ⓒ Ⓓ	163	Ⓐ Ⓑ Ⓒ Ⓓ	183	Ⓐ Ⓑ Ⓒ Ⓓ
104	Ⓐ Ⓑ Ⓒ Ⓓ	124	Ⓐ Ⓑ Ⓒ Ⓓ	144	Ⓐ Ⓑ Ⓒ Ⓓ	164	Ⓐ Ⓑ Ⓒ Ⓓ	184	Ⓐ Ⓑ Ⓒ Ⓓ
105	Ⓐ Ⓑ Ⓒ Ⓓ	125	Ⓐ Ⓑ Ⓒ Ⓓ	145	Ⓐ Ⓑ Ⓒ Ⓓ	165	Ⓐ Ⓑ Ⓒ Ⓓ	185	Ⓐ Ⓑ Ⓒ Ⓓ
106	Ⓐ Ⓑ Ⓒ Ⓓ	126	Ⓐ Ⓑ Ⓒ Ⓓ	146	Ⓐ Ⓑ Ⓒ Ⓓ	166	Ⓐ Ⓑ Ⓒ Ⓓ	186	Ⓐ Ⓑ Ⓒ Ⓓ
107	Ⓐ Ⓑ Ⓒ Ⓓ	127	Ⓐ Ⓑ Ⓒ Ⓓ	147	Ⓐ Ⓑ Ⓒ Ⓓ	167	Ⓐ Ⓑ Ⓒ Ⓓ	187	Ⓐ Ⓑ Ⓒ Ⓓ
108	Ⓐ Ⓑ Ⓒ Ⓓ	128	Ⓐ Ⓑ Ⓒ Ⓓ	148	Ⓐ Ⓑ Ⓒ Ⓓ	168	Ⓐ Ⓑ Ⓒ Ⓓ	188	Ⓐ Ⓑ Ⓒ Ⓓ
109	Ⓐ Ⓑ Ⓒ Ⓓ	129	Ⓐ Ⓑ Ⓒ Ⓓ	149	Ⓐ Ⓑ Ⓒ Ⓓ	169	Ⓐ Ⓑ Ⓒ Ⓓ	189	Ⓐ Ⓑ Ⓒ Ⓓ
110	Ⓐ Ⓑ Ⓒ Ⓓ	130	Ⓐ Ⓑ Ⓒ Ⓓ	150	Ⓐ Ⓑ Ⓒ Ⓓ	170	Ⓐ Ⓑ Ⓒ Ⓓ	190	Ⓐ Ⓑ Ⓒ Ⓓ
111	Ⓐ Ⓑ Ⓒ Ⓓ	131	Ⓐ Ⓑ Ⓒ Ⓓ	151	Ⓐ Ⓑ Ⓒ Ⓓ	171	Ⓐ Ⓑ Ⓒ Ⓓ	191	Ⓐ Ⓑ Ⓒ Ⓓ
112	Ⓐ Ⓑ Ⓒ Ⓓ	132	Ⓐ Ⓑ Ⓒ Ⓓ	152	Ⓐ Ⓑ Ⓒ Ⓓ	172	Ⓐ Ⓑ Ⓒ Ⓓ	192	Ⓐ Ⓑ Ⓒ Ⓓ
113	Ⓐ Ⓑ Ⓒ Ⓓ	133	Ⓐ Ⓑ Ⓒ Ⓓ	153	Ⓐ Ⓑ Ⓒ Ⓓ	173	Ⓐ Ⓑ Ⓒ Ⓓ	193	Ⓐ Ⓑ Ⓒ Ⓓ
114	Ⓐ Ⓑ Ⓒ Ⓓ	134	Ⓐ Ⓑ Ⓒ Ⓓ	154	Ⓐ Ⓑ Ⓒ Ⓓ	174	Ⓐ Ⓑ Ⓒ Ⓓ	194	Ⓐ Ⓑ Ⓒ Ⓓ
115	Ⓐ Ⓑ Ⓒ Ⓓ	135	Ⓐ Ⓑ Ⓒ Ⓓ	155	Ⓐ Ⓑ Ⓒ Ⓓ	175	Ⓐ Ⓑ Ⓒ Ⓓ	195	Ⓐ Ⓑ Ⓒ Ⓓ
116	Ⓐ Ⓑ Ⓒ Ⓓ	136	Ⓐ Ⓑ Ⓒ Ⓓ	156	Ⓐ Ⓑ Ⓒ Ⓓ	176	Ⓐ Ⓑ Ⓒ Ⓓ	196	Ⓐ Ⓑ Ⓒ Ⓓ
117	Ⓐ Ⓑ Ⓒ Ⓓ	137	Ⓐ Ⓑ Ⓒ Ⓓ	157	Ⓐ Ⓑ Ⓒ Ⓓ	177	Ⓐ Ⓑ Ⓒ Ⓓ	197	Ⓐ Ⓑ Ⓒ Ⓓ
118	Ⓐ Ⓑ Ⓒ Ⓓ	138	Ⓐ Ⓑ Ⓒ Ⓓ	158	Ⓐ Ⓑ Ⓒ Ⓓ	178	Ⓐ Ⓑ Ⓒ Ⓓ	198	Ⓐ Ⓑ Ⓒ Ⓓ
119	Ⓐ Ⓑ Ⓒ Ⓓ	139	Ⓐ Ⓑ Ⓒ Ⓓ	159	Ⓐ Ⓑ Ⓒ Ⓓ	179	Ⓐ Ⓑ Ⓒ Ⓓ	199	Ⓐ Ⓑ Ⓒ Ⓓ
120	Ⓐ Ⓑ Ⓒ Ⓓ	140	Ⓐ Ⓑ Ⓒ Ⓓ	160	Ⓐ Ⓑ Ⓒ Ⓓ	180	Ⓐ Ⓑ Ⓒ Ⓓ	200	Ⓐ Ⓑ Ⓒ Ⓓ

성명	
학급	
응답	

혼자서도 할 수 있는

신新토익,
모의고사만으로
700점 넘기

정답 및 해설

혼자서도 할 수 있는

신新토익 모의고사만으로 700점 넘기

정답 및 해설

다락원

Actual Test 01

p.29

● 정답

PART 1
1	(D)	2	(B)	3	(B)	4	(B)	5	(D)
6	(C)								

PART 2
7	(B)	8	(C)	9	(A)	10	(B)	11	(C)
12	(A)	13	(C)	14	(B)	15	(A)	16	(C)
17	(C)	18	(B)	19	(A)	20	(B)	21	(B)
22	(A)	23	(A)	24	(C)	25	(B)	26	(A)
27	(C)	28	(C)	29	(A)	30	(B)	31	(A)

PART 3
32	(A)	33	(C)	34	(A)	35	(D)	36	(A)
37	(B)	38	(D)	39	(B)	40	(B)	41	(A)
42	(D)	43	(C)	44	(B)	45	(C)	46	(A)
47	(A)	48	(B)	49	(D)	50	(B)	51	(C)
52	(B)	53	(C)	54	(B)	55	(D)	56	(C)
57	(A)	58	(B)	59	(B)	60	(B)	61	(A)
62	(C)	63	(A)	64	(B)	65	(C)	66	(B)
67	(C)	68	(B)	69	(C)	70	(B)		

PART 4
71	(A)	72	(C)	73	(C)	74	(D)	75	(C)
76	(B)	77	(B)	78	(B)	79	(A)	80	(D)
81	(C)	82	(B)	83	(C)	84	(A)	85	(D)
86	(A)	87	(B)	88	(B)	89	(A)	90	(D)
91	(C)	92	(D)	93	(C)	94	(B)	95	(B)
96	(A)	97	(B)	98	(C)	99	(D)	100	(A)

PART 5
101	(B)	102	(D)	103	(C)	104	(B)	105	(C)
106	(B)	107	(A)	108	(A)	109	(C)	110	(B)
111	(A)	112	(C)	113	(C)	114	(C)	115	(D)
116	(D)	117	(B)	118	(C)	119	(A)	120	(A)
121	(C)	122	(C)	123	(C)	124	(B)	125	(C)
126	(B)	127	(C)	128	(D)	129	(B)	130	(A)

PART 6
131	(B)	132	(B)	133	(C)	134	(D)	135	(D)
136	(C)	137	(D)	138	(A)	139	(D)	140	(B)
141	(B)	142	(A)	143	(C)	144	(D)	145	(A)
146	(B)								

PART 7
147	(D)	148	(B)	149	(B)	150	(D)	151	(A)
152	(C)	153	(B)	154	(B)	155	(C)	156	(B)
157	(A)	158	(C)	159	(C)	160	(B)	161	(B)
162	(C)	163	(D)	164	(C)	165	(D)	166	(B)
167	(A)	168	(C)	169	(C)	170	(A)	171	(C)
172	(A)	173	(B)	174	(C)	175	(A)	176	(A)
177	(B)	178	(D)	179	(D)	180	(B)	181	(B)
182	(A)	183	(B)	184	(C)	185	(A)	186	(A)
187	(C)	188	(D)	189	(B)	190	(B)	191	(B)
192	(C)	193	(B)	194	(C)	195	(A)	196	(D)
197	(C)	198	(A)	199	(B)	200	(B)		

● **PART 1**　　　　　　　　　　　　　　　　　　p.30

1 (A) A lecture is being given in a boardroom.
　 (B) The woman has gotten up from the chair.
　 (C) A diagram is being drawn on the board by the woman.
　 (D) Some documents have been placed on the table.

　 (A) 회의실에서 강연이 이루어지고 있다.
　 (B) 여자가 의자에서 일어나 있다.
　 (C) 여자에 의해 보드에 도표가 그려지고 있다.
　 (D) 테이블 위에 문서가 놓여 있다.

lecture 강연, 강의 | **boardroom** (중역) 회의실 | **diagram** 도표 | **document** 문서 | **place** 놓다

| 해설 | 회의실에서 여자가 리모컨을 들고 화면을 바라보고 있다. (A)와 (C)는 각각 사진으로부터 연상할 수 있는 boardroom(회의실)과 board(보드)라는 단어를 이용한 함정이며, 여자가 '의자에서 일어나 있는 것'(has gotten up from the chair)도 아니므로 (B) 역시 정답이 될 수 없다. 따라서 테이블 위에 놓여 있는 '서류'(documents)를 언급한 (D)가 정답이다.

☑ **700점 넘기 포인트**　전통적으로 1인 등장 사진에서는 사람의 동작을 설명하는 보기가 정답이 되는 경우가 많았으나, 이 문제에서 볼 수 있듯이 최근에는 1인 등장 사진에서도 주변 사물을 설명하는 보기가 정답이 되는 경우가 많아졌다.

2 (A) Several passengers are getting off the train.
　 (B) The subway has arrived at the station.
　 (C) Tickets are being sold to passengers.
　 (D) There are no seats available in any of the cars.

　 (A) 몇몇 승객들이 기차에서 내리고 있다.
　 (B) 지하철이 역에 도착했다.
　 (C) 승객들에게 승차권이 판매되고 있다.
　 (D) 어느 차량에도 비어 있는 자리가 없다.

passenger 승객 | **get off** (차량 등에서) 내리다, 하차하다 | **seat** 자리, 좌석 | **available** 이용할 수 있는

| 해설 | 지하철역에서 승객들이 지하철에 타고 있는 모습을 볼 수 있다. 따라서 정답은 '지하철이 역에 도착했다'고 설명한 (B)이다. 승객들이 서 있는 방향을 고려해 볼 때 승객들이 '기차에서 내리고 있다'(are getting off the train)고 볼 수는 없으므로 (A)는 정답이 될 수 없고, '승차권'(tickets)이나 '좌석'(seats) 역시 사진에서 찾아볼 수 없으므로 (C)와 (D) 또한 오답이다.

3 (A) Customers are trying on some new shirts in the store.

(B) A large number of shirts are being displayed on hangers.
(C) The clothes are currently on sale for low prices.
(D) A picture is hanging from the wall above the clothes.

(A) 매장에서 고객들이 새 셔츠를 입어 보고 있다.
(B) 여러 벌의 셔츠들이 옷걸이에 진열되어 있다.
(C) 의류들이 현재 염가로 판매되고 있다.
(D) 의류 위쪽의 벽에 사진이 걸려 있다.

try on (옷 등을) 입어 보다 | **a large number of** 많은, 다수의 | **hanger** 옷걸이 | **currently** 현재

| 해설 | 옷걸이에 여러 벌의 셔츠들이 진열되어 있는 장면을 볼 수 있으므로 이를 정확히 묘사한 (B)가 정답이다. 사진에서는 사물만 보이기 때문에 '고객'(customers)이 옷을 입고 있다고 묘사한 (A)는 정답이 될 수 없고, 현재 '염가 판매'(sale for low prices)가 진행 중인지는 사진만으로 파악할 수 없으므로 (C)도 오답이다. 사진에서 찾아볼 수 없는 '사진'(picture)을 언급한 (D) 또한 정답이 될 수 없다.

4 (A) Several participants in the meeting appear to be bored.
(B) All of the chairs have been pushed under the table.
(C) A computer has been placed in the center of the table.
(D) The decision to hold the meeting has been tabled.

(A) 회의에 참석한 몇몇 사람들은 지루해 보인다.
(B) 모든 의자들이 테이블 밑에 들어가 있다.
(C) 테이블의 중앙에는 컴퓨터가 놓여 있다.
(D) 회의 개최에 관한 결정은 연기되었다.

participant 참가자, 참여자 | **bored** 지루한 | **table** 테이블; (회의 등을) 미루다, 연기하다 | **hold a meeting** 회의를 개최하다

| 해설 | 사진에서 '참여자'(participants)와 '컴퓨터'(computer)는 보이지 않으므로 (A)와 (C)는 정답이 될 수 없고, 사진을 통해 '회의의 개최 여부'(the decision to hold the meeting)에 관해서도 알 수 없으므로 (D) 또한 적절한 설명이 될 수 없다. 따라서 정답은 '의자가 테이블 아래에 들어가 있다'고 진술한 (B)이다. 참고로 (D)의 table은 '미루다', '연기하다'라는 뜻의 동사로 사용되었다.

> ✔ **700점 넘기 포인트** PART 1에서 주관적인 판단을 요하는 보기는 일단 오답이라고 가정하자. (A)의 appear to be bored(지루해 보인다)와 같은 표현이 들어간 보기는 정답이 되는 경우가 거의 없다.

5 (A) There are several sheep in the field.
(B) One of the ships is sailing beneath the bridge.
(C) People are getting on board the ship.
(D) Pedestrians are walking alongside the waterway.

(A) 들판에 양이 몇 마리 있다.
(B) 배 한 척이 다리 아래를 통과하고 있다.
(C) 사람들이 승선하고 있다.
(D) 수로 옆을 따라 보행자들이 걸어가고 있다.

sheep 양 | **sail** 항해하다 | **bridge** 다리 | **get on board** ~에 타다, 승차하다 | **pedestrian** 보행자 | **alongside** ~을 따라

| 해설 | (A)는 ship(배)과 발음이 비슷한 sheep(양)을 이용한 함정이며, (B)는 ships(배)와 bridge(다리)라는 단어를 이용하여 혼동을 유발하고 있지만 '다리 아래'(beneath the bridge)를 통과하는 배는 보이지 않으므로 이 역시 적절한 묘사가 될 수 없다. 사람들은 길을 걸어가고 있을 뿐, 배에 올라타고 있지는 않기 때문에 (D)가 정답이고 (C)는 오답이다.

6 (A) The seated people are all facing the same direction.
(B) The outdoor dining area at the café is completely full.
(C) One man is walking in front of the seated individuals.
(D) Waiters are bringing plates of food to the diners.

(A) 앉아 있는 사람들은 모두 같은 방향을 바라보고 있다.
(B) 카페의 야외 좌석이 모두 채워져 있다.
(C) 한 남자가 앉아 있는 사람들 앞으로 걸어가고 있다.
(D) 웨이터들이 식당 손님들에게 요리를 가져다 주고 있다.

seat 좌석; 앉히다 | **face** 향하다 | **direction** 방향 | **outdoor** 야외의 | **dining area** 식사 공간 | **completely** 완전히 | **in front of** ~의 앞에 | **plate** 접시, 요리 | **diner** 식당 손님

| 해설 | 여러 명의 인물이 등장하는 사진이므로 각 인물들의 모습이나 행동을 잘 살피도록 한다. 신문을 보는 사람도 있고 거리를 바라보는 사람도 있기 때문에 사람들이 모두 '같은 방향을 바라보고 있다'(facing the same direction)고 진술한 (A)는 정답이 될 수 없다. 그리고 사진 중앙에 비어 있는 의자가 하나 보이므로 '자리가 꽉 차 있다'(completely full)고 설명한 (B)도 정답이 아니다. 사진에서는 손님들만 보일 뿐 '종업원'(waiters)은 찾아볼 수 없으므로 (D)도 오답이다. 따라서 식당 바깥쪽으로 걸어가고 있는 사람을 적절히 묘사한 (C)가 정답이다.

● PART 2 p.34

7 How much longer do you need on this project?
(A) About ten pages long.
(B) Roughly half an hour.
(C) In my office soon.

이 프로젝트에 시간이 얼마나 더 필요한가요?
(A) 약 10페이지 길이예요.
(B) 대략 30분이요.
(C) 곧 제 사무실에서요.

roughly 대략

| 해설 | how much longer라는 표현을 이용하여 필요한 '시간'이 얼마인지 묻고 있으므로 정답은 (B)이다. (A)는 길이나 분량을 묻는 질문에 적절한 대답이며, (C)는 장소를 묻는 질문에 이어질 수 있는 대답이다.

8 Why hasn't anyone responded to that complaint?
(A) That's the response she gave us.
(B) Yes, it looks a bit plain to me.
(C) I thought Ted already handled it.

저 불만 사항에 대해 왜 아무도 응답을 해 주지 않았나요?
(A) 그것이 그녀가 저희에게 한 대답이었어요.
(B) 네, 제게는 그것이 약간 평이해 보이는군요.
(C) Ted가 이미 처리했다고 생각했어요.

respond 반응하다, 응답하다 | **complaint** 불만 | **response** 반응 | **plain** 분명한; 평이한, 간단한

| 해설 | 의문사 why를 이용하여 불만 사항에 대처하지 않은 '이유'를 묻고 있다. (A)는 respond와 발음이 비슷한 response로, (B)는 complaint와 발음이 비슷한 plain to로 오답을 유도하고 있는 함정이다. 따라서 정답은 응답을 하지 않은 이유를 밝힌 (C)이다.

9 Do you want me to see if the item is still in stock?
(A) I would appreciate that a lot.
(B) I don't have stock in that company.
(C) This is the item that I purchased.

그 제품의 재고가 있는지 제가 확인해 볼까요?
(A) 그렇게 해 주면 정말 고맙겠어요.

3

(B) 저는 그 회사의 주식을 가지고 있지 않아요.
　　(C) 이것이 제가 구입한 제품이에요.

stock 재고; 주식 | **appreciate** 감사하다; 감상하다

| 해설 | 형식적으로는 일반의문문의 형태를 취하고 있지만, 실질적으로는 상대방에게 제안을 하고 있다. 따라서 제안에 대한 수락의 의사를 비친 (A)가 적절한 대답이다. (B)는 stock을 이용하여 오답을 유도하고 있는 함정으로, 여기서 stock은 '주식'이라는 의미로 사용되었다. (C)는 질문에서 사용된 item을 이용해서 만들어진 함정이다.

10 The picnic has been postponed until next week, hasn't it?
　　(A) Sometime last Friday.
　　(B) That's what I heard.
　　(C) I'm going to the picnic.

야유회가 다음 주로 연기되었죠, 그렇지 않나요?
　　(A) 지난 금요일에요.
　　(B) 저도 그렇게 들었어요.
　　(C) 저는 야유회에 갈 거예요.

picnic 소풍, 야유회 | **postpone** 연기하다, 미루다

| 해설 | 부가의문문을 이용하여 사실 여부를 확인하고 있다. 따라서 정답은 '나도 그렇게 들었다'고 말함으로써 긍정적인 반응을 보인 (B)이다. 과거의 시점을 이야기한 (A)와 야유회의 참석 여부를 밝힌 (C)는 주어진 질문에 전혀 어울리지 않는 답변들이다.

11 You'd better be on your best behavior at the meeting.
　　(A) He's behaving properly.
　　(B) That's the best product.
　　(C) I promise to do that.

당신은 회의에서 진중하게 행동하는 것이 좋겠어요.
　　(A) 그는 올바르게 행동하고 있어요.
　　(B) 그것이 가장 좋은 제품이에요.
　　(C) 그렇게 하겠다고 약속할게요.

had better ~하는 편이 낫다 | **be on one's best behavior** 진중하게 행동하다, 얌전히 있다 | **properly** 적합하게, 적절하게 | **promise** 약속하다

| 해설 | had better를 이용하여 상대방에게 충고를 하고 있다. (A)는 behavior의 동사형인 behave를 이용한 함정이고, (B)는 질문의 best를 중복 사용하여 혼동을 일으키려는 오답이다. 따라서 상대방의 충고에 따르겠다는 의사를 표시한 (C)가 정답이다.

12 Nobody can remember Ms. Carlyle's phone number, right?
　　(A) You should ask Jane for it.
　　(B) She called a while ago.
　　(C) No, I'm not on the phone.

Carlyle 씨의 전화번호를 아무도 기억하고 있지 않죠, 맞죠?
　　(A) 그것에 대해서는 Jane에게 물어보세요.
　　(B) 그녀가 조금 전에 전화를 했어요.
　　(C) 아니요, 저는 전화 통화를 하고 있지 않아요.

on the phone 통화 중인

| 해설 | 문장 끝에 right를 붙임으로써 Carlyle 씨라는 사람의 전화번호를 아는 사람이 있는지 묻고 있다. 따라서 정답은 Jane이라는 사람을 직접적으로 거론한 (A)이다. (B)는 phone number(전화번호)에서 연상될 수 있는 called(전화하다)를 이용한 함정이며, (C)는 phone을 중복 사용함으로써 오답을 유도하고 있다.

13 Where is the nearest gas station in this neighborhood?
　　(A) I'll fill up the car later today.
　　(B) We're in the Coldwater neighborhood.
　　(C) There's one right down the street.

이 근방에 가장 가까운 주유소가 어디에 있나요?
　　(A) 저는 오늘 늦게 주유를 할 거예요.
　　(B) 우리는 Coldwater 인근에 있어요.
　　(C) 길을 따라가면 있어요.

gas station 주유소 | **neighborhood** 인근, 근처; 지방 | **fill up** 채우다

| 해설 | 의문사 where를 놓치지 않고 들었다면 정답은 '장소'를 언급하고 있는 (C)임을 쉽게 알 수 있다. (A)는 gas station(주유소)과 관련이 있는 fill up(기름을 채우다, 주유하다)이라는 표현을, (B)는 질문에서 사용된 neighborhood(인근, 근처)라는 단어를 사용하여 오답을 유도하고 있는 함정이다.

14 What time should we expect Ms. Carter to arrive?
　　(A) On Monday or Tuesday.
　　(B) Sometime after six.
　　(C) Around forty minutes ago.

Carter 씨가 몇 시에 도착할 것으로 예상되나요?
　　(A) 월요일이나 화요일에요.
　　(B) 6시 이후요.
　　(C) 약 40분전에요.

| 해설 | what time으로 시작하는 의문사에는 '시각'으로 답을 해야 한다. 따라서 구체적인 시각을 언급하고 있는 (B)가 정답이다. (A)와 (C) 역시 시간과 관계된 답을 하고 있지만, (A)는 요일을 밝히고 있다는 점 때문에, (C)는 과거의 시간으로 대답했다는 점 때문에 이들은 모두 정답이 될 수 없다.

15 I believe you ought to see a doctor about that cough.
　　(A) That's what my husband said.
　　(B) He's been coughing all day.
　　(C) No, I don't want any coffee.

기침에 관해 당신이 진료를 받아야 한다고 생각해요.
　　(A) 제 남편이 말한 바와 같군요.
　　(B) 그는 하루 종일 기침을 하고 있어요.
　　(C) 아니요, 저는 커피를 원하지 않아요.

see a doctor 진찰을 받다 | **cough** 기침

| 해설 | ought to라는 표현을 이용해 상대방에게 충고를 하고 있다. 따라서 '남편에게서도 똑 같은 말을 들었다'고 답한 (A)가 가장 자연스러운 답변이다. (B)는 질문의 cough를 중복 사용하여 혼란을 일으키고 있고, (C)는 cough와 발음이 비슷한 coffee를 이용하여 오답을 유도하고 있다.

16 Who should we send on the business trip to Tokyo?
　　(A) About two weeks from now.
　　(B) To negotiate a new contract.
　　(C) How about Mark or Anna?

도쿄 출장에 누구를 보내야 할까요?
　　(A) 지금부터 약 2주 후에요.
　　(B) 새로운 계약에 관해 협상하기 위해서요.
　　(C) Mark나 Anna가 어때요?

business trip 출장 | **negotiate** 협상하다 | **contract** 계약

| 해설 | 의문사 who를 이용하여 '누구'를 출장보낼 것인지 묻고 있으므로 정답은 사람 이름을 직접적으로 거론하면서 상대방의 의견을 되묻은 (C)가 된다. (A)는 시간을 묻는 질문에, (B)는 목적이나 이유를 묻는 질문에 이어질 수 있는 답변이다.

17 Can you give me directions to the Wishbone Café?
　　(A) Yes, this is the map you asked for.

(B) You'll love the selection of teas there.
(C) Sorry, but I've never heard of it.

Wishbone 카페로 가는 길을 알려 주실 수 있나요?
(A) 네, 이것이 당신이 요청한 지도예요.
(B) 그곳에서 마실 수 있는 차를 좋아하게 될 거예요.
(C) 죄송하지만, 그에 대해서는 들어본 적이 없군요.

give directions 길을 알려 주다 | **ask for** ~을 요구하다, ~을 요청하다 | **selection** 선정, 선택; 선택된 것

| 해설 | 상대방에게 길을 알려 줄 수 있는지 묻고 있다. (A)는 give directions(길을 알려 주다)로부터 연상할 수 있는 map(지도)이라는 단어를 통해, (B)는 café라는 장소로부터 유추할 수 있는 teas(차)라는 단어를 통해 오답을 유도하고 있다. 따라서 '그에 대해 들어본 적이 없으니' 길을 알려 줄 수 없다는 점을 내포하고 있는 (C)가 가장 자연스러운 답변이다.

18 Which of these three proposals are we thinking of accepting?
(A) Yes, there are three of them.
(B) Probably the second one.
(C) We will accept the offer tomorrow.

이 세 가지 제안서 중에 우리가 어떤 것을 받아들일 건가요?
(A) 네, 세 개가 있어요.
(B) 아마도 두 번째 것이요.
(C) 우리는 내일 그 제안을 받아들일 거예요.

proposal 제안, 제안서 | **think of** ~에 대해 생각하다, ~을 고려하다 | **accept** 받아들이다, 수락하다 | **probably** 아마도

| 해설 | which of these three proposals에 유의하면 셋 중에 하나를 가리키는 (B)가 정답이라는 점을 쉽게 알 수 있다. (A)와 (B)는 각각 질문에서 사용된 three와 accept라는 단어를 이용한 함정이다.

19 Will Martin conduct the interviews, or is John doing them?
(A) Actually, Peter will be doing them.
(B) Martin and John are coworkers.
(C) Yes, that's correct.

Martin이 면접을 진행할 것인가요, 아니면 John이 그 일을 할 건가요?
(A) 실은, Peter가 그 일을 하게 될 거예요.
(B) Martin과 John은 동료예요.
(C) 네, 그것이 맞아요.

conduct 실시하다, 실행하다 | **interview** 인터뷰, 면접

| 해설 | 선택의문문을 이용하여 면접을 진행할 사람이 Martin인지 John인지를 묻고 있다. 정답은 두 사람 모두를 배제하고 제3의 인물을 지목한 (A)이다. (B)는 위의 두 사람이 '동료'(coworkers)라는 엉뚱한 답변을 했기 때문에, (C)는 선택의문문에 yes라고 대답하고 있으므로 정답이 될 수 없다.

20 There appears to be a problem with your car's engine.
(A) Thanks for fixing it for me.
(B) What exactly is wrong with it?
(C) How much do I owe you for it?

당신 차의 엔진에 이상이 있는 것 같군요.
(A) 저를 위해 수리해 주셔서 고마워요.
(B) 정확히 무엇에 문제가 있나요?
(C) 그에 대해 제가 얼마를 드려야 하죠?

exactly 정확히 | **owe** 빚지다

| 해설 | 평서문을 통해 '엔진에 이상이 있는 것 같다'는 의견을 제시하고 있다. 따라서 구체적으로 어떤 이상이 있는지를 되묻은 (B)가 대답으로서 가장 자연스럽다. (A)는 수리를 마친 후에 할 수 있는 말이고 (C)는 비용을 물을 때 할 수 있는 질문이다.

21 I can't recall where Ms. Hamilton's office is located.
(A) She's in Mr. Wilkin's office now.
(B) It's in the building by the Sultan Theater.
(C) No, I haven't located her yet.

Hamilton 씨의 사무실이 어디에 위치해 있는지 기억이 나지 않네요.
(A) 그녀는 지금 Wilkin 씨의 사무실에 있어요.
(B) Sultan 극장 옆 건물에 있어요.
(C) 아니요, 저는 아직 그녀의 위치를 알아내지 못했어요.

recall 회상하다, 기억하다 | **locate** 위치시키다, 위치를 찾아내다

| 해설 | 평서문의 형태를 띠고 있지만 실질적으로는 상대방에게 Hamilton 씨의 사무실 위치를 묻고 있는 문장이다. 따라서 사무실 위치를 직접적으로 언급한 (B)가 정답이다. 'Hamilton 씨의 위치'를 묻고 있는 것은 아니기 때문에 (A)는 정답이 될 수 없고, (C)는 locate를 중복 사용하여 오답을 유도하고 있는 함정이다.

22 The agenda for the staff meeting is already settled, isn't it?
(A) Not to the best of my knowledge.
(B) Yes, Jeff is a member of the staff here.
(C) I settled the problem this morning.

직원 회의의 안건이 이미 정해졌죠, 그렇지 않나요?
(A) 제가 아는 한 정해지지 않았어요.
(B) 네, Jeff는 이곳 직원 중 한 명이에요.
(C) 저는 오늘 아침에 그 문제를 해결했어요.

settle 놓다, 정착하다; 해결하다, 합의를 보다 | **to the best of** ~하는 한 | **knowledge** 지식

| 해설 | 안건의 확정 여부를 묻는 질문에 가장 자연스럽게 연결될 수 있는 답변은 (A)로, 여기에서 to the best of는 '~하는 한'이라는 의미를 나타낸다. (B)는 staff를 중복 사용함으로써, (C)는 settled를 중복 사용함으로써 각각 혼동을 일으키고 있는 오답이다.

23 How often does the subway come to this station?
(A) Five or six times an hour.
(B) On the number three line.
(C) Go out exit number nine.

이 역에는 지하철이 얼마나 자주 오나요?
(A) 한 시간에 대여섯 번이요.
(B) 3호선에서요.
(C) 9번 출구로 나가세요.

| 해설 | how often이 횟수나 빈도를 물을 때 사용되는 표현이라는 것을 알고 있으면 정답이 (A)라는 점을 쉽게 알 수 있다. (B)는 노선을 묻는 질문에, (C)는 출구를 묻는 질문에 이어질 수 있는 답변이다.

24 Would you prefer taking the train or flying to the conference?
(A) Yes, that's a good idea.
(B) We flew there last week.
(C) Either is fine with me.

콘퍼런스에 기차를 타고 갈까요, 아니면 비행기를 타고 갈까요?
(A) 네, 좋은 생각이에요.
(B) 우리는 지난 주에 비행기를 타고 그곳에 갔어요.

(C) 어느 쪽이든 좋아요.

prefer 선호하다 | **either** 둘 중 하나

| 해설 | 접속사 or를 이용하여 두 가지 교통편 중 어떤 것을 선호하는지 묻고 있다. (A)는 제안을 나타내는 말에 이어질 수 있는 답변이고, (B)는 과거에 어떤 교통편을 이용했는지 묻는 질문에 연결될 수 있는 답변이다. 따라서 정답은 '두 교통편 중 어떤 것이든 좋다'고 답한 (C)이다.

> ☑ **700점 넘기 포인트** 선택의문문을 이용하여 두 가지 사항 중 하나를 선택할 것을 요구하는 질문에서, 두 가지 모두를 취하거나 두 가지 모두를 배제하는 답변도 정답이 될 수 있음을 명심하자.

25 Did you remember to turn off the lights before you left?
 (A) Yes, I remember what they look like.
 (B) Oh, no. I totally forgot.
 (C) No, I haven't left the office yet.

떠나기 전에 불을 꺼야 한다는 점을 기억하고 있었나요?
 (A) 네, 그것이 어떻게 생겼는지 기억이 나요.
 (B) 오, 아니에요. 완전히 잊고 있었어요.
 (C) 아니요, 저는 아직 사무실을 떠나지 않았어요.

turn off ~을 끄다 | **totally** 완전히, 전부

| 해설 | 상대방에게 잊지 않고 불을 껐는지 묻고 있다. 따라서 정답은 '잊고 있었다'며 불을 끄지 않았다는 점을 암시한 (B)이다. (A)는 remember를, (C)는 left를 중복 사용함으로써 오답을 유도하고 있는 함정이다.

26 The interviews won't begin until this Friday, will they?
 (A) I believe that's correct.
 (B) Fred's going to interview then.
 (C) Friday's a busy day for her.

이번 주 금요일까지는 면접이 시작되지 않죠, 그렇죠?
 (A) 그런 것 같아요.
 (B) 그때 Fred가 면접을 볼 거예요.
 (C) 금요일은 그녀가 바쁜 날이에요.

| 해설 | 부가의문문을 통해 면접이 금요일 이후에 시작되는지 묻고 있다. 따라서 정답은 '그럴 것이다'라고 긍정적인 답변을 한 (A)이다. (B)는 면접을 진행할 사람 혹은 면접을 볼 사람이 누구인지를 묻는 질문에 이어질 수 있는 답변이고, (C)는 Friday라는 단어를 중복 사용하여 혼동을 유발하고 있는 함정이다.

27 Would you mind picking up a sandwich from the deli for me?
 (A) They are delighted to see you.
 (B) Sure, I can share my lunch with you.
 (C) Not at all. What would you like?

저를 위해 식품점에서 샌드위치를 사다 주실 수 있나요?
 (A) 그들이 당신을 만나서 기뻐하는군요.
 (B) 물론이에요, 제 점심을 나누어 먹으면 되어요.
 (C) 물론이죠, 어떤 것을 원하나요?

| 해설 | 형식적으로는 의문문의 형태를 갖추고 있지만, 실질적으로는 '상대방에게 샌드위치를 사다 달라'는 부탁을 하고 있다. (A)는 deli(식품점)라는 단어와 발음이 비슷한 delighted(기쁜)를 이용한 함정이며, (B)는 '점심을 나누어 먹자'는 제안에 이어질 수 있는 응답이다. 따라서 정답은 부탁에 대한 수락의 의미를 나타낸 (C)가 된다.

> ☑ **700점 넘기 포인트** 부탁을 할 때 자주 사용되는 동사인 mind는 원래 '꺼리다'라는 뜻이다. 따라서 부탁을 수락하는 답변에는 주로 부정적인 의미의 표현들이 등장한다.

28 I suggest calling the customer service hotline immediately.
 (A) Yes, you can borrow my telephone.
 (B) I'm expecting to get good service.
 (C) Do you know the telephone number?

즉시 고객 서비스 센터에 전화할 것을 제안드립니다.
 (A) 네, 제 전화를 쓰셔도 되어요.
 (B) 저는 좋은 서비스를 받게 될 것이라고 기대하고 있어요.
 (C) 전화번호를 알고 있나요?

hotline 상담 전화; 직통 전화 | **immediately** 곧장, 즉시 | **borrow** 빌리다

| 해설 | 평서문이지만 suggest라는 동사를 통해 일종의 제안을 하고 있는 문장이다. (A)는 전화를 빌려 달라는 요청에 이어질 수 있는 답변이고, (B)는 service라는 단어를 중복 사용하고 있는 함정이다. 따라서 '서비스 센터의 전화번호'를 되물어본 (C)가 답변으로서 가장 자연스럽다.

29 What do I need to do to open a new bank account here?
 (A) I need two forms of picture ID.
 (B) Fill out this form to withdraw money.
 (C) At the First National Bank branch.

이곳에서 은행 계좌를 신설하려면 어떻게 해야 하나요?
 (A) 사진이 들어 있는 두 개의 신분증이 필요해요.
 (B) 돈을 인출하기 위해서는 이 양식을 작성하세요.
 (C) First National 은행 지점에서요.

bank account 은행 계좌 | **picture ID** 사진이 들어 있는 신분증 | **fill out** (양식 등을) 작성하다, 기입하다 | **withdraw** 빼내다, 인출하다 | **branch** 가지; 지점, 지사

| 해설 | 은행 계좌 개설에 필요한 사항을 묻고 있으므로 two forms of picture ID(신분증 두 개)가 필요하다고 밝힌 (A)가 정답이다. 은행 계좌 개설에 대해 묻는 질문에 '인출'(withdraw money) 방법을 알려 준 (B)는 적절한 대답이 될 수 없고, 특정 지점을 언급한 (C) 역시 주어진 질문과 관련이 없는 답변이다.

30 Shouldn't we reserve a car for our trip to Los Angeles?
 (A) No, I haven't reserved a car yet.
 (B) We could just take public transportation.
 (C) On the morning of the thirtieth.

로스앤젤레스 출장을 위해 차를 예약해 두어야 하지 않나요?
 (A) 아니요, 저는 아직 차를 예약하지 않았어요.
 (B) 대중 교통을 이용하면 되어요.
 (C) 30일 아침에요.

reserve 예약하다 | **public transportation** 대중 교통

| 해설 | 의문문 형태를 갖추고 있지만 shouldn't를 이용하여 상대방의 의견을 묻고 있다. 따라서 '(차를 예약할 필요 없이) 대중 교통을 이용하면 된다'고 답변한 (B)가 가장 자연스러운 답변이다. (A)는 예약 여부를 묻는 질문에 적합한 답변이고, (C)는 시간이나 일정을 묻는 질문에 이어질 수 있는 답변이다.

31 We need to get in touch with the caterer regarding the event.
 (A) I'll instruct Ms. Johnson to do that.
 (B) Please be sure not to touch that.
 (C) I catered several meals in the past.

행사와 관련해서 음식 공급업체에 연락을 해야 해요.
 (A) 그렇게 하라고 Johnson 씨에게 지시해 놓을게요.
 (B) 그것을 만지면 안 된다는 점을 명심해 주세요.
 (C) 저는 과거에 몇 차례 음식을 공급해 보았어요.

get in touch with ~와 연락을 취하다 | caterer 음식 공급업체, 음식 공급업자 | regarding ~와 관련해서 | instruct 지시하다 | touch 만지다 | in the past 과거에

| 해설 | '음식 공급업체에 연락을 취해야 한다'는 사실을 알리고 있다. 따라서 'Johnson이라는 사람을 시켜서 그렇게 하도록 하겠다'고 답변한 (A)가 정답이다. (B)는 touch를 중복 사용함으로써, (C)는 caterer의 동사형인 catered를 사용함으로써 각각 오답을 유도하고 있는 함정이다.

PART 3
p.35

[32-34]

W Hello, Mr. Sanders. This is Julie Maple calling. I contacted you by e-mail this morning about a condo I'd like to look at. Do you have time to show me the place today?

M I sure do, Ms. Maple. You mentioned you'd prefer to check it out around 3:30. Is that time still satisfactory for you?

W Oh, no, it isn't. I've got a meeting scheduled at 4:00, so I'd like to see the place around 2:00 instead. That should give me plenty of time to check out the property.

M Fortunately, I've got time then, so I can comply with your request. Why don't we meet at 52 Jackson Avenue at that time?

W 안녕하세요, Sanders 씨. 저는 Julie Maple이에요. 오늘 아침 보고 싶은 아파트에 관해 제가 이메일로 연락을 드렸죠. 오늘 그곳을 보여 주실 시간이 있으신가요?

M 물론이죠, Maple 씨. 3시 30분경에 살펴보고 싶으시다고 말씀하셨죠. 아직도 그 시간이 좋으신가요?

W 오, 아니에요, 그렇지 않아요. 4시에 예정된 회의가 있어서, 그 대신 2시쯤에 그곳을 보고 싶어요. 그러면 부동산을 살펴볼 수 있는 시간이 충분할 거예요.

M 다행히, 저도 그때 시간이 있기 때문에, 고객님의 요청을 따를 수가 있어요. 그 시간에 Jackson 가 52번지에서 만나는 것이 어떨까요?

condo 콘도, 아파트 (= condominium) | mention 언급하다 | check out ~을 살펴보다; ~을 확인하다 | satisfactory 만족스러운 | plenty of 많은 | property 재산, 소유물; 부동산, 건물 | comply with ~에 따르다, ~에 순응하다

32 남자는 누구인 것 같은가?
(A) 부동산 중개인
(B) 여행 가이드
(C) 여행사 직원
(D) 항공사 직원

| 해설 | condo, place, property 등과 같은 단어를 통해 여자는 부동산에 관한 문의를 하고 있음을 알 수 있다. 따라서 문의에 답변하고 있는 남자는 (A)의 A real estate agent(부동산 중개인)일 것이다.

33 여자는 무엇을 하기를 원하는가?
(A) 계약서에 서명한다
(B) 집을 본다
(C) 사무실에 가구를 비치한다
(D) 주문을 한다

furnish (가구를) 비치하다

| 해설 | 남자가 여자의 통화 내용을 언급한 부분(you'd prefer to check it out)과 여자가 자신의 의향을 밝히고 있는 부분(I'd like to see the place)을 통해, 여자가 원하는 바는 (B)의 Look at a home임을 알 수 있다.

34 화자들은 언제 만날 것인가?
(A) 2시
(B) 3시 30분
(C) 4시
(D) 5시 20분

| 해설 | 대화 중반부에서 여자가 '4시에 회의가 있어서 2시에 집을 보고 싶다'(I've got a meeting scheduled at 4:00, so I'd like to see the place around 2:00 instead.)고 말하자, 남자도 이에 긍정적으로 답변을 하고 있다. 따라서 두 사람이 만날 시각은 (A)의 '2시'이다.

[35-37]

M I'm pleased we finally completed the interviews with the job candidates. I had no idea they were going to take nearly the entire day.

W I know what you mean. I was on the intern search committee last year, and the interviews only required about half the time that this year's did. So which of the applicants did you like the most? I thought Sarah Carpenter was impressive and believe we should strongly consider her for a position.

M She's definitely one of the leading candidates in my mind. We'll have to be sure to invite her back to conduct a second interview.

M 드디어 입사 지원자들과의 면접을 끝냈다니 기쁘네요. 거의 하루 종일 걸릴 것이라고는 생각하지 못했어요.

W 무슨 말인지 알아요. 저는 작년에 인턴 사원 모집 위원회에 있었는데, 당시 면접에는 올해의 절반 정도의 시간만이 필요했죠. 그래서 어떤 지원자가 가장 마음에 들었나요? 저는 Sarah Carpenter가 인상적이었다고 생각했고 그녀를 뽑는 것을 적극적으로 고려해야 한다고 생각해요.

M 제 생각으로도 그녀는 분명 우수한 지원자 중 한 명이었어요. 잊지 말고 그녀를 다시 오라고 해서 2차 면접을 실시해야 할 거예요.

job candidate 입사 지원자 | committee 위원회 | applicant 지원자 | impressive 인상적인 | leading 선도하는 | conduct 실시하다, 실행하다

35 화자들은 무엇을 논의하는가?
(A) 회사의 새로운 인턴 사원들
(B) 새로운 사장에 대한 느낌
(C) 다른 직원의 성과
(D) 면접 결과

| 해설 | 대화 초반부의 남자의 말에서 '면접이 모두 끝났다'(completed the interviews with the job candidates)는 사실을 알 수 있다. 이후 화자들은 우수한 지원자에 대해 이야기를 이어가고 있으므로 대화의 주제는 (D)의 '면접 결과'임을 알 수 있다.

36 여자는 작년의 활동에 대해 무엇을 말하는가?
(A) 마치는 데 시간이 덜 걸렸다.
(B) 더 우수한 지원자들이 있었다.
(C) 마치기까지 이틀이 걸렸다.
(D) 실행하기가 어려웠다.

| 해설 | 여자는 '(작년) 면접 시간은 올해 면접 시간의 절반 정도였다'(the interviews only required about half the time that this year's did)라고 말하고 있으므로 정답은 (A)이다.

37 Sarah Carpenter에 관한 남자의 의견은 무엇인가?
(A) 그녀는 즉시 고용되어야 한다.

(B) 그녀를 다시 면접할 가치가 있다.
(C) 그녀는 그가 예상했던 것 보다 더 좋은 결과를 보였다.
(D) 그녀는 모든 입사 지원자 중 가장 뛰어났다.

be worth –ing ~할 가치가 있다

| 해설 | 남자의 마지막 말인 'We'll have to be sure to invite her back to conduct a second interview.'를 통해 정답은 (B)임을 확인할 수 있다. Sarah Carpenter가 좋은 인상을 남기기는 했지만, 그녀가 즉시 고용되어야 한다던가 그녀가 가장 우수했다고 볼 수는 없기 때문에 (A)와 (D)는 정답이 될 수 없다. (C)의 경우, 남자가 Sarah Carpenter에 대해 기대했던 바는 대화에서 언급된 사항이 아니다.

[38-40]

M Lara, how is the work on the redesign of the Fargo Building progressing? Do you think that you're going to be able to finish everything by tomorrow's deadline?
W I'm afraid not, Mr. Ito. The work is taking much longer than I expected it to. However, I've started making good progress, so I am positive that I can submit the blueprints to you no later than noon on Friday.
M All right. I'll call the client now and request an extension. But you had better finish everything by the new due date. The client is eager to get a look at the plans, and I don't want to disappoint him.

M Lara, Fargo 빌딩의 재설계 작업은 어떻게 진행되고 있나요? 내일 마감 시간까지 모든 것을 다 끝낼 수 있을 것이라고 생각하나요?
W 그렇게 하지 못할 것 같아요, Ito 씨. 예상했던 것보다 작업에 훨씬 더 많은 시간이 들고 있어요. 하지만, 상당한 진전을 보이기 시작했기 때문에, 늦어도 금요일 정오까지는 제가 청사진을 제출할 수 있을 것으로 확신해요.
M 좋아요. 제가 지금 고객에게 전화를 해서 기한 연장을 요청할게요. 하지만 새로운 마감일까지는 모든 것을 끝내는 것이 좋을 거예요. 고객이 도면을 몹시 보고 싶어하고 있고, 저는 그를 실망시키고 싶지 않으니까요.

redesign 재설계 | **process** 과정, 절차; 진행하다 | **deadline** 마감일, 기한 | **make good progress** 진전을 보이다 | **positive** 긍정적인, 확신하는 | **blueprint** 청사진 | **extension** 연장 | **due date** 마감 일자 | **be eager to** ~하기를 열망하다 | **plan** 계획; 도면 | **disappoint** 실망시키다

38 화자들은 주로 무엇을 논의하고 있는가?
(A) 테스트 결과
(B) 남자가 완성시킨 설계
(C) 여자가 작성한 보고서
(D) 프로젝트의 마감 일자

| 해설 | 대화 전반에 걸쳐 남자와 여자는 재설계 작업의 일정에 관해, 특히 마감일에 대해 논의하고 있다. 따라서 정답은 (D)이다.

39 화자들은 어디에서 일하는 것 같은가?
(A) 건설 회사에서
(B) 건축 사무소에서
(C) 실내 장식용품 업체에서
(D) 컴퓨터 디자인 회사에서

architectural firm 건축 사무소 | **home decorating** 실내 장식

| 해설 | redesign of the Fargo Building(Fargo 빌딩의 재설계), plans(도면)과 같은 표현들을 고려할 때 화자들은 건축사임을 알 수 있다. 따라서 정답은 (B)이다. 원칙적으로 건설 회사는 설계 업무를 담당하지 않고 시공만 하기 때문에 (A)는 정답이 될 수 없다.

40 여자는 자신의 작업에 대해 무엇을 언급하는가?
(A) 그녀에게는 자신의 작업을 도와 줄 누군가가 필요하다.
(B) 그녀는 내일까지 작업을 끝낼 수 없다.
(C) 그녀는 작업에 관해 고객과 이야기하고 싶어한다.
(D) 그녀가 작업을 끝내기 위해서는 더 많은 예산이 필요하다.

be unable to ~할 수 없다 | **budget** 예산

| 해설 | 대화 초반에 남자가 내일까지 작업을 끝낼 수 있는지 묻자, 여자는 'I'm afraid not, Mr. Ito.'라고 답한 후 시간이 더 필요하다고 말한다. 따라서 (B)가 정답이다.

[41-43]

M Did you happen to read the news about promotions on the bulletin board? The list was just posted a few minutes ago. I can't believe Alice Milton got promoted to director.
W You've got to be kidding me. I heard she was probably going to get transferred to another branch or maybe even be fired. Do you mean she's going to be our boss now?
M That's right. According to what I read, her promotion won't go into effect for another month though. I'm considering making a request a transfer to another office.

M 혹시 승진에 관한 소식을 게시판에서 읽어 보았나요? 명단이 몇 분 전에 개시되었어요. 저는 Alice Milton이 이사로 승진했다니 믿을 수가 없어요.
W 농담하지 말아요. 저는 그녀가 아마도 다른 지사로 전근을 가던가, 아니면 심지어 해고될 수도 있을 것이라는 이야기를 들었어요. 당신 말은 그녀가 이제 우리의 상사가 될 것이라는 건가요?
M 맞아요. 하지만 제가 읽은 바에 따르면, 그녀의 승진은 한 달 후에 효력을 갖게 되죠. 저는 다른 지사로 전근을 요청하는 것에 대해 생각 중이에요.

bulletin board 게시판 | **get promoted to** ~으로 승진하다 | **fire** 해고하다 | **go into effect** 효력을 갖다

41 무엇이 논의되고 있는가?
(A) 동료의 승진
(B) 다른 지사의 개설
(C) 매장에서의 특별 세일
(D) 전근을 요청하는 방법

| 해설 | 남자는 승진 대상자 명단에 Alice Milton이라는 사람이 들어 있다는 소식을 전하며 그에 대한 놀라움을 나타내고 있다. 따라서 대화의 주제는 (A)로 볼 수 있다.

42 화자들은 Alice Milton에 대해 무엇을 말하는가?
(A) 그녀는 회사의 새 대표 이사이다.
(B) 그녀는 최근에 다른 지사에서 전근을 왔다.
(C) 그녀는 이전 직장에서 해고되었다.
(D) 그녀는 그들의 관리자가 될 것이다.

| 해설 | 여자가 'Do you mean she's going to be our boss now?'라고 묻자 남자는 '그렇다'라고 대답한다. 이를 통해 Alice Milton은 화자들의 상사가 될 것이라는 점을 추측할 수 있으므로 정답은 (D)이다.

43 남자의 기분은 어떠한가?
(A) 그는 자신의 일자리에 대해 걱정한다.
(B) 그는 일어나고 있는 일에 대해 불안해한다.
(C) 그는 소식에 기분이 상했다.

(D) 그는 결과에 만족한다.

nervous 불안해하는, 두려워하는

| 해설 | Alice Milton이라는 사람의 승진 소식에 남자는 '다른 지사로의 전근'(a transfer to another office)이라고 고려 중이라고 말한다. 따라서 남자는 전근을 고려할 정도로 불쾌감을 느끼고 있는 상황이므로 정답은 (C)가 된다.

[44-46]

W Good morning. What can I assist you with today, sir?
M I'd like to open a checking account. How can I go about doing that?
W It's a very simple process. First, you have to fill out this form here, and then you need to show me two forms of identification.
M Should both of them be picture IDs? I've only got my driver's license with me.
W One has to have a picture, but the other can be something such as a library card. Would you happen to have a bill with your name and address on it as well?
M Yes, I do. Here's my most recent electricity bill.
W Thank you very much.
M You're welcome. All right, let me complete the form right now.

W 안녕하세요. 어떻게 도와 드릴까요, 고객님?
M 예금 계좌를 개설하고 싶어요. 제가 어떻게 하면 되죠?
W 매우 간단해요. 먼저, 여기 이 양식에 내용을 기입하신 후, 두 개의 신분증을 제게 보여 주셔야 해요.
M 두 개 모두가 사진이 들어 있는 신분증이어야 하나요? 수중에는 운전면허증만 있어요.
W 하나에는 사진이 있어야 하지만, 다른 것은 도서관 카드와 같은 것이어도 괜찮아요. 혹시 고객님의 성함과 주소가 적혀 있는 청구서도 가지고 계신가요?
M 네, 그래요. 여기 가장 최근의 전기 요금 영수증이 있어요.
W 정말 고맙습니다.
M 천만에요. 좋아요, 이제 양식을 작성할게요.

assist 돕다 | **checking account** 예금 계좌 | **process** 과정, 절차 | **fill out** (내용을) 채우다, 기입하다 | **identification** 신원 확인, 신분증 | **picture ID** 사진이 들어 있는 신분증 | **happen to** 혹시 ~하다 | **electricity bill** 전기 요금 청구서

44 대화는 어디에서 이루어지고 있는가?
(A) 도서관에서
(B) 은행에서
(C) 학교에서
(D) 운전면허 시험장에서

| 해설 | '예금 계좌'(checking account)를 개설하고 싶은 고객과 은행원 간의 대화이다. 따라서 대화가 이루어지고 있는 장소는 (B)이다.

45 여자는 어떤 종류의 신분증을 제안하는가?
(A) 여권
(B) 운전면허증
(C) 도서관 카드
(D) 학생증

passport 여권 | **student ID card** 학생증

| 해설 | 여자는 남자에게 두 개의 신분증을 요청한 후, 사진이 들어 있는 신분증은 하나만 필요하고 '다른 하나는 도서관 카드와 같은 것이면 된다'(but the other can be something such as a library card)고 설명한다. 따라서 보기 중 여자가 남자에게 제출을 제안한 신분증은 (C)이다. (B)의 '운전 면허증'은 남자가 가지고 있는 신분증일 뿐, 여자가 제안한 형태의 신분증은 아니다.

46 남자는 여자에게 무엇을 주는가?
(A) 공공요금 청구서
(B) 신청서
(C) 임대차 계약서 사본
(D) 폐기된 수표

utility bill 공공요금 청구서 | **lease** 임대차 계약(서) | **canceled check** (지불이 완료되어) 폐기된 수표, 지불필 수표

| 해설 | 여자가 남자에게 이름과 주소가 적혀 있는 영수증이 있는지 묻자 남자는 'Here's my most recent electricity bill.'이라고 말하면서 전기 요금 청구서를 건넨다. 따라서 남자가 여자에게 건넨 것은 (A)의 A utilities bill(공공 요금 청구서)이다.

[47-49]

W Did you attend last night's awards ceremony?
M I had planned to go, but I needed to work late to complete the budget reports for tomorrow's meeting.
W That's a shame. It was the most surprising event I've attended in my five years here.
M You can say that again. I heard about it from Steve Burgess in the IT Department. He dropped by this morning to inform me about what happened.
W Can you believe Andrew Simmons won the employee of the year award?
M I was positive Emily Hargraves was going to be the winner. What did Andrew do to deserve it?
W There's a rumor going around that he just landed a multimillion dollar contract. There hasn't been an official announcement though.
M If that's true, that would explain everything.

W 어젯밤 시상식에 참여했나요?
M 갈 계획이었지만, 내일 회의를 위한 예산 보고서를 작성하느라 늦게까지 일을 해야 했어요.
W 안타깝군요. 제가 이곳에서 5년 동안 참석해 본 것 중에 가장 놀라운 행사였어요.
M 당신 말이 맞아요. 저는 IT부의 Steve Burgess로부터 그에 관한 이야기를 들었어요. 그가 오늘 아침에 들러서 제게 어떤 일이 있었는지를 알려 주더군요.
W Andrew Simmons가 올해의 사원상을 수상했다는 점이 믿어지나요?
M 저는 Emily Hargraves가 수상자가 될 것이라고 확신하고 있었죠. Andrew가 무엇을 했길래 수상 자격을 얻었나요?
W 그가 얼마 전에 수백만 달러의 계약을 성사시켰다는 소문이 돌고 있어요. 하지만 공식적인 발표는 없었고요.
M 그것이 사실이라면, 모든 것이 설명되겠군요.

awards ceremony 시상식 | **shame** 수치심; 아쉬운 일 | **drop by** 들르다 | **inform** 알리다, 고지하다 | **positive** 확신하는; 적극적인 | **deserve** ~할만 하다, ~의 자격이 있다 | **rumor** 소문, 루머 | **land a contract** 계약을 따내다 | **official** 공식적인

47 남자는 왜 "You can say that again"이라고 말하는가?
(A) 여자의 말에 대한 동감을 표시하기 위해
(B) 누군가 실수를 했다는 점을 확인시키기 위해

(C) 여자에게 앞에 한 말을 반복해 달라고 요청하기 위해
(D) 시상식에 참여하고 싶었다는 자신의 바람을 나타내기 위해

previous 이전의 | **comment** 논평 | **desire** 바람

| 해설 | 'You can say that again.'은 '당신 말이 맞다' 혹은 '동감이다'라는 뜻이므로 정답은 (A)이다.

48 화자들은 왜 놀라는가?
(A) 사내 행사가 촉박한 통지로 취소되었다.
(B) 그들이 예상하지 못했던 누군가가 수상을 했다.
(C) 회사가 새로운 계약을 성사시키지 못했다.
(D) IT부의 사람이 실수를 했다.

on short notice 촉박한 통보로 | **fail to** ~하는 데 실패하다, ~하지 못하다

| 해설 | 대화 중후반부의 내용을 통해 화자들은 Andrew Simmons라는 사람의 수상에 대해 놀라고 있다는 점을 알 수 있다. 따라서 정답은 (B)이다.

49 여자는 Andrew Simmons에 대해 무엇을 말하는가?
(A) 그는 경쟁사에서 일을 하기 위해 퇴사를 했다.
(B) 그는 복권으로 백만 달러를 탔다.
(C) 그는 자신이 중대한 계약에 서명을 했다고 발표했다.
(D) 그는 회사에서 상을 탔다.

lottery 복권

| 해설 | 대화 중반부의 여자의 말, 'Can you believe Andrew Simmons won the employee of the year award?'를 통해 Andrew Simmons는 올해의 사원상 수상자임을 알 수 있다. 따라서 정답은 (D)이다.

[50-52]

M Good evening. I wonder if you can give me some assistance.
W I'll do my best, sir. What do you require help with?
M I received this shirt as a birthday present yesterday, but it's not really my style. Would it be possible to exchange it for something else?
W You didn't take it out of the original plastic wrapping, right?
M Yeah, that's correct. But because it was a gift, I don't have the receipt. I'm really sorry about that.
W That's perfectly all right. We handle requests like this on occasion. And since I know that the shirt was sold here, I'm permitted to let you exchange it for something else costing the same price or lower.
M That's great news. Can you show me where the men's shirts are, please?

M 안녕하세요. 제게 도움을 주실 수 있는지 궁금하군요.
W 최선을 다하겠습니다, 고객님. 어떤 것에 도움이 필요하신가요?
M 저는 어제 생일 선물로 이 셔츠를 받았는데, 정말로 제 스타일이 아니에요. 다른 것으로 교환이 가능할까요?
W 원래 있던 비닐 포장을 뜯지는 않으셨죠, 그렇죠?
M 네, 맞아요. 하지만 선물이었기 때문에, 영수증을 가지고 있지는 않아요. 그에 대해서는 정말로 유감이에요.
W 괜찮습니다. 저희는 때때로 이번 일과 같은 요청을 처리해 드리고 있죠. 그리고 셔츠가 이곳에서 판매되었다는 점을 제가 알고 있기 때문에, 같은 가격이나 더 낮은 가격의 다른 것으로 교환해 드릴게요.
M 좋은 소식이군요. 남성용 셔츠가 어디에 있는지 알려 주시겠어요?

original 원래의, 본래의 | **plastic wrapping** 비닐 포장 | **perfectly** 완벽하게 | **handle** 다루다, 처리하다 | **on occasion** 때때로, 가끔

50 남자는 왜 도움을 요청하는가?
(A) 그는 돈을 돌려받고 싶어한다.
(B) 그는 교환에 관심이 있다.
(C) 그는 친구를 위한 선물을 사고 싶어한다.
(D) 그는 자신이 찾고 있는 셔츠를 찾을 수가 없다.

| 해설 | 남자의 말, 'Would it be possible to exchange it for something else?'를 통해, 남자는 생일 선물로 받은 셔츠를 교환하고자 한다는 점을 알 수 있다. 따라서 정답은 (B)이다.

51 남자는 왜 제품을 싫어하는가?
(A) 자신에게 잘 맞지 않는다.
(B) 소매가 너무 짧다.
(C) 스타일이 자신에게 어울리지 않는다.
(D) 너무 정장 차림에 가깝다

fit (몸에) 맞다 | **sleeve** 소매 | **suit** 어울리다 | **formal** 정식의, 형식을 갖춘, 정장의

| 해설 | 남자는 '셔츠 스타일이 자신에게 맞지 않는다'(it's not really my style)며 교환 이유를 밝히고 있다. 따라서 (C)가 정답이다.

52 화자들은 아마도 이다음에 무엇을 할 것인가?
(A) 환불 처리를 한다
(B) 다른 옷을 본다
(C) 비닐 포장을 벗긴다
(D) 영수증을 찾는다

| 해설 | 대화의 마지막 부분에서 남자는 'Can you show me where the men's shirts are, please?'라고 말하면서 여자에게 남성용 셔츠가 있는 곳을 보여 달라고 요청한다. 따라서 화자들은 남성용 셔츠 코너로 가게 될 것이므로 정답은 (B)이다.

[53-55]

Man A I'm nervous about the new boss we're getting tomorrow. Have either of you met him?
Woman I had lunch with Dave Thompson last week.
Man B What was your impression of him?
Man A Yeah, what was he like? Do you think he'll make a good boss?
Woman It's hard to tell.
Man B How come?
Woman He didn't say much at all. There were four of us dining together, but he mostly sat quietly and listened to us talk.
Man A I heard he's planning to restructure the department and that there might be layoffs.
Man B I hope your news is wrong, but I'm afraid you're right. Still, none of us has been performing up to expectations lately, so it makes sense that he's coming here to shake things up.
Woman And that's why all of us are worried.

Man A 내일 오실 새 사장님 때문에 긴장이 되는군요. 두 사람 중에 그분을 만나본 사람이 있나요?
Woman 제가 지난 주에 Dave Thompson과 점심 식사를 했어요.
Man B 그분에 대한 인상이 어땠나요?

Man A 예. 그분은 어떻던가요? 좋은 사장님이 되실 것 같다고 생각하나요?
Woman 말하기가 힘들군요.
Man B 왜요?
Woman 말씀을 많이 하지 않으셨거든요. 넷이서 함께 식사를 했지만, 그분은 주로 조용히 앉아 계시면서 우리가 이야기하는 것을 들으셨어요.
Man A 그분이 부서를 구조 조정해서 정리 해고가 있을 수도 있다고 들었어요.
Man B 당신 뉴스가 틀리기를 바라지만, 맞을까 두렵군요. 하지만, 최근 우리 중 누구도 기대에 부응하는 성과를 내지 못하고 있기 때문에, 그분이 변화를 주기 위해 여기에 올 것이라는 점이 이치에 맞아요.
Woman 그리고 그것이 우리 모두가 걱정하는 이유죠.

nervous 긴장되는, 초조한 | **impression** 인상 | **how come** 왜, 어째서 | **dine** 식사하다 | **restructure** 구조 조정하다 | **layoff** 해고 | **expectation** 예상, 기대 | **make sense** 말이 되다, 이치에 맞다 | **shake up** ~을 개혁하다, ~을 개편하다

53 화자들은 주로 무엇을 논의하는가?
(A) 그들의 업무 성과
(B) 최근의 점심 회동
(C) 곧 오게 될 관리자
(D) 부서의 구조 조정

| 해설 | 대화 초반부의 내용을 통해 화자들은 '새로운 사장'(new boss)인 Dave Thompson에 대해 이야기하고 있음을 알 수 있다. 따라서 정답은 (C)이다.

54 여자가 "It's hard to tell"이라고 말할 때 그녀는 무엇을 의미하는가?
(A) 그녀는 질문에 대답하고 싶지가 않다.
(B) 그녀는 Thompson 씨가 어떤 사람일지 잘 모른다.
(C) 그녀가 남자들에게 이야기하는 것은 허용되지 않는다.
(D) 그녀는 언제 Thompson 씨를 만날지 확신하지 못한다.

| 해설 | Thompson 씨가 좋은 사장이 될 것 같은지를 묻는 질문에 여자는 'It's hard to tell.'이라고 말한 후 그 이유를 그와 이야기를 많이 나누지 못했기 때문이라고 밝히고 있다. 따라서 주어진 문장을 통해 그녀가 의미한 바는 (B)로 볼 수 있다.

55 화자들은 무엇에 관해 걱정하는가?
(A) 직원들의 급여가 삭감될 수도 있다.
(B) 그들은 강등될 위험이 있다.
(C) 직원 중 누구도 보너스를 받지 못할 것이다.
(D) 그들 중 일부가 곧 일자리를 잃을 수도 있다.

in danger of ~할 위험이 있는 | **demote** 강등시키다, 좌천시키다

| 해설 | restructure(구조 조정하다)와 layoff(일시적인 해고) 같은 단어에 주의하면 화자들은 '해고될 가능성'에 대해 걱정하고 있음을 알 수 있다. 따라서 정답은 (D)이다.

[56-58]

M Good afternoon. Is this the number I should call regarding subscriptions to the *Daily Herald*?
W That's correct, sir. Are you interested in subscribing to the paper?
M Actually, I already get the newspaper delivered to my home each day, but my subscription is about to expire, and I'd like to renew it. My name is Charles Anderson.
W Okay . . . Are you the Charles Anderson living at 58 Oak Street?
M That's right. I'd like to receive the paper for six more months, please.
W No problem, Mr. Anderson. You know, we're running a special offer this month only. If you renew for one year, it will cost the same as it would if you paid for eight months. Are you interested?
M That's a pretty good deal. How about signing me up for it, please?

M 안녕하세요. 이 번호가 *Daily Herald*의 구독과 관련해서 전화를 걸어야 하는 번호인가요?
W 맞습니다, 고객님. 신문 구독에 관심이 있으신가요?
M 실은, 이미 제 집에서 매일 신문을 구독하고 있는데, 구독 기간이 곧 소멸될 예정이라 갱신을 하고 싶어서요. 제 이름은 Charles Anderson이에요.
W 좋아요… Oak 가 58번지에 사시는 Charles Anderson 씨인가요?
M 맞아요. 저는 6개월 더 신문을 받고 싶어요.
W 문제 없습니다, Anderson 씨. 아시는 대로, 저희는 이번 달에만 특별 할인을 제공해 드리고 있어요. 1년을 갱신하시면, 8개월 동안 내야 하는 금액과 동일한 비용이 들 거예요. 관심이 있으신가요?
M 상당히 좋은 조건이군요. 저를 위해 등록을 해 주시겠어요?

subscription 구독 | **subscribe** 구독하다 | **be about to** 막 ~하려고 하다 | **expire** 소멸하다 | **special offer** 특가 상품 | **renew** 갱신하다 | **deal** 거래

56 남자는 왜 여자에게 전화를 하는가?
(A) 주문을 취소하기 위해
(B) 배달물이 실종된 것에 대한 불만을 표현하기 위해
(C) 구독을 갱신하기 위해
(D) 요금 지불 방법을 알아내기 위해

| 해설 | 대화 초반에 남자는 신문의 구독 기간이 만료될 예정이라 '갱신을 하고 싶어서'(I'd like to renew it) 전화를 걸었다고 말한다. 따라서 정답은 (C)이다.

57 여자는 왜 남자의 주소를 말하는가?
(A) 남자의 신원을 확인하기 위해
(B) 남자의 주문품을 어디로 보내야 하는지 알아내기 위해
(C) 자신이 남자의 새로운 주소를 알고 있는지 확인하기 위해
(D) 어디로 청구서를 보내야 할지 묻기 위해

| 해설 | 남자가 자신의 이름을 밝히자 여자는 주소로 남자의 신원을 확인하고 있다. 따라서 정답은 '신원을 확인하기 위해'라는 의미의 (A)이다.

58 여자는 남자에게 무엇에 관해 이야기하는가?
(A) 무료 잡지
(B) 할인 금액
(C) 온라인 서비스
(D) 증정품

complimentary 무료의

| 해설 | 대화 후반부에서 여자는 남자에게 '특가 상품'(special offer)을 안내하면서 8개월치의 구독료를 납부하면 1년간 구독이 가능하다는 점을 설명한다. 따라서 여자가 이야기한 것은 '구독료 할인'에 관한 정보이므로 정답은 (B)이다.

[59-61]

W Do you know why the shipment from Dyson

Manufacturing has failed to arrive yet?
M I called Mr. Sykes this morning, and he explained the problem to me.
W Yes?
M Apparently, there was a bad snowstorm in Montana last week, so no trucks were able to leave the factory for three days.
W Did he indicate when our shipment is going to make it here?
M He informed me that he spoke with the driver and that we can expect it first thing tomorrow morning.
W That's a relief. Without the items in that delivery, we will have to shut down the assembly lines. Would you mind calling him back to confirm when the products are arriving?
M Not at all. I can give him a call once I return to my office.

W Dyson Manufacturing의 선적물이 왜 아직도 도착하지 않았는지 알고 있나요?
M 오늘 아침에 Sykes 씨에게 전화를 걸었더니, 그가 제게 문제를 설명해 주더군요.
W 네?
M 듣자 하니, 지난 주에 몬태나에 심한 눈보라가 쳐서, 3일 동안 어떤 트럭도 공장을 나설 수가 없었다더군요.
W 그가 우리 선적물이 언제 여기에 올 것인지도 알려 주었나요?
M 그가 기사에게 이야기를 해서 내일 오전 일찍 우리가 받을 수 있을 것이라고 알려 주었어요.
W 다행이군요. 그 선적품에 들어 있는 물품이 없으면, 우리는 조립 라인을 정지시켜야 할 거예요. 그에게 다시 전화를 해서 제품이 언제 도착할 것인지 확인해 줄래요?
M 그럴게요. 사무실로 돌아가서 그에게 전화를 할게요.

shipment 선적, 선적물 | **snowstorm** 눈보라 | **indicate** 가리키다, 나타내다 | **make it** 시간에 맞춰 가다 | **first thing** 아침 일찍 | **shut down** 폐쇄하다, 중지시키다 | **assembly line** 조립 라인 | **confirm** 확인하다

59 문제가 무엇인가?
  (A) 배달된 일부 부품들이 제대로 만들어지지 않았다.
  (B) 날씨 때문에 선적물이 늦게 발송되었다.
  (C) 눈보라로 인해 직원들이 출근을 하지 못했다.
  (D) 조립 라인의 가동이 3일 동안 중단되었다.

| 해설 | 대화 시작 부분에서 여자가 '물품이 왜 아직 도착하지 않았는지'(why the shipment from Dyson Manufacturing has failed to arrive yet) 묻자 남자는 bad snowstorm(심한 눈보라) 때문이었다고 답한다. 따라서 대화에서 논의되고 있는 문제는 (B)이다.

60 여자는 왜 "That's a relief"라고 말하는가?
  (A) 남자가 결과를 다시 한 번 확인해야 한다고 말하기 위해
  (B) 자신이 남자의 말에 기뻐한다는 점을 나타내기 위해
  (C) 몇몇 소식에 관한 자신의 실망감을 표현하기 위해
  (D) 어떤 문제에 대해 자신이 할 수 있는 것이 없다고 주장하기 위해

double-check 재확인하다 | **comment** 논평

| 해설 | 'That's a relief.'는 '다행이다'라는 의미이다. 바로 앞 문장에서 남자가 '내일 아침 일찍 물건을 받게 될 것'(we can expect it first thing tomorrow morning)이라고 말하자 여자가 안도감을 나타내고 있다. 정답은 (B)이다.

61 여자는 남자에게 무엇을 할 것을 요청하는가?

  (A) 공급업체에 연락한다
  (B) 계약을 재협상한다
  (C) 우체국에 연락한다
  (D) 조립 라인 작업자에게 이야기한다

| 해설 | 여자의 마지막 말, 'Would you mind calling him back to confirm when the products are arriving?'을 통해, 여자가 남자에게 요청하는 바는 (A)임을 알 수 있다.

[62-64]

Woman A I've considered all the proposals, but I can't make up my mind. Which vendor should we hire?
Man I'm in favor of selecting the Powell Corporation.
Woman B Why?
Man It has a proven track record of providing outstanding customer support. If anything goes wrong, Powell will handle it immediately.
Woman A That's a strong endorsement. Have you worked with Powell before?
Man Not personally. However, I know people who have, and they're unanimous in praising the company's dedication to service.
Woman B Well, I think we should go with the BYR Company. Its prices are the lowest, and we have financial constraints to worry about.
Woman A Hmm . . . You're right about that. Let me think about everything for a while. I'll inform you of my choice by 5:00 P.M.

Woman A 모든 제안서를 고려해 보았지만, 결정을 내릴 수가 없군요. 어떤 업체를 이용해야 할까요?
Man 저는 Powell 사를 선정하는 것에 찬성이에요.
Woman B 왜요?
Man 그곳은 우수한 고객 지원 서비스를 제공한다는 실적을 입증했어요. 무언가 잘못이 생기면, Powell이 즉시 처리해 줄 거예요.
Woman A 강력한 추천 발언이군요. 전에 Powell과 일을 해 본 적이 있나요?
Man 개인적으로는 없어요. 하지만, 일을 해 본 사람들을 알고 있는데, 그들은 만장일치로 서비스에 대한 그 업체의 헌신을 높이 평가하고 있죠.
Woman B 음, 저는 우리가 BYR 사와 일을 해야 한다고 생각해요. 가격이 가장 낮고, 우리에게는 고려해야 할 금전적인 제약이 있으니까요.
Woman A 음… 그에 대해서는 당신 말이 맞아요. 모든 것에 대해 잠시 생각을 해 볼게요. 오후 5시까지 제가 선택한 것을 알려 드리죠.

proposal 제안, 제안서 | **make up one's mind** 결정하다 | **vendor** 행상인; 납품업체 | **in favor of** ~을 찬성하여 | **select** 선정하다 | **track record** 실적 | **outstanding** 뛰어난, 우수한 | **endorsement** 지지, 승인; 추천의 말 | **unanimous** 만장일치의 | **dedication** 헌신 | **go with** ~와 어울리다, ~와 협력하다 | **constraint** 제약

62 무엇이 논의되고 있는가?
  (A) 어떻게 더 많은 고객들을 유인할 수 있는지
  (B) 어떤 사람이 면접을 잘 봤는지
  (C) 어떤 업체를 선정해야 하는지
  (D) 제안서에 무엇을 나타내야 하는지

| 해설 | 대화 시작 부분에서 여자A는 'Which vendor should we hire?'라

고 말하면서 업체 선정에 관해 나머지 두 사람의 의견을 묻고 있다. 따라서 논의의 주제는 (C)이다.

63 남자는 Powell 사에 대해 무엇을 말하는가?
(A) 고객들을 잘 지원해 준다.
(B) 그는 전에 그 업체와 일을 해 본 적이 있다.
(C) 그곳에서 제공한 가격이 경쟁자들보다 낮다.
(D) 그 업체는 재정적인 어려움을 겪고 있다.

| 해설 | 대화 중반부의 남자의 말, 'It has a proven track record of providing outstanding customer support.'에서 Powell 사의 고객 지원 서비스의 실적은 입증된 것임을 알 수 있다. 따라서 (A)가 Powell 사에 관한 내용이다. (B)는 사실과 반대되는 내용이고, (C)는 Powell 사가 아니라 BYR 사에 해당되는 이야기이다.

64 오후 5시에 어떤 일이 일어날 것인가?
(A) 발표가 이루어질 것이다.
(B) 결정이 내려질 것이다.
(C) 면접 일정이 정해질 것이다.
(D) 계약서에 서명이 이루어질 것이다.

| 해설 | 대화의 마지막 말인 'I'll inform you of my choice by 5:00 P.M.'에서 여자A는 5시에 자신이 결정한 사항을 나머지 두 사람에게 알려 줄 것임을 알 수 있다. 따라서 (B)가 정답이다.

[65-67]

M Excuse me. I'm looking to buy a blender.
W The top-of-the-line model is this one here by Nelson Electronics. However, unless you're employed as a cook, you probably don't need it. It's also a bit pricy.
M I intend to use it a couple of times each week, so it doesn't need to be anything special.
W In that case, I recommend this one. It's our bestselling blender.
M It looks fine, and the price isn't too bad either.
W Just so you know, we've got a special sale going on at the moment. Depending upon how much money you spend, you can get anywhere between five and twenty-percent off.
M Sounds great. So how much of a discount will I get for buying this one?
W You'll receive an extra fifteen percent off.
M Excellent.

M 실례합니다. 저는 믹서기를 구입하려고 하는데요.
W 최신 모델은 여기에 있는 Nelson 전자의 것이에요. 하지만, 요리사로 고용되어 있지 않은 이상, 아마도 이것이 필요하지는 않으실 거예요. 또한 가격도 다소 비싸고요.
M 매주 두어 번 정도 사용할 생각이기 때문에, 특별한 것일 필요는 없어요.
W 그런 경우라면, 이것을 추천해 드릴게요. 저희 매장에서 제일 잘 팔리는 믹서기예요.
M 좋아 보이고, 가격도 그렇게 나쁘지는 않군요.
W 아시겠지만, 현재 특별 세일이 진행 중이에요. 얼마를 지출하시느냐에 따라, 5퍼센트에서 20퍼센트 사이의 할인을 받으실 수 있어요.
M 잘 되었군요. 이것을 구입하면 얼마의 할인을 받게 되나요?
W 추가적으로 15%를 받으실 거예요.
M 굉장하군요.

blender 믹서기 | **top-of-the-line** 최신식의, 최고급의 | **a bit** 약간, 다소 | **pricy** 비싼 | **recommend** 추천하다 | **depending upon** ~에 따라서 | **extra** 여분의, 추가적인

65 여자는 Nelson 전자의 믹서기에 관해 무엇을 암시하는가?
(A) 매장에서 가장 잘 팔리는 모델이다.
(B) 다른 믹서기보다 가격이 덜 나간다.
(C) 전문 요리사에게 유용하다.
(D) 환불 보증을 해 준다.

professional 전문적인, 프로의 | **money-back guarantee** 환불 보증

| 해설 | 여자는 Nelson 전자의 믹서기를 소개하면서 '요리사가 아닌 이상 필요하지 않을 것'(unless you're employed as a cook, you probably don't need it)이라고 말한다. 이를 통해 Nelson 전자의 믹서기는 전문 요리사를 위한 제품임을 추측할 수 있으므로 정답은 (C)이다.

66 남자는 믹서기를 얼마나 자주 사용할 것인가?
(A) 매일
(B) 일주일에 두세 번
(C) 한 달에 한두 번
(D) 특별한 경우에만

| 해설 | 남자는 믹서기를 '일주일에 두어 번'(a couple of times each week) 사용할 것이라고 했으므로 (B)가 정답이다.

67 도표를 보아라. 남자는 제품 구입에 얼마를 소비할 것인가?
(A) 1-50달러
(B) 51-100달러
(C) 101-200달러
(D) 201달러 이상

| 해설 | 대화의 마지막 부분에서 남자는 15%의 할인을 받게 될 것이라는 점을 알 수 있다. 도표에서 15%의 할인을 받을 수 있는 소비 금액은 세 번째 줄의 $101-$200로 나타나 있으므로 정답은 (C)이다.

> ☑ **700점 넘기 포인트** 토익 LC에 시각 자료가 제시된다고 해서 크게 걱정할 필요는 없다. 일반적으로 RC에서보다 단순한 형태의 도표가 제시되며, 대화를 듣기에 앞서 도표를 먼저 간략히 살펴보면 오히려 어느 부분을 집중해서 들어야 할지를 가늠할 수 있다. 이 문제의 경우에도 표에 지출 금액과 할인율이 제시되어 있으므로 대화에서 이와 관련된 부분을 조금 더 주의해서 듣도록 하자.

[68-70]

M What a great speech that Dr. Apu just gave. I'm glad I decided to attend it at the last moment.
W I fully agree with you. His discussion on those new medical procedures was quite instructive.
M So, uh, what are you planning to do next?
W I'm attending the speech by Dr. Archer. He's a world-renowned expert on vaccinations.
M That doesn't appeal to me very much. Instead, I'm going to the lecture being given by Dr. Probst. I took a class with him at med school, so it will be nice to see him again.
W All right. They both finish at the same time, so how about meeting here at 1:30 and having lunch when the talks are over?
M Good thinking. I'll see you in a while.

M　Apu 박사가 조금 전에 했던 강연은 대단했어요. 마지막 순간에 참석하겠다는 결정을 내려서 기쁘네요.
W　전적으로 당신 말에 동감이에요. 새로운 치료 과정에 관한 그의 논의는 상당히 유익했어요.
M　그러면, 어, 이다음에 무엇을 할 계획인가요?
W　저는 Archer 박사의 강연에 참석할 거예요. 그는 예방 접종에 관해 세계적으로 유명한 전문가죠.
M　저에게는 그다지 매력적으로 들리지 않는군요. 대신, 저는 Probst 박사가 하는 강연에 가겠어요. 저는 의대에서 그분의 수업을 들었기 때문에, 그분을 다시 만나게 되면 좋을 것 같아요.
W　좋아요. 둘 다 같은 시간에 끝나기 때문에, 강연이 끝나면 1시 30분에 이곳에서 만나서 점심을 먹는 것이 어떨까요?
M　좋은 생각이군요. 잠시 후에 만나요.

at the last moment 마지막 순간에 | fully 완전히, 전적으로 | medical 의료의, 의학의 | instructive 유익한 | world-renowned 세계적으로 유명한 | vaccination 예방 접종 | appeal 호소하다; 관심을 끌다 | med school 의과대학 | in a while 잠시 후에

68　화자들은 어디에 있는 것 같은가?
　　(A) 병원에
　　(B) 의학 콘퍼런스에
　　(C) 의과 대학에
　　(D) 진료소에

| 해설 | 화자들은 본인들이 들었던 강연과 이후에 들을 강연에 대해 이야기하고 있는데 그 주제가 new medical procedures(새로운 치료 과정) 및 vaccinations(예방 접종)에 관한 것이다. 따라서 화자들이 있는 곳은 (B)의 '의학 콘퍼런스'임을 알 수 있다. 남자는 의대에 다닐 때 Probst 박사의 수업을 들었다고 말한 점에서 (C)의 '의과 대학'은 화자들이 있는 곳이 될 수 없다.

69　도표를 보아라. 여자는 어떤 룸에 있게 될 것인가?
　　(A) 106호
　　(B) 210호
　　(C) 309호
　　(D) 404호

| 해설 | 여자는 Archer 박사의 강연을 들을 것이며, 그가 '백신'(vaccinations)의 전문가라고 이야기한다. 따라서 도표 상 Vaccinations의 강연 장소를 찾으면 여자가 있게 될 곳이 (C)의 '309호'라는 점을 알 수 있다.

70　남자는 Probst 박사에 관해 무엇을 암시하는가?
　　(A) 그는 인근 병원에서 의사로 일한다.
　　(B) 그 두 사람은 개인적으로 아는 사이이다.
　　(C) 그는 최근에 교직에서 물러났다.
　　(D) 새로운 치료 과정이 그에 의해 만들어졌다.

personally 개인적으로 | acquainted 알고 있는, 안면이 있는

| 해설 | 남자는 의대 시절 Probst 박사의 수업을 들었다고 언급한 뒤, '그분과 다시 만나면 기쁠 것이다'(it will be nice to see him again)라고 말한다. 따라서 두 사람은 서로 아는 사이임을 알 수 있으므로 정답은 (B)이다.

● **PART 4**　　　　　　　　　　　　　　　　　p.41

[71-73]

W　Before we close this meeting, there's one more thing I'd like to cover. I'm well aware of the problems at the Dayton factory. A team of inspectors was sent there to look at the problems this morning, so none of you needs to worry about that anymore since we're handling the issue. I would, however, like to thank all of you who reported the problems to me. Your observations may have helped us avoid a catastrophe. And that's something I'd like to remind everyone to do: When you see something wrong, let a supervisor know immediately. That's how we can prevent small issues from transforming into major problems.

W　이번 회의를 끝내기 전에, 다루고 싶은 사항이 한 가지 더 있습니다. 저는 Dayton 공장의 문제를 잘 알고 있습니다. 오늘 아침에 문제를 살펴보기 위해 한 팀의 조사관들이 그곳으로 파견되었고, 우리가 문제를 해결하고 있기 때문에 여러분들 중 어느 누구도 그에 대해 더 이상 걱정하실 필요가 없습니다. 하지만 저는, 제게 문제를 보고해 주신 여러분 모두에게 감사를 드리고 싶습니다. 여러분들의 주의는 우리가 재앙을 피하는데 도움을 주었습니다. 그리고 그것은 제가 모든 사람들께 해야 한다고 상기시키는 일이기도 합니다: 무언가 잘못된 것을 보면, 즉시 감독관에게 알리십시오. 그것이 작은 문제가 커다란 문제로 변하는 것을 막을 수 있는 방법입니다.

be aware of ~을 알다 | inspector 조사관 | observation 관찰, 주시 | catastrophe 재앙 | remind 상기시키다 | supervisor 감독관 | prevent A from B A가 B하는 것을 막다 | transform 변하다

71　담화는 어디에서 이루어지고 있는 것 같은가?
　　(A) 사무실에서
　　(B) 실험실에서
　　(C) 매장에서
　　(D) 공장에서

| 해설 | 담화 첫 문장 중 before we close this meeting이라는 표현에 유의하면 담화가 이루어지고 있는 장소는 회의 공간인 (A)의 '사무실'임을 알 수 있다. 공장의 문제에 대해 이야기하고 있다고 해서 정답을 (D)로 고르는 실수는 하지 말아야 한다.

72　화자는 Dayton 시설에 대해 무엇을 말하는가?
　　(A) 그곳에서 폭발이 보고되었다.
　　(B) 그곳의 몇몇 사람들이 고용되었다.
　　(C) 그곳을 살펴보기 위해 사람들이 파견되었다.
　　(D) 그곳은 가까운 미래에 폐쇄될 것이다.

explosion 폭발 | in the near future 가까운 미래에

| 해설 | 담화 초반부에 화자는 'Dayton 공장의 문제를 조사하기 위해 조사관들이 파견되었다'(A team of inspectors was sent there to look at the problems,)고 언급한다. 따라서 정답은 (C)이다.

73　화자는 청자들에게 무엇을 하라고 말하는가?
　　(A) 더 빨리 일을 끝내기 시작한다
　　(B) 감독관들과 더욱 긴밀하게 협조한다
　　(C) 문제를 보면 보고를 한다
　　(D) 평소보다 일찍 출근한다

show up 모습을 나타내다

| 해설 | 담화 후반부의 'When you see something wrong, let a supervisor know immediately.'라는 문장에서 화자는 청자들에게 문제 발생 시 즉시 보고해야 한다는 메시지를 전달하고 있다. 따라서 (C)가 정답이다.

14

[74-76]

W Hello, Mr. Russell. This is Mandy Jenkins from Winston's. I'd like you to know that your laptop has been repaired, so you can come here to pick it up anytime we're open. We'll be closing our doors at 8:30 tonight and reopening them at 9:00 tomorrow morning. By the way, the problem with your computer wasn't as severe as we had initially feared. We didn't have to replace the hard drive. Instead, we just reinstalled some software, and that cleared the problem right up. So you'll only be charged $50 for the work we did.

W 안녕하세요, Russell 씨. 저는 Winston's의 Mandy Jenkins입니다. 귀하의 노트북 컴퓨터가 수리되었다는 점을 알려 드리며, 귀하께서는 영업 시간 중 어느 때나 이곳으로 오셔서 가져 가실 수 있습니다. 오늘 밤에는 8시 30분에 문을 닫을 것이고 내일은 오전 9시에 다시 문을 열 것입니다. 그건 그렇고, 귀하의 컴퓨터 문제는 처음에 저희가 우려했던 것만큼 심각한 것은 아니었습니다. 하드 드라이브는 교체할 필요가 없었습니다. 대신, 일부 소프트웨어를 다시 설치했고, 그로써 문제가 깨끗이 해결되었습니다. 저희가 한 작업에 대해서는 50달러의 비용만 내시면 됩니다.

as ~ as ~만큼 ~한 | **severe** 심각한 | **initially** 처음에, 초기에 | **fear** 두려워하다 | **replace** 교체하다 | **reinstall** 다시 설치하다

74 화자는 Russell 씨에게 무엇을 할 것을 요청하는가?
   (A) 결제를 한다
   (B) 답신을 한다
   (C) 피드백을 준다
   (D) 매장을 방문한다

make a payment 지불하다, 결제하다 | **feedback** 반응, 의견, 피드백

| 해설 | 여자는 컴퓨터가 수리되어 '매장에 와서 찾아 가면 된다'(you can come here to pick it up)는 점을 알려 준다. 따라서 여자가 요청한 바는 (D)이다.

75 Winston's는 내일 언제 문을 여는가?
   (A) 오전 8시
   (B) 오전 8시 30분
   (C) 오전 9시
   (D) 오전 9시 30분

| 해설 | 'We'll be closing our doors at 8:30 tonight and reopening them at 9:00 tomorrow morning.'이라는 문장을 통해 여자의 매장이 저녁 8시 30분에 문을 닫고 아침 9시에 문을 연다는 사실을 알 수 있다. 따라서 정답은 (C)이다.

76 화자의 말에 따르면, 문제가 어떻게 해결되었는가?
   (A) 새로운 스피커를 설치함으로써
   (B) 일부 소프트웨어를 다시 설치함으로써
   (C) 컴퓨터를 철저히 청소함으로써
   (D) 컴퓨터의 하드 드라이브를 교체함으로써

put back ~을 제자리에 다시 가져다 놓다

| 해설 | 여자는 처음의 우려와 달리 '소프트웨어를 다시 설치함으로써'(we just reinstalled some software) 문제가 간단히 해결되었다고 언급한다. 따라서 정답은 (B)이다. hard drive라는 용어만 듣고 (D)를 정답으로 선택해서는 안 된다.

[77-79]

M Now that the renovations on Fred's Diner are complete, we are once again ready to open our doors to the public. With more than 500 square feet of space added, we can fit more customers than ever before. That means you won't have to wait long to get a table. This weekend only, we're having a special sale to celebrate our reopening. Order one entrée, and you can get a second one of equal or lesser value for free. Come down to 76 Dansby Avenue and check us out. You won't regret it.

M Fred's Diner의 보수 공사가 끝났으므로, 저희는 사람들에게 다시 문을 열 준비를 마쳤습니다. 500평방피트가 넘는 공간이 추가됨으로써, 전보다 많은 고객분들을 수용할 수 있습니다. 이는 자리를 얻기 위해 오래 기다리실 필요가 없음을 의미합니다. 이번 주말을 한정으로, 다시 문을 연 것을 기념하기 위해 특별 세일을 실시할 예정입니다. 메인 요리를 하나 주문하시면, 그와 가격이 같거나 낮은 두 번째 요리를 무료로 드릴 수 있습니다. Dansby 가 76번지로 오셔서 저희를 찾아 주십시오. 후회하지 않으실 것입니다.

now that ~이므로 | **be ready to** ~할 준비가 되다 | **public** 대중, 공중 | **fit** 적합하다, 어울리다 | **celebrate** 경축하다, 기념하다 | **entrée** 메인 요리 | **equal** 동등한, 같은 | **value** 가치, 가격 | **for free** 무료로 | **regret** 후회하다

77 식당은 무엇을 기념할 것인가?
   (A) 새로운 지점의 오픈
   (B) 보수 공사를 끝냄
   (C) 개업 1주년
   (D) 5,000명 이상을 접대

| 해설 | 담화 중반부에서 특별 세일의 목적이 to celebrate our reopening(다시 문을 연 것을 기념하기 위해)이라고 언급되고 있으므로 정답은 (B)가 된다.

78 식당은 언제 세일을 할 것인가?
   (A) 월요일부터 금요일까지
   (B) 주말에
   (C) 다음 주 내내
   (D) 한 달 동안

| 해설 | this weekend only라는 문구를 통해 세일은 (B)의 '주말에만' 이루어질 것임을 알 수 있다.

79 고객들은 세일 기간 동안 무엇을 얻을 수 있는가?
   (A) 무료 음식
   (B) 상품권
   (C) 특별상
   (D) 무료 음료 쿠폰

| 해설 | 담화의 마지막 부분에서 메인 요리를 하나 주문하면 '금액이 그와 같거나 낮은 요리'(a second one of equal or lesser value)가 무료로 제공된다는 점을 알 수 있다. 따라서 고객이 얻을 수 있는 것은 (A)의 '무료 음식'이다.

[80-82]

M May I have your attention, please? It looks like the snow has been cleaned off the runway, so planes are being cleared for takeoff. We're fifth in line, so we've got a few minutes before it's our turn. In the meantime, would everyone please be sure your seatbelts are buckled and your baggage is stowed properly? Once we get airborne, we'll rise quickly to get above these storm clouds. After that, I expect to make up for lost time. We should have constant tailwinds the entire trip, which should help us make the flight to Moscow faster than normal.

M 주목해 주시겠습니까? 활주로의 눈이 제거된 것으로 보임에 따라, 비행기들의 이륙이 허가되고 있습니다. 저희 순서는 5번째이기 때문에, 저희 차례가 되기까지는 몇 분이 남아 있습니다. 그 동안, 모든 분들께서는 안전 벨트가 채워져 있는지, 그리고 수하물이 적절하게 놓여 있는지 확인해 주시겠습니까? 이륙을 하면, 저희는 먹구름 위로 빠르게 올라갈 것입니다. 그 후에는, 지체된 시간을 만회할 수 있을 것으로 예상됩니다. 비행 내내 순풍을 타게 될 것이며, 이로써 평소보다 빨리 모스크바로 비행할 수 있을 것입니다.

clean off ~을 치우다 | **runway** 활주로 | **clear for** ~을 허가하다 | **takeoff** 이륙 | **turn** 차례 | **in the meantime** 그 동안 | **buckle** (벨트 등을) 채우다 | **stow** 집어넣다 | **get airborne** 이륙하다 | **storm cloud** 먹구름 | **make up for** ~을 보상하다 | **tailwind** 순풍

80 무엇이 지연을 일으켰는가?
(A) 기계적인 문제
(B) 날개 위의 얼음
(C) 실종된 승객
(D) 활주로의 눈

| 해설 | 담화의 초반부에 화자는 '활주로의 눈이 제거되어'(the snow has been cleaned off the runway) 비행기 이륙이 허가되었다고 말한다. 따라서 지연의 원인은 (D)의 '눈'으로 볼 수 있다.

81 화자는 승객들에게 무엇을 할 것을 요청하는가?
(A) 좌석을 수직으로 세운다
(B) 승무원의 말에 귀를 기울인다
(C) 안전 벨트를 맨다
(D) 전자 기기의 전원을 끈다

upright 수직의 | **flight attendant** 항공기 승무원 | **fasten** 매다, 채우다

| 해설 | 화자는 승객들에게 '안전 벨트를 맬 것'(your seatbelts are buckled)과 '수하물이 제대로 들어가 있는지'(your baggage is stowed properly)를 확인하라고 당부하고 있다. 따라서 정답은 이 중 전자를 가리키고 있는 (C)이다.

82 화자가 "After that, I expect to make up for lost time"이라고 말할 때 화자는 무엇을 의미하는가?
(A) 비행기가 정시에 이륙할 것이다.
(B) 비행이 평소보다 빠를 것이다.
(C) 조종사가 보다 빠른 루트를 이용할 것이다.
(D) 몇 시간 후에 비행기가 도착할 것이다.

on time 정시에, 제때에 | **pilot** 조종사 | **route** 경로, 루트

| 해설 | make up for는 '~을 보상하다'라는 뜻이므로, 주어진 문장은 '지체된 시간을 만회할 것이다'라는 의미를 나타낸다. 따라서 주어진 문장에서는 평상시보다 빠른 속도로 비행기가 이동할 것임을 암시하고 있으므로 정답은 (B)이다.

[83-85]

W Good evening, listeners. This is Kate Charles at the WTRO news desk with a breaking news report for you. The East Bay Bridge has been closed to traffic. About twenty minutes ago, the bridge was struck by a barge passing beneath it. There are apparently cracks in one of the bridge's columns, so no vehicles or pedestrians are being allowed on it. Motorists are being redirected to other bridges in the city. This has understandably created serious traffic issues throughout the city. I'll keep you updated as soon as anything new comes across my desk. And now back to Earl Jenkins with today's sports news.

W 안녕하세요, 청취자 여러분. 저는 WTRO 뉴스 데스크의 Kate Charles로, 여러분들을 위한 속보를 가지고 왔습니다. East Bay 교의 교통이 통제되고 있습니다. 약 20분 전에, 그 아래를 지나가던 바지선이 다리와 충돌했습니다. 다리의 기둥 중 하나에 금이 간 것으로 보이기 때문에, 어떤 차량이나 보행자도 통행이 허가되지 않고 있습니다. 운전자들은 시내의 다른 다리로 방향을 돌리고 있습니다. 이는 당연하게도 시 전체에 심각한 교통 문제를 일으키고 있습니다. 새로운 소식이 데스크에 도착하는 대로 최신 정보를 알려 드리겠습니다. 그리고 이제 오늘의 스포츠 뉴스를 전할 Earl Jenkins에게 돌아가도록 하겠습니다.

breaking news 속보, 특보 | **bridge** 다리, 교각 | **barge** 바지선 | **apparently** 보아 하니, 듣자 하니 | **crack** 갈라짐, 금 | **column** 기둥 | **pedestrian** 보행자 | **motorist** 운전자 | **redirect** 방향을 바꾸다 | **understandably** 당연히 | **keep ~ updated** ~에게 최신 정보를 알려 주다

83 다리에 어떤 일이 일어났는가?
(A) 다리 일부가 강으로 떨어졌다.
(B) 조금 전에 모든 운전자들에게 개방되었다.
(C) 금이 생겼다.
(D) 두 대의 차량이 그 위에서 충돌했다.

fall into ~으로 떨어지다 | **collide** 충돌하다

| 해설 | 바지선이 교각에 충돌하여 '교각 하나에 금이 갔다'(cracks in one of the bridge's columns)는 소식을 전하고 있다. 따라서 정답은 (C)이다.

84 화자는 교통에 대해 무엇을 언급하는가?
(A) 천천히 움직이고 있다.
(B) 개선되고 있다.
(C) 정상적이다.
(D) 평소보다 낫다.

| 해설 | 'This has understandably created serious traffic issues throughout the city.'라는 화자의 말에서 다리의 폐쇄로 시내의 교통 상황이 심각해졌다는 점을 알 수 있다. 따라서 (A)가 정답이다.

85 청자들은 이다음에 무엇을 들을 것인가?
(A) 광고
(B) 최신 뉴스 속보
(C) 지역 뉴스
(D) 스포츠 뉴스

commercial 상업 광고

| 해설 | 뉴스의 마지막 부분에서 today's sports news를 전할 사람의 이름을 언급하고 있으므로 청자들이 듣게 될 것은 (D)의 '스포츠 뉴스'이다.

[86-88]

M I'm really proud of the way everybody in this room contributed to the conference we held here last weekend. Thanks to your efforts, it was a complete success. We had more than 250 people attend the conference, and the feedback we've received thus far has been unanimous. The attendees felt that the event was educational and well worth their time. As an added bonus, more than 30 of them registered for the seminar we're holding next month. So it's time for us to initiate our preparations for that event. How about taking a look at the handouts in front of you?

M 지난 주 이곳에서 열렸던 콘퍼런스에 헌신을 해 주신, 이 방에 계신 모든 분들이 너무나 자랑스럽습니다. 여러분들의 노력 덕분에, 콘퍼런스는 완전한 성공을 거두었습니다. 콘퍼런스에는 250명 이상의 사람들이 참석했고, 현재까지 우리가 받은 피드백은 모두 같은 내용이었습니다. 참가자들은 행사가 교육적이었으며 시간을 낼 만한 가치가 있다고 생각했습니다. 추가적으로, 그중 30명 이상은 다음 달에 열릴 세미나에 참가 신청을 했습니다. 따라서 이제 그 행사를 위한 준비를 시작해야 할 때입니다. 여러분 앞에 있는 유인물을 봐 주시겠습니까?

be proud of ~을 자랑스럽게 여기다 | **contribute** 기여하다, 헌신하다 | **thanks to** ~덕분에 | **effort** 노력 | **feedback** 반응, 의견, 피드백 | **unanimous** 만장일치의, 모두 의견이 같은 | **educational** 교육적인 | **worth** ~의 가치가 있는 | **register for** ~에 등록하다, ~을 신청하다 | **initiate** 시작하다 | **preparation** 준비 | **handout** 유인물 | **in front of** ~의 앞에

86 담화의 주된 목적은 무엇인가?
(A) 청자들에게 성과에 대한 축하를 하기 위해
(B) 청자들에게 열심히 일해야 한다는 점을 당부하기 위해
(C) 청자들이 충분히 열심히 일하지 않는다는 점을 비판하기 위해
(D) 청자들에게 몇몇 불만 사항에 대한 경고를 하기 위해

congratulate 축하하다 | **encourage** 고무시키다, 격려하다 | **criticize** 비판하다 | **warn** 경고하다

| 해설 | 담화의 첫 부분에서 화자는 '청자들을 자랑스럽게 생각한다'(I'm really proud of the way everybody in this room)라고 말한 후, 콘퍼런스의 성과에 대해 이야기하고 있다. 따라서 담화의 목적은 (A)로 볼 수 있다.

87 참가자들은 행사에 대해 무엇을 언급했는가?
(A) 그들은 행사 시간이 더 길어지기를 원했다.
(B) 그들은 행사에서 많은 것을 배웠다.
(C) 그들은 행사에 가격만한 가치가 있다고 생각했다.
(D) 그들은 연사들로부터 더 많은 피드백을 받고 싶어했다.

| 해설 | 콘퍼런스에 대한 참가자들의 평가는 담화 중반의 'The attendees felt that the event was educational and well worth their time.'이라는 문장에서 확인할 수 있다. 정답은 (B)이며, 참가비와 관련된 평가는 찾아볼 수 없으므로 (C)는 정답이 될 수 없다.

88 화자는 이다음에 무엇을 할 것 같은가?
(A) 청자들에게 양식을 작성하도록 시킨다
(B) 유인물을 나누어 준다
(C) 청자들에게 상을 수여한다
(D) 다가 올 세미나에 관해 이야기한다

| 해설 | 담화 후반부의 handouts(유인물)만 듣고 (B)를 정답으로 선택해서는 안 된다. 유인물은 이미 배포되어 있는 상황이다. 정답은 (D)인데, 화자는 담화의 후반부에서 '이제 다음 행사, 즉 세미나 준비를 할 시간이다'(it's time for us to initiate our preparations for that event)라고 말한다.

[89-91]

W I'd like to provide an update regarding the branch openings in Europe and Asia. Our stores in Europe are attracting large numbers of customers. They're performing according to our expectations. In fact, due to the revenue they're bringing in, we're considering opening several more stores on the continent later this year. On the other hand, our sales in Asia are much lower than we had hoped. We're not sure what's wrong since our products are popular in many Asian countries. On Monday, we hired an advertisement agency with expertise in Asian markets to improve our image there.

W 저는 유럽과 아시아에서 개설된 지점에 관한 소식을 알려 드리고자 합니다. 유럽의 매장은 많은 고객들을 유인하고 있습니다. 우리가 기대한 바대로 운영되고 있습니다. 사실, 그들이 거두어들이는 수입 때문에, 저희는 올해 후반기에 유럽 대륙에서 몇 개의 매장을 더 개설할 것을 고려하고 있습니다. 반면, 아시아에서의 매출은 기대했던 것보다 훨씬 낮습니다. 다수의 아시아 국가에서 우리 제품의 인기가 높기 때문에, 무엇이 문제인지 잘 모르겠습니다. 월요일에, 그곳에서의 우리 이미지를 향상시키기 위해서 우리는 아시아 시장에 관한 전문 지식을 갖추고 있는 광고 업체를 고용했습니다.

update 업데이트, 최신 정보 | **perform** 수행하다; 공연하다; 돌아가다 | **according to** ~에 따라 | **expectation** 예상, 기대 | **due to** ~ 때문에 | **revenue** 세수, 수입 | **continent** 대륙 | **advertisement agency** 광고 회사 | **expertise** 전문 지식

89 화자는 주로 무엇을 논의하고 있는가?
(A) 신규 매장들이 어떻게 운영되고 있는지
(B) 회사의 향후 계획
(C) 회사가 어디로 확장하고 있는지
(D) 가장 최근의 회사 수익

profit 이윤, 수익

| 해설 | 화자는 유럽과 아시아 매장의 상황을 서로 비교하면서 설명하고 있다. 따라서 담화의 주제는 (A)이다.

90 화자가 "They're performing according to our expectations"라고 말할 때 화자는 무엇을 의미하는가?
(A) 신제품들이 고객들에게 인기가 높다.
(B) 아시아 지점들은 운영이 잘 된다.
(C) 제품들이 모든 곳에서 잘 팔리고 있다.
(D) 유럽 내 매장에는 많은 고객들이 있다.

| 해설 | 주어진 문장은 '예상대로 잘 되고 있다'라는 뜻이다. 바로 앞 문장에서 '많은 고객들이 유럽 매장을 찾고 있다'고 했으므로 결국 주어진 문장을 통해 화자가 의미하는 바는 (D)가 된다.

91 이번 주에 회사는 무엇을 했는가?
(A) 내년 계획을 발표했다.
(B) 광고를 선보였다.
(C) 광고 회사를 고용했다.
(D) 마케팅 업체와의 계약을 취소했다.

announce 발표하다 | **commercial** 상업 광고 | **ad agency** 광고 회사 | **marketer** 마케팅 담당자, 마케팅 전문 업체

| 해설 | 담화의 마지막 문장, 'On Monday, we hired an advertisement agency with expertise in Asian markets to improve our image there.'에서 화자의 회사는 아시아 시장에서의 회사 이미지를 향상시키기 위해 월요일에 광고 업체를 고용했다는 점을 알 수 있다. 따라서 정답은 (C)이다.

[92-94]

W Good morning, Mr. Jackson. This is Cynthia Watson from the Two Towers Resort. We received your e-mail regarding your desire to book a double room with us. Unfortunately, the weekend you intend to stay with us is extremely busy because we're hosting a conference. As of this moment, there's only one room available to reserve. It's a junior suite, so it will cost a bit more than the room you requested. If you're interested in booking this room, please contact me as quickly as you can at 692-5768. I doubt this room will remain available for much longer.

W 안녕하세요, Jackson 씨. 저는 Two Towers 리조트의 Cynthia Watson입니다. 저희는 2인실을 예약하고 싶으시다는 귀하의 의향과 관련된 이메일을 받았습니다. 안타깝게도, 귀하께서 숙박하시고자 하는 주말은, 저희가 콘퍼런스를 주최할 예정이라, 객실을 구하기가 매우 어렵습니다. 현재 시간을 기준으로, 예약이 가능한 객실은 단 하나만 있습니다. 그 객실은 주니어 스위트이기 때문에, 귀하께서 요청하신 객실보다 약간 더 가격이 높을 것입니다. 이 객실을 예약하는 데 관심이 있으시면, 가능한 빨리 692-5768로 저에게 연락을 주십시오. 이 객실이 한참 후까지 계속해서 남아 있을 것으로 생각되지 않습니다.

desire 바람 | **book** 예약하다 | **double room** 2인실 | **intend to** ~할 의도가 다 | **extremely** 극도로, 매우 | **busy** 바쁜, 분주한; (방이) 사용 중인 | **host** 주최하다, 주관하다 | **as of** ~일자로 | **as ~ as one can** 가능한 ~하게 | **doubt** 의심하다

92 화자는 왜 Jackson 씨에게 전화를 걸었는가?
 (A) 예약을 취소하기 위해
 (B) 업그레이드를 해 주기 위해
 (C) 사과를 하기 위해
 (D) 제안을 하기 위해

apology 사과 | **suggestion** 제안, 제의

| 해설 | 화자는 '2인실'(double room)을 예약하려고 하는 고객에게 그 방은 예약이 불가능하다는 점을 설명한 후, '주니어 스위트'(junior suite)로 예약할 것을 권하고 있다. 따라서 정답은 (D)이다.

93 도표를 보아라. Jackson 씨는 얼마를 더 지불해야 하는가?
 (A) 20달러
 (B) 30달러
 (C) 40달러
 (D) 50달러

| 해설 | 원래 예약을 하려고 했던 2인실 요금은 1박에 130달러이고, 현재 예약이 가능한 객실인 주니어 스위트의 요금은 1박에 170달러이다. 따라서 두 금액의 차액인 (C)의 '40달러'가 정답이다.

94 화자는 왜 Jackson 씨에게 다시 전화를 달라고 이야기하는가?
 (A) 특가 상품이 오늘까지이다.
 (B) 곧 호텔에 남아 있는 방이 없을 것이다.
 (C) 그가 예약 신청서를 적절히 작성하지 않았다.
 (D) 언제 도착할 것인지 알려 주어야 한다는 점을 그가 잊었다.

| 해설 | 담화의 마지막 부분에서 화자는 '빨리 연락을 달라'고 당부한 후, 'I doubt this room will remain available for much longer.'라고 그 이유를 밝히고 있다. 따라서 (B)가 정답이다.

[95-97]

M Welcome to the Museum of National History. My name's Peter, and I'll be showing you some of the exhibits here today. First, I'd like to tell you about something that isn't covered on the tour. This morning, we opened a new exhibit featuring numerous items more than 300 years old. This exhibit provides a fascinating glimpse at life in colonial times, and you'll be sure to love it. It's in the west wing of the museum. You can purchase tickets for it at the booth beside the museum's front doors. Now, let's get started. If you'll look straight behind me, you can see the first exhibit.

M National History 박물관에 오신 것을 환영합니다. 제 이름은 Peter이고, 저는 오늘 이곳에서 여러분들께 몇몇 전시물들을 보여 드릴 것입니다. 먼저, 투어에 포함되어 있지 않은 사항에 대해 말씀을 드리고 싶습니다. 오늘 아침, 저희는 300년 이상 된 여러 전시품들을 주제로 한 새로운 전시를 시작했습니다. 이 전시는 식민지 시대의 삶에 대한 매혹적인 측면을 보여 주는데, 여러분들께서는 분명히 이를 좋아하시게 될 것입니다. 이는 박물관의 서쪽 건물에 있습니다. 그에 대한 티켓은 박물관의 정문 옆에 있는 부스에서 구입하실 수 있습니다. 자, 시작해 봅시다. 제 뒤쪽을 정면으로 바라보시면, 첫 번째 전시를 보실 수 있습니다.

exhibit 전시, 전시품 | **feature** ~을 특색으로 삼다 | **fascinating** 매혹적인 | **glimpse** 힐끗 봄 | **colonial times** 식민지 시대 | **wing** 날개; 부속 건물 | **booth** 부스

95 남자의 직업은 무엇인가?
 (A) 티켓 판매원
 (B) 가이드
 (C) 큐레이터
 (D) 번역가

| 해설 | 화자는 박물관에서 진행되고 있는 전시에 대해 설명한 후, 청자들을 데리고 박물관 관람을 시작하려고 하고 있다. 따라서 화자의 직업은 (B)의 '가이드'일 것이다. (B)의 '큐레이터'는 박물관이나 미술관의 전시, 운영, 홍보 등의 업무를 담당하는 직원으로, 큐레이터가 일반인을 대상으로 전시를 안내하는 경우는 거의 없다.

96 도표를 보아라. 방문객들은 어디에서 특별 전시 티켓을 구입할 수 있는가?
 (A) 1번 부스
 (B) 2번 부스
 (C) 3번 부스
 (D) 4번 부스

| 해설 | 담화 후반부의 'You can purchase tickets for it at the booth beside the museum's front doors.'가 정답의 단서이다. 정문 옆에 있는 부스에서 구입이 가능하다고 했으므로 정답은 (A)가 된다.

97 화자는 이다음에 무엇을 할 것인가?
 (A) 청자들에게 티켓을 준다
 (B) 전시에 대해 이야기한다
 (C) 팜플렛을 나누어 준다
 (D) 식민지 시대에 관한 전시를 관람한다

display 전시, 진열 | **hand out** 나누어 주다, 배포하다 | **pamphlet** 팜플렛

| 해설 | 화자의 마지막 말, 'If you'll look straight behind me, you can see the first exhibit.'을 통해 화자는 청자들에게 전시를 안내할 것이라는 점을 알 수 있다. 따라서 정답은 (B)이다. '식민지 시대에 관한 전시'는 특별 전시로, 투어에는 포함되어 있지 않은 사항이라는 점에 유의하도록 한다.

[98-100]

W All right, let's get this meeting started. Today, we received the figures from the first quarter, and they're somewhat worse than we had expected. So I'm going to discuss each type of item we sell starting with the worst-selling one first. However, before I do that, I'd like to introduce our newest employee to you. Her name is Sheila Roberts, and she's an assistant manager in the Marketing Department. Today is Sheila's first day on the job, so I imagine this is the first time most of you are meeting her. Sheila, how about standing up and taking a couple of moments to introduce yourself, please?

> W 좋아요, 이번 회의를 시작합시다. 오늘, 우리는 1분기의 수치들을 받았으며, 수치들은 예상과 달리 다소 좋지 않습니다. 그래서 저는 먼저 가장 적게 팔린 것을 시작으로 우리가 판매하고 있는 각각의 제품에 대해 논의하고자 합니다. 하지만, 그렇게 하기에 앞서, 여러분들께 신입 직원을 소개해 드리고 싶습니다. 그녀의 이름은 Sheila Roberts이며, 그녀는 마케팅부의 차장입니다. 오늘은 그녀가 처음으로 근무하는 날이기 때문에, 저는 여러분들과 그녀가 만난 것이 이번이 처음일 것으로 생각합니다. Sheila, 일어서서 자신을 소개하는 시간을 잠시 갖는 것이 어떨까요?

assistant manager 차장, 대리

98 도표를 보아라. 화자는 어떤 제품에 대해 처음으로 이야기할 것인가?
 (A) 전자레인지
 (B) 믹서
 (C) 가스 오븐
 (D) 토스터

| 해설 | 화자는 1분기 실적이 좋지 못하다는 점을 지적한 후, '제일 먼저 가장 많이 팔리지 않은 제품'(the worst-selling one first)에 대해 이야기하겠다고 말한다. 따라서 그래프상 가장 판매량이 적은 것을 찾으면 정답은 (C)의 '가스 오븐'이 된다.

99 Sheila Roberts는 누구인가?
 (A) 인턴 사원
 (B) 영업 사원
 (C) 회사의 대표 이사
 (D) 신입 직원

| 해설 | 화자는 Sheila Roberts를 '신입 직원'(our newest employee)이라고 소개한 후, '마케팅부의 차장'(assistant manager in the Marketing Department)이라고 소속 부서와 그 직위까지 알려 주고 있다. 정답은 (D)이다.

100 이다음에 어떤 일이 일어날 것인가?
 (A) 회의에서 한 사람이 다른 사람들에게 인사를 한다.
 (B) 그래프의 내용에 대해 논의가 이루어질 것이다.
 (C) 판매 촉진을 위한 제안이 있을 것이다.
 (D) 입사 지원자와의 면접이 실시될 것이다.

contents 내용물

| 해설 | 여자의 마지막 말, 'Sheila, how about standing up and taking a couple of moments to introduce yourself, please?'에서 담화 이후에는 Sheila라는 신입 직원이 자기 소개를 할 것이라는 점을 짐작할 수 있다. 따라서 (A)가 정답이다.

● **PART 5** p.46

101 조립 라인의 기계가 수리되었기 때문에 공장이 완전 가동되고 있다.
 (A) 가능성
 (B) 능력
 (C) 외관
 (D) 유사함

plant 공장 | **at full capacity** 전면 가동 중인, 전력으로 | **machinery** 기계류 | **assembly line** 조립 라인 | **availability** 유용성; 가능성 | **capacity** 능력, 수용력 | **resemblance** 비슷함, 유사함

| 해설 | '전력으로' 혹은 '전면 가동 중인'이라는 의미는 at full capacity로 나타낸다. 따라서 정답은 (B)이다.

102 제품의 적시 배송이 보장되기 위해서는, 구입 시에 결제가 이루어져야 합니다.
 (A) ~에 대하여
 (B) ~와 어울려
 (C) ~와 관련하여
 (D) ~하기 위해

in order to ~하기 위해 | **guarantee** 보장하다, 보증하다 | **timely** 시기 적절한 | **with respect to** ~에 대하여 | **in tune with** ~와 어울려 | **regarding** ~에 관하여

| 해설 | 종속절과 주절의 관계를 파악하면 정답을 쉽게 찾을 수 있다. '제때 배송이 이루어지기 위해서는 구입 시에 결제가 이루어져야 한다'는 의미가 완성되어야 하므로 정답은 '~하기 위해서'라는 의미의 (D)이다. 품사를 통해서도 정답을 찾을 수 있는데, (A), (B), (C) 다음에는 명사(구)가 와야 하므로 이들은 정답이 될 수 없다.

103 Wilson 꽃집은 고객 증가에 대응할 목적으로 2월 동안 영업 시간을 연장했다.
 (A) 수용하다
 (B) 숙소
 (C) 대응
 (D) 유순하게

extend 확장하다 | **operating hours** 운영 시간, 영업 시간 | **for the purpose of** ~을 목적으로 | **accommodate** 수용하다; (요구 등에) 부응하다 | **accommodation** 숙박, 거처 | **accommodatingly** 유순하게

| 해설 | 빈칸 앞의 of가 전치사이기 때문에 빈칸에는 명사나 명사구를 이끌 수 있고 동시에 빈칸 뒤의 the increase in customers를 목적어로 취할 수 있는 단어가 들어가야 한다. 이 두 가지 조건을 만족시키는 것은 동명사인 (C)의 accommodating이다.

104 Wellman 씨는, 이사회 위원 중 한 명인데, 신제품의 개발 상황에 관한 최신 정보를 제공받았다.
 (A) 주었다
 (B) 받았다
 (C) 받았다
 (D) 주었다

board of directors 이사회 | **give ~ an update** ~에게 최신 정보를 제공하다 | **process** 과정, 절차

| 해설 | one of the members of the board of directors가 Ms. Wellman과 동격이라는 점을 파악하면 이 문장은 수동태 문장이 되어야 한다는 점을 알 수 있다. 보기 중 Ms. Wellman을 주어로 삼으면서 수동태를 만들 수 있는 것은 (B)의 was 뿐이므로 정답은 (B)이다.

105 George Thacker는 Ellison 건설에 입사 지원을 했지만 경력 부족으로 불합격되었다.
 (A) 고용하다
 (B) 고려하다
 (C) 불합격시키다
 (D) 면접하다

due to ~ 때문에 | lack 부족, 결핍

| 해설 | 접속사 but과 due to lack of experience(경력 부족 때문에)라는 어구에 유의하면 빈칸에는 (C)의 rejected(거부하다, 불합격시키다)가 들어가야 한다.

106 펑크가 난 타이어를 교체하는데 승객들 자신이 버스 기사에게 도움을 주었다.
(A) 그들은
(B) 그들 자신이
(C) 그들의
(D) 그들을

offer 제공하다, 제의하다 | assist 돕다 | deflated 펑크가 난, 바람이 빠진

| 해설 | 문장 성분 중 빠져 있는 성분이 없으므로 빈칸에는 강조 용법의 재귀대명사가 들어가야 한다. 따라서 정답은 (B)의 themselves이다.

107 육류 가공 공장을 조사했던 조사관들은 시설 내부의 비위생적인 상태 때문에 공장주에게 벌금을 부과했다.
(A) 조사관
(B) 기자
(C) 조립공
(D) 정치인

inspector 조사관, 감독관 | fine 벌금을 부과하다 | on account of ~ 때문에 | unsanitary 비위생적인 | assembler 조립공 | politician 정치인

| 해설 | '벌금을 물릴 수 있는'(fined) 주체가 누구인지 생각해 보면 정답을 쉽게 유추할 수 있다. 정답은 '조사관'이라는 의미인 (A)의 Inspectors이다.

108 Hamilton 씨는 보이시의 콘퍼런스에 참석하기로 예정되어 있었지만 일정이 겹쳐서 갈 수가 없었다.
(A) 충돌
(B) 싸움
(C) 갈등을 겪는
(D) 대립하는

be supposed to ~하기로 예정되어 있다 | make it 도착하다, 오다 | scheduling conflict 일정 상의 충돌 | confliction 싸움

| 해설 | due to라는 전치사구로 인해 빈칸에는 명사가 들어가야 함을 알 수 있다. 보기 중에서 scheduling과 함께 '일정 상의 충돌'이라는 의미의 복합명사를 완성시킬 수 있는 것은 conflict(갈등, 충돌)이므로 정답은 (A)이다. 참고로 (B)의 confliction은 conflict의 구체적인 상태, 즉 '다툼'이나 '싸움'을 의미한다.

109 설문 조사에 응한 전체 고객 중 극소수만이 Shop Right의 가격이 너무 높다고 생각했다.
(A) 비율
(B) 변수
(C) 소수
(D) 조각

poll 투표하다, 여론 조사를 하다 | fraction 일부, 소수, 소량 | proportion 비율, 부분 | variable 변수; 가변적인

| 해설 | 문맥상 빈칸에는 '일부'라는 의미가 들어가야 하는데, 보기 중 (A), (C), (D)가 모두 '일부' 혹은 '부분'이라는 뜻으로 사용될 수 있으므로 상당한 주의를 기울여야 하는 문제이다. 여기에서 정답의 단서는 only에서 찾을 수 있는데, only의 수식을 받을 수 있는 것은 '소수', '소량'이라는 의미를 가진 (C)의 fraction 뿐이므로 정답은 (C)가 된다.

110 개업 당일날 밤에 식당이 너무나 분주했기 때문에 많은 식당 손님들은 자리에 앉기까지 한 시간 이상을 기다려야 했다.
(A) 따라서
(B) 때문에
(C) ~한 곳
(D) 만약 ~이라면

diner 식당 손님 | establishment 기관, 시설; 사업장

| 해설 | '식당이 분주했다'는 의미와 '사람들이 오래 기다려야 했다'라는 의미는 일종의 인과 관계로 묶일 수 있다. 따라서 정답은 '~이므로' 혹은 '~ 때문에'라는 의미를 지닌 (B)의 since이다.

111 기기에 중대한 결함이 생겨서 결코 수리될 수 없을 것처럼 보인다.
(A) 고장
(B) 고장이 난
(C) 고장
(D) 고장이 나는

as though 마치 ~인 것처럼 | suffer ~을 겪다 | malfunction 고장, 기능 불량

| 해설 | 빈칸에는 관사를 취하면서 major의 수식을 받을 수 있는 명사가 들어가야 한다. 따라서 정답은 (A), (C), 그리고 (D) 중에 하나인데, 관사 a 때문에 빈칸에는 복수형인 (C)는 들어갈 수 없다. 또한 동명사인 malfunctioning이 빈칸에 들어가기 위해서는 malfunctioning의 의미상 목적어가 있어야 하기 때문에 이 역시 정답이 될 수 없다. 따라서 정답은 (A)이다.

112 매장의 누군가가 도움을 주겠다는 제안을 하기 전까지 그 고객은 한 시간 이상 기다리고 있었다.
(A) 기다릴 것이다
(B) 기다리고 있다
(C) 기다리고 있었다
(D) 기다려 왔다

| 해설 | 종속절의 시제에 유의하여 정답을 찾도록 한다. before가 이끄는 부사절의 시제가 과거이므로 주절의 시제는 과거나 과거완료가 되어야 한다. 보기 중 여기에 해당되는 시제는 (C)의 had been waiting뿐이므로 (C)가 정답이다.

113 비록 7월에 지원서를 제출했지만, Erica는 아직까지 회사로부터 아무런 소식을 듣지 못하고 있다.
(A) 받다
(B) 승인하다
(C) 제출하다
(D) 응대하다

application 지원, 지원서 | firm 회사 | approve 승인하다 | respond 응대하다, 답장하다

| 해설 | although의 의미에 유의하면 정답을 쉽게 찾을 수 있다. '제출을 했음에도 불구하고 아무런 소식을 듣지 못했다'는 의미가 완성되어야 하기 때문에 정답은 '제출하다'라는 의미인 (C)의 submitted이다.

114 도서관 이용객들은 한 번에 최대 6권의 책을 2주 동안 빌리는 것이 허용된다.
(A) 기부자
(B) 이용객
(C) 쇼핑객
(D) 식당 손님

library patron 도서관 이용객 | permit 허락하다, 허가하다 | up to ~까지 | at a time 한 번에 | donor 기부자, 기증자 | diner 식당 손님

| 해설 | (B)의 patron은 '후원자'라는 의미로도 쓰이지만, '도서관 이용객'을 나타낼 때에도 사용될 수 있다.

115 고객의 불만 사항을 처리하는 일은 새로 온 인턴 사원에게 주어진 업무 중 하나이다.
(A) 처리하다
(B) 처리된

(C) 처리하다
(D) 처리하는 일

handle 다루다, 처리하다 | duty 임무 | intern 인턴 사원

| 해설 | 문장에 주어가 빠져 있으므로 빈칸에는 complaints by customers와 함께 명사구를 만들 수 있는 동명사가 들어가야 한다. 따라서 정답은 (D)의 Handling이다.

116 택배 기사가 택배를 들고 도착했을 때, 사무실에는 택배를 받았다는 서명을 해 줄 사람이 없었다.
(A) 싸다
(B) 열다
(C) 받다
(D) 서명하다

deliveryman 배달원, 택배 기사 | package 소포 | sign for ~을 받았다고 서명하다 | pack (짐을) 싸다, 꾸리다

| 해설 | '~을 받았다고 서명하다'라는 표현은 sign for로 나타낸다.

117 시상식에서 Trellis 씨는 자신에게 도움을 준 모든 직원들에게 감사를 표했다.
(A) 그녀는
(B) 그녀를
(C) 그들은
(D) 그들을

awards ceremony 시상식 | entire 전체의 | staff 직원 | assistance 도움, 원조 | provide 제공하다

| 해설 | 빈칸에 들어갈 알맞은 대명사를 묻는 문제이다. 문맥상 빈칸에는 Ms. Trellis를 가리키면서 동시에 provided의 목적어 역할을 할 수 있는 단어가 들어가야 한다. 따라서 정답은 (B)의 her이다. 참고로 빈칸 앞의 they는 her entire staff를 나타낸다.

118 양측간의 협상이 곧 완료될 것으로 보인다.
(A) 가까워지다
(B) 가까워질 것이다
(C) 가까워지고 있다
(D) 가까워지다

negotiation 협상 | side 측, 면 | near 가까워지다 | completion 완료, 완성

| 해설 | 내용상 '양측의 협상이 마무리에 이를 것이다'라는 의미를 전하고 있으므로 빈칸에는 가까운 미래의 의미를 나타내는 현재진행형 형태인 (C)의 are nearing이 들어가야 한다.

119 다음 몇 시간 동안 날씨가 개지 않는다면, 올해 회사의 야유회 행사는 실내로 옮겨질 것이다.
(A) ~하지 않는다면
(B) ~에도 불구하고
(C) 비록 ~이지만
(D) 따라서

clear up (날씨가) 개다 | outing 야유회 | indoors 실내에 | consequently 그 결과, 따라서

| 해설 | '날씨가 개지 않으면'이라는 부정의 의미 및 조건의 의미가 동시에 들어가야 자연스러운 문맥이 완성된다. 보기 중에서 이러한 두 가지 조건을 모두 충족시키는 것은 (A)의 Unless이다.

120 신차를 구입하려는 사람에게 시승을 하는 것은 흔한 행동이다.
(A) 테스트
(B) 테스트하는
(C) 테스트하는 사람
(D) 테스트된

test drive 시승, 시운전 | common 일반적인, 흔한

| 해설 | test drive(시승, 시운전)라는 복합 명사를 알고 있어야 문제를 풀 수 있다. 정답은 (A)의 test이다.

121 맨 위층에서 물이 새어서 한 사무실 내의 전자 기기들이 막대한 손상을 입었다.
(A) 부상
(B) 상처
(C) 손상
(D) 장애

leak 누수 | cause 일으키다, 야기하다 | electronic item 전자 제품 | impairment 장애

| 해설 | 언뜻 보기에 모든 보기들이 비슷한 의미를 가지고 있다고 생각할 수 있으나, 이 중 사물이나 재산에 가해진 '손해'를 의미할 수 있는 것은 (C)의 damage뿐이다. 나머지 보기들은 주로 사람이나 동물들을 수식할 때 쓰이는 단어들이다.

122 Leo 미술관의 현대 미술 전시회가 8월 2일부터 9월 14일까지 열릴 것이다.
(A) 열다
(B) 열리는
(C) 열릴 것이다
(D) 열리고 있다

exhibition 전시, 전시회 | hold 붙잡다; 열다, 개최하다 | from A to B A에서 B까지

| 해설 | 주어가 exhibition(전시회)이기 때문에, hold(열다, 개최하다)라는 동사가 쓰이기 위해서는 수동형이 되어야 한다. 보기 중 수동의 형식을 갖추고 있는 것은 (C)의 be held뿐이므로 (C)가 정답이다.

123 비가 많이 내린 결과, 그 지역의 여름 과일 수확량은 평년보다 훨씬 더 좋지 못할 것으로 예상된다.
(A) 몇몇의
(B) 매우
(C) 훨씬
(D) 그처럼

as a result of ~의 결과로 | rainy 비가 많이 오는 | harvest 수확 | than usual 평소보다, 평상시보다

| 해설 | '훨씬'이라는 의미로 비교급을 강조할 수 있는 표현은 much, even, still, less, by far, a lot 등이다. 따라서 보기 중 빈칸 다음의 poorer를 수식할 수 있는 것은 (C)의 much뿐이다. 참고로 최상급을 수식할 경우에는 very가 쓰인다.

124 그 박물관은 9월을 시작으로 고대 중국 유물 전시회를 개최할 것이다.
(A) 전시하다
(B) 전시회
(C) 전시하는
(D) 전시된

host 개최하다, 주최하다 | exhibition 전시회 | relics 유물 | ancient 고대의

| 해설 | 빈칸에는 host의 목적어 역할을 하는 동시에 전치사구인 of relics의 수식을 받을 수 있는 명사가 들어가야 한다. 보기 중 이러한 조건을 만족시키면서 '전시회'라는 의미를 나타내는 것은 (B)의 exhibition뿐이다. (A)의 exhibits를 명사로 생각하는 경우, 일단 이것이 복수 형태이기 때문에 (A)는 정답이 될 수 없고, 게다가 exhibit는 '전시품'이라는 의미이다.

125 건물 소유주들은 각층에 경사로 및 기타 시설들을 추가로 설치함으로써 장애인들이 보다 쉽게 건물을 이용할 수 있도록 만들었다.
(A) 접근할 수 있는

(B) 명백한
(C) 이용이 가능한
(D) 이용할 수 있는

handicapped-accessible 장애인이 이용할 수 있는, 장애인이 입장할 수 있는 | **add** 더하다, 추가하다 | **ramp** 경사로 | **approachable** 접근할 수 있는 | **apparent** 명백한

| 해설 | handicapped-accessible(장애인이 이용할 수 있는)이라는 표현을 알고 있어야 정답이 (C)임을 쉽게 알 수 있다. 참고로 이 문장은 5형식 문장인데, 여기에서 목적어 it은 the building을 가리킨다.

126 자격 요건을 갖춘 모든 분들은 연령, 성, 혹은 인종에 상관없이 그 직위에 지원하시기 바랍니다.
(A) ~에 관하여
(B) ~에 상관없이
(C) 간주된
(D) 간주하다

qualified 자격 요건을 갖춘, 자질이 있는 | **encourage** 권장하다, 장려하다 | **regardless of** ~에 상관없이 | **gender** 성 | **race** 인종 | **regard** 여기다, 간주하다

| 해설 | '~에 상관없이'라는 의미는 regardless of로 나타낸다. 따라서 정답은 (B)이다.

127 프로젝트에 너무나 많은 문제들이 있었기 때문에, 새로운 매니저가 임명되어 모든 것을 관리하게 되었다.
(A) 드러내다
(B) 구상하다
(C) 투자하다
(D) 임명하다

appoint 지명하다, 임명하다 | **reveal** 드러내다, 밝히다 | **conceive** (생각 등을) 마음에 품다, 구상하다 | **invest** 투자하다

| 해설 | 문맥상 '새로운 매니저가 임명되었다'라는 의미가 완성되어야 하므로 정답은 (D)의 appointed이다.

128 그 나라가 경제적으로 어려움을 겪고 있기는 하지만, Vertigo 주식회사의 매출은 역대 최고였다.
(A) 경제학
(B) 경제적인
(C) 경제학자
(D) 경제적으로

even though 비록 ~일 지라도 | **suffer** 고통을 겪다, 고생하다 | **have never been better** 더할 나위 없이 좋다, 최고이다

| 해설 | 이 문제에서 suffer는 '고통을 겪다'라는 의미의 자동사로 쓰이고 있다. 따라서 빈칸에는 suffer를 수식할 수 있는 부사인 (D)의 economically(경제적으로)가 들어가야 한다.

☑ **700점 넘기 포인트** 참고로, economy의 형용사형으로 economical과 economic이 있는데, economic은 '경제의'라는 의미를, economical은 '절약되는', '알뜰한'이라는 의미를 나타낸다.

129 Centerville 오케스트라의 야외 공연은 우천으로 인해 다음 주로 연기되었다.
(A) ~까지
(B) ~까지
(C) ~ 동안
(D) 아직도

outdoor 실외의, 야외의 | **postpone** 연기하다 | **due to** ~ 때문에

| 해설 | '~ 이후로 연기하다'라는 의미는 postpone과 until을 이용해서 나타낼 수 있다. 따라서 정답은 (B)이다.

130 시의회는 그 기업이 시내 중심가에 아파트를 건설하는 것을 허가해야 할 것인지, 불허해야 할 것인지에 관해 투표를 실시할 것이다.
(A) 허가하다
(B) 수여하다
(C) 합의하다
(D) 동의하다

city council 시의회 | **intend to** ~할 의도이다 | **vote** 투표하다 | **grant** 주다, 수여하다 | **consent** 합의하다, 동의하다

| 해설 | '투표'의 주제가 무엇일 지 생각해 보면 정답을 쉽게 찾을 수 있다. 정답은 '허가하다' 혹은 '허락하다'라는 의미를 갖는 (A)의 permit이다.

● **PART 6** p.50

[131-134]

Delmont 제지는 1878년부터 사업을 시작했습니다. 이 기간 동안, 저희는 전국에서 판매되고 있는 온갖 종류의 제지를 만들어 왔습니다. 저희는 올해 말까지 제지 생산량을 약 25% 증가시키기 위해 시설을 확장하고 있습니다. 확장이 끝나면, 제지 공장에 보다 많은 원료들이, 특히 종이 펄프가, 필요할 것입니다. 저희는 현재 공급업체의 입찰을 받고 있습니다. 저희가 필요로 하는 원료와 필요한 양에 관한 목록을 얻고 싶으시면, www.delmontpaper.com/supplies로 저희 웹사이트를 방문해 주십시오. 아셔야 할 모든 정보들을 그곳에서 찾으실 수 있습니다. 공급업체 선정을 위한 입찰에 관심이 있으신 분들은 850-3043으로 Peter Hopkins 씨에게 연락을 주십시오. 입찰 서류는 늦어도 10월 1일까지 제출되어야 합니다. 낙찰을 받은 업체와는 10월 10일이나 그 전후로 계약이 이루어질 것입니다. 신규 공급업체로 선정된 기업은 반드시 12월 중순 경에 공급 물품들을 납품하기 시작해야 합니다.

process 과정, 절차 | **facility** 시설 | **so that ~ can** ~하기 위하여 | **approximately** 대략 | **raw material** 원료 | **pulp** 펄프 | **mill** 제조소 | **bids** 입찰 | **B as well as A** A뿐만 아니라 B도 | **party** 당사자

131 (A) 디자인
(B) 확장
(C) 계획
(D) 융자

| 해설 | '생산량을 증가시키기 위해' 시설을 어떻게 해야 할지 생각해 보면 정답을 쉽게 찾을 수 있다. 정답은 '확장하다'라는 의미인 (B)의 expanding이다.

132 (A) 더 많은 정보를 얻기 위해 저희에게 전화를 주지는 마십시오.
(B) 아셔야 할 모든 정보들을 그곳에서 찾으실 수 있습니다.
(C) 공급업체는 저희에게 전화를 함으로써 필요한 원료에 대해 아실 수 있습니다.
(D) 입찰 절차는 11월에 종료될 것입니다.

| 해설 | 바로 앞 문장에서 필요한 정보는 웹사이트에서 확인할 수 있다고 설명했다. 따라서 그 이후에는 그에 대한 부연 설명이 이어지는 것이 가장 자연스러우므로 정답은 (B)가 된다.

133 (A) 낙찰을 받다
(B) 낙찰을 받은 업체
(C) 낙찰을 받은
(D) 낙찰을 받은 업체들

| 해설 | 빈칸에는 parties를 수식할 수 있는 형용사가 들어가야 한다. 따라서 형용사 역할을 할 수 있는 현재분사 형태의 (C)의 winning이 정답이다.

134 (A) 시작했다
(B) 시작했다
(C) 시작할 것이다
(D) 시작해야 한다

| 해설 | 동사 begin의 알맞은 형태를 묻는 질문이다. 12월이라는 '미래'에 대해 이야기하고 있으므로 (A)와 (B)는 정답이 될 수 없다. 또한 업체를 선정한 기업이 낙찰을 받을 업체가 해야 할 일을 알려 주고 있으므로 문맥상 (C)보다는 (D)가 보다 자연스러운 답이 된다.

[135-138]

12월 10일
친애하는 Thompson 씨께,

Savers' 은행에서 예금 계좌를 개설해 주신 점에 대해 감사를 드립니다. 저희는 고객들에게 35년 이상 양질의 서비스를 제공해 오고 있으며, 귀하에게도 똑같이 해 드릴 것입니다.
저희는 현재 귀하의 수표를 발행하고 있습니다. 늦어도 12월 15일까지는 받게 되실 것입니다. 수표로 상품이나 서비스를 구매하시는 경우에는 시내 대부분의 장소에서 사진이 들어 있는 신분증을 제출해 달라는 요청을 받게 될 것이라는 점을 유념해 주십시오. 보통의 경우, 대부분의 상점에서 운전 면허증이 받아들여 질 것으로 생각됩니다. 또한, 한도가 초과된 계좌로 수표를 끊으시는 경우에는 40달러의 수수료가 부과됩니다.
계좌에 관해 질문이나 하고 싶으신 말씀이 있는 경우에는 주저하지 마시고 언제라도 808-4243으로 저희 고객 서비스 담당 직원에게 연락을 주십시오. 귀하와 상호 이익이 되는 관계를 오랫동안 유지하고 싶습니다.

Carla Hampton 드림
Savers' 은행 부사장

checking account 예금 계좌 | **provide A with B** A에게 B를 제공하다 | **check** 수표 | **no later than** 늦어도 ~까지 | **note** 주목하다 | **fee** 요금, 수수료 | **overdrawn** 초과 인출된 | **feel free to** 자유롭게 ~하다, 마음껏 ~하다 | **regarding** ~에 관하여 | **look forward to** ~을 고대하다 | **mutually** 상호적으로, 서로

135 (A) 존경하다
(B) 요구하다
(C) 기다리다
(D) 의도하다

| 해설 | '귀하에게도 똑같은 서비스를 제공해 주겠다'는 일종의 의지를 나타내고 있으므로 정답은 (D)의 intend(의도하다)이다.

136 (A) ~으로부터
(B) ~ 이내에
(C) ~ 보다
(D) ~까지

| 해설 | '늦어도 ~까지'라는 표현은 no later than으로 나타낸다. 따라서 정답은 (C)이다.

137 (A) 예를 들어, 귀하의 이름이 들어 있는 전기 요금 청구서가 받아들여질 것입니다.
(B) 이러한 사업장에서 계산을 하기 위해서는, 저희에게 전화를 주셔서 더 많은 정보를 얻으십시오.
(C) 지급을 받기 위해서는, 적합한 신분증을 가지고 있어야 한다는 점을 명심하십시오.
(D) 대부분의 경우, 상점에서 운전 면허증이 받아들여 질 것으로 생각됩니다.

| 해설 | 바로 앞 문장에서 '신분증이 필요할 수도 있다'는 점을 상기시키고 있다. 따라서 구체적인 신분증의 종류를 언급하고 있는 (D)가 빈칸에 들어가는 것이 가장 자연스럽다.

electricity bill 전기 요금 청구서 | **make payments to** ~에게 지불하다 | **get paid** 지급을 받다 | **identification** 신원 확인, 신분증 | **vendor** 행상인, 노점상

138 (A) 이익이 되는
(B) 명백한
(C) 각각의
(D) 의심스러운

| 해설 | mutually라는 부사가 빈칸 앞에 있다는 점을 감안하면 (A)의 beneficial(이익이 되는)이 정답임을 알 수 있다.

apparent 명백한 | **respective** 각각의 | **suspicious** 의심스러운

[139-142]

자원봉사자 모집

Greenbrier 주민 센터에서 여름 동안 일을 하실 자원봉사자들을 찾고 있습니다. 저희가 제공하려고 하는 몇몇 수업들을 맡아 주실 분들이 필요하며, 안내 데스크에서 일하실 분도 필요합니다. 시간이 있으시고 회화, 공예, 자수, 그리고 재봉 수업을 맡으실 능력이 있는 분들이 절실히 필요합니다. 스포츠 팀을 지도해 주실 분들이나 심판을 봐 주실 분도 필요합니다. 더 많은 정보를 얻기 위해서는 382-8594로 Mary Ashford에게 전화를 주십시오.
Greenbrier 주민 센터의 자원봉사자들은 시간에 대한 어떠한 금전적인 보상도 받지 못하지만, 다른 방법으로 보상을 받게 될 것입니다. 일주일에 10시간 이상 자원봉사를 한 사람은 1년 회원비의 50%를 할인 받게 될 것입니다. 매주 20시간 이상 자원 봉사를 한 사람은 연간 회원권을 무료로 받게 될 것입니다.
Greenbrier 주민 센터의 자원봉사자가 되어 주십시오. 약간의 시간을 내 주셔서 지역 사회의 주민들의 삶을 향상시킬 수 있도록 도와 주십시오.

volunteer 자원봉사자 | **arts and crafts** 공예 | **needlepoint** 자수 | **sewing** 재봉, 바느질 | **compensation** 보상 | **reward** 보상하다, 보답하다 | **resident** 주민, 거주자 | **community** 지역 사회, 커뮤니티

139 (A) 그들은
(B) 그들을
(C) 이것들
(D) ~한 사람들

| 해설 | those가 수식어나 관계대명사와 함께 쓰이면 '~한 사람들'이라는 뜻을 나타낸다. 여기에서도 빈칸 뒤의 전치사구를 고려하면 (D)의 Those가 빈칸에 들어가야 한다. 보기 중 나머지 대명사들은 그와 같은 수식어의 수식을 받지 못한다.

140 (A) 귀하께서는 저희와 함께 보낸 시간에 대해 후한 보상을 받게 될 것입니다.
(B) 스포츠 팀을 지도해 주실 분들이나 심판을 봐 주실 분들도 필요합니다.
(C) 또한 누군가가 최근에 사임하신 Ashford 씨를 대체해 주시기를 바랍니다.
(D) 이번 여름에는 공예 수업이 진행되지 않을 것입니다.

coach 코치; 지도하다 | **act as** ~으로 활동하다 | **resign** 사임하다 | **referee** 심판

| 해설 | 앞 문장에서 구체적으로 필요한 사람들이 거론되고 있으므로 이와 가장 자연스럽게 연결될 수 있는 (B)가 빈칸에 들어가야 한다. 공고의 첫 번째 단락과 두 번째 단락을 통해 (A)와 (D)는 사실과 맞지 않는 내용이라는 점을 알 수 있으며, (C)의 Ashford 씨는 공고와 관련해 문의 전화를 받는 주민 센터 직원으로 소개되고 있으므로 이 역시 정답이 될 수 없다.

141 (A) 금융
(B) 금전적인
(C) 융자
(D) 금융업자

| 해설 | 빈칸에는 명사 compensation(보상)을 가장 자연스럽게 수식할 수 있는 형용사가 들어가야 한다. 따라서 정답은 (B)의 financial이다. (C)의 financing을 finance(자금을 조달하다)의 형용사형으로 볼 수도 있지만, 이는 의미상 compensation과 어울리지 않으므로 (C)는 오답이다.

142 (A) 향상시키다
(B) 기부하다
(C) 헌신하다
(D) 접근하다

| 해설 | 보기 중에서 their lives를 목적어로 받을 수 있는 동사는 (A)의 improve(향상시키다)뿐이다.

donate 기부하다, 기증하다 | **dedicate** 헌신하다 | **approach** 접근하다, 다가가다

[143-146]

받는 사람: 회계부 전 직원
보낸 사람: 회계부 이사 Darren Smith
제목: 구조 조정
날짜: 11월 4일

지난 2주 동안, 회계부 직원 중 세 명이 다른 회사에 입사하기 위해 퇴사를 했습니다. 안타깝게도, 인사부는 그러한 자리 중 단 한 자리만 신규 직원으로 충원을 하겠다는 결정을 내렸습니다. 그 결과, 우리는 모두 Jeb Marconi와 Jenna Wilkins가 했던 일을 처리하기 위해 추가적인 업무를 떠맡게 될 것입니다.
우리는 11월 6일 금요일에 이러한 문제를 논의하기 위해 직원 회의를 하게 될 것입니다. 오전 9시에 시작해서 모든 문제를 다룬 후에 회의가 끝날 것입니다. 저는 최소 2시간 동안 진행될 것으로 예상합니다. 회의 참석은 의무이기 때문에, 그 시간에 예정되어 있는 다른 계획이나 약속은 모두 취소하시기 바랍니다. 이번 문제에 대해서 제안할 것이 있으면 주저하지 마시고 회의에서 언급해 주십시오. 저는 업무 부담을 과도하게 만들지 않고 어떻게 추가 업무를 맡을 수 있을지에 대해 모든 사람들의 아이디어를 듣고자 합니다.

take on ~을 떠맡다 | **additional** 추가적인 | **duty** 임무 | **used to** ~하곤 했다 | **attendance** 출석 | **mandatory** 강제적인, 의무적인 | **mention** 언급하다 | **assume** 가정하다; 맡다 | **workload** 업무량

143 (A) 전근하다
(B) 변경하다
(C) 보류하다
(D) 사임하다

alter 변경하다 | **suspend** 매달다; 보류하다

| 해설 | '다른 곳에서 일하기 위해' 현재의 '일자리'(their positions)를 어떻게 했을지 생각해 보면 정답이 (D)라는 사실을 쉽게 알 수 있다. 이후에도 퇴사한 사람들의 업무 분담 이야기가 회람의 주제가 되고 있다.

144 (A) 채우고 있다
(B) 채울 것이다
(C) 채워졌다
(D) 채워질 것이다

| 해설 | 동사 fill의 알맞은 형태를 묻는 문제이다. 주어가 only one of those positions이므로 수동형의 문장이 완성되어야 하며, 아직 충원이 된 것은 아니기 때문에 미래시제가 오는 것이 자연스럽다. 따라서 이 두 가지 조건을 모두 만족시키는 (D)의 will be filled가 정답이다.

145 (A) 저는 최소 2시간 동안 진행될 것으로 예상합니다.
(B) 회의의 안건은 아직 정해지지 않았습니다.
(C) 시간이 된다면 회의에 참석해 주시기 바랍니다.
(D) 회의에서 말을 할 사람은 저 혼자가 될 것입니다.

| 해설 | 바로 앞에서 회의의 시작 시각과 종료 시각에 대해 언급하고 있으므로 이에 대해 자신이 예상하고 있는 회의 시간을 밝힌 (A)가 빈칸에 들어가는 것이 가장 자연스럽다. 참고로 회람의 내용을 통해 (B), (C), (D)는 모두 사실이 아니라는 점을 알 수 있다.

146 (A) 일정
(B) 업무 부담
(C) 약속
(D) 일

| 해설 | make의 목적보어로 사용된 heavy와 자연스럽게 어울릴 수 있는 명사는 (B)의 workloads(업무 부담, 업무량)뿐이다.

● PART 7 p.54

[147-148]

하와이에서 인사드립니다!

시내 최고의 하와이안 레스토랑인 Ono가 기념 행사를 열 예정입니다. 새로 온 헤드 셰프인 Hanale Akoni가 저희의 메뉴 전체를 조정하여 곧 태평양 전체에서 가장 훌륭한 진미를 준비해 드릴 것입니다. 새롭게 선보이는 메뉴를 여러분과 함께 나누기 위해, 저희는 놀라운 할인 메뉴를 선보일 것입니다. 타로 칩과 토마토, 양파, 후추, 코코넛, 그리고 바다 소금으로 만들어진 하와이안 살사로 구성된 맛있는 애피타이저와 함께 식사를 시작하십시오. 그런 다음 청새치 바비큐나 당면을 곁들인 칼루아 돼지 고기로 메인 요리를 맛보십시오. 식사의 마무리는 말라사다 디저트, 즉 설탕으로 덮인 하와이안 도넛으로 하십시오. 이러한 메뉴는 단 22달러라는 저렴한 가격으로 제공될 것입니다. 하지만 이번 세일은 이 달 말까지만 진행되기 때문에 서두르십시오.

celebration 기념 행사 | **revise** 수정하다, 개정하다 | **delicacy** 별미, 진미 | **remarkable** 주목할 만한 | **appetizer** 애피타이저, 전채 요리 | **entrée** 앙트레, 메인 요리 | **blue marlin** 청새치 | **long rice** 당면 | **coated with** ~으로 덮인, ~으로 싸인

147 식당은 왜 특별 세일을 실시할 것인가?
(A) 개업을 할 것이다.
(B) 식당에 새로운 주인이 들어 왔다.
(C) 10주년을 기념할 것이다.
(D) 제공되는 음식이 변경되었다.

grand opening 개장, 개업 | **celebrate** 경축하다, 기념하다 | **anniversary** 기념일

| 해설 | 광고에는 Ono라는 식당이 새로운 헤드 셰프를 영입해서 그가 '전체 메뉴를 손본 후'(has revised our entire menu) 특별 세일을 실시할 것이라고 광고하고 있다. 따라서 새로운 주방장의 영입에 따른 새로운 메뉴 출시가

세일의 원인이므로 정답은 (D)가 된다.

148 제공될 식사의 일부로 언급되지 않은 것은 무엇인가?
(A) 메인 요리
(B) 샐러드
(C) 애피타이저
(D) 디저트

| 해설 | 애피타이저, 메인 요리, 그리고 디저트가 순서대로 소개되고 있으나, (B)의 '샐러드'는 언급된 바 없으므로 (B)가 정답이다. 참고로 광고에서 사용된 salsa(살사)나 malasada(말라사다)를 salad로 잘못 읽으면 정답을 놓칠 수 있으니 주의해야 한다.

[149-150]

Cooper, Bruce   4:15 P.M.
입찰 과정이 끝났어요. 앞으로 2분 정도 지난 후에 그들이 결정을 내릴 거예요.

Irwin, Catherine   4:17 P.M.
우리가 일을 땄으면 좋겠군요.

Cooper, Bruce   4:25 P.M.
믿을 수가 없어요. 그들이 Tyler 프로젝트에 다른 모든 사람들을 제치고 우리가 제시한 금액을 선택했어요.

Irwin, Catherine   4:26 P.M.
축하해요. 당신이 해낼 줄 알았어요.

Cooper, Bruce   4:28 P.M.
이번 건은 우리가 지난 3년 동안 성사시키려고 힘써왔던 계약이에요.

Irwin, Catherine   4:30 P.M.
곧 정말로 바빠질 것 같군요. 사무실로 몇 시에 돌아올 건가요? 우리가 다음에 무엇을 해야 할지 논의하기 위해 제가 팀을 소집해 둘까요?

Cooper, Bruce   4:34 P.M.
좋은 생각이에요. 저는 5시 30분에 돌아갈 거예요. 우리는 계약서의 세부 사항들을 검토하고 어떤 일이 진행되어야 하는지에 관해 간략히 이야기할 수 있을 거예요.

bidding 입찰 | **land a job** 일을 얻다 | **bid** 응찰, 호가 | **assemble** 모으다, 조립하다 | **so that ~ can** ~하기 위해 | **specifics** 세부 사항 | **in brief** 간략히, 짧게

149 오후 4시 28분에, Cooper 씨는 왜 "This is the kind of contract we've been trying to get for the past three years"라고 썼는가?
(A) 프로젝트에 관해 Irwin 씨가 한 일을 축하하기 위해
(B) 거래를 성사시켰다는 점에 대한 기쁨을 표현하기 위해
(C) 회사가 곧 이윤을 낼 것이라는 점을 말하기 위해
(D) 지난 3년이 얼마나 힘들었는지를 언급하기 위해

award 수여하다 | **turn a profit** 이익을 내다

| 해설 | 계약을 성사시켜서 축하한다는 상대방의 말에 대한 답변이다. Cooper 씨는 주어진 문장을 통해 계약 성사에 대한 기쁨을 표현하고 있으므로 정답은 (B)가 된다. 참고로 (D)는 '지난 3년이 전체적으로 힘들었다'의 의미로, '3년 동안 노력했다'는 표현을 '3년 동안 힘들었다'는 뜻으로 받아들이기에는 무리가 있다.

150 5시 30분경에 어떤 일이 일어날 것인가?
(A) 계약서에 서명이 이루어질 것이다.
(B) 입찰 가격이 정해질 것이다.
(C) 업무가 주어질 것이다.
(D) 회의가 열릴 것이다.

| 해설 | 질문의 핵심어구인 around 5:30가 언급되고 있는 부분을 지문에서 찾으면 정답을 쉽게 찾을 수 있다. 지문의 맨 마지막 부분에 Cooper 씨는 5시 30분에 사무실로 되돌아 갈 것이라고 한 후, 이어서 'We can go over the specifics of the contract and talk in brief about what needs to be done.'이라고 말한다. 따라서 5시 30분경에는 (D)의 '회의가 이루어질 것'임을 짐작할 수 있다.

[151-152]

받는 사람: 전 직원
보낸 사람: Melissa Jenkins
날짜: 4월 10일
제목: 구조 조정

회사에서 영업부, 마케팅부, 그리고 회계부와 관련된 대규모 구조 조정을 실시할 것이라는 점을 알려 드립니다. 영업부와 마케팅부는 하나의 단일 부서로 통합되어 무역부로 불리게 될 것입니다. 현재 영업부 부장인 George Jenkins가 이 부서의 수장을 맡게 될 것입니다. 또한, 회계부는 25% 축소될 것입니다. 이 세 부서의 전 직원들은 이번 주 금요일 오전에 이곳에서의 향후 지위를 통보받게 될 것입니다. (여러분 중 일부는 해고되지만, 승진이나 이동을 하는 사람도 있을 것입니다.) 모든 변화는 5월 1일부로 효력을 갖습니다. 우리는 회사의 운영을 효율화하고 장래의 수익을 확보하기 위해 이러한 변화들을 이행시킬 것입니다. 보다 군더더기 없는, 하지만 수익성은 높은 회사로서 현재의 경기 침체로부터 빠져 나오기 위해, 이처럼 어려운 시기에는 모두가 힘을 모았으면 좋겠습니다.

restructuring 구조 조정 | **undergo** 겪다 | **involving** ~와 관련된 | **combine** 합치다 | **take over** 인수하다, 인계하다 | **downsize** 줄이다, 축소하다 | **notify** 통보하다 | **status** 지위 | **go into effect** 효력을 발휘하다 | **implement** 실행하다, 이행하다 | **streamline** 효율화하다 | **profitability** 수익성 | **pull together** 협력하다, 힘을 합치다 | **emerge** 나타나다, 출현하다 | **recession** 경기 침체 | **lean** 군살이 없는

151 회람에 따르면, 어떤 일이 일어날 것인가?
(A) 새로운 부서가 만들어질 것이다.
(B) George Jenkins가 대표 이사가 될 것이다.
(C) 한 부서의 모든 직원들이 해고될 것이다.
(D) 회사는 직원의 25%를 정리 해고할 것이다.

fire 해고하다 | **lay off** 해고하다 | **workforce** 노동력

| 해설 | 회람에서는 구조 조정에 대한 소식을 전한 후, 구체적인 구조 조정 조치에 대해 이야기하고 있다. 영업부와 마케팅부가 '무역부'(Commerce Department)로 통합된다고 했으므로 (A)가 정답이다. (B)의 George Jenkins는 무역부의 부장이 될 인물이며, 부서 전체의 직원이 해고된다는 언급 역시 찾아볼 수 없으므로 (C) 역시 정답이 아니다. '회계부가 25% 축소될 것이다'는 언급이 있기는 하지만, 이것이 '전체 직원의 25%를 감원하겠다'는 뜻은 아니므로 (D) 또한 오답이다.

152 [1], [2], [3], 그리고 [4]로 표시된 위치 중에 다음 문장이 들어가기에 가장 알맞은 곳은 어디인가?

"여러분 중 일부는 해고되지만, 승진이나 이동을 하는 사람도 있을 것입니다."

(A) [1]
(B) [2]
(C) [3]
(D) [4]

| 해설 | '해고', '승진', '자리 이동'은 모두 future status(앞으로의 지위)와 직접적으로 연관된 표현들이다. 따라서 주어진 문장은 (C)의 [3]에 들어가야 가장 자연스러운 문맥이 완성된다.

[153-155]

Falcon 항공
일정표

승객 성명: Naomi Strauss   예약 코드: ERE6095

출발지	항공편	좌석	출발 시간	도착지	도착 시간
취리히	FA394	이코노미	2:15 P.M.	바르셀로나	4:05 P.M.
바르셀로나	FA211	이코노미	10:30 A.M.	파리	12:25 P.M.
파리	FA95	비즈니스	4:20 P.M.	코펜하겐	6:10 P.M.
코펜하겐	FA575	이코노미	7:10 P.M.	취리히	8:50 P.M.

이 문서를 출력하셔서 탑승 수속대에 제시해 주십시오. 2개의 가방을 부치실 수 있는데, 이들의 무게는 총 20킬로그램까지입니다. 추가로 부치셔야 할 가방이 있는 경우에는, 각각에 대해 50유로의 요금이 부과될 것입니다. 무게 허용량을 초과하는 경우에는, 킬로그램당 7유로를 추가적으로 지불하셔야 합니다.

이 티켓은 티켓에 그 이름이 적혀 있는 승객에 의해서만 사용될 수 있습니다. 양도될 수 없습니다. 이것은 환불이 되지 않는 티켓이지만, 금전적인 불이익 없이 1회 변경이 가능합니다.

document 문서 | **check-in counter** 탑승 수속대 | **weigh** 무게가 나가다 | **up to** ~까지 | **exceed** 초과하다 | **allowance** 허용량 | **transfer** 옮기다, 이동하다; 이전하다 | **nonrefundable** 환불이 되지 않는 | **penalty** 처벌

153 어떤 비행기편이 오전에 출발하는가?

(A) FA95
(B) FA211
(C) FA394
(D) FA576

| 해설 | 표에서 출발 시간 항목을 살펴보면 오전에 출발하는 항공편은 10시 30분에 출발하는 (B)의 FA211뿐임을 알 수 있다.

154 승객은 몇 킬로그램의 화물을 무료로 부칠 수 있는가?

(A) 7킬로그램
(B) 20킬로그램
(C) 40킬로그램
(D) 50킬로그램

| 해설 | 'You may check in 2 bags weighing up to a total of 20 kilograms.'라는 문장을 통해 무료로 부칠 수 있는 가방의 개수는 두 개이며, 이들의 총 무게는 20킬로그램을 넘지 말아야 한다는 사실을 알 수 있다. 따라서 정답은 (B)이다.

155 티켓에 의하면, 어떤 진술이 사실인가?

(A) 승객은 모든 항공편에서 동일한 선실에 앉게 될 것이다.
(B) 승객은 다른 사람과 함께 여행할 것이다.
(C) 승객은 티켓으로 항공편을 변경할 수 있다.
(D) 승객은 티켓에 대해 전액 환불을 받을 수 있다.

cabin 객실, 선실 | **full refund** 전액 환불

| 해설 | FA95 항공편에서는 다른 경우와 달리 비즈니스석을 이용할 것이므로 (A)는 사실이 아니며, (B)의 내용은 지문에서 전혀 언급된 바 없는 사항이다. 정답은 (C)인데, 맨 마지막 부분의 it may be changed 1 time with no financial penalty(금전적인 불이익 없이 1회 변경이 가능하다)라는 부분에서 이를 확인할 수 있다. 티켓의 종류가 nonrefundable ticket(환불이 불가능한 티켓)이라고 했으므로 (D) 역시 오답이다.

[156-158]

Whitman 사의 Safety Pro 카시트를 구입해 주셔서 고맙습니다. 카시트는 적절하게 설치되었을 때만 아이들을 보호할 수 있으니, 아래 설명을 주의 깊게 읽으시고 따라 주시기 바랍니다.

* 이 카시트를 차량 앞 좌석에 설치하지 마십시오. 뒷좌석에만 설치되도록 고안되었습니다.
* 아이의 몸무게가 10킬로그램 미만이든가 혹은 월령이 18개월 미만인 경우, 카시트는 뒤쪽을 바라보고 있어야 합니다. 18개월 이상인 아이와 몸무게가 10킬로그램 이상 나가는 아이는 모두 앞쪽을 바라보고 있는 시트에 앉을 수 있습니다.
* 꼬임이 없는지 확인하면서 벨트가 지나가는 통로로 안전벨트를 통과시켜 주십시오. 그런 다음, 안전벨트를 채우십시오.
* 안전벨트를 조여서 카시트를 안전하게 장착시키십시오. 옆으로 흔들리면 카시트의 효과가 감소됩니다.
* 아이를 카시트에 앉히신 후 스트랩을 조정하여 아이가 시트 안에 편안히 있도록 해 주십시오. 아이가 카시트에 앉아 이동 중일 때에는 재킷을 입지 말아야 합니다.

단계별 설명이 들어 있는 동영상을 포함하여 보다 많은 정보를 원하시면 저희 웹사이트인 www.safetyprocarseat.com을 방문해 주십시오. Safety Pro 카시트와 관련된 질문이 있으신 경우에는 수신자 부담 전화, 1-888-555-4938로 연락을 주셔도 좋습니다.

protect 보호하다 | **properly** 적절하게, 적합하게 | **instruction** 설명, 지시 | **install** 설치하다 | **rear** 뒤쪽 | **forward** 앞으로 | **path** 길 | **twist** 꼬임, 비틀기 | **lock** 잠그다 | **in place** 제자리에 | **tightly** 단단히, 꽉 | **side-to-side** 좌우로의, 옆으로의 | **effectiveness** 유효성, 효과 | **adjust** 조정하다 | **strap** 스트랩, 끈 | **snugly** 편안하게, 아늑하게 | **step-by-step** 단계적인

156 이 설명은 어디에서 찾아볼 수 있을 것 같은가?

(A) 웹사이트에서
(B) 사용설명서에서
(C) 신문에서
(D) 편지에서

| 해설 | 지문의 시작 부분에서 이 지문은 카시트에 포함되어 있는 카시트 사용 설명서임을 알 수 있다. 이후에도 카시트 장착법 및 주의 사항 등에 대해 안내하고 있으므로 지문의 출처는 (B)로 볼 수 있다.

157 설명에 따르면 사실이 아닌 것은 무엇인가?

(A) 아이는 시트에서 좌우로 움직일 수 있어야 한다.
(B) 시트에 앉아 있는 아이가 재킷을 입는 것은 용인되지 않는다.
(C) 7킬로그램의 몸무게가 나가는 아이는 뒤쪽을 바라 보아야 한다.
(D) 안전벨트를 체결할 때에는 꼬임이 없어야 한다.

| 해설 | (B)는 다섯 번째 항목에서, (C)는 두 번째 항목에서, (D)는 세 번째 항목에서 언급되어 있다. 시트가 좌우로 움직이면 안 된다는 내용은 찾아볼 수 있지만, (A)의 내용은 전혀 언급된 바가 없다.

158 카시트 설치 동영상을 확인하기 위해서는 무엇을 해야 하는가?

(A) 전화 번호로 전화를 한다
(B) 비디오테이프를 시청한다
(C) 웹사이트를 방문한다
(D) 문자 메시지를 보낸다

| 해설 | 후반부의 'For more information, including a video with step-by-step instructions, please visit our Web site at www.safetyprocarseat.com.'이라는 문장에서 동영상 등의 정보는 웹사이트에서 얻을 수 있다고 나와 있다. 따라서 (C)가 정답이다.

[159-161]

받는 사람: James Walker 〈jwalker@ssuncorp.com〉
보낸 사람: Helen Trent 〈htrent@westing.com〉
제목: 수리 작업
날짜: 6월 16일

친애하는 Walker 씨께,

저는 지난 주에 귀사의 팀이 본사의 에어컨 시스템을 수리한 것과 관련하여 이메일을 작성하고 있습니다. 목요일에 작업이 끝난 이후로, 저는 에어컨에서 나오는 과도한 소음에 관해 직원들로부터 몇몇 불만 사항을 받았습니다. 수리공들이 떠난 후에야 문제가 발생했기 때문에, 저는 소음이 에어컨 작업과 관련이 있다고 생각합니다. 귀하께서도 분명 이해하시겠지만, 높은 수준의 소음은 모든 사람들로 하여금 일에 집중하는 것을 어렵게 만들고 있으며, 그렇기 때문에 저희는 에어컨을 꺼야만 합니다. 당연하게도, 모두가 계속되는 무더위로 심한 더위를 느끼고 있으므로, 저희는 에어컨을 가동시켜야 할 필요가 있습니다. 계약서에 따라, 귀사는 귀사가 실시한 모든 작업을 보증하기 때문에, 저는 귀사의 수리공들이 가능한 빨리 저희 회사로 다시 와야 한다고 요청드립니다. 그것이 언제 가능할지 제게 알려 주시겠습니까? 곧 귀하로부터 연락을 받게 되기를 고대하겠습니다.

Helen Trent 드림
Westing 사

with regard to ~와 관련해서 | main office 본사 | firm 회사 | air conditioning system 에어컨 | excessive 과도한, 초과적인 | assume 가정하다 | have something to do with ~와 관계가 있다 | concentrate on ~에 집중하다 | ongoing 진행 중인 | heatwave 혹서, 무더위 | in need of ~가 필요한 | as per ~에 따라

159 Trent 씨는 왜 Walker 씨에게 글을 썼는가?
(A) 이루어진 작업에 대해 칭찬하기 위해
(B) 자신에게 청구서를 보내 달라고 요청하기 위해
(C) 문제에 관해 알리기 위해
(D) 날씨에 대해 불평하기 위해

| 해설 | Trent 씨는 에어컨 수리 작업 이후 발생한 소음 문제를 수리 업체의 직원인 Walker 씨에게 알리고 있다. 따라서 그녀가 이메일을 작성한 이유는 (C)로 볼 수 있다.

160 7줄의 "concentrate"라는 단어와 그 의미가 가장 유사한 것은?
(A) 결정하다
(B) 집중하다
(C) 연습하다
(D) 강조하다

| 해설 | concentrate는 '집중하다'라는 뜻이므로 (B)의 focus가 정답이다. 참고로 두 동사 모두 전치사 on과 결합되어 사용되는 경우가 많다.

161 Trent 씨는 Walker 씨에게 무엇을 하라고 요청하는가?
(A) 에어컨을 교체한다
(B) 소음 문제를 처리하기 위해 팀을 보낸다
(C) 문제를 어떻게 해결해야 하는지 그녀에게 알려 준다
(D) 전화를 해서 약속을 잡는다

| 해설 | 이메일 후반부에서 Trent 씨는 소음 문제 해결을 위해 '가능한 빨리 수리공들이 사무실로 올 것을 요청한다'(I request that your repairmen return to my firm as soon as possible)고 말하고 있으므로 정답은 (B)이다. 문제가 심각할 경우 에어컨을 교체할 수도 있지만, 이메일에서 1차적으로 요청하고 있는 사항은 정황상 '교체'가 아니라 '수리'이기 때문에 (A)는 정답이 아니다.

[162-164]

일상을 벗어나 Bendburg 스키 리조트로 오십시오

눈이 내리기 시작했는데, 이는 스키를 탈 시기가 되었음을 의미합니다. Bendburg 스키 리조트는 겨울을 맞아 얼마 전에 개장을 했으며 예약을 받고 있습니다. 주에서 가장 멋진 스키장의 놀라운 최신 시설을 놓치지 마십시오. 여름 동안, Green Mountain Run이라는 슬로프가 추가되었습니다. Green Mountain Run은 저희의 가장 길고 가장 스릴있는 슬로프입니다. 여러분들께서는 또한 새롭게 바뀐 스키 리프트를 이용하여 산에 있는 시간을 극대화하실 수 있습니다. 그리고 스키를 타신 후 핫 초콜릿, 에스프레소, 혹은 간식을 먹을 수 있고, 주변 경치를 가장 잘 감상할 수 있는, 새로 생긴 카페인 Ricardo's를 방문하는 것도 잊지 마십시오. 스키가 처음이시라고요? Bendburg는 초보자들과 베테랑 스키어들에게 똑같이 도움을 줄 수 있는 네 명의 강사도 보유하고 있습니다. 미리 예약하셔서 최저가로 교습을 받으십시오. 152번 고속도로의 밀튼에서 남쪽으로 30분 거리에 있는 Bendburg 스키장은 밀튼 중심가까지 매일 셔틀 버스를 운행합니다. 더 많은 정보를 얻거나 예약을 하시려면 953-8201로 전화를 주십시오.

escape 탈출하다, 도피하다 | slope 슬로프 | challenging 도전 의식을 불러 일으키는 | take advantage of ~을 이용하다 | maximize 극대화하다 | stop by ~에 들르다 | instructor 강사 | novice 초보자 | veteran 베테랑, 전문가 | in advance 미리, 앞서 | make a booking 예약하다

162 안내의 목적은 무엇인가?
(A) 보수 공사에 대해 상세히 설명하기 위해
(B) 리조트에 가는 법을 논의하기 위해
(C) 사업장을 광고하기 위해
(D) 리조트를 다른 곳과 비교하기 위해

| 해설 | Bendburg 스키 리조트에 관한 광고이다. 따라서 스키 리조트를 a place of business(사업장)으로 바꾸어 표현한 (C)가 정답이다.

163 Green Mountain Run에 대해 언급되어 있는 것은 무엇인가?
(A) 초보자들은 그곳에서 스키를 타야 한다.
(B) Ricardo's는 그곳 아래에 있다.
(C) 새 스키 리프트가 그곳으로 이어져 있다.
(D) 최근에 만들어졌다.

bottom 맨 아래, 바닥 | lead to ~으로 이어지다

| 해설 | 광고에서는 '놀라운 최신 시설'(the excellent new facilities)을 놓치지 말라고 한 후, 여름에 Green Mountain Run이라는 슬로프가 만들어졌다고 언급한다. 따라서 '최신 시설'이 가리키는 것은 다름아닌 Green Mountain Run이므로 정답은 (D)가 된다.

164 방문객들은 Bendburg 스키 리조트에서 무엇을 할 수 있는가?
(A) 산이 보이는 방을 대여할 수 있다
(B) 그 지역을 도보로 여행할 수 있다
(C) 스키 실력을 향상시키기 위해 교습을 받을 수 있다
(D) 리조트의 웹사이트에서 방을 예약할 수 있다

| 해설 | 'Bendburg has four instructors able to help novices and veteran skiers alike.'라는 문장을 통해 방문객들은 자신의 실력에 맞는 스키 강습을 받을 수 있다는 점을 알 수 있다. 따라서 정답은 (C)이다.

[165-167]

친애하는 Kristin에게,

오늘 아침 *Business Today*의 최신호를 펼쳐 보았는데, 당신 사진을 보고 제가 얼마나 놀랐을지 상상해 보세요. 잡지 기사에 실린 것을 축

하해요. 그리고 Pinewood 주식회사의 부사장으로 승진했다니 잘 되었군요. 저는 우리가 Ceti 중공업에서 동료로 있었을 때를 기억해요. 그곳의 모든 사람들은 당신이 대단한 일을 해낼 것이라는 점을 알고 있었죠. 그리고 당신이 잠재력을 발휘한 것 같아 보이는군요.
기사에 따르면, 당신은 곧 오마하로 전근을 갈 것이더군요. 우연하게도, 그곳은 제가 지금 일을 하고 있는 곳이에요. 당신과 만날 기회가 생겨서 서로 못다한 이야기를 하게 되면 좋을 것 같아요. 기회가 있을 때 daveb@tristan.com으로 제게 이메일을 보내서 서로가 편한 시간으로 만날 시간을 정하는 것이 어떨까요? 또한, 시에 대해 알아야 할 것이 있거나 살 집을 구하는데 도움이 필요한 경우, 주저하지 말고 저를 이용해 주세요. 저는 지난 6년 동안 이곳에 있었기 때문에, 이 지역에 대해서는 꽤 잘 알고 있어요.

조만간 또 연락해요.

그럼 안녕히,
Dave Babson

imagine 상상하다 | article 기사, 글 | feature 특징을 이루다 | remember back 회상하다 | be destined for ~할 운명이다 | as though 마치 ~인 것처럼 | potential 잠재력 | as luck would have it 우연하게도, 공교롭게도 | get caught up 따라잡다; 못다한 이야기를 나누다 | mutually 상호적으로 | reference 참고, 문의, 조회 | be familiar with ~와 친숙하다

165 Babson 씨는 *Business Today*에 대해 무엇을 언급하는가?
(A) 그것은 Kristin에 의해 작성된 기사를 싣고 있다.
(B) 그는 매주 그 잡지를 읽는다.
(C) 그는 그것을 연간 구독한다.
(D) 그 안에 Kristin에 관한 기사가 실려 있다.

subscription 구독

| 해설 | 편지의 첫 문장에서 Babson 씨는 *Business Today*라는 잡지에 실린 Kristin의 사진을 보고 놀랐다고 말한다. 따라서 잡지에 관해 언급된 사항은 (D)이다. 잡지를 봤다고 해서 반드시 그 잡지를 '(정기) 구독'하고 있다고 볼 수는 없으므로 (B)와 (C)는 정답이 될 수 없다.

166 Kristin은 현재 어디에서 일을 하는가?
(A) Ceti 중공업에서
(B) Pinewood 주식회사에서
(C) *Business Today*에서
(D) Tristan Corporation에서

| 해설 | Kristin이 Pinewood, Inc.에서 부사장(vice president)으로 승진했다는 소식에 축하를 보내고 있으므로 그녀의 현재 직장은 (B)의 'Pinewood 주식회사'이다.

167 Babson 씨에 대해 무엇이 언급되어 있는가?
(A) 그는 현재 오마하에서 산다
(B) 그는 전에 Pinewood 주식회사에서 일을 한 적이 있다.
(C) 그는 부동산 중개소에서 일한다
(D) 그는 최근에 Kristin을 만났다.

reside 거주하다, 살다 | **used to** ~하곤 했다 | **real estate agency** 부동산 중개소

| 해설 | 마지막 문장에서 Babson 씨는 '이곳(오마하)에 6년째 살고 있다'(I've been here for the past 6 years)고 적고 있으므로 그에 관해 언급된 사항은 (A)이다.

[168-171]

Cash, Leona — 1:30 P.M.
토론토에서 오는 사람들이 두어 시간 후에 공항에 도착할 거예요. 그들이 내일 하게 될 시설 시찰에 대한 준비는 다 끝났나요?

Bergeron, Neil — 1:33 P.M.
제게 요청하신 것은 다 했어요.

Alderson, John — 1:35 P.M.
저도 마찬가지예요. 저는 내일 오전에 그들에게 공장을 보여 줄 준비도 할 거예요.

Cash, Leona — 1:38 P.M.
좋은 소식이군요. 두 분 중 누가 공항으로 마중을 가서 그분들을 호텔까지 데리고 갈 계획인가요?

Alderson, John — 1:39 P.M.
저희가 그 일을 하기 바라신다는 점은 몰랐어요.

Bergeron, Neil — 1:40 P.M.
저도 몰랐어요. 당신이 지난 주에 당신과 Harold가 그 일을 할 것이라고 말씀하신 것으로 알고 있었거든요.

Cash, Leona — 1:42 P.M.
오… 제가 일정상 변경 사항에 대해 이야기해야 한다는 것을 잊은 것 같군요. 저는 오늘 오후에 영업부 차장님과 만나야 하고, Harold는 오늘 아침에 코스타리카로 떠났어요. 두 분 중에 시간이 되는 사람이 있나요?

Bergeron, Neil — 1:45 P.M.
저는 4시에 Irene Chang과 만나기로 예정되어 있어요. 하지만 그녀에게 다른 날 오라고 말할 수도 있을 것 같아요.

Alderson, John — 1:48 P.M.
그러지 말아요, Neil. 제가 그곳에 가서 그들을 만날 수 있어요. 저는 몇 차례 Claude Messier와 이야기를 나누어 보았기 때문에, 제가 직접 그를 만나는 것이 좋을 거예요. 그들의 비행기편 정보를 제게 보내 주시겠어요? Leona?

Cash, Leona — 1:50 P.M.
2분 후에 이메일을 확인해 보세요. 고마워요, John. 제가 신세를 졌군요.

inspection 조사, 시찰 | **facility** 시설 | **pick up** 마중하다, 차에 태우러 가다 | **be aware that** ~을 알다 | **in person** 몸소, 직접 | **info** 정보 (= information) | **owe** 빚지다; 신세를 지다

168 온라인 메시지 글은 주로 무엇에 관한 것인가?
(A) 곧 이루어질 비행기 여행
(B) 다음 날 행사 일정
(C) 방문객들의 도착을 위한 준비
(D) 각자가 참석하게 될 회의

| 해설 | 토론토에서 오는 사람들의 공장 시찰을 위한 준비 상황에 대해 이야기를 나누고 있다. 따라서 메시지 창의 주제는 (C)로 볼 수 있다.

169 오후 1시 35분, Alderson 씨가 "Same here"라고 말할 때 그는 무엇을 의미하는가?
(A) 그는 Bergeron 씨의 의견에 동의한다.
(B) 그는 고객들을 만나기를 고대하고 있다.
(C) 그는 그가 하기로 되어 있던 모든 일을 끝냈다.
(D) 그는 현재 Bergeron 씨와 함께 있다.

opinion 의견 | presently 현재, 지금

| 해설 | Bergeron 씨가 'I've done everything you asked of me.'(당신이 요청한 것은 다 했다)라고 말한 후에 Alderson 씨가 'Same here.'라고 말했으므로 그 역시 '나도 요청받은 것은 다 했다'는 의미를 전하고 있다. 따라서 정답은 (C)이다.

170 Messier 씨에 관해 무엇이 암시되어 있는가?
(A) 그는 토론토에서 오고 있는 중이다.
(B) 그는 Alderson 씨와 친한 친구 사이이다.
(C) 그는 곧 코스타리카로 갈 것이다.
(D) 그는 내일 오전에 Cash 씨와 만날 것이다.

| 해설 | 메시지 글의 후반부에서 Alderson 씨는 자신이 공항으로 마중을 가겠다고 이야기하면서 'I've spoken with Claude Messier several times, so it will be nice to get a chance to see him in person.'이라고 말한다. 이를 통해 Claude Messier라는 인물은 공항에 도착할 사람 중 한 명, 즉 토론토에서 오고 있는 사람 중 한 명이라는 사실을 알 수 있다. 따라서 (A)가 정답이다.

171 Alderson 씨는 아마도 이다음에 무엇을 할 것인가?
(A) 공장을 시찰한다
(B) 공항으로 간다
(C) 이메일을 확인한다
(D) Bergeron 씨에게 이야기한다

| 해설 | 메시지 글 마지막 부분에서 Bergeron 씨가 방문객들의 항공편 정보를 요구하자 Alderson 씨는 'Check your e-mail in two minutes.'라고 말한다. 따라서 Alderson 씨가 하게 될 일은 (C)이다. 참고로 (B)의 '공항으로 간다'는 이메일을 확인한 후에 하게 될 일이다.

[172-175]

문해 능력 관심의 달이 곧 끝납니다

문해 능력 관심의 달이 곧 끝날 예정입니다. 끝나기에 앞서, 저희는 아이들에게 변화를 만들어 주신 커뮤니티의 모든 회원분들께 경의를 표하고 싶습니다. 저희 Kent 독서회(RCK)는 아이들과 부모 모두에게 글 읽기를 권장하는 행사를 매일 주최함으로써 빈곤 아동들의 문맹률에 대처하고 있습니다. 올해 프로그램은 자원봉사자들의 헌신으로 큰 성공을 거두었습니다. (220명 이상의 사람들이 이번 달에 시간과 노력을 바쳐 다른 사람들이 글을 배우는 데 도움을 주었습니다.)

읽기가 교육에 있어서 핵심이라는 점과 교육은 가난을 쫓을 수 있는 근본이라는 점을 알고 있기 때문에, RCK는 Kent 공공 도서관에서 읽기 수업을 주관해 왔습니다. 시내 초등학교 학생들은 이곳에 와서 책을 읽고, 지역 운동 선수들, 가수들, 배우들, 그리고 기타 저명인사들이 큰 소리로 재미있는 이야기를 읽어 주는 것을 들었습니다. 총 2,500명 이상의 아이들이 이러한 행사에 참여했습니다.

RCK는 Joseph Stack과 그의 가족들에 의해 설립되었습니다. Stack가는 1892년에 켄트로 이주를 했고, 글을 읽지 못하는 아이들의 수에 걱정을 하게 되었습니다. 그래서 그들은 켄트 및 인근 지역의 문맹률과 싸우기로 맹세했습니다. 그 이후로, RCK는 가난하게 살고 있는 아이들에게 20,000권 이상의 책을 기증해 왔으며 매년 이번과 같은 특별 행사들을 개최하고 있습니다.

literacy 문자 해독률 | awareness 의식, 관심 | be about to 막 ~하려고 하다 | salute 거수 경례를 하다, 경의를 표하다 | make a difference to ~에 차이를 주다, ~에 영향을 주다 | battle 싸우다, 전투하다 | illiteracy 문맹률 | impoverished 가난한, 빈곤한 | host 주최하다 | volunteer 자원봉사자 | key 열쇠; 비결 | fundamental 근본적인 | poverty 가난, 빈곤 | session 기간, 회기 | celebrity 저명인사 | establish 설립하다 | resettle 재정착하다, 이주하다 | disturb 방해하다; 불안하게 만들다 | vow 맹세하다 | on an annual basis 매년

172 기사는 어디에서 볼 수 있는 것 같은가?
(A) 주간 소식지에서
(B) 역사 서적에서
(C) 전국지에서
(D) 구인용 팜플렛에서

| 해설 | 기사의 첫 번째 단락에서 글쓴이는 '커뮤니티의 모든 회원들'(all of the members of the community)에게 감사를 표하고 싶다고 한 후, RCK라는 단체의 활동을 소개하고 있다. 따라서 보기 중에서 이러한 독자층을 대상으로 삼을 수 있는 매체는 (A)의 '주간 소식지'뿐이므로 (A)가 정답이다.

173 문해 능력 관심의 달 기간 중 어떤 일이 일어났는가?
(A) 가난한 사람들에게 책이 무료로 나누어졌다.
(B) 유명한 사람들이 아이들에게 책을 읽어 주었다.
(C) 성인을 위한 읽기 수업이 개최되었다.
(D) 책 구입을 돕기 위해 모금 행사가 열렸다.

fundraiser 모금 행사

| 해설 | 두 번째 단락에서 '지역 사회의 유명 인사들이 아이들에게 책을 읽어 주었다'(to listen to local athletes, singers, actors, and other celebrities read their favorite stories aloud)는 내용을 찾아볼 수 있으므로 행사 기간 중 일어난 일은 (B)이다.

174 Joseph Stack은 누구인가?
(A) 켄트 시의 설립자
(B) 문해 능력 관심의 달 행사의 자원봉사자
(C) RCK의 원년 멤버
(D) Kent 공공 도서관 직원

| 해설 | 마지막 단락에서 RCK를 설립한 사람이 Joseph Stack과 그의 가족이라고 소개되어 있다. 따라서 정답은 (C)이다.

175 [1], [2], [3], 그리고 [4]로 표시된 위치 중에 다음 문장이 들어가기에 가장 알맞은 곳은 어디인가?

"220명 이상의 사람들이 이번 달에 시간과 노력을 바쳐 다른 사람들이 글을 배우는데 도움을 주었습니다."

(A) [1]
(B) [2]
(C) [3]
(D) [4]

| 해설 | 주어진 문장이 무엇에 관한 설명인지 생각해 보면 정답을 쉽게 찾을 수 있다. 주어진 문장의 내용은 [1] 바로 앞문장의 the hard work of our volunteers를 부연 설명하고 있는 것이므로 (A)의 [1]에 들어가야 가장 자연스러운 문맥이 완성된다.

[176-180]

Outdoorsman
384 E. Atlantic 가, 뱅고르, 메인
(804) 434-8594

주문 날짜: 9월 30일   주문 번호: 505954
고객 성명: Thomas Heckbert
배송 주소: Lansing 가 34번지, 트렌턴, 뉴저지

제품 번호	제품 설명	수량	가격
606-544	남성용 블랙 캐시미어 스웨터 (L)	1	$125.00
204-994	남성용 청바지 (L)	2	$45.00
766-121	여성용 그린 블라우스 (S)	1	$80.00
653-476	남성용 레드 윈드브레이커 (L)	1	$22.00

소계	$ 272
Outdoorsman 실버 클럽 할인	- $ 27.20
세금	$ 14.69
배송료*	$ 15.00
합계	**$ 274.49**

* 특급 배송을 선택하셨습니다. 주문품은 영업일 기준으로 2일 내에 도착할 것입니다.

Outdoorsman 에서 쇼핑해 주셔서 감사합니다. 질문이 있으신 경우에는 저희에게 전화를 주시거나 customerservice@outdoorsman.com 으로 이메일을 보내 주십시오.

받는 사람: customerservice@outdoorsman.com
보낸 사람: theckbert@marketmail.com
제목: 주문 번호 505954
날짜: 10월 21일
첨부: 사진

담당자분께,

제 이름은 Thomas Heckbert입니다. 저는 Outdoorsman에서 오랫동안 쇼핑을 해 왔습니다. 제 실버 클럽 멤버쉽 번호는 49A0433입니다. 저는 지난 달에 제가 주문했던 것과 관련하여 글을 쓰고 있습니다. 항상 그랬듯이, 제품은 완벽한 상태로 도착했고, 제 아내와 저는 모두 옷이 몸에 잘 맞아서 기뻐하고 있습니다. Outdoorsman에서 판매하는 제품의 품질은 제가 사실상 한 달에 한 번 꼴로 귀하의 웹사이트에서 무언가를 구입하는 주된 이유입니다.

하지만 문제는 제가 산 제품에 청구된 금액과 관련이 있습니다. 제품과 함께 받은 청구서에는 제가 10%의 할인을 받았다고 나와 있었지만, 신용 카드 사용 내역서를 받았을 때 저는 실제로 할인이 적용되지 않았다는 점을 알게 되었습니다. 따라서 저는 구매 물품에 대해 과도한 비용을 청구받았습니다. 제가 얼마만큼의 할인을 받았어야 하는지를 아실 수 있도록 청구서 사진을 첨부해 두었습니다. 그 돈을 되돌려 주시겠습니까? 제가 이번 주 목요일이나 금요일에 또 한 번 주문할 계획을 가지고 있기 때문에, 제게 포인트를 주셔도 좋습니다. 문제가 있다면, 주저하지 마시고 제게 답장을 주십시오.

곧 긍정적인 답변을 듣게 되기를 기대하겠습니다.

Thomas Heckbert 드림

with regard to ~에 관하여 | **as always** 항상 그랬듯이 | **be pleased with** ~에 기뻐하다 | **main** 주요한 | **concern** ~와 관계가 있다 | **invoice** 송장, 청구서 | **note** 주목하다; 언급하다 | **credit card bill** 신용 카드 청구서 | **apply** 적용하다 | **attach** 부착하다; 첨부하다 | **store credit** (해당 매장에서 쓸 수 있는) 포인트 | **feel free to** 마음껏 ~하다 | **look forward to** ~을 고대하다

176 청구서에 언급되어 있지 않은 것은 무엇인가?
   (A) 지불 방법
   (B) 수신인의 주소
   (C) 구입된 각 제품의 번호
   (D) 회사 전화번호

| 해설 | 나머지 항목들은 청구서에서 모두 확인이 가능한 반면, (A)의 '지불 방법'은 적혀 있지 않다. 참고로 지불 방법은 예컨대 현금으로 결제 했는지 혹은 신용 카드로 결제 했는지 등에 관한 것이다.

177 Heckbert 씨는 어떤 제품에 가장 많은 비용을 지불했는가?
   (A) 204-994
   (B) 606-544

   (C) 653-476
   (D) 766-121

| 해설 | 제품의 '금액'(Price) 항목을 서로 비교해 보면 (B)의 606-544 제품에 125달러라는 가장 큰 금액이 지출되었음을 알 수 있다.

178 Heckbert 씨는 자신이 주문한 제품 중 하나에 대해 무엇을 암시하는가?
   (A) 그에 대해 과다한 요금이 청구되었다.
   (B) 그것이 몸에 맞지 않는다.
   (C) 세일 중에 그것을 구입했다.
   (D) 아내를 위해 그것을 구입했다.

| 해설 | 첫 번째 지문인 주문서에 여성용 의류가 하나 포함되어 있고 두 번째 지문인 이메일에서는 Heckbert 씨가 '아내와 자신 모두' 옷이 잘 맞아서 만족한다고 밝히고 있다. 따라서 주문품 중 하나는 아내를 위한 것임을 알 수 있으므로 정답은 (D)이다. 전체적인 할인이 적용되지 않은 것이 문제이지, 개별 제품에 과다한 요금이 청구된 것은 아니므로 (A)는 정답이 될 수 없고, (B)는 사실과 반대되는 내용이며, (C)는 주어진 지문만으로는 알 수 없는 내용이다.

179 Heckbert 씨는 얼마의 금액을 돌려 받고 싶어하는가?
   (A) 15달러
   (B) 14.69달러
   (C) 22.00달러
   (D) 27.20달러

| 해설 | 이메일에서 Heckbert 씨는 적용되어야 할 할인 금액이 실제로 적용되지 않았다고 했으므로, 첫 번째 지문인 청구서에서 할인 금액을 확인하면 그가 돌려받고자 하는 금액을 알 수 있다. 정답은 Outdoorsman Silver Club Discount 항목에서 확인할 수 있듯이 (D)의 '27.20달러'이다.

180 Heckbert 씨는 이메일과 함께 무엇을 보냈는가?
   (A) 새 의류 주문서
   (B) 청구서 사본
   (C) 하자 제품의 사진
   (D) 신용 카드 사용 내역서가 포함된 파일

faulty 흠이 있는, 잘못된 | **merchandise** 상품 | **contain** 포함하다

| 해설 | 이메일 두 번째 단락에서 Heckbert 씨는 'I have attached a picture of the invoice so that you can see how much of a discount I should have received.'라고 말하며 청구서 사진 파일을 첨부했음을 밝히고 있다. 따라서 정답은 (B)이다.

[181-185]

Templeton Manufacturing에서
올해 송년회를 개최할 예정입니다

12월 29일, 금요일

오후 6시 30분부터 오후 10시까지

Rose 연회장
Garden 호텔

다음과 같은 행사들이 열릴 예정입니다:
오후 6시 30분 – James Lambert 대표 이사의 되돌아보는 한 해
오후 7시 – 다섯 코스의 저녁 식사
오후 8시 30분 – 시상식
오후 9시 – 라이브 공연

Templeton Manufacturing의 전 직원들과
배우자 혹은 연인분들을 환영합니다.
참석 여부를 확인할 수 있도록 Virginia Snyder 씨에게
vsnyder@templetonmanu.com으로 연락을 주십시오.

end-of-the-year 연말 | **take place** 일어나다, 발생하다 | **review** 검토 | **live entertainment** 라이브 공연 | **spouse** 배우자 | **significant** 중요한, 의미가 있는 | **attendance** 참석

받는 사람: Elisa Standish
보낸 사람: Percy Wilson
제목: 12월 29일 행사
날짜: 12월 20일

다음 주 중요 행사를 위해 모든 것이 준비된 것처럼 보이는군요. 저는 Garden 호텔의 Kevin Crawford와 이야기를 나누었고, 그는 우리가 요청한 음식이 모두 제공 가능하다는 점을 제게 확인시켜 주었어요. 그는 이번 주 금요일인 12월 22일에 호텔에 들러서 시식을 해 보라고 저를 초대했어요. 저와 같이 가고 싶으면, 제게 알려 주세요. 저는 5시 회의에 맞춰 사무실로 돌아올 수 있도록 약 2시 30분에 이곳에서 나설 거예요. 하지만 일정상 한 가지 변경 사항이 있어요. Connie Parker 씨께서는 Lambert 씨가 연설을 한 후에 상을 수여하고 싶어하세요. 그래서 우리는 인쇄소에 연락을 해서 인쇄된 일정에 행사 순서가 올바르게 되어있는지를 확인해야 해요. 당신이 인쇄소와의 연락 담당자이기 때문에, 그 일을 해 줄래요? 제가 Connie에게 알릴 수 있도록 그렇게 하는 대로 제게 알려 주세요. 이번 행사는 그녀가 처음으로 담당하는 시상식이어서, 그녀는 정말로 실수를 하고 싶어하지 않거든요. 작년 Todd Seager가 책임을 맡았을 때 일이 어떻게 진행되었는지 기억하죠, 그렇지 않나요? 우리는 그런 일이 반복되는 것을 원하지 않아요.

assure 확신시키다 | **drop by** ~에 들르다 | **sample** 견본, 샘플; 시식하다 | **accompany** 동반하다 | **printer** 인쇄업자, 인쇄소 | **order** 순서 | **as soon as** ~하자마자 | **be responsible for** ~을 책임지다 | **be eager to** ~하기를 열망하다 | **in charge** 담당하는, 책임지는 | **repeat** 반복

181 공지의 목적은 무엇인가?
(A) 일정상의 변경 사항을 언급하기 위해
(B) 회사 직원들을 행사에 초대하기 위해
(C) 몇몇 직원들의 연락처를 알려 주기 위해
(D) 몇몇 상의 수상자를 발표하기 위해

| 해설 | 송년회에 관한 안내문으로, 안내문 하단에 직원들과 배우자 혹은 연인을 초대하는 문구를 발견할 수 있다. 따라서 정답은 (B)이다.

182 공지의 15줄의 "confirm"이라는 단어와 그 의미가 가장 비슷한 것은?
(A) 확인하다
(B) 반박하다
(C) 구매하다
(D) 인정하다

certify 확인하다 | **refute** 반박하다

| 해설 | confirm은 '확인하다' 혹은 '확정시키다'라는 의미이므로 보기 중에서는 (A)의 certify(확인하다)가 이와 가장 유사한 의미를 나타낸다.

183 메모에 따르면, 상은 언제 수여될 것인가?
(A) 6시 30분에
(B) 7시에
(C) 8시 30분에
(D) 9시에

| 해설 | 두 번째 지문인 메모의 'Connie Parker wants to present the awards right after Mr. Lambert gives his talk.'라는 문장에서 Lambert 씨의 연설 후에 시상식이 이루어져야 한다는 점을 알 수 있다. 첫 번째 지문의 공지에서 Lambert 씨의 연설 이후에 예정된 행사는 '7시' 저녁 식사 시간이므로, 시상식은 이때 이루어질 것이다. 따라서 (B)가 정답이다.

184 Wilson 씨는 Standish 씨에게 무엇을 할 것을 요청하는가?
(A) 그를 대신해서 Garden 호텔에 간다
(B) Snyder 씨에게 이메일을 보낸다
(C) 일정이 변경되도록 한다
(D) Parker 씨와 협력한다

in one's place ~을 대신하여 | **arrange** 마련하다, 준비하다 | **coordinate with** ~와 협력하다

| 해설 | 이메일에서 Wilson 씨는 수신자인 Standish 씨에게 일정상 변경 사항이 생겼다는 소식을 전한 후, 'You're the contact person for the printer, so would you mind doing that?'이라고 말한다. 즉 그가 요청한 사항은 인쇄소에 연락해서 변경 사항이 반영되었는지를 확인하라는 것이므로 정답은 (C)이다.

185 Todd Seager에 대해 무엇이 암시되어 있는가?
(A) 그는 작년에 자신의 임무를 잘 해내지 못했다.
(B) 그는 올해의 수상자 중 한 명이다.
(C) 그는 Garden 호텔에 고용되어 있다.
(D) 그는 Parker 씨와 긴밀히 협력한다.

duty 임무, 업무 | **work closely with** ~와 긴밀히 협력하다

| 해설 | 이메일 후반부 중 'You remember how things went last year with Todd Seager in charge, don't you?'라는 문장에서 Todd Seager라는 이름이 거론되고 있다. 여기에서 그는 작년에 송년회를 맡았던 사람임을 알 수 있는데, 그 다음 문장에서 '작년 송년회가 되풀이 되지 않기를 바란다'고 적혀 있으므로 작년 송년회는 잘 진행되지 못했을 것으로 추측할 수 있다. 따라서 (A)가 정답이다.

[186-190]

AI's 전자 제품 매장으로 오셔서 특가 상품을 구입하십시오

"오래된 것은 버리고 새로운 것을 맞이하라."는 말을 자주 들으실 것입니다. AI's 전자 제품 매장은, 새로운 것과 함께 오래된 것도 가지고 있어야 한다고 믿습니다. 이번 주말을 한정으로, 오래되고 고장 난 라디오, CD 플레이어, 토스터, 그리고 기타 전자 제품들을 매장으로 가지고 오십시오. 가지고 오시면 저희가 무상으로 수리해 드리겠습니다. TV, 노트북 컴퓨터, 그리고 히터도 수리하실 수 있습니다. 각 고객들께서는 최대 50달러 상당의 수리를 무료로 받으실 수 있습니다. 여러분께서 하셔야 할 일은 100달러 이상의 환불이 되지 않는 제품을 구입하시는 것입니다. 그러니 여러분의 차고, 다락, 혹은 창고로 가셔서 수리를 받아야 하는 물건들을 찾으십시오. 이번 주 토요일이나 일요일인 5월 7일과 8일에 Vernon 가 549번지에 있는 AI's 전자 제품 매장을 방문하시면, 저희가 즉시 작동을 하도록 만들겠습니다. 더 많은 정보가 필요하시면 675-9303으로 전화를 주십시오.

phrase 어구 | **along with** ~와 함께 | **absolutely** 절대적으로, 꼭 | **worth** ~의 가치가 있는 | **nonrefundable** 환불이 되지 않는 | **garage** 차고 | **attic** 다락 | **toolshed** 공구 창고 | **in no time** 즉시

AI's 전자 제품 매장
Vernon 가 549번지
피츠버그, 펜실베니아
675-9303

날짜: 5월 8일
고객명: Eric Simpson
전화번호: 509-4485

제품 번호	설명	수량	가격
685-5542	64GB 썸드라이브	2	12.00달러
054-1022	Sidewinder 토스터 (모델명 RT40)	1	52.00달러
966-6854	Pampas DVD 플레이어 (모델명 600TE)	1	65.00달러
N/A	수리 작업 (비디오 게임기)	1	0.00달러
	소계		129.00달러
	세금		6.45달러
	총계		135.45달러

참고: 수리 작업은 Jason Hampton이 담당

Al's 전자 제품 매장에서 쇼핑해 주셔서 고맙습니다. 곧 다시 뵙기를 바라겠습니다.

5월 10일

관계자분께,

제 이름은 Eric Simpson입니다. 5월 8일, 저는 귀하의 매장을 방문하여 두 개의 제품을 구입했습니다. 저는 그곳에 있는 동안 오래된 비디오 게임기를 수리할 수 있는 기회를 이용했습니다. 기기를 수리한 사람이 작업을 매우 잘 했다고 말씀드려야 할 것 같습니다. 기기는 10년이 넘도록 작동을 하지 않았지만, 지금은 완벽하게 작동하고 있습니다. 제 남동생과 저는 지난 이틀 동안 1990년대의 비디오 게임을 하면서 즐거운 시간을 보내고 있습니다. 잊지 마시고 수리를 맡아 주신 분께 감사의 말을 전해 주십시오. 그분의 이름은 기억이 나지 않지만, 그분이 그곳 관리자 중 한 명이라는 점은 알고 있습니다. 저는 오래되고 상태가 꽤 좋지 않은 녹음기를 가지고 있습니다. 아마도 다음 주에 수리를 받으러 방문을 하게 될 것 같습니다. 비용이 들 것이라는 점은 알고 있지만, 오래된 몇몇 테이프들을 듣고 싶기 때문에, 요금을 내는 것은 개의치 않습니다.

Eric Simpson 드림

take advantage of ~을 이용하다 | **chance** 기회 | **have a time –ing** ~을 하면서 시간을 보내다 | **tape recorder** 녹음기

186 어떤 서비스가 광고되고 있는가?
  (A) 무료 서비스를 받을 수 있는 기회
  (B) 선정된 제품에 대한 할인
  (C) 기존 제품을 새 제품으로 교환할 수 있는 기회
  (D) 구입과 관련된 무료 상담

| 해설 | 첫 번째 지문은 주말을 한정으로 일정 조건을 충족시키는 경우 오래된 전자 제품을 무료로 수리해 준다는 광고다. 따라서 광고되고 있는 내용은 (A)이다.

187 서비스에 대해 언급된 것은 무엇인가?
  (A) 일부 제품에 대해서는 적용되지 않는다.
  (B) 5월 내내 계속될 것이다.
  (C) 고객들은 구입을 해야 한다.
  (D) 회원들에게만 제공된다.

| 해설 | 첫 번째 지문에서 '100달러 이상의 환불 불가 상품을 구입하는'(make a nonrefundable purchase of $100 or more) 경우에 무상 수리 서비스가 제공된다고 나와 있다. 따라서 언급된 사항은 (C)이다.

188 주문서에 암시되어 있는 것은 무엇인가?
  (A) Simpson 씨는 자신이 구입한 제품을 교환할 수 있다.
  (B) 토스터는 할인된 금액으로 구입했다.
  (C) 제품을 배송하기 위해서는 배송비가 부과된다.
  (D) 비디오 게임 수리 비용은 50달러 미만이었다.

| 해설 | 첫 번째 지문의 'Each shopper can receive up to $50 worth of free repairs.'라는 문장에서 무상 수리는 수리비가 50달러 이하일 때 가능하다는 점을 알 수 있으므로 비디오 게임의 수리 비용 역시 50달러 이하였을 것으로 예상할 수 있다. 따라서 정답은 (D)이다. 참고로, 무상 수리 서비스는 100달러 이상의 반품 불가 상품을 구입했을 때 제공되는 것이므로 (A)는 사실과 반대되는 내용이다.

189 Simpson 씨는 왜 편지를 썼는가?
  (A) 자신이 소유하고 있는 제품의 수리에 대해 문의하기 위해
  (B) 그가 받은 서비스에 대한 만족감을 나타내기 위해
  (C) 비디오 게임기가 어떻게 고쳐졌는지 알기 위해
  (D) 수리 작업의 질에 대해 불만을 표시하기 위해

| 해설 | 자신의 비디오 게임기를 고쳐준 직원에 대한 칭찬의 말을 건네고 있으므로 편지를 작성한 목적은 (B)로 볼 수 있다.

190 Simpson 씨는 Al's 전자 제품 매장에 대해 무엇을 암시하는가?
  (A) 곧 또 한 번의 특별 세일을 실시할 것이다.
  (B) 매니저로 Jason Hampton을 고용하고 있다.
  (C) 녹음기는 수리할 수 없었다.
  (D) 그가 구매한 제품에 과도한 요금을 청구했다.

overcharge 과도한 요금을 청구하다

| 해설 | 편지에서 Simpson 씨는 비디오 게임기를 고친 직원이 누구인지는 모르겠지만 그가 매니저 중 한 명이었다고 언급한다. 한편 두 번째 지문의 주문서를 보면 수리를 담당했던 직원의 이름이 Jason Hampton이라고 적혀져 있으므로 그는 매니저일 것이다. 따라서 지문의 내용으로 추론할 수 있는 사항은 (B)이다.

[191-195]

부은행장님께서 곧 퇴임하십니다

Chamberlain 저축 은행에서 11월 28일 금요일에 부은행장님이신 Sebastian Brown 씨께서 퇴임하신다는 점을 알려 드리고자 합니다. Brown 씨께서는 지난 43년 동안 이곳의 직원이셨습니다. 대학을 나오자마자 은행 창구 직원으로 시작하여, 곧 자신의 가치를 보여 주고 관리자로 승진하셨습니다. 이곳에서 세 개의 다른 직위에 임명되셨다가, 14년 전에 부은행장으로 임명되셨습니다. Brown 씨께서 부은행장으로 재임해 계셨던 기간 동안, Chamberlain 저축 은행은 작은 지역 은행에서, 7개의 주에 34개의 지점을 보유하고 있는, 중서부 지역에서 가장 큰 민간 은행 중 하나로 변모했습니다. Brown 씨께서는 존경받는 직원이자 유명한 박애주의자이며, 애정이 많은 아버지였고, 우리는 그의 존재를 그리워하게 될 것입니다. 마지막으로 근무를 하시는 날 오후 3시에 그분을 위한 퇴임식이 열릴 예정입니다. 퇴임식은 세인트루이스 Cutler 가 56번지에 있는 Chamberlain 저축 은행 지점에서 열릴 것입니다.

bank teller 은행 창구 직원 | **swiftly** 신속히, 빨리 | **value** 가치 | **appoint** 임명하다, 지명하다 | **tenure** 재임 기간 | **transition** 이행하다, 변천하다 | **privately owned** 개인 소유의, 민영의, 민간의 | **beloved** 사랑받는 | **philanthropist** 박애주의자, 자선가

받는 사람: Chamberlain 저축 은행 전 직원
보낸 사람: Kelly Rudolph 이사, Cutler 가 56번지 지점
제목: 은퇴 기념 파티
날짜: 11월 7일

Sebastian Brown을 위해 열리는 은퇴 기념 파티에 여러분들을 초대합니다. Brown 씨의 은퇴일의 하루 앞에 있는 추수 감사절 연휴 때문에, Brown 씨를 위한 파티는 1주일 앞당겨졌습니다. 따라서 추수 감사절 이전 금요일에 열릴 것입니다. 하지만 행사 시간과 장소는 변경되지 않았습니다.

은행의 소유주이신 David Chamberlain께서 Brown 씨에게 선물을 주실 생각이시지만, 몇몇 직원들은 우리 스스로도 그에게 무언가를 주어야 한다고 생각합니다. 그래서 우리는 그를 위한 모금 활동을 하고 있습니다. Brown 씨께서 골프를 좋아하시기 때문에, 우리는 그분께 새 골프채 세트를 사 드리려고 합니다. 저에게 돈을 주시거나 관리자에게 내시면, 관리자들이 저에게 전달해 줄 것입니다. 모금된 돈은 모두 Brown 씨의 선물을 사는데 사용될 것입니다. 16일에 골프채를 주문할 예정이니, 돈을 내실 계획이 있으시면, 그때까지 내시기 바랍니다.

prior to ~에 앞서 | **move up** (일정을) 당기다 | **take up a collection** 모금을 하다 | **club** 동호회; 곤봉, 골프채 | **donation** 기부, 기증

받는 사람: Kelly Rudolph <krudolph@chamberlainsavings.com>
보낸 사람: Susan Walters <susan_walters@redbirdsportinggoods.com>
날짜: 11월 17일
제목: 주문 번호 204-KL-505

친애하는 Rudolph 씨께,

저희는 어제 웹사이트에서 귀하의 주문을 받았습니다. 귀하를 새로운 고객으로 맞이하게 되어 기쁘게 생각하며 앞으로도 계속해서 저희 물건들을 구입하시기 바랍니다.
귀하께서 주문하신 Delmar's Deluxe 골프채 세트(제품 번호 59505594)는 배송 준비 중이라는 점을 알려 드리고자 합니다. 안타깝게도, 귀하께서 주문하신 Delmar's 검정색 골프 가방(제품번호 68586965)은 현재 재고가 없으며 앞으로 7일 이후에나 도착을 할 것입니다. 귀하께서는 특급 배송을 요청하셨기 때문에, 저희는 귀하의 주문품이 급히 필요한 것으로 추측하고 있습니다. 없는 제품은 제품 번호 69658494나 23420534 중 하나로 대체를 하시는 것이 어떨까요? 각각의 번호를 클릭만 하시면 제품에 대한 설명을 보실 수 있습니다. 가격이 약간 더 비싸기는 하지만, 저희는 추가 요금은 부과하지 않을 것이니, 주문 가격은 여전히 3,500달러가 될 것입니다.

Susan Walters 드림, Redbird Sporting Goods

assume 가정하다, 추측하다 | **in a hurry** 급히, 서둘러 | **substitute** 대체하다

191 공지는 누구를 대상으로 작성된 것 같은가?
(A) 세인트루이스 주민
(B) 은행 직원
(C) 은행 고객
(D) Brown 씨의 가족

| 해설 | 부은행장의 은퇴 소식을 알리면서 아울러 은퇴 기념 행사의 일정에 대해서도 소개하고 있다. 따라서 공지를 볼 사람은 해당 은행의 직원일 가능성이 높으므로 (B)의 '은행 직원'이 정답이다.

192 Brown 씨에 대해 언급되지 않은 것은 무엇인가?
(A) 은행 직원들은 그를 좋아한다.
(B) 그는 40년 동안 은행에서 일을 했다.
(C) 그는 세인트루이스 지점을 설립했다.
(D) 그가 그곳에서 근무한 이후로 은행의 성과가 좋았다.

| 해설 | 첫 번째 지문을 유심히 살펴보면 정답을 찾을 수 있다. (A)는 Brown 씨를 beloved employee(사랑받는 직원)라고 칭했다는 점에서, (B)는 그가 '43년 동안'(for the past 43 years) 근무했다는 점에서, 그리고 (D)는 그의 재임 기간 동안 은행이 '작은 지역 은행에서 가장 큰 민간 은행 중 하나로'(from a small local bank to one of the largest privately owned banks in the Midwest) 성장했다는 점에서 모두 언급된 사항임을 알 수 있다. 하지만 세인트루이스 지점의 설립자에 관한 내용은 찾아볼 수 없으므로 언급되지 않은 내용은 (C)이다.

193 회람에 따르면, 은퇴 기념 파티는 언제 열릴 것인가?
(A) 11월 7일에
(B) 11월 21일에
(C) 11월 27일에
(D) 11월 28일에

| 해설 | 첫 번째 지문에서 은퇴 날짜는 11월 28일로 나와 있고 퇴임식은 근무 마지막 날에 이루어진다고 했으므로 원래 예정되었던 은퇴 기념 파티는 11월 28일에 열릴 계획이었다는 점을 알 수 있다. 하지만 두 번째 지문인 회람에서 추수 감사절 연휴 때문에 파티가 1주일 앞당겨졌다고 했으므로 실제 파티가 열릴 날짜는 (B)의 '11월 21일'일 것이다.

194 Walters 씨는 왜 이메일을 썼는가?
(A) 특급 배송을 이용하라는 제안을 하기 위해
(B) 주문품에 대해 할인을 적용하기 위해
(C) 제품과 관련된 문제를 논의하기 위해
(D) 일부 제품들이 배송되었다는 점을 알리기 위해

| 해설 | Rudolph 씨의 주문품 중 골프 가방의 재고가 없어서 다른 모델을 추천하고 있으므로 Walter 씨가 이메일을 작성한 이유는 (C)로 볼 수 있다.

195 은행 직원들에 관해 무엇이 암시되어 있는가?
(A) Brown 씨의 선물을 사기 위해 3,500달러를 모았다.
(B) Brown 씨의 은퇴 기념 파티에 전원 참석할 것이다.
(C) Rudolph 씨에게 무엇을 살 것인지 제안했다.
(D) 새로운 부은행장을 만나고 싶어한다.

be eager to ~하기를 열망하다

| 해설 | 두 번째 지문인 회람에서 은행 직원들이 선물을 사기 위해 모금을 했다는 점과 모금된 돈은 모두 선물을 사는 데 쓰일 것이라는 점이 나타나 있다. 한편 세 번째 지문인 이메일의 마지막 문장에서 Rudolph 씨가 주문한 제품의 총액이 3,500달러라고 적혀 있는데, 이러한 사실들을 종합하면 직원들은 총 3,500달러를 모금했음을 알 수 있다. 따라서 정답은 (A)이다.

[196-200]

Sussex 샐러드 믹싱 볼

Sussex 샐러드 믹싱 볼을 구입해 주셔서 고맙습니다. 건강에 좋고 영양 많은 음식들을 이것으로 혼합해서 드시기 바랍니다. 새로운 기기를 사용하시기 전에, 아래 지시 사항을 주의 깊게 읽어 주십시오.

* 볼을 씻은 후 그 안에 무언가를 넣기 전에 볼이 완전히 말랐는지 확인 하십시오.
* 반드시 작은 조각으로 썰린 신선한 채소만을 사용하십시오. 커다란 조각은 믹싱 장치를 방해하여 기계적인 결함을 일으킬 수 있습니다.
* 볼 위에 덮개를 덮고 믹싱 장치의 손잡이를 잡으십시오. 그런 다음, 손잡이를 천천히 반시계 방향으로 10번까지 돌리십시오.
* 뚜껑을 열고 샐러드를 살펴보십시오. 더 섞여야 하는 경우에는 위 과정을 반복하십시오.
* 음식이 완성되면, 볼, 뚜껑, 그리고 믹싱 장치를 온수와 주방 세제로 청소하십시오. 볼을 식기 세척기에 넣지 마십시오.

질문이 있는 경우에는 information@sussex.com으로 연락을 주십시오. 지시 사항을 따르지 않으면 보증의 효력이 없어집니다.

healthy 건강에 좋은 | **nutritious** 영양이 많은 | **appliance** 가정용 기기 | **add** 더하다, 첨가하다 | **block** 막다, 방해하다 | **mechanism** 기구, 기계 장치 | **mechanical** 기계적인 | **grasp** 쥐다, 붙잡다 | **gently** 온화하게, 부드럽게 | **counterclockwise** 시계 반대 방향으로 | **inspect** 조사하다 | **dishwashing detergent** 주방 세제 | **dishwasher** 식기 세척기 | **void** 무효로 하다 | **warranty** 품질 보증서

받는 사람: information@sussex.com
보낸 사람: trussell@sunmail.com
날짜: 6월 12일
제목: Sussex 샐러드 믹싱 볼

담당자님께,

일주일 전, 저는 인근 백화점에서 Sussex 샐러드 믹싱 볼을 구입했습니다. 그곳의 판매 사원은 제가 만들려고 하는 여름철 샐러드에 그 제품이 적합할 것이라고 저를 설득시켰습니다. 저는 45달러를 지불하여 하나를 구입해서 매장을 나섰습니다. 그날 밤 집에 돌아왔을 때, 저는 가족들을 위한 맛있는 샐러드를 만들기로 결심했습니다. 그래서 상추, 당근, 피망, 그리고 토마토를 볼에 넣고 그 위에 약간의 드레싱을 부었습니다. 그런 다음, 모든 것을 섞으려고 시도했습니다. 볼이 야채들을 섞지 못할 뿐만 아니라 자르지도 못했을 때 제가 얼마나 놀랐을지 상상해 보십시오. 게다가, 볼은 더 이상 작동을 하지 않았습니다. 저는 구입품에 대해 크게 실망하고 있으며 돈을 돌려 받고 싶습니다. 백화점에서는 환불을 해 주지 않기 때문에, 저는 귀하께서 돈을 돌려 주셔야 한다고 생각합니다. 구매를 입증할 수 있도록, 영수증 사본을 첨부해 두었습니다.

그럼 이만 줄이겠습니다.

Tina Russell

---

salesclerk 판매원 | **convince** 설득하다 | **delicious** 맛있는 | **lettuce** 상추 | **pepper** 피망 | **dressing** 드레싱, 소스 | **to top it off** 그 외에도, 게다가 | **verify** 입증하다, 증명하다

받는 사람: trussell@sunmail.com
보낸 사람: mmartin@sussex.com
날짜: 6월 13일
제목: 회신: Sussex 샐러드 믹싱 볼

친애하는 Russell 씨께,

저희 Sussex는 Sussex 샐러드 믹싱 볼에 관하여 귀하께서 작성하신 이메일을 받았습니다. 귀하께서 볼을 사용하신 방법에 관한 설명에 따르면, 귀하께서는 볼에 포함되어 있는 지시 사항을 따르지 않으셨습니다. 그 결과, 저희는 환불을 해 드릴 수도, 무상 수리를 해 드릴 수도 없습니다.
하지만, 저희 Sussex는 고객을 돕는데 자부심을 가지고 있으며, 귀하께서 저희 제품으로 실망하시는 것을 원하지 않습니다. 그래서 저는 다운로드 할 수 있는 30달러짜리 쿠폰을 포함시켰습니다. 이를 사용하셔서 저희 웹사이트에서 판매 중인 어떤 제품이든 구입하실 수 있습니다. www.sussexinc.com을 방문하시면, 저희가 판매하는 모든 제품을 보실 수 있습니다.
질문이 있으신 경우에는 주저하지 마시고 제게 연락을 주십시오. 제가 기꺼이 도와 드리도록 하겠습니다.

Matthew Martin 드림
고객 서비스 담당
Sussex 주식회사

---

description 설명, 묘사 | **include** 포함하다 | **at no cost** 무상으로, 무료로 |

---

take pride in ~에 자부심을 갖다

196 지시 사항의 목적은 무엇인가?
　(A) 제품을 수리하는 법을 설명하기 위해
　(B) 제품을 조립하는 법을 보여 주기 위해
　(C) 제품을 분해하는 법을 보여 주기 위해
　(D) 제품을 사용하는 법을 설명하기 위해

assemble 조립하다 | **take apart** 분해하다

| 해설 | 첫 번째 지문은 제품의 사용법과 주의 사항에 대해 알려 주고 있는 제품 설명서로 볼 수 있다. 따라서 이 글의 목적은 (D)이다.

197 첫 번째 이메일에 따르면, Russell 씨는 어떻게 부적절하게 볼을 사용했는가?
　(A) 그녀는 손잡이를 잘못된 방향으로 돌렸다.
　(B) 그녀는 볼을 식기 세척기로 세척했다.
　(C) 그녀는 잘리지 않은 채소를 넣었다.
　(D) 그녀는 볼을 제대로 청소하지 않았다.

| 해설 | 'Imagine my surprise when not only did the bowl fail to mix the vegetables, but it also did not cut them.'이라는 문장이 정답의 단서이다. 지시 사항에서는 야채들을 잘게 자른 후 볼에 넣으라고 안내되어 있는데, Russell 씨는 오히려 볼에서 야채들이 잘리지 않았다고 불만을 표시하고 있다. 따라서 그녀의 잘못은 (C)가 된다.

198 Russell 씨는 이메일에 무엇을 함께 보냈는가?
　(A) 영수증 사본
　(B) 볼의 사진
　(C) 작성을 끝낸 고객 설문지
　(D) 사용 설명서 사본

| 해설 | 첫 번째 이메일의 마지막 문장, 'I have attached a copy of the receipt so that you can verify my purchase.'에서 (A)의 '영수증 사본'이 이메일에 첨부되었음을 알 수 있다.

199 Martin 씨는 왜 Russell 씨에게 환불을 거부하는가?
　(A) 그녀는 Sussex의 웹사이트에서 제품을 구입하지 않았다.
　(B) 그녀가 볼을 사용한 방식이 보증을 무효화시켰다.
　(C) Sussex는 환불을 금지하는 정책을 펴고 있다.
　(D) 그녀는 한 달 이전에 제품을 구입했다.

| 해설 | 두 번째 이메일의 'According to the description of how you used the bowl, you failed to follow the instructions that should have been included in the bowl.'이라는 설명에서, 환불이 불가능한 이유는 사용자의 잘못된 사용법 때문이라는 점을 짐작할 수 있다. 따라서 (B)가 정답이다.

200 Martin 씨는 Russell 씨에게 무엇을 하라고 제안하는가?
　(A) 앞으로 문제가 발생하면 자신에게 연락을 한다
　(B) 쿠폰을 사용하여 다른 제품을 구입한다
　(C) 매장을 방문해서 환불을 요청한다
　(D) 볼을 스스로 수리한다

| 해설 | 두 번째 이메일에서 Martin 씨는 Russell 씨에게 '다운로드할 수 있는 30달러상당의 쿠폰'(downloadable coupon for $30)을 제공하면서 이를 이용하여 회사의 웹사이트에서 제품을 구입할 것을 권유하고 있다. 따라서 그가 제안한 사항은 (B)이다.

Actual Test 02

p.75

● 정답

PART 1
1	(B)	2	(D)	3	(B)	4	(C)	5	(A)
6	(C)								

PART 2
7	(A)	8	(B)	9	(C)	10	(A)	11	(A)
12	(C)	13	(B)	14	(B)	15	(C)	16	(C)
17	(A)	18	(C)	19	(B)	20	(B)	21	(A)
22	(B)	23	(C)	24	(B)	25	(B)	26	(A)
27	(C)	28	(A)	29	(A)	30	(C)	31	(A)

PART 3
32	(C)	33	(A)	34	(B)	35	(C)	36	(B)
37	(A)	38	(D)	39	(C)	40	(A)	41	(C)
42	(B)	43	(D)	44	(C)	45	(D)	46	(A)
47	(D)	48	(C)	49	(B)	50	(C)	51	(A)
52	(B)	53	(A)	54	(C)	55	(B)	56	(B)
57	(A)	58	(A)	59	(C)	60	(C)	61	(A)
62	(A)	63	(D)	64	(C)	65	(B)	66	(A)
67	(A)	68	(D)	69	(B)	70	(C)		

PART 4
71	(A)	72	(B)	73	(B)	74	(C)	75	(A)
76	(A)	77	(B)	78	(A)	79	(A)	80	(B)
81	(C)	82	(D)	83	(B)	84	(B)	85	(A)
86	(B)	87	(A)	88	(C)	89	(B)	90	(C)
91	(B)	92	(B)	93	(D)	94	(B)	95	(C)
96	(A)	97	(D)	98	(C)	99	(D)	100	(C)

PART 5
101	(A)	102	(C)	103	(C)	104	(D)	105	(C)
106	(C)	107	(A)	108	(B)	109	(A)	110	(A)
111	(B)	112	(C)	113	(C)	114	(B)	115	(D)
116	(B)	117	(A)	118	(D)	119	(C)	120	(B)
121	(B)	122	(A)	123	(C)	124	(B)	125	(D)
126	(B)	127	(A)	128	(C)	129	(C)	130	(A)

PART 6
131	(B)	132	(C)	133	(C)	134	(D)	135	(A)
136	(D)	137	(B)	138	(C)	139	(D)	140	(B)
141	(A)	142	(A)	143	(C)	144	(A)	145	(A)
146	(C)								

PART 7
147	(C)	148	(A)	149	(C)	150	(B)	151	(B)
152	(A)	153	(C)	154	(A)	155	(D)	156	(D)
157	(A)	158	(A)	159	(B)	160	(B)	161	(A)
162	(D)	163	(B)	164	(C)	165	(B)	166	(A)
167	(C)	168	(B)	169	(D)	170	(B)	171	(D)
172	(D)	173	(B)	174	(C)	175	(C)	176	(B)
177	(D)	178	(D)	179	(B)	180	(A)	181	(D)
182	(C)	183	(C)	184	(A)	185	(B)	186	(B)
187	(C)	188	(D)	189	(B)	190	(B)	191	(C)
192	(C)	193	(A)	194	(C)	195	(B)	196	(A)
197	(C)	198	(B)	199	(D)	200	(C)		

● PART 1

p.76

1 (A) Attendance at the event is higher than it normally is.
(B) Several people are focusing on the man standing up.
(C) The professor is lecturing to the students in his class.
(D) Notes are being taken about the lessons being learned.

(A) 행사의 출석률이 평소보다 높다.
(B) 몇몇 사람들이 일어나 있는 사람에게 시선을 맞추고 있다.
(C) 교수가 수업 시간에 학생들에게 강의를 하고 있다.
(D) 학습되고 있는 교과 내용에 대해 필기가 이루어지고 있다.

attendance 출석, 출석률 | **normally** 보통, 평소에 | **focus on** ~에 초점을 맞추다, ~에 집중하다 | **lecture** 강의, 강의하다 | **take notes** 필기하다, 메모하다

| 해설 | 서 있는 사람은 이야기를 하고 나머지 사람들은 그의 말을 듣고 있다. 따라서 이를 적절히 설명하고 있는 (B)가 정답이다. 주어진 사진만으로는 '출석률'(attendance)에 대해 알 수 없으므로 (A)는 정답이 될 수 없고, 말을 하는 사람이 '교수'(professor)인지 역시 불명확하기 때문에 (C)도 정답이 아니다. 앉아 있는 사람들은 이야기를 듣고 있을 뿐, '필기'(notes)를 하고 있지는 않으므로 (D) 또한 적절한 진술이 될 수 없다.

2 (A) Several passengers are getting on the bus.
(B) Pedestrians are crossing the street at the crosswalk.
(C) The sprinters are having a race downtown.
(D) Some cyclists are riding in a line on the street.

(A) 몇몇 승객들이 버스에 타고 있다.
(B) 보행자들이 횡단보도로 길을 건너고 있다.
(C) 달리기 선수들이 도심에서 경주를 하고 있다.
(D) 자전거를 탄 사람들이 거리에서 일렬로 지나가고 있다.

cross 가로지르다, 건너다 | **crosswalk** 횡단보도 | **sprinter** 단거리 주자 | **have a race** 경주를 하다 | **downtown** 시내에서 | **cyclist** 자전거 선수, 자전거를 타는 사람 | **in a line** 한 줄로

| 해설 | 사진에서 버스에 오르내리는 '승객'(passengers)이나 거리를 지나가는 '보행자'(pedestrians)는 보이지 않으므로 (A)와 (B)는 정답이 아니다. 또한 자전거를 타고 있는 사람만 있을 뿐, '달리기를 하는 사람'(sprinters)은 찾아볼 수 없으므로 (C) 역시 오답이다. 따라서 정답은 '자전거를 탄 사람들이 일렬로 지나가고 있다'고 진술한 (D)이다.

> ☑ **700점 넘기 포인트** cyclist가 '자전거 선수'를 의미할 때도 있지만, 일반적으로는 '자전거를 탄 사람'을 가리킨다. 또 다른 예로서 singer 역시 '가수'라는 전문적인 직업의 의미보다는 '노래를 하는 사람'이라는 의미로 자주 사용된다.

3 (A) The chef is preparing meals for all of the customers.
(B) Plates of food have been placed in front of the diners.
(C) All of the seats at the restaurant are currently occupied.
(D) A waiter is taking an order from one of the customers.

35

(A) 주방장이 모든 고객들을 위해 식사를 준비하고 있다.
(B) 식당 손님들 앞에 요리가 놓여 있다.
(C) 현재 식당의 모든 자리가 채워져 있다.
(D) 종업원이 한 명의 고객으로부터 주문을 받고 있다.

chef 주방장 | **prepare** 준비하다 | **occupied** 사용 중인, 점령된 | **take an order** 주문을 받다

| 해설 | 식당이라는 장소로부터 유추할 수 있는 chef(주방장)와 meal(식사) 그리고 waiter(종업원)와 order(주문)라는 단어를 이용한 (A)와 (D)는 함정이다. 사진 속에는 빈 의자가 하나 보이기 때문에 '모든 좌석'(all of the seats)이 차 있다고 진술한 (C) 역시 정답이 아니다. 따라서 '사람들 앞에 모두 접시가 놓여 있다'고 사진 속 상황을 적절히 설명한 (B)가 정답이다.

4 (A) Shoppers are heading up the escalator.
   (B) Some people are waiting to get on the elevator.
   (C) Everyone is heading in the same direction.
   (D) Both sides of the escalator are currently in use.

(A) 쇼핑객들이 에스컬레이터를 타고 올라가고 있다.
(B) 몇몇 사람들이 엘리베이터를 타기 위해 기다리고 있다.
(C) 모든 사람들이 같은 방향으로 가고 있다.
(D) 현재 에스컬레이터의 양방향 모두가 사용되고 있다.

head 향하다 | **escalator** 에스컬레이터 | **elevator** 엘리베이터 | **in use** 사용 중인

| 해설 | 사진 속 사람들이 서 있는 방향을 고려해 볼 때, 모두가 '같은 방향을 향하고 있다'(is heading in the same direction)고 진술한 (C)가 정답이며, 사람들이 '위로 올라가고 있다'(are heading up the escalator)고 설명한 (A)는 적절하지 못하다. (B)는 escalator(에스컬레이터)와 기능이 유사한 elevator(엘리베이터)라는 단어를 이용한 함정이고, 올라가는 방향의 에스컬레이터를 타고 있는 사람은 보이지 않기 때문에 (D) 또한 오답이다.

5 (A) Merchandise has been stocked on several shelves.
   (B) The customer is putting items in the grocery cart.
   (C) The prices of some of the items have been reduced.
   (D) Fresh produce is being placed in the refrigerators.

(A) 선반에 상품들이 채워져 있다.
(B) 고객이 쇼핑 카트에 상품을 담고 있다.
(C) 일부 상품의 가격이 인하되었다.
(D) 신선한 농산물들이 냉장고에 들어가고 있다.

merchandise 상품 | **stock** 재고; 채우다 | **grocery cart** 식료품점의 카트, 쇼핑 카트 | **reduce** 줄이다, 감소하다 | **fresh produce** 신선한 농산물, 청과물

| 해설 | 음료 등의 상품들이 선반 위에 올려져 있는 모습을 적절히 설명한 (A)가 정답이다. (B)와 (D)는 각각 식료품점으로부터 유추할 수 있는 grocery cart(쇼핑 카트)와 fresh produce(신선 식품)라는 표현을 이용해 오답을 유도하고 있는 함정이며, 상품의 가격 인하 여부에 대해서 사진만으로는 확인할 수 없으므로 (C) 또한 정답이 될 수 없다.

6 (A) There are paintings on all of the room's walls.
   (B) Cushions are being placed on the sofa.
   (C) A table is in between the couch and the television.
   (D) One of the doors in the room has been opened.

(A) 거실의 모든 벽면에 그림이 걸려 있다.
(B) 소파 위에 쿠션이 놓아지고 있다.
(C) 소파와 텔레비전 사이에 테이블이 하나 있다.
(D) 거실의 문 하나가 열려 있다.

cushion 쿠션 | **between A and B** A와 B 사이에 | **couch** 긴 의자, 소파

| 해설 | '모든 벽면'(all of the room's walls)에 그림이 걸려 있는 것은 아니므로 (A)는 오답이며, 쿠션이 놓아지고 있는 광경은 보이지 않기 때문에 (B)

도 정답이 아니다. 사진 속 문은 모두 닫혀 있으므로 (D) 또한 정답이 될 수 없다. 따라서 정답은 테이블의 위치를 적절히 설명하고 있는 (C)이다.

> ☑ **700점 넘기 포인트** 현재진행형을 사용하고 있는 (B)는 '상태'가 아니라 '동작'을 설명하는 보기이다. 만약 어떤 사람이 소파 위에 쿠션을 놓고 있는 모습을 보여 주는 사진이 문제로 제시되었다면 (B)가 정답이 될 수 있을 것이다.

● PART 2 p.80

7 The files have all been submitted, haven't they?
   (A) Yes, about two hours ago.
   (B) I'll submit my application then.
   (C) Mr. Peters wants to see them.

파일이 모두 제출되었죠, 그렇지 않나요?
(A) 네, 약 2시간 전에요.
(B) 그러면 제가 지원서를 제출할게요.
(C) Peters 씨께서 보고 싶어 하세요.

submit 제출하다 | **application** 신청, 신청서

| 해설 | 부가의문문을 통해 파일의 제출 여부를 묻고 있으므로, '두 시간 전에 제출되었다'라고 답한 (A)가 정답이다. (B)는 질문의 submit를 중복 사용하여 오답을 유도하고 있는 함정이고, (C)는 주어진 질문과 전혀 관련이 없는 답변이다.

8 I recommend applying for a job at Ermine Consulting.
   (A) A low-level employee there.
   (B) That's what I'm planning to do.
   (C) No, you didn't recommend that.

Ermine 컨설팅에 입사 지원을 할 것을 추천드려요.
(A) 그곳에서 지위가 낮은 직원이요.
(B) 그것이 바로 제가 계획하고 있는 바예요.
(C) 아니요, 당신은 그것을 추천하지 않았어요.

recommend 추천하다 | **low-level** 지위가 낮은

| 해설 | 평서문의 형식을 취하고 있지만, 동사 recommend를 통해 추천 혹은 제안을 하고 있는 문장이다. 따라서 '그것이 바로 내가 생각하던 바였다'라고 답변한 (B)가 가장 자연스러운 대답이다. (A)는 문제의 applying for(지원하다)라는 표현으로부터 연상이 가능한 employee라는 단어를 이용한 오답이고, (C)는 recommend를 중복 사용하여 혼동을 일으키고 있는 함정이다.

9 How long do you intend to wait for Mr. Schnell?
   (A) I've known him for years.
   (B) Several months from now.
   (C) Until the workday ends.

Schnell 씨를 얼마나 기다리실 생각인가요?
(A) 저는 여러 해 동안 그를 알아 왔어요.
(B) 지금부터 몇 개월 후에요.
(C) 일과가 끝날 때까지요.

intend to ~할 의도이다 | **workday** 근무일, 근무 시간

| 해설 | how long은 주로 기간이나 경과 시간을 물을 때 사용되는 표현이므로 '근무 시간이 끝날 때 까지'라고 구체적인 기간을 밝힌 (C)가 가장 적절한 답변이다. (A)는 주어진 질문과 전혀 관련이 없는 답변이고, (B)는 기간이 아니라 '시점'을 밝힌 대답으로 주어진 질문에 대한 적절한 답변이 될 수 없다.

10 What time is the flight supposed to land?
   (A) Let me check the schedule.
   (B) We're landing in San Francisco.
   (C) It's Flight TR492.

비행기가 언제 착륙할 예정인가요?
(A) 시간표를 확인해 볼게요.
(B) 우리는 샌프란시스코에 착륙할 거예요.
(C) TR492 비행기편이에요.

be supposed to ~할 예정이다 | **flight** 비행, 비행기편 | **land** 땅, 육지; 착륙하다, 상륙하다

| 해설 | what time은 시각을 물을 때 사용되는 표현이므로 시각과 관련된 답변을 찾도록 한다. (B)는 착륙할 장소를 묻는 질문에, (C)는 비행기편을 묻는 질문에 이어질 수 있는 답변이다. 따라서 정답은 '(시각을 알기 위해) 시간표를 확인해 보겠다'고 답한 (A)이다.

11 Shouldn't you submit the application form at once?
(A) Actually, I already did.
(B) Apply it to the surface.
(C) Yes, he has very good form.

지금 당장 지원서를 제출해야 하지 않나요?
(A) 실은, 이미 했어요.
(B) 표면에 바르세요.
(C) 네, 그는 매우 잘 하고 있어요.

application form 신청서, 지원서 | **at once** 즉시, 당장 | **apply** 지원하다; 바르다 | **surface** 표면 | **form** 양식; 형태; 기량, 솜씨

| 해설 | shouldn't를 사용해 상대방에게 지원서 제출을 제안하고 있다. 따라서 '이미 제출했다'고 대답한 (A)가 답변으로서 가장 자연스럽다. (B)는 질문의 application의 동사형인 apply를 이용한 함정으로, 여기에서 apply는 '지원하다'가 아니라 '바르다'라는 의미로 사용되었다. (C) 역시 질문의 form을 중복 사용하여 오답을 유도하고 있는 함정인데, 여기에서의 form은 '기량, 솜씨'라는 의미로 사용되었다.

12 Do you happen to know who the head accountant is?
(A) He works in the Accounting Department.
(B) Get ahead by working hard.
(C) His name is Fred Marshall.

혹시 회계부의 장이 누구인지 알고 있나요?
(A) 그는 회계부에서 일을 해요.
(B) 열심히 일함으로써 앞서 나가세요.
(C) 그의 이름은 Fred Marshall이에요.

head 머리; 책임자, 수장 | **accountant** 회계사, 회계 직원 | **get ahead** 앞서 나가다

| 해설 | 간접의문문이 제시될 때에는 실제로 무엇을 묻는지 잘 살펴야 한다. 이 문제의 경우에는 '회계부의 장이 누구인지'가 핵심 내용이므로 정답은 직접적으로 해당 인물의 이름을 언급한 (C)가 된다.

13 Can you please file these documents for me?
(A) There's the file cabinet.
(B) Sorry, but I'm too busy now.
(C) No, they haven't been documented.

이 문서들을 정리해 줄 수 있나요?
(A) 파일 캐비닛이 있어요.
(B) 미안하지만, 제가 지금 너무 바쁘군요.
(C) 아니요, 그것들은 기록되지 않았어요.

file 파일; (정리하여) 보관하다 | **document** 서류; 기록하다, 문서화하다

| 해설 | 형식적으로는 의문문의 형태를 갖추고 있지만 please 등을 감안하면 이 문장은 부탁의 의미를 담고 있음을 알 수 있다. 따라서 거절의 의사를 밝힌 (B)가 정답으로서 가장 적절하다. (A)는 file을 중복 사용한 오답이고, (C)는 document(문서)의 동사형인 document(기록하다)를 이용하여 혼동을 일으키고 있는 함정이다.

14 Where did Jenny put the stapler after she finished using it?
(A) The staples are in the drawer.
(B) She left it on the counter.
(C) I'm sitting at my desk now.

Jenny가 스테이플러를 사용한 뒤에 어디에 놓았나요?
(A) 스테이플은 서랍 안에 있어요.
(B) 카운터에 놓았어요.
(C) 저는 지금 제 책상에 앉아 있어요.

stapler 스테이플러 | **staple** 스테이플 (스테이플러의 알) | **drawer** 서랍

| 해설 | 의문사 where를 이용해 스테이플러가 있는 곳을 묻고 있다. (A)는 stapler와 발음이 비슷한 staples을 이용한 함정이고, (C)는 at my desk라는 장소 표현으로 혼란을 일으키고 있지만 스테이플러의 위치를 묻는 질문에 자신의 위치로 대답한 것은 적절하지 않다. 따라서 정답은 (B)이다.

15 How much does it cost to purchase a box of paper?
(A) I bought some paper.
(B) 5,000 sheets per box.
(C) I'm not quite sure.

용지 한 박스를 구입하는데 비용이 얼마나 드나요?
(A) 제가 용지를 샀어요.
(B) 박스당 5,000장이요.
(C) 잘 모르겠어요.

purchase 구입하다 | **sheet** 장 | **per** ~당

| 해설 | how much와 cost가 함께 쓰여 용지의 '가격'을 묻고 있다. (A)는 purchase와 의미가 비슷한 buy를 이용하여 오답을 유도하고 있고, (B)는 가격을 묻는 질문에 용지의 용량으로 답하고 있으므로 이 역시 정답이 될 수 없다. 정답은 '(가격을) 잘 모르겠다'는 의미인 (C)이다.

16 There appears to be a mistake on this report.
(A) Why am I mistaken?
(B) Didn't he report it?
(C) What's wrong with it?

이 보고서에 실수가 있는 것 같아요.
(A) 제가 왜 잘못 알고 있죠?
(B) 그가 그것을 보고하지 않았나요?
(C) 무엇이 문제인가요?

mistake 실수 | **mistaken** 잘못 알고 있는

| 해설 | 평서문을 이용하여 보고서에 대한 일종의 우려를 나타내고 있다. (A)는 명사 mistake(실수)의 형용사형인 mistaken(잘못 알고 있는)을 이용한 함정이며, (C)의 report는 '보고하다'라는 의미로서 이는 주어진 질문과 전혀 관련이 없는 답변이다. 따라서 정답은 우려의 이유가 무엇인지를 되물은 (C)이다.

17 Could you please send me the itinerary by e-mail?
(A) I'll do that after lunch.
(B) That's my e-mail address.
(C) It's our schedule for the conference.

여행 일정표를 제게 이메일로 보내 주시겠어요?
(A) 점심 식사 후에 보낼게요.
(B) 그것은 제 이메일 주소예요.
(C) 그것은 콘퍼런스 일정이에요.

itinerary 여행 일정표

| 해설 | could와 please를 이용하여 상대방에게 부탁을 하고 있다. 따라서 '점심 시간 후에 그렇게 하겠다'며 긍정적인 답변을 한 (A)가 정답이다. (B)는

37

e-mail을 중복 사용하고 있는 오답이며, (C)는 itinerary와 의미가 상통하는 schedule이라는 단어로 혼동을 유발하고 있는 함정이다.

18 Why don't we meet Mr. Richardson at the restaurant after work?
(A) I'd like a menu, please.
(B) No, he doesn't work there.
(C) I already have plans tonight.

퇴근 후에 식당에서 Richardson 씨를 만나는 것이 어떨까요?
(A) 메뉴를 가져다 주세요.
(B) 아니요, 그는 그곳에서 일하지 않아요.
(C) 오늘 밤에는 이미 약속이 있어요.

| 해설 | 「Why don't we ~」는 제안을 할 때 자주 사용되는 표현이다. (A)는 restaurant에서 연상할 수 있는 menu라는 단어로 오답을 유도하고 있는 함정이고, (B)는 근무 여부를 묻는 질문에 이어질 수 있을 만한 답변이다. 따라서 상대방의 제안에 '다른 약속이 있다'며 간접적으로 거절 의사를 밝힌 (C)가 정답이다.

19 Was that Mr. Murphy's boss who just called him on the phone?
(A) His boss is Ms. Sanderson.
(B) No, it was a client of his.
(C) Call me at 407-4994.

그와 전화 통화한 사람이 Murphy 씨의 상사였나요?
(A) 그의 상사는 Sanderson 씨예요.
(B) 아니요, 그의 고객 중 한 명이었어요.
(C) 제게 407-4994로 전화를 주세요.

boss 상사, 사장

| 해설 | '전화를 건 사람이 Murphy 씨의 상사인지' 묻고 있으므로 정답은 '그렇지 않다'고 답한 (B)이다. (A)와 (C)는 각각 질문의 boss와 called를 중복 사용하여 혼동을 유발하고 있는 함정이다.

20 What's your opinion of that article on the front page?
(A) Yes, I'm reading it.
(B) I haven't read it yet.
(C) He wrote a short article.

제1면에 실린 기사에 관해 어떻게 생각하나요?
(A) 네, 제가 읽고 있어요.
(B) 저는 아직 읽어보지 못했어요.
(C) 그가 짧은 기사를 썼어요.

opinion 의견 | **article** (짧은) 글, 기사 | **front page** (신문의) 제1면

| 해설 | what's your opinion of라는 표현을 이용하여 기사에 대한 상대방의 의견을 묻고 있다. 따라서 '아직 읽어보지 못해서 판단할 수 없다'는 의미를 담고 있는 (B)가 가장 자연스러운 답변이다. 의견을 묻는 질문에 yes로 대답한 (A)는 정답이 될 수 없고, (C)는 article을 중복 사용하여 오답을 유도하고 있는 함정이다.

21 When did Ms. Jackson send the contract to be signed?
(A) By courier, I believe.
(B) Both your name and hers.
(C) Two or three days ago.

서명을 받아야 하는 계약서를 Jackson 씨가 언제 보냈나요?
(A) 제가 알기로는 택배 기사 편으로요.
(B) 당신 이름과 그녀의 이름 둘 다요.
(C) 이틀이나 사흘 전에요.

contract 계약, 계약서 | **sign** 서명하다 | **courier** 급사, 택배 기사

| 해설 | 의문사 when에 착안하면 정답은 시점을 언급한 (C)임을 쉽게 알 수 있다. (A)는 전달 방법을 묻는 질문에 어울릴법한 답변이고, (B)는 질문의 to be signed(서명을 받다)라는 표현에서 유추할 수 있는 내용으로 오답을 유도하고 있는 함정이다.

22 Let me give you a hand with all of those folders.
(A) Fold the items carefully.
(B) I really appreciate it.
(C) We gave the performers a hand.

저 폴더들 전부를 정리하는데 제가 도움을 드릴게요.
(A) 제품을 조심해서 접어 주세요.
(B) 정말 고마워요.
(C) 우리는 배우들에게 박수를 보냈어요.

give a hand 돕다; 박수를 보내다 | **fold** 접다 | **performer** 배우, 연주자

| 해설 | 동사 let을 이용한 간접명령문 형태를 띄고 있지만, 실제로는 도움을 주겠다는 호의를 나타내고 있는 문장이다. 따라서 이에 대해 고마움을 표시한 (B)가 대답으로서 가장 적절하다. (A)는 folder(폴더)라는 단어에서 연상할 수 있는 fold(접다)를 이용한 함정이고, (C)의 give a hand는 '돕다'라는 의미가 아니라 '박수를 보내다'라는 의미로 사용되었다.

23 What time did Mr. Butters say he is going to contact us?
(A) Five days ago.
(B) I'll get in contact.
(C) No later than seven.

Butters 씨가 몇 시에 우리에게 연락할 것이라고 말했나요?
(A) 5일 전에요.
(B) 제가 연락해 볼게요.
(C) 늦어도 7시 전에요.

contact 연락하다 | **get in contact** 연락하다

| 해설 | what time이라는 표현을 이용하여 'Butters 씨가 몇 시에 연락할 것인지'를 묻고 있다. (A)는 과거의 날짜를 언급하고 있기 때문에 자연스러운 답변이 될 수 없고, (B)는 get in contact라는 표현을 통해 혼동을 유발시키고 있는 오답이다. 정답은 '7시'라는 구체적인 시각을 언급한 (C)이다.

24 Weren't we supposed to turn right at the last intersection?
(A) Yes, let's turn right here.
(B) No, at the next one.
(C) Yeah, the streets intersect here.

지나친 교차로에서 우회전을 하기로 되어 있지 않았나요?
(A) 네, 여기에서 우회전을 하죠.
(B) 아니요, 다음 교차로에서예요.
(C) 예, 도로들이 이곳에서 교차해요.

intersection 교차로

| 해설 | 부정의문문을 이용하여 '우회전을 해야 하지 않았는지' 묻고 있다. 따라서 정답은 '다음 교차로에서 우회전해야 한다'는 뜻을 밝힌 (B)이다. (A)와 (C)는 각각 turn right와 intersect라는 어구와 단어로 오답을 유도하고 있는 함정이다.

25 Why can't we connect to the Internet right now?
(A) We're not connected to it.
(B) There's a problem of some sorts.
(C) I'll call the repairman now.

지금 왜 인터넷에 연결을 할 수가 없나요?
(A) 우리는 그것과 관련이 없어요.
(B) 일종의 문제가 있어요.

(C) 제가 지금 수리 기사를 부를게요.

connect ~와 연결하다; ~와 연관되다 | repairman 수리공

| 해설 | 의문사 why를 이용하여 인터넷 연결이 되지 않는 '이유'를 묻고 있다. (A)의 connect는 '연관이 있다'라는 의미로 주어진 질문에 대한 답변이 될 수 없고, (C) 역시 구체적인 이유를 언급하고 있지 않기 때문에 정답이 아니다. 따라서 정답은 '문제가 있어서 그렇다'고 그 이유를 밝힌 (B)이다.

26 Has the shipment from Murray Office Supplies arrived yet?
(A) It won't be here until tomorrow.
(B) Several boxes of pens and paper.
(C) Not by ship but by plane.

Murray 사무용품점의 선적품이 도착했나요?
(A) 내일 이후에야 올 거예요.
(B) 펜과 용지 몇 박스요.
(C) 배편이 아니라 비행기편이에요.

shipment 선적, 선적품 | not A but B A가 아니라 B인

| 해설 | 현재완료를 사용하고 있는 일반의문문이다. 따라서 '내일 이후에야 도착할 것이다'라고 부정적인 답변을 제시한 (A)가 정답이다. (B)는 질문의 Murray Office Supplies(Murray 사무용품점)로부터 연상할 수 있는 boxes of pens and paper를, (C)는 질문의 shipment로부터 연상할 수 있는 by ship이라는 표현을 이용한 함정이다.

27 How many times this week has the machine broken down?
(A) It's the latest model.
(B) It's time to take a break.
(C) Twice according to my count.

이번 주에 그 기기가 몇 번 고장이 났죠?
(A) 그것은 최신 모델이에요.
(B) 휴식을 취해야 할 시간이군요.
(C) 제 계산에 따르면 두 번이에요.

break down 고장이 나다 | latest 최신의 | take a break 쉬다, 휴식을 취하다 | according to ~에 의하면 | count 셈, 계산

| 해설 | how many times가 빈도나 횟수를 물어볼 때 사용되는 표현이라는 점을 알면 정답을 쉽게 찾을 수 있다. (A)는 질문의 machine과 연관성이 있는 latest model(최신 모델)이라는 표현을, (B)는 broken의 명사형인 break(휴식)을 이용하여 혼동을 유발하고 있지만 모두 질문에는 어울리지 않는 답변들이다. 따라서 정답은 직접적으로 고장 횟수를 언급한 (C)이다.

28 You ought to renew your magazine subscription by July.
(A) Thanks for the reminder.
(B) It's a daily newspaper.
(C) Yes, I read it every month.

당신은 7월까지 잡지 구독을 갱신해야 해요.
(A) 알려 줘서 고마워요.
(B) 그것은 일간지예요.
(C) 네, 저는 매달 그것을 읽고 있어요.

renew 갱신하다 | subscription 구독, 구독료 | reminder 상기시키는 것 | daily newspaper 일간지

| 해설 | ought to라는 표현을 이용해서 상대방에게 충고를 하고 있다. 따라서 충고에 따른 고마움을 표시한 (A)가 정답이다. (B)와 (C)는 각각 질문의 magazine으로부터 연상할 수 있는 daily newspaper와 read라는 표현을 이용한 함정이다.

29 Doesn't this contract require three people's signatures?
(A) Yes, yours and two other individuals'.
(B) Sign on the dotted line, please.
(C) You're not required to sign it.

이 계약서에는 세 명의 서명이 필요하지 않나요?
(A) 네, 당신과 다른 두 사람의 서명이요.
(B) 점선 위에 서명해 주세요.
(C) 당신은 서명할 필요가 없어요.

require 요구하다 | signature 서명 | dotted line 점선

| 해설 | 부정의문문으로 묻고 있으므로 기본적으로 yes/no의 의미를 나타내는 보기가 정답이다. 보기 중에서 그러한 의미는 (A)에 명확히 드러나 있으므로 정답은 (A)이다.

30 Do you mind taking a look at this budget form?
(A) We went over budget last month.
(B) Yes, we are minding our own business.
(C) Can I do that after the conference?

이 예산 문서를 살펴봐 주시겠어요?
(A) 우리는 지난 달에 예산을 검토했어요.
(B) 네, 우리는 우리 일에 신경을 쓰고 있어요.
(C) 콘퍼런스가 끝난 후에 해도 될까요?

mind 꺼리다 | take a look at ~을 보다 | go over ~을 검토하다 | mind one's business ~의 일에 신경을 쓰다

| 해설 | 일반의문문의 형태를 갖추고 있지만 mind라는 동사를 이용하여 실질적으로는 부탁을 하고 있는 문장이다. 따라서 조건부로 승낙의 의미를 나타내고 있는 (C)가 정답이다. 보기 중 '예산 문서를 봐 달라는 부탁'에 '지난 달에 검토했다'는 의미인 (A)는 적절한 답변이 될 수 없고, (B)는 mind를 이용한 함정으로 여기에서의 mind는 '돌보다', '신경쓰다'라는 의미로 사용되었다.

31 How did you enjoy your meal at the Spanish restaurant?
(A) It was a bit too spicy for me.
(B) I look forward to trying the food there.
(C) Jeff paid for everyone's meal.

스페인 식당에서의 식사는 어땠나요?
(A) 제게는 다소 매웠어요.
(B) 저는 그곳에서의 식사를 기대하고 있어요.
(C) Jeff가 모든 사람의 식대를 계산했어요.

spicy 양념 맛이 강한, 매운 | look forward to ~을 고대하다

| 해설 | how가 enjoy 혹은 like 등의 동사와 같이 사용되면 일반적으로 상대방의 의견을 묻는 경우가 많다. 여기에서도 '스페인 식당의 음식'에 대한 의견을 구하고 있으므로 '매웠다'고 답한 (A)가 가장 자연스러운 답변이다.

● PART 3
p.81

[32-34]

M We've just arrived at the Cumberland House. This was the home of John Cumberland, who founded our city more than 200 years ago. It's now been turned into a museum. Why don't you all take a look around it for an hour or so?

W Are there any pamphlets we can get to learn more about the house and its history?

M Yes, there are. You can pick up some free pamphlets at the information desk right beside the front door. They'll tell you everything you need to know about this place. Be sure to be back at the bus by 11:30 so that we can

39

depart here and visit the Landers Art Gallery next.

M 우리는 조금 전에 Cumberland House에 도착했습니다. 이곳은 John Cumberland의 집으로, 그는 200년 전에 우리 도시를 설립했죠. 현재는 박물관으로 바뀌어 있습니다. 모두들 한 시간 정도 둘러 보시는 것이 어떨까요?
W 주택과 그 역사에 대해 더 많은 것을 알려 주는 팜플렛이 있을까요?
M 네, 있습니다. 정문 바로 옆의 안내 데스크에서 무료 팜플렛을 가져 가시면 됩니다. 이곳에 대해 아셔야 할 모든 것들을 알려 줄 것입니다. 여기를 떠나 그 이후에 Landers 미술관을 방문할 수 있도록, 잊지 마시고 11시 30분까지 버스로 돌아와 주십시오.

found 세우다, 설립하다 | **turn A into B** A를 B로 바꾸다 | **depart** 떠나다, 출발하다

32 남자의 직업은 무엇인가?
(A) 박물관 큐레이터
(B) 버스 기사
(C) 여행 가이드
(D) 화가

| 해설 | 남자는 Cumberland House에 대해 소개한 후, 이후 미술관 관람 일정에 대해 이야기하고 있다. 따라서 남자의 직업은 (C)의 '여행 가이드'일 것이다.

33 여자는 무엇에 대해 묻는가?
(A) 팜플렛을 얻을 수 있는지
(B) 티켓 요금
(C) 건물의 역사
(D) John Cumberland의 일생

availability 유용성, 입수 가능성

| 해설 | 여자는 팜플렛이 있는지 묻고 있으므로 정답은 (A)가 된다. 직접적으로 '주택과 그 역사'를 묻는 것이 아니라 이를 알려 줄 수 있는 팜플렛이 있는지를 묻고 있으므로 (C)를 정답으로 골라서는 안 된다.

34 11시 30분에 어떤 일이 일어날 것인가?
(A) 박물관을 방문한다.
(B) 버스가 떠날 것이다.
(C) 방문객들이 미술관에 들어갈 것이다.
(D) 역사 강연이 이루어질 것이다.

| 해설 | 남자는 대화의 마지막 부분에서 '11시 30분까지 버스로 돌아올 것'(be back at the bus by 11:30)을 당부하고 있다. 따라서 정답은 (B)이다. 참고로 11시 30분에 버스가 이동한 후 미술관 관람이 이루어질 것이므로 (C)는 11시 30분 이후에 일어날 일이다.

[35-37]

W Hello. My name is Wendy Sanders, and I'd love to dedicate some time to your organization. What's the process for becoming a volunteer?
M Thanks for calling, Ms. Sanders. We at the Seaside Charity Organization are always willing to accept offers to work. We're having a fundraiser for orphans this Saturday and could use some more volunteers. Are you interested?
W That sounds perfect. I have nothing scheduled for then, so I'd be glad to be of assistance.
M If you visit our Web site, you can learn about the event, and you'll also see what kinds of volunteers we need. How about checking out our Web site and then calling me right back to tell me what you'd like to do?

W 안녕하세요. 제 이름은 Wendy Sanders로, 저는 당신 조직에 시간을 바치고 싶습니다. 자원봉사자가 되기 위한 과정이 어떻게 되나요?
M 전화 주셔서 고맙습니다, Sanders 씨. 저희 Seaside 자선 단체는 항상 봉사하겠다는 제안을 기꺼이 받아들이죠. 이번 주 토요일에 고아를 위한 기금 마련 행사가 있는데 자원봉사자들을 더 많이 고용했으면 해요. 관심이 있으신가요?
W 완벽하군요. 일정상 그 시간에 잡힌 일이 없기 때문에, 제가 도움이 된다면 기쁠 것 같아요.
M 저희 웹사이트를 방문하시면, 행사에 대해 아실 수 있고, 저희가 어떤 유형의 자원 봉사자를 필요로 하는지도 알게 되실 거예요. 저희 웹사이트를 보시고 제게 바로 다시 전화를 주셔서 어떤 일을 하고 싶으신지 말씀해 주는 것이 어떨까요?

dedicate 헌신하다, 바치다 | **process** 과정, 절차 | **volunteer** 자원봉사자 | **be willing to** 기꺼이 ~하다 | **fundraiser** 모금 행사 | **orphan** 고아 | **assistance** 도움

35 여자가 전화를 건 목적은 무엇인가?
(A) 남자에게 도움을 달라고 요청하기 위해
(B) 면접 일정을 정하기 위해
(C) 무료로 일을 하겠다고 제안하기 위해
(D) 다가 오는 행사에 대해 알기 위해

| 해설 | 대화 초반부에 여자는 '당신 조직에 시간을 바치고 싶다'(I'd love to dedicate some time to your organization)고 말한 후 자원봉사에 지원하는 법을 묻는다. 따라서 여자가 전화를 건 이유는 (C)이다.

36 토요일에 무엇이 계획되어 있는가?
(A) 해변 파티
(B) 자선 행사
(C) 특별 만찬
(D) 독서

| 해설 | 남자는 토요일에 '고아를 위한 기금 마련 행사'(a fundraiser for orphans)가 진행될 것이어서 자원봉사자가 필요하다고 말한다. 따라서 토요일에 예정된 사항은 (B)의 '자선 행사'이다.

37 남자는 여자에게 무엇을 할 것을 요청하는가?
(A) 자신의 단체의 웹페이지를 방문한다
(B) 사무실에서 자신을 만난다
(C) 내일 오후에 자신에게 전화한다
(D) 계좌 이체를 통해 기부금을 보낸다

donation 기부, 기증 | **bank transfer** 계좌 이체

| 해설 | 남자의 마지막 말에서 정답의 단서를 찾을 수 있다. 그는 여자에게 '웹사이트를 살펴보고'(checking out our Web site) 자신에게 다시 연락을 줄 것을 부탁하고 있다. 따라서 그가 요청한 사항은 (A)이다.

[38-40]

W Excuse me, but I have a ticket for the express train to Boston. Can you tell me which gate it's leaving from?
M I'm very sorry, ma'am, but it pulled out of the station about three minutes ago. I'm afraid you need to wait for the next train for Boston to depart. I think that's going to be around 7 o'clock.

W Oh, no. I can't believe I missed my train. It's my first time to visit this station, so I got lost on my way here. Anyway, it looks like I've got to wait for an hour. I guess I've got time to grab a bite to eat.

W 죄송하지만, 저는 보스턴행 특급 열차 티켓을 가지고 있어요. 기차가 어느 게이트에서 출발하는지 알려 주실 수 있나요?
M 고객님, 정말 죄송하지만, 그 기차는 약 3분전에 역을 빠져 나갔어요. 안타깝게도 이다음에 출발하는 보스턴행 열차를 기다리셔야 할 것 같군요. 7시 정도에 출발하는 것으로 알고 있어요.
W 오, 이런. 제가 기차를 놓쳤다니 믿기지가 않아요. 이 역에 온 것이 이번이 처음이라, 도중에 길을 잃었거든요. 어쨌든, 제가 한 시간 동안 기다려야 할 것으로 보이네요. 간단히 식사를 할 시간이 생긴 것 같군요.

express train 특급 열차 | **pull out of** ~에서 빠져 나가다, ~에서 철수하다 | **on one's way** 도중에 | **grab a bite to eat** 간단히 먹다

38 대화가 어디에서 이루어지고 있는가?
(A) 지하철에서
(B) 버스 터미널에서
(C) 공항에서
(D) 기차역에서

| 해설 | 언뜻 들으면 (A)와 (D) 모두가 정답이 될 수 있을 것 같지만, '보스턴행 특급 열차'(express train to Boston)라는 표현과 '다음 기차가 1시간 후에 출발할 것'이라는 내용에 착안하면 정답은 (D)임을 알 수 있다.

39 여자의 문제는 무엇인가?
(A) 티켓을 잘못 샀다.
(B) 충분한 돈을 가지고 있지 않다.
(C) 목적지에 늦게 도착했다.
(D) 어디로 가야 하는지 잊었다.

destination 목적지

| 해설 | 대화의 후반부에서 여자는 자신이 기차를 놓친 이유가 '길을 잃었기 때문'(I got lost on my way here)이라고 말한다. 따라서 정답은 (C)인데, (C)에서 destination은 기차역을 의미한다.

40 여자는 이다음에 무엇을 할 것인가?
(A) 음식을 먹는다
(B) 티켓을 구입한다
(C) 환불을 요청한다
(D) 쇼핑을 한다

| 해설 | 여자의 마지막 말, 'I guess I've got time to grab a bite to eat.'에서 여자는 기다리는 시간 동안 식사를 할 것이라는 점을 알 수 있다. 따라서 정답은 (A)이다.

[41-43]

M Elaine, nobody here in the office can access the Internet again. This is the third time in four days that we've lost the connection. We'd better consider changing Internet providers.
W I couldn't agree more. To be honest, I was going to suggest the same thing at the staff meeting this afternoon. I even went ahead and found a company I believe would be a good fit for us.
M Way to show initiative, Elaine. Which company is it?
W It's Info Solutions. The law firm I was employed at prior to coming here used its services, and we never had any problems during the five years I worked there.

M Elaine, 또 다시 여기 사무실에서 인터넷 연결이 되지 않아요. 4일 동안 연결이 끊긴 것이 이번이 벌써 세 번째예요. 인터넷 업체를 바꾸는 것을 고려해 보는 것이 좋겠어요.
W 전적으로 동감이에요. 솔직히 말해서, 저는 오늘 오후 직원 회의에서 같은 사항을 제안하려고 했어요. 심지어 제 생각에 우리에게 적합한 업체를 미리 찾아 보기도 했고요.
M 추진력이 있군요, Elaine. 어떤 업체인가요?
W Info Solutions예요. 제가 이곳에 오기 전 일했던 법률 사무소에서 그곳 서비스를 이용했는데, 제가 거기서 일했던 5년 동안 아무런 문제가 없었어요.

access 접근하다 | **connection** 연결 | **to be honest** 솔직히 말해서 | **fit** (옷 등이) 맞다; 맞는 것 | **initiative** 독창성, 진취성 | **prior to** ~에 앞서

41 화자들은 어디에 있는 것 같은가?
(A) 법률 사무소에
(B) 컴퓨터 연구소에
(C) 사무실에
(D) 회의실에

| 해설 | 대화 첫 부분의 nobody here in the office can access the Internet again을 놓치지 않고 들었다면 정답은 (C)라는 사실을 알 수 있다. 참고로 (A)의 '법률 사무소'는 여자의 전 직장이다.

42 남자는 왜 여자를 칭찬하는가?
(A) 그녀는 한 회사와 계약을 협상했다.
(B) 그녀가 문제에 대한 해결 방법을 찾았다.
(C) 그녀는 회사의 경비를 절약했다.
(D) 그녀가 직원 회의의 일정을 조정했다.

solution 해결, 해결 방안

| 해설 | 인터넷 연결 문제를 해결하기 위해 여자가 '적합한 다른 업체'(a company I believe would be a good fit for us)를 찾아 보았다고 말하자 남자가 이에 대해 칭찬을 한다. 따라서 칭찬한 이유는 (B)로 볼 수 있다.

> ☑ **700점 넘기 포인트** 최근 토익에서는 구어체 표현을 자주 들을 수 있는데 이 대화에서도 way to show initiative라는 표현이 사용되고 있다. 이는 직역하면 '(그것은) 추진력을 보일 수 있는 방법이다'라는 뜻이지만, 보통 칭찬을 할 때 많이 쓰이는 표현이다. 구어체 표현에 익숙하지 않은 경우에는, 문맥이나 화자의 톤으로 구어체 표현의 의미를 짐작해야 한다.

43 여자는 Info Solutions에 대해 무엇을 말하는가?
(A) 그곳에 근무하는 변호사가 있다.
(B) 낮은 요금을 부과한다.
(C) 최고의 관리 요원들이 있다.
(D) 효과적인 서비스를 제공한다.

lawyer 변호사 | **maintenance staff** 관리 요원, 정비 직원

| 해설 | 여자는 Info Solutions에 대해 '자신이 그곳에서 일했을 때 어떤 문제도 겪지 않았다'(we never had any problems during the five years I worked there)고 평가한다. 따라서 정답은 (D)이다.

[44-46]

W Hello. This is the Rosedale Community Center. How may I be of assistance?
M Hi. Um, I'm calling to find out about the classes you're offering this winter.

W Which one are you interested in?
M Is it true that Cathy Pollard will be teaching a class on painting?
W Yes, it is. But there's only one spot left, so if you want to take it, you'd better sign up right now.
M This must be my lucky day. I'd definitely like to reserve that seat. What do you need to know?
W Your name and telephone number. And I have to get your credit card information so that you can pay the $100 fee. Just so you know, the price includes the cost of the materials you're going to use.

W 안녕하세요. Rosedale 주민 센터입니다. 어떻게 도와 드릴까요?
M 안녕하세요. 음, 저는 이번 겨울에 제공되는 수업에 대해 알아보려고 전화를 드렸어요.
W 어떤 수업에 관심이 있으신가요?
M Cathy Pollard가 회화 수업을 담당할 것이라는 점이 사실인가요?
W 네, 그래요. 하지만 단 한 자리만이 남아 있기 때문에, 수강을 원하시면, 지금 바로 등록을 하시는 것이 좋을 것 같군요.
M 정말로 운이 좋은 날이군요. 지금 그 자리를 꼭 예약하고 싶어요. 무엇을 알려드리면 될까요?
W 성함과 전화번호요. 그리고 100달러의 수업료를 지불하기 위해서는 제가 고객님의 신용 카드 정보도 알아야 해요. 아시겠지만, 수업료에는 고객님께서 사용하실 재료에 관한 비용도 포함되어 있어요.

---

spot 자리, 장소 | **definitely** 분명히; 반드시 | **material** 물질; 재료

44 남자가 전화한 목적은 무엇인가?
  (A) 등록을 취소하기 위해
  (B) 강사와의 통화를 요청하기 위해
  (C) 수업에 관해 문의하기 위해
  (D) 수업이 언제 실시되는지 알기 위해

inquire 묻다, 문의하다

| 해설 | 대화 초반부에서 남자는 '수업에 관해 알아보려고 전화했다'(I'm calling to find out about the classes)고 말한다. 따라서 남자가 전화를 한 목적은 (C)이다.

45 Pollard 씨에 대해 무엇이 암시되어 있는가?
  (A) 그녀는 많은 그림을 팔았다.
  (B) 그녀는 주민 센터에서 정규직으로 일을 한다.
  (C) 그녀는 유화 수업을 담당한다.
  (D) 그녀는 유명한 강사이다.

work full time 정규직으로 일하다, 전임으로 일하다 | **oil painting** 유화

| 해설 | Pollard 씨의 수업이 한 자리만 남아 있다는 점, 그리고 그러한 이야기를 듣고 남자가 'This must be my lucky day.'라고 말한 점에서 Pollard 씨 수업은 듣기가 힘든 수업임을 알 수 있다. 이를 통해 Pollard 씨는 '유명 강사'일 것이라고 추측할 수 있으므로 정답은 (D)이다.

46 남자가 "This must be my lucky day"라고 말할 때 남자는 무엇을 의미하는가?
  (A) 수업에 자리가 있어서 그는 운이 좋다.
  (B) 수업료를 지불할 충분한 돈이 있어서 그는 운이 좋다.
  (C) 전에 Pollard 씨를 만난 적이 있어서 그는 기쁘다.
  (D) 겨울에 시간이 있어서 그는 기쁘다.

| 해설 | 여자가 '한 자리만 남아 있다'(there's only one spot left)고 말하자 그에 대한 반응으로 남자가 한 말이다. 따라서 정답은 (A)로, 이는 남자의 그 다음 말, 'I'd definitely like to reserve that seat.'를 통해서도 확인이 가능하다.

[47-49]

W Why haven't the wastebaskets been emptied? Didn't the cleaning crew come last night?
M They did, but they don't appear to have done a thorough job.
W Uh-oh. Aside from not taking out the trash, what else didn't they do?
M The carpet in the Sales Department wasn't vacuumed, and the employee lounge is an absolute mess.
W Didn't we change cleaning services recently? We never had any problems with the previous company.
M That's true, but B&G, Inc. raised its rates too much. That's why we hired the new company.
W Well, I'm going to give the person in charge there a call and insist that the work crews do a better job from now on. This kind of shoddy work is simply not acceptable.

W 왜 쓰레기통이 비어 있지 않죠? 어젯밤에 청소부가 오지 않았나요?
M 오기는 했지만, 일을 철저히 하지는 않은 것 같군요.
W 이런. 쓰레기를 버리지 않은 것 외에도, 또 무엇을 하지 않았나요?
M 영업부의 카펫을 진공청소기로 청소하지 않았고, 직원 휴게실은 완전히 엉망이에요.
W 최근에 청소 용역업체를 바꾸지 않았나요? 기존 업체와는 아무런 문제가 없었어요.
M 그건 사실이지만, B&G 주식회사가 요금을 너무 많이 올렸어요. 그것이 새로운 업체를 선정한 이유죠.
W 음, 그곳 담당자에게 전화를 해서 지금부터는 청소 직원들이 일을 더 잘해야 한다고 요구할게요. 이처럼 제대로 되지 않은 작업은 받아들일 수 없어요.

---

wastebasket 쓰레기통 | **empty** 비우다 | **cleaning crew** 청소부 | **thorough** 철저한 | **aside from** ~을 제외하고 | **vacuum** 진공청소기로 청소하다 | **employee lounge** 직원 휴게실 | **absolute** 완전한, 완벽한 | **mess** 엉망인 상태 | **in charge** 담당하고 있는 | **insist** 주장하다 | **shoddy** 조잡한, 부당한

47 여자는 왜 화가 났는가?
  (A) 그녀의 카펫이 진공청소기로 청소되지 않았다.
  (B) 그녀의 사무실이 청소되지 않았다.
  (C) 욕실이 엉망이다.
  (D) 쓰레기통이 비워지지 않았다.

| 해설 | 여자의 첫 번째 말인 'Why haven't the wastebaskets been emptied?'를 통해, 여자는 쓰레기통이 비워 있지 않아 기분이 상했음을 알 수 있다. 따라서 정답은 (D)이다. (A)의 경우, 진공청소기로 청소되지 않은 카펫은 영업부 카펫이며, (B)는 직접적으로 언급된 사항이 아닐뿐만 아니라 너무 포괄적인 내용이라 정답으로 보기 힘들다.

48 남자는 B&G 주식회사에 관해 무엇을 암시하는가?
  (A) 곧 파산할 것이다.
  (B) 일을 잘하는 사람들을 고용하지 않는다.
  (C) 현 청소 업체보다 더 많은 요금을 부과한다.
  (D) 성과가 좋지 못해서 선정 업체가 되지 않았다.

go out of business 파산하다

| 해설 | 남자는 'B&G 주식회사가 요금을 과도하게 인상시켰다'(B&G, Inc. raised its rates too much)고 말한 후, 그것이 새 업체를 선정하게 된 이유라고 밝힌다. 따라서 현 업체의 요금은 B&G 보다 낮을 것으로 생각해 볼 수 있

으므로 정답은 (C)가 된다.

49 여자는 아마도 이다음에 무엇을 할 것인가?
(A) 모임을 주선한다
(B) 전화를 건다
(C) 이메일을 보낸다
(D) 업체를 방문한다

| 해설 | 대화의 마지막 부분에서 여자는 '업체의 담당자에게 전화를 걸어'(I'm going to give the person in charge there a call) 불만을 표시할 것이라고 말한다. 따라서 (B)가 정답이다.

[50-52]

W My computer just got disconnected from the Internet again. Do you know what the problem is?
M I haven't the slightest idea. The same thing has also happened to me several times this morning.
W We ought to do something about this.
M Let's speak with the Maintenance Department. We can get a repairman here to determine the cause of the problem.
W Okay. How about if you call them while I ask around to see if anyone else is having connectivity issues?
M Good thinking. Oh, do you happen to know the number for the Maintenance Department?
W Sorry, but I've never called anyone there before. Just dial 0, and the receptionist can connect you.
M Right. Why didn't I think of that?

> W 조금 전 제 컴퓨터에서 또 다시 인터넷 연결이 끊겼어요. 문제가 무엇인지 알고 있나요?
> M 전혀 모르겠어요. 오늘 아침 똑같은 일이 제게도 여러 차례 일어났어요.
> W 그에 대해 무언가 조치를 취해야겠군요.
> M 관리부에 얘기해 볼게요. 여기로 수리 기사를 불러서 문제의 원인을 알아볼 수 있어요.
> W 좋아요. 다른 누군가가 연결 문제를 겪고 있는지 제가 확인해 보는 동안 당신이 전화를 하는 것이 어떨까요?
> M 좋은 생각이군요. 오, 혹시 관리부의 전화번호를 알고 있나요?
> W 미안하지만, 저는 그곳에 전화를 걸어본 적이 없어요. 0번을 누르면, 접수 직원이 연결시켜 줄 거예요.
> M 맞아요. 제가 왜 그 생각을 못했을까요?

disconnect 연결을 끊다 | **determine** 결심하다; 알아 보다 | **connectivity** 연결 | **issue** 문제 | **receptionist** 접수 직원

50 무엇이 문제인가?
(A) 한 컴퓨터가 작동을 멈추었다.
(B) 전기가 나갔다.
(C) 인터넷에 연결을 할 수 없다.
(D) 소프트웨어에 문제가 있다.

| 해설 | 대화 초반부에 여자가 '인터넷 연결이 되지 않는다'(got disconnected from the Internet)는 문제를 제기하고 있으므로 정답은 (C)이다.

51 남자는 무엇을 하는 것을 원하는가?
(A) 수리 기사의 서비스를 요청한다
(B) 관리자에게 보고서를 제출한다
(C) 상사에게 새로운 장비를 구입할 것을 요청한다
(D) 인터넷에 한 번 더 연결을 시도해 본다

file a report 보고서를 제출하다

| 해설 | 문제를 해결하기 위해 조치를 취해야 한다는 여자의 말에 남자는 관리부에 연락할 것을 제안하면서 'We can get a repairman here to determine the cause of the problem.'이라고 말한다. 즉 남자가 원하는 것은 관리부를 통해 수리 기사를 부르는 것이므로 정답은 (A)가 된다.

52 여자는 남자에게 무엇을 하라고 말하는가?
(A) 관리부를 방문한다
(B) 접수 직원과 이야기한다
(C) 올바른 내선 번호를 찾아 본다
(D) 문제를 해결하기 위한 노력을 중단한다

extension 내선 번호 | **look up** (자료 등을) 찾아보다

| 해설 | 대화 후반부의 여자의 말, 'Just dial 0, and the receptionist can connect you.'에서 여자는 남자에게 접수 직원과 이야기하라고 말하고 있다. 따라서 (B)가 정답이다.

[53-55]

Man A Here are your schedules for next week. Please note that both of you are working slightly different shifts than normal.
Man B Why did they change?
Man A We've got many new employees, and you're our most experienced workers. I want you two working different shifts to provide as much assistance as possible for the inexperienced people.
Woman Um, Brad, there's a slight problem here.
Man A What is it?
Woman I can't work on Wednesday evening. My sister is flying in from Sydney, and I have to pick her up then. Did you forget I mentioned this to you earlier in the week?
Man A Yeah, it completely slipped my mind.
Man B I can switch shifts with you on Wednesday, Stacy.
Woman Thanks so much, Dean. You're a lifesaver.

> Man A 다음 주 당신들의 일정이 여기에 있어요. 두 사람 모두 평소와 약간 다른 근무 시간에 일을 하게 될 거예요.
> Man B 왜 바뀌었죠?
> Man A 신입 직원들이 많아졌는데, 당신들은 가장 경험이 많은 직원이에요. 경험이 없는 사람들을 위해 두 사람이 가능한 많은 도움을 줄 수 있도록 서로 다른 근무 시간에 일을 했으면 좋겠어요.
> Woman 음, Brad, 여기에 사소한 문제가 하나 있군요.
> Man A 그것이 무엇인가요?
> Woman 저는 수요일 저녁에는 일을 할 수 없어요. 제 동생이 시드니에서 올 텐데, 제가 그때 그녀를 마중가야 하죠. 제가 주 초반에 이러한 사실을 당신에게 언급했다는 점을 잊었나요?
> Man A 예, 완전히 잊고 있었네요.
> Man B 제가 수요일 근무를 바꾸어 줄 수 있어요, Stacy.
> Woman 정말 고마워요, Dean. 당신이 저를 살렸군요.

note 주목하다 | **shift** 교대 근무 시간 | **normal** 평소의; 정상적인 | **inexperienced** 경험이 없는, 숙련되지 않은 | **slip one's mind** 잊어 버리다 | **switch** 바꾸다, 전환하다 | **lifesaver** 생명의 은인

53 화자들은 무엇을 논의하는가?
(A) 새로운 일정
(B) 직원 교육

(C) 회사의 신입 직원
(D) 휴가 계획

| 해설 | 근무와 관련된 서로의 일정에 대해 논의하고 있으므로 정답은 (A)이다.

54 여자의 말에 따르면, 문제가 무엇인가?
(A) 그녀의 여행 계획이 연기되었다.
(B) 그녀는 동생과 잘 지내지 못한다.
(C) 그녀의 근무 시간에 경험이 없는 사람들이 너무 많다.
(D) 일정 상의 시간에 일을 할 수가 없다.

| 해설 | 여자는 'I can't work on Wednesday evening.'이라고 말한 후, 그 이유가 동생을 마중가야 하기 때문이라고 밝힌다. 따라서 문제는 예정되어 있는 근무 시간에 그녀가 일을 할 수 없다는 점이므로 (D)가 정답이다.

55 여자는 왜 기뻐하는가?
(A) 그녀는 여러 해 동안 동생을 보지 못했다.
(B) Dean이 수요일 저녁에 일을 할 수 있다.
(C) 그녀가 직원들을 교육시키는 것을 Brad가 도울 것이다.
(D) 그녀는 곧 시드니로 여행을 갈 것이다.

| 해설 | 남자B의 말, 'I can switch shifts with you on Wednesday, Stacy.'를 듣고 여자가 고마움을 표시하며 안도하고 있다. 따라서 그녀 대신 Dean이 수요일 근무를 하게 되어 여자가 기뻐한 것이므로 정답은 (B)이다.

[56-58]

M   We need to add one more person to the negotiating team heading to Madrid tomorrow. Who would be ideal?
W   Ray Walker would make a great addition to the team. How about asking him?
M   I did, but he informed me that his passport has expired. I also considered asking Tina Andrews, but she doesn't speak the language there.
W   Oh . . . The person ought to speak Spanish. Well, I took a few semesters in college, and I've vacationed in Spain three times.
M   That's sufficient. You have a passport, don't you?
W   Yes, and it's not going to expire for a couple more years.
M   Great. You're on the team. I'll tell Diana Matthews that you're going with her. You'd better leave work immediately so that you can pack your bags.

> M   내일 마드리드로 가는 협상팀에 한 명을 더 추가시켜야 해요. 누가 이상적일까요?
> W   Ray Walker가 팀에 추가되면 좋을 것 같아요. 그에게 물어보는 것이 어떨까요?
> M   그랬는데, 그가 자신의 여권이 소멸되었다고 제게 알려 주더군요. Tina Andrews에게 물어보는 것도 생각해 보았지만, 그녀는 그곳 언어를 할 줄 몰라요.
> W   오… 스페인어를 할 수 있는 사람이어야 하군요. 음, 제가 대학에서 강의를 몇 번 들었고, 방학을 스페인에서 세 번 보냈어요.
> M   그것이면 충분해요. 여권을 가지고 있죠, 그렇지 않나요?
> W   네, 그리고 앞으로 2년간은 소멸되지 않을 거예요.
> M   잘 되었군요. 당신이 팀원이에요. Diana Matthews에게 당신이 함께 갈 것이라고 말을 할게요. 가방을 꾸릴 수 있도록 즉시 퇴근하는 편이 좋겠어요.

add 더하다, 추가하다 | **head to** ~으로 향하다 | **ideal** 이상적인 | **passport** 여권 | **expire** 소멸하다 | **vacation** 휴가, 방학; 휴가를 보내다 | **sufficient** 충분한

| **pack** (짐을) 꾸리다, 싸다

56 협상팀은 언제 마드리드로 갈 것인가?
(A) 퇴근 후에
(B) 내일
(C) 모레
(D) 이번 주말

| 해설 | 남자의 첫 번째 말에서 협상팀은 '내일' 마드리드로 떠날 것임을 알 수 있다. 따라서 정답은 (B)이다.

57 남자는 왜 "That's sufficient"라고 말하는가?
(A) 여자의 발언에 대한 만족감을 나타내기 위해
(B) 여자에게 더 많은 정보를 달라고 요청하기 위해
(C) 여자가 한 제안을 거절하기 위해
(D) 여자의 해결 방안의 문제점을 지적하기 위해

| 해설 | 스페인어 구사 능력에 대한 여자의 발언을 듣고 남자가 보인 반응이다. 이후 여권도 가지고 있다는 여자의 말에 남자는 'Great.'라고 말하면서 여자가 스페인 출장팀에 합류할 것을 지시하고 있으므로 그가 'That's sufficient.'라고 말한 이유는 (A)로 볼 수 있다.

58 남자는 여자에게 무엇을 할 것을 제안하는가?
(A) 곧 퇴근을 한다
(B) Diana Matthews에게 전화한다
(C) 스페인어 공부를 시작한다
(D) 여권을 갱신한다

| 해설 | 대화 마지막 부분에서 남자는 'You'd better leave work immediately so that you can pack your bags.'라고 말하면서 여자에게 곧바로 퇴근을 해서 짐을 싸라고 이야기한다. 따라서 남자가 제안한 사항은 (A)이다.

[59-61]

W   Good morning, sir. Where are you headed today?
M   I'm going on a business trip to Tokyo. Here are my ticket and passport.
W   Thank you very much. Do you have any luggage to check?
M   I've got one bag here that I need to check in, and I'm carrying my laptop on board with me.
W   Okay. Let me get a luggage tag for you . . . Oh, I'm sorry, sir, but your bag weighs too much. You're only allowed 20 kilograms, but it weighs 23 kilograms.
M   Should I remove some of my belongings?
W   You can either do that, or you can pay an overweight bag fee.
M   I'll pay the fee. How much do I owe?
W   That will be forty-five dollars, please.

M 요금을 낼게요. 얼마를 드려야 하죠?
W 45달러입니다.

luggage 짐, 수화물 | **check in** (짐을) 부치다 | **on board** 승선하여 | **weigh** 무게가 나가다 | **remove** 제거하다 | **belonging** 소지품, 재산 | **overweight** 과체중의, 용량 초과의 | **owe** 빚지다

59 대화가 어디에서 이루어지고 있는 것 같은가?
 (A) 출입국 심사 데스크에서
 (B) 수화물 찾는 곳에서
 (C) 탑승 수속 창구에서
 (D) 탑승구에서

immigration desk 출입국 심사 데스크 | **baggage claim area** 수화물 찾는 곳 | **check-in counter** 탑승 수속 창구

| 해설 | 부칠 수화물의 무게를 재는 곳은 (C)의 '탑승 수속 창구'이므로 (C)가 정답이다. 참고로 (A)는 여권과 비자 등을 확인함으로써 적법한 출입국이 이루어지도록 하는 곳이고, (D)는 비행기에 탑승하기 직전에 해당 항공사에서 항공권 등을 확인하는 곳이다.

60 남자는 무엇을 제안하는가?
 (A) 가방을 가지고 탑승한다
 (B) 분실된 가방에 대해 항의를 한다
 (C) 가방에서 몇몇 물품들을 꺼낸다
 (D) 가방을 X레이로 검사한다

file a claim 항의를 하다, 클레임을 걸다

| 해설 | 남자는 'Should I remove some of my belongings?'라고 말하면서 가방에 있는 물건을 꺼내야 하는지 묻고 있다. 따라서 남자가 제안한 것은 (C)이다.

61 여자는 남자에게 무엇을 하라고 요청하는가?
 (A) 추가 요금을 낸다
 (B) 탑승권을 보관한다
 (C) 가방에 이름을 쓴다
 (D) 가방을 잠근다

| 해설 | 남자가 가방의 무게를 줄여야 하는지 묻자 여자는 'You can either do that, or you can pay an overweight bag fee.'라고 답한다. 따라서 여자가 요청한 바는 가방의 무게를 줄이거나 추가 요금을 내는 것이므로 정답은 이들 중 후자를 가리키고 있는 (A)가 된다.

[62-64]
Woman Now that you've seen my presentation, do you have any questions about the DV5000?
Man A How is our product different from the other ones on the market?
Woman It's capable of ironing clothes in less time than any other products.
Man B How does it do that?
Woman Simple. It uses more heat than other irons, so that lets it remove wrinkles from clothes more quickly.
Man A Can't that hurt the people using it? We don't want anyone getting severe burns.
Woman That's a distinct possibility. However, we're planning to market it to dry cleaners and other professionals. They know how to take the proper precautions.
Man B So the DV5000 isn't for home use?
Woman Precisely. We anticipate 98% of all sales will be to professional users.

Woman 제 발표를 보셨으니, DV5000에 관해 하실 질문이 있으신가요?
Man A 저희 제품이 시중에 나와 있는 다른 것들과는 어떻게 다르죠?
Woman 다른 어떤 제품보다 빠른 시간 내에 옷을 다림질 할 수 있어요.
Man B 어떻게 그런가요?
Woman 간단해요. 다른 다리미들보다 더 많은 열을 사용하기 때문에, 의류의 구김을 보다 빠르게 제거하죠.
Man A 그러면 사용하는 사람이 다칠 수도 있지 않을까요? 누군가가 심한 화상을 입는 것은 원하지 않거든요.
Woman 분명 그럴 가능성이 있습니다. 하지만, 우리는 이것을 세탁업자나 기타 전문가들을 대상으로 마케팅할 계획입니다. 그들은 적절히 주의하는 법을 알고 있죠.
Man B 그렇다면 DV5000은 가정용이 아니죠?
Woman 정확히 그렇습니다. 우리는 전체 판매의 98%가 전문적인 사용자에 의해 이루어질 것으로 예상하고 있습니다.

different from ~와 다른 | **be capable of** ~을 할 수 있다 | **iron** 다리미; 다림질하다 | **wrinkle** 주름 | **severe** 심한 | **burn** (불에) 타다; 화상 | **distinct** 분명한, 명백한 | **possibility** 가능성 | **dry cleaner** 세탁업자 | **precaution** 주의 | **precisely** 정확하게 | **anticipate** 예상하다

62 화자들에 관해 무엇이 암시되어 있는가?
 (A) 그들은 같은 회사에서 일한다.
 (B) 그들은 합동 발표를 하고 있다.
 (C) 그들은 엔지니어로 고용되어 있다.
 (D) 그들은 DV5000을 디자인하는 데 도움을 주었다.

joint 합동의, 공동의

| 해설 | 남자A가 DV5000을 our product으로 지칭하고 있다는 점에서, 그리고 화자들이 주어로 we를 사용하고 있다는 점에서 화자들은 모두 같은 회사의 직원임을 짐작할 수 있다. 따라서 정답은 (A)이다.

63 여자가 "That's a distinct possibility"라고 말할 때 여자는 무엇을 의미하는가?
 (A) 엔지니어들은 DV5000의 재설계를 원할 수도 있다.
 (B) DV5000은 아마도 잘 팔릴 것이다.
 (C) DV5000을 마케팅하는데 문제가 있을 수 있다.
 (D) DV5000을 사용하는 사람들이 다칠 수도 있다.

| 해설 | 'That's a distinct possibility.'는 '분명 그럴 가능성이 있다'라는 뜻으로 일종의 동의를 나타내는 표현인데, 앞서 남자A가 고열로 사람들이 다칠 수 있음을 지적하자 여자가 그와 같이 답변했다. 따라서 주어진 문장을 통해 여자가 의미한 바는 (D)이다.

64 DV5000에 대해 언급된 것은 무엇인가?
 (A) 시중에서 가장 비싼 다리미이다.
 (B) 98%의 만족도를 보인다.
 (C) 대부분의 구매자들은 그것을 올바르게 사용할 것이다.
 (D) 회사는 젊은 성인들에게 마케팅을 할 것이다.

satisfaction rate 만족도

| 해설 | DV5000이 더 높은 열을 사용한다는 언급은 있었지만 가장 비싸다는 언급은 없었으므로 (A)는 정답이 아니며, 98%라는 수치는 예상되는 구매자의 직업을 거론할 때 나온 말이므로 (B) 역시 정답이 될 수 없다. 또한 마케팅 대상은 세탁업자와 전문가일 것이라고 했으므로 (D)도 사실과 다르다. 따라서 정답은 (C)인데, 이는 'They know how to take the proper precautions.'라는 여자의 말을 통해 확인할 수 있다.

[65-67]

W Pardon me, but would you happen to know this part of town well? I'm visiting this neighborhood for the first time, and I'm afraid I've gotten lost.
M I should be able to provide some assistance. Where are you heading?
W I'm looking for the local branch of Trust Bank. I thought it was here on State Street, but that doesn't seem to be the case.
M Ah, it used to be here, but it moved to another building in November.
W I see. Does that building happen to be nearby?
M Yes, you can walk there easily. Go straight to the corner and take a right on Carter Street. You want the second building on the left-hand side of the street.
W Thank you for your assistance. You've been a tremendous help.

W 죄송하지만, 혹시 이 구역에 대해 잘 아시나요? 저는 이곳 방문이 처음이라, 제가 길을 잃었는지 걱정이 되는군요.
M 제가 도움을 드릴 수 있을 거예요. 어디로 가시는 중인가요?
W 저는 Trust 은행의 지점을 찾고 있어요. 여기 State 가에 있는 것으로 생각했지만, 그렇지가 않아 보이네요.
M 아, 전에 여기 있었는데, 하지만 11월에 다른 건물로 이전을 했어요.
W 그렇군요. 혹시 그 빌딩이 근처에 있나요?
M 네, 그곳까지 쉽게 걸어가실 수 있어요. 모퉁이까지 직진하신 다음에 Carter 가에서 우회전하세요. 찾으시는 곳은 거리의 왼쪽에 있는 두 번째 건물이에요.
W 도와 주셔서 고마워요. 정말로 큰 도움이 되었어요.

---

get lost 길을 잃다 | **local branch** 지점, 지사 | **be the case** 그러하다 | **used to** ~하곤 했다 | **nearby** 인근의, 근처의 | **tremendous** 막대한

65 화자들은 어디에 있는 것 같은가?
(A) 은행에
(B) 거리에
(C) 사무실에
(D) 버스 정류장에

| 해설 | 거리에서 흔히 들을 수 있는, 길을 묻는 내용의 대화이다. 정답은 (B)이다.

66 남자는 은행에 대해 무엇을 말하는가?
(A) 그곳 위치가 바뀌었다.
(B) 그는 그곳에 돈을 보관하고 있다.
(C) 여자는 거기까지 버스를 타고 가야 한다.
(D) 그곳은 곧 문을 닫을 것이다.

| 해설 | 남자는 여자가 찾는 은행 지점이 한때 State 가에 있었지만, '다른 곳으로 이전을 했다'(it moved to another building)고 알려 준다. 따라서 정답은 (A)이다.

67 도표를 보아라. 여자의 최종 목적지는 어디인가?
(A) 1
(B) 2
(C) 3
(D) 4

| 해설 | 남자는 모퉁이까지 직진한 후 Carter 가에서 우회전하면 왼쪽 두 번째 건물에서 은행 지점을 찾을 수 있다고 안내한다. 지도에서 이에 해당되는 곳은 (A)의 1이다.

[68-70]

M How were our sales during the past seven days?
W As you can see on the graph, we sold more than $25,000 in clothes last week.
M That's incredible. We've never had a week that good before, have we?
W I don't believe so. We appear to be gaining popularity with many shoppers in the mall.
M And it looks like we sold more men's clothes than anything else. I never imagined that would happen.
W Actually, there's a mistake on the graph you're looking at.
M What's wrong with it?
W The figure you're looking at has been labeled incorrectly. We need to reverse the numbers for men's and women's clothes.
M I see. Okay, the new numbers make a lot more sense now.
W You're right. Still, the numbers are all positive and have been improving recently.

M 지난 7일 동안 매출이 어땠나요?
W 그래프에서 볼 수 있듯이, 지난 주에는 의류를 25,000달러 이상 판매했어요.
M 놀랍군요. 전에는 그만큼 좋았던 주가 없었잖아요, 그렇죠?
W 없었다고 생각해요. 우리가 쇼핑몰의 많은 쇼핑객들에게 인기를 얻고 있는 것 같아요.
M 그리고 다른 어떤 것보다도 남성 의류를 더 많이 판매한 것으로 보이는군요. 그런 일이 일어나리라고는 상상도 못했어요.
W 실은, 당신이 보고 있는 그래프에는 한 가지 잘못된 점이 있어요.
M 무엇이 잘못되었나요?
W 당신이 보고 있는 수치에 항목 이름이 잘못 적혀져 있어요. 남성과 여성 의류의 숫자들을 서로 바꾸어야 해요.
M 알았어요. 좋아요, 새로운 숫자들로 바꾸니 훨씬 이해가 잘 되는군요.
W 맞아요. 그래도 수치들이 모두 긍정적이고 최근에 올라가고 있어요.

---

incredible 믿을 수 없는, 놀라운 | **gain** 얻다 | **popularity** 인기 | **figure** 수치 | **label** 라벨; 상표를 붙이다 | **reverse** 뒤바꾸다 | **make a sense** 말이 되다, 이치에 맞다

68 화자들은 주로 무엇을 논의하는가?
(A) 더 많은 의류를 판매해야 할 필요성
(B) 남성용 의류의 저조한 매출
(C) 판매되고 있는 의류의 스타일
(D) 매장의 주간 매출

| 해설 | 대화 초반부의 during the past seven days와 last week라는 표현에 주의하면 화자들은 지난 주 매출에 대한 이야기를 하고 있음을 쉽게 알 수 있다. 따라서 논의의 주제는 (D)이다.

69 매장에 대해 무엇이 암시되어 있는가?
(A) 신입 판매 직원들을 몇 명 고용했다.
(B) 쇼핑 센터 내에 위치해 있다.
(C) 몇 개월 전에 문을 열었다.
(D) 유명 브랜드 제품을 판매한다.

brand-name 유명 상표가 붙은, 유명 브랜드의

| 해설 | 대화 중반부에서 여자는 자신들이 '쇼핑몰 내 쇼핑객들에게 인기가 높아지고 있다'(gaining popularity with many shoppers in the mall)고 설명한다. 이를 통해 화자들의 매장은 쇼핑몰 내에 위치해 있을 것이라고 예상할 수 있으므로 정답은 (B)이다.

70 도표를 보아라. 지난 주 남성용 의류의 매출액은 얼마인가?
(A) 3,500달러
(B) 4,000달러
(C) 5,500달러
(D) 13,000달러

| 해설 | 여자는 도표상 남성용 의류와 여성용 의류의 수치가 서로 바뀌어야 한다는 점을 지적하고 있으므로 남성용 의류의 수치는, 13,000달러가 아닌, (C)의 '5,500달러'이다.

PART 4   p.87

[71-73]

W My next guest on tonight's show is one of the city's most popular residents. One year ago, Jeff Gonzalez was a guy who sometimes sang at weddings to earn a few extra dollars. But when he performed at a wedding last August, a music producer happened to be in attendance. Fascinated by his voice, the producer signed Jeff to a contract on the spot. In the following ten months, Jeff has produced two number-one singles and sold more than 2 million copies of his debut album. He's going to be here in my studio performing his latest song right after we listen to a few words from our sponsors.

W 오늘 방송의 다음 게스트는 시내에서 가장 유명한 사람 중 한 명입니다. 1년 전, Jeff Gonzalez는 몇 달러의 용돈을 벌기 위해 결혼식에서 때때로 노래를 부르던 사람이었습니다. 하지만 지난 8월 그가 어떤 결혼식에서 공연을 했을 때, 한 음악 프로듀서가 우연히 그곳에 참석을 하고 있었습니다. 그의 목소리에 매료되어, 그 프로듀서는 그 자리에서 Jeff와 계약을 체결했습니다. 10개월 후, Jeff는 1위를 차지한 두 개의 싱글 음반을 제작했고 그의 데뷔 앨범은 2백만 장 이상 판매되었습니다. 광고주들의 광고를 몇 개 들은 후에 이곳 스튜디오에서 그가 본인의 최신곡을 부를 것입니다.

wedding 결혼식 | **in attendance** 참석한 | **fascinate** 매혹시키다 | **voice** 목소리 | **on the spot** 그 자리에서, 즉석에서 | **number-one** 1등의, 1위의 | **debut album** 데뷔 앨범 | **latest** 최신의 | **sponsor** 후원자, 광고주

71 화자는 누구인 것 같은가?
(A) 라디오 진행자
(B) 음악 프로듀서
(C) 음악 비평가
(D) 가수

| 해설 | 화자는 Jeff Gonzalez라는 게스트를 소개한 후 앞으로 방송에서 진행될 내용을 안내하고 있다. 따라서 보기 중 이러한 일을 하는 사람은 (A)의 '라디오 진행자'밖에 없으므로 정답은 (A)이다.

72 작년에 Jeff Gonzalez에게 어떤 일이 일어났는가?
(A) 그는 결혼을 했다.
(B) 그는 계약을 체결했다.
(C) 그는 노래 수업을 들었다.

(D) 그는 두 번째 앨범을 발표했다.

| 해설 | 담화에서 '작년'(last year)에 일어났던 일이 언급되는 부분에 집중한다. 화자는 Jeff Gonzalez가 '지난 8월'(last August)에 결혼식장에서 노래를 부르던 중, 우연히 프로듀서에 의해 발탁되어 '그와 계약을 체결했다'(the producer signed Jeff to a contract)고 설명한다. 따라서 작년에 일어났던 일은 (B)의 '계약 체결'이다.

73 청자들은 이다음에 무엇을 들을 것인가?
(A) 라이브 공연
(B) 광고
(C) 교통 정보
(D) 녹음된 음악

| 해설 | 담화의 마지막 문장, 'He's going to be here in my studio performing his latest song right after we listen to a few words from our sponsors.'에서 화자들은 (B)의 '광고'를 듣게 될 것임을 알 수 있다. (A)의 '라이브 공연'은 광고를 들은 후에 일어날 일이다.

[74-76]

W If everyone would look at the handout I gave you, you'll see the results of last month's online survey. We received responses from more than 1,400 customers, and the results were mixed. Apparently, customers were highly satisfied with the prices we charge for our services. So we don't need to make any adjustments there. We also scored well on our speed and friendliness. On the negative side, many customers expressed a strong dislike for our Web site, calling it outdated, user unfriendly, and poorly designed. Customers additionally criticized the knowledge of our staff. Let's discuss these negatives and how we can fix them.

W 모두들 제가 드린 유인물을 살펴보시면, 지난 달 온라인 설문 조사의 결과를 보실 수 있습니다. 1,400명 이상의 고객들로부터 응답을 받았는데, 결과는 복합적입니다. 고객들은 서비스에 부과되는 요금에 대해서는 매우 만족한 것으로 보입니다. 따라서 그 부분에 관해서는 조정을 해야 할 필요가 없습니다. 또한 속도와 친절함에 대해서도 점수가 높았습니다. 부정적인 측면으로, 많은 고객들은 저희 웹사이트가 구식이고, 사용자 중심적이 아니며, 디자인이 좋지 못하다고 말하면서, 그에 대한 강한 불만을 나타냈습니다. 게다가 고객들은 직원들의 지식에 대해서도 비판을 했습니다. 이러한 부정적인 면과 이를 어떻게 해결할 수 있을지에 관해 논의해 봅시다.

handout 유인물 | **result** 결과 | **survey** 설문 조사 | **response** 반응, 대답 | **mixed** 섞인, 혼합된 | **highly** 매우 | **charge** (요금 등을) 부과하다 | **adjustment** 조정, 조절 | **score** 점수를 기록하다 | **negative** 부정적인 | **outdated** 구식의 | **user unfriendly** 사용자 중심적이지 않은 | **additionally** 게다가, 추가적으로 | **criticize** 비판하다 | **knowledge** 지식

74 담화의 목적은 무엇인가?
(A) 업무에 대해 참석자들을 칭찬하기 위해
(B) 신제품의 출시에 관해 이야기하기 위해
(C) 설문 결과에 관해 논의하기 위해
(D) 회사의 새로운 웹사이트에 대해 언급하기 위해

| 해설 | 담화의 초반부에서 담화의 주제가 '지난 달 온라인 설문 조사의 결과'(results of last month's online survey)임을 짐작할 수 있다. 따라서 정답은 (C)이다.

75 여자가 "So we don't need to make any adjustments there"라고

말할 때 여자는 무엇을 의미하는가?
(A) 회사는 가격을 변경하지 않을 것이다.
(B) 더 이상 직원이 고용되지 않을 것이다.
(C) 웹사이트는 업데이트될 필요가 없다.
(D) 직원들은 교육을 더 받을 필요가 없다.

| 해설 | 바로 앞 문장을 통해 there가 가리키는 것은 '가격 부문'임을 알 수 있으므로, 화자는 주어진 문장을 이용하여 '가격을 조정할 필요가 없다'는 의미를 전달하고 있다. 따라서 화자가 의미하는 바는 (A)이다.

76 화자는 무엇을 할 것을 제안하는가?
(A) 비판적으로 이루어진 언급에 대해 이야기한다
(B) 회사 직원들을 더 잘 교육한다
(C) 회사의 웹사이트를 개선시키기 위해 업체를 고용한다
(D) 다음 달에 또 다시 설문 조사를 실시한다

critical 비판적인 | **remark** 언급, 발언 | **educate** 교육시키다 | **conduct** 행하다, 실시하다

| 해설 | 담화 마지막 부분의 'Let's discuss these negatives and how we can fix them.'이라는 문장에서 화자는 부정적인 설문 결과에 대해 논의할 것을 제안하고 있다. 따라서 정답은 (A)이다.

[77-79]

M Good morning. I'm Paul Yoder from Goalpost Cable. I'm trying to reach Mr. Steve Marino. Mr. Marino, I'd like to inform you of a special that Goalpost Cable is offering this week only. If you upgrade your cable service to the Gold or Platinum level, you can get the first three months for free. We'll also slash the cost of the installation fee in half, so you'll only have to pay $40. Imagine receiving double or even triple the number of television stations that you currently do. This offer expires at midnight on Friday, so go to our Web site soon to sign up and to make the arrangements.

M 안녕하세요. 저는 Goalpost 케이블의 Paul Yoder입니다. Steve Marino 씨께 연락을 드리고자 합니다. Marino 씨, 저는 귀하께 Goalpost 케이블에서 이번 주에만 제공하는 특별 행사에 관해 알려 드리고자 합니다. 케이블 TV 서비스를 골드 혹은 플래티넘 등급으로 업그레이드하시면, 첫 3개월 동안 무료로 시청을 하실 수 있습니다. 저희는 또한 설치비를 반값으로 대폭 낮춰 드릴 것이기 때문에, 귀하께서는 40달러만 내시면 됩니다. 현재 보고 계시는 텔레비전 방송국의 숫자가 두 배 혹은 심지어 세 배까지 늘어날 것이라고 상상해 보십시오. 이번 행사는 금요일 자정에 종료될 것이므로, 빨리 저희 웹사이트를 방문하셔서 등록을 하시고 일정을 잡으십시오.

reach ~에 이르다, 닿다; 연락을 취하다 | **inform A of B** A에게 B에 대해 알리다 | **slash** 대폭 낮추다 | **installation fee** 설치비 | **in half** 절반으로 | **imagine** 상상하다 | **triple** 3배로 만들다 | **television station** 텔레비전 방송국 | **expire** 소멸하다

77 화자는 왜 전화를 하고 있는가?
(A) 주문을 확인하기 위해
(B) 특별 행사에 대해 설명하기 위해
(C) 구인 광고를 하기 위해
(D) 청구액 납부를 요청하기 위해

describe 묘사하다, 설명하다 | **special offer** 특가 판매 | **payment** 지불, 납부

| 해설 | 담화 초반부에서 화자는 'Goalpost Cable에서 이번 주에만 제공하는 특별 행사'(a special that Goalpost Cable is offering this week only)를 홍보하고 있다. 따라서 전화를 건 목적은 (B)이다.

78 Marino 씨는 40달러로 무엇을 얻을 수 있는가?
(A) 케이블 TV의 설치
(B) 영화 채널을 세 배로 늘리기
(C) 3개월간 케이블 TV 시청
(D) 스포츠 채널을 두 배로 늘리기

| 해설 | '40달러'는 담화 중반부의 'We'll also slash the cost of the installation fee in half, so you'll only have to pay $40.'라는 문장에서 찾을 수 있다. 이에 따르면 40달러만 내면 케이블 TV의 설치가 가능하므로 정답은 (A)이다.

79 전화를 건 사람은 Marino 씨에게 무엇을 할 것을 요청하는가?
(A) 온라인으로 양식을 작성한다
(B) 그의 회사를 방문한다
(C) 답신 전화를 한다
(D) 설문지를 작성한다

| 해설 | 담화의 마지막 부분에서 화자는 '등록을 해서 일정을 잡기 위해'(to sign up and to make the arrangements) 웹사이트를 방문할 것을 요청하고 있다. 즉 화자가 요청한 사항은 온라인으로 가입 신청을 하라는 것이므로 정답은 (A)가 된다.

[80-82]

M Now that the computers have been installed, let me provide you with some instructions regarding using them. Firstly, you may not install any software on them without the permission of the IT Department. Too many programs have malware and viruses, so we don't want our computers to get infected. Next, please keep in mind that these computers are strictly for work usage. You may not check your personal e-mail accounts with them or use them to surf the Internet. Those activities are banned. The computers will also be monitored, and everything you do on them will be recorded.

M 컴퓨터가 설치되었으므로, 컴퓨터 사용에 관한 몇 가지 방침을 알려 드리고자 합니다. 먼저, IT부의 허가 없이는 어떠한 소프트웨어도 설치하면 안 됩니다. 너무나 많은 프로그램에 악성 코드 및 바이러스가 들어 있기 때문에, 우리는 컴퓨터가 감염되는 것을 원하지 않습니다. 다음으로, 이 컴퓨터들은 엄격하게 업무용으로만 사용해야 한다는 점을 명심하십시오. 컴퓨터로 개인 이메일 계정을 확인하거나 인터넷 서핑을 위해 컴퓨터를 사용하시면 안 됩니다. 그러한 행위는 금지됩니다. 또한 컴퓨터는 감시가 될 것이며, 여러분이 컴퓨터로 하는 모든 일이 기록될 것입니다.

install 설치하다 | **instruction** 지시 | **permission** 허락, 허가 | **malware** 악성 코드, 악성 프로그램 | **virus** 바이러스 | **infect** 감염시키다 | **keep in mind** ~을 명심하다 | **strictly** 엄격하게 | **usage** 사용, 용법 | **surf the Internet** 인터넷 서핑을 하다 | **activity** 활동 | **ban** 금지하다 | **monitor** 감시하다, 모니터하다

80 담화의 목적은 무엇인가?
(A) 몇 가지 규정을 검토하기 위해
(B) 도움을 요청하기 위해
(C) 설명을 하기 위해
(D) 사과를 요구하기 위해

go over ~을 검토하다 | **explanation** 설명

| 해설 | 새로 설치된 컴퓨터의 사용에 관한 방침을 안내하고 있다. 따라서 담

화의 목적은 (A)로 볼 수 있다.

81 청자들은 컴퓨터에 소프트웨어를 설치하기에 앞서 무엇을 해야 하는가?
(A) 컴퓨터와 호환되는지 확인한다
(B) 정품으로 구입한다
(C) 허가를 받는다
(D) 업무에 중요하다는 점을 입증한다

be compatible with ~와 양립하다, ~와 호환되다

| 해설 | 화자는 'IT부의 허락 없이'(without the permission of the IT Department) 소프트웨어를 함부로 설치하면 안 된다는 점을 이야기하고 있다. 따라서 소프트웨어를 설치하려면 사전에 허락을 받아야 하므로 정답은 (C)가 된다.

82 화자는 컴퓨터에 대해 무엇을 언급하는가?
(A) 매일 밤 전원을 꺼야 한다.
(B) 가장 최근에 출시된 모델이다.
(C) 매일 바이러스 검사를 받아야 한다.
(D) 업무용으로만 사용되어야 한다.

| 해설 | 화자는 'Next, please keep in mind that these computers are strictly for work usage.'라고 말하면서, 컴퓨터가 업무용으로만 사용되어야 한다는 점을 강조한다. 따라서 컴퓨터에 대해 언급된 사항은 (D)이다.

[83-85]

M May I have your attention, please? The train from South Hampton scheduled to arrive at 6:45 has been delayed. Apparently, a tree fell on the tracks, so a work crew has been sent to remove it. They expect to finish the work within the next half hour, so then the train can complete its journey. It should arrive around one hour from now. For anyone who wishes to seek an alternative mode of transportation, please see the agent in the departure lounge, and she will provide you with a reimbursement. We apologize for the delay and will keep you updated on the progress of the train.

M 주목해 주시겠습니까? 6시 45분에 도착 예정이었던 사우스 햄턴 발 열차가 연착되고 있습니다. 나무 한 그루가 선로에 떨어진 것으로 보이며, 작업 인부들이 이를 제거하기 위해 현장으로 보내졌습니다. 앞으로 30분 이내에 작업이 끝날 것으로 예상되기 때문에, 그 후에는 열차가 운행을 재개할 수 있을 것입니다. 열차는 지금부터 약 한 시간 후에 도착할 예정입니다. 다른 교통 수단을 찾으시는 분들께서는, 출발 라운지의 직원을 찾아 주시면 그녀가 보상을 해 드릴 것입니다. 연착에 대해 사과 말씀을 드리며 열차의 진행 상황에 대해서는 계속 소식을 전해 드리도록 하겠습니다.

apparently 듣자 하니, 보아 하니 | **work crew** 작업 인부 | **remove** 제거하다 | **journey** 여행, 여정 | **seek** 찾다, 추구하다 | **alternative** 대안의 | **transportation** 교통, 운송 | **agent** 대리인, 요원, 직원 | **departure lounge** 출발 라운지 | **reimbursement** 배상, 변제 | **keep ~ updated** ~에게 최신 정보를 알려 주다 | **progress** 진전, 진행

83 열차는 왜 연착되었는가?
(A) 선로에서 차량과 충돌했다.
(B) 선로에 물체가 있다.
(C) 열차가 기계적인 문제를 겪었다.
(D) 악천후로 서행을 하고 있다.

collide with ~와 충돌하다 | **object** 물체, 물건

| 해설 | 화자는 연착 이유를 a tree fell on the tracks 때문이라고 말하고 있다. 즉 선로에 나무가 쓰러졌기 때문에 열차가 연착되고 있으므로 (B)가 정답이다.

84 열차는 언제 도착할 것으로 예상되는가?
(A) 30분 후에
(B) 한 시간 후에
(C) 한 시간 반 후에
(D) 두 시간 후에

| 해설 | 담화 중반부의 'It should arrive around one hour from now.'라는 문장에서 한 시간 후에 열차가 도착할 것임을 알 수 있다. 따라서 정답은 (B)이다. 참고로 (A)의 '30분'은 나무를 제거하는 작업에 필요한 시간이다.

85 청자들은 출발 라운지에서 무엇을 받을 수 있는가?
(A) 환불
(B) 무료 업그레이드
(C) 무료 간식
(D) 새로운 티켓

complimentary 무료의

| 해설 | 화자는 담화의 후반부에서 다른 교통 수단을 이용할 승객에게 출발 라운지의 직원이 '보상을 해 줄 것'(provide you with a reimbursement)이라고 말한다. 따라서 청자들은 '환불'을 받게 될 것이므로 (A)가 정답이다.

[86-88]

W Hello. This is Brenda Marston. I've got an appointment for a haircut on Thursday at 3:30, but I can't go there on that day. I have to go out of town and won't be back for a few days. Would it be possible to reschedule my appointment for next week? I've got time next Wednesday in the morning. 11 would be perfect for me. In addition, I don't just want to get a cut, but I want to get a perm as well. Please call me back at 675-4855 to let me know if this is possible. Thank you. Goodbye.

W 안녕하세요. 저는 Brenda Marston이에요. 저는 목요일 3시 30분에 커트 예약을 했는데, 그날 갈 수가 없게 되었어요. 시외로 가야 해서 며칠 동안은 돌아오지 않을 거예요. 제 예약을 다음 주로 조정하는 것이 가능할까요? 저는 다음 주 수요일 오전에 시간이 있어요. 저로서는 11시가 가장 좋을 것 같군요. 게다가, 저는 커트만 원하는 것이 아니고 파마도 하고 싶어요. 675-4855로 제게 전화를 주셔서 그것이 가능한지 알려 주세요. 고마워요. 안녕히 계세요.

haircut 머리 깎기, 이발 | **perfect** 완벽한 | **in addition** 게다가, 또한 | **get a perm** 파마를 하다

86 화자의 문제는 무엇인가?
(A) 예약을 잊었다.
(B) 딸의 예약을 취소해야 한다.
(C) 예약 시간에 늦을 것이다.
(D) 예약한 시간에 갈 수가 없다.

make it (시간에 맞춰) 가다

| 해설 | 담화 초반부에 화자는 시외로 나가야 해서 예약 시간에 갈 수가 없게 되었다는 사실을 알리고 있다. 따라서 화자의 문제는 (D)이다.

87 화자는 언제 시간이 있는가?
(A) 수요일 오전 9시에
(B) 수요일 오후 3시에
(C) 목요일 오전 11시에

(D) 화요일 오후 1시에

| 해설 | 담화 중반부의 'I've got time next Wednesday in the morning.'이라는 문장에서 화자가 시간을 낼 수 있는 때는 '수요일 오전'이라는 점을 알 수 있다. 보기 중 수요일 오전에 해당되는 시간은 (A)뿐이다.

88 화자는 예약 사항을 어떻게 변경하고 싶어하는가?
(A) 머리만 자름으로써
(B) 염색을 함으로써
(C) 파마를 함으로써
(D) 스트레이트 파마를 함으로써

dye 염색하다 | **straighten** 곧게 하다

| 해설 | 담화 후반부에서 화자는 'I don't just want to get a cut, but I want to get a perm as well.'이라고 말하면서 커트 이외에 파마도 요청하고 있다. 따라서 정답은 (C)이다.

[89-91]

M All right, we've given out every award tonight, so there's one more thing to do before we can get to the entertainment part of tonight's event. We had an eventful year full of ups and downs. Overall, however, we at Hartford Construction earned our largest profit ever, and we expanded our business as well. Now, we'd like to inform you about our plans for the future. It's time to listen to our CEO, Gregory O'Connell. He's going to take five minutes to tell us what's in store for the next twelve months. Let's give a big hand to our CEO.

M 좋아요, 오늘밤 상은 모두 수여했지만, 오늘밤 행사의 일부인 연회를 시작하기에 앞서 해야 할 일이 한 가지 더 있습니다. 우리는 기복이 크고 다사다난했던 한 해를 보냈습니다. 하지만 전체적으로, 우리 Hartford 건설은 어느 때보다도 높은 수익을 거두었으며, 사업도 확장시켰습니다. 이제, 여러분들께 미래에 대한 우리의 계획에 대해 알려 드리고자 합니다. 대표 이사인 Gregory O'Connell 씨의 이야기를 들을 시간이 되었군요. 그분께서는 내년 12개월 동안 우리에게 어떤 일이 일어날 것인지를 5분 동안 말씀해 주실 것입니다. 큰 박수로 대표 이사님을 맞이하여 주십시오.

give out 나누어 주다 | **entertainment** 여흥, 오락; 연회 | **eventful** 다사다난한 | **ups and downs** 오르내림, 기복 | **in store** 기다리고 있는 | **give a hand to** ~에게 박수를 치다

89 청자들은 어디에 있는 것 같은가?
(A) 회의에
(B) 시상식에
(C) 은퇴 기념 파티에
(D) 오리엔테이션에

awards ceremony 시상식 | **retirement** 은퇴 | **orientation session** 오리엔테이션

| 해설 | 담화의 시작 부분 중 we've given out every award tonight이라는 어구에서 청자들이 있는 곳을 짐작할 수 있다. 보기 중 상을 수여하는 행사를 가리키는 것은 (B)의 '시상식'이다.

90 화자가 "We had an eventful year full of ups and downs"라고 말할 때 화자는 무엇을 의미하는가?
(A) 회사가 지출한 돈보다 많은 돈을 벌었다.
(B) 긍정적인 일보다 부정적인 일들이 더 많이 일어났다.
(C) 좋은 일과 나쁜 일이 모두 일어났다.

(D) 미래는 부정적이기보다 긍정적일 것이다.

negative 부정적인 | **positive** 긍정적인

| 해설 | eventful은 '다사다난한' 혹은 '파란만장한'이라는 뜻을 나타내며 ups and downs는 말 그대로 '오르내림'이라는 의미를 갖는다. 따라서 화자가 주어진 문장을 통해 말하려고 하는 바는 '좋은 일과 나쁜 일이 많았던 한 해를 보냈다'는 것이므로 정답은 (C)가 된다.

91 이다음에 어떤 일이 일어날 것인가?
(A) 연설이 있을 것이다.
(B) 음악이 연주될 것이다.
(C) 저녁 식사가 제공될 것이다.
(D) 상이 수여될 것이다.

| 해설 | 담화의 후반부에서 화자는 대표 이사의 연설이 있을 것이라고 말한 후 대표 이사를 소개하고 있다. 따라서 담화 이후에 벌어질 일은 (A)이다.

[92-94]

W Something important has just been brought to my attention. Apparently, the brownies which we ordered for the company picnic have peanuts in them, and there may be people at the event who have nut allergies. We need to arrange for some kind of new dessert. Including the brownies, we ordered four types of desserts. I think that we ought to find something else that we can order in order to replace the food that some people are allergic to. I've got a few copies of the menu from the caterer, so why don't we take a look at them and come to a decision right now?

W 중요한 사항이 떠올랐습니다. 아마도, 우리가 회사 야유회를 위해 주문했던 브라우니에 땅콩이 들어 있을 것 같은데, 땅콩 알레르기가 있는 사람들이 행사에 올 수도 있습니다. 새로운 디저트를 마련해야 할 필요가 있습니다. 브라우니를 포함하여, 우리는 네 종류의 디저트를 주문했습니다. 저는 사람들이 알레르기 반응을 보이는 음식을 대체하기 위해 우리가 주문할 수 있는 다른 것을 찾아보아야 한다고 생각합니다. 제가 음식 공급업체로부터 온 메뉴의 사본을 몇 장 가지고 있기 때문에, 이를 살펴본 후 지금 바로 결정을 내리는 것이 어떨까요?

attention 주의, 주목 | **peanut** 땅콩 | **nut allergy** 땅콩 알레르기 | **arrange for** ~을 마련하다, ~을 준비하다 | **include** 포함하다 | **in order to** ~하기 위해 | **replace** 대체하다, 대신하다 | **caterer** 음식 공급업체 | **decision** 결정

92 왜 문제가 생겼는가?
(A) 일부 사람들은 채식주의자이다.
(B) 일부 사람들은 특정 종류의 음식을 먹지 못한다.
(C) 일부 사람들은 설탕이 든 음식을 싫어한다.
(D) 일부 사람들은 초콜릿을 먹는 것을 좋아하지 않는다.

vegetarian 채식주의자 | **sugary** 설탕이 든, 단맛이 나는

| 해설 | 담화 초반부에 화자는 땅콩이 들어 있을 수 있는 브라우니를 주문했다고 말하고 '땅콩 알레르기가 있는 사람이 있을 수 있다'(there may be people at the event who have nut allergies)는 점을 지적한다. 따라서 문제가 생긴 이유는 (B)로 볼 수 있다. 참고로 (B)에서 certain types of food는 '땅콩이 들어 있는 음식'을 바꾸어 표현한 것이다.

93 도표를 보아라. 얼마나 많은 제품이 대체되어야 하는가?
(A) 35
(B) 45
(C) 50

(D) 70

| 해설 | 땅콩이 들어 있는 브라우니를 대체할 것이므로 도표에서 브라우니의 수량을 확인하면 된다. 정답은 (D)의 '70개'이다.

94 청자들은 이다음에 무엇을 할 것 같은가?
(A) 음식 제공업체에 연락한다
(B) 메뉴를 본다
(C) 시식을 한다
(D) 빵집을 방문한다

sample 견본, 샘플; 시식하다, 시음하다 | **bakery** 빵집, 베이커리

| 해설 | 담화의 마지막 부분에서 화자는 '메뉴를 살펴보고 결정을 내리자'(why don't we take a look at them and come to a decision right now)고 제안한다. 따라서 청자들은 메뉴를 본 후 결정을 내릴 것으로 예상되므로 정답은 (B)이다.

[95-97]

M The chart on the screen shows how our franchises in different states are doing. The restaurants in the southeastern part of the country are clearly profiting. We're considering expanding the number of restaurants in Alabama, Georgia, and Tennessee. We're getting numerous requests by people who want to become franchise owners, so we'll have to select the ones who look the most promising. We're also doing well in the Midwest as our restaurants in Iowa, Indiana, and Ohio are popular. But sales in Oklahoma are so low that we've decided to shut down every franchise there since none of them is profitable.

M 화면의 차트는 서로 다른 주에 있는 우리의 프랜차이즈 매장이 어떻게 운영되고 있는지를 보여 줍니다. 우리 나라의 동남부에 있는 매장들은 확실히 수익을 내고 있습니다. 우리는 앨라배마, 조지아, 그리고 테네시에서 식당 수를 늘리는 것을 고려해 보고 있습니다. 프랜차이즈 점주가 되고 싶어하는 사람들의 많은 요청을 받고 있기 때문에, 가장 유망해 보이는 사람들을 선정해야 할 것입니다. 또한 아이오아, 인디애나, 그리고 오하이오의 식당들의 인기가 높기 때문에, 미드웨스트 지역에서도 운영이 잘 되고 있습니다. 하지만 오클라호마의 매출은 너무 낮아서, 그들 중 어느 곳도 수익을 내지 못하고 있기 때문에, 저희는 그곳에 있는 모든 프랜차이즈 매장을 폐점할 것이라는 결정을 내렸습니다.

franchise 프랜차이즈, 가맹점 | **profit** 이윤; 이윤을 내다 | **expand** 확장하다, 확대하다 | **numerous** 많은 | **select** 선정하다 | **promising** 전도 유망한, 장래성이 있는 | **shut down** 문을 닫다, 폐쇄시키다 | **profitable** 수익을 내는

95 화자는 앨라배마의 식당에 대해 무엇을 언급하는가?
(A) 폐점될 것이다.
(B) 확장하고 있다.
(C) 수익을 내고 있다.
(D) 손실을 보고 있다.

close down 폐쇄하다, 폐점하다 | **make money** 돈을 벌다 | **lose money** 돈을 잃다, 손실을 보다

| 해설 | 담화 초반부에 화자는 동남부의 매장들이 수익을 내고 있다고 말하면서 앨라배마, 조지아, 그리고 테네시에서 매장 수를 늘릴 것을 고려하고 있다고 말한다. 따라서 화자가 앨라배마에 관해 언급한 사항은 (C)이다.

96 화자는 무엇이 실시되어야 한다고 말하는가?
(A) 새 프랜차이즈 점주들이 선정되어야 한다.
(B) 새로운 메뉴가 선정되어야 한다.
(C) 새로운 위치가 결정되어야 한다.
(D) 새로운 가격이 책정되어야 한다.

location 위치 | **establish** 설립하다

| 해설 | 화자는 프랜차이즈 점주가 되고 싶어하는 사람들이 많다는 점을 언급한 후, '가장 장래성이 높은 사람을 선택해야 할 것이다'(we'll have to select the ones who look the most promising)라고 주장한다. 따라서 정답은 (A)이다.

97 도표를 보아라. 얼마나 많은 식당이 잘 운영되고 있는가?
(A) 17
(B) 31
(C) 37
(D) 51

| 해설 | 오클라호마의 매장들을 제외한 나머지 매장들은 모두 수익을 내고 있다고 보인다. 따라서 오클라호마 매장을 제외한 나머지 매장들의 수를 합하면 (D)의 '51'이 된다.

[98-100]

W Good afternoon, Ms. Kimball. This is Heather Dobbins from Dr. Russell's clinic. You're scheduled to have a physical exam with Dr. Russell on Tuesday at 10:30 A.M. Unfortunately, Dr. Russell will be out of the office to attend a training session the entire week. However, some other doctors have agreed to fill in for him. You therefore have a choice. You can come here at your regularly scheduled time, but you won't see Dr. Russell. Or you can reschedule your appointment. Dr. Russell hopes to return to the office by next Monday, so anytime starting then will be sufficient. How about calling me to let me know your decision?

W 안녕하세요, Kimball 씨. 저는 Dr. Russell's 병원의 Heather Dobbins입니다. 고객님은 화요일 오전 10시 30분에 Russell 박사님에게 건강 검진을 받기로 예약이 되어 있습니다. 안타깝지만, Russell 박사님께서는 일주일 내내 교육에 참가하셔야 해서 사무실에 계시지 않을 것입니다. 하지만, 다른 의사 선생님들께서 그 분을 대신하시기로 하셨습니다. 따라서 고객님께서는 선택을 하실 수 있습니다. 정상적으로 예약된 시간에 여기로 오셔도 좋지만, Russell 박사님은 만나 뵙지 못할 것입니다. 아니면 예약 시간을 변경하실 수도 있습니다. Russell 박사님께서는 다음 주 월요일에 사무실로 돌아오실 생각이기 때문에, 그 이후로는 언제든지 괜찮을 것입니다. 제게 전화를 주셔서 결정 사항을 알려 주시는 것이 어떨까요?

clinic 병원, 진료소 | **physical exam** 신체 검사, 건강 검진 | **training session** 교육 | **fill in for** ~을 대신하다 | **therefore** 따라서 | **sufficient** 충분한

98 Russell 박사는 왜 사무실에 없을 것인가?
(A) 그는 가족들과 휴가를 갈 것이다.
(B) 그는 너무나 아파서 일을 할 수가 없다.
(C) 그는 교육에 참석할 것이다.
(D) 그는 다른 병원에서 일을 할 것이다.

too ~ to 너무 ~해서 ~하다 | **educational** 교육의

| 해설 | 화자는 Russell 박사의 부재 이유를 '일주일 동안 교육에 참석해야 하기 때문'(to attend a training session the entire week)이라고 밝히고 있다. 따라서 정답은 (C)이다. 참고로 (C)에서는 training session이

educational event로 바꾸어 표현되었다.

99 도표를 보아라. Kimball's 씨의 임시 의사는 누가 될 것인가?
(A) Fuji 박사
(B) DeLorean 박사
(C) Brandt 박사
(D) Murphy 박사

| 해설 | 대화 초반부에서 Kimball 씨의 검진 예약 시간은 '화요일 오전 10시 30분'(on Tuesday at 10:30 A.M.)이라고 했으므로 '화요일' 의사 명단을 살펴면 정답을 찾을 수 있다. 정답은 (D)이다.

100 화자는 Kimball 씨에게 무엇을 하라고 요청하는가?
(A) 자신에게 이메일을 보낸다
(B) 온라인으로 양식을 작성한다
(C) 전화를 건다
(D) 다른 병원을 방문한다

| 해설 | 마지막 문장인 'How about calling me to let me know your decision?'에서 화자는 전화로 Kimball 씨의 결정 사항을 알려 달라고 요청하고 있다. 따라서 화자가 요청한 것은 (C)의 '전화를 건다'이다.

● PART 5   p.92

101 새 카페의 매력 중 하나는 야외 좌석에 앉으면 인근의 호수가 보인다는 점이다.
(A) 매력
(B) 동의
(C) 기준
(D) 모델

appeal 호소; 매력 | **overlook** 간과하다; 바라보다 | **nearby** 근처의, 인근의 | **consent** 동의, 합의 | **standard** 기준, 표준

| 해설 | '인근의 호수가 보인다'는 점은 카페의 장점 중 하나일 것이다. 따라서 정답은 '매력'이라는 의미를 가진 (A)의 appeal이다.

102 Blaire 씨는 사무실 내의 근무 환경을 개선시키기 위해 끊임없이 일을 하고 있다.
(A) 작업된
(B) 작업자
(C) 작업
(D) 작업하다

tirelessly 지칠 줄 모르고, 끊임없이 | **working environment** 작업 환경, 근무 환경

| 해설 | '작업 환경' 혹은 '근무 환경'이라는 의미는 복합 명사인 working environment로 나타낸다. 따라서 정답은 (C)의 동명사 working이다.

103 결정되어야 할 것은 그 부서의 예산에 얼마나 많은 금액이 할당되어야 하는지이다.
(A) ~인 것
(B) ~하는 방법
(C) ~인 것
(D) ~인 것

determine 결정하다 | **allocate** 할당하다

| 해설 | 주어가 determined까지라는 점을 파악하면 빈칸에는 명사절을 이끌 수 있는 단어가 들어가야 한다. 보기 중 그러한 역할을 할 수 있는 것은 선행사를 포함한 관계대명사인 (C)의 What뿐이다. 관계대명사 (A)나 (D)가 정답이 되기 위해서는 빈칸 앞에 선행사 역할을 하는 단어가 있어야 한다.

104 Thompson 씨의 비서는 그가 점심 식사를 마치고 돌아오는 대로 부사장에게 전화를 해야 한다고 그에게 말했다.
(A) 돌아오다
(B) 전화하다
(C) 머무르다
(D) 돌아오다

secretary 비서 | **vice president** 부회장, 부사장 | **as soon as** ~하자마자 | **arrive back** 돌아오다 | **stay** 머물다, 체류하다

| 해설 | 빈칸 다음의 back을 보지 못하면 정답을 (A)로 선택하는 실수를 범할 수 있다. return 자체에 back의 의미가 담겨 있기 때문에 (A)는 정답이 될 수 없다. 정답은 (D)의 arrived로, arrive back은 '돌아오다'라는 의미를 나타낸다.

105 Hampton 씨는 가족과 함께 해외 여행을 가기 위해 8월 첫 주에 휴가를 내기로 결심했다.
(A) 가다
(B) 가는
(C) 가기 위해
(D) 갈 것이다

| 해설 | 내용상 '~하기 위해'라는 목적의 의미를 나타내는 말이 빈칸에 들어가야 자연스러운 문장이 완성된다. 보기 중 목적의 의미는 (C)의 to부정사로 나타낼 수 있다.

106 무대 근처에 앉고 싶은 사람들에게는 표를 미리 구입할 것이 권장된다.
(A) 앉히다
(B) 앉히는
(C) 앉은
(D) 인승

in advance 미리, 사전에 | **recommend** 추천하다

| 해설 | seat는 '(~을) 앉히다'라는 의미의 타동사이다. 따라서 '앉고 싶은 사람들'이라는 의미를 나타내기 위해서는 수동형을 완성시킬 수 있는 (C)의 seated가 빈칸에 들어가야 한다.

107 승진이 모두 확정되면, 이름과 직위가 회사 웹페이지에 게시될 것이다.
(A) ~하면
(B) 따라서
(C) ~에도 불구하고
(D) ~에 관하여

confirm 확정하다, 확인하다 | **post** 게시하다 | **in spite of** ~에도 불구하고 | **with regard to** ~에 관하여

| 해설 | 주절과 종속절의 의미를 파악하면 빈칸에는 '조건'이나 '시간'의 의미를 나타내는 접속사가 들어가야 함을 알 수 있다. 따라서 정답은 (A)이다. (C)와 (D) 다음에는 절이 아니라 구가 이어져야 한다는 점을 통해서도 이들이 오답임을 알 수 있다.

108 경쟁사들보다 높은 경쟁력을 확보하기 위해, 그 회사의 관리자들은 대학원 과정을 밟기로 결심했다.
(A) 경쟁하다
(B) 경쟁력이 있는
(C) 경쟁
(D) 경쟁하는

in order to ~하기 위해 | **gain** 얻다 | **advantage** 장점 | **rival** 경쟁자 | **pursue** 쫓다, 추구하다 | **graduate studies** 대학원 과정, 대학원에서의 연구

| 해설 | 빈칸에는 advantage를 수식할 수 있는 형용사가 들어가야 한다. 보기 중 형용사는 (B)와 (D)인데, 이 중 '경쟁력이 있는'이라는 의미의 (B)가 빈칸에 들어가야 보다 자연스러운 의미가 완성된다.

109 Eager 여행사의 Jameson 씨가 사무실에 전화를 해서 곧 있을 Smith 씨의 출장에 대한 여행 일정을 알려 주었다.

(A) 여행 일정
(B) 당번표
(C) 표
(D) 임대차 계약

itinerary 여행 일정(표) | **roster** 당번표, 근무자 명단 | **lease** 임대차 계약

| 해설 | Eager Travel(Eager 여행사), business trip(출장)과 같은 표현들에 유의하면 빈칸에는 '여행 일정(표)'라는 뜻의 (A)가 들어가야 함을 쉽게 알 수 있다.

110 컴퓨터 시스템이 오작동을 일으켜서 사용자들이 인터넷에 로그온하는 것을 허용하지 않았다.

(A) 허락하다
(B) 보고하다
(C) 들어가다
(D) 제출하다

malfunction 제대로 작동하지 않다, 오작동하다 | **allow A to B** A가 B하는 것을 허락하다

| 해설 | '컴퓨터 시스템이 고장 난' 결과로 인터넷 사용자들에게 벌어질 수 있는 일을 생각해 보면 정답은 (A)의 allow임을 알 수 있다.

111 McGregor 씨는 20년 이상 Ernst Welding을 위해 기기들을 수리해 왔다.

(A) 수리하고 있다
(B) 수리해 왔다
(C) 수리되었다
(D) 수리되었다

| 해설 | for more than two decades(20년 이상)라는 부사구를 고려하면 빈칸에는 현재완료 시제가 들어가야 한다. 또한 주어가 Mr. McGregor이고 목적어가 machines이므로 동사 repair(수리하다)는 능동형이어야 한다. 보기 중 이러한 조건을 모두 만족시키는 것은 (B)의 has been repairing이다.

112 Murray 씨의 기차가 10분 내로 도착하지 않는다면, 그는 회의에 늦을 것이다.

(A) ~까지
(B) ~ 동안
(C) ~ 이내에
(D) 약

| 해설 | the next ten minutes와 가장 자연스럽게 연결될 수 있는 전치사는 (C)의 within이다. (A)의 by 다음에는 구체적인 시각이, (B)의 for 다음에는 경과 시간이 이어져야 한다.

113 시카고 지역의 시계가 좋지 않기 때문에, 비행기가 다른 공항으로 가고 있다고 기장이 안내했다.

(A) 시력
(B) 보이는
(C) 시계
(D) 눈에 띄게

captain 기장, 선장 | **visibility** 시계, 눈에 잘 보임 | **vision** 시력, 시야 | **visible** 눈에 보이는 | **visibly** 눈에 띄게, 분명히

| 해설 | 비행기가 다른 공항으로 간 이유가 무엇일지 생각해 보면 정답은 (C)의 visibility(시계)임을 알 수 있다.

114 밤에 라이트를 켜지 않고 운전하는 것은 다른 운전자들뿐만 아니라 보행자들에게도 위험한 일이다.

(A) 그래서
(B) ~에게도
(C) ~도 아닌
(D) ~으로

hazardous 위험한 | **pedestrian** 보행자

| 해설 | not only A but also B(A뿐만 아니라 B도)라는 구문을 알고 있으면 정답이 (B)임을 쉽게 알 수 있다.

115 주말에 반드시 초과 근무를 해야 한다는 점에 많은 직원들이 실망감을 나타냈다.

(A) 좌절시키다
(B) 좌절감을 주는
(C) 좌절한
(D) 좌절감

express 표현하다, 나타내다 | **frustration** 좌절감 | **be obligated to** 반드시 ~해야 한다, ~해야 할 의무가 있다 | **work overtime** 초과 근무를 하다, 시간외 근무를 하다 | **frustrate** 좌절감을 주다

| 해설 | their의 수식을 받으면서 expressed의 목적어 역할을 할 수 있는 것은 명사이다. 따라서 정답은 '좌절감'이라는 의미인 (D)의 frustration이다.

▣ **700점 넘기 포인트** (B)를 동명사로 생각해서 (B)가 정답이라고 오인할 수도 있다. 하지만 동명사에서는 명사보다 상대적으로 동사의 의미, 즉 '동작'이나 '행위'의 의미가 부각된다.

116 지원 절차의 첫 번째 단계를 통과한 모든 사람들은 본사에서 면접을 보도록 초청될 것이다.

(A) ~한 것
(B) ~한 사람
(C) ~한 곳
(D) ~한 사람

invite 초청하다, 초대하다 | **headquarters** 본부, 본사

| 해설 | 빈칸 이후의 내용을 고려할 때 빈칸 앞의 those는 사람을 나타낸다는 점을 알 수 있다. 또한 종속절 내에 빠져 있는 문장 성분이 주어라는 점을 파악하면 정답은 사람을 나타내는 주격 관계대명사인 (B)의 who가 되어야 한다. 통상적으로 those who는 '~하는 사람들'이라는 의미를 나타낸다.

117 Wilkins 씨는 직원들이 팀워크를 향상시키는 데 도움이 되도록 직원들이 서로 소통할 것을 격려한다.

(A) 소통하다
(B) 논의하다
(C) 결합하다
(D) 드러내다

interact with ~와 상호 작용을 하다, ~와 소통하다 | **teamwork** 팀워크, 단체 정신

| 해설 | '~와 교감하다', '~와 소통하다'라는 의미는 interact with로 나타낸다. 따라서 정답은 (A)이다. 참고로 (B)의 discuss(논의하다)는 목적어를 취하는 타동사로, 전치사 with와는 쓰이지 않는다.

118 새로운 제조 시설이 공식적으로 문을 열기 하루 전에 대표 이사가 시설을 견학할 예정이다.

(A) 공무를 수행하다
(B) 공식적인
(C) 사무실
(D) 공식적으로

be scheduled to ~할 예정이다 | **take a tour of** ~을 견학하다 | **manufacturing facility** 제조 시설 | **officially** 공식적으로 | **officiate** 공무를 수행하다

| 해설 | before가 이끄는 부사절에 빠져 있는 문장 성분이 없으므로 빈칸에는 동사 opens를 수식할 수 있는 부사가 들어가야 한다. 따라서 정답은 (D)이다.

119 Davis 컨설팅의 고객들은 긍정적이거나 부정적인 성격의 피드백을 제공해 달라는 요청을 받는다.
(A) 응답
(B) 판촉
(C) 피드백
(D) 반응

either A or B A나 B 중 하나 | **positive** 긍정적인 | **negative** 부정적인 | **nature** 자연; 성격, 특성 | **response** 반응, 응답 | **reaction** 반응, 반작용

| 해설 | 제품이나 서비스에 대한 소비자의 반응이나 의견은 (C)의 feedback으로 나타낸다. 참고로 (A)의 response는 '자극'에 대한 반응을, (D)의 reaction은 '사건이나 상황'에 대한 반응이나 '반발', '반작용'이라는 의미를 나타낸다.

120 정비공은 자동차가 심각한 엔진 문제를 겪고 있어서 수리되기까지 1주일이 걸릴 것이라고 안내했다.
(A) 걸릴 것이다
(B) 걸릴 것이다
(C) 걸렸다
(D) 걸렸다

mechanic 정비공 | **indicate** 나타내다, 가리키다

| 해설 | '(시간이) 걸리다'라는 표현은 동사 take로 나타내며, 이 문장의 경우 주절의 시제가 과거이기 때문에 시제 일치의 법칙에 따라 빈칸에는 과거나 대과거의 시제가 들어가야 한다. 따라서 take의 알맞은 형태는 (B)의 would take이다.

121 최소 10명의 사람들이 주말 연휴에 초과 근무를 하라는 매니저의 요구를 거절했다.
(A) ~만큼
(B) 최소한
(C) 대략
(D) 약

no fewer than 최소한, ~만큼 | **reject** 거절하다, 거부하다 | **request** 요청, 요구 | **holiday weekend** 주말 연휴

| 해설 | 빈칸에는 ten people을 수식할 수 있는 말이 들어가야 한다. (A)의 as much as는 셀 수 없는 명사와 함께 쓰이는 표현이고, (C)와 (D)는 각각 at과 with를 삭제했을 경우에 정답이 될 수 있다. 따라서 정답은 '최소한'이라는 의미의 (B)의 no fewer than이다. 참고로 as many as도 정답이 될 수 있다.

122 뮤지컬 티켓은 온라인으로 혹은 509-5430으로 매표소에 전화를 걸어 구매할 수 있다.
(A) 구매하다
(B) 요구하다
(C) 검토하다
(D) 기증하다

review 검토하다 | **donate** 기부하다, 기증하다

| 해설 | 뮤지컬 티켓의 구입 방법에 대해 이야기하고 있으므로 정답은 '구매하다'라는 의미를 지닌 (A)의 purchased이다.

123 Katmandu 여행사는 동남아시아의 가장 멋진 곳으로 떠나는, 가이드 동반 여행을 전문으로 한다.
(A) 전문으로 하는
(B) 전문화되었다
(C) 전문으로 하다
(D) 전문화되었다

specialize in ~을 전문으로 하다, ~에 특화되다 | **guided tour** 안내원을 동반하는 여행 | **fascinating** 매력적인, 놀라운

| 해설 | 빈칸에는 문장 전체의 동사 역할을 할 수 있는 단어가 들어가야 한다. 정답은 (C)의 specializes로, specialize in은 '~을 전문으로 하다', '~에 특화되다'라는 의미를 나타낸다.

124 권한이 있는 직원만이 수행원 없이 연구 시설의 저층을 통과할 수 있다.
(A) 권한
(B) 권한이 있는
(C) 권한을 부여하다
(D) 권한을 주는

authorized 권한이 있는 | **personnel** 직원 | **level** 수준; 층 | **escort** 호위자, 수행원

| 해설 | 빈칸에는 personnel(직원)이라는 명사를 수식할 수 있는 형용사가 들어가야 한다. 따라서 (B)와 (D) 중 하나가 정답인데, authorize가 '권한을 부여하다'라는 뜻이므로, 빈칸에는 '권한을 부여받은'이라는 의미의 과거분사, 즉 (B)의 authorized가 들어가야 한다.

125 두 직원이 서로 다른 점을 가지고 있기는 하지만, 상당히 많은 유사점도 공유하고 있다.
(A) ~ 때문에
(B) 따라서
(C) 만약 ~이라면
(D) ~이긴 하지만

difference 차이, 차이점 | **share** 공유하다 | **a large number of** 많은 | **similarity** 유사함, 유사점

| 해설 | difference와 similarities의 의미에 유의하면, 빈칸에는 양보의 의미를 나타내는 (D)의 While이 들어가야 한다는 점을 알 수 있다.

126 Rabbit 택배가 높은 요금을 부과하기는 하지만, 그곳에서 배달하는 택배는 정시에 도착할 것이 보장된다.
(A) ~하는 것
(B) ~인 것
(C) ~하는 것
(D) ~할 때

charge (요금을) 부과하다 | **guarantee** 보장하다, 보증하다 | **on time** 정시에

| 해설 | 빈칸 앞에 별도의 선행사가 보이지 않고 빈칸 이후의 절에 빠져 있는 문장 성분이 없으므로 관계대명사나 관계부사는 정답이 될 수 없다. 따라서 명사절을 이끄는 (B)의 that이 정답이다.

127 마케팅 캠페인이 성공적인 것으로 널리 알려졌지만, 사실 지난 분기에 J. Gilman 주식회사의 수익은 감소했다.
(A) 수익
(B) 판매
(C) 제품
(D) 수량

marketing campaign 마케팅 캠페인 | **hail** 환호하여 맞이하다 | **revenue** 수익, 세수 | **quantity** 수량

| 해설 | '마케팅 캠페인(marketing campaign)이 성공적으로 평가되었지만, 실제로는 그렇지 못했다'라는 의미가 완성되어야 한다. 따라서 빈칸에는 동사 declined의 목적어로 (A)의 revenue(수익)가 들어가는 것이 가장 적절하다. sales(매출, 판매량)도 정답이 될 수 있으나 (B)의 sale(판매)은 정답이 될 수 없다.

128 매출을 증가시키는 첫 번째 단계는 고객층과 확고한 관계를 설정하는 것이다.
(A) 증가시키다

(B) 증가되는
(C) 증가시키는
(D) 증가되고 있다

step 단계 | **solid** 단단한, 견고한 | **connection** 관계 | **client base** 고객층

| 해설 | step을 이용하여 '~으로 가는 단계'라는 의미를 전달하고자 할 때에는 전치사 to가 수반된다. 따라서 정답은 (C)to improving이다.

129 Ervin Textiles는 국내에서 생산된 우수한 품질의 제품을 누구나 구입할 수 있는 합리적인 가격으로 판매한다.
(A) 추론
(B) 이성
(C) 합리적인
(D) 합리적으로

high-quality 품질이 우수한 | **domestically** 국내에서 | **reasonable** 합리적인 | **afford** 여력이 있다, 여유가 있다 | **reasoning** 추론 | **reason** 이유, 근거; 이성

| 해설 | 보기 중에서 명사 prices를 수식할 수 있는 것은 형용사인 (C)의 reasonable뿐이므로 정답은 (C)이다.

130 그 회사는 모든 문제의 원인이 무엇인지 알아내기 위해 몇몇 외부 전문가들을 영입할 것이다.
(A) 알아내다
(B) 접근하다
(C) 규제하다
(D) 논의하다

bring in ~을 도입하다, ~을 데리고 오다 | **outside expert** 외부 전문가 | **determine** 결정하다; 알아내다 | **cause** 원인 | **regulate** 규제하다

| 해설 | 외부 전문가를 영입하려는 목적이 무엇일지 생각해 보면 정답을 쉽게 찾을 수 있다. 정답은 (A)인데, determine은 '결정하다', '결심하다'라는 뜻으로도 쓰일 수 있지만 '알아내다'라는 뜻으로도 사용될 수 있다. 이 문제에서도 후자의 의미로 사용되었다.

PART 6
p.96

[131-134]

Darby's 인쇄소

시내에 새로운 인쇄소가 생겼고, 저희는 여러분께 서비스를 제공해 드리고자 합니다. Darby's 인쇄소가 얼마 전에 개업을 했습니다. 저희는 Washburn 가 67번지에 위치해 있으며 Whitman Steakhouse의 길 건너편에 있습니다. 새로 생긴 업체이지만, 저희 직원들은 인쇄 업계의 베테랑들입니다. 사장인 Clarence Darby는 해당 분야에서 50년 이상의 경력을 가지고 있으며, 그의 직원들은 각각 20년 이상 일해 오고 있습니다.
인쇄소의 개업을 축하하기 위해, 개업 첫 주 동안 저희가 제공하는 모든 서비스를 약 40% 할인된 금액으로 이용하실 수 있습니다. 그러니 오셔서 귀사의 보고서를 인쇄하십시오. 혹은 새로운 명함을 의뢰하십시오. 저희는 간판, 광고물, 그리고 포스터도 인쇄합니다. 인쇄와 관련된 것이라면, 저희가 전문가입니다. 701-7649로 전화를 주시거나 저희 웹사이트인 www.darbysprinting.com을 방문하셔서 저희에 관해 더 알아보시고 서비스 요금이 얼마인지 확인하십시오. 곧 만나 뵙기를 바라겠습니다.

old hand 노련한 사람, 베테랑 | **celebrate** 경축하다, 축하하다 | **sign** 표지판, 간판 | **have something to do with** ~와 관계가 있다

131 (A) Darby's 인쇄소가 다시 문을 열 것입니다.

(B) 시내에 새로운 인쇄소가 생겼고, 저희는 여러분께 서비스를 제공해 드리고자 합니다.
(C) 개업 첫 주를 성공적으로 만들어 주셔서 감사합니다.
(D) Darby's 인쇄소가 개업 10주년을 축하할 것입니다.

| 해설 | 빈칸 바로 뒤의 문장, 'Darby's Printing Services has just opened for business.'를 통해 Darby's Printing Services라는 업체가 새로 생겼다는 점을 알 수 있다. 따라서 정답은 (B)이며, 나머지 보기들은 모두 이전부터 영업을 하던 업체를 광고할 때 사용될 수 있는 문구이다.

132 (A) ~인 반면에
(B) 하지만
(C) ~이므로
(D) 만약 ~이라면

| 해설 | '새로 오픈했다'는 의미와 '직원들이 베테랑이다'라는 의미는 서로 상반되는 것이므로 빈칸에는 '반면에'라는 뜻을 지닌 (A)의 While이 들어가야 한다. (B)의 However는 접속부사이기 때문에 정답이 될 수 없다.

133 (A) 일부의
(B) ~인 것
(C) 모든
(D) ~인 것

| 해설 | 빈칸에는 단수 명사인 service를 수식할 수 있는 형용사가 들어가야 한다. 따라서 정답은 (C)의 every이다.

134 (A) 판매자
(B) 디자이너
(C) 건축가
(D) 전문가

architect 건축가

| 해설 | if it has anything to do with printing 이라는 부사절과 어울려 자신들을 광고하기에 적합한 단어가 무엇일지 생각해 보자. 보기 중 빈칸에 들어가기에 가장 적합한 단어는 (D)의 experts(전문가)이다.

[135-138]

오데사 봄축제가 끝나다

오데사 (5월 10일) – 5일을 끝으로, 어제 오데사 봄축제가 종료되었다. 축제는 어젯밤 늦게까지 계속된 Big Bass 호수에서의 불꽃놀이와 함께 막을 내렸다.
올해 축제는 근래에 가장 성공적인 것이었다고 널리 평가받았다. 축제 5일 동안 연일 맑은 날씨를 보인 것은 2011년 이후로 이번이 처음이었다. 기온 또한 계절에 맞지 않게 높았는데, 이로 인해 대부분의 참석자들은 보다 즐거운 경험을 할 수 있었다. 축제 기획자인 Diane Armstrong은 "올해에는 잘못된 것을 단 하나도 찾을 수가 없어요. 멋진 축제를 만들었다는 점과 정말로 많은 지역 주민분들께서 오셔서 도움을 주셨다는 점에 기분이 좋습니다."라고 말했다.
축제의 마지막 날에는 해마다 열리는 낚시 대회가 열렸다. 우승자는 Pete Wellman으로, 그는 합산 무게가 11.4킬로그램에 이르는 6마리의 물고기를 낚았다. 그는 이 대회에서 세 차례 우승을 했는데, 6년 전과 작년에도 수상을 했다.

come to an end 끝나다 | **firework** 불꽃놀이 | **unseasonably** 계절에 맞지 않게 | **make for** ~에 기여하다 | **attendee** 참석자 | **organizer** 기획자 | **combined** 합쳐진

135 (A) 결말
(B) 결승전
(C) 멈춤

55

(D) 끝난

final 마지막의; 결승전

| 해설 | 보기 중에서 동사 come과 함께 '끝나다'라는 의미를 완성시킬 수 있는 것은 (A)의 conclusion(결말, 결론)뿐이다.

136 (A) 축제의 기획자들은 맑은 하늘로 인해 많은 사람들이 오기를 바라고 있다.
(B) 폭우로 인해 예상했던 것보다 적은 사람들이 축제를 방문했다.
(C) 특히 날씨 때문에, 축제에 여러 가지 문제가 생겼다.
(D) 올해 축제는 근래에 가장 성공적인 것이었다고 널리 평가받았다.

| 해설 | 두 번째 단락 전체에 걸쳐 올해 축제가 날씨 덕분에 성공적이었다는 내용을 다루고 있다. 따라서 이에 가장 부합되는 문장인 (D)가 빈칸에 들어가야 한다.

137 (A) 시도
(B) 경험
(C) 시각화
(D) 모습

visualization 시각화, 구상화

| 해설 | 보기 중에서 more pleasant의 수식을 가장 자연스럽게 받을 수 있는 명사는 (B)의 experience(경험)이다.

138 (A) 무게가 나가다
(B) 무게를 잰
(C) 무게가 나가는
(D) 무게가 나가다

| 해설 | 빈칸에는 형용사절을 이끌어 six fish을 수식할 수 있는 현재분사가 들어가야 한다. 따라서 정답은 (C)의 weighing이다.

[139-142]

받는 사람: Wilma Arlington <wilma_a@trr.com>
보낸 사람: Chad Silva <csilva@trr.com>
제목: 오리엔테이션
날짜: 8월 24일

Wilma,

알고 있겠지만, 신입 직원을 위한 오리엔테이션이 다음 주 월요일 8월 31일로 예정되어 있어요. 안타깝게도, 작은 문제가 하나 생겼어요. Matt Powell이 교육을 진행할 계획이었죠. 하지만, 그가 오늘 아침에 사직서를 제출했기 때문에, 대표 이사님께서 그에게 프로그램 진행을 맡기고 싶어 하지 않으세요. 대신 Jenkins 씨께서 당신이 모든 것을 책임지게 하자는 제안을 하셨죠.

저는 당신이 전에 이와 같은 일을 해 본 적이 없다고 알고 있지만, 이는 상당히 쉬운 과정이에요. 저는 당신이 해야 하는 모든 일에 대해 알려 줄 수 있고 다음 주 월요일 전에 무엇이 되어 있어야 하는지도 알려 줄 수 있어요. 조만간 우리가 직접 만나는 것이 좋을 것 같아요. 오늘 만나는 것은 어떨까요? 제가 오늘 오후 약 2시까지는 사무실 밖에 있을 거예요. 하지만 그때부터 저녁 6시까지는 언제라도 시간이 괜찮아요. 제가 사무실 밖에 있는 동안에는 이메일을 확인할 수 없으니 제 휴대 전화로 문자 메시지를 남기는 것이 어떨까요? 제 번호는 (205) 365-8434예요.

답장을 기다릴게요.

Chad Silva로부터

aware 알고 있다 | **slight** 작은, 사소한 | **resignation** 사직(서), 사임 | **be responsible for** ~을 책임지다 | **fairly** 꽤, 상당히 | **straightforward** 쉬운,

평이한 | **get ~ up to speed** ~에게 최신 정보를 주다, ~에게 상황을 이해시키다 | **get together** 모이다, 만나다

139 (A) 이끄는
(B) 이끌었다
(C) 이끌기로
(D) 이끌었다

| 해설 | be supposed to(~하기로 예정되어 있다)라는 표현을 알고 있으면 정답을 쉽게 찾을 수 있다. 정답은 to부정사 형태인 (C)의 to lead이다.

140 (A) 협상
(B) 프로그램
(C) 의식
(D) 직장

negotiation 협상 | **ceremony** 의식 | **workplace** 직장, 일터

| 해설 | 문맥상 빈칸에는 orientation session을 가리키는 말이 들어가야 한다. 오리엔테이션은 일종의 '교육 프로그램'이므로 정답은 (B)의 program이다.

141 (A) 과정
(B) 행진
(C) 가공된
(D) 가공하는

| 해설 | process는 명사로 '과정', '절차'라는 의미를 나타내며 동사로는 '가공하다', '처리하다'라는 의미를 나타내기 때문에, 정답은 '과정'이라는 의미의 (A)가 된다. 한편 process가 동사로서 '행진하다'라는 뜻을 나타내기도 하는데, 이때 명사형인 procession은 '행진'이라는 뜻이다.

142 (A) 조만간 우리가 직접 만나는 것이 좋을 것 같아요.
(B) 세부적인 것들을 모두 다루기 위해 전화로 이야기해요.
(C) 저는 내일까지 사무실 밖에 있을 거예요.
(D) 우리는 지난번처럼 실수가 발생하는 것을 원하지 않아요.

| 해설 | 빈칸 다음 문장에서 'Why don't we get together today?'라고 말하며 만나자는 제안을 하고 있다. 따라서 (A)의 내용이 그 앞에 들어가는 것이 가장 자연스럽다.

[143-146]

받는 사람: 전 직원
보낸 사람: 인사부 Rachel Hunter
제목: 부서 이동
날짜: 10월 2일

인사부에서 현재 부서 이동 지원자를 받고 있습니다. 지원 양식은 인사부에서 가져가실 수도 있고 회사 웹사이트인 www.jacksons.com/transfers에서 다운로드받으실 수도 있습니다. 모든 항목이 채워져야 하며, 직속 상관의 서명이 들어가야 하고, 늦어도 10월 10일까지는 제출이 되어야 합니다. 기타 필요한 문서들은 지원서와 함께 제출되어야 합니다. 반드시 어떤 부서 혹은 어떤 지사에 지원할 것인지, 그리고 왜 그곳에서 일을 하고 싶으신지를 밝히셔야 합니다.

올해 우리가 몇몇 해외 지사를 신설했다는 점에 주목해 주십시오. 현재 브라질, 남아프리카, 싱가포르, 중국, 그리고 호주에 지사가 있습니다. 이러한 지사 중 한 곳으로의 이동에 관심이 있다면, 그러한 특정 국가에서 사용되는 1차 언어에 능숙해야 합니다. 이동과 관련해서 질문이나 관심이 있으시면 내선 번호 33번으로 언제든지 제게 연락을 주십시오.

internal 내부의 | **direct supervisor** 직속 상사 | **turn in** ~을 제출하다 | **state** 진술하다, 말하다 | **branch** 지점, 지사 | **note** 주목하다 | **primary language** 1차 언어 | **particular** 특정한 | **extension** 내선 번호 | **concerns**

걱정: 관심사

143 (A) 우리는 몇몇 신입 직원들을 고용했습니다.
(B) 승진 대상자를 고려하기 시작할 때입니다.
(C) 인사부에서 현재 부서 이동 지원자를 받고 있습니다.
(D) 해마다 실시되는 직원 평가를 준비하셔야 합니다.

employee evaluation 직원 평가

| 해설 | 회람의 제목이나 빈칸 이후의 내용을 통해, 이 글이 부서 이동이나 전근을 원하는 사람을 위한 안내임을 알 수 있다. 따라서 빈칸에는 (C)가 들어가는 것이 가장 적절하다.

144 (A) ~ 대신에
(B) ~와 상관없이
(C) ~와 함께
(D) ~에 관하여

in lieu of ~ 대신에 | **regardless of** ~와 상관없이

| 해설 | '지원서와 함께' 다른 서류들도 제출되어야 한다는 의미가 완성되어야 한다. 따라서 정답은 (C)의 along with(~와 함께)이다.

145 (A) 유창한
(B) 말이 많은
(C) 알고 있는
(D) 준비된

talkative 말하는 것을 좋아하는, 말이 많은

| 해설 | 빈칸 이후의 내용에 주목하면 빈칸에는 '(언어에) 능숙한' 혹은 '유창한'이라는 의미의 형용사가 들어가는 것이 가장 자연스럽다. 따라서 정답은 (A)이다.

146 (A) 간주하다
(B) 상관하지 않고
(C) ~에 관하여
(D) 간주된

| 해설 | regarding은 전치사로 '~에 관하여'라는 뜻을 나타낸다. 동사 regard(여기다, 간주하다)와는 별도의 단어로 생각해야 한다.

● PART 7   p.100

[147-148]

받는 사람: Joan Jackson <jjackson1@gumpers.com>
보낸 사람: Marvin White <mwhite@gumpers.com>
제목: 경비 지급
날짜: 2월 16일

친애하는 Jackson 씨께,

저는 당신의 최근 출장에 대한 당신의 경비 지급 요청서가 불완전하다는 점을 알게 되었습니다. 당신은 몇 장의 영수증을 지급 요청서와 함께 제출하지 않았습니다. 우선, 데번포트의 Old Country 숙소에서 3박을 했다고 적었지만, 2박짜리의 영수증을 제출했습니다. 또한 식당에서 했다고 한 몇 차례 식사에 관한 영수증과, 방문했다고 한 주유소의 영수증도 빠져 있습니다. 경비 지급에 관한 회사의 방침은 명확합니다. 모든 영수증이 요청서 안에 포함되어 있어야 합니다. 당신이 요청한 금액을 전액 지급받기 위해서는 제게 주말까지 빠져 있는 영수증을 주어야 합니다. 이번 문제에 관해 질문이 있는 경우에는 언제라도 제 사무실(509호실)을 방문해 주시기 바랍니다.

Marvin White 드림
회계부 부장
Gumpers 주식회사

reimbursement 상환, 변제 | **come to one's attention** ~의 주의를 끌다 | **sales trip** 출장 | **along with** ~와 함께 | **turn in** ~을 제출하다 | **policy** 정책, 방침 | **include** 포함하다 | **in order to** ~하기 위하여

147 Jackson 씨에 관해 무엇이 언급되어 있는가?
(A) 그녀는 이번 주 금요일에 양식을 제출할 것이다.
(B) 그녀는 곧 데번포트로 이사할 것이다.
(C) 그녀는 최근에 출장을 다녀왔다.
(D) 그녀는 출장 중에 자동차를 대여했다.

| 해설 | 이메일 첫 문장에서 White 씨는 Jackson 씨에게 '최근 출장에 관한 경비 지급 요청서'(your request for reimbursement for your latest sales trip)에 문제가 있다는 점을 지적하고 있다. 이를 통해 Jackson 씨는 '최근에 출장을 다녀왔다'는 점을 알 수 있으므로 정답은 (C)이다.

148 Jackson 씨는 어떻게 문제를 해결할 수 있는가?
(A) 빠진 영수증을 제출함으로써
(B) 양식을 올바르게 작성함으로써
(C) 그녀가 한 주장을 변경함으로써
(D) 은행 계좌 정보를 알려 줌으로써

| 해설 | White 씨는 'You must give me the missing receipts by the end of the week in order to receive the full amount you are requesting.'이라고 말하면서 경비를 전액 환불받기 위해서는 영수증을 모두 제출해야 한다고 안내한다. 따라서 정답은 (A)이다.

[149-150]

Grasshopper 350 노트북 컴퓨터 보증서

이 제품에 대한 보증은 영수증에 있는 구입 날짜 이후로 2년간 유효합니다. 이 보증서의 안내 사항을 주의 깊게 읽어 주십시오. 어느 것이라도 지시 사항을 따르지 않는다면 즉시 보증이 무효화됩니다.

* 언제라도 컴퓨터의 케이스를 열지 마십시오.
* 혼자서 기기를 수리하거나 부품을 교체하려고 시도하지 마십시오.
* Grasshopper 이외의 회사가 제조한 전력 케이블을 컴퓨터에 연결하지 마십시오.
* 제품을 물이나 기타 액체에 담그지 마십시오.
* 컴퓨터를 오븐과 같이 고온이 발생하는 곳과, 냉장고와 같이 극도의 추위가 발생하는 곳 근처에 두지 마십시오.
* 불법적으로 다운로드한 소프트웨어를 사용하지 마십시오.

보증 사항에 대한 질문이 있으신 경우에는 www.grasshopper.com/350laptopwarranty를 방문하시거나 가장 가까운 Grasshopper 대리점으로 연락을 주십시오.

valid 유효한 | **instruction** 설명, 지시 사항 | **instantly** 즉시 | **invalidate** 무효화하다 | **by oneself** 혼자서 | **immerse** (물 등에) 담그다 | **liquid** 액체 | **source** 출처, 근원 | **illegally** 불법적으로 | **dealer** 중개인, 딜러, 대리점

149 이 지시 사항은 누구를 위한 것인가?
(A) 컴퓨터 디자이너
(B) 컴퓨터 대리점
(C) 컴퓨터 소유자
(D) 컴퓨터 수리 기사

| 해설 | 첫 문장에서 '구입 후 2년간'(for two years after the date of

purchase on your receipt) 보증이 유효하다고 했으므로 보증의 대상은 '노트북 컴퓨터의 구입자들', 즉 (C)임을 알 수 있다.

150 지시 사항에서 언급되지 않은 것은 무엇인가?
(A) 컴퓨터를 온도가 낮은 곳 주변에 두어서는 안 된다.
(B) 컴퓨터에는 Grasshopper가 제작한 소프트웨어만이 사용되어야 한다.
(C) 보증 사항에 관한 더 많은 정보는 웹사이트에서 찾아볼 수 있다.
(D) 컴퓨터의 문제를 수리하려고 시도해서는 안 된다.

| 해설 | '극도로 추운'(extreme cold) 곳에 두어서는 안 된다고 했으므로 (A)는 언급된 사항이며, 맨 마지막 문장을 통해 (C)의 '기타 정보는 웹사이트에서 찾아볼 수 있다'는 점도 확인이 가능하다. 또한 두 번째 지시 사항에서 (D)와 관련된 '수리나 부품 교체도 허용되지 않는다'는 점이 언급되어 있기 때문에 이 역시 사실이다. 따라서 정답은 (B)로, 합법적인 소프트웨어가 반드시 Grasshopper의 소프트웨어일 필요는 없다.

[151-152]

Treadway, Peter 1:24 P.M.
저희 제안을 수락해 줘서 고마워요. 저희 Trueheart 병원은 당신과 함께 일하기를 고대하고 있어요.

Grant, Marcus 1:26 P.M.
우리가 곧 동료가 된다니 기쁘군요.

Treadway, Peter 1:29 P.M.
그러면 보수에 관해서 질문이 있으신가요? 급여와 수당은 괜찮으시죠, 그렇죠?

Grant, Marcus 1:31 P.M.
그래요. 저는 오늘 만난 자리에서 당신이 제시한 모든 것에 만족하고 있어요. 제가 계약서나 혹은 그와 같은 것에 서명을 해야 하나요?

Treadway, Peter 1:32 P.M.
네, 제가 오늘 늦게 이메일로 보내 드릴게요.

Grant, Marcus 1:35 P.M.
잘 되었군요. 아시다시피, 당신은 제가 4월 28일에 일을 시작하기를 바란다고 말씀하셨지만, 저는 필요하다면 4월 20일에도 일을 시작할 수 있어요.

Treadway, Peter 1:38 P.M.
그에 대해서는 제가 다시 연락을 드려야 할 것 같군요. 하지만 조금 전에 하신 말씀은 Hearst 박사님께 알려 드리죠.

colleague 동료 | **compensation package** 보수 | **benefit** 혜택; 수당 | **get back to** ~에게 나중에 다시 연락하다

151 무엇이 주로 논의되고 있는가?
(A) 계약 협상
(B) 새로운 일자리의 조건
(C) 곧 있을 승진
(D) 새로운 지사로의 전근

terms 조건

| 해설 | '제안'(offer)을 수락함으로써 서로 '직장 동료'(colleagues)가 될 사람들 간의 대화이다. 이후에도 근무 조건 등에 관한 내용이 이어지고 있으므로 대화의 주제는 (B)로 볼 수 있다.

152 오후 1시 28분에, Treadway 씨는 왜 "I'll have to get back to you on that"이라고 썼는가?
(A) 그는 Grant 씨에게 일을 시작해야 할 시점을 말할 수 없다.
(B) 그는 Grant 씨에게 부정적인 답을 주고 싶어하지 않는다.
(C) 그는 Grant 씨에게 더 높은 급여나 더 많은 수당을 제안할 수 없다.
(D) 그는 만나기로 한 날짜를 나중에 알려 줄 것이다.

| 해설 | 근무 시작일을 언제로 할 것인지를 묻는 질문에 대한 답변이다. Treadway 씨는 주어진 문장과 같이 말한 후, 'But I'll let Dr. Hearst know what you just told me.'라고 적고 있으므로 실제 근무 시작일에 관한 결정은 본인이 아니라 Hearst 박사라는 사람이 내릴 것이라는 점을 알 수 있다. 따라서 주어진 문장의 의미는 (A)로 볼 수 있다.

[153-155]

Good Times 스튜디오

Good Times 스튜디오는 사람들의 인생에서 기념할만한 순간을 포착하는데 전문인, 가족에 의해 운영되는 사진 스튜디오입니다. 저희 사진사들은 야외 사진의 세세한 측면까지도 이해하고 있기 때문에, 생일, 졸업식, 결혼식, 그리고 기념일과 같은 행사에서 귀중한 순간을 기록해 드릴 수 있습니다. 그들이 찍는 사진은 여러분들께 일생 동안 지속될 기억을 제공해 드릴 것입니다. 저희의 노력은 행사가 시작되기 전부터 시작됩니다. Good Times의 전문가들은 태양, 날씨, 그리고 배경이 최고의 사진을 만들어 낼 수 있도록 행사 장소를 어디로 정해야 하는지에 관한 조언도 해 드릴 것입니다. 저희의 목표는 여러분들의 최고의 모습을 모든 사람이 볼 수 있도록 만드는 것입니다. 사진 촬영을 위해 저희 스튜디오를 방문하시는 분들께, 저희는 여러분들에게 필요한 모든 것을, 여권 및 신분증용 사진에서 가족 사진에 이르기까지, 제공해 드릴 수 있습니다. 스튜디오에 예약을 하지 않으셔도 되지만, 특별한 행사를 위해서는 통상적으로 일주일 전에 연락을 주셔야 합니다. 하지만 보다 일찍 예약하시는 것을 권해 드립니다. 예약이나 가격 정보가 더 필요하시면 737-3921로 전화를 주십시오.

family-owned 가족에 의해 운영되는 | **specialize in** ~을 전문으로 하다 | **capture** 포획하다, 포착하다 | **monumental** 기념비적인 | **minute** 극미한, 상세한 | **precious** 소중한 | **anniversary** 기념일 | **stage** 무대; 개최하다 | **contribute to** ~에 기여하다, ~에 이바지하다 | **passport** 여권 | **portrait** 초상화 | **walk-in** 예약을 하지 않은 | **notice** 통지, 고지

153 누가 Good Times 스튜디오의 서비스를 필요로 할 것 같은가?
(A) 그림이 그려지기를 원하는 가족
(B) 일자리를 구하는 사진사
(C) 신분증을 만들어야 하는 학생
(D) 신혼 여행을 떠날 신혼 부부

newlyweds 신혼 부부

| 해설 | 전반적인 내용을 통해 Good Times 스튜디오는 생일, 졸업, 결혼, 기념일 사진과 여권 및 신분증용 사진, 그리고 가족 사진을 취급한다는 점을 알 수 있다. 보기 중에서 이러한 카테고리의 사진이 필요한 사람은 (C)의 '신분증이 필요한 학생'뿐이다. 참고로 (A)의 picture는, paint라는 동사와 함께 쓰인 것을 감안할 때 '사진'이 아니라 '그림'을 나타낸다.

154 광고에 의하면, Good Times의 전문가들은 무엇을 하는가?
(A) 행사의 위치를 선정한다
(B) 행사가 열리는 시간을 정한다
(C) 고객과 날씨 상황에 대해 논의한다
(D) 행사에 무엇을 입고 가야 할지 알려 준다

| 해설 | 전문가들이 하는 일은 광고의 중간 부분, 'Good Times specialists will provide advice on where to stage your events to ensure that the sun, weather, and background will contribute to taking the best shots possible.'에 드러나 있다. 그러므로 정답은 (C)이다. 장소에 관해 '조언'을 한다고 했지, 장소를 '결정'한다는 언급은 찾아볼 수 없으므로 (A)를 정답으로 선택해서는 안 된다.

155 Good Times 스튜디오에 관해 언급되지 않은 것은 무엇인가?
  (A) 전화로 예약을 받는다.
  (B) 스튜디오 안과 기타 장소에서 사진을 촬영한다.
  (C) 일부 행사에 대해서는 사전 예약이 필요하다.
  (D) 스튜디오 밖에서 찍는 사진에는 추가 요금이 부과된다.

| 해설 | 예약 및 가격에 정보에 관해서는 전화로 문의해 달라고 했으므로 (A)는 언급된 사항이고, 야외 사진 및 스튜디오 사진을 촬영한다는 내용도 찾아볼 수 있기 때문에 (B)도 사실임을 알 수 있다. 또한 최소 1주일 전에 미리 예약을 하는 것이 권장된다고 했으므로 (C) 역시 올바른 사항이다. 언급되지 않은 내용은 (D)인데, 사진 요금에 관한 정보는 광고에 나타나 있지 않다.

[156-158]

전근 신청

최근 몇 개월간 해외 전근 신청이 크게 늘고 있기 때문에, 인사부(HR)는 차후 요청과 관련하여 즉시 효력을 지니는 몇 가지 규칙을 시행하기로 결정했습니다. 먼저, 모든 신청서는 적절한 양식에 작성되어 제출되어야 합니다. 양식은 인사부 인트라넷 사이트에서 찾으실 수 있습니다. 지금부터 이메일로 제출된 비공식적인 요청은 더 이상 받아들여지지 않고 무시될 것입니다. 둘째, 전근 신청서는 전체적으로 적절하게 작성되어야 하며, 그렇지 않을 경우에는 거부될 것입니다. (신청서 중 빈칸이 있다던가 부적절하게 작성된 부분이 있으면 그 신청서는 폐기될 것입니다.) 셋째, 각 부서의 직원들이 할 수 있는 전근의 수를 제한시키자는 결정이 내려졌습니다. 6개월 이내에, 같은 부서 내 두 명 이상의 직원은 해외로 전근을 할 수 없습니다. 마지막 규칙은 올해 남은 기간에만 시행될 것입니다. 멕시코와 이탈리아는 모두 직원이 꽉 차있는 상태이므로 직원들은 더 이상 이곳으로 전근을 갈 수 없습니다. 하지만, 스웨덴, 폴란드, 그리고 독일의 지점은 여전히 인원이 부족한 상태이므로 도움이 필요할 수 있습니다. 전근을 신청하려는 지역에서 사용되는 언어에 재능이 있는 경우, 선택될 기회가 크게 높아질 것이라는 점에 주목해 주십시오. 항상 그렇듯이, 전근이 실제로 이루어지기 위해서는 부서장과 사장님께서 전근 신청을 최종적으로 승인해야 한다는 점도 기억해 주십시오.

overseas 해외의 | **implement** 실행하다, 시행하다 | **effective** 효과가 있는, 효력이 있는 | **intranet** 내부 전산망, 인트라넷 | **disregard** 무시하다 | **in one's entirety** 전체적으로, 전부 | **remainder** 나머지 | **staff** 직원; 직원을 제공하다 | **undermanned** 인원이 부족한 | **facility** 시설; 재능 | **as always** 항상 그렇듯이 | **final approval** 최종 승인 | **go into effect** 효력을 나타내다

156 직원들은 어떻게 전근 신청을 할 수 있는가?
  (A) 이메일로 요청서를 제출함으로써
  (B) 부서장에게 이야기를 함으로써
  (C) 인사부를 방문함으로써
  (D) 컴퓨터로 양식을 다운로드함으로써

| 해설 | 첫 번째 규칙에서 전근 신청은 인사부 인트라넷에서 다운로드한 양식을 통해 이루어져야 한다는 점을 알 수 있으므로 정답은 (D)이다.

157 어떤 규칙이 정해진 기간 동안만 효력을 나타내는가?
  (A) 직원들은 특정 지사로의 전근을 신청할 수 없다.
  (B) 부서장이 직원의 전근을 승인해야 한다.
  (C) 2개월마다 한 부서 내의 두 직원만이 전근을 할 수 있다.
  (D) 전근을 할 직원들은 하나의 외국어를 할 수 있어야 한다.

| 해설 | 마지막 규칙이 한시적으로 적용되는 규칙이므로 이에 대한 내용을 살펴보도록 한다. 마지막 규칙은 멕시코와 이탈리아로의 전근을 '올해 남은 기간 동안만'(for the remainder of the calendar year) 불허하는 것이므로 정답은 (A)가 된다.

158 [1], [2], [3], 그리고 [4]로 표시된 위치 중에 다음 문장이 들어가기에 가장 알맞은 곳은 어디인가?
"신청서 중 빈칸이 있다던가 부적절하게 작성된 부분이 있으면 그 신청서는 폐기될 것입니다."
  (A) [1]
  (B) [2]
  (C) [3]
  (D) [4]

| 해설 | 주어진 문장은 두 번째 규칙의 구체적인 사례로 볼 수 있기 때문에 정답은 (A)가 된다.

> ✓ **700점 넘기 포인트** 영어에서는 일반적인 내용이 앞선 다음에 구체적인 사례가 이어지는 경우가 많다. 이 문제의 경우에도, 'Second, the transfer request form must be properly filled out in its entirety, or it will be rejected.'라는 일반적인 규칙이 소개된 뒤에는 그에 관한 예시로 'If any part of the form happens to be left blank or is filled in improperly, it will be discarded.'라는 문장이 이어져야 한다.

[159-161]

Columbus 주간 소식지

6월 15일에 시작되는 한 주 동안 콜럼버스에서 예정된 행사들은 다음과 같습니다.

6월 16일 월요일
Columbus 공공 수영장에서 오전 8시와 오전 10시 사이에 수영 강습을 실시할 예정입니다. 4세에서 13세까지의 어린이들이 강습을 받을 수 있으며, 수강료는 무료입니다. 수영장 회원이 되고 싶으신 가족분들은 이날 가입을 하시면 연간 회원권에 대해 30%의 할인을 받게 될 것입니다.

6월 19일 목요일
오후 1시에 West Street 도서관에서 낭독회가 열릴 예정입니다. 저명한 아동 문학 작가인 Dee Matthews가 자신의 최신 도서인 *나의 애완용 용*을 읽을 것입니다. 아이들과 부모 모두 환영합니다. 낭독회는 1층 어린이 코너에서 열릴 것입니다. 가벼운 다과가 제공될 예정입니다.

6월 21일 토요일
매년 열리는 10킬로미터 여름 도로 경주가 오전 9시에 시청에서 시작될 것입니다. 코스를 따라 주자들은 역사적인 콜럼버스의 시내를 관통하게 될 것이며, 코스는 Broadway 공원에서 끝날 것입니다. 더 많은 정보가 필요하시거나 달리기 경주의 참가를 원하시면 495-3939로 전화를 주십시오. 오전 11시에는, 제1회 여름 야유회가 Broadway 공원에서 열릴 예정입니다. 게임, 라이브 음악, 그리고 기타 재미있는 활동들이 예정되어 있습니다. 햄버거, 핫도그, 치킨, 그리고 그 밖의 수많은 간식 거리들도 제공될 것입니다. 점심 식사 비용으로 성인은 5달러, 아동은 3달러를 내셔야 합니다.

be eligible for ~의 자격이 있다 | **noted** 저명한 | **light refreshments** 다과, 가벼운 스낵 | **historic** 역사적인 | **entertainment** 오락, 여흥 | **numerous** 많은 | **side dish** 곁들여 내는 요리

159 일정은 누구를 위해 의도된 것 같은가?
  (A) 지역 고등학교 학생들
  (B) 콜럼버스 주민들
  (C) 콜럼버스 내의 쇼핑객들
  (D) 여름 방학을 맞은 학생들

| 해설 | 콜럼버스라는 도시에서 일주일 동안 진행될 행사, 즉 수영 강습, 낭독회, 달리기 대회, 그리고 야유회에 대해 안내하고 있다. 이러한 행사들은 주

160 6월 19일 행사의 참가자들은 무엇을 하게 될 것인가?
(A) 작가에게 질문을 한다
(B) 작가가 책을 읽는 것을 듣는다
(C) 사인을 받는다
(D) 책을 쓰는 법을 배운다

autograph 자필 서명, 사인

| 해설 | '6월 19일'에 이루어질 행사에 관해 묻고 있다. 6월 19일에 예정된 일을 살펴 보면 저명한 아동 문학 작가의 낭독회가 열릴 것이라는 점을 알 수 있으므로 정답은 (B)가 된다. (A)와 (C)는 낭독회에서 있을 수 있는 일이기는 하지만, 지문에서는 언급된 바 없는 사항들이다.

161 일정에 따르면, 6월 21일 행사에서 참가자들이 할 수 없는 것은 무엇인가?
(A) 야구 경기에 참여한다
(B) 음악이 연주되는 것을 듣는다
(C) 달리기 경주에 참가한다
(D) 음식을 구입한다

| 해설 | '6월 21일' 행사를 살펴보면 달리기 대회와 야유회가 계획되어 있다는 점을 알 수 있는데, 야유회 활동으로는 games, live music, 그리고 other entertainment가 예정되어 있다. 따라서 보기 중 참가자들이 할 수 없는 활동은 (A)의 '야구 경기'이다.

[162-164]

받는 사람: 회계부 Stan Erickson
보낸 사람: 영업부 Mika Oh
제목: 교육
날짜: 3월 14일

일부 영업 사원들을 교육시킬 수 있도록 영업부에서 공식적으로 추가적인 자금 지원을 요청합니다. 구체적으로 말하면, 저희는 4월 5일과 6일에 로스앤젤레스에서 Walter Perkins가 주관하는 특별 행사에 세 명의 직원을 참석시키기 위해 자금을 지원받고자 합니다. 저는 당신이 검토할 수 있도록 이틀간의 세미나에 관한 브로셔를 첨부했습니다. Perkins 씨는 영업 전략 및 거래 성사 기법의 전문가입니다. 과거 그의 세미나에 참석한 사람들은 자신들이 얻은 정보의 가치를 입증해 냈습니다. 우리는 영업팀의 세 명의 팀원(Jodie Welch, Alana Monroe, and Jeff Stevens)을 보냄으로써, 그들이 개별적인 혜택을 보게 될 것으로 믿습니다. 게다가, 그 세 팀원들은, 부서 내에서 가장 우수한 직원들인데, Perkins의 방식에 관해 자신들이 배운 내용을 바탕으로 다른 직원들을 교육시키겠다고 했습니다. 세 명 모두에 대한 비용은, 교통비, 숙박비, 식비, 그리고 등록비를 포함하여, 5천 달러를 초과하지 않을 것입니다. 3월 22일이 행사 등록이 가능한 마지막 날이기 때문에, 늦어도 그때까지 응답을 주시기를 요청합니다. 정보가 더 필요하시면 내선 번호 798로 제게 전화를 주십시오.

officially 공식적으로 | **funding** 재정 지원, 자금 지원 | **to be specific** 구체적으로 말하면, 상세히 말하면 | **brochure** 소책자, 브로셔 | **examine** 검사하다, 검토하다 | **strategy** 전략 | **attest** 입증하다 | **value** 가치 | **acquire** 얻다, 획득하다 | **based on** ~에 근거하여 | **method** 방법, 방식 | **accommodations** 숙박

162 Oh 씨는 왜 회람을 작성했는가?
(A) 곧 있을 세미나의 이점에 대해 설명하기 위해
(B) 직원들에게 행사 등록을 장려하기 위해
(C) 일부 직원들이 세미나에 가는 것을 허가하기 위해
(D) 사람들이 행사에 참여할 수 있도록 돈을 요청하기 위해

| 해설 | 회람의 첫 문장에서 요청 사항이 extra funding to be able to train some of our sales staff임을 알 수 있다. 즉 교육에 필요한 자금 지원이 회람을 작성한 목적이므로 정답은 (D)이다.

163 Alana Monroe는 누구인가?
(A) 특별 강사
(B) 영업부 직원
(C) 회계부 직원
(D) 영업 방식에 관한 교육 담당자

| 해설 | Alana Monroe라는 이름은 회람 중반부의 three members of our sales team 중 한 명으로 언급되고 있다. 따라서 Alana Monroe는 (B)의 '영업부 직원'이다.

164 세미나에 관해 언급되지 않은 것은 무엇인가?
(A) 그것을 설명하는 브로셔가 출간되어 있다.
(B) 그것은 이틀 동안 로스앤젤레스에서 열릴 것이다.
(C) 단체로 등록하는 사람들에게 할인이 제공된다.
(D) 등록에 관한 마감 시간이 존재한다.

| 해설 | 브로셔를 첨부했다는 말을 통해 (A)의 내용을, 세미나의 개최 날짜 및 장소에 관한 정보에서 (B)의 내용을, 그리고 회신을 바라는 날짜를 언급하는 부분에서 (D)의 내용을 확인할 수 있다. 하지만 '등록비 할인'에 관한 언급은 찾아볼 수 없으므로 언급되지 않은 내용은 (C)이다.

[165-167]

회생의 기미를 보이는 경제

레이크랜드힐스 (10월 25일) – 전국 각지에서, 침체된 경제를 극복하기 위한 노력의 일환으로 수많은 도시와 주들이 최저 임금을 인상하고 있다. 하지만 이곳 레이크랜드힐스에서는, Rush Nelson 시장과 시의회가 또 다른 전략을 구사하고 있는데, Mark Sanders가 시장이었을 때 시작된 장기적인 경기 침체로부터 시가 벗어나려는 모습을 보임에 따라, 이는 성과를 올리고 있는 것처럼 보인다.
Nelson 시장은 약 6개월 전에 시의회로 하여금, 시의 판매세와 재산세를 포함하여, 지방세를 대폭 삭감하도록 유도했다. 몇몇 시의원들과 지역 주민들이 그러한 결정에 항의했지만, Nelson 시장의 행보는 옳았던 것으로 보인다. 몇몇 지역 기업들이 신규 직원들을 고용하기 시작했을 뿐만 아니라, 인근 지역의 몇몇 사업장들은 문을 닫고 레이크랜드힐스의 기업 친화적인 테두리 안으로 이전을 했다. 이러한 기업들의 소유주들은 특히 시의 낮은 세율이 이전을 하게 된 주요 원인이었다고 언급했다.
지난 4개월 동안, 실업률은 꾸준히 하락했고 현재 단 4.2%만을 나타내고 있다. 이는 주 전체의 실업률보다 7.4%보다 훨씬 낮은 것이다. 시의 경기 호황으로, 세율이 감소했음에도 불구하고 세수는 증가했다. 이로써 시는 오랫동안 필요했던 기간 시설의 개선에 자금을 쓰고 있다. 이러한 프로젝트에는 Main 가와 Oak 가의 일부 도로를 다시 포장하는 공사와 Golden 강에 다리를 하나 더 건설하는 공사가 포함되어 있다.

signs of life 소생의 기미 | **countless** 수많은 | **minimum wage** 최저 임금 | **in an effort to** ~하려는 노력의 일환으로 | **struggling** 분투하는; 어려운, 힘든 | **city council** 시의회 | **strategy** 전략 | **pay off** 성공하다, 성과를 올리다 | **emerge** 나타나다, 등장하다 | **lengthy** 오랜 | **recession** 경기 침체 | **slash** 베다; 대폭 삭감하다 | **property tax** 재산세 | **protest** 항의하다 | **not only ~ but also** ~뿐만 아니라 ~도 | **shutter** 셔터; 문을 닫다 | **business-friendly** 기업 친화적인 | **confine** 테두리, 범위 | **specifically** 특히 | **steadily** 꾸준히 | **booming** 급속히 발전하는 | **tax revenue** 세수 | **infrastructure** 사회 기반 시설 | **repave** 다시 포장하다

165 Sanders 씨가 시장이었을 때 어떤 일이 일어났는가?
(A) 레이크랜드힐스의 실업률이 개선되었다.

(B) 레이크랜드힐스의 경기가 악화되었다.
(C) 레이크랜드힐스의 많은 주민들이 떠났다.
(D) 세금이 평소보다 더 많이 인상되었다.

| 해설 | Sanders 시장에 대한 언급은 첫 번째 단락의 마지막 문장에서 찾아볼 수 있는데, 여기에서는 '장기 경기 침체가 그가 시장이었을 때 시작되었다'(the lengthy recession that began when Mark Sanders was mayor)고 밝히고 있다. 따라서 그가 시장이었을 당시 경제가 악화되기 시작했다고 볼 수 있으므로 정답은 (B)이다.

166 Nelson 시장은 6개월 전에 무엇을 했는가?
(A) 시의 세금을 인하할 것을 요구했다
(B) Sanders 씨를 상대로 선거에서 승리했다
(C) 레이크랜드힐스에서 자신의 회사를 개업했다
(D) 재산세 징수를 중단하기로 결정했다

election 선거 | **collecting** 모으다; 징수하다

| 해설 | six months ago와 같은 뜻을 나타내는 어구는 두 번째 단락의 첫 문장 중 around half a year ago이다. 따라서 이때 Nelson 시장이 한 일은 (A)의 '(시의회에) 세금 감소를 요청한 일'이다.

167 레이크랜드힐스의 현재 경제 상황에 대해 언급된 것은 무엇인가?
(A) 사업체들이 그 지역을 떠나 인근 도시로 가고 있다.
(B) 지역 실업률이 7.4%이다.
(C) 거리 개선에 사용할 자금이 충분히 있다.
(D) 평소보다 낮은 세수가 걷히고 있다.

| 해설 | 사업체들이 레이크랜드힐스로 이전하고 있으므로 (A)는 사실과 반대되는 진술이며, (B)의 7.4%의 실업률은 레이크랜드힐스의 실업률이 아니라 주 전체의 실업률이다. 세율은 낮지만 세수는 증가했다는 점을 통해 (D)도 사실이 아님을 알 수 있다. 세수 증가로 도로 포장 및 교각 건설 등 사회 기반 시설을 위한 자금이 사용되고 있다고 했으므로 정답은 (C)이다.

[168-171]

받는 사람: Emily Williams 〈ewilliams@tayloraccounting.com〉
보낸 사람: Gwen Scott 〈gwen_s@tayloraccounting.com〉
제목: 고마워요
날짜: 4월 28일

Emily,

제가 하와이로 신혼 여행을 떠나 있는 동안 제 고객들을 상대해 주기로 해서 정말로 고마워요. 모든 사람들이 당신의 유능한 손 안에 있게 될 것이라는 점을 알게 되니 정말로 마음이 편하군요.
일을 가능한 매끄럽게 진행시키기 위해, 당신이 상대하게 될 몇몇 고객들과 관련된 사항들을 당신에게 알려 주어야 한다고 생각했어요. 먼저, Westside Bakery 세금 보고서 파일에 대한 검사는 Thompson 씨가 저희에게 모든 정보를 제출하지 않아서 아직 하지 못했어요. 그는 5월 1일까지 그 일을 해 주겠다고 했어요. 검사는 5월 3일에 시작될 예정이었지만, 이틀 뒤로 미루어졌죠. 하지만 같은 장소와 같은 시간에 이루어질 거예요. 둘째, Douglas 은행 파일은 잠시 대기시킬 수 있기 때문에, 제가 돌아와서 그 일을 하도록 할게요. 은행의 누군가로부터 전화가 오면, 제가 Alicia Franks와 이야기를 해서 제 계획을 확인시켜 주었다는 점을 상기시켜 주세요. 마지막으로, 그리고 가장 중요한 일인데, Baker 건설의 회계 장부는 처음부터 끝까지 다시 검토해야 해요. 시 조사관이 Lincoln 경기장의 공사를 조사하고 있는데, 이곳은 Baker가 시공하고 있는 곳이어서, 특이한 점이 없는지 확인하기 위해서 파일에 있는 모든 내용을 당신이 읽어 보아야 해요. 이 일을 당신에게 떠넘겨서 미안하지만, 그에 대해서는 저도 오늘 아침에야 알게 되었어요.
당신이 알아야 하는 것은 이것이 다예요. 저는 모레 출발을 해서 열흘 후에 돌아올 거예요. 문제가 생기는 경우, 제게 어떻게 연락해야 하는지는 당신이 알고 있을 거예요. 다시 한 번 고마워요. 큰 신세를 지는군요.

그럼 이만,

Gwen

handle 다루다, 처리하다 | **honeymoon** 신혼 여행 | **capable** 유능한 | **smoothly** 매끄럽게, 원활하게 | **examination** 검사 | **bump** 부딪히다; 이동시키다 | **remind** 상기시키다 | **account** 회계 장부 | **reexamine** 다시 검사하다 | **from top to bottom** 샅샅이 | **inspector** 조사관, 감독관 | **investigate** 조사하다 | **dump** 버리다; 떠넘기다 | **owe** 빚지다

168 이메일은 왜 작성되었는가?
(A) 회의 일정을 정하자고 요청하기 위해
(B) 업무 지시 사항을 알려 주기 위해
(C) 그녀가 한 일에 대한 감사를 표하기 위해
(D) 많은 업무량에 대해 사과하기 위해

workload 업무량

| 해설 | 이메일 초반부 내용을 통해 신혼 여행을 가게 될 직원이 자신의 업무를 다른 사람에게 맡기기 위해 이메일을 작성하고 있다는 점을 알 수 있다. 따라서 정답은 (B)이다.

169 Scott 씨에 대해 무엇이 암시되어 있는가?
(A) 그녀는 회계부를 운영한다.
(B) 그녀는 오늘 Douglas 은행을 방문할 것이다.
(C) 그녀는 Alicia Franks와 만나야 한다.
(D) 그녀는 곧 결혼을 할 것이다.

| 해설 | Scott 씨는 이메일을 작성한 사람으로, 그녀는 곧 하와이로 '신혼 여행'(honeymoon)을 떠날 것이라는 점이 첫 번째 단락에서 언급되어 있다. 따라서 정답은 (D)이다. 참고로 신혼 여행의 구체적인 기간은 이메일의 마지막 단락에서 찾을 수 있다.

170 Westside Bakery에 대한 업무는 왜 연기되었는가?
(A) 소유주가 Scott 씨하고만 일하는 것을 원한다.
(B) 일부 정보가 빠져 있다.
(C) 아직 돈이 지급되지 않았다.
(D) 고객을 만날 수가 없다.

| 해설 | Westside Bakery에 관한 업무에 대해서는 일정이 연기되었다고 말한 후 그 이유를 'Thompson 씨가 정보를 모두 제출하지는 않았기 때문'(because Mr. Thompson hasn't submitted all of his information to us)이라고 밝히고 있다. 따라서 (B)가 정답이다.

171 Scott 씨는 Baker 건설에 대해 무엇을 언급하는가?
(A) 가장 최근에 알게 된 고객 중 하나이다.
(B) 얼마 전에 경기장 건설 계약을 체결했다.
(C) 파산할 위기에 처해 있다.
(D) 정부에 의해 감사를 받고 있다.

in danger of ~의 위험에 처한 | **go out of business** 파산하다

| 해설 | Scott 씨는 Baker 건설의 회계 장부를 전체적으로 다시 검토해야 한다고 말하면서, '시 공무원'(city inspectors)이 Baker 건설이 시공중인 경기장에 대한 조사를 실시하고 있다는 점을 알리고 있다. 따라서 Baker 건설에 대해 언급되어 있는 사항은 (D)이다.

[172-175]

Ortega, Pedro   2:12 P.M.
모두들, 좋은 소식이 있어요. Butler 씨가 조금 전에 우리 팀을 선택해서 Madison과의 거래를 맡도록 했어요.

Atwell, Gary   2:15 P.M.
진심인가요? 놀라운 소식이네요. 저는 Samantha 팀에 주어질 것으로 예상하고 있었거든요.

Struthers, Lucy   2:16 P.M.
저도 그랬어요. 우리가 어떻게 그 일을 얻게 되었나요?

Ortega, Pedro   2:19 P.M.
저는 Butler 씨와 오랫동안 이야기를 해서 우리가 그 업무를 감당할 수 있다고 알려 주었죠. 그러니 저를 실망시키지 말아 주세요. 회사는 이번 건에 대해 큰 기대를 하고 있어요.

Struthers, Lucy   2:21 P.M.
최선을 다할게요. 오… 우리가 조만간 회의를 해야 하나요?

Ortega, Pedro   2:23 P.M.
네, 그것이 바로 제가 두 분 모두에게 글을 쓰고 있는 이유예요. 저는 4시 30분이 넘어서 사무실로 돌아올 것이기 때문에, 우리가 5시에 만나서 이번 주에 어떤 일을 해야 하는지 논의해 보는 것이 어떨까요?

Atwell, Gary   2:24 P.M.
그래요. 저는 그럴 수 있어요. 당신은 어떤가요, Lucy?

Struthers, Lucy   2:24 P.M.
저도 좋아요.

Atwell, Gary   2:25 P.M.
제가 Denise와 이야기를 해서 3층의 소회의실을 예약해 둘까요? 그러면 우리가 조용한 장소에서 모일 수 있을 거예요.

Ortega, Pedro   2:27 P.M.
그렇게 해 주면 고맙겠어요, Gary. Lucy, 제 사무실로 가서 제 책상에 놓여 있는 보고서를 세 부 복사해 줄래요? "Madison"이라고 라벨이 붙어 있는 노란색 폴더에 있어요. 찾기 쉬울 거예요.

Struthers, Lucy   2:30 P.M.
맡겨만 주세요. 두어 시간 후에 만나요, Pedro.

select 선정하다 | **account** 계좌; 고객, 거래처 | **awesome** 놀라운 | **manage to** 가까스로 ~하다, 그럭저럭 ~하다 | **up to** ~까지; ~의 수준에 이르는 | **task** 과제, 일 | **let down** ~을 실망시키다 | **expectation** 기대, 예상

172 주로 무엇이 논의되고 있는가?
(A) 새로운 프로젝트에 관해 이루어진 업무
(B) Samantha 팀과의 경쟁
(C) Madison 업체와의 거래에 필요한 요건
(D) 새로운 거래처에 관한 회의 준비

competition 경쟁 | **requirement** 요건 | **preparation** 준비

| 해설 | 새로운 거래처를 확보했다는 소식과 함께 그에 따른 회의 준비에 관한 이야기들이 오가고 있다. 따라서 메시지 창의 주제는 (D)의 '새로운 거래처에 관한 회의 준비'로 볼 수 있다.

173 Ortega 씨는 어떻게 Madison이라는 업체와 거래를 하게 되었는가?
(A) Madison 주식회사의 대표 이사를 직접 만남으로써
(B) 프로젝트를 자신에게 맡겨 달라고 Butler 씨를 설득함으로써
(C) Samantha 팀보다 더 열심히 일을 함으로써
(D) 회사의 다른 팀들보다 성과를 더 많이 냄으로써

| 해설 | 어떻게 거래처를 확보했는지 묻는 질문에 Ortega 씨는 'I had a long chat with Mr. Butler and informed him that we're up to the task.'라고 답한다. 이를 통해 그가 'Butler라는 인물을 설득하여' 일을 맡게 되었음을 알 수 있으므로 (B)가 정답이다.

174 Atwell 씨는 아마도 이다음에 무엇을 할 것인가?
(A) Ortega 씨의 사무실을 방문한다
(B) Madison과의 거래에 관한 파일을 읽는다
(C) 회의실을 예약한다
(D) Struthers 씨와 만난다

| 해설 | Atwell 씨의 마지막 말, 'Shall I talk to Denise and have her reserve the small conference room on the third floor?'를 통해, 그는 회의실을 예약할 것으로 예상할 수 있다. 따라서 (C)가 정답이다.

175 오후 2시 30분에, Struthers 씨가 "Consider it done"이라고 적었을 때 그녀는 무엇을 의미하는가?
(A) 그녀는 이미 Ortega 씨의 요청을 받아들였다.
(B) 그녀는 Madison 업체와의 거래에 최선을 다할 것이다.
(C) 그녀는 Ortega 씨가 요청한 파일을 복사할 것이다.
(D) 그녀는 새로운 업무에 대해 논의하기를 고대하고 있다.

comply with ~에 순응하다, ~을 지키다

| 해설 | 주어진 문장을 직역하면 '그 일은 다 되었다고 생각하라'이다. 이는 '복사를 해 달라'는 부탁에 대한 답변이므로, 주어진 문장은 곧 '맡겨만 달라' 혹은 '그렇게 할 테니 걱정하지 말아라'는 뜻으로 받아들일 수 있다. 따라서 정답은 (C)이다.

[176-180]

받는 사람: Fairview 컨벤션 센터 전 직원
보낸 사람: Helga Matzner
제목: 예정된 콘퍼런스
날짜: 10월 12일

10월 15일부터 17일까지 열릴 예정인 올해 National Geologists' 콘퍼런스가 시작되기까지 단 3일만이 남아 있습니다. 참석자들이 내일 장소를 확인하기 위해 도착하기 시작할 것이므로 우리는 모든 것이 준비되어 있는지 확인해야 합니다. 대부분의 참석자들은 Emporium 호텔이나 Marconi 호텔에 머물 것이라는 점을 기억해 주십시오. Marconi 호텔은 컨벤션 센터의 맞은 편 거리에 있기 때문에, 그쪽 사람들은 아무런 문제 없이 여기에 올 수 있습니다. 하지만 콘퍼런스가 열리는 3일 내내 오전 8시부터 오후 10시 사이에는, 30분마다 Emporium 호텔까지 무료 셔틀 버스가 운행될 예정입니다. 그 호텔에서 이곳으로 오기까지 대략 25분이 걸리기 때문에, 우리는 직행 버스를 두어 대 운행할 것입니다. 전자 기기를 담당하는 분들께서는 작은 문제도 없도록 모든 것을 이중으로 확인하셔야 합니다. 그리고 스낵, 샌드위치, 그리고 음료 등이 이곳에 있어야 할 시간에 정확히 도착할 것인지도 음식 제공업체에게 확인해야 합니다. 최선을 다해서 이번 행사를 성공적인 콘퍼런스로 만듭시다.

prepare 준비하다 | **check out** 확인하다, 둘러 보다 | **premise** 구역, 부지 | **individual** 개인 | **complimentary** 무료의 | **shuttle bus** 셔틀 버스 | **nonstop** 직행의, 직항의 | **double-check** 이중으로 확인하다 | **glitch** 작은 결함, 실수

**Fairview 컨벤션 센터
설문지**

Fairview 컨벤션 센터의 행사에 참여해 주셔서 고맙습니다. 저희가 제공해 드리는 서비스의 질을 향상시키기 위해, 잠시 시간을 내셔서 이 설문지를 작성하시고 모든 질문에 대답해 주시기 바랍니다.

이름: Rupert Helmond
행사: National Geologist' 콘퍼런스
참석 날짜: 10월 15일-17일
전화 번호: (064) 455-5847

다음에 대해 어떻게 생각하십니까:

	콘퍼런스 조직	직원들의 전문성	셔틀 버스	전체적인 콘퍼런스의 수준
매우 우수		V	V	
우수	V			V
나쁨				
매우 나쁨				

의견: 귀하의 컨벤션 센터의 행사에 참석을 한 것은 이번이 처음이었습니다. 하지만 비슷한 다른 센터에서는 여러 차례 콘퍼런스에 참석을 해 보았습니다. 귀하의 직원들은 다른 곳에서 일하는 사람들과 비교해 볼 때 손색이 없습니다. 문제가 생길 때마다, 직원이 거의 즉시 저에게 도움을 줄 수 있었습니다. 셔틀 버스 또한 인상적이었습니다. 저는 여러 차례 버스를 탔는데, 한 번도 버스가 늦은 적이 없었습니다. 하지만 강연 도중 전자 기기의 오작동과 관련된 문제가 두어 번 있었습니다. 예를 들어, 한 사람이 강연을 하던 도중에 마이크가 10분 정도 작동을 멈추었습니다. 하지만 콘퍼런스는 전체적으로 상당히 잘 진행되었습니다.

in order to ~하기 위해 | **similar** 비슷한, 유사한 | **compare favorably to** ~와 비교해도 손색이 없다 | **assist** 돕다 | **malfunction** 오작동하다 | **microphone** 마이크 | **overall** 전체적으로

176 Matzner 씨는 왜 회람을 작성했는가?
(A) 콘퍼런스가 얼마나 잘 진행되었는지 검토하기 위해
(B) 몇 가지 최종 준비 사항을 논의하기 위해
(C) 그날의 행사를 대략적으로 설명하기 위해
(D) 계획상의 변경 사항을 언급하기 위해

review 검토하다 | **overview** 개요, 대략적인 설명

| **해설** | 회람 초반부에서 Matzner 씨는 3일 후에 행사가 시작될 것임을 상기시킨 후, '모든 것이 준비가 되었는지 확인해야 한다'(need to make sure everything is prepared)고 말한다. 따라서 회람을 작성한 이유는 (B)로 볼 수 있다.

177 회람에 따르면, 콘퍼런스 참가자에 대해 사실인 것은 무엇인가?
(A) 대부분의 참석자들이 전에 Fairview를 방문한 적이 없다.
(B) 참석자들은 모두 Marconi 호텔에 묵을 것이다.
(C) 참석자 중 소수는 아직 등록을 하지 않았다.
(D) 참석자 중 일부는 10월 13일에 도착할 것이다.

| **해설** | '일부 참석자들은 장소 확인을 위해 내일 도착할 것'(the attendees are going to begin arriving to check out the premises tomorrow)이라는 언급을 통해, 일부 참석자들은 회람 작성일의 다음 날, 즉 '10월 13일'에 도착할 것이라는 점을 알 수 있으므로 (D)가 사실인 내용이다.

178 회람에서 콘퍼런스에 관해 언급되지 않은 것은 무엇인가?
(A) 지리학에 관심이 있는 사람들이 참석할 것이다.
(B) 승객들을 위한 셔틀 버스는 무료이다.
(C) 3일 동안 지속될 것이다.
(D) 참석자들은 제공되는 음식에 대해 비용을 지불해야 한다.

geology 지리학 | **free of charge** 무료의

| **해설** | (A)는 콘퍼런스의 명칭이 National Geologists' Conference라는 점에서, (B)는 complimentary shuttle bus라는 어구에서, 그리고 (C)는 개최 기간이 '10월 15일부터 17일까지'라는 언급을 통해 확인할 수 있다. 음식에 대한 비용 문제는 회람에서 찾아볼 수 없으므로 (D)가 정답이다.

179 Helmond 씨는 Fairview 컨벤션 센터의 직원들을 어떻게 생각하는가?
(A) 그들은 그다지 잘 알지 못했다.
(B) 그들은 그에게 많은 도움을 주었다.
(C) 그들은 때때로 참석자들에게 무례하게 행동했다.
(D) 그들은 콘퍼런스를 성공적으로 만들었다.

| **해설** | Comments(의견란)에 'Anytime I had a problem, a staff member was able to assist me almost immediately.'라고 적은 것으로 보아 Helmond 씨는 직원들에게 많은 도움을 받았다는 점을 알 수 있다. 따라서 정답은 (B)이다. 컨퍼런스가 전체적으로 잘 진행되었다는 말은 있지만, 그것이 직원들 때문이라고는 하지 않았으므로 (D)는 정답이 되기 힘들다.

180 Helmond 씨에 대해 무엇이 암시되어 있는가?
(A) 그는 Emporium 호텔에 묵었다.
(B) 그는 지리학과 교수이다.
(C) 그는 Fairview의 주민이다.
(D) 그는 전자 기기에 관심이 있다.

| **해설** | 의견란에 셔틀 버스가 좋았다고 했으므로 Helmond 씨는 셔틀 버스가 운행된 호텔, 즉 Emporium 호텔에 묵었다는 사실을 알 수 있다. 따라서 (A)가 정답이다. 지리학자라고 해서 반드시 지리학과 교수일 필요는 없으므로 (B)는 정답이 될 수 없다.

[181-185]

Morrell 은행에서 신규 행원을 구합니다

텍사스 주에서 가장 오래된 은행 중 하나인 Morrell 은행이 웨이코 Gila가 지점을 관리할 자격이 있는 분을 찾고 있습니다.

업무: 지점장은 은행의 일상적인 업무에 대한 책임을 지게 될 것입니다. 지점장은 은행의 재정 안정성을 관리하는 책무를 맡게 될 것이고 모든 대출금 신청에 관해 최종 승인을 내리게 될 것입니다. 지점장은 또한 지점 직원들이 수준 높은 서비스를 제공하는지, 그리고 Morrell 은행의 가치를 충분히 대표하는지를 확인해야 할 것입니다.

자격 조건: 지점장은 다음의 자격 조건을 갖추고 있어야 합니다:
* 은행에서 최소 5년간의 관리직 경력을 가지고 있을 것
* 사교적이고 다른 사람들과 잘 어울릴 것
* 은행 업계, 금융업, 그리고 경제에 관한 상세한 지식을 가지고 있을 것
* 뛰어난 기획자일 것

지원 방법: 자격을 갖춘 지원자는 이력서, 자기 소개서, 그리고 3명의 전문가 추천인 명단과 그들의 연락처를 텍사스 주 댈러스 Alamo 로 46번지 주소로, 인사부 이사인 Urania Desmond에게 보내야 합니다. udesmond@morrellbank.com으로 질문을 하시면 Desmond 씨와 연락을 하실 수 있을 것입니다.

Morrell 은행은 평등한 고용 기회를 제공하는 업체이며 개인의 나이, 성별, 혹은 인종에 근거하여 차별을 하지 않습니다.

qualified 자격이 있는 | **operation** 운영, 가동 | **in charge of** ~을 책임지는, ~을 담당하는 | **stability** 안전성 | **loan application** 대부 신청 | **sufficiently** 충분하게 | **represent** 대표하다 | **value** 가치 | **supervisory position** 관

리직 | **outgoing** 외향적인, 사교적인 | **get along well with** ~와 잘 어울려 지내다 | **thorough** 철저한 | **cover letter** 자기 소개서 | **equal opportunity employer** 평등한 고용 기회를 보장하는 고용주 | **discriminate** 차별하다 | **on the basis of** ~을 기반으로 | **gender** 성 | **ethnicity** 민족성

Urania Desmond
인사부 이사
Morrell 은행
Alamo 로 46번지
댈러스, 텍사스

8월 2일

Harry Astley
Rio Grande 로 302번지
웨이코, 텍사스

친애하는 Astley 씨께,

웨이코의 Morrell 은행 지점의 지점장 직위에 지원서를 제출해 주셔서 고맙습니다. 보통의 경우라면, 귀하께서 지난 2년 동안만 Freedom 은행을 관리하셨기 때문에 제가 연락을 드리지 않았을 것입니다. 하지만, 저는 귀하의 은행이 얼마나 잘 운영되었는지 알고 있기 때문에, 저는 실례를 무릅쓰고 귀하께서 알려 주셨던 두 명의 추천인들과 이야기를 나누었습니다. 두 분 모두가 당신에 대해 찬사를 보냈습니다. 그들은 귀하께서 날카로운 금융 마인드를 소유하고 있을 뿐만 아니라 사람들과 잘 어울린다는 점을 강조했고, 귀하의 직원들 모두 당신을 좋아했다는 점도 강조했습니다.

귀하께서는 Morrell 은행에서도 탁월하게 일을 하실 것 같습니다. 따라서, 저는 해당 직위에 대해 귀하께 면접을 제안하고 싶습니다. 일자리는 웨이코에 있지만, 1차 면접은 댈러스의 본사에서 진행될 것입니다. 토요일인 8월 16일 오전 10시에 귀하의 면접 일정을 정해 두었습니다. 그때 면접을 보실 수 있다면, 웨이코에서 댈러스까지 일등석 왕복 항공편을 예약해 드릴 것이며, 또한 Emerson 호텔의 객실도 예약하도록 하겠습니다. 면접을 잘 보시면, 귀하께서 일을 하시게 될 웨이코 지점에서 2차 면접을 실시할 것이라는 점을 유의해 주십시오. 이 면접은 8월 30일에 이루어질 것입니다.

(382) 634-6468로 제게 전화를 주셔서 면접을 보시겠다는 점을 확인시켜 주시기 바랍니다.

그럼 이만 줄이겠습니다.

Urania Desmond
Morrell 은행 인사부 이사

---

submit 제출하다 | **branch manager** 지점장 | **normal** 보통의, 정상적인 | **situation** 상황 | **be aware of** ~을 알다 | **take the liberty of** 실례를 무릅쓰고 ~하다 | **glowing terms** 찬사 | **stress** 강조하다 | **possess** 소유하다 | **keen** 예리한, 날카로운 | **excel** 뛰어나다, 탁월하다 | **headquarters** 본사, 본부 | **round-trip** 왕복의 | **conduct** 수행하다, 실시하다

181 은행 지점장은 무엇을 할 것으로 예상되는가?
(A) 대출을 요청하는 사람들을 면접한다
(B) 직원 교육을 기획한다
(C) 인사와 관련된 모든 문제들을 감독한다
(D) 직원들이 자신의 업무를 하고 있는지 확인한다

organize 조직하다, 기획하다 | **oversee** 감독하다 | **personnel** 직원

| 해설 | 첫 번째 지문인 구인 광고 중 Responsibilities 항목에서 정답의 단서를 찾을 수 있다. 지점장은 직원들이 수준 높은 서비스를 하고 있는지, 그리고 은행의 가치를 충분히 대표하고 있는지를 확인해야 한다고 했으므로 정답은 (D)이다.

182 사람들은 어떻게 직위에 지원할 수 있는가?

(A) 웹 페이지의 지원서를 작성함으로써
(B) 이메일로 지원서를 제출함으로써
(C) 지원서를 우편으로 보냄으로써
(D) 지원서를 직접 제출함으로써

turn in ~을 제출하다 | **in person** 몸소, 직접

| 해설 | 지원 방법은 구인 광고의 How to Apply 항목에서 확인할 수 있는데, 여기에서는 지원자들에게 해당 주소로 이력서 등의 서류를 보낼 것을 요청하고 있다. 따라서 정답은 (C)가 된다.

183 Desmond 씨에 의하면, Astley 씨는 왜 해당 직책에 대한 자격 조건을 갖추고 있지 않은가?
(A) 그는 기획력이 부족하다.
(B) 그는 경제학 학위를 가지고 있지 않다.
(C) 그는 5년 미만의 경력을 가지고 있다.
(D) 그는 전에 은행에서 일을 해 본 적이 없다.

| 해설 | 정답의 단서는 편지의 첫 번째 단락에서 찾을 수 있다. Desmond 씨는 정상적인 경우라면 연락을 드리지 않았을 것이라고 말한 후, 그 이유를 'Freedom 은행의 관리 경험이 2년밖에 없기 때문'(since you have only managed Freedom Bank for the past couple of years)이라고 말한다. 따라서 Astley 씨가 채용 공고상의 자격 조건, 즉 5년 이상의 경력을 보유하고 있지 않으므로 (C)가 정답이다.

184 편지에서, 1단락 5줄의 "keen"이라는 단어와 그 의미가 가장 유사한 것은?
(A) 날카로운
(B) 호기심이 많은
(C) 적절한
(D) 정확한

adequate 적절한, 적합한 | **precise** 정확한

| 해설 | keen은 '예리한' 혹은 '날카로운'이라는 의미를 나타내므로 보기 중에서는 (A)의 sharp(날카로운)와 가장 뜻이 비슷하다.

185 Astley 씨는 무엇을 하라는 요청을 받는가?
(A) 댈러스행 비행기표를 예약한다
(B) 8월 16일에 면접을 볼 수 있는지 확인시킨다
(C) Desmond 씨에게 이메일을 보낸다
(D) 8월 30일 면접을 위해 웨이코를 방문한다

| 해설 | 편지의 마지막 부분에서 Desmond 씨는 Astley 씨에게 면접을 볼 수 있는지에 관해 확인 전화를 요청하고 있다. 따라서 정답은 (B)이다. (D)의 '8월 30일 면접'은 1차 면접에 통과했을 경우에 볼 수 있는 2차 면접으로, 이것이 직접적인 요청 사항은 될 수 없다.

[186-190]

Harper 부동산
Peachtree 로 86번지
애틀란타, 조지아
Tel: 731-4932   Fax: 731-4931

Harper 부동산을 통해 귀하에게 이상적인 사업 혹은 상업 장소를 찾으십시오. 무엇을 찾고 계신지 말씀해 주시면, 저희 직원들이 귀하에게 필요한 적정 가격의 장소를 정확히 찾아 드릴 것입니다. 매매 혹은 임대용으로 저희가 보유하고 있는 부동산은 다음과 같습니다.

Main 가 498번지 – 12층 건물 내 1,200평방미터의 상업 공간; 2층; 의류 매장과 같은 상점에 최적; 월세만 가능; 월 4,500달러
16번가 84번지 – 800평방미터; 20층 건물의 1층; 식당 시설; 매매나 임대용; 250,000달러 혹은 월 2,000달러

7번가 590번지 – 5층 건물; 매매만 가능; 가격 협의
Pine 가 15번지 – 10층 건물의 3층 전체; 소규모 및 중간 규모 기업에 적합; 임대만 가능; 월 10,500달러

매물로 나온 부동산에 대해 문의를 하시거나 한 곳에 대한 방문 일정을 정하고 싶으시면 전화나 이메일(information@harperrealtor.com)로 저희에게 연락을 주십시오. 모든 가격은 협상이 가능합니다. 귀하와 거래를 하게 되기를 바랍니다.

ideal 이상적인 | **commercial** 상업적인 | **locate** 위치시키다; 장소를 찾다 | **property** 재산 | **inquire** 문의하다, 묻다 | **negotiable** 협상이 가능한

받는 사람: Greg Turner 〈gturner@hamilton.com〉
보낸 사람: Marcie Aybar 〈marcie@harperrealtor.com〉
제목: 방문
날짜: 4월 16일

친애하는 Turner 씨께,

저희 웹사이트에서 보신 부동산에 관해 이메일을 보내 주셔서 감사합니다. 저는 귀하께 그곳이 매물로 나와 있다는 점을 알려 드리고 싶습니다. 귀하께서 제게 말씀하신 바에 따르면, 그곳은 식당 손님에게 이상적인 장소로 보입니다. 저는 그곳이 속해 있는 건물을 매우 잘 알고 있습니다. 건물에는 많은 수의 사무 직원들이 있습니다. 또한, 주변 지역에 보행자들이 많이 지나다니므로, 귀하께서 소비자들을 유인하시는데 전혀 어려움이 없을 것입니다.

제가 부동산을 보여 드리는 것이 어떨까요? 저는 이번 주 어느 때나 시간이 됩니다. 애틀란타 지역에 익숙하시면, 부동산 바로 앞에서 만날 수 있습니다. 그곳이 어디인지 잘 모르시는 경우에는, 저와 어디에서 만날 것인지 말씀해 주시면, 제가 귀하를 모시러 가서 차를 타고 그곳으로 같이 가는 것이 어떨까요? 어떤 방법이 더 좋으신지 알려 주시기 바랍니다.

Marcie Aybar 드림
Harper 부동산

diner 식당 손님 | **be familiar with** ~에 친숙하다 | **pedestrian** 보행자 | **traffic** 교통량 | **attract** 유인하다 | **option** 선택, 옵션

받는 사람: Marcie Aybar 〈marcie@harperrealtor.com〉
보낸 사람: Greg Turner 〈gturner@hamilton.com〉
제목: 제안
날짜: 4월 20일

친애하는 Aybar 씨께,

어제 시간을 내 주셔서 저와 만나 주신 점에 대해 감사드립니다. 제게 보여 주셨던 부동산은 제가 개업을 생각 중인 사업에 완벽한 곳처럼 보입니다. 저는 그 부동산을 임대하는데 큰 관심이 있고, 가능한 빠른 시간 안에 2년 계약을 체결했으면 좋겠습니다.

하지만 한 가지 문제가 있습니다. 저는 부동산 내 시설이 다소 낡았다는 점을 알게 되었습니다. 제 추측으로는 모든 것을 보수하는 데 약 4,000달러에서 5,000달러가 필요할 것 같습니다. 통상적으로, 그것은 소유주의 책임이 될 것입니다. 하지만 이번 경우에는, 제가 지불하게 될 월세가 삭감될 수 있다면, 제가 모든 보수 비용을 기꺼이 지불하도록 하겠습니다. 제가 매달 500달러를 덜 낼 수 있다면, 내일 귀하의 사무실을 방문해서 계약서에 서명하도록 하겠습니다. 그것이 가능한지 궁금합니다.

Greg Turner 드림

notice 주목하다 | **require** 요구하다 | **normally** 보통은, 정상적으로는 | **responsibility** 책임 | **reduction** 감소, 축소

186 Harper 부동산에 대해 언급되지 않은 것은 무엇인가?
(A) 매매용 부지를 가지고 있다.
(B) 고객들이 은행 대출을 받는 것을 돕는다.
(C) 가격에 대해 기꺼이 협상을 한다.
(D) 상업 부지를 취급한다.

loan 대부, 대출

| 해설 | 첫 번째 지문인 광고를 통해 정답을 찾을 수 있다. 매매 및 임대용 부동산을 보유하고 있다고 했으므로 (A)는 맞는 내용이고, 'All prices are negotiable.'이라는 문장과 find the ideal business or commercial space 라는 어구에서 각각 (C)와 (D)의 내용 역시 사실임을 알 수 있다. 따라서 언급되지 않은 사항은 (B)이다.

187 광고에서, 9줄의 "ideal"이라는 단어와 그 의미가 가장 비슷한 것은?
(A) 흥미로운
(B) 독특한
(C) 완벽한
(D) 가능한

| 해설 | ideal은 '이상적인'이라는 의미이므로 (C)의 perfect가 정답이다.

188 Turner 씨는 어떤 부동산에 관심이 있는가?
(A) Pine 가 15번지
(B) Main 가 498번지
(C) 7번가 590번지
(D) 16번가 84번지

| 해설 | 두 번째 지문인 이메일의 'According to what you told me, it appears to be the ideal location for your diner.'라는 문장이 정답의 단서이다. diner(식당 손님)를 위한 이상적인 장소는 식당일 것이므로, 첫 번째 지문인 광고에서 식당 용도의 부동산을 찾도록 한다. 식당용으로 적합한 부지는 (D)의 '16번가 84번지'이다.

189 Aybar 씨는 Turner 씨에게 무엇을 하라고 제안하는가?
(A) 자신의 사무실을 방문해서 계약서에 서명한다
(B) 자신과 함께 부동산을 보러 간다
(C) 부동산 소유자에게 수정 제안을 한다
(D) 자신을 차에 태워서 부동산에 간다

counteroffer 수정 제안

| 해설 | Aybar 씨가 작성한 이메일 후반부에서 그녀는 Turner 씨가 지리를 잘 모르는 경우, '자신이 그를 차에 태워서 부동산까지 가겠다'(I can pick you up and drive you there)는 제안을 하고 있다. 따라서 (B)가 정답이다.

190 Turner 씨는 임대료로 얼마를 지불하고 싶어하는가?
(A) 월 500달러
(B) 월 1,500달러
(C) 월 4,000달러
(D) 월 4,500달러

| 해설 | 두 번째 이메일에서 Turner 씨는 '월세를 500달러 삭감해 주면'(if I could pay $500 less per month) 보수 비용을 자신이 부담하겠다고 말한다. 한편 그가 원하는 매물은 '16번가 84번지'로, 첫 번째 광고에서 이곳의 월세는 2,000달러로 나타나 있다. 따라서 결국 그가 지불하고자 하는 월세는 (B)의 '1,500달러'이다.

[191-195]

깜짝 합병이 발표되다

리치몬드 (10월 3일) – 오늘 오전, Pennington's의 대표 이사인 Amy Emery가 기자 회견을 열고 자신의 회사와 Rosebud 주식회사가 합병을 할 것이라고 말했다. 두 기업은 네바다, 캘리포니아, 그리고 애리조나 주에서 가장 유명한 식료품점에 속한다. Pennington's는 이 세 개의 주에서 186개의 매장을 보유하고 있고, Rosebud는 190개의 매장을 보유하고 있다. 이들 회사가 합병을 하면, Rosebud라는 명칭은 사라질 것이며, 모든 매장들은 Pennington's로 이름이 바뀔 것이다. Rosebud는 3년 전에 설립되었으나 낮은 가격으로 판매되는 높은 품질의 식품 때문에 인기가 급속도로 증가했다. Emery 씨는 Pennington's가 Rosebud의 상업적 관습 중 다수를 채택할 것이라고 주장했다. 또한 그녀는 두 개의 매장이 서로 인접해 있는 몇몇 지역에서는 중복을 피하기 위해 일부 매장들이 폐점될 것이라고 언급했다. 합병은 11월 1일에 완료될 것으로 예상된다.

press conference 기자 회견 | **merge** 합병하다 | **found** 설립하다 | **popularity** 인기 | **dramatically** 극적으로 | **adopt** 채택하다 | **business practice** 상업적 관행 | **redundancy** 중복, 반복

Rosebud 매장이 문을 닫습니다

10월 31일, 애리조나 피닉스의 Sedona 가 494번지에 위치한 Rosebud 식료품점이 자정을 끝으로 문을 닫을 예정입니다. 이는 Rosebud 주식회사와 Pennington's 간의 합병과 관련이 있으며, 매장의 재정 상태와는 전혀 관련이 없는 것으로, 매장의 재정 상태는 상당히 탄탄합니다. 저희는 Rosebud의 고객분들께 Pennington's에서의 쇼핑을 권해 드리는데, 이곳에서는 현재 Rosebud에서 누리실 수 있는 것과 동일한 놀라운 품질과 낮은 가격을 기대하셔도 좋습니다.
매장이 문을 닫을 것이기 때문에, 매장 안의 모든 것이 소진되어야 합니다. 10월 30일과 31일, 저희는 특별 세일을 실시할 것입니다. 저희가 판매하는 모든 것들을 정가의 절반 가격으로 구입하실 수 있습니다. 저희는 또한 고객분들께서 쇼핑을 최대한 오래 하실 수 있도록 양일간 하루 종일 문을 열 것입니다.

for the last time 마지막으로, 끝으로 | **be related to** ~와 관계가 있다 | **have nothing to do with** ~와 관계가 없다 | **urge** 재촉하다, 촉구하다 | **fantastic** 환상적인, 멋진 | **regular price** 정가 | **maximize** 극대화하다

11월 1일

친애하는 Rosebud 골드 카드 회원님께,

Rosebud 주식회사라는 기업은 더 이상 존재하지 않지만, 귀하께서는 그곳에서 하셨던 것과 동일한 쇼핑을 하실 수 있습니다. 가장 가까운 Pennington's 슈퍼마켓을 방문하십시오. 새로운 식료품점에서의 쇼핑에 익숙해지기까지 얼마간의 시간이 필요할 수도 있다고 생각하기 때문에, 저희는 귀하께서 보다 쉽게 적응하실 수 있도록 만들어 드리고자 합니다.
먼저, 인근 Pennington's를 방문하셔서 Rosebud 골드 카드를 Pennington's 골드 카드로 변경하십시오. Rosebud에서 누리셨던 모든 혜택과 그 이상의 혜택을 받으시게 될 것입니다. 지금부터 11월 15일까지, 모든 구매 물품에 대해 20%의 할인을 받으시게 될 것입니다. 또한, 이 편지에 동봉된 쿠폰을 확인해 주십시오. 이들은 Rosebud에서 판매되었던 가장 인기 있는 제품들을 할인해 드립니다.
저희는 Pennington's를 귀하의 새로운 주거래 식료품점으로 만들어 드리고자 합니다. 저희가 할 수 있는 일이 있다면, 주저하지 마시고 요청해 주십시오. 1-888-559-5768로 전화를 주셔서 어떤 질문이나 하시고 싶은 말씀을 해 주십시오.

Amy Emery 드림
Pennington's 대표 이사

exist 존재하다 | **corporation** 기업 | **get used to** ~에 익숙해지다 | **transition** 이행, 변화 | **trade** 거래하다, 교환하다 | **qualify for** ~에 대한 자격이 있다 | **hesitate** 주저하다, 망설이다

191 기사는 왜 작성되었는가?
(A) 문제에 대한 해결책을 제안하기 위해
(B) 세일을 광고하기 위해
(C) 사업적 거래를 설명하기 위해
(D) 새로운 대표 이사의 영입을 알리기 위해

| 해설 | Pennington's와 Rosebud의 합병 소식을 알리는 기사이다. 따라서 기사가 작성된 이유는 (C)로 볼 수 있다.

192 Sedona 가 494번지의 Rosebud에 대해 무엇이 암시되어 있는가?
(A) 최초로 문을 연 Rosebud 매장이었다.
(B) 회사의 본사가 그곳에 있다.
(C) 그 근처에 Pennington's 매장이 위치해 있다.
(D) 매장이 고객들을 유치하지 못하고 있다.

| 해설 | 두 번째 지문인 광고에서 Sedona 가 494번지의 Rosebud 매장이 곧 문을 닫을 것이라는 점을 제목과 내용을 통해 확인할 수 있다. 한편 첫 번째 지문 기사의 마지막 부분에서는 '합병 대상인 기업의 매장이 서로 인접해 있는 경우에는 일부 매장이 폐쇄될 것'(some stores will be closed to avoid redundancy in certain areas where two stores are located close to each other)이라고 나와 있으므로, Sedona 가 494번지의 Rosebud 매장의 인근 지역에는 Pennington's 매장이 존재할 것이라는 점을 추측할 수 있다. 따라서 정답은 (C)이다.

193 10월 30일에 어떤 일이 일어날 것인가?
(A) 슈퍼마켓이 문을 닫지 않을 것이다.
(B) 몇몇 신입 직원들이 채용될 것이다.
(C) 매장이 파산할 것이다.
(D) 모든 제품들이 24% 할인 가격으로 판매될 것이다.

| 해설 | 두 번째 지문인 광고의 두 번째 단락에서 10월 30일과 31일 이틀 동안은 '하루 종일 문을 열 것'(remain open all day and night)이라고 안내되어 있으므로 정답은 (A)가 된다. 매장이 문을 닫을 것이기는 하지만, 이는 '파산'이 아닌 '합병'의 결과라는 점이 강조되고 있으므로 (C)를 정답으로 선택해서는 안 된다.

194 Rosebud 골드 카드 회원들이 받지 못하는 것은 무엇인가?
(A) 할인
(B) 새 카드
(C) 무료 상품
(D) 쿠폰

| 해설 | 세 번째 지문인 편지를 통해 기존 Rosebud 골드 카드의 회원들은, '새 카드', '한시적 할인', 그리고 '쿠폰'을 받게 될 것이라는 점을 알 수 있다. 따라서 이 중 언급되지 않은 것은 (C)의 '무료 상품'이다.

195 Emery 씨는 Rosebud 골드 카드 회원들에게 무엇을 할 것을 권하는가?
(A) 그녀에게 직접 전화를 걸어 질문을 한다
(B) Pennington's에서 쇼핑을 시작한다
(C) 그녀 회사의 웹사이트에 등록한다
(D) 고객 설문 카드를 작성한다

| 해설 | 세 번째 지문인 편지의 마지막 단락에서 Emery 씨는 'We'd like to make Pennington's your new home for grocery shopping.'이라고 말한 후 필요한 점이 있으면 연락을 달라고 당부한다. 따라서 그녀가 권유하는 것은 (B)로 볼 수 있다.

[196-200]

받는 사람: Ryan Crisp <ryancrisp@privatemail.com>
보낸 사람: Jessica Peabody <j_peabody@ytp.com>
제목: 관리직
날짜: 9월 9일

친애하는 Crisp 씨께,

충분한 검토를 거친 끝에, 이사회는 귀하께 YTP 사의 IT부 관리직을 제안드리고자 합니다. 저희는 귀하께서 가능한 빨리, 늦어도 10월 1일을 넘기지 않는 선에서 업무를 시작하시기를 바랍니다.
귀하의 초봉은 1년에 74,000달러가 될 것이며, 한 달에 두 번 급여가 지급될 것입니다. 귀하께서는 1년 동안 2주간의 유급 휴가, 6일간의 병가, 그리고 3일간의 연차를 받게 되실 뿐만 아니라 종합적인 복지 혜택도(첨부 문서를 다운로드하시면 어떤 것을 받을 수 있는지 확인하실 수 있습니다) 받게 되실 것입니다.
귀하의 직위에서, 귀하께서는 IT부의 일상적인 업무들을 책임지시게 될 것입니다. 여기에는, 이것에만 국한되는 것은 아니지만, 직원의 채용 및 해고, 그리고 부서 예산의 관리가 포함됩니다.
이번 제안에 대해 이틀 내로 답변을 주실 것을 요청드립니다. 제안의 수락 여부에 대해 알려 주십시오.

Jessica Peabody 드림
인사부 부장
YTP 사

consideration 고려 | **board of directors** 이사회 | **starting salary** 초봉 | **comprehensive** 종합적인, 포괄적인 | **benefits package** 복지 혜택 | **operation** 작동, 가동

받는 사람: Jessica Peabody <j_peabody@ytp.com>
보낸 사람: Ryan Crisp <ryancrisp@privatemail.com>
제목: 회신: 관리직
날짜: 9월 10일

친애하는 Peabody 씨께,

채용 제안에 감사를 드립니다. 저는 복지 혜택을 검토해 보았고 그에 만족하지만, 제안하신 급여는 너무 낮습니다. 제가 참석했던 2차 면접에서, 저는 85,000달러 이하의 연봉은 받지 않게 될 것이라는 확언을 들었습니다. YTP의 일자리를 수락한다는 것은 현재 거주하고 있는 곳보다 더 많은 생계비가 드는 주로 제가 가족과 함께 이사를 가야 한다는 것을 의미합니다. 현재 저는 연봉으로 70,000달러를 받고 있기 때문에, 제가 요구하는 급여 조건이 충족되지 않으면 저에게는 직위 제안을 받아드릴 동기가 전혀 없습니다. 따라서 저는 제안을 조건부로 수락하고자 합니다. 위에서 언급한 수치대로 제 급여를 인상시켜 주신다면, 이사 준비를 시작해서 9월 24일에 업무를 시작할 수 있습니다. 그러한 수준을 맞춰 주실 수 없다면, 안타깝지만 귀하의 제안은 거절해야만 하겠습니다.

Ryan Crisp 드림

assure 확언하다 | **cost of living** 생계비 | **incentive** 동기, 유인 | **demand** 요구 | **meet** 충족시키다 | **conditionally** 조건부로 | **match** 어울리다, 맞다; 맞추다

받는 사람: IT부 전 직원
보낸 사람: IT부 차장 Helga Martinez
제목: Ryan Crisp
날짜: 9월 21일

마침내 IT부의 새로운 수장을 맞이하게 되었다는 점을 알리게 되어 기쁘게 생각합니다. Ryan Crisp께서 제안을 수락하셔서 다음 주 월요일에 첫 근무를 시작하시게 될 것입니다. Crisp 씨께서는 Texas 대학을 다니셨는데, 그곳에서는 물리학과 경제학을 복수 전공하셨습니다. 졸업 후 3년 동안은 Fairmount Manufacturing에서 근무를 하셨으며, 그 후 4년 동안은 Haverford 주식회사에서 근무를 하셨습니다. 마지막으로 근무를 하신 곳은 Landers 사였는데, 이곳에서는 3년 동안 일을 하셨습니다.
월요일 오전 10시에, 그분을 위한 환영회가 열릴 예정입니다. 부서 내의 모든 분들께서는 참석하셔야 합니다. 또한 12시에는 Benson's에서 함께 점심 식사를 할 것입니다. 근무 첫날, 여러분의 문제들로 Crisp 씨를 성가시게 만들지는 마십시오. 그분께서는 수요일과 목요일에 여러분 모두와 개별적으로 면담을 하실 것이니, 사안이나 여러분께서 하시고 싶은 프로젝트에 관한 논의는 그때 하실 수 있습니다.

double-major in ~을 복수 전공하다 | **physics** 물리학 | **economics** 경제학 | **reception** 리셉션, 환영회 | **bother** 귀찮게 하다 | **individually** 개별적으로, 개인적으로

196 IT부의 관리자 직위에 있는 사람은 무엇을 해야 하는가?
  (A) 재정적인 문제들을 처리한다
  (B) 과학적인 연구를 실시한다
  (C) 직원을 승진시킨다
  (D) 전근을 돕는다

| 해설 | 첫 번째 지문인 이메일의 세 번째 단락에서 IT부 관리직의 일상적인 업무로 '직원 채용 및 해고'(hiring and firing of employees) 그리고 '부서 예산 관리'(managing of the departmental budget)가 예시되어 있다. 따라서 정답은 이 중 두 번째 업무를 가리키고 있는 (A)이다.

197 Peabody 씨는 Crisp 씨에게 무엇을 보내는가?
  (A) 서명을 받을 계약서
  (B) 검토할 이력서
  (C) 읽어야 할 파일
  (D) 검토할 예산

| 해설 | '종합적인 복지 혜택'(comprehensive benefits package)의 내용 확인을 위해서는 '첨부 문서를 다운로드 해 달라'(please download the attachment to see what you qualify for)고 말하고 있다. 따라서 이메일에 첨부된 것은 (C)이다.

198 Crisp 씨는 직위를 수락하기 전에 무엇을 필요로 하는가?
  (A) 이사에 대한 금전적인 보상
  (B) 11,000달러가 더 높은 연봉
  (C) 1주일 더 많은 유급 휴가
  (D) 이사 후의 정착 지원

compensation 보상

| 해설 | 두 번째 이메일에서 Crisp 씨는 자신이 2차 면접에서 최소 '85,000달러' 이상의 연봉을 보장받았다는 점을 상기시키면서 그러한 수준의 연봉을 맞춰 주면 관리직을 수락하겠다고 말한다. 한편 첫 번째 이메일을 통해서는 YTP 사가 Crisp 씨에게 '74,000달러'의 연봉을 제안했다는 사실을 알 수 있으므로 결국 Crisp 씨가 요구한 조건은 (B)로 볼 수 있다.

199 회람에 따르면, 9월 24일에 일어나지 않을 일은 무엇인가?

(A) 직원들이 함께 식사를 한다.
(B) 새로 온 직원이 일을 시작할 것이다.
(C) 특별 환영 행사가 열릴 것이다.
(D) 개인 면담이 실시될 것이다.

| 해설 | 회람의 세 번째 단락의 마지막 문장에서 '개인 면담'은 수요일과 목요일, 즉 26일과 27일에 이루어질 것이라는 점을 알 수 있다. 따라서 24일에 일어나지 않을 일은 (D)이다.

200 Crisp 씨에 관해 무엇이 암시되어 있는가?

(A) 그는 이미 모든 동료들을 만났다.
(B) 그는 10월에 출장을 갈 것이다.
(C) 그는 연봉으로 85,000달러를 받을 것이다.
(D) 그는 자신이 하고 싶어하는 프로젝트를 몇 개 가지고 있다.

| 해설 | 두 번째 지문인 이메일에서 Crisp 씨는 연봉으로 85,000달러를 요구했는데, 세 번째 지문인 회람에서 그를 위한 환영식에 대한 안내가 이루어지고 있다. 이를 종합해 보면, 결국 그의 요구가 관철되었을 것이라는 점을 짐작할 수 있으므로 (C)가 정답이다.

Actual Test 03

p.123

● 정답

PART 1
1	(C)	2	(C)	3	(A)	4	(D)	5	(A)
6	(C)								

PART 2
7	(B)	8	(B)	9	(C)	10	(A)	11	(C)
12	(B)	13	(C)	14	(A)	15	(C)	16	(C)
17	(B)	18	(A)	19	(C)	20	(A)	21	(C)
22	(C)	23	(B)	24	(B)	25	(A)	26	(A)
27	(A)	28	(B)	29	(C)	30	(A)	31	(B)

PART 3
32	(A)	33	(D)	34	(A)	35	(C)	36	(B)
37	(B)	38	(D)	39	(A)	40	(A)	41	(B)
42	(A)	43	(A)	44	(B)	45	(D)	46	(D)
47	(A)	48	(C)	49	(D)	50	(B)	51	(A)
52	(D)	53	(D)	54	(A)	55	(B)	56	(C)
57	(A)	58	(C)	59	(C)	60	(A)	61	(B)
62	(B)	63	(C)	64	(B)	65	(B)	66	(A)
67	(B)	68	(C)	69	(C)	70	(A)		

PART 4
71	(B)	72	(B)	73	(D)	74	(C)	75	(D)
76	(D)	77	(A)	78	(B)	79	(D)	80	(D)
81	(A)	82	(C)	83	(C)	84	(A)	85	(B)
86	(B)	87	(A)	88	(C)	89	(B)	90	(C)
91	(A)	92	(D)	93	(A)	94	(B)	95	(A)
96	(A)	97	(B)	98	(D)	99	(C)	100	(C)

PART 5
101	(B)	102	(D)	103	(C)	104	(C)	105	(A)
106	(B)	107	(C)	108	(A)	109	(A)	110	(A)
111	(B)	112	(C)	113	(B)	114	(A)	115	(D)
116	(C)	117	(D)	118	(D)	119	(C)	120	(A)
121	(C)	122	(B)	123	(B)	124	(C)	125	(D)
126	(B)	127	(D)	128	(A)	129	(C)	130	(A)

PART 6
131	(C)	132	(B)	133	(C)	134	(B)	135	(A)
136	(D)	137	(D)	138	(C)	139	(B)	140	(A)
141	(C)	142	(C)	143	(C)	144	(B)	145	(A)
146	(D)								

PART 7
147	(A)	148	(C)	149	(D)	150	(B)	151	(A)
152	(C)	153	(C)	154	(B)	155	(C)	156	(C)
157	(A)	158	(A)	159	(C)	160	(C)	161	(D)
162	(A)	163	(B)	164	(C)	165	(D)	166	(B)
167	(B)	168	(D)	169	(D)	170	(B)	171	(A)
172	(B)	173	(A)	174	(C)	175	(C)	176	(D)
177	(B)	178	(A)	179	(C)	180	(B)	181	(A)
182	(A)	183	(D)	184	(B)	185	(D)	186	(B)
187	(B)	188	(C)	189	(D)	190	(D)	191	(D)
192	(C)	193	(A)	194	(B)	195	(A)	196	(B)
197	(B)	198	(B)	199	(D)	200	(C)		

● PART 1

p.124

1 (A) The farmer is sowing some crops in the field.
   (B) The sewing machine is being used.
   (C) The woman is cutting something with scissors.
   (D) The clothes are being stitched by the woman.

   (A) 농부가 들판에서 곡식 씨앗을 심고 있다.
   (B) 재봉틀이 사용되고 있다.
   (C) 여자가 가위로 무언가를 자르고 있다.
   (D) 여자에 의해 옷이 꿰매지고 있다.

   sow (씨를) 뿌리다, 심다 | **crop** 작물 | **sewing machine** 재봉틀 | **scissors** 가위 | **stitch** 꿰매다

   | 해설 | 여자가 가위로 천을 자르고 있으므로 이를 가장 적절히 설명한 (C)가 정답이다. (A)는 사진 속 장면으로부터 연상할 수 있는 sew(바느질하다)라는 단어와 발음이 같은 sow(씨를 뿌리다)를 이용한 함정이고, '재봉틀'(sewing machine)이 보이기는 하지만 이것이 사용 중이지는 않으므로 (B)도 오답이다. 여자가 '꿰매는'(are being stitched) 동작을 하고 있는 것도 아니기 때문에 (D) 역시 정답이 될 수 없다.

2 (A) Vehicles are being parked by the attendants.
   (B) Several cars are waiting for the light to change.
   (C) Cars have been parked along the side of the road.
   (D) Some cards are being set down beside the road.

   (A) 차량들이 주차 안내원에 의해 주차되고 있다.
   (B) 여러 대의 자동차가 신호가 바뀌기를 기다리고 있다.
   (C) 자동차들이 도로 가장자리에 주차되어 있다.
   (D) 도로에 몇 장의 카드가 놓이고 있다.

   vehicle 차량 | **attendant** 종업원, 안내원 | **along** ~을 따라

   | 해설 | 자동차들이 이미 주차된 상태이기 때문에 '주차 중'(are being parked)이라고 설명한 (A)와 신호 변경을 '기다리고 있다'(are waiting for the light to change)고 진술한 (B)는 정답이 될 수 없다. 따라서 사진을 적절히 묘사한 것은 (C)인데, (D)는 cars(자동차)와 발음이 비슷한 cards(카드)로 오답을 유도하고 있는 함정이다.

3 (A) People are holding glasses in their hands.
   (B) They are eating toast at the dinner table.
   (C) Diners are helping themselves to the buffet.
   (D) Some people are whining about the meal.

   (A) 사람들이 손에 잔을 들고 있다.
   (B) 그들은 식탁에서 토스트를 먹고 있다.
   (C) 식사를 하는 사람들이 마음껏 뷔페 음식을 먹고 있다.
   (D) 몇몇 사람들이 식사에 대해 투덜대고 있다.

   toast 토스트; 건배 | **help oneself to** ~을 마음껏 먹다 | **buffet** 뷔페 | **whine** 투덜대다, 칭얼거리다

   | 해설 | 사람들이 손에 잔을 들고 있는 모습을 적절히 설명한 (A)가 정답이다. (B)는 사진에서 연상할 수 있는 toast(건배; 건배하다)라는 단어를 사용하고 있지만, 여기서 toast는 '토스트'라는 의미이며, (D)역시 사진 속 wine과 발음은 같으나 뜻은 전혀 다른 whine(투덜대다)이라는 동사를 이용하여 혼동을 유발하고 있다. (C)는 사진에서 볼 수 있는 diners(식당 손님)라는 단어로 오답을 유도하고 있는 함정이다.

4 (A) Boxes are being loaded onto delivery vans.
   (B) Many of the items are being boxed up by employees.
   (C) Workers are moving the crates from place to place.
   (D) Packages have been stacked on top of one another.

   (A) 상자들이 화물 트럭에 실리고 있다.
   (B) 많은 제품들이 직원들에 의해 포장되고 있다.
   (C) 직원들이 상자를 이곳저곳으로 옮기고 있다.
   (D) 상자들이 겹겹이 쌓여 있다.

load (짐을) 싣다 | **delivery van** 화물 트럭 | **box** 상자; 상자에 넣다, 포장하다 | **crate** 상자 | **from place to place** 이곳저곳, 여기저기 | **stack** 쌓다 | **on top of one another** 겹겹이, 차곡차곡

| 해설 | 사진에서 '화물 트럭'(delivery vans), '직원'(employees), 그리고 '일꾼'(workers) 등은 보이지 않으므로 (A), (B), (C)는 모두 정답이 될 수 없다. 정답은 상자들이 '차곡차곡'(on top of one another) 쌓여 있다고 진술한 (D)이다.

✓ **700점 넘기 포인트** 이처럼 사물만 등장하는 사진 문제에서는 동작을 나타내는 진행형 문장이 정답이 되는 경우가 거의 없다. 사진에 사물만 등장하는 경우에는 현재완료 시제가 사용된 보기를 보다 유심히 듣도록 하자.

5 (A) The customer is receiving change from the employee.
   (B) The cashier is handing some bags to the customer.
   (C) Shoppers are browsing through the items in the store.
   (D) The items have all been placed in a single bag.

   (A) 고객이 직원으로부터 잔돈을 받고 있다.
   (B) 계산원이 고객에게 봉투를 건네고 있다.
   (C) 쇼핑객들이 매장 물품들을 살펴보고 있다.
   (D) 물품들이 모두 하나의 봉투 안에 놓여 있다.

change 변화; 잔돈, 거스름돈 | **hand** 건네다, 주다 | **browse through** ~을 훑어보다

| 해설 | 고객이 점원으로부터 '잔돈을 받고 있다'(is receiving change)고 설명한 (A)가 정답이다. '봉투'(some bags)를 건네고 있지는 않으므로 (B)는 정답이 될 수 없고, 제품들을 살펴보는 다른 사람들은 찾아볼 수 없으므로 (C)도 적절한 설명이 아니다. 사진에서 물품들은 여러 개의 봉투에 나누어 담겨 있으므로 (D) 역시 오답이다.

6 (A) Rocks are being moved by construction workers.
   (B) The performers are all moving in concert.
   (C) People are gathered in front of a stage.
   (D) An orchestra is performing for an audience.

   (A) 건설 인부들에 의해 바위가 옮겨지고 있다.
   (B) 연주자들 모두가 일제히 이동하고 있다.
   (C) 사람들이 무대 앞에 모여 있다.
   (D) 오케스트라가 관객들을 위해 연주를 하고 있다.

rock 바위; 록 음악 | **in concert** 일제히, 동시에 | **gather** 모으다, 모이다 | **audience** 청중, 관객

| 해설 | (A)와 (B)는 각각 rock과 concert라는 단어를 이용한 함정인데, (A)의 rock은 '바위'라는 의미를, (B)의 in concert는 '일제히', '동시에'라는 의미를 나타낸다. 연주는 '오케스트라'(orchestra)가 아니라 밴드가 하고 있으므로 (D) 또한 오답이다. 따라서 정답은 '무대 앞에 사람들이 모여 있다'고 묘사한 (C)이다.

● **PART 2** p.128

7 Who is interested in working overtime this weekend?
   (A) It won't go over well with them.
   (B) I don't mind coming in on Saturday.
   (C) Jason's meeting his friends on the weekend.

   누가 이번 주말의 특근에 관심이 있나요?
   (A) 그것은 그들의 마음에 들지 않을 거예요.
   (B) 저는 토요일에 나와도 상관없어요.
   (C) Jason은 주말에 친구들을 만날 거예요.

be interested in ~에 관심이 있다 | **work overtime** 초과 근무를 하다 | **go over well with** ~의 마음에 들다

| 해설 | 의문사 who를 이용하여 주말에 근무할 의향이 있는 사람이 누구인지 묻고 있다. 정답은 '나는 토요일에 나오는 것을 꺼리지 않는다'며 자기 자신을 지목한 (B)이다. who로 물었다고 해서 무조건 사람 이름으로 시작하는 (C)와 같은 보기를 정답으로 골라서는 안 된다.

✓ **700점 넘기 포인트** 무엇을 가리키는지 불분명한 대명사가 들어 있는 보기는 오답일 가능성이 높다. 위 문제의 보기 (A)에서도 대명사 it과 them을 이용하여 오답을 유도하고 있다.

8 It appears as though there's heavy traffic on this road.
   (A) The item is heavier than I thought.
   (B) We'd better take a detour then.
   (C) I rode on the rollercoaster there.

   이 도로에는 심한 정체 현상이 있는 것 같아요.
   (A) 그 제품은 제가 생각했던 것보다 무거워요.
   (B) 그러면 우회하는 것이 좋겠군요.
   (C) 저는 그곳에서 롤러코스터를 탔어요.

as though 마치 ~인 것처럼 | **heavy traffic** 교통 체증 | **take a detour** 우회하다 | **ride** 타다 | **rollercoaster** 롤러코스터

| 해설 | 평서문을 이용해 상대방에게 교통 상황에 관한 정보를 제공하고 있다. 교통 체증이 일어나고 있는 상황이므로 '우회하는 것이 좋겠다'고 답한 (B)가 가장 자연스러운 답변이다. (A)는 heavy의 비교급인 heavier로, (C)는 road와 발음이 같은 rode(ride의 과거형)를 이용한 함정이다.

9 Could you please mail this letter sometime before noon?
   (A) She wrote that she's doing well.
   (B) About ten minutes to twelve.
   (C) I'll take care of it right now.

   이 편지를 12시 이전에 우편으로 보내 줄 수 있나요?
   (A) 그녀는 자신이 잘 지낸다고 썼어요.
   (B) 약 11시 50분예요.
   (C) 제가 바로 지금 처리할게요.

mail 우편으로 부치다 | **take care of** ~을 돌보다; ~을 처리하다

| 해설 | 조동사 could를 이용하여 상대방에게 우편 발송을 부탁하고 있으므로 '바로 처리하겠다'는 의미를 전달한 (C)가 정답이다. (A)는 letter(편지)에서 연상할 수 있는 wrote(편지를 쓰다)라는 동사를 이용함으로써, (B)는 noon(정오)에서 연상할 수 있는 twelve(12시)라는 시각을 이용함으로써 각각 혼동을 일으키고 있다.

10 How are nonmembers supposed to reserve seats?
   (A) Try calling the box office.
   (B) We're in the front row.
   (C) I'll reserve a car later today.

   비회원은 어떻게 좌석을 예매하도록 되어 있나요?

(A) 매표소에 전화해 보세요.
(B) 우리는 지금 앞줄에 있어요.
(C) 제가 오늘 늦게 차를 예약할게요.

nonmember 비회원 | **box office** 매표소 | **front** 앞면, (건물의) 정면

| **해설** | 의문사 how를 이용하여 '예약 방법'에 대해 묻고 있다. 이에 대한 우회적인 답변으로 '(자신은 모르니) 매표소에 전화해 보아라'는 의미를 전한 (A)가 정답이다. (B)는 자신의 위치를, (C)는 자동차 예약 시점을 알리고 있는 답변으로, 모두 주어진 질문과는 전혀 어울리지 않는 답변들이다.

11 Why didn't you answer the phone when I called you?
(A) That's right. I called you twice.
(B) I always answer my phone.
(C) I was in a meeting with my boss.

제가 전화를 걸었을 때 왜 전화를 받지 않았나요?
(A) 맞아요. 제가 당신에게 두 번 전화했어요.
(B) 저는 항상 전화를 받아요.
(C) 상사와 회의 중이었어요.

| **해설** | why를 이용하여 상대방이 전화를 받지 않은 '이유'를 묻고 있으므로 정답은 '상사와의 회의 때문'이라고 그 이유를 밝힌 (C)이다. why didn't you를 제안을 나타내는 표현인 「Why don't you ~」 구문으로 잘못 들으면 (B)를 정답으로 고르는 실수를 할 수 있다.

12 What seems to be the problem with the new intern?
(A) Yes, it's rather problematic.
(B) He isn't very energetic.
(C) She applied for that position.

새로 온 인턴 사원에게 무슨 문제가 있는 것 같나요?
(A) 네, 다소 문제가 많은 편이에요.
(B) 그가 그다지 의욕적이지 않아요.
(C) 그녀는 그 자리에 지원했어요.

seem to ~처럼 보이다 | **intern** 인턴 | **problematic** 문제가 많은 | **energetic** 활동적인, 정력적인

| **해설** | 인턴 사원에게 어떤 문제가 있는지 묻고 있다. (A)는 problem의 형용사형인 problematic을 이용한 함정으로, what으로 시작되는 질문에 yes로 대답을 하고 있기 때문에 이는 정답이 될 수 없다. (C)는 intern으로부터 연상할 수 있는 표현인 that position으로 혼란을 유도하고 있을 뿐, 주어진 질문과는 전혀 관련이 없는 답변이다. 따라서 정답은 '의욕적이지 않다'는 문제점을 지적한 (B)이다.

13 I may be mistaken, but I believe the seminar will start at three.
(A) Steak and potatoes for dinner.
(B) At least three more people.
(C) Yes, that seems to be correct.

제가 잘못 들었을 수도 있지만, 저는 세미나가 3시에 시작하는 것으로 알고 있어요.
(A) 저녁 식사로 스테이크와 감자요.
(B) 최소한 3명 이상의 사람들이요.
(C) 네, 맞는 것 같아요.

at least 적어도, 최소한

| **해설** | 세미나의 시작 시각에 대한 정보를 전달하고 있다. (A)는 메뉴를 물었을 때 이어질 수 있는 답변이고 (B)는 참석 인원을 묻는 질문에 어울릴법한 답변이다. 따라서 '당신 말이 맞을 것이다'라는 동의의 의미를 나타낸 (C)가 정답이다.

14 Have you heard who's getting promoted this quarter?
(A) Either Tina or May.
(B) A brand-new promotion.
(C) Several of our products.

이번 분기에 누가 승진할 것인지 들었나요?
(A) Tina나 May 중 한 명이요.
(B) 새로운 프로모션이요.
(C) 몇몇 제품이요.

get promoted 승진하다 | **quarter** 분기 | **either A or B** A와 B 중 하나 | **brand-new** 새로운 | **promotion** 승진; 판촉, 프로모션

| **해설** | 승진 대상자에 대해 묻고 있으므로 대상자의 이름을 직접적으로 거론한 (A)가 정답이다. 참고로 (B)의 promotion은 '승진'이 아니라 '판촉', '프로모션'의 의미를 나타낸다.

> ☑ **700점 넘기 포인트** 간접의문문이 제시된 경우에는 문장의 후반부를 보다 집중해서 들어야 한다. 위 문제의 경우에도 결국 질문자가 묻는 것은 '승진 대상자가 누구인지'(who's getting promoted this quarter)이다.

15 When is the new employee orientation session being held?
(A) For a couple of hours.
(B) It's being led by Mr. Morrison.
(C) This Thursday morning.

신입 직원을 위한 오리엔테이션이 언제 열리나요?
(A) 2시간 동안이요.
(B) 그것은 Morrison 씨가 주관할 거예요.
(C) 이번 주 목요일 오전에요.

orientation session 오리엔테이션

| **해설** | 의문사 when을 이용하여 오리엔테이션의 개최 시기를 묻고 있다. (A)는 기간을 묻는 질문에, (B)는 행사의 주최자를 묻는 질문에 어울릴법한 답변들이다. 따라서 정답은 직접적으로 개최 시기를 언급한 (C)이다.

16 Could I borrow some money to pay for these items, please?
(A) Who did you borrow it from?
(B) Yes, I'll pay for everything.
(C) Sure. How much do you need?

이 제품을 사기 위해 제가 돈을 빌려도 될까요?
(A) 그것을 누구에게서 빌렸나요?
(B) 네, 제가 모두 계산할게요.
(C) 물론이죠. 얼마가 필요한가요?

borrow 빌리다 | **pay for** ~에 대한 값을 치르다

| **해설** | 조동사 could를 이용해 상대방에게 돈을 빌려 달라는 부탁을 하고 있으므로 정답은 수락이나 거절의 의미를 나타내고 있는 것이어야 한다. (A)는 borrow를, (B)는 pay for를 중복 사용함으로써 혼란을 일으키고 있는 함정이다. 따라서 정답은 수락의 의사를 표시한 후 필요한 금액을 되묻은 (C)가 된다.

17 Isn't Washington Consulting helping us with the ad campaign?
(A) The ad will be airing for the first time tonight.
(B) No, we couldn't reach an agreement with them.
(C) He's a new addition to the workforce.

Washington 컨설팅이 우리의 광고를 돕고 있지 않나요?
(A) 그 광고는 오늘 밤에 처음으로 방송을 타게 될 거예요.
(B) 네, 그들과 계약을 체결할 수가 없었어요.

71

(C) 그는 새로 온 직원이에요.

ad campaign 광고 | **air** 방송되다 | **for the first time** 처음으로 | **reach an agreement** 합의에 도달하다 | **addition** 추가 | **workforce** 노동력

| 해설 | 부정의문문을 이용해 'Washington 컨설팅이 돕고 있는지'의 여부를 묻고 있다. (A)는 질문의 ad를 그대로 사용하고 있는 함정이며, (C)는 ad와 발음이 비슷한 addition을 이용하여 오답을 유도하고 있다. 따라서 '합의에 이르지 못해 돕고 있지 않다'는 의미를 전달한 (B)가 가장 자연스러운 답변이다.

18 What was the reason that sales dropped so dramatically?
 (A) The quality of the product.
 (B) It's a drama on television.
 (C) Sorry for dropping it.

매출이 이처럼 급격히 하락한 이유가 무엇이었나요?
 (A) 품질이요.
 (B) 그것은 텔레비전 드라마예요.
 (C) 떨어뜨려서 미안해요.

drop 떨어지다, 떨어뜨리다 | **dramatically** 극적으로

| 해설 | 의문사 what으로 시작하고 있지만, 이 질문은 사실 매출 감소의 '이유'를 묻고 있다. 따라서 '품질'이라는 이유를 밝힌 (A)가 정답이다. (B)는 dramatically(극적으로)와 발음이 비슷한 drama(드라마)로, (C)는 drop을 중복 사용하여 혼란을 일으키고 있는 오답들이다.

19 How is the real estate market in the suburbs around the city?
 (A) A house in the downtown area.
 (B) Three bedrooms, at least.
 (C) It could be a lot better.

시 외곽의 부동산 시장은 어떤가요?
 (A) 시내 중심가의 주택이요.
 (B) 최소 3개의 침실이요.
 (C) 다소 좋지가 않아요.

real estate 부동산 | **suburbs** 교외

| 해설 | 의문사 how를 이용하여 부동산 시장의 상황을 묻고 있다. (A)와 (B) 모두 부동산과 관련이 있는 어휘로 답하고 있지만, 주어진 질문에는 전혀 어울리지 않는 답변이다. 따라서 정답은 '좋지가 못하다'는 의미를 전하고 있는 (C)이다.

> **✓ 700점 넘기 포인트** 가정법을 이용한 답변은 항상 주의를 해서 들어야 한다. 위 문제의 보기 (C)는 가정법을 이용하여 '훨씬 더 좋을 수도 있었을 텐데'라는 뜻을 나타낸다. 이처럼 가정법 문장의 조동사 could, would, should가 사용되면 아쉬움이나 후회의 의미가 들어 있지 않은지 확인하도록 하자.

20 Will the package be delivered by the end of the day?
 (A) That's what the courier told me.
 (B) You can go ahead and sign for it.
 (C) Yes, let's have a pizza delivered.

일과가 끝나기 전에 소포가 배달될까요?
 (A) 택배 기사가 제게 그렇게 이야기해 주었어요.
 (B) 계속 진행시켜서 서명을 하셔도 좋아요.
 (C) 네, 피자를 배달시키죠.

deliver 배달하다 | **courier** 배달원, 택배 기사

| 해설 | 소포가 오늘 내로 도착할 것인지의 여부를 묻고 있으므로 '택배 기사로부터 그렇게 들었다'는 의미를 나타낸 (A)가 가장 자연스러운 답변이다. (B)는 package와 연관이 있는 sign이라는 단어로 오답을 유도하고 있는 함정

이며, (C)는 질문의 delivered라는 단어를 중복 사용하여 혼동을 유발하고 있다.

21 Would you like to apply for a membership card?
 (A) He's a member of this gym.
 (B) This is an application form.
 (C) Actually, I already have one.

멤버십 카드를 신청하시겠어요?
 (A) 그는 이곳 체육관의 회원이에요.
 (B) 이것이 신청서예요.
 (C) 실은 이미 하나를 가지고 있어요.

gym 체육관

| 해설 | 「Would you like to ~」는 의향을 묻거나 제안을 할 때 사용되는 표현이다. (A)와 (B)는 각각 가리키는 대상이 불분명한 he와 this로 대답하고 있으므로 정답이 될 수 없고, 따라서 '이미 가지고 있다'며 거절의 의사를 간접적으로 밝힌 (C)가 가장 적절한 답변이다.

22 Mr. Thomas should give you a call soon, shouldn't he?
 (A) Sure, go ahead.
 (B) Call me later.
 (C) I sure hope so.

Thomas 씨가 곧 당신에게 전화를 하겠죠, 그렇지 않나요?
 (A) 물론이에요, 그렇게 하세요.
 (B) 나중에 전화를 주세요.
 (C) 그랬으면 좋겠어요.

give ~ a call ~에게 전화하다 | **later** 나중에, 후에

| 해설 | 부가의문문을 이용해 전화가 올 것인지의 여부를 확인하고 있다. (A)는 제안에 대한 답변으로 적절하며 (B)는 질문에서 사용된 call을 이용한 함정이다. 가장 자연스러운 답변은 '그러기를 바란다'는 의미인 (C)이다.

23 Where should we put all of these empty bottles?
 (A) I'll take a bottle of soda, please.
 (B) In the recycling bin over there.
 (C) I just put them over there.

이 빈 병들은 어디에 두어야 하나요?
 (A) 저는 소다 한 병을 마실게요.
 (B) 저쪽에 있는 재활용품 통이에요.
 (C) 저는 그것들을 저쪽에 두었어요.

empty 빈 | **bottle** 병 | **recycling bin** 재활용품 용기

| 해설 | 의문사 where를 이용하여 병을 둘 곳을 묻고 있으므로 재활용품 통이라는 '장소'로 대답한 (B)가 가장 적절한 답변이다. (A)는 주문을 할 때 쓰일 수 있는 표현이고, 과거시제로 대답한 (C)는 주어진 질문에 대한 적절한 답변이 될 수 없다.

24 To whom was the letter Mr. Daniels sent addressed?
 (A) I'm not sure how to spell that.
 (B) Alice Kenworth, I believe.
 (C) His address is 22 Wilson Street.

Daniels 씨가 보낸 편지에는 누구의 주소가 적혀 있었나요?
 (A) 철자를 어떻게 쓰는지 잘 모르겠어요.
 (B) 제가 알기로는 Alice Kenworth예요.
 (C) 그의 주소는 Wilson 가 22번지예요.

address 주소; 주소를 쓰다, (편지 등을) ~에게 보내다 | **spell** 철자를 쓰다

| 해설 | '누구에게'(to whom) 편지를 보냈는지 묻고 있으므로 수신인을 직접적으로 밝힌 (B)가 정답이다. 질문의 letter를 편지가 아닌 글자로 이해하면

(A)를 정답으로 고르는 실수를 하기 쉽다. Daniels 씨의 주소를 물은 것은 아니므로 (C)도 적절한 답변이 아니다.

25 We ought to attend the conference in New Orleans this month.
(A) That's what I told Mr. Barnes.
(B) From August 10 to 14.
(C) On new marketing techniques.

우리는 이번 달에 뉴올리언스에서 열리는 콘퍼런스에 참석해야 해요.
(A) 저도 Barnes 씨에게 그렇게 말했어요.
(B) 8월 10일부터 14일까지요.
(C) 새로운 마케팅 기법에 관해서요.

| 해설 | 이 평서문과 같이 진술에 대한 전형적인 답변이 없는 문제는 상당히 까다로운 문제라 할 수 있다. 이러한 경우는 오답을 소거하는 방식으로 문제를 푸는 것이 보다 수월하다. (B)는 기간을 묻는 질문에 이어질 수 있는 답변이며, (C)는 콘퍼런스의 주제를 물을 때 답할 수 있는 내용이다. 따라서 '나도 그렇게 이야기했다'는 (A)가 다른 보기에 비해 가장 자연스러운 답변이 된다.

26 Can you help me process all of these order forms this afternoon?
(A) I'd love to, but I've got a meeting.
(B) I'm going to order them in a few minutes.
(C) Yes, I always help her with her work.

오늘 오후에 이 주문 양식을 모두 처리하는 것을 도와 줄 수 있나요?
(A) 그렇게 하고 싶지만, 회의가 있어서요.
(B) 저는 몇 분 후에 주문을 할 거예요.
(C) 네, 저는 항상 그녀의 일을 도와 주고 있죠.

process 처리하다

| 해설 | 조동사 can을 이용하여 업무 처리에 대한 도움을 요청하고 있다. 따라서 '회의가 있다'며 완곡하게 거절 의사를 밝힌 (A)가 정답이다. (B)에서 order는 '주문하다'라는 뜻의 동사로 쓰였으며, (C)는 대화와 무관한 her를 언급하고 있으므로 적절하지 못한 답변이다.

27 How long does it take to get from here to the theater district?
(A) Somewhere around twenty minutes.
(B) No more than three kilometers away.
(C) The show starts at a quarter past seven.

여기서 극장가까지 가는 데 시간이 얼마나 걸리나요?
(A) 약 20분쯤이요.
(B) 3킬로미터 이상 떨어져 있지는 않아요.
(C) 쇼는 5시 15분에 시작해요.

from A to B A에서 B까지 | **theater district** 극장가 | **somewhere** 어딘가; 대략 | **quarter** 4분의 1, 15분

| 해설 | how long이 동사 take와 함께 사용되면 주로 '시간의 길이'를 묻는다. 따라서 직접적으로 '20분'이라는 시간을 밝힌 (A)가 가장 적절한 답변이다. (B)는 '거리'로 답함으로써, (C)는 공연이 시작되는 '시각'으로 답하고 있기 때문에 이들은 모두 정답이 될 수 없다.

28 Isn't Ms. Carpenter supposed to be joining us for breakfast?
(A) Bacon and eggs with toast.
(B) No, for lunch this afternoon.
(C) We thoroughly enjoyed it.

Carpenter 씨가 우리와 함께 아침 식사를 하기로 되어 있지 않았나요?
(A) 베이컨과 달걀을 곁들인 토스트요.

(B) 아니요, 오늘 오후 점심 식사예요.
(C) 우리는 정말로 그것이 마음에 들었어요.

join 합류하다 | **bacon** 베이컨 | **thoroughly** 철저히, 완전히

| 해설 | Carpenter 씨가 오찬에 동석할 것인지의 여부를 묻고 있다. (A)는 메뉴를 물은 경우에, (C)는 의견을 물은 경우에 이어질 수 있는 답변으로 이들은 모두 정답이 될 수 없다. 정답은 오찬이 아니라 '점심 식사' 때 동석할 것이라고 상대방의 정보를 정정해 준 (B)이다.

29 I hear that Danielson's is having a special promotion this weekend.
(A) I relaxed at home last Saturday.
(B) She's trying to promote her new book.
(C) That's right. Everything's on sale.

Danielson이 이번 주말에 특별 프로모션을 한다고 들었어요.
(A) 저는 지난 주 토요일에 집에서 쉬었어요.
(B) 그녀는 자신의 책을 홍보하고 있어요.
(C) 맞아요. 모든 것이 세일되죠.

promotion 판촉 활동, 프로모션; 승진 | **relax** 쉬다, 휴식하다

| 해설 | 세일 소식을 듣고 가장 자연스럽게 이어질 수 있는 답변을 고르도록 한다. (A)는 주말 세일 소식에 '자신의 지난 주말에 했던 일'을 언급하고 있으므로 적절하지 못하고, (B)는 문제의 Danielson을 사람 이름으로 잘못 들었을 경우에 선택할 수 있는 오답이다. 정답은 세일 소식에 호응을 한 (C)이다.

30 Would you rather shop online or visit the shopping mall?
(A) Let's do our shopping in person today.
(B) I spend a few hours a day on the Internet.
(C) A new mall just opened downtown last week.

온라인으로 쇼핑을 하겠어요, 아니면 쇼핑몰을 방문하실 건가요?
(A) 오늘은 직접 쇼핑을 하죠.
(B) 저는 인터넷을 하는데 하루에 몇 시간 정도를 보내요.
(C) 지난 주 중심가에서 새로운 쇼핑몰이 문을 열었어요.

in person 몸소, 직접 | **spend** 소비하다, 쓰다

| 해설 | 접속사 or를 이용하여 두 가지 방안 중 선호하는 것을 묻고 있다. 정답은 (A)인데, 여기서 do our shopping in person(직접 쇼핑을 하다)은 결국 visit the shopping mall과 같은 의미로 사용되었다. (B)는 질문의 online으로부터 연상이 가능한 Internet이라는 단어로, (C)는 mall이라는 단어를 중복 사용함으로써 오답을 유도하고 있는 함정이다.

31 Did you answer all of the questions on the application form?
(A) I got questions two and nine wrong.
(B) I'm pretty sure that I did.
(C) Show me the answers you got.

지원서의 모든 질문에 답을 했나요?
(A) 2번하고 9번 문제를 틀렸어요.
(B) 그런 것 같아요.
(C) 당신이 쓴 답을 제게 보여 주세요.

| 해설 | 일반의문을 이용해 모든 질문에 답을 했는지 묻고 있으므로, '그랬다'라는 긍정의 의미를 전한 (B)가 정답이다. (A)와 (C)는 각각 질문의 questions와 answer를 이용한 오답이다.

● **PART 3** p.129

[32-34]

W We've finally finished rearranging the desks in the office,

73

Mr. Moreno. Does everything look satisfactory?
M The way you set up everything is fine. It appears as though you've made efficient use of space. In fact, there's a large area over by the windows that doesn't have any desks or equipment in it. What are your plans for utilizing that space?
W We intend to set up some cubicles there next week. When the summer interns arrive, that's where they're going to be put.
M Good thinking. We didn't have a place for them last year, and they got in everyone's way.

W 드디어 사무실 책상의 재배치 작업을 끝냈군요, Moreno 씨. 모든 것이 만족스러워 보이시나요?
M 모든 것을 배치한 방식이 마음에 들어요. 공간을 효과적으로 사용하신 것처럼 보이는군요. 실은, 책상이나 기기가 들어 있지 않은 커다란 공간이 창가에 있어요. 그러한 공간을 활용하기 위한 계획은 무엇인가요?
W 다음 주에 그곳에 칸막이 공간을 설치할 생각이에요. 여름에 인턴 사원들이 도착하면, 그들이 있게 될 곳이죠.
M 좋은 생각이군요. 작년에는 그들을 위한 공간이 없어서, 모든 사람들에게 방해가 되었어요.

---

rearrange 재배치하다 | **satisfactory** 만족스러운 | **as though** 마치 ~인 것처럼 | **efficient** 효율적인, 효과적인 | **space** 공간 | **equipment** 장비, 기기 | **utilize** 활용하다 | **cubicle** 칸막이로 구분된 공간 | **get in one's way** ~에게 방해가 되다

32 화자들은 주로 무엇을 논의하는가?
   (A) 사무실의 새로운 배치
   (B) 인턴 사원들이 하게 될 일
   (C) 그들에게 필요한 사무 기기
   (D) 그들의 여름 계획

| 해설 | 화자들은 사무실의 가구 배치 작업에 대해, 그리고 공간 활용 문제에 대해 이야기를 나누고 있다. 따라서 정답은 (A)이다.

33 여자는 창가에 무엇을 할 것인가?
   (A) 자신의 책상을 그쪽으로 옮긴다
   (B) 그곳에 컴퓨터를 설치한다
   (C) 그곳에 복사기를 설치한다
   (D) 그곳에 칸막이 공간을 만든다

| 해설 | 남자가 창가의 공간 활용 방안에 대해 묻자 여자는 'We intend to set up some cubicles there next week.'라고 답한다. 따라서 그녀가 하게 될 일은 (D)이다.

34 남자의 말에 따르면, 작년 인턴 사원에게 어떤 일이 일어났는가?
   (A) 다른 직원들을 방해했다.
   (B) 모두가 자신의 책상을 가지고 있었다.
   (C) 임무를 잘 수행했다.
   (D) 복사를 담당했다.

interfere 방해하다

| 해설 | 대화의 마지막 부분에서 남자는 인턴 사원들의 자리가 없어서 '인턴 사원들이 모두에게 방해가 되었다'(they got in everyone's way)고 말한다. 따라서 get in one's way를 interfere로 바꾸어 표현한 (A)가 정답이다.

[35-37]

M Tina, these contracts have be delivered to our firm's attorney in his office on the other side of town no later than 4 P.M. Can you take the bus there to deliver them?
W I'd love to assist you, Steve, but Ms. Parker insisted that I finish working on the presentation she's giving tomorrow morning, so I can't leave the office.
M Well, I'm meetings clients all day. How do you suggest we get the contracts to Mr. Murphy?
W What about trying the local courier service? It guarantees two-hour delivery of packages anywhere in the city limits. Why don't I call and arrange a pickup?

M Tina, 이 계약서들은 늦어도 오후 4시까지 시 반대편에 있는, 회사의 변호사 사무실로 배달되어야 해요. 버스를 타고 그곳으로 가서 전달해 줄 수 있나요?
W 도와 주고 싶지만, Steve, Parker 씨께서 내일 오전에 하실 프레젠테이션과 관련된 작업을 제가 끝내야 한다고 하셔서, 저는 사무실을 떠날 수가 없어요.
M 음, 저는 하루 종일 고객들을 만나게 될 거예요. Murphy 씨에게 어떻게 계약서들을 가져다 주는 것이 좋을까요?
W 인근 택배 서비스를 이용하는 것이 어때요? 시내 한정으로 어디든지 2시간 이내의 택배를 보장해 주죠. 제가 전화를 해서 가지러 오라고 할까요?

---

attorney 변호사 | **insist** 주장하다 | **courier service** 택배 서비스 | **guarantee** 보장하다, 보증하다 | **city limit** 시의 경계 | **pickup** (물건 등을) 가지러 옴

35 남자는 여자에게 무엇을 할 것을 요청하는가?
   (A) 계약서에 서명한다
   (B) 프레젠테이션 관련 작업을 한다
   (C) 문서를 배달한다
   (D) 고객과 이야기한다

| 해설 | 대화의 초반부에 남자는 'Can you take the bus there to deliver them?'이라고 말하면서 여자에게 계약서 전달을 요청하고 있다. 따라서 정답은 (C)이다.

36 Murphy 씨는 누구인가?
   (A) 배달원
   (B) 변호사
   (C) 고객
   (D) 발표자

| 해설 | 대화의 첫 부분에서 남자는 계약서를 '회사의 변호사'(our firm's attorney)에게 가져다 주어야 한다고 말하고 중반부에서는 'How do you suggest we get the contracts to Mr. Murphy?'라고 여자에게 묻는다. 따라서 Murphy 씨는 서류를 받아야 할 '변호사'임을 알 수 있으므로 정답은 (B)이다.

37 여자는 무엇을 제안하는가?
   (A) 기한 연장을 요청한다
   (B) 택배 회사를 이용한다
   (C) 고객과 재협상한다
   (D) 몇 가지 항목들을 팩스로 보낸다

| 해설 | 대화 후반부에서 여자는 'What about trying the local courier service?'라고 말하면서 남자에게 택배 서비스 이용을 제안하고 있다. 따라서 (B)가 정답이다.

[38-40]

W What was your opinion of the items delivered by

Lewis Manufacturing? Was the quality of the products sufficient?
M Even better, it was outstanding. The workers who used those products to assemble ours uniformly praised them for being engineered so well. We'd better come to an agreement with Lewis to supply us with products on a weekly basis. Would you mind working on that?
W Not at all. I'll give Jeff Lambert over there a call as soon as lunch ends. We used to be colleagues at another firm, so I'll see if he can get us a good deal.

W Lewis Manufacturing에서 보낸 제품들에 대해 어떻게 생각하나요? 제품의 품질이 괜찮던가요?
M 훨씬 더 좋아서, 뛰어났어요. 그 제품을 이용해서 우리 제품을 조립한 작업자들은 한결같이 그것들이 매우 잘 제작되었다고 칭찬했죠. 일주일 단위로 우리에게 제품을 공급할 수 있도록 Lewis와 계약을 체결하는 것이 좋겠어요. 그렇게 하는 것이 어떨까요?
W 좋아요. 점심 시간이 끝나는 대로 그쪽의 Jeff Lambert에게 제가 전화를 할게요. 한때 다른 회사에서 동료 사이였기 때문에, 그가 우리에게 좋은 조건을 제시할 수 있는지 알아볼게요.

opinion 의견 | **quality** 질, 품질 | **sufficient** 충분한 | **outstanding** 뛰어난 | **assemble** 조립하다 | **uniformly** 한결같이 | **engineer** 제작하다 | **come to an agreement with** ~와 합의에 이르다, ~와 계약을 체결하다 | **on a weekly basis** 매주, 주 단위로 | **as soon as** ~하자마자 | **colleague** 직장 동료

38 남자와 여자는 무엇에 대해 이야기하고 있는가?
  (A) 회사의 제품이 언제 출시될 것인지
  (B) 직원들을 대상으로 한 설문의 결과
  (C) 최근에 구입한 제품의 가격
  (D) 다른 회사로부터 구입한 제품

release 놓아 주다, 풀어 주다; 출시하다

| 해설 | Lewis Manufacturing으로부터 구입한 물품의 품질에 대해 이야기하고 있다. 따라서 정답은 (D)이다.

39 남자는 여자에게 무엇을 하라고 말하는가?
  (A) 공급업체와 거래를 한다
  (B) 조립 라인 작업자들과 이야기한다
  (C) Lewis Manufacturing에게 편지를 쓴다
  (D) 고객의 공장을 방문한다

make a deal 거래를 하다

| 해설 | 'We'd better come to an agreement with Lewis to supply us with products on a weekly basis.'라는 말을 통해 남자는 여자에게 계약을 체결할 것을 제안하고 있다. 따라서 (A)가 정답이다.

40 Jeff Lambert에 관해 여자가 암시하는 것은 무엇인가?
  (A) 그녀는 그와 아는 사이이다.
  (B) 그는 고위 경영진이다.
  (C) 그는 공학 석사 학위를 가지고 있다.
  (D) 그녀는 그와 협력하는 것을 좋아한다.

be acquainted with ~을 알다, ~와 아는 사이이다 | **upper management** 고위 경영진 | **collaborate** 협력하다, 협동하다

| 해설 | 대화의 마지막 부분에서 여자는 Jeff Lambert라는 사람과 '다른 회사에서 동료였다'(used to be colleagues at another firm)라는 점을 밝히고 있으므로 그녀가 암시하는 바는 (A)로 볼 수 있다.

[41-43]
M Hello. My name is Harold Reynolds, and I'm calling regarding the room service bill I received for lunch this afternoon. I believe there was an error.
W I'm very sorry to hear that, Mr. Reynolds. Could you please tell me what the problem is?
M Of course. I ordered a steak sandwich, some fries, and a can of cola, but the price on my receipt reads $50. That can't possibly be right, can it?
W It most definitely isn't, sir. You were charged too much for your meal. I'll contact the kitchen immediately and have someone there send you a new bill in just a few minutes.

M 안녕하세요. 제 이름은 Harold Reynolds인데, 저는 오늘 오후 점심 시간에 받았던 룸서비스 청구서에 관해 전화를 드렸어요. 제 생각에는 착오가 있는 것 같아요.
W 그런 이야기를 들으니 매우 유감이군요, Reynolds 씨. 문제가 무엇인지 말씀해 주시겠어요?
M 물론이죠. 저는 스테이크 샌드위치, 감자 튀김, 그리고 콜라 한 캔을 주문했지만, 영수증에는 50달러로 적혀 있어요. 제대로 된 것이 아니죠, 그런가요?
W 분명히 잘못 되었네요, 고객님. 식사에 대해 너무 많은 요금이 청구되었군요. 제가 즉시 주방에 연락을 해서 그곳 누군가에게 곧 새로운 청구서를 가져다 드리라고 할게요.

error 잘못, 실수 | **bill** 청구서 | **receipt** 영수증 | **definitely** 분명 | **immediately** 즉시 | **in just a few minutes** 잠시 후에

41 여자는 어디에서 일하는 것 같은가?
  (A) 식당에서
  (B) 호텔에서
  (C) 음식 공급 업체에서
  (D) 슈퍼마켓에서

| 해설 | 대화 초반에서 남자가 전화를 건 이유는 room service bill(룸서비스 청구서) 때문임을 알 수 있다. 따라서 정답은 (B)이다.

☑ 700점 넘기 포인트 문제 해결의 단서가 대화의 여러 곳에서 등장하는 경우도 있지만, 짧은 대화인 경우에는 정답의 단서가 하나만 등장하는 경우도 있다. 예컨대 만약 위 문제에서 남자의 첫 대사를 놓치면 (A)를 정답으로 선택하는 실수를 범하게 된다.

42 남자는 어떤 문제를 언급하는가?
  (A) 식비가 과도하게 청구되었다.
  (B) 주문한 음식이 도착하지 않았다.
  (C) 음식이 제대로 준비되지 않았다.
  (D) 구입한 음식이 상했다.

overcharge 과도하게 요금을 청구하다 | **improperly** 부적절하게 | **spoil** 망치다; (음식을) 상하게 하다

| 해설 | 문제가 무엇인지 묻는 여자의 말에 남자는 영수증에 적힌 룸서비스 가격을 언급한 후, 가격이 제대로 된 것인지를 되묻는다. 이에 대해 여자가 'You were charged too much for your meal.'이라고 말하고 있으므로 남자의 문제는 (A)의 '과도하게 청구된 식비'이다.

43 여자는 아마도 이다음에 무엇을 할 것인가?
  (A) 전화를 건다
  (B) 주방장과 이야기한다
  (C) 남자를 위해 새 영수증을 준비한다

(D) 남자에게 환불을 해 준다

chef 주방장 | **refund** 환불하다

| 해설 | 여자의 마지막 말에서 여자는 '즉시 주방에 연락할 것'(I'll contact the kitchen immediately)이라고 말한다. 따라서 정답은 (A)이다. (B)의 경우, 주방에 연락한다고 해서 '주방장'(chef)과 이야기할 것이라는 보장이 없으며, 새 영수증을 본인이 직접 준비할 것이라는 언급은 찾아 볼 수 없기 때문에 (C)도 정답이 될 수 없다.

[44-46]

M Hi. I'd like two tickets for the 5:30 showing of *African Adventure*.
W I regret to say that there aren't any tickets available at that time.
M Hmm . . . Well, uh, what about the 7:00 show then?
W You're out of luck. Sorry about that.
M Are there any times today when it's possible to see the film?
W Let me check . . . Yes, there are a few tickets left for the 4:00 show, but those are all single seats, so you can't sit together with your companion. Or you could get two tickets next to each other if you watch the show at 9:15.
M I'll take two tickets for the late show then. I don't want to sit apart from my friend.
W Great. That will be $22 for two tickets.

M 안녕하세요. *African Adventure*의 5시 30분 티켓을 두 장 사고 싶어요.
W 안타깝게도 그 시간대에는 구하실 수 있는 티켓이 없어요.
M 흠… 음, 어, 그러면 7시 상영은 어떤가요?
W 운이 나쁘시군요. 그에 대해서는 유감이에요.
M 오늘 영화를 볼 수 있는 시간대가 있나요?
W 확인해 볼게요… 네, 4시 상영의 티켓이 몇 장 남아 있기는 하지만 모두 1인석이라 일행이 있는 경우에는 함께 앉으실 수 없어요. 아니면 9시 15분 상영을 보신다면 서로 붙어 있는 좌석의 표를 두 장 구입하실 수 있죠.
M 그러면 늦은 시간대로 두 장 주세요. 제 친구와 떨어져 앉고 싶지는 않거든요.
W 잘 되었군요. 두 장 가격은 22달러예요.

regret 후회하다, 유감이다 | **out of luck** 운이 없는 | **single seat** 1인석 | **companion** 동반자, 동행인 | **apart from** ~와 떨어져서

44 대화는 어디에서 이루어지고 있는가?
  (A) 전화로
  (B) 매표소에서
  (C) 무대에서
  (D) 구내 매점에서

box office 매표소 | **concession stand** 구내 매점

| 해설 | 영화 표를 구매하려는 고객과 매표소 직원 간의 대화이다. 따라서 대화가 이루어지고 있는 장소는 (B)의 '매표소'이다.

45 남자는 무엇을 보고 싶어하는가?
  (A) 뮤지컬
  (B) 콘서트
  (C) 연극
  (D) 영화

| 해설 | 원하는 시간대에 남아 있는 좌석이 없다는 이야기를 듣고 남자는 'Are there any times today when it's possible to see the film?'이라고 말한다. 이를 통해 남자가 보고자 하는 것은 '영화'(film)임을 알 수 있으므로 정답은 (D)이다.

46 남자는 몇 시에 영화를 관람할 것인가?
  (A) 4시에
  (B) 5시 30분에
  (C) 7시에
  (D) 9시 15분에

| 해설 | 여자가 4시와 9시 15분에 상영되는 영화의 좌석에 대해 설명하자 남자는 'I'll take two tickets for the late show then.'라고 말하며 '늦은 시간'의 티켓을 주문한다. 따라서 남자가 영화를 관람하게 될 시간은 (D)의 '9시 15분'이다.

[47-49]

M We've completed our estimate of the repair work to be done on your home, Ms. Chen.
W Great. How much is it going to cost?
M We can do everything you requested for $3,500.
W That's a bit out of my price range. Is there any way you can charge me less?
M I'm afraid not. I spoke with the work crew, and they remarked that they anticipate some problems because your house is so old.
W Why is that an issue?
M As a general rule, older houses have large amounts of wiring that need to be replaced. There are typically problems with pipes, too.
W I see. Well, I need some time to consider this. Can I contact you tomorrow?
M Sure. Please give me a call once you make a decision.

M 귀하의 주택에 실시될 보수 공사의 견적 작업이 끝났습니다, Chen 씨.
W 잘 되었군요. 비용이 얼마나 들까요?
M 요청하신 모든 작업을 3,500달러에 해 드릴 수 있습니다.
W 제가 생각했던 가격대에서 약간 벗어나는군요. 요금을 낮춰 주실 수는 없나요?
M 없을 것 같습니다. 작업 인부들과 이야기해 보았는데, 귀하의 주택이 너무 오래되어서 몇 가지 난관이 예상된다고 언급하더군요.
W 그것이 왜 문제가 되나요?
M 일반적으로, 오래된 주택일수록 교체가 필요한 전선들이 많아요. 또한 전형적으로 배관과 관련된 문제들도 있고요.
W 알겠어요. 음, 그에 대해 생각해 볼 시간이 필요해요. 제가 내일 연락을 드려도 될까요?
M 물론이죠. 결정을 내리시면 제게 전화를 주세요.

estimate 추산, 견적 | **price range** 가격대 | **remark** 언급하다 | **anticipate** 예상하다 | **as a general rule** 일반적으로 | **make a decision** 결정하다, 결심하다

47 남자가 "I'm afraid not"이라고 말할 때 남자는 무엇을 의미하는가?
  (A) 그는 견적 금액을 변경시킬 수 없다.
  (B) 그의 인부들이 여자의 집에서 일을 할 수 없다.
  (C) 그의 팀은 다음 주까지 일을 시작할 수 없다.
  (D) 그는 여자가 원하는 수리를 할 수 없을 것이다.

| 해설 | 남자의 말을 완전한 문장으로 바꾸어 써 보면 'I'm afraid that there isn't any way I can charge you less.'가 된다. 따라서 남자가 의미한 바는

(A)이다.

48 남자의 말에 따르면, 여자의 집의 문제는 무엇인가?
(A) 전선 작업이 제대로 되지 않았다.
(B) 누수가 되는 수도관이 있다.
(C) 매우 오래되었다.
(D) 바닥을 교체할 필요성이 있다.

| 해설 | 요금을 낮춰 달라는 여자의 요구에 남자는 거절의 의사를 표시하면서 '집이 낡아서'(because your house is so old) 많은 문제가 예상된다는 답변을 하고 있다. 따라서 정답은 (C)이다. 참고로 전선이나 배관의 문제가 있을 수 있다는 가능성은 제기되었지만, (A)와 (B)가 직접적인 문제로서 언급되지는 않았다.

49 여자는 남자에게 자신이 무엇을 할 것이라고 말하는가?
(A) 그에게 내일 수표를 보낸다
(B) 다른 업체와 이야기한다
(C) 그가 이야기한 금액을 지불한다
(D) 이후에 결정한다

check 수표 | **contractor** 계약자, 도급업체

| 해설 | 여자는 남자의 답변에 '생각할 시간이 필요하다'(I need some time to consider this)고 말하면서 자신의 결정을 미루고 있다. 따라서 정답은 (D)이다.

[50-52]

W Jackson Hardware. This is Lucy speaking.
M Hello, Lucy. My name is Gunther Heinz. I purchased a few items at your store yesterday and had them delivered this morning.
W Was everything all right with the delivery?
M Unfortunately, no. Several things which I ordered weren't included.
W I'm sorry to hear that. Could you tell me what's missing?
M Sure. I purchased three screwdrivers, a power saw, and some lumber. None of them arrived.
W Hold on a minute, please . . . Ah, I've got a note here about you, Mr. Heinz. Apparently, your order was divided in two shipments. The remaining items will be sent this afternoon.
M I see. Thanks for clearing everything up for me.

W Jackson 철물점입니다. 저는 Lucy입니다.
M 안녕하세요, Lucy. 제 이름은 Gunther Heinz예요. 어제 당신네 매장에서 몇 가지 제품을 구입해서 오늘 오전에 배송을 시켰어요.
W 배송에 아무런 문제가 없었나요?
M 안타깝게도, 있었어요. 제가 주문한 몇 가지 제품들이 포함되어 있지 않았죠.
W 그런 말씀을 들으니 유감이군요. 무엇이 빠져 있는지 말씀해 주시겠어요?
M 물론이죠. 저는 드라이버 3개, 전기 톱, 그리고 기타 몇 가지 물품들을 구입했어요. 이 중 어떤 것도 도착을 하지 않았고요.
W 잠시만 기다려 주세요… 아, 당신에 대한 메모가 있군요. Heinz 씨. 보아 하니, 주문품이 두 개로 나눠져서 배송되었어요. 나머지 물품들은 오늘 오후에 발송될 거예요.
M 그랬군요. 모든 것을 명확히 알려 줘서 고마워요.

include 포함하다 | **screwdriver** 드라이버 | **power saw** 전기 톱 | **lumber** 잡동사니 | **divide** 나누다, 구분하다

50 남자는 누구인 것 같은가?
(A) 건축가
(B) 고객
(C) 전화 교환원
(D) 철물점 직원

architect 건축가 | **telephone operator** 전화 교환원

| 해설 | 철물점에서 자신이 구입한 제품의 배송에 관해 문의하고 있으므로 남자는 (B)의 '고객'이다. 참고로 만약 여자의 직업을 물었다면 정답은 (D)가 될 것이다.

51 남자는 무엇에 대해 묻는가?
(A) 오지 않은 물품들
(B) 다가 올 세일
(C) 특별 할인
(D) 그가 받은 청구서

| 해설 | 대화 중반부의 남자의 말, 'Several things which I ordered weren't included.'를 통해 남자가 문의하는 것은 '배송되지 않은 물품'임을 알 수 있으므로 (A)가 정답이다.

52 여자는 오늘 오후에 어떤 일이 일어날 것이라고 말하는가?
(A) 매장에 몇 가지 제품들이 도착할 것이다.
(B) 웹사이트가 업데이트될 것이다.
(C) 매장의 세일이 끝날 것이다.
(D) 남자의 주문품이 발송될 것이다.

| 해설 | 여자의 마지막 말인 'The remaining items will be sent this afternoon.'을 통해, 정답은 (D)임을 알 수 있다.

[53-55]

Woman A Brian, is your team prepared to fly to L.A. to meet Drexel Industries tomorrow?
Man We sure are. I'm positive we can seal the deal and land a big contract.
Woman A That's the kind of upbeat attitude I like to hear.
Man But . . . There's a slight problem. James Hooper, whom I was counting on to do some of the negotiating, has been hospitalized after getting in a motor vehicle accident last night.
Woman B Who's his replacement?
Man I haven't decided yet. Do either of you have any suggestions?
Woman A How do you feel about Greg Randolph?
Man He does outstanding work, but we get along poorly.
Woman B I'd suggest Mark Nelson, but he's still at the tradeshow in Toronto.
Man It looks like we just might be shorthanded.

Woman A Brian, 당신 팀은 내일 L.A.로 가서 Drexel Industries와 회의를 할 준비가 되었나요?
Man 물론이죠. 저희가 거래를 성사시켜서 중대한 계약을 수주할 수 있을 것으로 저는 확신해요.
Woman A 제가 듣고 싶었던 긍정적인 유형의 발언이군요.
Man 하지만… 작은 문제가 하나 있어요. James Hooper가, 협상을 하기 위해 제가 의지하고 있는 사람인데, 어젯밤 자동차 사고를 당한 후 입원해 있어요.
Woman B 그를 대신할 사람이 누구인가요?
Man 아직 결정하지 못했어요. 두 분 중에 제안하실 것이 있으신가요?

Woman A Greg Randolph에 대해서는 어떻게 생각하나요?
Man 그는 일을 잘하지만, 저희는 친하지가 않아요.
Woman B 저는 Mark Nelson을 추천하고 싶은데, 하지만 그는 아직 토론토의 무역 박람회에 있어요.
Man 일손이 부족한 것 같군요.

seal the deal 합의에 이르다, 계약을 체결하다 | land a contract 계약을 성사시키다, 계약을 따내다 | upbeat 긍정적인, 낙관적인 | count on ~을 믿다, ~에 의지하다 | replacement 대체 | get along 어울려 지내다 | tradeshow 무역 박람회 | shorthanded 일손이 부족한

53 남자는 내일 무엇을 할 것인가?
(A) L.A.에서 관광을 한다
(B) 동료를 찾아간다
(C) 면접을 본다
(D) 잠재적 고객을 만난다

go sightseeing 관광을 하러 가다 | potential 잠재적인

| 해설 | 내일 출장을 떠날 준비가 되었는지를 묻는 여자A의 질문에 남자는 그렇다고 대답한 후, 'I'm positive we can seal the deal and land a big contract.'라고 말한다. 이를 통해 남자는 거래를 성사시키기 위해 출장을 떠날 것이라는 사실을 알 수 있으므로 그가 하게 될 일은 (D)이다.

54 James Hooper에 관해 무엇이 언급되는가?
(A) 그는 사고로 부상을 당했다.
(B) 그는 남자와 동행할 것이다.
(C) 그는 토론토에서 행사에 참석 중이다.
(D) 그와 남자는 친한 사이가 아니다.

accompany 동반하다, 동행하다 | on friendly terms 사이가 좋은, 친한

| 해설 | 남자는 자신이 의지하고 있는 James Hooper라는 사람이 '자동차 사고로 병원에 입원했다'(has been hospitalized after getting in a motor vehicle accident)고 말한다. 따라서 언급된 사항은 (A)이다.

55 남자는 왜 "It looks like we just might be shorthanded"라고 말하는가?
(A) 회사에서 더 이상 신입 직원을 고용하지 않을 것이라는 점을 말하기 위해
(B) 대체할 수 있는 직원이 없을 것이라는 점을 나타내기 위해
(C) 그의 팀원 중 한 명이 퇴사를 했다는 점을 언급하기 위해
(D) 그의 팀 스스로 업무를 처리할 수 있다고 주장하기 위해

| 해설 | 여자A와 여자B는 James Hooper를 대신할 수 있는 사람의 이름을 거론하지만 모두 대안이 되기 힘든 인물이다. 따라서 남자는 shorthanded(일손이 부족한)라는 단어를 이용하여 '(그를) 대체할 수 있는 사람이 없다'는 (B)의 의미를 나타내고 있다.

[56-58]

W Your total comes to $85, sir.
M Oh, hold on just a moment, please. I completely forgot that I have some coupons to give you. I've got them right here.
W No problem. Let me scan them . . . Hmm . . . This coupon for laundry detergent has expired, so I'm afraid you can't use it.
M Are you sure about that? What's the expiration date on it?
W It's January 15. You came here one day too late.
M Oh, well. That's my mistake. But what about the other ones? They're still valid, aren't they?
W They are, so you just saved a total of $12. That brings your new total to $73. How would you like to pay for that?
M Here's my debit card.

W 총 85달러 나왔습니다, 고객님.
M 오, 잠시만 기다려 주세요. 보여 드릴 쿠폰이 있다는 것을 완전히 잊고 있었네요. 여기에 있어요.
W 문제 없어요. 제가 확인해 볼게요… 흠… 이 세제용 쿠폰은 기간이 만료되었기 때문에, 안타깝지만 사용하실 수 없을 것 같군요.
M 확실한가요? 유효 기간이 어떻게 되는데요?
W 1월 15일이요. 하루 늦게 오셨어요.
M 오, 이런. 제 실수군요. 하지만 다른 것들은 어떤가요? 아직 유효하죠, 그렇지 않나요?
W 그것들은 유효하기 때문에, 총 12달러를 절약하셨어요. 그래서 새로운 합계가 73달러이죠. 어떻게 결제를 하시겠어요?
M 여기 직불 카드를 드릴게요.

scan 살피다, 훑어보다 | laundry detergent 세탁용 세제 | expire (기간이) 소멸하다 | expiration date 유효 기간, 유통 기한 | valid 유효한, 효력이 있는 | debit card 직불 카드, 현금 카드

56 여자는 어디에서 일을 하는 것 같은가?
(A) 세탁소에서
(B) 약국에서
(C) 슈퍼마켓에서
(D) 인쇄소에서

dry cleaner's 세탁소 | pharmacy 약국 | grocery store 식료품점, 잡화점, 슈퍼마켓

| 해설 | 유효 기간이 만료된 쿠폰이 'laundry detergent 구입용'이라는 점을 통해 여자가 일하는 곳은 (C)의 '슈퍼마켓'이라고 추측할 수 있다. 참고로 (C)의 grocery store는 기본적인 생필품을 판매하는 식료품점이나 잡화점을 가리킨다.

57 무엇이 문제인가?
(A) 남자의 쿠폰 중 한 장이 유효하지 않다.
(B) 남자가 찾는 제품이 매장에 없다.
(C) 남자는 충분한 돈을 가지고 있지 않다.
(D) 세일이 그 전날 끝났다.

good 유효한 | previous 이전의

| 해설 | 여자는 남자가 제시한 쿠폰 중 세제용 쿠폰의 기간이 만료되어 쓸 수 없다고 말하고 있으므로 남자의 문제는 (A)로 볼 수 있다.

58 남자는 여자에게 무엇을 주는가?
(A) 수표
(B) 운전면허증
(C) 은행 카드
(D) 상품권

gift certificate 상품권

| 해설 | 대화의 마지막 부분에서 결제 수단을 묻는 여자의 질문에 남자는 'Here's my debit card.'라고 답한다. 따라서 정답은 '직불 카드'를 지칭하는 (C)이다.

[59-61]

M Let's take a break and get something to eat.
W Actually, I'd rather finish writing this computer program first. It should only take about five more minutes.

M Well, I'm starving. Do you mind if I head out to lunch first? I skipped breakfast this morning.
W In that case, feel free to go ahead without me. I can catch up to you later if you tell me where you're going.
M I'm going to head to Papa Gino's, that new Italian restaurant. You know where it is, don't you?
W Actually, I haven't the slightest idea.
M Then I'll just wait for you so that we can go together. I can't believe you've never been there. It's one of the best restaurants in the neighborhood.
W Well, I suppose I'll get to experience its food in a few minutes.

M 잠시 일을 중단하고 무언가를 먹기로 하죠.
W 사실, 저는 먼저 이 컴퓨터 프로그램을 작성하는 일을 끝내는 것이 좋겠어요. 앞으로 약 5분 정도 걸릴 거예요.
M 음, 저는 배가 몹시 고파요. 제가 먼저 점심을 먹으러 가도 될까요? 오늘은 아침 식사도 걸렀거든요.
W 그런 경우라면, 주저하지 말고 저 없이 가도록 해요. 어디로 갈 것인지 제게 알려 주면 제가 나중에 쫓아 갈게요.
M 저는 새로 생긴 이탈리아 식당인 Papa Gino's로 갈 거예요. 어디에 있는지 알고 있죠, 그렇지 않아요?
W 실은, 전혀 모르고 있어요.
M 그러면 우리가 함께 갈 수 있도록 제가 기다리죠. 그곳에 가 본 적이 없다니 믿을 수가 없군요. 그곳은 근처 식당 중에서 최고의 식당 중 하나거든요.
W 음, 몇 분 후에는 저도 그곳 음식을 경험하게 되겠군요.

---

would rather 차라리 ~하겠다 | **starving** 몹시 배고픈, 굶주린 | **skip** 건너뛰다, 거르다 | **feel free to** 마음껏 ~하다 | **catch up to** ~을 따라잡다 | **so that ~ can** ~할 수 있도록 | **neighborhood** 인근, 근처 | **experience** 경험하다

59 여자는 무엇을 하고 싶어 하는가?
(A) 곧바로 점심을 먹으러 간다
(B) 컴퓨터 프로그램을 다운로드한다
(C) 자신이 하던 일을 마무리한다
(D) 잠시 휴식을 취한다

| 해설 | 점심을 먹으러 가자는 남자의 제안에 여자는 '먼저 컴퓨터 프로그램 작성을 끝내고 싶다'(I'd rather finish writing this computer program first)고 답하고 있다. 따라서 정답은 (C)이다.

60 여자가 "Actually, I haven't the slightest idea"라고 말할 때 여자는 무엇을 의미하는가?
(A) 그녀는 식당이 어디에 위치해 있는지 모른다.
(B) 그녀는 컴퓨터의 문제가 무엇인지 잘 모른다.
(C) 그녀는 남자가 아침 식사를 놓쳤다는 점을 모른다.
(D) 그녀는 자신과 남자가 무엇에 대해 이야기했는지 기억할 수 없다.

| 해설 | 식당의 위치를 알고 있는지 묻는 남자의 질문에 여자가 한 답변이다. 'Actually, I haven't the slightest idea.'를 직역하면 '아주 조금도 모른다'라는 뜻이므로, 여기에서는 (A)의 '위치를 전혀 모르겠다'는 의미를 나타낸다.

61 남자는 왜 놀라는가?
(A) 그의 컴퓨터가 정상적으로 작동을 하지 않는다.
(B) 여자가 Papa Gino's에서 식사를 한 적이 없다.
(C) 그는 프로그램이 이미 작성되었다고 생각했다.
(D) 여자는 새로운 곳으로 이사를 갈 계획이다.

| 해설 | 남자의 말, 'I can't believe you've never been there.'를 통해 남자는 여자가 Papa Gino's라는 식당에 가 본 적이 없다는 점 때문에 놀라고 있음을 알 수 있다. 따라서 정답은 (B)이다.

[62-64]

Woman Sorry to interrupt, but I wonder how you're enjoying your meal.
Man A Everything is perfect.
Man B I agree. My steak was cooked exactly the way I requested it. Please do me a favor and give my regards to the chef.
Woman I'll be sure to do that. So, uh, is there anything else I can get you?
Man A I'd appreciate another glass of tea if you don't mind.
Woman Not at all. What about you, sir? Would you care for some more coffee?
Man B That's all right. Two cups is my limit, or else I'll never get to sleep tonight. However, we could both go for some dessert. Could you please bring us two dessert menus?
Woman Of course. I'll be back with the drink and menus right after I visit the kitchen.

Woman 방해해서 죄송하지만, 식사가 어떠신지 궁금하군요.
Man A 모든 것이 완벽해요.
Man B 동감이에요. 제 스테이크는 제가 정확히 요청한대로 요리가 되었어요. 부탁합니다만, 주방장께 감사 인사를 전해 주세요.
Woman 잊지 않고 그렇게 하죠. 그러면, 어, 그밖에 제가 가져다 드릴 것이 있을까요?
Man A 괜찮으시면 차를 한 잔 더 가져다 주시면 고맙겠어요.
Woman 그럴게요. 손님께서는 어떠신가요? 커피를 더 드시고 싶으신가요?
Man B 괜찮아요. 두 잔이 제 한계라서, 그렇지 않으면 밤에 전혀 잠을 잘 수가 없을 거예요. 하지만, 우리 둘 모두 디저트를 원해요. 디저트를 두 개 가져다 주실 수 있으신가요?
Woman 물론이죠. 주방에 들러서 음료와 메뉴를 가지고 돌아오겠습니다.

---

interrupt 방해하다 | **perfect** 완벽한 | **do ~ a favor** ~의 부탁을 들어 주다 | **give one's regards to** ~에게 안부를 전하다 | **limit** 한계, 제한

62 여자의 직업은 무엇인가?
(A) 주방장
(B) 종업원
(C) 설거지하는 사람
(D) 계산원

| 해설 | 보기 중에서 음식에 대한 만족도를 묻고 주문을 받는 사람의 직업은 (B)의 '종업원'밖에 없다.

63 여자는 남자들에게 무엇을 가져다 줄 것인가?
(A) 커피
(B) 디저트
(C) 식당 메뉴
(D) 계산서

| 해설 | 대화 후반부에서 남자B가 'Could you please bring us two dessert menus?'라고 묻자 여자는 그렇게 하겠다고 답한다. 따라서 여자가 가지고 올 것은 '디저트'를 바꾸어 표현한 (C)의 '식당 메뉴'이다.

64 여자는 이다음에 아마도 무엇을 할 것인가?
(A) 음식을 준비한다

79

(B) 주방에 간다
(C) 음료를 따른다
(D) 음식을 배달한다

pour 따르다, 붓다

| 해설 | 여자의 마지막 말인 'I'll be back with the drink and menus right after I visit the kitchen.'을 통해 여자는 주방에 가서 음료와 메뉴를 가지고 돌아올 것임을 알 수 있다. 따라서 정답은 (B)이다.

[65-67]

M Julia, is it true that some of us in the department are going to change offices?
W That's right. Since we're getting a couple of new employees, we have to move people around.
M Do you know what's going to happen?
W Yes. Eric is going to move to office 305 while Susan will be moving to office 301.
M What about me?
W You're going to move from office 303 to the one right next to the elevator.
M That's perfect. It's quite a bit bigger than my current office.
W I thought you'd think that way. I specifically requested you be given that room.
M Why did you do that?
W You've been conducting numerous meetings with clients lately, so a bigger office will impress them more.

M Julia, 부서 내 우리 중 몇 명이 사무실을 바꾸게 될 것이라는 말이 사실인가요?
W 맞아요. 신입 직원이 두어 명 생길 것이기 때문에, 사람들의 자리를 조정해야 해요.
M 어떻게 될지 알고 있나요?
W 네, Eric이 305호실로 자리를 이동할 것이고, 반면에 Susan은 301호실로 자리를 이동할 것이에요.
M 저는 어떻게 되나요?
W 당신은 303호실에서 엘리베이터 바로 옆에 있는 곳으로 옮기게 될 거에요.
M 완벽하군요. 현재 사무실보다 상당히 큰 곳이죠.
W 당신이 그렇게 생각할 것이라고 생각했어요. 저는 당신이 그 사무실로 가야 한다고 특별히 요청을 해 두었죠.
M 왜 그렇게 했나요?
W 최근에 당신이 많은 고객들과 만나고 있어서, 사무실이 크면 그들에게 더 좋은 인상을 남기게 될 것이니까요.

move around 이동시키다, 자리를 바꾸다 | **from A to B** A에서 B로 | **current** 현재의 | **specifically** 특별히 | **conduct** 실행하다, 실시하다 | **numerous** 많은 | **lately** 최근에 | **impress** 각인시키다, 인상을 남기다

65 남자는 무엇에 관해 묻는가?
　　(A) 직원들과의 회의
　　(B) 부서의 자리 배치
　　(C) 신입 직원의 도착
　　(D) 사무실의 보수 공사

rearrange 재배열하다, 재배치하다 | **renovate** 개조하다, 보수하다

| 해설 | 대화의 시작 부분에서 남자는 '자리 배정'(change offices)에 대해 묻고 있다. 따라서 정답은 (B)이다.

66 도표를 보아라. 남자의 새로운 사무실은 어디인가?
　　(A) 1
　　(B) 2
　　(C) 3
　　(D) 4

| 해설 | 자신의 자리를 묻는 질문에 여자는 from office 303 to the one right next to the elevator라고 답한다. 따라서 엘리베이터 바로 옆 자리인 (A)의 1이 남자의 새 사무실이다.

67 남자는 왜 기뻐하는가?
　　(A) 그에게 특별 휴가가 주어졌다.
　　(B) 바이어와의 만남이 잘 진행되었다.
　　(C) 그는 자리를 옮길 필요가 없다.
　　(D) 그는 보다 큰 사무실로 가게 될 것이다.

extra 여분의, 추가적인 | **go well** 잘 진행되다, 잘 되다

| 해설 | 남자는 자신의 새로운 사무실 위치에 대한 소식을 듣고 반색하며 'It's quite a bit bigger than my current office.'라고 말한다. 따라서 남자가 기뻐하는 이유는 (D)이다.

[68-70]

M Hello. Gateway Travel. This is David speaking. How may I be of assistance?
W Hello, Mr. Parker. This is Yolanda DuPont calling.
M Good afternoon, Ms. DuPont. Do you have a question regarding the itinerary I e-mailed you this morning?
W Actually, there's something on it that has to be altered.
M Sure. What would you like for me to do?
W The first two legs of my trip are fine. However, I need to be in Oslo one day earlier than I had planned.
M I see. Well, I can change your departure date from London to the previous day. Would you prefer a morning or afternoon flight?
W The morning would be better.
M Great. Let me contact the airline. I'll give you a call once everything has been taken care of.

M 안녕하세요. Gateway 여행사입니다. 저는 David입니다. 어떻게 도와 드릴까요?
W 안녕하세요, Parker 씨. 저는 Yolanda DuPont이에요.
M 안녕하세요, DuPont 씨. 오늘 아침에 제가 이메일로 보내 드린 여행 일정표와 관련해서 질문이 있으신가요?
W 실은, 일정상 변경되어야 할 것이 있어요.
M 그러시군요. 제가 어떻게 해 드리면 될까요?
W 첫 번째 두 여정은 괜찮아요. 하지만, 저는 계획되어 있는 것보다 하루 일찍 오슬로에 가고 싶어요.
M 알겠습니다. 음, 런던에서 출발하는 날짜를 그 전날로 바꾸어 드릴 수 있어요. 오전 비행기편을 선호하시나요, 아니면 오후 비행기편을 선호하시나요?
W 오전이 더 좋을 것 같아요.
M 잘 되었군요. 제가 항공사에 연락을 할게요. 모든 일이 처리되면 제가 전화를 드리겠습니다.

itinerary 여행 일정(표) | **alter** 변경하다, 바꾸다 | **leg** 다리; 여정 | **previous** 이전의 | **airline** 항공사 | **take care of** ~을 돌보다; ~을 처리하다

68 남자는 어디에서 일을 하는 것 같은가?
　　(A) 항공사에서

80

(B) 기차역에서
(C) 여행사에서
(D) 렌터카 업체에서

rental car agency 렌터카 업체

| 해설 | 고객에게 '여행 일정표'(itinerary)를 보내고, 고객을 위해 '출발 일자를 조정하고'(change your departure date), 고객을 대신해서 '항공사에 연락을 취하는'(contact the airline) 일은 여행사 직원의 업무이다. 따라서 남자가 일하는 곳은 (C)의 '여행사'이다.

69 도표를 보아라. 여자는 어느 날짜의 여행 계획을 바꾸어야 하는가?
  (A) 10월 12일
  (B) 10월 16일
  (C) 10월 20일
  (D) 10월 22일

| 해설 | 대화 중반부의 여자의 말, 'However, I need to be in Oslo one day earlier than I had planned.'가 정답의 단서이다. 일정표 상에는 오슬로에 체류하는 기간이 21일에서 22일까지로 적혀 있지만, 여자가 하루 일찍 오슬로로 가야 한다고 말했기 때문에 여행 계획이 변경되어야 하는 날은 (C)의 '10월 20일'이다.

70 남자는 무엇을 하겠다고 제안하는가?
  (A) 항공사에 전화를 건다
  (B) 여자에게 새로운 여행 일정표를 보낸다
  (C) 청구서를 재검토한다
  (D) 여자의 좌석을 일등석으로 업그레이드한다

recalculate 다시 계산하다, 재검토하다 | first class 일등석

| 해설 | 대화의 마지막 부분에서 남자는 'Let me contact the airline.'이라고 말하며 자신이 항공사에 전화를 걸어 항공편을 변경할 것이라는 점을 암시하고 있다. 따라서 정답은 (A)이다.

● **PART 4** p.135

[71-73]

M Phillipe, this is Fred Reynolds in Marketing. I'm calling regarding the work I'm doing on the Simpson project. I'm afraid I'm going to require an extension. Instead of finishing the work on Friday as we had originally discussed, I'd like to change the due date to next Wednesday. I apologize for requesting this change, but Tina Westerly, the head of my department, just assigned me to work with Dave Powers in Accounting on his project. Apparently, Dave is progressing slowly and is way behind schedule, and she wants it done no later than Thursday. Once we complete it, I can resume working on our project.

M Phillipe, 저는 마케팅부의 Fred Reynolds예요. Simpson 프로젝트에 관해 제가 하고 있는 일 때문에 전화를 했어요. 아쉽게도 제가 기한 연장을 요청해야 할 것 같아요. 원래 우리가 논의했던 대로 금요일에 일을 마감하는 것 대신, 저는 마감 날짜를 다음 주 수요일로 변경했으면 해요. 이와 같이 변경을 요청하게 되어 미안하지만, 저희 부서장이신 Tina Westerly 씨께서 제게 회계부의 Dave Powers와 함께 그의 프로젝트 업무를 하라고 시키셨어요. 듣자 하니, Dave가 일을 느리게 해서 일정이 크게 뒤져지고 있는데, 그녀는 늦어도 목요일까지는 일을 끝내기를 바라고 있어요. 그 일이 끝나면, 저는 우리 프로젝트 업무를 재개할 수 있을 거예요.

extension 연장 | instead of ~ 대신에 | originally 원래, 본래 | due date 마감 일자 | apologize for ~에 대해 사과하다 | assign 맡기다, 할당하다 | progress 진행하다, 진전을 보이다 | way behind schedule 예정보다 많이 뒤쳐진 | resume 다시 시작하다, 재개하다

71 전화를 건 목적은 무엇인가?
  (A) 회의 일정을 취소시키기 위해
  (B) 기한 연장을 요청하기 위해
  (C) 보고서에 관한 도움을 요청하기 위해
  (D) 진행 중인 프로젝트를 검토하기 위해

later 나중의, 이후의 | go over ~을 검토하다 | ongoing 진행 중인

| 해설 | 담화 초반부에 화자는 'I'm afraid I'm going to require an extension.'이라고 말하며 마감 일자를 늦춰 줄 것을 요청하고 있다. 따라서 전화를 한 목적은 (B)이다.

72 Tina Westerly는 어디에서 일을 하는 것 같은가?
  (A) 영업부
  (B) 마케팅부
  (C) 회계부
  (D) 선적부

| 해설 | 담화 중반부에서 화자는 Tina Westerly를 the head of my department라고 소개하고 있다. 따라서 그녀가 일하는 곳은 Fred Reynolds와 같은 부서인 (B)의 '마케팅부'이다. 참고로 (C)의 '회계부'는 Dave Powers가 소속된 부서이다.

73 화자는 자신이 무엇을 해야 한다고 말하는가?
  (A) 다른 부서로 이동한다
  (B) 상사와의 회의에 참석한다
  (C) 자신의 업무를 보다 빨리 처리한다
  (D) 동료의 프로젝트를 도와 준다

| 해설 | 화자는 마감 기한을 연장해야 하는 이유로 자신의 상사가 '회계부의 Dave Powers와 함께 프로젝트를 진행할 것을 지시했으며'(assigned me to work with Dave Powers in Accounting on his project) 상사는 프로젝트가 빨리 끝나기를 원한다고 언급한다. 따라서 화자가 해야 할 일은 (D)이다.

[74-76]

M Are you tired of high prices and poor quality? Then you should visit West Side Auto Repairs. We'll provide you with the highest quality in auto care, but we won't overcharge you. In fact, our rates are much lower than those of our competitors. The mechanics here have several years of experience and are qualified to work on automobiles, trucks, motorcycles, and even buses. Before they make any repairs to your vehicle, they'll tell you exactly what needs to be done and how much it will cost. So come to West Side Auto Repairs for top-quality service. We're located at 899 Beacon Street and never close.

M 높은 가격과 낮은 품질에 넌더리가 나십니까? 그렇다면, West Side 자동차 정비소를 방문하셔야 합니다. 저희는 자동차 관리에 있어서 최고의 품질을 제공해 드리지만, 과도한 요금을 부과하지는 않습니다. 실제로, 저희 요금은 경쟁업체들보다 훨씬 낮습니다. 이곳 정비사들은 다년간의 경력을 가지고 있으며 자동차, 트럭, 오토바이, 그리고 버스에 관해서도 정비 자격을 갖추고 있습니다. 귀하의 차량을 수리하기 전에, 그들은 어떤 조치가 취해져야 하고 비용은 얼마가 들 것인지를 귀하께 정확히 알려 드립니다. 그러니 최고

의 서비스를 받으시려면 West Side 자동차 정비소로 오십시오. 저희는 Beacon 가 899번지에 위치해 있으며 연중무휴입니다.

be tired of ~에 싫증나다 | **overcharge** 과도하게 요금을 부과하다 | **rate** 요금 | **competitor** 경쟁자 | **mechanic** 정비사 | **qualified** 자격이 있는

74 화자는 West Side 자동차 정비소의 정비사들에 관해 무엇을 말하는가?
(A) 매년 특별 교육을 받는다.
(B) 자동차와 트럭에 관한 정비 자격만을 갖추고 있다.
(C) 오랫동안 업계에서 일했다.
(D) 검사하는 모든 차량들에 둘씩 짝을 이루어 작업한다.

training 훈련, 교육 | **in pairs** 둘씩 짝을 이뤄

| 해설 | 화자는 담화 중반에 자기 업체의 정비사들이 첫째 '다년간의 경력을 가지고 있고'(have several years of experience) 둘째 '다양한 차량의 정비 능력을 갖추고 있다'(are qualified to work on automobiles, trucks, motorcycles, and even buses)고 말한다. 따라서 정답은 이 중 전자의 설명과 관련이 있는 (C)이다.

75 정비사들은 차량에 관한 작업을 하기 전에 무엇을 하는가?
(A) 고객에게 계약서에 서명하라고 요청한다
(B) 왜 작업이 이루어져야 하는지에 대해 설명한다
(C) 고객에게 수리에 관한 선택권을 준다
(D) 그들이 하게 될 작업의 비용에 대해 언급한다

option 선택, 선택권

| 해설 | 'Before they make any repairs to your vehicle, they'll tell you exactly what needs to be done and how much it will cost.'라는 문장에서, 정비사들은 정비에 앞서 실시될 조치와 가격을 안내할 것이라고 나와 있다. 따라서 정답은 (D)이다.

76 West Side 자동차 정비소에 대해 언급된 것은 무엇인가?
(A) 교외에 위치해 있다.
(B) 5대의 차량을 위한 공간이 있다.
(C) 오토바이를 전문으로 한다.
(D) 일년 내내 문을 연다.

suburbs 교외 | **space** 공간 | **specialize in** ~을 전문으로 하다, ~에 특화되다 | **all year round** 일년 내내

| 해설 | 담화 마지막 부분에서 화자의 정비소는 '문을 닫지 않는다'(never close)는 사실을 알 수 있으므로 정비소에 대해 언급된 내용은 (D)이다.

[77-79]

W We've taken on more than 75 new employees in the past two months since we've been expanding recently. Not everyone's working out well though. We've been receiving complaints from other employees about the low quality of work several individuals are doing. So those of you here now have an additional duty. You need to work closely with the new employees in your department and act as mentors for them. Train them properly so that we can reduce the number of errors they're making. I'd appreciate it if you would do that for me. Otherwise, we'll be obligated to terminate some of them.

W 우리는 최근 사업을 확장한 이후로 지난 2개월간 75명의 직원을 새로 고용했습니다. 하지만 모든 이들이 일을 잘하고 있는 것은 아닙니다. 우리는 몇몇 사람들이 하고 있는 낮은 질의 업무에 대해 다른 직원들로부터 불만을 받고 있습니다. 따라서 여기에 계신 여러분들에게는 이제 추가적인 업무가 생겼습니다. 부서 내 신입 직원들과 긴밀히 협력해야 하며 그들의 멘토로서 활동하셔야 합니다. 그들이 저지르는 실수를 줄이기 위해 그들을 적절하게 교육시키십시오. 저를 위해서 그렇게 해 주시면 고맙겠습니다. 그렇지 않은 경우, 우리는 그중 일부를 해고해야 할 것입니다.

expand 확장하다, 확대하다 | **recently** 최근에 | **complaint** 불만 | **additional** 추가적인 | **duty** 임무 | **act as** ~으로서 기능하다, ~으로서 활동하다 | **mentor** 멘토 | **properly** 적절하게 | **reduce** 줄이다, 감소시키다 | **be obligated to** ~해야 한다, ~해야 할 의무가 있다 | **terminate** 제거하다

77 화자는 주로 무엇에 대해 논의하고 있는가?
(A) 일부 직원들의 업무 성과
(B) 더 많은 직원을 고용해야 할 필요성
(C) 실시될 교육 과정
(D) 고객들의 불만 사항을 감소시키는 법

| 해설 | 담화 전반에 걸쳐 화자는 일부 신입 사원들의 업무 능력이 좋지 못하다는 점과 이를 해결하기 위한 대책에 대해 논의하고 있다. 따라서 대화의 주제는 (A)로 볼 수 있다.

78 화자가 "I'd appreciate it if you would do that for me"라고 말할 때 화자는 무엇을 의미하는가?
(A) 그녀는 청자들이 자신의 일을 더 열심히 하기를 원한다.
(B) 그녀는 청자들이 다른 직원을 돕기를 원한다.
(C) 그녀는 청자들이 고객들에게 보다 공손하기를 원한다.
(D) 그녀는 청자들이 자신의 업무를 더 잘 해낼 것을 원한다.

polite 공손한

| 해설 | 주어진 문장에서 if you would do that for me가 구체적으로 무엇을 의미하는지 파악해야 문제를 풀 수 있다. 앞 부분에서 화자는 청자들에게 '신입 직원들과 긴밀히 협력하라'(work closely with the new employees)고 당부한 후 '신입 직원들을 훈련시킬 것'(train them properly)을 요청하고 있다. 따라서 주어진 문장이 의미하는 바는 (B)가 된다.

79 화자는 어떤 일이 일어날 수도 있을 것이라고 암시하는가?
(A) 몇몇 매장이 문을 닫을 수도 있다.
(B) 서비스 가격이 오를 수도 있다.
(C) 오리엔테이션이 취소될 수도 있다.
(D) 몇몇 사람들이 일자리를 잃을 수도 있다.

| 해설 | 담화의 마지막 문장에서 화자는 개선이 이루어지지 않으면 '몇 명을 해고해야 할 수도 있다'(we'll be obligated to terminate some of them)고 언급하고 있으므로 (D)가 정답이다.

[80-82]

M Ladies and gentlemen, your attention, please. It has been brought to our attention that a black SUV has been parked right in front of the shop. This is a no-parking zone, and we request that the owner of the vehicle immediately move it. The vehicle's license plate is 595-M87. If the car is not moved within the next five minutes, we will call a tow truck, and the vehicle will be removed at the owner's expense. Once again, will the owner of the black SUV parked in front of the front doors please return to your vehicle and park it elsewhere? Thank you.

M 신사 숙녀 여러분, 주목해 주십시오. 검정색 SUV 차량이 매장 바로 앞에 주차되어 있다는 소식이 들어왔습니다. 이곳은 주차 금지 구역이며, 저희는 차량 소유주께 즉시 차량을 이동시켜 주실 것을 요청드립니다. 차량 번호는 595-M87입니다. 지금부터 5분 내로 차가 이동하지 않으면, 견인 차량을 불러서 차주의 비용으로 차량을 이동시킬 것입니다. 다시 한 번 말씀드리면, 정문 앞에 주차되어 있는 검정색 SUV 차량의 소유주께서는 차량으로 돌아가셔서 다른 곳에 주차를 해 주시겠습니까? 감사합니다.

no-parking zone 주차 금지 구역 | **immediately** 즉시 | **vehicle's license plate** 차량 번호판 | **tow truck** 견인 차량 | **expense** 비용, 경비

80 이 담화는 어디에서 이루어지고 있는 것 같은가?
(A) 주차장에서
(B) 사무실에서
(C) 공원에서
(D) 매장에서

| 해설 | 담화의 시작 부분에서 화자는 '매장 앞에'(in front of the shop) 주차되어 있는 차량을 이동시킬 것을 요구한다. 따라서 방송이 이루어지고 있는 곳은 (D)의 '매장'임을 알 수 있다.

81 무엇이 문제인가?
(A) 자동차가 잘못된 장소에 있다.
(B) 주차 공간이 없다.
(C) 정문이 잠겨 있다.
(D) 사람들이 건물 밖으로 나갈 수 없다.

| 해설 | '주차 금지 구역'(no-parking zone)에 차량이 주차되어 있다는 사실을 알리고 있으므로 정답은 (A)이다.

82 화자는 무엇을 요청하는가?
(A) 요금이 지불되어야 한다
(B) 문이 열려야 한다
(C) 차량을 이동시켜야 한다
(D) 사람이 조용해야 한다

| 해설 | 담화의 초반부와 후반부에서 화자는 주차 금지 구역에 주차되어 있는 차량의 차주에게 차량을 즉시 이동시켜 줄 것을 요청하고 있다. 따라서 (C)가 정답이다.

[83-85]

W The numbers for the month of July are in, and they're worse than expected. Revenues declined by more than 25%, and we posted a loss of nearly half a million dollars. That's the worst month we've had in the past 6 years. The reason for this decline has to do with the negative response of consumers to our newest product line. It's widely considered user unfriendly, and people think it's overpriced as well. That's having a negative effect on our other products because consumers are avoiding buying anything made by us. How about brainstorming on how to solve this problem right now?

W 7월 수치가 입수되었는데, 예상보다 좋지가 않습니다. 수입은 25% 이상 감소했고, 우리는 거의 5백만 달러의 손실을 보았습니다. 지난 6년 동안 가장 좋지 않은 달입니다. 이러한 감소의 이유는 우리의 최신 제품에 대한 소비자들의 부정적인 반응과 관계가 있습니다. 사용자 중심적이 아니라고 널리 생각되고 있으며, 사람들은 가격도 너무 비싸다고 생각합니다. 소비자들이 우리가 만든 어떤 것도 사려고 하지 않기 때문에, 그러한 점은 우리의 다른 제품에도 부정적인 영향을 미치고 있습니다. 이러한 문제를 어떻게 해결해야 할지에 대해 지금 당장 브레인스토밍을 하는 것이 어떨까요?

revenue 수입 | **decline** 쇠퇴하다; 쇠퇴, 감소 | **post** 게시하다, 발표하다 | **have to do with** ~와 관계가 있다 | **negative** 부정적인 | **overpriced** 값이 너무 비싼 | **effect** 효과 | **avoid** 피하다 | **brainstorm** 브레인스토밍하다

83 화자는 회사의 최근 실적에 대해 무엇을 언급하는가?
(A) 5백만 달러를 벌었다.
(B) 6개의 신제품을 출시했다.
(C) 전보다 수입이 적었다.
(D) 수년 동안 최고의 달이었다.

| 해설 | 담화 초반부에 화자는 7월 실적이 예상보다 낮아서, 수입은 25% 감소했고 500백만 달러의 손실이 발생했다고 지적한다. 따라서 실적과 관련된 내용은 (C)이다.

84 소비자들은 신제품에 대해 어떻게 생각하는가?
(A) 너무 비싸다고 생각한다.
(B) 사용하기가 쉽다고 생각한다.
(C) 긍정적으로 반응했다.
(D) 잘 만들어지지 않았다고 생각한다.

| 해설 | 신제품에 대한 고객의 평가는 'It's widely considered user unfriendly, and people think it's overpriced as well.'에서 알 수 있다. 즉 소비자들은 신제품이 사용자 중심적이 아니며 제품 가격이 너무 높다고 생각하고 있기 때문에 정답은 (A)가 된다.

85 화자는 청자들에게 무엇을 할 것을 요청하는가?
(A) 신제품을 더 많이 팔려고 노력한다
(B) 해결 방안에 대해 생각한다
(C) 대안이 될 수 있는 제품을 제안한다
(D) 몇몇 고객들과 이야기한다

solution 해결책, 해결 방안 | **alternative** 대안의

| 해설 | 담화의 마지막 부분에서 화자는 'How about brainstorming on how to solve this problem right now?'라고 말하면서 청자들에게 문제 해결을 위한 브레인스토밍을 제안하고 있다. 따라서 화자가 요청한 것은 (B)이다.

[86-88]

M Hi, Amy. This is Sam Chu. It was just brought to my attention that you weren't invited to the staff dinner we're having after work tonight. I apologize for the oversight. I'm not sure how that happened. Anyway, we'd love for you to be in attendance. We're getting together at the Mesa Steakhouse at 6:30. If you don't know where it is, ask Cathy or me, and one of us can provide you with directions. Or you can ride along with someone else who's driving. Would you mind calling me back at extension 689 to confirm that you can make it to tonight's event? I'd appreciate that.

M 안녕하세요, Amy. 저는 Sam Chu예요. 오늘 밤 퇴근 후에 예정되어 있는 직원 저녁 식사에 당신이 초대되지 않았다는 점을 조금 전에야 알게 되었어요. 실수에 대해 사과를 할게요. 왜 그런 일이 일어났는지 잘 모르겠어요. 하여튼, 우리는 당신이 참석하기를 바라

요. 우리는 6시 30분에 Mesa Steakhouse에서 모일 거예요. 그곳이 어디에 있는지 모르는 경우에는, Cathy나 저에게 물어보면, 우리 중 한 명이 당신에게 길을 알려 줄 수 있을 거예요. 아니면 차를 몰고 갈 사람과 함께 차를 타고 올 수도 있죠. 내선 번호 689로 제게 전화를 해서 당신이 오늘 밤 행사에 올 수 있는지 확인시켜 줄래요? 그러면 고맙겠어요.

invite 초대하다 | **oversight** 간과, 실수 | **in attendance** 참석한 | **get together** 모이다 | **direction** 방향 | **confirm** 확인하다 | **make it** (시간 내에) 오다 | **appreciate** 감사하다

86 6시 30분에 어떤 일이 일어날 것인가?
 (A) 직원 회의가 열릴 것이다.
 (B) 저녁 식사가 시작될 것이다.
 (C) 사람들이 야유회를 떠날 것이다.
 (D) 시상식에 음식이 제공될 것이다.

cater 음식을 공급하다

| 해설 | '6시 30분'이라는 시각은 'We're getting together at the Mesa Steakhouse at 6:30.'라는 문장에서 들을 수 있다. 이를 통해 6시 30분은 모임이 시작되는 시간임을 알 수 있으므로 정답은 (B)이다.

87 화자는 왜 "I'm not sure how that happened"라고 말하는가?
 (A) Amy가 초대되지 않은 점에 대한 변명을 하기 위해
 (B) Amy가 길 안내를 받지 못한 것을 설명하기 위해
 (C) Amy가 상을 받지 못해서 사과를 하기 위해
 (D) 행사가 왜 변경되었는지 그가 모른다는 점을 설명하기 위해

excuse 변명, 구실

| 해설 | 앞서 Amy가 초대되지 못한 점에 대해 사과를 한 후, 주어진 문장을 통해 그에 대한 일종의 변명을 하고 있다. 따라서 (A)가 정답이다.

88 화자는 Amy에게 무엇을 하라고 제안하는가?
 (A) 웹사이트에서 길 안내 지도를 다운로드한다
 (B) 퇴근 전에 그에게 이메일을 보낸다
 (C) 동료 중 한 명과 함께 차를 타고 간다
 (D) 그녀가 전근을 원한다는 점을 확인시켜 준다

get a ride (자동차 등에) 타다

| 해설 | 담화의 후반부에서 화자는 모임 장소로 오는 길을 모르는 경우에는 자신이나 Cathy에게 길을 물어보던가, 아니면 '운전을 하고 올 사람의 차를 얻어 타라'(you can ride along with someone else who's driving)고 말한다. 따라서 정답은 화자가 두 번째로 제안한 내용을 가리키는 (C)이다.

[89-91]

W Thank you for coming, ladies and gentlemen. I'm pleased with the turnout to today's event. I hope those of you in the back can hear me all right. It's now time for the main event. David Hooper, the author of the recently released novel *Winters End*, is going to read some excerpts from his book. After he completes that, Mr. Hooper has agreed to answer some of your questions for a few minutes. And please be aware that all of Mr. Hooper's books are available for purchase at the front counter. Now, won't you please give a big round of applause for Mr. David Hooper?

W 신사 숙녀 여러분, 와 주셔서 고맙습니다. 오늘 행사에 참여해 주신 분들의 숫자가 만족스럽군요. 뒤쪽에 계신 여러분께서도 제 말이 잘 들리시기를 바랍니다. 이제 본행사를 할 시간입니다. 최근에 발표된 *겨울이 끝나다*의 작가인 David Hooper 씨께서 자신의 책에서 발췌한 내용을 읽어 주실 것입니다. 이것이 끝나면, Hooper 씨께서는 몇 분 동안 여러분들의 질문에 답변을 해 주시기로 동의하셨습니다. 그리고 Hooper 씨의 모든 책들은 앞 계산대에서 구입이 가능하다는 점을 알려 드립니다. 자, David Hooper 씨를 큰 박수로 맞이해 주시지 않겠습니까?

turnout 참가자 수 | **author** 작가 | **excerpt** 발췌 | **a round of applause** 박수 갈채

89 이 담화는 어디에서 이루어지고 있는 것 같은가?
 (A) 도서관에서
 (B) 서점에서
 (C) 학교에서
 (D) 출판사에서

| 해설 | 화자는 David Hooper라는 '작가'를 소개하고 있고, 담화 후반부에서는 '이 작가의 책을 계산대에서 구입할 수 있다'(all of Mr. Hooper's books are available for purchase at the front counter)고 말한다. 보기 중에서 책을 판매할 수 있는 곳은 (B)의 '서점'뿐이므로 (B)가 정답이다.

90 Hooper 씨는 제일 먼저 무엇을 할 것인가?
 (A) 질문에 답변한다
 (B) 강연을 한다
 (C) 책을 읽는다
 (D) 책에 사인을 한다

copy 복사; 한 권, 한 부

| 해설 | Hooper 씨가 하게 될 일은 첫째가 '책에서 발췌한 내용을 읽는 것'(read some excerpts from his book)이고 둘째가 '질문에 대답하는 것'(answer some of your questions)이다. 따라서 제일 먼저 할 일은 (C)이고, 그 다음에 할 일은 (A)이다.

91 화자는 Hooper 씨의 책에 대해 무엇을 말하는가?
 (A) 판매를 한다.
 (B) 모두 대출되었다.
 (C) 비소설 작품이다.
 (D) 대출이 가능하다.

| 해설 | 담화의 후반부에 화자는 'Hooper 씨의 모든 책은 계산대에서 구입할 수 있다'(all of Mr. Hooper's books are available for purchase at the front counter)고 말한다. 따라서 정답은 (A)이다.

[92-94]

W This is Crystal Wallace in the WTRE helicopter providing you with a bird's-eye view of traffic in the city. Right now, traffic on Main Street is moving fairly well considering that it's rush hour. It's backed up about five minutes on both Oak Street and Wadley Road though. And there's a four-car accident on Gold Street right now, so traffic moving northbound is stopped for several blocks. I highly recommend that drivers seek alternative routes and avoid that part of the city. I'll be back in fifteen minutes with another rush hour update.

W 시내 교통의 전경을 제공해 드리는 WTRE 헬기의 Crystal Wallace 입니다. 현재, Main 가의 교통은, 러시아워임을 감안할 때, 상당히 원활하게 이루어지고 있습니다. 하지만 Oak 가와 Wadley 로는 모두 5분 정도 지체되고 있습니다. 그리고 현재 Gold 가에서는 4중 추돌 사고가 있었기 때문에, 북쪽 방향으로 이동하는 차량들이 몇 블록에 걸쳐 움직이지를 못하고 있습니다. 운전자분들께서는 우회 도로를 찾으셔서 시내의 해당 부분을 피해가실 것을 강력히 권해 드립니다. 저는 또 다른 러시아워 소식을 가지고 15분 후에 돌아오겠습니다.

helicopter 헬리콥터 | bird's-eye view 전경 | fairly 상당히, 패 | be backed up 지체되다, 막히다 | northbound 북쪽을 향하는 | alternative route 우회 도로 | update 최신 정보; 업데이트

92 Wallace 씨는 어디에 있는가?
(A) 뉴스 차량에
(B) 스튜디오에
(C) 라디오 방송국에
(D) 헬리콥터에

| 해설 | 담화 첫 문장 중 in the WTRE helicopter라는 부분을 놓치지 않고 들으면 Wallace 씨가 있는 곳은 (D)의 '헬리콥터 안'이라는 사실을 쉽게 알 수 있다.

93 도표를 보아라. 시내의 어떤 부분에 교통 사고가 있었는가?
(A) 1번
(B) 2번
(C) 3번
(D) 4번

| 해설 | 담화 중반의 there's a four-car accident on Gold Street right now라는 어구를 통해 Gold 가에서 교통 사고가 있었음을 알 수 있다. 정답은 (A)이다.

94 Wallace 씨는 언제 또 다시 교통 안내 방송을 할 것인가?
(A) 5분 후에
(B) 15분 후에
(C) 30분 후에
(D) 1시간 후에

| 해설 | 마지막 문장에서 화자는 'I'll be back in fifteen minutes with another rush hour update.'라고 말하며 15분 후에 다시 교통 소식이 안내될 것이라는 점을 암시하고 있다. 따라서 '15분 후'를 의미하는 (B)가 정답이다.

[95-97]

M Hello. My name is Nick Tenaglia. I'm calling regarding order number 985020. I purchased several items two days ago, and they just arrived in the mail a few minutes ago. I must admit that I'm highly impressed with the speed of the delivery. Unfortunately, it appears as though the person who packed the order wasn't particularly careful. I ordered some 10-inch dinner plates, but only a dozen of them were actually in the box. How do I go about getting the other plates that I bought and paid for? I would appreciate receiving a call to inform me about this issue. Thank you. Goodbye.

M 안녕하세요. 제 이름은 Nick Tenaglia에요. 저는 주문 번호가 985020인 건에 대해 전화를 드려요. 저는 이틀 전에 몇 개의 제품을 구입했고, 제품들은 몇 분 전에 우편으로 도착을 했죠. 배송 속도에 대해서는 크게 감명을 받았다는 점을 인정해야만 할 것 같아요. 안타깝게도, 주문품을 포장한 사람은 그다지 주의가 깊지 않았던 것으로 보여요. 저는 10인치의 접시를 주문했는데, 실제로 그중 12개만이 상자에 들어 있었죠. 제가 주문을 해서 결제한 다른 접시들에 대해서는 어떻게 해야 하나요? 전화를 받고서 제가 이 문제에 대해 어떻게 해야 할지 알려 주시면 고맙겠어요. 감사합니다. 안녕히 계세요.

mail 우편물 | admit 인정하다 | be impressed with ~에 감명을 받다 | dinner plate 정찬용 접시 | dozen 12개

95 화자는 배송에 대해 무엇을 언급하는가?
(A) 매우 빨랐다.
(B) 비용이 너무 많이 들었다.
(C) 평소보다 느렸다.
(D) 평소보다 빨랐다.

| 해설 | 화자는 I'm highly impressed with the speed of the delivery라고 말하면서 배송 속도에 대해서는 만족감을 나타내고 있다. 따라서 정답은 (A)이며, 배송 속도가 기존과 비교해서 빠른 것인지는 주어진 담화에서 언급된 바 없기 때문에 (D)는 정답이 되기 힘들다.

96 도표를 보아라. Tenaglia 씨는 몇 개의 새로운 제품을 필요로 하는가?
(A) 8개
(B) 10개
(C) 12개
(D) 14개

| 해설 | 대화 중후반부의 화자의 말, 'I ordered some 10-inch dinner plates, but only a dozen of them were actually in the box.'가 정답의 단서이다. 먼저 '정찬용 접시'(dinner plates)를 주문했다고 했으므로 이를 도표에서 찾으면 주문 수량은 20개였음을 알 수 있다. 그리고 '12개'만이 상자에 있었다고 했으므로, 화자가 더 받아야 할 접시는 (A)의 '8개'임을 알 수 있다.

97 화자는 무엇을 원하는가?
(A) 그가 방문했던 지점 주소
(B) 받지 못한 제품을 어떻게 받아야 하는지에 관한 정보
(C) 파손된 제품에 대한 전액 환불
(D) 잘못 온 제품을 회사로 돌려보내는 방법

missing 분실된, 실종된

| 해설 | 화자는 담화의 후반부에서 '주문을 했으나 받지 못한 제품에 대해 어떻게 해야 하는지' 물은 후 그에 관해 전화로 알려 달라고 요청하고 있다. 따라서 화자가 원하는 바는 (B)로 볼 수 있다.

[98-100]

W Welcome, everyone, to the fifth annual workshop for creative writers. We've got a great day filled with exciting events in store for you. In a few minutes, we're going to start today's workshop with a short talk by Mary Lattimore, one of the best-known poets in the state. She's going to talk about how to develop a creative mindset. After she's done, we'll listen to Ronald Devers, who's going to chat about making outlines for essays. There's one change to the schedule though. Lisa Delacruz's train has been delayed, so she's going to switch times with Mark Haverford.

> W 창의적인 작가들을 위한 제5회 워크숍에 오신 모든 분들을 환영합니다. 여러분들을 위해 흥미로운 행사들로 가득한 멋진 하루가 준비되어 있습니다. 몇 분 후, 우리는 주에서 가장 유명한 시인 중 한 명인 Mary Lattimore의 짧은 강연으로 오늘 워크숍을 시작할 것입니다. 그녀는 창의적인 사고방식을 기르는 방법에 대해 이야기를 할 것입니다. 그것이 끝나면, 우리는 Ronald Devers의 말을 듣게 될텐데, 그는 에세이의 개요 작성에 관해 이야기할 것입니다. 하지만 일정표상 한 가지 변경 사항이 있습니다. Lisa Delacruz의 강연은 연기가 되어서, 그녀는 Mark Haverford와 시간대를 서로 바꾸게 될 것입니다.

annual 연례의, 연1회의 | **creative** 창의적인, 창의력이 있는 | **in store** 준비가 된 | **poet** 시인 | **develop** 발전시키다 | **mindset** 사고방식 | **chat** 이야기하다 | **outline** 개요 | **switch** 바꾸다, 전환하다

98 담화의 목적은 무엇인가?
(A) 관객들의 전면적인 참여를 요청하기 위해
(B) 기조 연설자를 소개하기 위해
(C) 사람들이 서명을 하도록 장려하기 위해
(D) 행사의 손님들을 환영하기 위해

full participation 전면적인 참여, 적극적인 참여 | **keynote speaker** 기조 연설자 | **encourage** 고무시키다, 격려하다

| 해설 | 대화의 첫 부분에서 화자는 참석자들에게 환영 인사를 건넨 후, 앞으로의 일정에 대해 이야기하고 있다. 따라서 보기 중 담화의 목적으로 볼 수 있는 것은 (D)이다.

99 Mary Lattimore는 누구인가?
(A) 소설가
(B) 창작 지도 교수
(C) 시인
(D) 주최자

host 주인, 주최자

| 해설 | 담화 중반부에서 화자는 그녀를 one of the best-known poets in the state라고 소개하고 있으므로 그녀의 직업은 (C)의 '시인'이다.

100 도표를 보아라. Lisa Delacruz는 몇 시에 강연을 할 것인가?
(A) 10시 30분에
(B) 11시 15분에
(C) 1시에
(D) 2시에

| 해설 | 담화의 마지막 부분에서 화자는 Lisa Delacruz의 강연 시간이 'Mark Haverford의 강연 시간과 서로 바뀔 것'(she's going to switch times with Mark Haverford)이라고 언급한다. 도표에서 Mark Haverford의 강연 시간은 2시에 시작된다고 적혀 있으므로, 결국 Lisa Delacruz가 강연을 하게 될 시간은 (D)의 '2시'가 된다.

● **PART 5** p.140

101 예산에 자금이 추가되지 않는다면, 그 프로젝트는 제때에 완료되지 못할 것이다.
(A) 연구실
(B) 예산
(C) 선거
(D) 제안

fund 자금, 재원 | **add** 더하다, 추가하다 | **budget** 예산 | **on time** 제때에, 정시에 | **election** 선거

| 해설 | 보기 중 funds(자금, 재원)가 추가될 수 있는 것은 (B)의 budget(예산)뿐이다.

102 내년도 마케팅 캠페인을 준비하기 위해서는 신차 생산에 관한 결정이 빨리 내려져야 한다.
(A) 준비하다
(B) 준비하는
(C) 준비할 것이다
(D) 준비하기 위해

| 해설 | 빠져 있는 문장 성분이 없으므로 빈칸에는 부사구를 이끌 수 있는 표현이 들어가야 한다. 보기 중 그러한 역할을 할 수 있는 것은 (D)의 to prepare로, 여기에서 to부정사는 부사적 용법 중 '목적'의 의미로 사용되었다.

103 시내에 새로운 호텔을 건설하는 일이 예상했던 것보다 오래 걸리고 있어서 예정보다 늦게 완공이 될 것이다.
(A) 건설하다
(B) 건설적인
(C) 건설
(D) 구성하는

behind schedule 예정보다 늦게

| 해설 | 빈칸에는 문장의 주어 역할을 하면서 on으로 시작하는 전치사구의 수식을 받을 수 있는 명사가 들어가야 한다. 따라서 정답은 (C)의 Construction이다. 참고로 (D)를 동명사로 보는 경우, 그 다음에는 동명사의 목적어 역할을 할 수 있는 명사가 이어져야 한다.

104 Hall 씨는 관광객들에게 시골에 있는 호텔보다 차라리 공항에서 가까운 호텔을 찾으라는 제안을 했다.
(A) ~에 반대하여
(B) ~에 따라
(C) 차라리 ~ 보다
(D) ~의 결과로

rather than 차라리 ~ 보다는 | **countryside** 시골

| 해설 | '공항에서 가까운 호텔'과 '시골에 있는 호텔'의 관계를 생각해 보면 보기 중에서 가장 자연스러운 문장을 완성시킬 수 있는 것은 (C)의 rather than(차라리 ~ 보다)임을 알 수 있다.

105 해외 지사로의 전근 신청서는 늦어도 11월 셋째 주 금요일까지 제출되어야 한다.
(A) 전근
(B) 옮겨진
(C) 이동할 수 있는
(D) 이동

overseas branch 해외 지사 | **transferable** 이동할 수 있는, 양도할 수 있는 | **transference** 이동

| 해설 | '해외 지사로의 전근'이라는 의미를 완성하기 위해서는 (A)의 transfer(전근)가 빈칸에 들어가야 한다. (D)의 transference도 '이동'이라는 뜻을 가지고 있지만, 이는 사물의 이동을 나타낼 때에만 쓰인다.

106 영업부 이사나 부사장인 Karen Wolf 중 한 사람이 직원 회의에 참석할 것이다.
(A) 그리고
(B) 혹은
(C) 또한
(D) 그래서

| 해설 | 'A와 B 중 하나'라는 의미는 either A or B 구문으로 나타낼 수 있다. 정답은 (B)의 or이다.

107 그 제품이 전 연령대의 사람들에게 매력적이어서 예상보다 높은 매출이 발생했다.
(A) 승인하다
(B) 간주하다
(C) 예상하다
(D) 해결하다

result in (결과로) ~이 되다 | **anticipate** 예상하다 | **resolve** 해결하다; 결심하다

| 해설 | '예상보다 높은 매출'이라는 의미가 완성되어야 자연스러운 문장이 될 수 있으므로 정답은 '예상하다'라는 의미를 가진 (C)의 anticipated이다.

108 온라인 상점에서 첫 번째 구매를 하는 모든 고객들은 주문품에 대해 15%의 할인을 받는다.
(A) 받다
(B) 기다리다
(C) 구입하다
(D) 교환하다

first-time 처음으로 해 보는

| 해설 | 15% off와 가장 자연스럽게 연결될 수 있는 동사를 찾도록 한다. '15%의 할인을 받다'라는 의미는 (A)의 receive를 이용하여 만들 수 있다.

109 성수기에는 투숙객들이 호텔에 예약 사항을 확인해 보아야 한다는 점이 강력히 권고된다.
(A) 확인하다
(B) 확인하는
(C) 확인했다
(D) 확인하기 위해

highly 매우 | **peak season** 성수기

| 해설 | suggest와 같이 제안이나 권고를 나타내는 동사의 목적어 역할을 하는 that절 내에서는 조동사 should가 사용된다. 하지만 이러한 should는 생략될 수 있기 때문에 빈칸에는 should confirm이나 confirm이 들어갈 수 있다. 따라서 보기 중 정답은 (A)이다.

110 Dynasty 호텔의 보수 공사는 늦어도 여름이 시작되기 전에 끝날 것이다.
(A) ~ 보다
(B) ~인 것
(C) ~할 때
(D) 그러한

renovation 수선, 보수 | **no later than** 늦어도 ~ 전에

| 해설 | '늦어도 ~ 전에'라는 의미는 no later than으로 나타낸다. 따라서 정답은 (A)이다.

> **☑ 700점 넘기 포인트** no later than이라는 어구의 뜻을 모르더라도 비교급이 사용되었다는 점에서 빈칸에는 than이 들어가야 한다는 점을 알 수 있다. 빈칸 앞에 비교급이 있다면 우선적으로 than이 빠져 있는지를, 빈칸 뒤에 than이 있다면 비교급이 빠져 있는지를 먼저 살피도록 하자.

111 일정표에 따르면, Harper 씨가 보이시 콘퍼런스에서 개회사를 할 것이다.
(A) 열다
(B) 시작
(C) 오프너
(D) 열려 있는

opening speech 개회사, 기조 연설

| 해설 | '개회사', '기조 연설'은 복합 명사인 opening speech로 나타낸다. 따라서 정답은 (B)의 opening이다.

112 두 회사 간의 합병이 끝나자마자, 몇몇 직원들이 해고될 것이라는 통보를 받았다.
(A) 접근하다
(B) 보고하다
(C) 통보하다
(D) 기대하다

merger 합병 | **notify** 통지하다, 알리다 | **lay off** 해고하다 | **approach** 접근하다

| 해설 | '합병의 결과로 직원들이 해고될 것이라는 통보를 받았다'는 의미가 완성되어야 한다. 따라서 정답은 '통보하다'라는 의미를 지닌 (C)의 notified이다.

113 관광객들이 자주 방문하는 시내 지역에 많은 기념품 상점들이 위치해 있다.
(A) ~할 때
(B) ~하는 것
(C) ~하는 방법
(D) 그때

numerous 많은 | **souvenir shop** 기념품 가게 | **commonly** 흔히, 자주

| 해설 | 빈칸에는 형용사절을 이끌면서 the part of the city를 수식할 수 있는 관계대명사가 들어가야 한다. 선행사가 사물이므로 빈칸에는 that이나 which가 들어갈 수 있다. 보기 중 여기에 해당하는 것은 (B)의 which이다.

114 Murrell 씨의 서명이 들어가면, 문서들은 법무팀에 보내질 것이다.
(A) 문서
(B) 다큐멘터리
(C) 기록된
(D) 기록하는

document 문서; 기록하다, 문서로 보관하다 | **take A to B** A를 B에 데리고 가다, A를 B로 보내다 | **documentary** 다큐멘터리, 기록물

| 해설 | 빈칸에는 관사 the의 수식을 받으면서 once가 이끄는 부사절의 주어 역할을 할 수 있는 명사가 들어가야 한다. 따라서 정답은 (A)와 (B) 중 하나인데, (B)의 documentary는 보통 '다큐멘터리 방송 프로그램'를 의미하므로 정답은 '문서'라는 의미를 가진 (A)의 documents이다. 빈칸 뒤의 동사가 have이기 때문에 단수형인 (B)는 오답임을 다시 한 번 확인할 수 있다.

115 악천후로 비행기편이 취소되자 많은 승객들은 하룻밤 동안 공항에 발이 묶였다.
(A) 탑승하다
(B) 기다리다
(C) 이동하다
(D) 발이 묶이다

stand 가닥, 줄; 발을 묶다, 움직이지 못하게 하다 | **overnight** 밤새, 하룻밤 동안 | **board** 탑승하다

| 해설 | 악천후로 인해 승객들이 어떻게 되었을지 생각해 보면 정답을 쉽게 찾을 수 있다. 정답은 (D)의 stranded인데, be stranded는 보통 '발이 묶이다' 혹은 '꼼짝 못하다'라는 뜻을 나타낸다.

116 Lakewood 씨는 부동산 중개업자가 보여 준 주택에 감명을 받아서 그곳 주택을 구입하기로 결심했다.
(A) 감명을 주다
(B) 감명을 받을 것이다
(C) 감명을 받았다
(D) 감명을 주었다

realtor 부동산 중개인 | property 재산; 부동산 | spot 장소, 자리

| 해설 | impress의 정확한 뜻은 '감명을 주다'이다. 내용상 Lakewood 씨가 '감명을 받은' 것이므로 정답은 수동태 형식을 갖춘 (C)의 was impressed이다. and 이후의 시제가 과거이므로 (B)의 will be impressed는 정답이 될 수 없다.

117 매장 매니저가 오늘 내로 가구를 사무실로 배달해 주겠다고 약속했다.
(A) ~까지
(B) ~ 동안
(C) ~에
(D) ~까지

| 해설 | '~까지 배달해 주겠다'는 의미를 나타내기 위해서는 빈칸에 (D)의 by가 들어가야 한다. 참고로 (B)의 for는 보통 '경과 시간' 앞에, (C)의 on은 '날짜'나 '요일' 앞에 쓰인다.

> ✓ 700점 넘기 포인트　전치사 by와 until은 모두 '~까지'라는 의미를 나타내지만, by는 '완료'의 뉘앙스를, until은 '계속'의 뉘앙스를 갖는다. 다음 두 문장의 의미 차이를 생각해 보자.
> They should finish their project by 5 o'clock tomorrow.
> (내일 5시전까지 마쳐야 한다)
> They should work on the project until 5 o'clock tomorrow.
> (내일 5시까지 일을 해야 한다)

118 연구에 참여한 사람들에게는 지역 상점에서 사용할 수 있는 상품권이 지급될 것이다.
(A) 참가자
(B) 참가의
(C) 참가하고 있는
(D) 참가하다

participate in ~에 참여하다 | gift certificate 상품권 | redeem 만회하다; 상품[현금]으로 바꾸다 | participant 참가자

| 해설 | 빈칸에는 관계대명사 who의 동사 역할을 할 수 있는 단어가 들어가야 한다. 따라서 정답은 (D)의 participate인데, participate in은 '~에 참여하다'라는 뜻이다.

119 매년 봄마다 Westside 건설은 여러 공사 현장에서 새로 생기는 직책에 사람들을 모집한다.
(A) 해고하다
(B) 전근시키다
(C) 모집하다
(D) 제의하다

fire 해고하다 | recruit (신입 직원을) 모집하다 | various 다양한 | worksite 일터, 작업 현장

| 해설 | for new positions라는 어구에 유의하면 보기 중 빈칸에 들어갈 가장 적절한 동사는 (C)의 recruits(모집하다)임을 쉽게 알 수 있다.

120 만약 마감 시간을 연장해야 한다면, 가능한 빨리 저희에게 알려 주십시오.
(A) 알리다
(B) 알리기 위해
(C) 알리고 있는
(D) 알려지다

extension 연장, 확장 | deadline 마감, 기한 | inform 알리다

| 해설 | 이 문장이 명령문이라는 점을 파악하면 정답은 동사 원형인 (A)의 inform임을 쉽게 알 수 있다. please 앞 부분은 if it should be necessary to receive an extension on the deadline이라는 가정법 절에서 if가 생략되어 있는 형태이다.

121 Worthy 씨는 언제 고용 계약서에 서명이 이루어질 것인지에 대해 전혀 아는 내색을 하지 않았다.
(A) 알다
(B) 지식
(C) 앎
(D) 알 수 있는

give indication of ~의 징후를 보이다, ~을 내색하다 | employment contract 고용 계약서 | knowledge 지식

| 해설 | 전치사 of에 유의하면 빈칸에는 명사가 들어가야 함을 알 수 있는데, (B)의 knowledge는 '지식'이라는 뜻으로 이 문장의 의미와는 어울리지 않고, 빈칸 다음에 when이 이끄는 명사절을 목적어로 받을 수도 없다. 따라서 정답은 know의 동명사 형태인 (C)의 knowing이다.

122 Travis Bean이 그 회사의 새로운 회계부 책임자로 임명되었다는 발표가 있었다.
(A) 고용하다
(B) 임명하다
(C) 제안하다
(D) 동의하다

announcement 발표 | name 지명하다, 임명하다

| 해설 | 문장의 의미상 빈칸에는 (A)의 hired와 (B)의 named가 들어갈 수 있을 것으로 보인다. 하지만 빈칸 이후의 the company's newest head of Accounting이 보어 역할을 하고 있다는 점에서 빈칸에는 (B)의 named가 들어가야 한다. 즉 that절 이하를 능동태 문장으로 바꾸어 보면 'They had named Travis Bean the company's newest head of Accounting.'이라는 5형식 문장이 만들어진다. 참고로 만약 빈칸 뒤에 as와 같은 단어가 있었다면 3형식 동사인 (A)의 hired가 정답이 될 것이다.

123 참석자 중 아무도 기조 연설자인 Judy Garcia가 아직 도착하지 않았다는 점을 알지 못했다.
(A) 아무도
(B) 아무도
(C) 많은
(D) 많은

attendee 참석자 | aware 알고 있는 | keynote speaker 기조 연설자

| 해설 | nobody나 none 모두 부정문에서 '아무도'라는 뜻을 나타내지만, of로 시작되는 전치사구와 함께 '~중에 아무도'라는 의미로 쓰일 수 있는 것은 none뿐이다. 따라서 정답은 (B)이다. 부정의 의미를 지닌 yet에 유의하면 (C)의 Many가 오답임이 분명해진다.

124 Limnos 주식회사는 다음 주 뉴올리언스에서 열리는 판매 전시회에서 최신 가전 제품들을 소개할 것이다.
(A) 소개했다
(B) 소개했다
(C) 소개할 것이다
(D) 소개될 것이다

latest 최신의 | appliance 가정용 기기

| 해설 | next week(다음 주)라는 부사구 때문에 빈칸에는 미래시제를 나타내는 동사가 들어가야 한다. 보기 중에서 미래의 의미를 나타낼 수 있는 것은 (C)와 (D)인데, 수동태 형식의 (C)는 답이 될 수 없다. 따라서 정답은 현재진행형으로 미래의 의미를 나타내고 있는 (C)의 is introducing이다.

125 노조 위원장인 Dirk Powers가 정치인에게 뇌물을 주었다는 혐의로 체포되었다.
(A) 뇌물
(B) 뇌물

(C) 뇌물을 받은
(D) 뇌물 수수

labor union 노동 조합 | **arrest** 체포하다 | **on suspicion of** ~의 혐의로 | **bribe** 뇌물; 뇌물을 주다. 매수하다 | **bribery** 뇌물 수수

| 해설 | 빈칸에는 making의 목적어 역할을 할 수 있는 명사가 들어가야 한다. 따라서 (A)와 (B)가 정답이 될 수 있는데, 빈칸 뒤의 to politicians(정치인들에게)라는 어구에 주의하면 빈칸에 들어갈 말은 단수 명사보다 복수 명사가 더 적합하다. 따라서 정답은 복수 명사인 (B)의 bribes가 된다.

126 불시 점검으로 다수의 공장 노동자들이 안전 규정을 지키지 않는다는 점이 드러났다.
(A) 경고하다
(B) 드러내다
(C) 의심하다
(D) 완료하다

surprise inspection 불시 점검 | **reveal** 드러내다, 밝히다 | **adhere to** ~을 고수하다; ~을 지키다 | **safety standard** 안전 기준, 안전 규정

| 해설 | surprise inspection(불시 점검)의 결과로 밝혀진 내용이 언급되고 있다. 따라서 (B)의 revealed가 빈칸에 들어가야 가장 자연스러운 문장이 완성된다.

127 Dawson 씨는 동료들에게 이사회의 임원이 되려는 자신의 시도를 지지해 달라고 설득했다.
(A) 선출하다
(B) 간주하다
(C) 접근하다
(D) 설득하다

persuade 설득하다 | **colleague** 동료 | **attempt** 시도 | **board of directors** 이사회

| 해설 | to support him in his attempt(자신의 시도를 지지해 달라)가 정답의 단서이다. 이와 가장 자연스럽게 어울릴 수 있는 동사는 '설득하다'라는 뜻의 (D)의 persuade이다.

128 승진과 상당히 많은 급여 인상을 제의받았음에도 불구하고, Lansing 씨는 퇴사를 해서 다른 회사에 입사했다.
(A) ~에도 불구하고
(B) 사실
(C) 그럼에도 불구하고
(D) ~에 관하여

sizable 상당히 큰, 상당히 많은 | **raise** 급여 인상 | **resign** 사임하다, 사퇴하다

| 해설 | 문장의 전반부 내용과 후반부의 내용이 서로 상반되는 의미를 나타내고 있으므로 빈칸에는 전치사인 (A)의 Despite가 들어가야 한다. (C) 역시 '그럼에도 불구하고'라는 유사한 뜻을 나타내지만, 이는 접속부사로서 부사구를 이끌 수 없다.

129 Weber 주식회사의 제품 설계에 대해 다수의 고객들이 불만을 제기하자 몇몇 엔지니어들이 교체되었다.
(A) 제기하고 있다
(B) 제기했다
(C) 제기했다
(D) 제기되었다

replace 교체하다 | **large numbers of** 많은, 다수의 | **file a complaint** 불만을 제기하다

| 해설 | 시제 일치에 유의하여 정답을 고르도록 한다. 주절에 과거 시제가 쓰였으므로 when이 이끄는 종속절에도 과거나 과거완료 시제가 사용되어야 한다. 따라서 (C)와 (D) 중에 하나가 정답인데, 수동태 문장이 쓰일 이유가 없으므로 정답은 (C)가 된다.

130 매장 관리자는 남성 의류 코너를 정문 바로 옆에 위치시키기 위해 매장의 레이아웃을 변경했다.
(A) 레이아웃
(B) 예산
(C) 광고
(D) 일정

layout 배치, 레이아웃

| 해설 | place가 정답의 단서이다. '남성 의류 코너를 정문 옆에 놓기 위해서' 무엇을 변경해야 할 것인지 생각해 보면 빈칸에 들어갈 단어는 (A)의 layout(배치, 레이아웃)임을 알 수 있다.

PART 6

p.144

[131-134]

공항에 새로운 터미널이 문을 엽니다

Springfield 국제 공항에서 최신 터미널이 곧 문을 열 것이라는 점을 알려 드리게 되어 기쁘게 생각합니다. 30개월의 공사 끝에, 제2터미널이 승객들을 전 세계 목적지로 보낼 준비를 마쳤습니다. 새 터미널은 서로 다른 9개의 항공사가 사용할 25개의 게이트를 갖추고 있습니다. 지역 저가 항공사인 Ace 항공이 10개 이상의 게이트를 통제할 것이기 때문에, 터미널의 주요한 사용자가 될 것입니다. 제2터미널은 매일 수천 명의 승객들을 처리할 수 있을 것입니다. 또한 면세점과 수많은 프랜차이즈 식당을 포함하여, 온갖 종류의 시설들도 들어설 것입니다. 이들은 매년 수백만 달러의 수입을 거두어 들일 것으로 예상됩니다. 게이트는 또한 전 세계에서 가장 큰 여객기들을 수용할 수 있을 것입니다. 터미널은 4월 10일 목요일에 문을 열 것으로 예정되어 있습니다. 오전 7시에 조촐한 기념식이 열릴 것이며 그 후에는 승객들이 비행기편을 이용할 수 있도록 게이트로의 입장이 허가될 것입니다.

be proud to ~하게 되어 자랑스럽게 생각하다 | **terminal** 터미널 | **destination** 목적지 | **airline** 항공사 | **occupant** 사용자, 점유자 | **duty-free shop** 면세점 | **handle** 다루다, 처리하다 | **airliner** 여객기 | **so that ~ can** ~하기 위하여

131 (A) ~을 넘어
(B) ~ 안에
(C) ~ 주변에
(D) ~ 안에

| 해설 | in the world라는 표현과 around the world라는 표현 모두 자주 사용되는 것들이기 때문에 주의를 요한다. 만약 destinations 앞에 various와 같은 형용사가 있다면 in the world가 더 적합한 표현이 될 것인데, 그 이유는 around라는 전치사에 various라는 의미가 이미 내포되어 있기 때문이다. 하지만 이 문장에서는 destinations가 단독으로 쓰였으므로 (C)의 around가 보다 자연스러운 의미를 완성시킨다.

132 (A) 영장류
(B) 주요한
(C) 준비가 된
(D) 기폭제

primate 영장류 | **primed** 준비가 된 | **priming** 기폭제

| 해설 | occupant(점유자, 사용자)를 가장 자연스럽게 수식할 수 있는 단어를 고르도록 한다. 정답은 (B)의 primary(주요한)이다.

133 (A) 승객들은 이미 그곳에서 판매되는 제품의 질에 찬사를 보내고 있습니다.
(B) 게다가, 게이트는 소규모 통근용 비행기를 위해 특별히 설계되었

89

(C) 연간 수입으로 수백만 달러를 거두어 들일 것으로 예상됩니다.
(D) 하지만 승객들이 식사를 하거나 쇼핑을 할 수 있는 곳은 아직 없습니다.

compliment 칭찬하다 | **specifically** 특별하게

| 해설 | 빈칸 앞 문장에서 면세점 등 상업 시설에 대해 이야기하고 있으므로 그 다음에는 상업 시설의 경제적 효과에 대한 내용이 이어지는 것이 자연스럽다. 따라서 정답은 (C)이며, (A)는 현재로서는 알 수 없는 내용을, (B)는 언급되지 않은 내용을, (D)는 사실과 다른 내용을 언급하고 있다.

134 (A) 부과하다
(B) 허가하다
(C) 발송하다
(D) 예약하다

dispatch 발송하다 | **book** 예약하다

| 해설 | '게이트로 가기 위해서는'(so that they can start going to their gates) 승객들이 어떠한 절차를 거쳐야 하는지 생각해 보면 정답을 쉽게 찾을 수 있다. 정답은 '(입장을) 허가하다'라는 뜻인 (B)의 admitted이다.

[135-138]

받는 사람: Bluebird Tower의 입주자 전체
보낸 사람: 건물 관리인 Cliff Samuels
제목: 임대료 인상
날짜: 8월 2일

9월 1일부로 건물의 임대료가 모두 10% 인상될 것이라는 점을 아시기 바랍니다. 이번 인상은 아파트를 임대하고 있는 개인, 그리고 사무용 및 상업용 공간을 임대하고 계신 모든 분들께 적용됩니다. 임대료는 최근 공공요금의 상승을 반영하기 위해 인상될 것입니다. 제가 영업일 기준으로 5일 이내에 모든 입주자분들께 새로운 계약서를 보내 드릴 것입니다. 여기에 서명하셔서 늦어도 8월 15일까지 계약서를 1층에 있는 제 사무실로 다시 보내 주셔야 합니다. 인상된 임대료를 납부하고 싶지 않은 분들께서는 8월 31일까지 공간을 비워 주셔야 합니다. 보증금은 귀하의 공간에 손상된 부분이 없는지를 저희 관리실에서 확인하는 대로 반환해 드릴 것입니다. 임대료 인상이나 기타 신경이 쓰이는 점에 대해서는 자유롭게 저에게 말씀해 주셔도 좋습니다. 정규 근무 시간에 856-4584로 제게 전화를 주십시오.

tenant 입주자, 세입자 | **as of** ~일자로 | **rent** 임대료, 월세 | **apply to** ~에 적용되다 | **commercial** 상업의 | **contract** 계약(서) | **vacate** 비우다 | **premise** 부지, 용지 | **security deposit** 보증금 | **on one's mind** 마음 속에 둔, 마음에 걸리는 | **regular** 정규의

135 (A) 그리고
(B) 그래서
(C) 혹은
(D) 저것

| 해설 | both A and B(A와 B 모두) 구문을 알고 있어야 한다. 정답은 (A)의 and이다.

136 (A) 안타깝게도 현재 임대를 할 수 있는 장소는 없습니다.
(B) 원하지 않는 이상 여러분들 중 누구도 새로운 임대 계약서에 서명할 필요는 없습니다.
(C) 모든 입주자들은 이번 주 내로 지불하고 있는 임대료에 관해 재협상을 해야 합니다.
(D) 임대료는 최근 공공요금의 상승을 반영하기 위해 인상될 것입니다.

lease 임대차 계약 | **renegotiate** 재협상하다

| 해설 | 빈칸 앞 부분에서는 임대료 인상에 대한 안내를, 빈칸 뒷부분에서는 새로운 계약서 발송에 대한 안내를 하고 있기 때문에 빈칸에는 인상 이유를 밝힌 (D)가 들어가는 것이 바람직하다. (A)는 임대료 인상과 무관한 내용이며 (B)는 새로운 계약서를 소개한 후에 이어질 수 있는 내용이고 (C)의 재협상은 공지에서 찾아볼 수 없는 사항이다.

137 (A) 제거하다
(B) 팔다
(C) 수리하다
(D) 비우다

remove 제거하다, 없애다

| 해설 | 건물 관리인이 '임대료 인상을 원하지 않는 사람들'(those of you who do not wish to pay the higher rent)에게 요구하는 것이 무엇인지를 생각해 보면 정답을 쉽게 찾을 수 있다. 정답은 '비우다'라는 뜻인 (D)의 vacate이다.

138 (A) 반환되었다
(B) 반환했다
(C) 반환될 것이다
(D) 반환되었다

| 해설 | 동사 return의 알맞은 형태를 묻는 문제이다. 주어가 사물인 '보증금'(your security deposit)이라는 점에서 수동태가, as soon as가 이끄는 부사절 내에서 현재시제가 사용되고 있다는 점에서 미래시제가 필요하다. 따라서 정답은 이 두 가지 조건을 만족시키는 (C)이다.

[139-142]

3월 15일
친애하는 Auto Mechanics 협회 회원들께,

Auto Mechanics 협회(AAM)에서 9월 14일과 15일에 연례 콘퍼런스를 개최할 예정입니다. 이번 행사는 테네시의 멤피스에서 열릴 것입니다. 이곳은 작년 행사 장소와 같은 곳입니다. 작년에 콘퍼런스가 큰 성공을 거두었기 때문에, 한 번 더 멤피스에서 행사를 가져야 한다는 점이 AAM 임원진에 의해 만장일치로 결정되었습니다.

올해 콘퍼런스에서는, 연설, 워크숍, 그리고 세일즈 페어 등 다수의 행사들이 열릴 것입니다. 기조 연설자는 저명한 정비 기사인 Robert McGuffin이 될 것인데, 그는 클래식 차량 수리의 전문가입니다. AAM의 회원으로서, 여러분들께서는 할인이 적용된 등록비인 75달러만 지불하시면 됩니다. 이로써 콘퍼런스에서 열리는 모든 행사에 참가하실 수 있습니다. 일부 항공사와 호텔들은 저희 회원들에게 할인을 제공해 줄 것입니다. 그에 대해 더 많은 정보를 알고 싶으시면 (405) 326-8695로 전화를 주십시오. 9월에 뵙게 되기를 바라겠습니다.

Tim Matterhorn 드림
Auto Mechanics 협회장

location 위치 | **tremendous** 막대한 | **unanimously** 만장일치로 | **executive staff** 임원, 간부 | **a large number of** 많은 | **mechanic** 정비공 | **antique** 골동품 | **be entitled to** ~할 자격을 얻다 | **registration rate** 등록비 | **access** 접근

139 (A) 성공하다
(B) 성공
(C) 연속
(D) 계속되는

succeed 성공하다; 잇다, 계승하다 | **succession** 연속 | **succeedding** 계속해서 일어나는, 계속되는

| 해설 | succeed는 '성공하다'라는 뜻과 '잇다', '계승하다'라는 뜻을 갖고 있는데, 각각의 명사형은 success(성공)와 succession(연속, 계승)이다. 여기에서는 '성공'이라는 뜻인 (B)success가 빈칸에 들어가야 자연스러운 문장이 완성된다.

140 (A) 유명한
(B) 모조품
(C) 초보자
(D) 무능한

imitation 모방, 모조품 | **novice** 초보자 | **incompetent** 무능한

| 해설 | '기조 연설자'(keynote speaker)의 자격을 나타낼 수 있는 단어는 (A)의 famed(유명한)뿐이다.

141 (A) 제외되다
(B) 회피되다
(C) 자격이 있다
(D) 보고되다

| 해설 | '~할 자격이 있다'라는 표현은 be entitled to로 나타낸다. 따라서 정답은 (C)이다. 참고로 entitle은 원래 '~할 자격을 부여하다'라는 뜻의 동사이다.

142 (A) 행사에 참석해 주셔서 감사합니다.
(B) 모든 사람들이 멋진 시간을 보냈습니다.
(C) 9월에 뵙게 되기를 바라겠습니다.
(D) 이 문제와 관련된 전화 통화는 무시될 것입니다.

| 해설 | 초청장의 마지막 인사로 올 수 있는 문장을 생각해 보자. 정답은 (C)이고, (A)와 (B)는 행사를 마친 후에 사용될 수 있는 문장이다.

[143-146]

올해의 펄 시민이 지명되다

펄 (12월 28일) — 어젯밤 시청에서 열린 시상식에서 Jason O'Brien이 Anna Harper 시장에 의해 올해의 시민으로 지명되었다. O'Brien 씨는 어렸을 때 시내로 이사온 이후 40년 넘게 펄에서 살고 있는데, 올해 여러 번 기사감이 되고 있다. 먼저, 봄에 토네이도가 시를 휩쓸었을 때, O'Brien 씨는 주민들을 규합해 도움이 필요한 사람들을 구조했다. 그의 노력으로 20명 이상의 사람들이 무너진 주택에서 구조되었다. 그는 또한 시의 구호 활동을 위해 많은 돈을 기부하였다. 여름에 Red 강이 범람하여 도시 절반이 2피트 수위의 물에 잠겼을 때 그는 다시 한 번 구조 활동을 벌였다. 마지막으로 O'Brien 씨는 지역 주민 센터의 설립을 위해 2백만 달러를 제공했는데, 지금부터 14개월 후 공사가 완료되면 주민들은 다양한 레저 활동을 즐길 수 있게 될 것이다. Harper 시장에 따르면, 그 외의 누구도 수상자로 고려되지 않았다.

name 지명하다 | **be in the news** 기사감이 되다 | **tornado** 토네이도 | **sweep through** ~을 휩쓸다 | **organize** 조직하다 | **rescue** 구조하다 | **relief effort** 구호 활동 | **bank** 둑 | **go for** ~을 좋아하다 | **various** 다양한 | **leisure activity** 레저 활동

143 (A) 추천하다
(B) 보고하다
(C) 지명하다
(D) 진술하다

nomiate 추천하다, 지명하다 | **state** 진술하다

| 해설 | (A)의 nominate와 (C)의 name 모두 '지명하다'라는 뜻을 나타내지만, nominate는 주로 '후보자를 지명하다', '후보로 추천하다'라는 뜻을 갖는다. 이 문장에서는 후보가 아니라 '수상자의 이름을 발표하다'라는 의미가 완성되어야 하기 때문에 정답은 (C)가 된다.

144 (A) 그는 홍수가 시 전체에 영향을 미치는 것을 막은 팀에 소속되어 있었다.
(B) 그의 노력으로 20명 이상의 사람들이 무너진 주택에서 구조되었다.
(C) 그 사람들은 토네이도에 관해 지역 주민들에게 경고를 해서 주민들을 안전하게 만들었다.
(D) 그가 제공한 돈은 화재로 소실된 주택을 수리하는데 도움을 주었다.

stop A from B A가 B하는 것을 막다 | **warn** 경고하다 | **lead A to B** A를 B로 이끌다 | **safety** 안전

| 해설 | 빈칸 앞뒤 문장을 살펴볼 때, 빈칸에는 앞 문장에 대한 부연 설명이나 그에 관한 구체적인 사례가 들어가는 것이 바람직하다. 따라서 정답은 (B)이다. (A)의 '홍수' 이야기는 이후에 언급되고 있는 내용이며 (B)의 내용을 '구조 활동'으로 보기는 힘들다. (D)의 '화재'는 기사와 상관이 없는 내용이다.

145 (A) 기부하다
(B) 예금하다
(C) 투자하다
(D) 계약하다

deposit 예금하다 | **invest** 투자하다 | **contract** 계약하다

| 해설 | '많은 돈'(a large amount of money)이라는 목적어와 '구조 활동에'(to relief efforts)라는 부사구와 자연스럽게 어울릴 수 있는 동사는 보기 중 (A)의 donated(기부하다)뿐이다.

146 (A) 모두가
(B) 어떤 사람도
(C) 누군가
(D) 아무도

| 해설 | '(O'Brien 씨를 제외한) 그 밖의 누구도 수상자로 고려되지 않았다'는 의미를 나타내기 위해서는 빈칸에 부정어가 들어가야 한다. 따라서 정답은 (D)의 nobody이다.

PART 7

p.148

[147-148]

받는 사람: customerservice@perseusmart.com
보낸 사람: amcclain@personalmail.com
제목: 프리포트 매장
날짜: 7월 11일

관계자님께,

제 이름은 Alice McClain입니다. 어제, 제 남편과 저는 프리포트에 있는 Perseus 마트를 방문했는데, 그곳에서 저희는 그곳 직원과 관련하여 불쾌한 경험을 하게 되었습니다. 저희는 가습기를 사려 했고 Tim Nelson에게 도움을 요청했습니다. 겨울 동안 건조하지 않은 지역에서 이사를 왔기 때문에, 저희는 기기의 기본적인 기능과 작동법에 대해 많은 질문을 했습니다. Tim은 우리 질문에 대답을 하지 못했을 뿐만 아니라, 몇몇 답변을 통해서는 모순되는 말을 했습니다. 제 남편이 그러한 점을 지적하자, Tim은 무례하게 굴었고, 자신이 아니라, 저희가 제품에 대해 몰라서 잘못 생각하고 있는 것이라고 말했습니다. 저희는 즉시 매장을 떠나 맞은 편에 있는 Electromart로 갔는데, 그곳에서는 정중한 대우를 받았고 질문에 대한 답도 얻을 수 있었습니다. 저희는 올버니에 있었을 때처럼 저희가 Perseus 마트의 단골 고객이 되기를 기대했지만, 그럴 수는 없을 것으로 보입니다.

그럼 이만 줄이겠습니다.
Alice McClain

humidifier 가습기 | **function** 기능 | **operate** 작동시키다, 가동시키다 | **contradict oneself** 모순되는 말을 하다, 자가당착에 빠지다 | **point out** ~을 지적하다 | **rude** 무례한, 버릇없는 | **insinuate** 넌지시 말하다, 암시하다 | **fault** 잘못 | **loyal customer** 단골 고객 | **be the case** 사실이 그러하다

147 McClain 씨는 왜 이메일을 작성했는가?
(A) 그녀가 받은 서비스에 대해 불만을 표시하기 위해
(B) Perseus 마트에서 판매한 제품에 대해 문의하기 위해
(C) 프리포트 내 Perseus 마트의 위치를 알기 위해
(D) 직원의 행동에 대해 칭찬하기 위해

| 해설 | 이메일의 시작 부분에서 이메일을 작성한 이유가 '직원과 관련된 불쾌한 경험'(an unpleasant experience involving an employee there) 때문이라는 점을 알 수 있다. 이후로도 매장 직원의 잘못에 대해 설명하고 있으므로 정답은 (A)가 된다.

148 이메일에서 언급되어 있는 것은 무엇인가?
(A) McClain 씨는 또 다시 Perseus 마트를 방문할 계획이다.
(B) Electromart는 Perseus 마트보다 가격이 저렴하다.
(C) McClain 씨는 올버니에서 프리포트로 이사를 왔다.
(D) Tim Nelson은 Perseus 마트의 매니저이다.

| 해설 | 이메일의 마지막 문장에서 McClain 씨는 Perseus 마트를 다시 방문하지 않을 것이라고 썼기 때문에 (A)는 사실과 다른 내용이며 (B)는 언급된 바 없는 사항이다. Tim Nelson은 매장 직원의 이름이므로, (D) 역시 잘못된 내용이다. 따라서 정답은 (C)인데, McClain 씨는 이메일의 후반부에서 자신이 올버니에서 이사를 왔음을 암시하고 있다.

[149-150]

Harvey's Home Appliances에서 세일을 실시합니다!

이번 주 토요일인 9월 24일, Harvey's Home Appliances가 처음으로 문을 열 예정입니다. 저희는 Wellman 극장 옆의 Grandview 쇼핑몰 2층에 위치해 있습니다. 방문하셔서, 냉장고, 전자레인지, 오븐, 식기세척기, 토스터, 그리고 커피메이커를 포함하여, 최신 가전 제품들을 살펴보십시오. 개업을 축하하기 위해, 150달러 이상의 물건을 구매하시는 선착순 20명의 고객분들께서는 30%의 할인을 받게 되실 것입니다. 그 외에도, 저희는 저녁 6시 30분에 신제품인 Jenkins 냉장고가 경품으로 걸린 추첨 행사를 실시할 것입니다. 구매를 하시는 모든 고객분들께서는 자동으로 응모가 되실 것입니다. 저희는 오전 9시에 문을 열 것이며 오후 7시 30분에 문을 닫을 것입니다. 반드시 이번 특별 행사를 놓치지 마십시오.

for the first time 처음으로, 최초로 | **latest** 최신의 | **home appliance** 가전제품 | **dishwasher** 식기세척기 | **on top of** ~이외에 | **hold a drawing** 추첨을 하다 | **automatically** 자동적으로

149 세일의 목적은 무엇인가?
(A) 매장이 폐업할 것이다.
(B) 기념일을 축하할 것이다.
(C) 작년 물품들이 처분되어야 한다.
(D) 매장이 개장을 할 것이다.

go out of business 폐점하다, 파산하다 | **anniversary** 기념일

| 해설 | 첫 문장에서 Harvey's Home Appliances라는 매장이 '개업 할 것'(going to be opening our doors for the first time)이라는 소식을 전한 후 그에 따른 세일을 안내하고 있다. 따라서 세일의 목적은 (D)로 볼 수 있다.

150 9월 24일에 구매를 한 모든 고객은 무엇을 받게 될 것인가?
(A) 할인
(B) 당첨 기회
(C) 상품권
(D) 쿠폰

win a prize 상을 타다, 당첨 되다 | **gift certificate** 상품권

| 해설 | 광고 후반부에서 경품 추첨에 대한 안내를 한 후, 개업 당일 구매 고객은 '여기에 자동으로 응모가 될 것이다'(All customers who make a purchase will be automatically entered.)라고 설명한다. 따라서 정답은 (B)이다. 참고로 (A)의 '할인'은 일정 금액 이상을 소비한 '선착순 20명의 고객들만' 받을 수 있는 혜택이다.

[151-152]

Davis, Erica   9:45 A.M.
Alicia, 어려운 부탁이 하나 있어요.

Chin, Alicia   9:46 A.M.
무엇이 필요한가요?

Davis, Erica   9:48 A.M.
저는 Hammer Engineering의 Swanson 씨를 만나러 가고 있는 중이에요. 하지만 제 책상 위에 있는 보고서를 가져 와야 한다는 것을 완전히 잊고 있었어요.

Chin, Alicia   9:49 A.M.
제가 가져다 주기를 원하는 것은 아니죠, 그런가요? 저는 사무실에서 보고서를 작성하느라 바쁘거든요.

Davis, Erica   9:51 A.M.
아니에요, 하지만 첫 네 페이지를 스캔해서 제게 이메일로 보내 줄 수 있나요? 제가 회의에 가기 전에 카피 센터에 들를 수 있을 거예요.

Chin, Alicia   9:53 A.M.
문제가 되지는 않겠군요. 언제까지 필요한가요? Chatterley 씨가 원하는 것을 제가 끝낼 때까지 기다려 줄 수 있나요?

Davis, Erica   9:54 A.M.
빠를수록 좋아요. 회의가 10시 30분에 시작하거든요.

huge 거대한, 큰 | **favor** 부탁 | **totally** 완전히 | **scan** 살피다; 스캔하다 | **copy center** 카피 센터(간단한 사무 업무를 할 수 있도록 마련된 공간)

151 오전 9시 49분에, Chin 씨는 왜 "You don't need me to deliver it, do you"라고 적었는가?
(A) Davis 씨를 만날 시간이 없다는 점을 암시하기 위해
(B) 물건을 배달해 달라는 요청을 거절하기 위해
(C) 물건 배달은 자신의 업무 사항에 포함되지 않는다는 점을 지적하기 위해
(D) Davis 씨와 어디에서 만나야 하는지를 묻기 위해

turn down ~을 거절하다 | **job description** 직무 해설서 | **point out** 가리키다, 지적하다

| 해설 | 물건을 잊고 나왔다는 말에 대한 반응이다. 주어진 문장의 바로 뒷문장을 살펴보면, '바빠서 가져다 줄 시간이 없다'는 의사를 표시하고 있기 때문에, 주어진 문장의 의미는 (A)로 볼 수 있다. Davis 씨가 직접적으로 '요청'을 한 것은 아니므로 (B)를 정답으로 선택해서는 안 된다.

152 Chin 씨는 이다음에 무엇을 할 것인가?
(A) 이메일을 확인한다
(B) Chatterley 씨를 방문한다
(C) 문서를 스캔한다
(D) 회의에 참석한다

| 해설 | 요청 사항이 '보고서의 일부를 스캔해서 이메일로 보내달라'(would you mind scanning the first four pages and e-mailing them to me)는 것이므로 Chin 씨가 하게 될 일은 (C)이다.

[153-155]

도시 가스 점검을 실시합니다

7월 10일과 11일 오전 7시와 9시 사이에 그린우드 주민들의 가스 계량기를 대상으로 정기 점검이 있을 예정입니다. 점검은, 반년마다 이루어지는데, Elm 가와 Pike 로 사이에 위치한 주택들과 12번가의 동쪽과 28번가의 서쪽에 있는 주택들을 대상으로 실시될 것입니다. 점검을 받게 될 주택의 주민분들께서는 인도에서 가스 계량기까지의 도로를 깨끗하고 안전하게 만들어 줌으로써 협조를 하셔야 하는데, 가스 계량기는 주택의 측면에 설치되어 있습니다. 모든 방해물들은 치워져야 하고, 개와 기타 동물들은 줄에 묶여야 하며, 울타리는 잠기지 않고 열려 있어야 합니다. (이에 따르지 않음으로써 도시 가스 직원들로 하여금 자신의 업무를 하지 못하게 만드는 주민들께는 벌금이 부과될 것입니다.) 도시 가스 담당자들이 예고 없이 도착할 수도 있습니다. 시 규정에 따라, 가스 회사 직원들은 점검을 목적으로 사유지에 출입할 수 있습니다. 하지만, 항상 거주지에 들어갈 수 있는 것은 아닙니다. 더 많은 정보를 원하시면 849-1042로 전화를 주십시오.

routine inspection 정기 점검 | **gas meter** 가스 계량기 | **biannually** 반년 마다 | **conduct** 실시하다, 실행하다 | **cooperate** 협동하다, 협조하다 | **path** 길, 통로 | **affix** 부착하다, 붙이다 | **obstacle** 방해물, 장애물 | **official** 공무원, 관리 | **without notice** 통보 없이, 예고 없이 | **regulation** 규정 | **private property** 사유 재산 | **for the purpose of** ~을 목적으로

153 점검은 얼마나 자주 실시되는가?
(A) 매달
(B) 4개월마다
(C) 6개월마다
(D) 매년

| 해설 | biannually(반년마다)라는 단어를 알고 있으면 쉽게 풀 수 있는 문제이다. 정답은 (C)의 '6개월마다'이다.

154 주민들은 무엇을 할 것을 요구받는가?
(A) 계량기 문제를 도시 가스에 보고한다
(B) 담당자들이 계량기를 점검하는 것을 용이하게 만든다
(C) 가스 계량기 아래에 가스 사용량을 기록해 둔다
(D) 마당에 애완 동물이 있다는 점을 알리는 표지판을 세운다

usage 사용 | **put up** ~을 세우다 | **sign** 표지판, 사인 | **pet** 애완 동물

| 해설 | 공지는 주민들에게 '계량기로 이어지는 통로를 정비해 달라'(by creating a clear and safe path from the sidewalk to the gas meter)는 협조를 구하면서, 구체적으로 도로 청소, 애완 동물 관리, 그리고 잠금 장치에 대한 이야기를 꺼내고 있다. 따라서 주민들이 요구받은 사항은 (B)이다.

155 [1], [2], [3], 그리고 [4]로 표시된 위치 중에 다음 문장이 들어가기에 가장 알맞은 곳은 어디인가?
"이에 따르지 않음으로써 도시 가스 직원들로 하여금 자신의 업무를 하지 못하게 만드는 주민들께는 벌금이 부과될 것입니다."
(A) [1]
(B) [2]
(C) [3]
(D) [4]

| 해설 | '따르지 않는'(who fail to comply) 주민들이 '무엇'을 따르지 않는 주민인지 생각해 봄으로써 정답을 찾을 수 있다. 여기서 '무엇'이란 도로를 청소하고, 애완 동물에게 목줄을 채우고, 잠금 장치를 해제하는 것이므로, 주어

진 문장은 (C)의 [3] 위치에 들어가야 가장 자연스러운 문맥이 완성된다.

[156-158]

Robert Shaver
Magnolia 대로 491번지
롬, 조지아
8월 3일

친애하는 Robert Shaver에게,

축하합니다! 당신이 7월 Knight's Home Repair Warehouse의 이달의 직원으로 지명되었습니다. 이 상은 매장 매니저들의 투표로 결정됩니다. 당신은 만장일치로 수상자로 선정되었습니다. 또한, 가장 최근의 고객 만족도 조사에서, 가장 친절하고 가장 많은 도움을 준 직원으로 당신 이름이 리스트의 가장 상단에 적혀 있습니다. 우리 Knight's Home Repair Warehouse는 당신의 노고와 의지를 자랑스럽게 생각합니다. 보상으로, 당신은 8월 내내 매장 앞 주차 공간을 사용할 수 있으며, 8월 10일 금요일을 유급 휴가로 보낼 수 있습니다. 또한 당신이 선택한 (100달러 이하의) 제품도 받게 될 것입니다. 우리가 판매하는 모든 제품 중에서 선택이 가능합니다. 정문 옆에 당신의 사진을 걸고 싶기 때문에, 가능한 빨리 Betty Smith를 찾아 주십시오. 사진을 찍을 때에는 회사 셔츠를 입고 있어야 합니다. 다시 한 번 축하를 드리며, 우수한 직원이 되어 주어서 고맙습니다. 앞으로 당신으로부터 더 큰 일을 기대하게 될 것입니다.

David Knight 드림
Knight's Home Repair Warehouse 사장

determine 결정하다 | **vote** 투표 | **unanimously** 만장일치로 | **customer satisfaction survey** 고객 만족도 조사 | **be proud of** ~을 자랑스럽게 생각하다 | **reward** 보상, 보답 | **paid holiday** 유급 휴가 | **hang** 걸다, 매달다 | **outstanding** 뛰어난, 탁월한

156 편지에 따르면, Shaver 씨에 대해 사실인 것은 무엇인가?
(A) 그는 2년 동안 Knight's Home Repair Warehouse에서 일했다.
(B) 그는 경영진으로 고용되어 있다.
(C) 그는 7월 수상자로서 모든 사람들의 표를 얻었다.
(D) 그는 최근에 고객 만족도 조사를 실시하는데 도움을 주었다.

| 해설 | 편지 초반부의 내용을 통해 Shaver 씨는 '만장일치로'(unanimously) 7월의 '이달의 직원'(the employee of the month)으로 선정되었음을 알 수 있다. 따라서 정답은 (C)이다.

157 Shaver 씨가 수상을 이유로 받지 않는 것은 무엇인가?
(A) 상금
(B) 무료 상품
(C) 주차 공간
(D) 일일 휴가

| 해설 | Shaver 씨가 받게 될 것은 100달러 이하의 제품, 8월 한 달간의 주차 공간, 그리고 하루짜리 유급 휴가이다. 하지만 여기에 (A)의 '상금'은 포함되어 있지 않다.

158 Smith 씨에 대해 무엇이 암시되어 있는가?
(A) 그녀가 Shaver 씨의 사진을 찍을 것이다.
(B) 그녀는 홍보부에서 일을 한다.
(C) 그녀는 이전 수상자이다.
(D) 그녀는 Knight 씨와 긴밀하게 협조한다.

| 해설 | 편지 후반에서 Knight 씨는 Shaver 씨에게 Betty Smith를 찾아가라고 한 후, 'You need to wear your company shirt when you take the photo.'라고 당부한다. 이를 통해 Betty Smith라는 사람이 사진 촬영을 담당

할 것이라고 추측할 수 있으므로 정답은 (A)가 된다.

[159-161]

Pandemonium 부동산 중개업소
Dobson 가 409번지
메사, 애리조나 85204
(805) 281-5632

Pandemonium 부동산 중개업소는 메사 내 최고의 매물을 보유하고 있습니다. 이번 주에 매물로 나온 주택들을 확인해 보십시오:

Guadalupe 로 32번지 – 침실 4개, 욕실 3개; 최근에 주방을 새로 꾸밈; 수영장이 딸린 커다란 뒷마당; 마당에 오렌지 나무와 레몬 나무가 몇 그루 있음; 인근 초등학교 및 고등학교로부터 도보 5분거리; 320,000달러

Desert 가 483번지 – 침실 2개, 욕실 1개; 울타리가 쳐져 있는 마당; 골프장 주변의 조용한 지역; 작은 집을 원하는 은퇴자에게 적합; 205,000달러

Erickson 로 904번지 – 침실 3개, 욕실 2개; 커다란 주방; 태양 전지판에 의해 모든 전기가 공급됨; 뒷마당에 수영장 및 온수 욕조가 있음; 사생활이 크게 보장됨; 상점가 근처에 위치; 380,000달러

Hidalgo 길 1954번지 – 4개의 침실, 2개의 욕실; 커다란 앞마당과 뒷마당; Superstition 고속도로 옆; 업무 지구와 가까움; 428,000달러

더 많은 목록을 원하시면, www.pandemoniumrealestate.com을 방문해 주십시오. 저희 직원들은 여러분들이 꿈꾸는 주택을 찾아 드릴 준비가 되어 있습니다. 전 과정을 통해 도움을 드릴 것입니다. 주 밖에서 이사를 하신다고요? 걱정하지 마십시오. 이주를 하는데 저희가 도움을 드릴 수 있습니다. 수많은 분들께 해 드렸던 일이니까요.

go on sale 판매하다 | **refurbish** 새로 꾸미다 | **fenced-in** 울타리가 쳐진 | **retiree** 은퇴자 | **downsize** 줄이다, 축소하다 | **solar panel** 태양 전지판 | **hot tub** 온수 욕조 | **privacy** 사생활, 프라이버시 | **shopping district** 상가, 상가 지구 | **business district** 사업 지구, 업무 지구 | **settle** 정착하다

159 이 광고는 어디에서 찾아볼 수 있을 것 같은가?
(A) 지역 신문에서
(B) 경제 잡지에서
(C) 전국지에서
(D) 주민 자치 센터의 소식지에서

| 해설 | 메사라는 도시에 있는 부동산 중개업소의 광고이다. 따라서 (A)의 '지역 신문'을 정답으로 생각할 수도 있지만, 광고 마지막 부분의 'Moving from out of state? Don't worry. We can help you get settled.'라는 부분에 주의하면 (C)의 '전국지'에 실려 있을 가능성이 훨씬 더 높다.

160 어린 아이들이 있는 가정은 어떤 주택에 가장 큰 관심을 가질 것 같은가?
(A) Erickson 로 904번지
(B) Hidalgo 길 1954번지
(C) Guadalupe 로 32번지
(D) Desert 가 483번지

| 해설 | 아이들이 있으면 '학교와의 거리'가 주택 구입을 결정하는데 큰 요인으로 작용할 수 있으므로 (C)의 'Guadalupe 로 32번지' 주택이 가장 매력적으로 보일 것이다.

161 매매할 수 있는 다른 주택에 대해 알아 보려면 어떻게 할 것이 권장되는가?
(A) 전화 번호로 전화를 함으로써
(B) 직접 중개업소를 방문함으로써
(C) 편지를 작성함으로써
(D) 웹사이트를 방문함으로써

| 해설 | 마지막 단락의 첫 번째 문장, 'For more listings, visit www.pandemoniumrealestate.com.'에서 더 많은 매물 정보는 웹사이트에서 확인이 가능하다는 점을 알 수 있다. 따라서 정답은 (D)이다.

[162-164]

받는 사람: Peter Carter 〈pcarter@worldmail.com〉
보낸 사람: William Folsom 〈willfolsom345@viscount.com〉
제목: 지원
날짜: 9월 28일

친애하는 Mr. Carter 씨께,

저는 이곳 Viscount 출판사의 보조 편집자 직위에 대한 귀하의 입사 지원서를 받았습니다. 안타깝게도, 그 직은 오늘 아침 내부 채용에 의해 채워졌다는 소식을 알려 드립니다.

하지만 저는 귀하의 지원서를 모두 살펴보았고, 귀하의 지원서와 함께 제출된 이력서와 추천서 모두에 제가 큰 감명을 받았다는 점을 인정해야 할 것 같습니다. 귀하께서는 아동 서적 편집에 관한 오랜 경력을 지니고 계시고, 저는 귀하께서 Milton 주식회사에 있으면서 작업하고 계신 세 권의 책에 대해서도 잘 알고 있습니다.

우연하게도 Viscount는 아동 부서를 신설하는 과정에 있으며, 저희는 현재 직원들을 새로 모집하고 있습니다. 귀하께서 청소년 소설 편집 직에 지원하셨다는 점은 알고 있지만, 귀하의 경력 때문에 귀하께서는 신설 부서의 직책에 매우 유력한 후보가 되고 있습니다. 관심이 있으시면, 제가 기꺼이 귀하의 이력서를 Mary Farnsworth 씨에게 넘기도록 하겠습니다.

하지만, 아동 부서는 뉴욕이 아니라 보스턴에 있게 될 것이라는 점과, 누구를 면접해야 할지에 관한 결정이 곧 이루어질 예정이므로 늦어도 내일 오후까지는 제게 답장을 주셔야 한다는 점을 말씀드리고 싶습니다. 시간이 매우 중요하기 때문에, 제게 빨리 답변을 주시기 바랍니다.

William Folsom 드림
Viscount 출판사

editor 편집자 | **regret** 후회하다, 유감이다 | **internal hire** 내부 채용 | **admit** 인정하다 | **packet** 소포, 꾸러미 | **be familiar with** ~에 친숙하다 | **it just so happens that** 우연히도 | **division** 부, 부서 | **young adult** 청소년 | **fiction** 소설, 픽션 | **candidate** 후보 | **of the essence** 매우 중요한

162 Folsom 씨는 왜 Carter 씨에게 이메일을 썼는가?
(A) 다른 직으로의 지원을 제안하기 위해
(B) Viscount 출판사의 일자리를 제안하기 위해
(C) 아동 서적에 대한 그의 제안을 거부하기 위해
(D) 그가 원고 작성을 했던 작품을 칭찬하기 위해

proposal 제안 | **compliment** 칭찬하다 | **author** 작가; 원고를 쓰다

| 해설 | Folsom 씨는 Carter 씨에게 지원한 직책은 채용이 끝났으나 신설 부서에 관심이 있으면 그쪽에 지원서를 넘기겠다는 제안을 하고 있다. 따라서 정답은 (A)이다. '신설 부서의 일자리에 지원해 볼 것'을 제안하는 것이지 '일자리 자체를 제안하는 것'은 아니므로 (B)를 정답으로 선택해서는 안 된다.

163 Carter 씨에 대해 언급된 것은 무엇인가?
(A) 그는 아동용 도서의 작가이다.
(B) 그는 현재 청소년용 소설에 관한 작업을 하고 있다.
(C) 그는 Milton 주식회사에서 편집자로 일을 한다.
(D) 그는 Mary Farnsworth의 동료이다.

| 해설 | Carter 씨에게 '아동 서적 편집 경험'(experience editing children's

books)이 많다고 나와 있을 뿐, 작가로서의 그의 활동에 대해서는 언급된 바 없으므로 (A)는 정답이 될 수 없다. (B)의 '청소년 소설에 관한 작업'은 그가 하고 있는 일이 아니라 그가 지원한 직책과 관련이 있는 일이므로 이 역시 오답이다. (D)의 Mary Farnsworth는 신설 부서의 직원 채용을 담당하고 있는 인물로 소개되어 있다. 따라서 정답은 (C)로, three of the books that you have worked on while at Milton, Inc.라는 어구를 통해 그가 Milton 주식회사의 편집자임을 알 수 있다.

164 Carter 씨는 9월 29일까지 무엇을 해야 하는가?
(A) 그가 받은 일자리 제안에 대해 답장을 한다
(B) 면접을 볼 시간과 날짜를 정한다
(C) Milton 주식회사의 누군가에게 이력서를 제출한다
(D) 그가 직위의 후보로 고려되기를 원하는지 결정한다

| 해설 | 이메일이 작성된 날짜가 9월 28일이므로, 9월 29일은 28일을 기준으로 '내일'이 된다. 이메일의 마지막 단락에서 Folsom 씨는 Carter 씨에게 '늦어도 내일 오후까지' 신설 부서에 지원할 의사가 있는지를 자신에게 알려 달라고 했으므로, Carter 씨가 29일까지 해야 할 일은 (D)이다.

[165-167]

12월 3일

Clive Robertson
Walker Resources
11번가 495번지
버밍햄, 앨라배마

친애하는 Robertson 씨께,

시간을 내 주셔서 저희 회사를 방문해 주신 점과 귀사의 제품에 대해 발표를 해 주신 점에 대해 감사를 드립니다. 귀하의 강연은 활기차고 즐거웠으며, 그로써 저희는 귀하의 신제품에 관한 식견을 갖게 되었습니다. 저희 RX Products는, 그것이 바로 우리에게 필요한 것이라고 생각하기 때문에, 특히 귀하께서 간략히 언급하신 용기 밀봉 기계에 관심이 있습니다. 저희는 브라질에서 Ramos Manufacturing과 함께 공장 문을 열 예정인데, 저희는 그곳의 습기에 관해 우려를 하고 있습니다. 아시다시피, 높은 습도는 용기를 적절하게 밀봉하는 일을 어렵게 만듭니다. 저희는 현재 Robinson 주식회사에서 제조한 밀봉 기계를 사용하고 있지만, 이 제품은 몇 개월 전에 해당 업체에 의해 생산이 중단되었습니다. 귀사의 밀봉 기계는 새 것일 뿐만 아니라 최첨단 기술을 사용하는 것으로 보이며, 이는, 저희가 예상하기에, 효율성을 증대시킬 것입니다. 귀사의 밀봉 기계의 구입과 관련하여 귀하와 논의를 시작하고 싶습니다. 하지만 현재로서는, 기계의 가격이 너무 높습니다. 저희가 상당 수의 기기를 주문하는 경우, 아마도 귀사가 가격에 대해 유연한 태도를 취할 수 있을 것입니다. 저는 귀하께서 얼마 전 버밍햄으로 돌아가셨다는 점은 알고 있지만, 다음 주에 펜사콜라로 다시 오시는 것은 어떠신지요? 공장이 1월 10일에 문을 열기로 되어 있어서 서둘러 협상을 해야 합니다.

James Matters 드림
구매부 차장, RX Products

lively 활기찬 | insight 통찰력 | container 용기, 그릇 | sealing machine 밀봉 기계 | in brief 짧게, 간략하게 | humidity 습기 | manufacture 제작하다, 제조하다 | discontinue 중단하다 | anticipate 예상하다 | efficiency 효율성 | flexible 유연한 | make a deal 거래를 하다, 협상을 하다

165 Matters 씨는 왜 Walker Resources의 제품을 구입하고 싶어하는가?
(A) 제품 가격이 시중에 나와 있는 다른 제품보다 낮다.
(B) 그의 회사는 과거에 Walker Resources와 일을 했다.
(C) 그는 그와 유사한 다른 회사의 제품을 구입할 수가 없다.
(D) 그 제품은 현재 그의 회사가 사용하고 있는 제품의 업그레이드 버전일 것이다.

| 해설 | Matters 씨는 현재 사용 중인 밀봉 기계의 생산이 중단되었는데, Walker Resources의 제품이 '새 것이고 최신 기술을 사용하고 있다'(is not only new but also appears to use the latest technology)는 점을 지적한다. 따라서 그가 구매를 하고자 하는 이유는 (D)로 볼 수 있다.

166 Ramos Manufacturing에 대해 언급된 것은 무엇인가?
(A) 버밍햄에 위치해 있다.
(B) RX Products와의 합작 투자에 관련되어 있다.
(C) 최근에 기계 생산을 중단했다.
(D) 최신 공장을 건설하는 데 문제를 겪고 있다.

| 해설 | Ramos Manufacturing은 두 번째 단락 중 we are opening a factory in Brazil together with Ramos Manufacturing이라는 어구에서 언급되고 있다. 이를 통해 Ramos Manufacturing은 발신인의 회사인 RX Products와 함께 공장을 설립하려는 회사임을 알 수 있으므로 정답은 (B)가 된다.

167 Matters 씨는 무엇을 요청하는가?
(A) 팜플렛
(B) 대량 구매에 따른 할인
(C) 무료 샘플
(D) 제품 시연

bulk discount 대량 구매에 따른 할인 | demonstration 시위; 시연

| 해설 | 마지막 단락에서 Matters 씨는 제품 가격이 너무 높다는 점을 지적한 후, 'Perhaps your company can be flexible on pricing if we order a significant number of machines.'라고 말한다. 여기에서 그가 요청한 사항은 '대량 구매 시 할인을 적용해 줄 수 있는지'이므로 (B)가 정답이다.

[168-171]

McCartney, Laurie   10:49 A.M.
방금 전에 Sanders 씨가 흥미로운 설명을 해 주었군요. 당신들에게 즉각적으로 떠오르는 생각을, 좋은 점과 나쁜 점 모두를 제게 알려 주는 것이 어떨까요?

Patrick, Rebecca   10: 52 A.M.
저는 그녀의 회사가 우리에게 도움을 주지 못할 것으로 생각해요.

Daniels, George   10:53 A.M.
저는 그녀가 했던 말이 마음에 들어요.

McCartney, Laurie   10:54 A.M.
놀랍군요. 당신 둘은 정반대의 결론에 도달했어요. 제게 보다 자세히 이야기해 줄래요? George, 당신이 먼저 하세요.

Daniels, George   10:56 A.M.
Whitewater 컨설팅은 많은 신규 업체들이 해외 시장으로 상품을 수출하는 일을 돕고 있어요. 그래서 업체들이 상당히 많은 제품을 판매해서 수입을 증대시키고 있죠. 간단해요.

Patrick, Rebecca   10: 57 A.M.
하지만 요점은 Whitewater가, 국내 시장이 아니라, 해외 시장에서 기업들을 돕는다는 점이에요.

McCartney, Laurie   10:59 A.M.
그에 대한 당신의 입장이 어떤지 알 것 같아요.

Patrick, Rebecca   11:02 A.M.
우리는 해외 시장으로의 진출을 시도하고 있지 않아요. 그것은 지금부터 몇 년 후에나 생각해 볼 사안이죠. 우리는 국내 시장에 제품을 출시해야 해요.

Daniels, George   11:04 A.M.
하지만 Sanders 씨는 자신의 회사가 이곳에서 일을 해 왔다고 말하지 않았나요? 그녀가 유럽 시장에 초점을 맞추고 있다는 점은 저도 알고 있지만, 그녀는 초반부에 미국에서의 회사 업무에 대해서도 이야기를 했어요.

Patrick, Rebecca   11: 07 A.M.
네, 그랬죠. 하지만 그녀가 미국에 초점을 맞추지 않는다는 점은 그녀가 이곳에서의 Whitewater의 성과를 논의하고 싶어하지 않는다는 점, 혹은 적절한 준비가 되어 있지 않다는 점 중에 하나를 나타내죠. 어느 쪽이든 매력적이지 않아요.

McCartney, Laurie   11:10 A.M.
두 명 모두 합당한 지적을 하고 있군요. 12시에 점심을 먹으러 만난 후, 우리가 마주 앉아서 이 문제에 대해 논의할 수 있을 거예요.

demonstration 시위; 설명, 시연 | **fascinating** 매력적인, 흥미로운 | **opposing** 반대되는 | **conclusion** 결론 | **startup** 신규 업체 | **revenue** 수입 | **domestic** 국내의 | **break into** 침입하다, 진입하다 | **focus on** ~에 집중하다 | **lack** 부족, 결여 | **appealing** 호소력이 있는, 매력적인 | **legitimate** 정당한, 타당한

168 무엇이 주로 논의되고 있는가?
(A) Whitewater 컨설팅과의 협력
(B) 회사의 성과를 향상시키는 법
(C) 발표에 관한 의견
(D) 해외 시장과 국내 시장의 중요성

| 해설 | 첫 번째 메시지에서 Sanders라는 인물의 설명에 대해 '즉각적으로 떠오르는 생각들'(immediate thoughts)이 논의될 것으로 예상할 수 있다. 이후에도 Sanders 씨 회사에 대한 각자의 의견을 교환하고 있으므로 메시지의 주제는 (C)로 볼 수 있다.

169 Daniels 씨는 발표에 대해 어떻게 느끼는가?
(A) 자신의 회사가 해외 시장으로 진출할 수 있다는 점을 입증해 주었다.
(B) Whitewater 컨설팅을 고용해야 한다는 확신을 심어 주었다.
(C) 국내 판매의 문제점을 설명해 주었다.
(D) Whitewater 컨설팅이 회사를 어떻게 도울 수 있는지를 보여 주었다.

| 해설 | Daniels 씨가 작성한 문장만 빠르게 살펴보면 그는 Sanders 씨의 회사에 우호적인 입장을 취하고 있음을 알 수 있다. 특히 많은 회사들이 '해외 시장으로 상품을 수출하는 데'(getting their products into foreign markets) 도움을 주고 있다는 글을 통해 발표에 대한 Daniels 씨의 생각은 (D)와 같을 것으로 생각해 볼 수 있다.

170 오전 10시 59분에, McCartney 씨가 "I think I see where you're going with this"라고 썼을 때 그녀는 무엇을 의미하는가?
(A) 그녀는 Patrick 씨와 회의를 하러 가야 한다.
(B) 그녀는 Patrick 씨가 다음에 어떤 글을 쓸지 알고 있다.
(C) 그녀는 곧 발표에 참석할 것이다.
(D) 그녀는 Patrick 씨가 보다 상세한 이야기를 하기를 원한다.

| 해설 | 주어진 문장을 직역하면 '당신이 그에 대해 어느 쪽으로 갈지 알 것 같다'는 뜻이다. Patrick 씨가 자신의 주장을 이야기한 후에 작성된 문장이므로, 이를 의역하면 '당신 입장이 무엇인지 알겠다'는 짐작의 의미가 드러나므로, 보기 중 이러한 의미와 상통하는 (B)가 정답이다.

171 Patrick 씨는 Sanders 씨에 관해 무엇을 암시하는가?
(A) Sanders 씨는 미국 시장을 무시함으로써 실수를 범했다.
(B) Sanders 씨의 발표는 중요한 점을 지적해 주었다.
(C) Sanders 씨의 회사는 그녀를 도울 수 있을 것이다.
(D) Sanders 씨는 자신이 한 주장을 명확히 해야 할 필요가 있다.

| 해설 | Patrick 씨는 메신저 글의 후반부에 'But her lack of focus on the U.S. shows she either didn't want to discuss Whitewater's performance here or she hadn't prepared properly.'라고 말하면서 Sanders 씨가 국내에서의 성과를 논의하고 싶어하지 않거나 적절한 준비가 되어 있지 않다고 비판한다. 따라서 보기 중에 그가 암시하는 바는 (A)로 볼 수 있다.

[172-175]

7월 28일

친애하는 Rice 씨께,

Evercrest Shipping의 직원들을 대표하여, 귀하에게 선임 가격 분석가의 직책을 제안하게 되어 기쁘게 생각합니다. 저희 모두는 귀하와 함께 일하는 것을 고대하고 있으며, 저는 귀하께서 이곳 일이 보람되면서도 매력적인 것이라고 생각하실 것으로 믿습니다. Evercrest Shipping은 직원들을 매우 소중히 여기는 기업이며 비즈니스 업계뿐만 아니라 샌페르난도 시에도 긍정적인 영향을 끼치기 위해 지역 사회와 협력하고자 노력하는 기업입니다.

저희 제안을 수락하시면, 근무 첫 날은 8월 31일이 될 것입니다. 귀하께서는 가격 책정 업무를 담당하는 부소장인 Rob Hamilton의 직접적인 감독 하에서 일을 하시게 될 것입니다. 연봉으로는 55,000달러를 받게 되실 것이며, 매년 4%의 인상분과, 연간 성과급도 받게 되실 것입니다. 다른 주에서 이사를 오실 것이기 때문에, 저희는 이사 비용으로 7,500달러도 지급할 것입니다. (이곳으로의 이사에 관해 보다 자세한 사항을 알고 싶으신 경우에는 950-1434로 Vince Hoover에게 연락하시면 됩니다.) 다른 모든 직원들과 마찬가지로, 1년에 유급 병가 10일을 받게 되실 것이며, 이중 절반은 다음 년도로 이월될 수 있습니다. 고용 첫 해에는, 10일간의 유급 휴가를 받게 되실 것입니다. 둘째 년도를 시작으로, 이는 매년 20일이 될 것입니다.

이 편지에 포함된 계약서를 살펴봐 주십시오. 위의 모든 조건들이 포함되어 있습니다. 조건이 받아들일 수 있는 것이면, 계약서에 서명하고 날짜를 적으셔서, 10일 이내에 제게 다시 보내 주십시오. 이 제안은 협상이 불가능하며 어떤 식으로도 변경될 수 없습니다.

Shirley Gathers 드림
Evercrest Shipping 인사부

on behalf of ~을 대신하여 | **analyst** 분석가 | **rewarding** 보람된 | **challenging** 도전 의식을 불러 일으키는 | **value** 소중히 여기다 | **strive to** ~하기 위해 노력하다 | **influence** 영향 | **deputy director** 부소장, 부국장 | **performance bonus** 성과급 | **contribute** 기부하다, 기여하다 | **sick day** 병가 | **roll over** 이월하다 | **terms** (계약) 조건 | **amenable** ~을 잘 받아들이는 | **nonnegotiable** 협상이 불가능한

172 Gathers 씨는 왜 편지를 작성했는가?
(A) Rice 씨에게 일자리에 지원할 것을 요청하기 위해
(B) 채용 제안을 하기 위해
(C) 입사 지원자에게 그녀의 회사를 홍보하기 위해
(D) Rice 씨의 업무 사항을 나열하기 위해

extend 확장하다; 제안하다 | **list** 열거하다, 나열하다

| 해설 | 편지의 첫 부분에서 Gathers 씨는 Rice 씨에게 head price analyst라는 직책을 제안하며 그녀의 근무 조건에 대해 상세히 밝히고 있다. 따라서 편지를 작성한 목적은 (B)이다.

173 다음 중 Rice 씨의 보수의 일부가 아닌 것은 무엇인가?
(A) 복지 혜택 가입

(B) 매년 인상되는 임금
(C) 유급 휴가와 병가
(D) 성과에 따른 보너스

enrollment 등록, 가입 | benefits plan 복지 제도

| 해설 | 근무 조건은 두 번째 단락에 자세히 나와 있는데, 구체적으로 a salary of $55,000 per year(55,000달러의 연봉), a yearly raise of 4%(매년 4%의 인상분), an annual performance bonus(성과급), 그리고 10 paid sick days(10일간의 병가)와 10 days of paid vacation(10일간의 유급 휴가)이 언급되고 있다. 따라서 보기 중 언급되지 않은 사항은 (A)의 '복지 혜택'이다.

174 편지에 언급되어 있는 것은 무엇인가?
(A) Evercrest Shipping은 샌페르난도 정치 문제에 적극적이다.
(B) Rice 씨는 두 차례의 면접을 보았다.
(C) 계약 조건은 변경될 수 없다.
(D) Gathers 씨는 모든 고용 결정에 대한 책임을 맡고 있다.

active 활동 중인, 적극적인 | in charge of ~을 맡고 있는, ~을 담당하는

| 해설 | 편지의 마지막 문장, 'This offer is nonnegotiable and cannot be changed in any way.'에서 제안 사항은 변경이 불가능하다는 점을 알 수 있다. 따라서 편지에서 언급된 사항은 (C)이다.

175 [1], [2], [3], 그리고 [4]로 표시된 위치 중에 다음 문장이 들어가기에 가장 알맞은 곳은 어디인가?
"이곳으로의 이사에 관해 보다 자세한 사항을 알고 싶으신 경우에는 950-1434로 Vince Hoover에게 연락하시면 됩니다."
(A) [1]
(B) [2]
(C) [3]
(D) [4]

| 해설 | transition이 이사를 의미하므로 주어진 문장은 이사에 관련된 내용이 언급된 이후에 등장하는 것이 가장 바람직하다. 정답은 (C)이다.

[176-180]

보낸 사람: Laurel Flanagan ⟨laurel_f@privatemail.com⟩
받는 사람: Customer Service ⟨customerservice@broadwayelectronics.com⟩
제목: 주문 65059697
날짜: 5월 6일

담당자님께,

저는 4월 20일에 했던 주문(주문 번호 65059697)과 관련해서 글을 쓰고 있습니다. 저는 1,100달러 이상을 썼지만, 제 주문에는 문제가 있었습니다. 우선, 구입 후 2주가 넘어서야 제품이 도착했습니다. 게다가, 저는 프린트용 잉크를 구입했습니다. 저는 TR440 검정색 잉크를 두 팩 주문했으나, TR687 검정색 잉크 두 팩이 배송되었습니다. 저는 그 잉크가 어떤 프린터와 호환되는지 확인해 보았는데, 제 것과는 호환이 되지 않습니다. 다른 문제는 제가 구입한 Montague P2000 디지털 카메라와 관계가 있습니다. 카메라는 양호한 상태로 도착했지만, 사용자 매뉴얼이 포함되어 있지 않았습니다. 그래서 저는 어떻게 새 카메라를 작동시키는지 모르고 있습니다.

저는 빠진 품목이 즉시 배송되기를 원하며 더 나아가 잉크를 반품하는 법도 알려 주실 것을 요청합니다. 저는 5일 후 해외 여행을 떠날 때 카메라를 가져 가고 싶기 때문에 가능한 빨리 이번 일을 처리해 주시기 바랍니다. 지난 7개월간 귀사가 저지른 실수는 이번이 벌써 세 번째입니다. 저는 낮은 가격 때문에 귀하의 온라인 상점에서 쇼핑하는 것을 좋아하지만, 잘못된 제품을 받고 주문이 불완전하게 이루어지는 것에 대해서는

넌더리가 납니다. 비슷한 일이 또 생기면, 저는 더 이상 귀하의 매장을 자주 이용하지 않을 것입니다.

그럼 이만 줄이겠습니다.

Laurel Flanagan

to begin with 우선, 먼저 | in addition 또한, 게다가 | be compatible with ~와 양립하다, ~와 호환되다 | concern ~와 관계가 있다 | manual 매뉴얼, 설명서 | include 포함하다 | therefore 그러므로 | operate 가동시키다, 작동시키다 | further 더 나아가, 더 멀리 | due to ~ 때문에 | be tired of ~에 넌더리가 나다 | incomplete 불완전한 | no longer 더 이상 ~ 않는 | frequent 빈번한

보낸 사람: Customer Service ⟨customerservice@broadwayelectronics.com⟩
받는 사람: Laurel Flanagan ⟨laurel_f@privatemail.com⟩
제목: 회신: 주문 65059697
날짜: 5월 6일

친애하는 Flanagan 씨께,

Broadway 전자의 모든 선적부 직원을 대신하여, 저희가 저지른 실수에 대해 진심으로 사과를 드립니다. 귀하의 주문에 더 이상 문제가 생기지 않도록 저희는 최선을 다할 것임을 약속드립니다. 실제로, 이제부터는 귀하께서 구입하시는 모든 제품을 확실히 받아 보실 수 있도록 제가 직접 귀하의 모든 주문품을 포장해서 발송하겠습니다. 또한 귀하의 주문품은 별도의 추가 비용 없이 프리미엄 특급 우편으로 발송될 것입니다. 그리고 이 다음에 귀하께서 저희의 제품을 구입하시는 경우, 쿠폰 코드 BIGSAVINGS를 사용하셔서 1,000달러 이하의 주문에 대해 50%의 할인을 받으시길 바랍니다. 저는 이러한 조치들이 앞으로 여러 해 동안 귀하께서 계속 저희 서비스를 이용하시는데 도움이 되기를 바랍니다.

빠진 품목에 대해 말씀을 드리면, 잉크는 택배 회사에 의해 선적이 되었고 내일 12시 이전에는 도착을 할 것입니다. 나머지 품목은 현재 재고가 없기 때문에, 제가 제조업체에 주문을 했습니다. 내일 이곳에 도착할 예정이어서, 그때 저희가 곧바로 귀하께 발송해 드리겠습니다. 따라서 귀하께서는 여행을 떠나시기 전에 받으시게 될 것입니다.

추후에 또 다시 문제를 겪으시는 경우, (403) 679-5495로 제게 직통 전화를 주시면 제가 최선을 다해 도움을 드리도록 하겠습니다.

Carmen Diego 드림

선적부 이사
Broadway 전자

on behalf of ~을 대신하여 | wholeheartedly 진심으로 | assure 장담하다, 확언하다 | do one's utmost 전력을 다하다 | personally 몸소, 직접 | absolutely 절대적으로, 틀림없이 | action 행동, 조치 | convince 설득시키다 | as for ~에 대해 말하자면 | courier 배달원, 택배 회사 | in stock 재고가 있는 | manufacturer 제조체, 제조업자 | straight 곧장, 곧바로 | directly 직접적으로 | do one's best 최선을 다하다

176 첫 번째 이메일의 목적은 무엇인가?
(A) 최근에 가격이 왜 인상되고 있는지 묻기 위해
(B) 몇몇 제품을 받았다는 점을 인정하게 위해
(C) 구입한 제품의 품질이 나쁘다는 점을 언급하기 위해
(D) 빠진 물품에 대해 불평을 하기 위해

lately 최근에 | acknowledge 인정하다 | receipt 받음; 영수증

| 해설 | 주문에 대한 두 가지 문제, 즉 '잘못 배송된 잉크'와 '설명서가 누락된 카메라'에 대한 불만을 제기하고 있다. 따라서 정답은 (D)이다.

177 Flanagan 씨는 앞으로 자신이 어떻게 할 것이라고 언급하는가?

(A) 친구들에게 좋지 못한 서비스에 관해 이야기한다
(B) Broadway 전자에서의 쇼핑을 중단한다
(C) 몇몇 구입품에 대해 환불을 요청한다
(D) Broadway 전자의 오프라인 매장을 방문한다

| 해설 | 첫 번째 이메일의 두 번째 단락 중 맨 마지막 문장, 'If something similar happens again, I will no longer frequent your store.'에서 화자는 문제가 재발될 경우 해당 전자 회사의 제품을 더 이상 구입하지 않겠다는 의지를 나타내고 있다. 따라서 그녀가 하게 될 행동은 (B)이다.

178 두 번째 이메일에서, 1단락 2줄의 "ensure"라는 단어와 그 의미가 가장 비슷한 것은?

(A) 보장하다
(B) 예측하다
(C) 인정하다
(D) 확인하다

guarantee 보장하다, 보증하다 | **predict** 예측하다, 예언하다

| 해설 | ensure는 '보장하다'라는 뜻으로 보기 중에서는 (A)의 guarantee와 그 의미가 가장 비슷하다.

179 Diego 씨는 제조업체로부터 어떤 제품을 주문했는가?

(A) TR440 검정색 잉크
(B) TR687 검정색 잉크
(C) Montague P2000 디지털 카메라
(D) Montague P2000 디지털 카메라 사용자 매뉴얼

| 해설 | 두 번째 이메일의 두 번째 단락 중 the other item이 무엇을 가리키는지 파악해야 정답을 찾을 수 있다. 문제가 된 주문품 중 첫 번째 것이 프린터용 잉크고, 두 번째 것은 디지털 카메라의 사용자 매뉴얼이다. 두 번째 단락의 첫 번째 문장에서 프린터용 잉크에 대한 조치를 언급했으므로 the other item이 가리키는 것은 (D)의 '디지털 카메라 사용자 매뉴얼'이다.

180 Flanagan 씨가 작성한 문제 중 Diego 씨가 이메일에서 답변을 하지 않은 것은 무엇인가?

(A) 잘못 발송된 제품을 더 이상 받지 않는 법
(B) 제품을 회사로 반품시키는 법
(C) 주문한 제품을 받는 법
(D) 제품을 보다 빨리 받는 법

| 해설 | Flanagan 씨의 문제 해결을 위해 Diego 씨는 자기가 직접 포장 및 배송을 할 것이라고 했으므로 (A)는 언급된 사항이며, 누락된 잉크와 설명서를 받게 될 방법에 대해서도 안내되고 있으므로 (C) 역시 언급된 사항이다. '프리미엄 특급 우편'을 이용하겠다는 약속을 통해 (D)와 관련된 내용도 확인할 수 있으므로, 언급되지 않은 사항은 (B)이다.

[181-185]

Carter Manufacturing
Reggie Simmons의 여행 일정표

날짜	시간	행사	숙박 장소
9월 14일 월요일	오후 4시 15분	• Chicago O'Hare 공항 도착 • Davis 렌터카에서 차량 렌트 • 호텔에서 체크인	Lakeside 호텔, 시카고
9월 15일 화요일	오전 9시 – 오후 3시	• Turner 주식회사에서 회의 • 새로운 시설 견학	Paradise 호텔, 피오리아
9월 16일 수요일	오후 1시 – 오후 4시	• MTR 주식회사에서 제품 설명	Traveler's Inn, 스프링필드
9월 17일 목요일	오후 1시 30분 – 오후 6시	• Riverside Tractors에서 협상	Royal Inn, 에임스
9월 18일 금요일	오후 2시 45분	• Davis Rentals에 자동차 반납 • Western 항공 카운터에서 탑승 수속 • Chicago O'Hare 공항에서 출발	해당 사항 없음

demonstration 시위; 실물 설명, 실연 | **N/A** 해당 사항 없음

Ted Lyons
Jade 여행사
Mountain 로 465번지
솔트레이크시티, 유타
9월 1일

Reggie Simmons
Cater Manufacturing
12번가 309번지
솔트레이크시티, 유타

친애하는 Simmons 씨께,

저는 곧 있을 귀하의 중서부 출장을 위해 귀하께서 요청하신 여행 계획을 세웠습니다. 저는 귀하에게 일정표 사본을 이메일로 보내 드렸지만, 이 편지에도 사본을 한 부 포함시켰습니다. 수정을 요청하시는 경우, 제게 알려 주시면, 제가 필요한 조치를 취하겠습니다.
시카고에 도착하시자마자, 3번 터미널에 있는 Davis Rentals로 가셔서 차량을 받으십시오. 평소에 중형차에 지불하셨던 비용과 같은 금액으로 차량을 고급형 세단으로 업그레이드해 드릴 수 있었습니다. 추가 요금을 지불하지 않기 위해서는 9월 18일에 연료를 채우셔서 차량을 반납하셔야 합니다.
호텔에 대해 말씀을 드리면, 귀하께서는 전에 한 곳을 제외하고는 모든 곳에서 숙박을 해 보셨습니다. 최근 스프링필드에서 문을 연 호텔이 하나 있는데, 저는 다른 고객들이 그곳에 관해 칭찬하는 말을 들었습니다. 그곳은 평소 묵으시던 Welcome Inn의 숙박 시설보다 더 새것이고 요금도 저렴하기 때문에, 저는 귀하께 그곳 객실을 예약해 드려야 한다고 생각했습니다. 하지만 Welcome Inn이 더 좋으시면, 기꺼이 그곳으로 예약을 해 드리겠습니다.
항공 요금, 자동차 요금, 그리고 호텔 숙박비의 청구서는 항상 하던 대로 회계부의 Thompson 씨께 보내 드리겠습니다. 즐거운 여행이 되시길 바랍니다.

Ted Lyons 드림
여행사 직원
Jade 여행사

arrangement 준비, 마련; 배치 | **along with** ~와 함께 | **modification** 수정, 변경 | **vehicle** 차량 | **luxury** 사치스러운, 호화로운 | **midsized** 중간 크기의, 중형의 | **excessive** 초과의 | **but** ~을 제외하고 | **complimentary** 칭찬의 | **remark** 언급, 발언 | **make a booking** 예약하다

181 Simmons 씨가 출장에서 하기로 예정되어 있지 않은 것은 무엇인가?

(A) 콘퍼런스에 참석한다
(B) 회사와 협상한다
(C) 견학을 한다
(D) 제품 사용법을 실연한다

| 해설 | 첫 번째 지문의 표의 Event(행사) 항목을 살펴보도록 한다. (B), (C),

(D)의 내용은 쉽게 찾을 수 있으나 (A)의 '콘퍼런스에 참석한다'는 것은 일정상 예정되어 있지 않다.

182 Simmons 씨는 9월 17일에 어디에 묵을 것인가?
(A) 에임스
(B) 시카고
(C) 스프링필드
(D) 피오리아

| 해설 | '9월 17일'(September 17) 일정은 표의 네 번째 줄에서 확인할 수 있다. 그가 묵을 지역은 (A)의 '에임스'이다.

183 Lyons 씨는 Mr. Simmons 씨에게 편지와 함께 무엇을 보냈는가?
(A) 청구서
(B) 비행기 티켓
(C) 확인용 코드
(D) 여행 일정표

| 해설 | 편지의 첫 번째 단락에서 Lyons 씨는 '여행 일정표'(itinerary)를 이메일로 보냈지만 '편지에도 사본 한 부를 동봉했다'(have included a paper copy along with this letter)고 밝히고 있다. 따라서 정답은 (D)이다. (A)의 '청구서'는 회계부의 Thompson 씨에게 보내질 것이다.

184 Lyons 씨는 Simmons 씨의 렌터카에 대해 무엇을 언급하는가?
(A) 연료가 가득 채워져서 나온다.
(B) 평소와 같은 가격이다.
(C) 평소보다 더 작은 것이다.
(D) 피오리아에서 받을 수 있다.

| 해설 | 이메일의 for the same price that you normal pay for a midsized vehicle이라는 어구를 통해 평소 이용하던 중형차의 렌터카 요금으로 고급형 세단을 이용할 수 있다는 안내를 하고 있다. 따라서 정답은 (B)이다.

185 Welcome Inn에 관해 무엇이 언급되었는가?
(A) 에임스에서 가장 최근에 생긴 호텔이다.
(B) 그곳 주인은 Paradise 호텔도 운영하고 있다.
(C) 그곳은 현재 예약이 꽉 차있다.
(D) Traveler's Inn보다 요금이 높다

| 해설 | 이메일의 세 번째 단락에서 Lyons 씨는 Traveler's 호텔에 대해 '평소에 묵던 Welcome Inn보다 새것이고 가격도 저렴하다'(newer and cheaper than your normal accommodations at the Welcome Inn)고 안내한다. 따라서 보기 중 Welcome Inn에 대해 언급된 사실은 (D)로 볼 수 있다.

[186-190]

저희와 함께 Seaside 리조트의 개장을 축하해 주십시오

플로리다 포트로더데일의 Seaside 리조트가 5월 1일에 개장을 함에 따라 모든 분들을 초대합니다. 전 객실에서 바다를 보실 수 있으며, 투숙객분들께는 해변에서의 조식 뷔페를 매일 무료로 제공해 드립니다. 숙박을 하시면 무료 와이파이와 5성급 식당에서의 할인 가격도 누리실 수 있습니다.

1인실: 퀸사이즈 침대 1개; 1박 129.99달러
2인실: 퀸사이즈 침대 2개 혹은 킹사이즈 침대 1개; 1박 159.99달러
주니어 스위트; 방 2개; 킹사이즈 침대 2개; 1박 209.99달러
럭셔리 스위트; 방 3개; 킹사이즈 침대 3개; 1박 259.99달러

www.seasideresort.com을 방문하시면 숙박 시설의 사진과 함께 객실 사진도 보실 수 있습니다. 저희는 프라이빗 비치, 야외 수영장, 피트니스 센터, 그리고 테니스장을 구비하고 있습니다. 또한 대서양에서의 스쿠버 다이빙, 낚시, 그리고 유람선 서비스도 제공해 드립니다.

지금부터 4월 30일까지 객실 예약을 하시면, 정가의 50%를 할인해 드립니다. 이번 특가를 놓치지 마십시오. 지금 reservations@seasideresort.com으로 연락주십시오.

ocean view 바다가 보이는 전망 | **complimentary** 무료의 | **buffet** 뷔페 | **facility** 시설 | **private beach** (호텔 등의) 전용 해수욕장 | **fitness center** 피트니트 센터, 헬스장 | **cruise** 유람선, 크루즈 | **pass up** 포기하다

보낸 사람: hwalker@homemail.com
받는 사람: reservations@seasideresort.com
제목: 예약 문의
날짜: 5월 2일

담당자님께,

저는 지역 신문에서 귀하의 리조트 광고를 보고, 그곳이 제가 가족들을 데리고 가서 여름 휴가를 보내고 싶은 곳이라는 점을 즉각적으로 알게 되었습니다. 저희는 네 명(아내와 두 딸이 있습니다)이기 때문에, 주니어 스위트에 머물고 싶습니다. 저희는 5월 28일에 도착할 예정이며 6월 5일에 떠날 것입니다. 저희는 할인 요금을 적용받게 될 것입니다, 그렇지 않나요?
제 아내와 저는 스쿠버 다이빙을 매우 좋아하기 때문에, 그곳에 있는 동안 스쿠버 다이빙을 두어 차례 하고 싶습니다. 난파선이나 산호초 주변에서 잠수할 기회를 가질 수 있으면 정말로 좋겠습니다. 제 딸들은 스쿠버 다이빙을 하지 않기 때문에, 저희가 바다에 있는 동안 딸들이 할 수 있는 활동이 있을까요? 또한, 유람선은 어디로 가는 건가요? 마지막으로, 리조트에 개가 입장하는 것이 허락되나요? 저희는 가능하다면 골든 리트리버인 Rusty를 데려 가고 싶습니다.

Henry Walker 드림

instantly 즉시 | **rate** 비율; 요금 | **avid** 열렬한, 열심인 | **opportunity** 기회 | **shipwreck** 난파선 | **coral reef** 산호초 | **premises** 부지, 구역

보낸 사람: reservations@seasideresort.com
받는 사람: hwalker@homemail.com
제목: Seaside 리조트에 오신 것을 환영합니다
날짜: 5월 2일

친애하는 Walker 씨께,

Seaside 리조트의 객실을 예약해 주셔서 감사합니다. 다음 사항이 확정되었습니다:

주니어 스위트 1실 – 5월 28일에서 6월 5일 (9일)

오후 2시에 체크인하십시오. 체크인을 일찍 하셔야 하는 경우에는 저희가 적절한 준비를 할 수 있도록 가능한 빨리 알려 주시기 바랍니다. 소액의 요금이 부과될 수 있습니다.
다이빙 강사는 Cliff Swan입니다. 포트로더데일에서의 스쿠버 다이빙에 관해서는 그가 귀하의 질문에 답변을 드릴 것입니다. 그는 그룹 다이빙과 개인 다이빙 모두를 진행합니다. cliffswan@seasideresort.com으로 연락을 하실 수 있습니다.
애완 동물의 리조트 출입이 허가되지 않는다는 점을 알려 드리게 되어 유감입니다. 또한, 특가 상품은 더 이상 제공되지 않기 때문에, 객실에 대해서는 정가를 지불하셔야 합니다. 아이들에 대해 말씀을 드리면, 아이들은 바닷가에 가거나, 소정의 요금으로 저희 직원 중 한 명과 낚시를 할 수 있습니다.

Christie McDougal 드림
Seaside 리조트

instructor 강사 | reach 연락하다 | regret 후회하다, 유감이다 | pet 애완 동물 | full price 전액

186 Seaside 리조트에 관해 다음 중 어떤 것이 언급되어 있는가?
(A) 투숙객들에게 무료 점심 뷔페를 제공한다.
(B) 여러 가지의 즐길 거리들을 제공한다.
(C) 일주일을 체류함으로써 보다 저렴한 요금을 누릴 수 있다.
(D) 시설들은 별 다섯 개의 등급을 받았다.

| 해설 | 첫 번째 지문에서 투숙객들은 '무료 조식 뷔페'를 먹을 수 있다고 나와 있으므로 (A)는 잘못된 내용이다. 요금 할인은 4월 30일 이전 예약 고객에 대해 적용된다고 안내되어 있을 뿐 (C)와 같은 할인 내용은 찾아볼 수 없다. 시설 등급에 대해서는 식당만 '5성급'이라고 광고되어 있으므로 (D) 역시 사실과 다르다. 따라서 정답은 (B)로, 광고에서는 스쿠버 다이빙 등 호텔에서 할 수 있는 여러 가지 활동들이 소개되어 있다.

187 Walker 씨는 왜 포트로더데일로 여행을 갈 것인가?
(A) 업무를 처리하기 위해
(B) 휴가를 보내기 위해
(C) 친지를 방문하기 위해
(D) 콘퍼런스에 참석하기 위해

| 해설 | 두 번째 지문인 이메일에서 Walker 씨는 '여름 휴가를 보내기 위해'(for our annual summer trip) 포트로더데일에 위치한 Seaside 리조트로에 가고 싶다고 적고 있다. 따라서 그가 여행을 하려는 목적은 (B)이다.

188 Walker 씨는 얼마를 지불하게 될 것인가?
(A) 1박에 129.99달러
(B) 1박에 159.99달러
(C) 1박에 209.99달러
(D) 1박에 259.99달러

| 해설 | 두 번째 지문과 세 번째 지문을 통해 Walker 씨가 예약한 객실의 종류는 '주니어 스위트'임을 알 수 있다. 한편 세 번째 지문에서는 그가 요금 할인을 받을 수 없다는 점이 통보되어 있으므로 결과적으로 그가 지불해야 할 숙박비는 주니어 스위트 1박 요금의 정가인 (C)의 '209.99달러'이다.

189 Walker 씨는 왜 Swan 씨에게 연락을 할 것 같은가?
(A) 테니스 교습을 받기 위해
(B) 수영하는 법을 배우기 위해
(C) 유람선 여행을 하기 위해
(D) 다이빙 교습을 받기 위해

| 해설 | 세 번째 지문인 이메일에서 Cliff Swan 씨는 스쿠버 다이빙 강사로, '그가 포트로더데일에서의 스쿠버 다이빙에 관한 질문에 답변을 할 수 있다'(He can answer your questions about scuba diving in the Fort Lauderdale area.)고 소개되어 있다. 따라서 Walker 씨가 그에게 연락할 경우는 (D)로 볼 수 있다.

190 Walker 씨의 어떤 질문에 대해 McDougal 씨가 답변을 하지 않는가?
(A) 그곳에서의 어떤 활동이 아이들을 위한 것인지
(B) 보다 저렴한 요금이 적용될 수 있는지
(C) 투숙객들이 동물을 데리고 올 수 있는지
(D) 승객들은 배를 타고 어디로 갈 수 있는지

| 해설 | 두 번째 지문과 세 번째 지문을 비교해야 정답을 찾을 수 있다. 유람선이 어디로 가는지에 대한 답변은 세 번째 지문에서 찾아볼 수 없으므로 정답은 (D)이다.

[191-195]

자기 계발: 가이드
Art Mooney의 리뷰

자립의 전문가인 Sabrina Lattimore가 최신 도서인 *자기 계발: 가이드*로 또 다시 일을 냈다. 이번 작품은, Nelson 출판사의 하드커버 도서로 출판되었는데, 그녀의 8번째이자, 개인적인 의견으로는, 최고의 책이다. 이 책은 개인의 일생의 모든 측면을 개선시키기 위한 단계별 방법을 소개하고 있다. 물론, 글은 재치 넘치는 논평과 흥미로운 개인 일화들로 채워져 있으며, 이러한 점은 책을 훨씬 더 재미있게 만들고 있다. 나는 이미 Lattimore 씨가 자기 계발을 위해 제안한 몇 가지 단계들을 나 스스로에게 적용시켜 보았고, 몇몇 친구들과 가족들에게는 이 책을 개인적으로 추천하기도 했는데, 이와 같은 일은 내가 결코 해 본 적이 없던 일이다. 사실상 이 책의 유일한 단점은 색인이 없다는 점으로, 이로 인해 나는 내가 찾는 부분으로 다시 돌아가는 일이 때때로 어려웠다. 그럼에도 불구하고, 기분이 상할 일은 거의 없다. 나는 진심으로 이 책을 추천하며 소매 가격인 19.99달러가 상당히 저렴한 가격이라고 생각한다. 즉시 나가서 구입을 하도록 하자.

self-improvement 자기 계발 | **self-help** 자립, 자조 | **guru** 그루, 권위자, 전문가 | **have done it** 완수하다, 해내다 | **hardback** 하드커버 | **aspect** 측면 | **witty** 재치 있는 | **anecdote** 일화 | **adopt** 채택하다 | **drawback** 단점, 결점 | **index** 색인 | **wholeheartedly** 진심으로 | **retail** 소매; 소매하다 | **bargain** 싸게 파는 물건 | **at once** 즉시

Sabrina Lattimore가 금요일에 강연을 합니다

8월 11일인 이번 주 금요일, Sabrina Lattimore가 오후 3시에 강당에서 강연을 할 예정입니다. Lattimore는 전국에서 수많은 강연을 해 온 유명한 동기 부여 강사입니다. 저희 Murray 컨설팅은 그녀가 우리에게 강연을 하기로 동의해 주셨다는 점을 기쁘게 생각합니다. 강연은 두 시간 동안 진행될 예정이며 *리더가 되는 법*에서 그녀가 쓴 내용들이 다루어질 것입니다. 강연이 끝날 무렵에는, Lattimore 씨가 질문에 답변을 할 것이며, 그 후에는 짧은 연회가 있을 것입니다. Murray 컨설팅의 전 직원분들을 환영합니다. 여러분들께서는 한 명의 게스트를 초청하셔도 좋습니다. 가족, 친구, 혹은 고객이어도 좋습니다. 늦어도 수요일인 8월 9일까지는 게스트의 이름과 본인의 참석 여부를 Julie Richardson(내선번호 564)에게 알려 주시기 바랍니다.

auditorium 강당 | **motivational** 동기 부여의 | **countless** 셀 수 없는, 많은 | **conclusion** 결말, 결론 | **reception** 리셉션, 연회 | **afterward** 그 후에

8월 14일

친애하는 Lattimore 씨께,

Murray 컨설팅의 모든 사람을 대신하여, 금요일 오후에 하신 강연에 대해 감사를 드립니다. 저도 많은 것을 배웠으며, 귀하께서는 저로 하여금 저녁에 퇴근을 하자마자 귀하의 최신 도서를 구입하기 위해 서점을 찾도록 만드셨습니다. 저는 몇 명의 동료들과 이야기를 나누어 보았는데, 그들 역시 연설에서 귀하께서 하신 조언에 감명을 받았습니다. 그들은 또한 귀하께서 강연 후 그들의 초대에 응하셔서 저녁 식사 자리에 오신 점과, 자상하게도 시간을 할애하셔서 모든 이들의 질문에 대답을 하셨다는 사실에 대해서도 감사를 표시했습니다. 저는 귀하께서 앞으로 약 6개월 후에 다시 오셔서 다른 주제로 강연을 하시는 것에 관심이 있으신지 궁금합니다. 과거에도 많은 강연을 하신 걸로 알고 있기 때문에, 아마도 논의하실 새로운 주제를 제안하실 수 있으실 것입니다. 기회가 되시면, 제게 알려 주시기 바랍니다.

Charles Murray 드림
Murray 컨설팅 사장

on behalf of ~을 대표하여 | **inspire** 영감을 주다, 고무시키다 | **invitation** 초대 | **gracious** 자비로운 | **memorable** 기억할 만한

191 Mooney 씨가 리뷰에서 언급한 것은 무엇인가?
  (A) *자기 계발: 가이드*는 페이퍼백으로 구입할 수 있다.
  (B) *자기 계발: 가이드*에 있는 이야기들이 가장 멋진 부분이다.
  (C) 그는 *자기 계발: 가이드*를 그의 친구들에게 주었다.
  (D) 그가 *자기 계발: 가이드*의 모든 측면을 좋아하지는 않는다.

paperback 페이퍼백 | **copy** 부, 권

| 해설 | 색인이 없다는 점을 '유일한 단점'(the only real drawback to this book)이라고 말하고 있으므로 (D)가 언급된 내용이다.

192 리뷰에서, 4줄의 witty라는 단어와 그 의미가 가장 유사한 것은?
  (A) 명백한
  (B) 도움이 되는
  (C) 재치 있는
  (D) 사려 깊은

obvious 명백한 | **clever** 영리한; 재치 있는 | **thoughtful** 사려 깊은, 친절한

| 해설 | witty는 '위트가 있는', '재치 있는'이라는 뜻이므로 (C)의 clever(영리한, 재치 있는)와 그 의미가 가장 비슷하다.

193 *리더가 되는 법*에 관해 무엇이 암시되어 있는가?
  (A) *자기 계발: 가이드*보다 먼저 발간되었다.
  (B) Lattimore 씨의 어떤 다른 책보다도 많이 팔렸다.
  (C) Lattimore 씨가 쓴 첫 번째 책이었다.
  (D) Murray 컨설팅의 모든 직원들이 읽어 보았다.

| 해설 | 첫 번째 지문의 첫 문장에서 *Self-Improvement: A Guide*를 'Lattimore 씨의 최신 도서'(her latest book)로 소개하고 있으므로 *How to Become a Leader*라는 도서는 그보다 먼저 출간된 책임을 예상할 수 있다. 따라서 암시되어 있는 내용은 (A)이다.

194 편지에 따르면, Murray 씨는 금요일 저녁에 무엇을 했는가?
  (A) 동료들과 저녁 식사를 했다
  (B) *자기 계발: 가이드*를 구입했다
  (C) 직장에서 특별 행사를 주최했다
  (D) Lattimore 씨에게 몇 가지 질문을 했다

| 해설 | 세 번째 지문인 편지의 초반부에서 Murray 씨는 금요일 강연을 들은 후 감명을 받고 '저녁에 퇴근을 하자마자 가장 최근에 나온 책을 구입했다'(I could purchase your newest work as soon as I left the office in the evening)고 말한다. 따라서 그가 금요일 저녁에 한 일은 (B)이다.

195 Murray 씨는 Lattimore에게 무엇을 할 것을 요청하는가?
  (A) 차후에 또 다른 강연을 한다
  (B) 자신의 책 몇 권에 사인을 한다
  (C) 그가 쓰고 있는 책에 관해 몇 가지 조언을 해 준다
  (D) 이메일로 몇 가지 질문에 답을 한다

autograph 자필 서명을 하다

| 해설 | 세 번째 지문에서 Murray 씨는 'I wonder if you would be interested in returning around six months from now and speaking about another topic.'이라고 말하며 Lattimore 씨에게 다른 주제로 강연을 한 번 더 해 줄 것을 요청하고 있다. 따라서 그가 요청한 사항은 (A)이다.

[196-200]

Best Value
고객 만족도 조사

Best Value에서 쇼핑해 주셔서 고맙습니다. 애용에 감사를 드립니다. 저희는 판매되는 제품과 제공되는 서비스의 품질을 향상시키고자 항상 노력하고 있습니다. 그러니 몇 분간 시간을 내 주셔서 이 양식을 작성해 주실 것을 요청드립니다. 모든 질문에 대답해 주시고 가지고 계신 의견을 남겨 주시기 바랍니다. 그런 다음, 이 설문지를 매장의 아무 직원에게나 제출하시고 다음 이곳을 방문할 때 사용하실 수 있는 10%의 할인 쿠폰을 받으십시오.

Best Value에서 다음 사항에 대해 어떻게 느끼셨습니까?

	매우 나쁘다	나쁘다	좋다	매우 좋다
가격				∨
물품		∨		
시간				∨
직원	∨			

의견: 많은 직원들이 손님에 대해 신경을 쓰지 않는 것으로 보입니다. 제가 질문을 하면, 그들은 모르고 있거나 부정확한 답변을 합니다. 조금 전에도, 저는 한 직원의 주의를 끌려고 했지만, 그녀는 완전히 저를 무시했습니다. 이곳 서비스의 품질을 개선시키기 위해 무언가 조치를 취하시기 바랍니다.

이름: Thaddeus Toole

patronage 후원, 지원; 애용 | **strive to** ~하려고 노력하다 | **attention** 주의, 주목 | **ignore** 무시하다

받는 사람: Best Value의 전 직원
보낸 사람: Best Value 부사장 Marcus Dupree
제목: 최근의 설문 조사
날짜: 11월 10일

지난 달 설문 조사를 시행하기 위해 우리가 고용했던 업체에서, 사람들이 남긴 의견과 함께 자료들을 제출했습니다. 저희는 가격과 판매 제품에 대해 매우 높은 점수를 받았습니다. 대부분의 쇼핑객들은 영업 시간도 마음에 들어 했지만, 소수는 우리가 하루 24시간 문을 열기를 바라고 있습니다. 하지만, 응답자 중 50% 이상이 직원들을 '나쁨'이나 '매우 나쁨'으로 평가했습니다. 의견들은 믿을 수 없을 정도로 냉혹했습니다. 우리에게 직원 문제가 있는 것으로 보이며, 우리는 이에 대한 조치를 취할 필요가 있습니다. 몇몇 고객들은 우리 직원이 자신을 무시하거나 질문에 답을 하지 못한다는 이유로 더 이상 이곳에서 쇼핑을 하지 않겠다고 진술했습니다. 우리는 이에 대해 시급히 조치를 취해야 합니다. 곧 연휴가 다가올 것이며, 우리는 매출이 하락하지 않도록 해야 합니다. 우리는 그때 대부분의 수익을 거두고 있으므로, 고객을 잃게 된다면 우리는 올해 목표를 달성하지 못하게 될 것입니다.

score (점수를) 얻다 | **respondent** 응답자 | **rate** 평가하다, 등급을 매기다 | **incredibly** 믿을 수 없을 정도로, 매우 | **harsh** 가혹한 | **revenue** 수입 | **cause** ~의 원인이 되다 | **objective** 목표

오래된 매장의 새로운 프로그램

트렌턴 (12월 5일) – 시내에서 가장 오래된 매장 중 한 곳에서 새로운 프로그램을 실시할 예정이다. Best Value는, 1852년 이래로 영업을 하고 있는데, 한 달 전 시행된 설문 조사의 결과를 접하고 자신들에게 문제가 있다는 점을 깨달았다. "우리 고객들은 만족하지 못하고 있었습니

다."라고 Travis Butler 사장이 말했다. "따라서 저희는 새로운 프로그램을 도입했고, 이는 성공적인 것으로 여겨집니다." Best Value의 전 직원은 현재 10시간 동안의 교육을 받고 있다. 그들은 고객 관계에 대해 배우고, 또한 매장에서 판매되는 모든 것에 대해 배우고 있다. "제가 이곳에서 일을 시작했을 때에는 어떤 질문에도 대답을 할 수 없었지만, 이제는 이곳에 있는 모든 제품들의 사용법을 알고 있어요."라고 매장에서 근무하는 Kimberly Charles가 말했다. "저는 이제 고객분들을 돕는 것이 좋고, 근무 시간이 끝나도 몇몇 기구들을 사용해 보면서 남아 있는 것도 좋아해요."라고 그녀는 덧붙였다.

realize 깨닫다 | **institute** 도입하다, 시작하다 | **relation** 관계 | **shift** 근무 (시간) | **practice** 연습하다 | **gadget** 도구, 기기

196 고객들은 설문 조사 작성의 대가로 무엇을 받을 수 있는가?
   (A) 사은품
   (B) 할인 쿠폰
   (C) 음료
   (D) 상품권

| 해설 | 첫 번째 지문인 설문지에서 설문을 작성하면 '다음 방문 시 사용할 수 있는 10%의 할인 쿠폰'(a coupon for 10% off on your next visit here)을 받을 수 있다고 나와 있기 때문에 정답은 (B)가 된다.

197 Toole 씨가 Best Value 직원에 대해 언급한 것은 무엇인가?
   (A) 그들은 교육을 더 받아야 한다.
   (B) 그들은 자신의 업무를 잘 수행하지 않는다.
   (C) 그들은 그의 질문에 답을 할 수 있다.
   (D) 그들은 때때로 그에게 무례하게 말을 했다.

| 해설 | Best Value 직원에 관한 Toole 씨의 구체적인 의견은 '의견란'을 살펴봄으로써 확인할 수 있다. 의견란에서 Toole 씨는 직원들이 고객에 대해 신경을 쓰지 않는다고 말하고, 본인의 질문에 직원들이 답을 하지 않거나 잘못된 답을 한다고 지적한다. 따라서 그가 언급한 사항은 (B)이다.

198 Toole 씨의 평가는 대다수의 응답자들과 어떤 항목에서 다른가?
   (A) 가격
   (B) 물품
   (C) 시간
   (D) 직원

| 해설 | 첫 번째 지문의 표와 두 번째 지문인 회람 내용을 비교하면 정답을 찾을 수 있다. 회람에서는 '가격'(prices)과 '물품'(selection of items)에 대해 높은 점수가 매겨졌으며, '영업 시간'(hours)에 대해서도 대부분의 쇼핑객들이 만족해 한다고 했고, 반면 '직원'(employees) 평가는 좋지 못하다고 했다. 따라서 이를 Toole 씨의 체크 표시와 비교해 보면 서로 차이를 보이는 항목은 (B)의 '물품'임을 알 수 있다.

199 Dupree 씨는 무엇을 하자고 제안하는가?
   (A) 새로운 프로그램을 실시한다
   (B) 제품을 할인 판매한다
   (C) 몇몇 직원들을 해고한다
   (D) 매출이 떨어지지 않도록 한다

| 해설 | 두 번째 지문인 회람에서 Dupree 씨는 '연휴 기간 동안 매출이 떨어지지 않도록 해야 한다'(we have to make sure sales don't suffer)고 강조하고 있으므로 그가 제안한 사항은 (D)로 볼 수 있다.

200 Kimberly Charles는 누구인가?
   (A) Best Value 매니저
   (B) Best Value 고객
   (C) Best Value 직원
   (D) Best Value 대표 이사

| 해설 | 마지막 지문인 기사에서 Kimberly Charles라는 인물은 'Best Value 매장에서 일하는 직원'(who works at the store)으로 소개되어 있다. 따라서 정답은 (C)이다.

Actual Test 04

p.171

● 정답

PART 1
1 (C) 2 (D) 3 (A) 4 (C) 5 (D)
6 (C)

PART 2
7 (C)   8 (B)   9 (C)   10 (C) 11 (A)
12 (B) 13 (B) 14 (A) 15 (C) 16 (C)
17 (B) 18 (C) 19 (B) 20 (A) 21 (B)
22 (B) 23 (A) 24 (C) 25 (C) 26 (A)
27 (B) 28 (C) 29 (A) 30 (A) 31 (C)

PART 3
32 (C) 33 (A) 34 (B) 35 (C) 36 (D)
37 (A) 38 (D) 39 (B) 40 (C) 41 (C)
42 (D) 43 (A) 44 (B) 45 (A) 46 (C)
47 (B) 48 (D) 49 (D) 50 (B) 51 (B)
52 (D) 53 (C) 54 (C) 55 (A) 56 (B)
57 (A) 58 (C) 59 (D) 60 (D) 61 (C)
62 (A) 63 (B) 64 (D) 65 (A) 66 (B)
67 (B) 68 (D) 69 (C) 70 (C)

PART 4
71 (B) 72 (D) 73 (B) 74 (B) 75 (A)
76 (C) 77 (D) 78 (D) 79 (C) 80 (A)
81 (B) 82 (D) 83 (C) 84 (C) 85 (A)
86 (C) 87 (A) 88 (B) 89 (C) 90 (A)
91 (B) 92 (B) 93 (A) 94 (D) 95 (C)
96 (B) 97 (D) 98 (B) 99 (C) 100 (D)

PART 5
101 (C) 102 (A) 103 (A) 104 (C) 105 (D)
106 (C) 107 (C) 108 (B) 109 (C) 110 (A)
111 (D) 112 (B) 113 (C) 114 (A) 115 (D)
116 (B) 117 (B) 118 (D) 119 (B) 120 (D)
121 (B) 122 (B) 123 (A) 124 (C) 125 (B)
126 (B) 127 (D) 128 (B) 129 (A) 130 (D)

PART 6
131 (D) 132 (B) 133 (B) 134 (C) 135 (C)
136 (C) 137 (A) 138 (B) 139 (D) 140 (A)
141 (D) 142 (C) 143 (C) 144 (C) 145 (A)
146 (B)

PART 7
147 (D) 148 (C) 149 (A) 150 (C) 151 (C)
152 (A) 153 (A) 154 (C) 155 (A) 156 (D)
157 (B) 158 (A) 159 (C) 160 (A) 161 (C)
162 (A) 163 (C) 164 (D) 165 (D) 166 (B)
167 (C) 168 (D) 169 (D) 170 (C) 171 (B)
172 (A) 173 (B) 174 (A) 175 (D) 176 (C)
177 (C) 178 (A) 179 (C) 180 (C) 181 (B)
182 (A) 183 (D) 184 (D) 185 (C) 186 (D)
187 (A) 188 (A) 189 (B) 190 (D) 191 (D)
192 (A) 193 (B) 194 (B) 195 (B) 196 (C)
197 (C) 198 (B) 199 (D) 200 (A)

● PART 1

p.172

1   (A) Firemen are spraying the fire with water from the hose.
    (B) The crops in the garden are being watered.
    (C) Workmen with tools are walking in the same direction.
    (D) People are enjoying playing in the water.

    (A) 소방관들이 호스로 불이 난 곳에 물을 뿌리고 있다.
    (B) 정원의 작물에 물이 뿌려지고 있다.
    (C) 도구를 지닌 일꾼들이 같은 방향으로 걸어가고 있다.
    (D) 사람들이 물속에서 놀고 있다.

fireman 소방관 | **spray** 분사하다, 뿌리다 | **crop** 작물 | **direction** 방향

| 해설 | 주어진 사진만으로는 물을 뿌리고 있는 사람이 '소방관'(firemen)인지 불확실하며, '불이 난 곳'(fire)도 보이지 않으므로 (A)는 정답이 아니다. 물이 뿌려지고 있는 곳은 '작물'(crops)이 아니라 '바닥'이기 때문에 (B)도 오답이고, water라는 단어를 이용해 혼동을 유발하고 있는 (D)는 사진과 전혀 관련이 없는 설명을 하고 있다. 따라서 정답은 (C)인데, 여기에서는 두 사람이 가지고 있는 '삽'과 '호스'가 tools(도구)로 표현되어 있다.

2   (A) Swimmers are having a good time at the beach.
    (B) People are lying on the beach and sunbathing.
    (C) Some people are making a sandcastle on the beach.
    (D) Bags have been set down in places on the beach.

    (A) 수영객들이 해변에서 즐거운 시간을 보내고 있다.
    (B) 사람들이 해변에 누워서 일광욕을 하고 있다.
    (C) 몇몇 사람들이 해변에서 모래성을 쌓고 있다.
    (D) 해변 곳곳에 가방이 놓여 있다.

sunbath 일광욕을 하다 | **sandcastle** 모래성 | **in places** 곳곳에

| 해설 | '수영을 하는 사람'(swimmers)은 보이지 않으므로 (A)는 오답이고, 사진 속 사람들은 옷을 입은 채 서 있거나 앉아 있기 때문에 (B)도 정답이 될 수 없다. '모래성'(sandcastle)을 쌓고 있는 사람 역시 찾아 볼 수 없으므로 (C)도 오답이다. 정답은 사람들 주변에 놓여 있는 가방들을 적절히 설명하고 있는 (D)이다.

3   (A) One of the men is going into the pastry store.
    (B) The customers are purchasing pastries at the bakery.
    (C) Two men are baking a cake together in the kitchen.
    (D) A shopper is selecting some desserts from the store window.

    (A) 한 남자가 제과점으로 들어가고 있다.
    (B) 손님들이 빵집에서 패스트리를 구입하고 있다.
    (C) 주방에서 두 사람이 함께 케이크를 굽고 있다.
    (D) 쇼핑객이 매장 진열장에서 디저트를 고르고 있다.

pastry store 제과점 | **pastry** 패스트리 | **bake** 굽다 | **select** 선정하다, 고르다 | **store window** (상점의) 진열장 유리

| 해설 | 제과점으로 보이는 상점 안에 한 남자가 들어가고 있으므로 (A)가 가장 적절한 설명이다. 제품을 구입하는 사람은 없으므로 (B)는 정답이 될 수 없고, 사진 속 두 사람은 손님으로 보이기 때문에 (C) 또한 오답이다. 상

103

점 밖에 있는 사람은 진열대를 바라보고 있을 뿐, 제품을 '고르고 있는'(is selecting) 것은 아니므로 (D) 역시 잘못된 설명이다.

4 (A) All of the passengers have boarded the subway.
(B) The mechanic is trying to repair the train.
(C) The subway doors have not been closed yet.
(D) The conductor is collecting tickets from passengers.

(A) 모든 승객들이 지하철에 탑승했다.
(B) 정비사가 열차를 수리하려고 노력 중이다.
(C) 지하철 문이 아직 닫히지 않았다.
(D) 안내원이 승객들로부터 표를 걷고 있다.

board 탑승하다 | **mechanic** 정비공 | **conductor** 지휘자; 안내원, 승무원

| 해설 | 한 승객이 열차 밖에 있으므로 '모든 승객'(all of the passengers)이 탑승했다는 (A)의 설명은 사실과 다르며, 사진에서 '수리를 하고 있는'(repair) 사람 역시 찾아볼 수 없으므로 (B)도 정답이 아니다. 정답은 열차의 문이 열려 있는 모습을 묘사한 (C)이다. (D)의 경우, 사진 왼쪽에 있는 사람이 '안내원'(conductor)일 수는 있지만, '표를 걷고 있지는'(is collecting tickets) 않으므로 (D)도 정답이 될 수 없다.

5 (A) The man is lifting a fork from his plate.
(B) They have arrived at a fork in the road.
(C) Some people are lifting weights in the gym.
(D) The forklift is parked beside some boxes.

(A) 남자가 접시에 있던 포크를 집어 올리고 있다.
(B) 그들은 도로 분기점에 도착했다.
(C) 몇몇 사람들이 체육관에서 역기를 들어 올리고 있다.
(D) 지게차가 상자들 옆에 주차되어 있다.

fork 포크; 분기점, 갈래 | **weight** 역기, 아령 | **gym** 체육관 | **forklift** 지게차

| 해설 | 이 문제의 경우 forklift(지게차)라는 단어를 알고 있으면 문제를 쉽게 풀 수 있고, 그렇지 않으면 forklift라는 단어를 이용한 함정에 빠지기 쉽다. (A)와 (B) 모두 fork라는 단어로 혼동을 유발하고 있는데, (A)의 fork는 '포크'를 (B)의 fork는 '분기점'을 의미한다. (C) 역시 lift라는 단어를 이용하여 오답을 유도하고 있는 함정으로, 여기에서의 lift는 '들어올리다'라는 의미의 동사로 사용되었다.

6 (A) People are holding umbrellas to keep from getting wet.
(B) The doors to the buildings are being closed.
(C) Each table has some chairs set up around it.
(D) The umbrellas above the tables are being put up.

(A) 사람들이 비를 맞지 않기 위해 우산을 쓰고 있다.
(B) 건물의 문이 닫히고 있다.
(C) 각 테이블 주위에 의자가 놓여 있다.
(D) 테이블 위의 파라솔이 세워지고 있다.

umbrella 우산, 파라솔

| 해설 | 노천 테이블을 보여 주는 전형적인 야외 사물 사진이다. 따라서 '사람'의 행동과 직간접적으로 연관이 있는 (A), (B), (D)는 모두 정답이 될 수 없다. 정답은 테이블과 의자들의 배치 방식을 올바르게 설명하고 있는 (C)이다.

● PART 2   p.176

7 How would you like me to prepare your coffee?
(A) She's making copies.
(B) From the local café.
(C) Black with no sugar.

커피를 어떻게 준비해 드릴까요?
(A) 그녀는 복사를 하고 있어요.
(B) 근처 카페로부터요.
(C) 설탕 없이 블랙으로요.

prepare 준비하다 | **make a copy** 복사하다 | **local** 지역의, 인근의

| 해설 | 의문사 how를 사용하여 원하는 커피의 종류를 묻고 있다. (A)는 coffee와 발음이 비슷한 copies(복사물)를 이용한 함정이고 (B)는 coffee로부터 연상이 가능한 café(카페)를 이용한 함정이다. 따라서 가장 자연스러운 답변은 (C)이다.

8 When will I be informed about the status of my application?
(A) A promotion within two months.
(B) Sometime around Thursday.
(C) You can do that on our Web site.

제 지원 상황에 관해 언제 통보를 받게 되나요?
(A) 2개월 내의 승진이요.
(B) 목요일 정도에요.
(C) 웹사이트에서 그렇게 하실 수 있어요.

inform 알리다, 통보하다 | **status** 상태 | **application** 지원

| 해설 | when을 이용하여 지원 상황에 관한 통보 일자를 묻는 질문이므로, '목요일'이라고 답한 (B)가 정답이다. 참고로 (C)는 지원 방법을 물었을 때 이어질 수 있는 답변이다.

9 Do you know where the office supplies happen to be?
(A) We buy from Alpha Stationery.
(B) It came as a total surprise.
(C) Look in the storage closet.

사무용품이 어디에 있는지 알고 있나요?
(A) 우리는 Alpha 문구점에서 구입했어요.
(B) 그것은 전혀 예상치 못한 일이었어요.
(C) 비품 수납장을 보세요.

storage closet 수납장

| 해설 | 간접의문문이 제시되면 후반부 내용에서 정답의 단서를 찾도록 한다. 이 질문은 결국 '사무용품이 있는 장소'를 묻는 것이므로 '비품 수납장'을 보라고 답한 (C)가 정답이다. (A)는 '구입처'를 묻는 질문에 적합한 답변이며, (B)는 supplies와 발음이 비슷한 surprise를 이용한 오답이다.

10 Shall I save a seat for you in the cafeteria?
(A) Yeah, the new café has great seats.
(B) That's fine. I'm already sitting here.
(C) No, I'm going to eat at my desk.

구내 식당에서 당신의 자리를 맡아 놓을까요?
(A) 네, 새로운 카페에는 멋진 좌석이 있어요.
(B) 괜찮아요. 저는 이미 여기에 앉아 있어요.
(C) 아니요, 저는 제 책상에서 식사를 할 거예요.

save a seat 자리를 맡다

| 해설 | 조동사 shall을 이용하여 '자리를 맡아 놓겠다'는 제안을 하고 있다. (A)는 질문의 seat를 중복 사용한 함정이며, (B)의 '이미 앉아 있다'는 말은 주어진 질문과 전혀 어울리지 않는 답변이다. 따라서 정답은 '책상에서 먹을 것이니 그럴 필요가 없다'며 거절의 의사를 밝힌 (C)이다.

11 Shouldn't you be heading to the conference room in a few minutes?
(A) No, the meeting got canceled.
(B) Sure, I'll call you in half an hour.
(C) Yes, we're ahead of our competitors.

몇 분 후에 콘퍼런스 룸으로 가지 않을 건가요?
(A) 네, 회의가 취소되었어요.
(B) 물론이에요, 제가 30분 후에 전화를 할게요.
(C) 네, 우리는 경쟁사들을 앞서고 있어요.

head to ~으로 향하다, ~으로 가다 | **cancel** 취소하다 | **ahead of** ~ 앞에 | **competitor** 경쟁자

| 해설 | 부정의문문을 통해 콘퍼런스의 참석 여부를 묻고 있으므로 '참석하지 않을 것이다'라고 밝힌 (A)가 정답이다. (B)는 전화를 달라는 부탁을 받았을 때 이어질 수 있는 답변이고, (C)는 질문의 heading과 발음이 비슷한 ahead를 이용한 오답이다.

12 Is it possible to have cable TV installed at my home?
(A) There's a game on channel 10.
(B) If you pay an installation fee.
(C) A house at 54 Rosemont Avenue.

저희 집에 케이블 TV를 설치하는 것이 가능한가요?
(A) 10번 채널에서 시합을 해요.
(B) 설치비를 지불하면요.
(C) Rosemont 가 54번지의 주택이요.

install 설치하다 | **installation fee** 설치비

| 해설 | '케이블 TV의 설치 여부'를 묻고 있으므로 이에 조건부로 가능하다고 답한 (B)가 가장 자연스러운 답변이다. (A)는 cable TV로 유추할 수 있는 channel이라는 단어로, (C)는 home과 의미가 유사한 house로 혼동을 일으키고 있는 답변이다.

13 Why did Mr. Martinson request Ms. Johnson's work file?
(A) She works in the Marketing Department.
(B) To review her performance last year.
(C) You'll have to file your own request.

Martinson 씨가 왜 Johnson 씨의 업무 파일을 요청했나요?
(A) 그녀는 마케팅 부서에서 일을 해요.
(B) 그녀의 작년 성과를 검토하기 위해서요.
(C) 당신은 당신의 요청서를 제출해야 할 거예요.

request 요구, 요청 | **file** 파일; (문서를) 보관하다, 제출하다 | **review** 검토하다 | **performance** 성과

| 해설 | 파일 요청의 '이유'를 묻고 있으므로 '성과를 검토하기 위해'라고 답한 (B)가 가장 적절한 답변이다. (A)는 근무 부서를 물었을 때 적합한 답변이고 (C)는 질문의 request와 file을 중복 사용한 함정이다.

14 Is it your turn to drive tomorrow, or is it mine?
(A) Neither. Jane's driving.
(B) I'll drive you home today.
(C) I'm pretty sure that's right.

내일은 당신이 운전할 차례인가요, 아니면 제가 할 차례인가요?
(A) 둘 다 아니에요. Jane이 운전할 거예요.
(B) 오늘은 제가 당신을 차로 집까지 데려다 줄게요.
(C) 그 말이 옳다고 생각해요.

turn 차례

| 해설 | 운전할 사람이 당신인지 나인지를 묻고 있는 선택의문문이다. 이에 대한 가장 적절한 답변은 제3자를 지목한 (A)이다. (B)는 drive를 중복 사용한 함정이며, (C)는 질문을 'Is it your turn to drive tomorrow?'로 잘못 들었을 경우에 선택할 수 있는 오답이다.

15 We had better order some more food for the event.
(A) Two large pizzas and a pitcher of soda.
(B) It's going to take place on Friday night.
(C) You're right. More people are attending it.

행사 음식을 더 주문하는 것이 좋겠어요.
(A) 라지 피자 두 개와 소다수 피처 하나요.
(B) 금요일 밤에 열릴 거예요.
(C) 당신 말이 맞아요. 더 많은 사람들이 참석할 거예요.

had better ~하는 편이 낫다 | **pitcher** 피처 | **take place** 일어나다, 발생하다

| 해설 | '~하는 편이 낫다'라는 의미의 had better를 사용하여 추가 주문의 필요성을 지적하고 있다. (A)는 식당에서 주문을 할 때 쓸 수 있는 표현이고, (B)는 행사가 시작되는 요일을 물었을 때 이어질 수 있는 답변이다. 따라서 정답은 상대방의 말에 호응을 한 (C)이다.

16 Why hasn't the appliance that I ordered been mailed yet?
(A) You can get a discount on it.
(B) I ordered it last Monday.
(C) It's not in stock at the warehouse.

제가 주문한 기기가 왜 아직도 발송되지 않았나요?
(A) 당신은 그에 대해 할인을 받을 수 있어요.
(B) 저는 지난 월요일에 주문을 했어요.
(C) 창고에 재고가 없어요.

appliance 기기 | **mail** 우편; (우편으로) 보내다 | **get a discount** 할인을 받다 | **in stock** 재고가 있는 | **warehouse** 창고

| 해설 | 의문사 why를 이용하여 주문품이 왜 아직 도착하지 않았는지를 묻고 있다. (A)는 질문의 order로부터 연상할 수 있는 표현인 get a discount를 이용한 함정이고, (B)는 order를 중복 사용함으로써 오답을 유도하고 있다. 정답은 '재고가 없어서'라는 이유를 밝힌 (C)이다.

17 You're picking the German delegation up at the airport, aren't you?
(A) They'll be here for the next two weeks.
(B) Jeremy volunteered to go there instead.
(C) She delegated several tasks to me.

당신이 독일 대표단을 마중하러 공항에 갈 거죠, 그렇지 않나요?
(A) 그들은 앞으로 2주 동안 이곳에 있을 거예요.
(B) 그 대신 Jeremy가 그곳에 가겠다고 자원했어요.
(C) 그녀는 제게 몇 가지 업무를 위임했어요.

pick up ~을 차에 태우러 가다, ~을 마중하다 | **delegation** 대표단, 파견단 | **volunteer** 자원하다 | **delegate** 위임하다

| 해설 | 공항에 마중 갈 사람이 당신인지 묻고 있다. (A)는 체류 기간을 물었을 때 이어질 수 있는 답변이고, (C)는 delegation의 동사형인 delegated로 오답을 유도하고 있는 함정이다. 정답은 '다른 사람이 갈 것이다'라며 간접적으로 no라는 의미를 전달한 (B)이다.

18 Who's giving the presentation at the staff meeting?
(A) It's going to start at eight o'clock sharp.
(B) We can open the presents later in the day.
(C) Ken told me that Ms. Ruiz is doing that.

직원 회의에서 누가 발표를 할 건가요?
(A) 8시 정각에 시작할 거예요.
(B) 오늘 오후에 선물을 개봉할 수 있어요.
(C) Ruiz 씨가 할 것이라고 Ken이 얘기해 주더군요.

presentation 발표 | **sharp** 날카로운; 정각 | **present** 발표하다; 선물

| 해설 | 의문사 who를 이용하여 발표를 할 사람이 '누구'인지 묻고 있다. (A)는 행사의 시작 시간을 묻는 질문에 적합한 답변이고, (B)는 presentation과 발음이 유사한 present로 오답을 유도하고 있는 함정이다. 따라서 'Ruiz가 할 것이라고 들었다'고 답변한 (C)가 정답이다.

105

19 How quickly can we get the fax machine repaired?
  (A) It was around several years ago.
  (B) Let's call the service provider and ask.
  (C) Sure, I'll send you my fax number.

팩스 기기를 얼마나 빨리 수리할 수 있을까요?
  (A) 대략 몇 년 전이었어요.
  (B) 서비스 제공 업체에 전화해서 물어보죠.
  (C) 물론이에요, 제가 당신에게 제 팩스 번호를 보내 줄게요.

service provider 서비스 제공자, 서비스 제공 업체

| 해설 | how quickly를 이용하여 수리 기간을 묻고 있다. 따라서 '(자신은 모르니) 서비스 제공 업체에 물어보자'고 답한 (B)가 가장 자연스러운 답변이다. (A)는 시점을 묻는 질문에, (C)는 팩스 번호를 묻는 질문에 어울릴 법한 답변이다.

20 What do you think about purchasing tickets for next Wednesday's concert?
  (A) Go ahead and buy a couple for me, please.
  (B) It's going to feature some popular bands.
  (C) Everyone on the team should act in concert.

다음 수요일 공연의 티켓을 구매하는 것을 어떻게 생각하나요?
  (A) 그렇게 해서 제 것도 두 장 사 주세요.
  (B) 인기 있는 몇몇 밴드들이 나올 거예요.
  (C) 팀 전체가 똑같이 움직여야 해요.

feature 특징; 특징을 이루다 | **in concert** 일제히, 소리를 맞추어

| 해설 | 「What do you think ~」는 상대방의 의견을 물어볼 때 사용되는 표현이다. 따라서 긍정적인 반응을 보인 한 후 '내 것도 구입해 달라'는 요청을 한 (A)가 답변으로서 가장 적절하다. (B)는 concert로부터 연상할 수 있는 popular bands를 이용한 함정이고, (C)는 concert를 반복 사용한 오답인데, 여기서 in concert는 '일제히'라는 의미이다.

21 Why haven't the survey results been published?
  (A) It hit the bestseller list after being published.
  (B) All the data is still being compiled.
  (C) Sure, I don't mind taking a survey.

설문 결과가 왜 발표되지 않고 있나요?
  (A) 그것은 출판된 후 베스트셀러 목록에 올랐어요.
  (B) 모든 자료들을 아직도 집계 중이에요.
  (C) 물론이에요, 저는 설문 조사를 꺼리지 않아요.

survey 설문 조사; 살펴 보기 | **result** 결과 | **publish** 공표하다, 출판하다 | **hit the bestseller list** 베스트셀러 목록에 오르다 | **compile** 편집하다; 종합하다, 집계하다 | **take a survey** 설문 조사를 받다

| 해설 | 설문 조사의 결과가 발표되지 않는 '이유'를 묻고 있다. (A)는 published로부터 연상할 수 있는 hit the bestseller list(베스트셀러 목록에 오르다)라는 표현으로 혼동을 일으키고 있고, (C)는 survey를 이용한 함정으로 여기서 take a survey는 '설문 조사를 받다'라는 의미로 사용되었다. 정답은 '자료가 집계 중이기 때문에'라고 그 이유를 밝힌 (B)이다.

22 Could you please direct me to the Marketing Department?
  (A) Take a right at the third intersection.
  (B) Follow me. I'm going there now.
  (C) He's quite an experienced marketer.

마케팅부로 가는 길을 알려 주시겠어요?
  (A) 세 번째 교차로에서 우회전하세요.
  (B) 저를 따라 오세요. 저도 지금 그곳에 가는 중이거든요.
  (C) 그는 상당히 경험이 많은 마케팅 전문가예요.

direct 지휘하다; 길을 안내하다 | **intersection** 교차로 | **experienced** 경력이 많은, 숙련된

| 해설 | direct(안내하다)라는 말만 듣고 정답을 (A)로 골라서는 안 된다. Marketing Department(마케팅부)를 야외에서 찾을 일은 없기 때문이다. 정답은 '자신을 따라오라'고 답변한 (B)이다.

23 Someone had better assist that customer who has been waiting.
  (A) I'm free, so I'll give her a hand.
  (B) It's our job to provide customer assistance.
  (C) I've been waiting for almost an hour.

기다리고 있는 저 고객을 누군가 도와 주는 것이 좋겠어요.
  (A) 제가 한가하니 제가 도움을 줄게요.
  (B) 고객을 돕는 것이 우리의 일이에요.
  (C) 저는 거의 한 시간째 기다리고 있어요.

assist 돕다 | **give ~ a hand** ~을 돕다 | **provide** 제공하다 | **assistance** 도움, 원조

| 해설 | 실질적으로 이 진술은 '고객을 도와 달라'는 요청의 의미를 담고 있다. 따라서 '내가 도와 주겠다'고 답한 (A)가 가장 적절한 답변이다. (B)는 assist의 명사형인 assistance를 이용함으로써, (C)는 waiting을 반복 사용함으로써 각각 오답을 유도하고 있다.

24 When is the commercial for the new product line going to air?
  (A) Sometime during the middle of the week.
  (B) It features all kinds of new cosmetics.
  (C) Yeah, she's done something new with her hair.

신제품들에 대한 광고가 언제 방송을 타게 되나요?
  (A) 주 중반쯤에요.
  (B) 그것은 온갖 종류의 새로운 화장품들을 다루어요.
  (C) 네, 그녀가 머리에 새로운 시도를 했어요.

commercial 상업 광고 | **product line** 제품 라인, 제품군 | **air** 방송되다 | **cosmetic** 화장품

| 해설 | 의문사 when을 이용하여 광고가 방송되는 '시점'을 묻고 있다. 따라서 정답은 '주 중반'이라고 답한 (A)이다. (B)는 질문과 전혀 관련이 없는 엉뚱한 대답이고, (C)는 air와 발음이 비슷한 hair로 오답을 유도하고 있는 함정이다.

25 What about purchasing a laptop instead of a desktop?
  (A) This one is too costly.
  (B) They bought it last week.
  (C) I'd prefer not to do that.

데스크톱 대신 노트북 컴퓨터를 구입하는 것은 어떤가요?
  (A) 이것은 너무 비싸요.
  (B) 그들은 지난 주에 그것을 샀어요.
  (C) 그렇게 하고 싶지는 않군요.

laptop 노트북 컴퓨터 | **instead of** ~ 대신에 | **desktop** 데스크톱 | **costly** 비싼

| 해설 | 「What about ~」는 「How about ~」와 마찬가지로 상대방의 의견을 물을 때 주로 사용되는 표현이다. 노트북 컴퓨터 구입에 대한 상대방의 '의견'을 묻고 있으므로 이에 대해 부정적인 반응을 보인 (C)가 정답이다. (A)의 this one은 가리키는 대상이 불분명하며, (B)는 purchasing(구입하다)과 의미가 같은 bought(사다)를 이용한 함정이다.

26 How much money do I owe you for these items?
  (A) Don't worry. It's my treat.
  (B) I deposited it in your account.

106

(C) There are five of them in total.

이 제품에 대해 제가 얼마를 드려야 하죠?
(A) 걱정하지 마세요. 제가 살게요.
(B) 제가 당신 계좌로 입금했어요.
(C) 총 5개가 있어요.

owe 빚지다 | **treat** 다루다, 취급하다; 대접, 한턱 | **deposit** 예금하다 | **account** 계좌 | **in total** 전부, 총

| 해설 | how much money를 이용하여 자신이 지불해야 할 금액을 묻고 있다. 이에 대해 '내가 내겠다'며 돈을 따로 줄 필요가 없음을 알린 (A)가 가장 적절한 답변이다. (B)는 '돈'과 관련이 있는 deposited와 account라는 단어를 이용해 혼동을 유발하고 있고, (C)는 '수량'을 물었을 때 이어질 수 있는 대답이다.

27 What caused the power to go out all over the city?
(A) I don't know why my phone has no power.
(B) Some electric lines got knocked down.
(C) There will be thunderstorms next week.

무엇 때문에 시 전체의 전기가 나갔나요?
(A) 제 전화기가 왜 방전되었는지 모르겠어요.
(B) 일부 전선들이 쓰러졌어요.
(C) 다음 주에 뇌우가 발생할 거예요.

cause 야기하다, ~의 원인이 되다 | **power** 힘; 전력 | **go out** (전기가) 나가다, 정전되다 | **electric line** 전선 | **knock down** 쓰러지다 | **thunderstorm** 뇌우

| 해설 | what에 동사 cause가 수반되는 의문문은 결국 이유를 묻는 질문이다. 따라서 정전의 이유를 직접적으로 밝힌 (B)가 정답이다. 시내의 정전 이유를 묻는 질문에 '휴대폰이 방전된 이유'를 언급한 (A)는 정답이 될 수 없고, (C)는 미래시제로 답함으로써 질문과 어울리지 않는다.

28 Don't forget to submit your nominations for the employee of the month.
(A) Thanks. I can't believe that I won.
(B) Yes, he was nominated again.
(C) I turned mine in to Clarice already.

이 달의 직원상 후보를 제출해야 한다는 점을 잊지 마세요.
(A) 고맙습니다. 제가 상을 탔다니 믿을 수가 없군요.
(B) 네, 그가 또다시 후보로 올랐어요.
(C) 제 것은 이미 Clarice에게 제출했어요.

nomination 지명, 추천 | **the employee of the month** 이 달의 직원 | **nominate** (후보로) 지명하다 | **turn in** 제출하다

| 해설 | 부정명령문을 이용하여 후보 명단을 제출할 것을 당부하고 있다. (A)는 수상 소감을 밝힐 때 어울리는 문장이며, (B)는 nominations의 동사형인 nominated를 이용한 함정이다. 따라서 정답은 '이미 제출했다'는 사실을 밝힌 (C)이다.

29 When can you send someone to look at the air conditioner?
(A) It's not very cool in this room.
(B) I can't find anything wrong with it.
(C) A repairman will be there by two.

언제 사람을 보내서 에어컨을 살펴보도록 할 건가요?
(A) 이 방은 그다지 시원하지 않군요.
(B) 잘못된 점을 찾을 수가 없어요.
(C) 수리 기사가 2시까지 그곳으로 갈 거예요.

air conditioner 에어컨

| 해설 | when을 이용하여 사람이 언제 올 것인지를 묻고 있으므로 '2시에 갈 것'이라고 답한 (C)가 가장 적절한 답변이다. (A)는 air conditioner(에어컨)로부터 연상할 수 있는 단어인 cool(시원한)을 이용한 함정이고, (B)는 질문과 전혀 상관이 없는 '점검 결과'를 알리고 있다.

30 I wonder what's taking Mr. Yeats so long.
(A) He called and said he's caught in traffic.
(B) This is much longer than I had expected.
(C) He's looking forward to meeting everyone.

Yeats 씨가 오는 데 왜 그처럼 시간이 오래 걸리는지 궁금하군요.
(A) 그가 전화를 해서 차가 꽉 막혔다고 말했어요.
(B) 이것은 제가 예상했던 것보다 훨씬 길군요.
(C) 그는 모두를 만나게 되기를 고대하고 있어요.

wonder 궁금하다 | **caught in traffic** 차가 꽉 막힌, 교통 체증에 걸린 | **look forward to** ~을 기대하다, ~을 고대하다

| 해설 | 간접의문문을 이용해서 Yeats 씨가 늦는 이유를 묻고 있으므로 정답은 '교통 체증' 때문이라고 답한 (A)이다. 참고로 질문에서 take는 '시간이 걸리게 하다'라는 의미로 사용되었다.

31 Which type of wallpaper would look best in this room?
(A) I've never put up wallpaper before.
(B) This is going to be my office.
(C) They all seem all right to me.

어떤 종류의 벽지가 이 방에 가장 잘 어울릴까요?
(A) 저는 전에 벽지를 발라본 적이 없어요.
(B) 이곳이 제 사무실이 될 거예요.
(C) 제게는 모두가 괜찮아 보이는군요.

wallpaper 벽지 | **put up wallpaper** 벽지를 바르다

| 해설 | 질문이 which type of wallpaper로 시작하고 있으므로, 답변 또한 벽지의 종류를 언급하고 있어야 한다. 어울리는 벽지를 묻는 말에 '나는 벽지를 발라본 적이 없다'고 대답한 (A)는 적절한 답변이 될 수 없고, '이곳이 내 사무실이 될 것이다'는 (B) 역시 질문과 전혀 어울리지 않는 엉뚱한 답변이다. 따라서 정답은 '모든 벽지가 좋아 보인다'고 본인의 의견을 밝힌 (C)이다.

● PART 3 p.177

[32-34]

M I'm so glad I decided to attend the seminar today. The talk which Mark Kenmore just gave on how to market products in foreign countries was brilliant.

W I couldn't agree with you more. He mentioned several things that seem obvious now but which had never previously occurred to me. I'm going to request that my firm implement some of his suggestions immediately.

M I'm glad I took comprehensive notes. I'm supposed to give a presentation on what I learned on Monday morning, and my coworkers should be pleased to hear what I have to tell them.

M 오늘 세미나에 참석하겠다는 결정을 내려서 정말 기쁘군요. 해외에 제품을 마케팅하는 법에 관한 Mark Kenmore의 강연은 정말 훌륭했어요.

W 전적으로 동감이에요. 지금은 명백해 보이지만 전에는 결코 제가 생각할 수 없는 몇 가지 사항들을 그가 언급했죠. 저는 회사에 그의 제안 중 몇 가지를 즉시 이행하자고 요청할 거예요.

M 전체적으로 필기를 해 두어서 다행이에요. 저는 월요일 오전에 제가 알게 된 내용에 대해 발표를 하기로 예정되어 있는데, 제 동료들은 제가 하는 말을 들으면 기뻐할 거예요.

brilliant 눈부신; 훌륭한, 멋진 | **obvious** 명백한 | **occur to** ~에게 떠오르다 | **implement** 시행하다 | **comprehensive** 포괄적인

32 화자들은 주로 무엇을 논의하고 있는가?
(A) Mark Kenmore와 그들의 관계
(B) 다가올 강연의 주제
(C) 그들이 참석했던 세미나
(D) 그날 오후의 계획

| 해설 | 화자들은 자신들이 들었던 Mark Kenmore라는 사람의 강연을 높이 평가하고 있다. 따라서 정답은 (C)이다.

33 여자는 무엇을 언급하는가?
(A) 그녀는 자신이 알게 된 지식을 차후에 활용할 계획이다.
(B) 그녀는 나중에 Mark Kenmore와 직접 만나고 싶어한다.
(C) 그녀는 Mark Kenmore가 강연에서 한 말을 메모해 두었다.
(D) 그녀는 다른 나라에서 제품을 마케팅할 것이다.

in the future 미래에, 장래에 | **in person** 직접, 몸소

| 해설 | 'I'm going to request that my firm implement some of his suggestions immediately.'라는 여자의 말에서 여자는 강연에서 들었던 내용을 회사에 적용시킬 것이라는 점을 알 수 있다. 따라서 정답은 (A)이다. 참고로 (C)는 여자가 아니라 남자가 한 일이다.

34 월요일에 어떤 일이 일어날 것인가?
(A) 여자가 발표를 할 것이다.
(B) 남자가 동료들에게 강연을 할 것이다.
(C) 남자가 특별 행사에 참석할 것이다.
(D) 여자가 관리자와 만날 것이다.

| 해설 | 대화의 마지막 부분에서 남자는 월요일 오전에 '자신이 알게 된 내용에 대해 발표할 것'(give a presentation on what I learned)이라고 언급하고, 이를 들으면 '동료들이 기뻐할 것'(my coworkers should be pleased)이라고 말한다. 따라서 월요일에는 남자가 동료들을 대상으로 발표를 할 것이므로 정답은 (B)이다. 남녀를 혼동하면 (A)를 정답으로 선택하는 실수를 범할 수 있으니 주의하도록 하자.

☑ **700점 넘기 포인트** 문제에 특정한 시간이나 장소를 나타내는 말이 있으면 대화를 들을 때 그와 관련된 부분을 특히 주의해서 듣도록 하자. 34번의 문제에서도 on Monday라는 시간을 나타내는 말이 등장하므로 대화에서 '월요일'과 관련된 내용에 집중을 해야 한다.

[35-37]

W I really appreciate your dropping by, Mr. Gardner. I want to show you exactly what's wrong with my apartment so that everything can be repaired.
M I came here as soon as I received your voicemail message, Ms. Woodrow. You indicated that there's a leaky pipe in the kitchen.
W Actually, that's happening in the bathroom. In the kitchen, the problem is that the light keeps blinking on and off, and it's driving me crazy.
M All right. Well, let me take a look at the pipe first since that's likely to be the more serious of the two issues.

W 들러 주셔서 정말 고맙습니다, Gardner 씨. 저는 모든 것이 수리될 수 있도록 제 아파트의 문제가 무엇인지를 정확히 알려 드리고 싶어요.
M 당신의 음성 메시지를 듣자마자 이리로 왔어요, Woodrow 씨. 주방에 물이 새는 파이프가 있다고 말씀하셨죠.

W 사실, 그것은 욕실에서 일어나고 있는 일이에요. 주방에서는, 조명이 계속 깜빡여서 제가 미칠 것 같아요.
M 좋아요. 음, 두 가지 문제 중에서는 파이프가 더 심각한 문제일 수 있으니 먼저 파이프를 살펴보도록 할게요.

drop by 들르다 | **as soon as** ~하자마자 | **voicemail message** 음성 메시지 | **leaky** 물이 새는, 누수의 | **blink on and off** 깜빡이다 | **be likely to** ~하기 쉽다 | **issue** 문제, 화제

35 여자는 왜 기뻐하는가?
(A) 남자가 그녀의 문제를 고쳐 주었다.
(B) 그녀에게는 수리할 것이 없다.
(C) 남자가 그녀의 아파트에 방문했다.
(D) 그녀가 스스로 문제를 해결했다.

| 해설 | drop by(들르다)라는 표현을 알고 있으면 정답이 (C)라는 사실을 쉽게 알 수 있다. 그녀가 문제를 알리기 위해 남자를 부른 것이므로 나머지 보기들은 사실과 전혀 다른 내용들이다.

36 주방의 문제는 무엇인가?
(A) 가스가 새는 곳이 있다.
(B) 냉장고가 작동을 멈추었다.
(C) 파이프에서 물이 떨어진다.
(D) 조명이 깜빡인다.

| 해설 | 주방의 문제와 욕실의 문제를 구분해서 들어야 한다. 정답은 (D)이고, (C)는 욕실의 문제이다.

37 남자는 아마도 이다음에 무엇을 할 것인가?
(A) 욕실의 문제를 해결한다
(B) 전구를 교체한다
(C) 바닥의 물기를 닦는다
(D) 음성 메시지를 남긴다

light bulb 전구

| 해설 | 대화의 마지막 부분에서 남자는 누수가 더 심각한 문제일 수 있기 때문에 '파이프를 먼저 보겠다'(let me take a look at the pipe first)고 말한다. 따라서 남자가 할 일은 누수 문제가 있는 욕실을 점검하는 것이므로 정답은 (A)가 된다.

[38-40]

M Hello, Ms. Desmond. This is Ian Carter calling from First-Class Furniture. We received your online order a few minutes ago, and we want to check on one thing.
W Yes? What do you need to know?
M You indicated that you'd like to have express shipping. However, while we have the table and chairs in our showroom, we have to acquire the sofa from our warehouse. That's going to take three days. Would you like us to go ahead and ship the table and chairs first?
W That would be ideal. I recently moved into a new home and don't have anywhere to sit since the movers haven't arrived with my possessions yet.

M 안녕하세요, Desmond 씨. 저는 First-Class 가구의 Ian Carter입니다. 몇 분전에 귀하의 온라인 주문을 받았는데, 한 가지 사항에 대해 확인을 하고 싶습니다.
W 네? 무엇을 알고 싶으신가요?

M 특급 배송을 원하신다고 하셨잖아요. 하지만, 테이블과 의자들은 전시실에 있는 반면, 소파는 저희가 창고에서 가지고 와야 합니다. 그러면 3일 정도가 걸릴 것이고요. 저희가 그대로 진행해서 테이블과 의자들을 먼저 배송해 드릴까요?

W 그러면 좋을 것 같군요. 저는 새 집으로 이사를 왔는데, 이삿짐 센터 직원들이 아직 가재 도구들을 가지고 오지 않아서 앉을 곳이 없어요.

express shipping 특급 배송 | **showroom** 전시실 | **warehouse** 창고 | **ship** (배에) 싣다, 운송하다 | **ideal** 이상적인 | **possession** 소유, 소유물, 재산

38 여자는 어떻게 제품을 주문했는가?
(A) 전화 통화를 함으로써
(B) 매장을 직접 방문함으로써
(C) 주문서를 우편으로 보냄으로써
(D) 웹사이트를 방문함으로써

| 해설 | 대화 초반부에 남자는 여자로부터 '온라인 주문'(online order)을 받았다고 이야기한다. 따라서 여자가 제품을 구입한 방법은 (D)이다.

39 매장은 여자에게 먼저 무엇을 보낼 것인가?
(A) 소파
(B) 테이블
(C) 침대
(D) 화장대

dresser 경대, 화장대

| 해설 | 남자는 현재 테이블과 의자는 가지고 있지만, 소파는 창고에서 가지고 와야 한다는 점을 안내한 후, '테이블과 의자만 먼저 배송하는 것'(ship the table and chairs first)에 대한 여자의 의견을 묻는다. 이에 대해 여자가 긍정적인 반응을 보이고 있으므로 배송이 먼저 이루어질 제품은 테이블과 의자이다. 따라서 정답은 이 중 하나를 가리키고 있는 (B)이다.

40 여자는 자신의 집에 대해 무엇을 말하는가?
(A) 최근에 보수되었다.
(B) 창고 근처에 위치해 있다.
(C) 가구가 들어오지 않았다.
(D) 현재 판매 중이다.

furnish 가구를 들이다

| 해설 | 대화의 마지막 부분에서 여자는 '가재 도구들이 도착을 하지 않아 앉을 곳이 없다(don't have anywhere to sit since the movers haven't arrived with my possessions yet)고 말한다. 따라서 정답은 (C)이다.

[41-43]

W Lionel, would you mind if one of my assistants accompanied me to our meeting this afternoon? I've got to show quite a few slides, and it would make it easier if someone else ran the projector.

M Sure, but what kinds of slides do you have? I wasn't expecting any type of visual aids.

W I visited the factory yesterday and took some pictures of the equipment which employees there have been complaining about. The pictures are quite revealing. Once you see how everything looks, you'll understand why the foremen there have been filling out forms requesting new machinery for the past three months.

W Lionel, 오늘 오후 회의에 제 보조 중 한 명을 데리고 가도 될까요? 저는 몇 장의 슬라이드를 보여 주어야 하는데, 다른 누군가가 프로젝터를 작동시키면 훨씬 편할 것 같아서요.

M 그래요, 하지만 어떤 종류의 슬라이드를 가지고 있나요? 저는 어떤 유형의 시각 자료도 예상하지 못하고 있었는데요.

W 저는 어제 공장을 방문해서 그곳 직원들이 불만을 가지고 있는 기기들의 사진을 몇 장 찍었어요. 사진들이 상당히 의미심장해요. 모든 것이 어떤 상태인지 알게 되면, 왜 그곳 작업반장들이 지난 3개월 동안 새로운 기기를 요청하는 양식을 작성했는지 이해가 될 거예요.

assistant 보조, 조수 | **accompany** 동반하다 | **projector** 영사기, 프로젝터 | **visual aid** 시각 보조 자료 | **revealing** 의미심장한, 흥미로운 점을 나타내는 | **foreman** 십장, 작업반장

41 여자는 무엇을 제안하는가?
(A) 내일 오후에 모임을 갖는다
(B) 공장의 작업반장 중 한 명에게 연락한다
(C) 다른 직원으로 하여금 자신을 돕도록 시킨다
(D) 프레젠테이션에 쓸 슬라이드를 만든다

| 해설 | 대화의 첫 부분에서 여자는 남자에게 '회의에 보조를 동반해도 되는지'(if one of my assistants accompanied me to our meeting this afternoon) 묻고 있다. 따라서 여자가 제안한 사항은 (C)이다.

42 화자들은 무엇을 할 계획인가?
(A) 입사 지원자들을 면접한다
(B) 양식을 작성한다
(C) 공장을 방문한다
(D) 회의를 한다

| 해설 | 화자들은 회의에서 선보일 슬라이드에 대해 이야기하고 있으므로 정답은 (D)이다. (B)는 작업반장들이 했던 일이고 (C)는 여자가 한 일이다.

43 여자는 무엇을 암시하는가?
(A) 그녀는 몇몇 기기의 교체를 찬성한다.
(B) 그녀는 몇 주 동안 공장을 방문하지 못했다.
(C) 그녀는 설비들이 근래에 고장 나지 않기를 바란다.
(D) 그녀는 오늘 오후에 주문서를 제출할 계획이다.

| 해설 | 대화의 마지막 부분에서 여자는 사진을 보면 기기 교체를 요청하는 작업반장들의 말을 이해할 수 있을 것이라고 말한다. 따라서 여자는 작업반장들의 주장에 일리가 있다는 점을 암시하고 있으므로 정답은 (A)이다.

[44-46]

M Pardon me, but I have a problem that I hope you can help me with.
W I'll do my best. What's the matter?
M I bought this radio yesterday, but when I tried using it, it wouldn't turn on.
W That's peculiar. Did you visit the Electronics Department to exchange it for another item?
M Yes, I was just there a few minutes ago, but the manager refused to help me.
W Hmm . . . Did you bring the receipt with you?
M No, but I brought the box with me, and the saleswoman who sold it to me remembers me. Can we just talk to her?
W Normally, we require a receipt. But I'll make an exception in this case. Why don't we visit the Electronics

Department together?
M　Sure. Let's go.

M　죄송하지만, 제게 문제가 생겨서 저를 도와 주셨으면 해요.
W　최선을 다할게요. 문제가 무엇인가요?
M　어제 이 라디오를 구입했는데, 사용하려고 하자 켜지지를 않네요.
W　이상하군요. 다른 제품으로 교환하기 위해 전자 제품 매장을 방문하셨나요?
M　네, 몇 분전에 그곳에 있었지만, 매니저가 도와 주기를 거부하더군요.
W　흠… 영수증을 가지고 오셨나요?
M　아니요, 하지만 박스를 가지고 왔고, 제게 판매를 한 판매원은 저를 기억하고 있어요. 그녀와 이야기를 나눌 수 있나요?
W　보통은, 영수증이 필요해요. 하지만 이번 경우만큼은 예외를 두도록 할게요. 함께 전자 제품 매장으로 가는 것이 어떨까요?
M　좋아요. 가시죠.

peculiar 이상한 | **refuse** 거부하다, 거절하다 | **normally** 평소에는, 보통은 | **make an exception** 예외를 두다

44　남자의 문제는 무엇인가?
(A) 그에게 무언가에 대한 너무 많은 비용이 부과되었다.
(B) 그가 구입한 제품이 정상적으로 작동하지 않는다.
(C) 매장 매니저가 그에게 영수증 발급을 거부했다.
(D) 그의 라디오가 어제 갑자기 작동이 되지 않았다.

| 해설 | 문제가 무엇인지 묻는 여자의 질문에 남자는 'I bought this radio yesterday, but when I tried using it, it wouldn't turn on.'이라고 답한다. 따라서 정답은 (B)이다. 라디오가 처음부터 작동이 되지 않았으므로 (D)는 정답이 될 수 없다.

45　여자가 "But I'll make an exception in this case"라고 말할 때 여자는 무엇을 의미하는가?
(A) 남자는 영수증 없이 제품을 교환할 수 있다.
(B) 남자는 그가 조금 전에 한 주문을 취소할 수 있다.
(C) 남자는 더 이상 양식을 작성하지 않아도 된다.
(D) 남자는 환불을 받게 될 것이다.

| 해설 | make an exception은 '예외를 두다'라는 뜻이다. 바로 앞 문장에서 '(물건을 교환하려면) 영수증이 필요하다'라고 언급했기 때문에, 여기에서 예외를 둔다는 의미는 '영수증 없이도 교환을 해 주겠다'는 의미로 받아들일 수 있다. 따라서 정답은 (A)이다.

46　화자들은 아마도 이다음에 무엇을 할 것인가?
(A) 매장 매니저에게 전화를 건다
(B) 고장이 난 제품을 수리한다
(C) 다른 코너에 간다
(D) 대체 부품을 찾는다

look for ~을 찾다 | **replacement part** 대체 부품

| 해설 | 대화의 마지막 부분에서 'Why don't we visit the Electronics Department together?'라는 여자의 제안을 남자가 수락하고 있다. 따라서 화자들은 전자 제품 매장에 갈 것이라고 예상할 수 있으므로 정답은 (C)이다.

[47-49]

M　Now that the interviews are complete, we need to determine who should be hired.
W　Eric Harrison is by far the most qualified applicant.
M　I agree, but he didn't perform very well on his interview. I wasn't particularly impressed with him.
W　I couldn't disagree more.
M　Yeah? Tell me why you think that way.
W　I thought the answers he gave were well thought out and showed sufficient knowledge of the pharmaceutical industry. Sure, he seemed a bit nervous, but he's only a college student. I don't blame him for being a bit jittery.
M　What you say makes sense, but I'd like to call him in for a second interview before we offer him the position. Can you set it up for some time next week?
W　Sure.

M　면접이 끝났으니, 누구를 채용해야 할지 결정을 내려야 해요.
W　단연코 Eric Harrison이 가장 적합한 지원자예요.
M　저도 동의하지만, 그는 면접을 잘 보지 못했어요. 저는 그로부터 깊은 인상을 받지는 않았어요.
W　저는 결코 동의할 수 없어요.
M　예? 왜 그렇게 생각하는지 말해 주세요.
W　저는 그가 한 대답이 심사 숙고해서 한 말이었고 그가 제약업계에 관한 충분한 지식을 보여 주었다고 생각했어요. 물론, 그가 다소 긴장한 것으로 보이기는 했으나, 그는 대학생일 뿐이에요. 그가 약간 초조해 했다고 해서 그를 비난하지는 않겠어요.
M　당신 말에 일리가 있기는 하지만, 저는 우리가 그에게 일자리를 제안하기에 앞서 그를 2차 면접에 부르고 싶어요. 다음 주 중으로 면접 일정을 잡아 줄래요?
W　그럴게요.

now that ~이므로 | **by far** 단연코 | **qualified** 자격이 있는 | **perform** 수행하다 | **particularly** 특히 | **well thought out** 심사 숙고한, 면밀히 계획한 | **sufficient** 충분한 | **pharmaceutical industry** 제약업계 | **nervous** 불안한, 초조한 | **blame** 비난하다 | **jittery** 초조한 | **make sense** 말이 되다, 이치에 맞다

47　화자들은 무엇을 논의하는가?
(A) 그들이 참석할 프레젠테이션
(B) 면접 결과
(C) 몇몇 프로젝트에 관한 그들의 업무
(D) 남자의 전근 신청

| 해설 | 화자들은 면접을 끝내고 누구를 고용해야 할지에 대해 이야기하고 있으므로 대화의 주제는 (B)로 볼 수 있다.

48　Eric Harrison은 누구인가?
(A) 대학 교수
(B) 약사
(C) 매니저
(D) 입사 지원자

pharmacist 약사

| 해설 | 대화 초반부에 여자는 'Eric Harrison is by far the most qualified applicant.'라고 말하면서 그가 지원자 중 가장 뛰어난 사람이라고 강조한다. 따라서 Eric Harrison의 신원은 (D)의 '입사 지원자'이다.

49　남자는 여자에게 무엇을 하라고 말하는가?
(A) 다른 사람들의 이력서를 살펴본다
(B) 제약업계에 대해 조사를 더 많이 한다
(C) 근무 중에 덜 긴장하는 법을 배운다
(D) 또 다른 면접 일정을 정한다

| 해설 | 남자는 여자에게 2차 면접을 실시하자고 제안한 후 'Can you set it up for some time next week?'라고 말한다. 따라서 남자가 지시한 사항은 2차 면접 일정을 정하라는 것이므로 정답은 (D)이다.

[50-52]

M Hi, Melanie. It's Ken from TWP, Inc.
W Hello, Ken. What can I do for you?
M I have a question for you regarding today's lunch get-together.
W Sure. Go ahead.
M I'm new in town, so I'm not quite sure how I should get to the restaurant. Can you tell me where it is?
W Of course. You know where my office is, don't you?
M Yes. I was there yesterday.
W From my office, go straight down Hampton Road two blocks and then take a left onto Lemon Street. The restaurant is the second building on the right.
M Okay, uh, I think I can do that.
W You know, on second thought, how about coming here first, and then we can go to Roberto's together?
M I think I'll take you up on your offer.

M 안녕하세요. Melanie. TWP 주식회사의 Ken이에요.
W 안녕하세요. Ken. 무엇을 도와 드릴까요?
M 오늘 점심 회동과 관련해서 질문이 있어요.
W 그렇군요. 말씀하세요.
M 저는 시내가 생소해서, 어떻게 식당에 가야 할지 잘 모르겠어요. 어디에 있는지 알려 줄 수 있으신가요?
W 물론이죠. 제 사무실이 어디인지 알고 계시죠, 그렇지 않나요?
W 알아요. 어제 그곳에 있었죠.
W 제 사무실에서, Hampton 로를 따라 두 블록 직진하신 다음에 Lemon 가에서 좌회전하세요. 식당은 오른쪽의 두 번째 건물이에요.
M 알겠어요, 어, 찾아갈 수 있을 것 같아요.
W 그러니까, 다시 생각해 보니, 먼저 여기로 오셔서, 우리가 함께 Roberto's에 가는 것이 어떨까요?
M 당신의 제안을 받아들일게요.

---

get-together 모임, 회동 | **on second thought** 다시 생각해 보니 | **take up on** ~을 수락하다

50 남자가 전화를 건 목적은 무엇인가?
(A) 회의를 확정시키기 위해
(B) 길을 안내받기 위해
(C) 방문 일정을 정하기 위해
(D) 시간을 더 요청하기 위해

| 해설 | 남자는 모임 장소가 어디인지 잘 모르겠다고 말한 후, 'Can you tell me where it is?'라며 여자에게 모임 장소의 위치를 묻고 있다. 따라서 남자가 전화를 건 이유는 (B)이다.

51 화자들은 오후에 무엇을 할 것인가?
(A) 프레젠테이션에 참석한다
(B) 함께 점심을 먹는다
(C) 부동산을 살펴본다
(D) 고객을 만난다

| 해설 | today's lunch get-together(오늘 오후의 점심 회동)와 restaurant(식당)가 정답의 단서다. 화자들은 식당에서 함께 점심을 먹게 될 것이므로 정답은 (B)이다.

52 남자는 어디에서 여자와 만날 예정인가?
(A) 자신의 사무실에서
(B) 식당에서
(C) Hampton 로에서
(D) 그녀의 사무실에서

| 해설 | 대화의 후반부에서 여자가 남자에게 '자신의 사무실로 올 것'(how about coming here first)을 제안하자 남자가 수락의 의사를 나타냈으므로 정답은 (D)이다. 대화의 초반부 내용만 듣고 정답을 (B)로 선택해서는 안 된다.

[53-55]

Man I just read the memo HR sent to everyone. I can't believe that Ted Martin is finally retiring.
Woman A I know what you mean. It will be strange not having him around anymore.
Woman B Are we going to have a party for him?
Woman A Yes, it's being held after work next Friday.
Man We should definitely buy him a retirement present. But what?
Woman B I've no idea.
Woman A I don't think we need to worry about that too much.
Man What makes you say that?
Woman A I'm positive the company will get Ted something. We might be asked to make donations, but when someone who's been employed here this long retires, the company always provides that person with a very nice gift.
Man Oh, right. That's what happened with Mary Burns.

Man 인사부에서 모두에게 보낸 회람을 조금 전에 읽어 보았어요. Ted Martin이 결국 은퇴를 할 것이라니 믿을 수가 없군요.
Woman A 무슨 의미인지 알겠어요. 그가 더 이상 주변에 있지 않으면 이상할 거예요.
Woman B 그를 위한 파티를 열 건가요?
Woman A 네, 다음 주 금요일 퇴근 시간 후에 열릴 거예요.
Man 그에게 반드시 은퇴 기념 선물을 사 주어야겠군요. 하지만 무엇을 사야 할까요?
Woman B 저는 모르겠어요.
Woman A 그에 대해서는 크게 걱정하지 않아도 될 것 같은데요.
Man 왜 그렇게 말을 하죠?
Woman A 저는 회사가 Ted에게 무언가를 줄 것이라고 확신해요. 돈을 모으자는 요청을 받을 수는 있겠지만, 이곳에서 오래 고용되었던 사람이 은퇴를 할 때에는, 회사가 항상 그 사람에게 매우 멋진 선물을 제공해 주죠.
Man 오, 맞아요. Mary Burns의 경우에도 그랬어요.

---

memo 메모, 회람 | **retire** 은퇴하다 | **retirement present** 은퇴 기념 선물 | **positive** 긍정적인; 확신하는 | **make a donation** 돈을 내다, 기부하다, 기증하다 | **provide A with B** A에게 B를 제공하다 | **gift** 선물

53 화자들은 무엇에 대해 이야기하고 있는가?
(A) 그들이 구입한 선물
(B) 새로운 관리자의 고용
(C) 그들이 받은 보너스
(D) 동료의 퇴사

resignation 사임, 사퇴

| 해설 | Ted Martin이라는 사람의 은퇴 소식에 대해 이야기를 나누고 있으므로 정답은 (D)가 된다.

54 다음 주 금요일에 무엇이 예정되어 있는가?
 (A) 시상식
 (B) 생일 파티
 (C) 고별 파티
 (D) 회사 야유회

farewell party 고별 파티

| 해설 | next Friday가 언급되고 있는 부분을 주의해서 듣는다. 여자B가 은퇴를 앞둔 직원의 파티가 열리는지 묻자 여자A는 '다음 주 금요일에 열릴 것'(it's being held after work next Friday)이라고 답한다. 따라서 다음 주 금요일에는 (C)의 '고별 파티'가 열릴 것이다.

55 남자는 Mary Burns에 대해 무엇을 암시하는가?
 (A) 그녀는 한때 화자들과 같이 일을 했다.
 (B) 그녀는 회사의 임원이다.
 (C) 그녀는 화자들에게 돈을 내라고 요청할 것이다.
 (D) 그녀는 최근에 접수 직원으로 고용되었다.

used to 한때 ~하곤 했다 | **executive** 중역, 임원

| 해설 | 장기 근속자가 은퇴를 하는 경우에는 회사가 선물을 마련했다는 이야기를 듣고 남자는 'That's what happened with Mary Burns.'라고 말한다. 따라서 Mary Burns 역시 같은 회사에서 일을 했던, 퇴직한 직원이라는 점을 알 수 있으므로 정답은 (A)이다.

[56-58]

W Good afternoon, Mr. Cutler. According to the request you filed, you're interested in transferring to another branch. You specifically mentioned St. Louis. May I ask why?
M That's where my parents live.
W Do you intend to live with them?
M No, but they're both elderly, so I would like to be near them in case they require assistance. My wife and I won't be living together with them though.
W Okay. Well, there happens to be an opening in the St. Louis office, but it's in the Marketing Department.
M I can handle that. Prior to being employed here, I did some marketing work for the company I previously worked at.
W Then it's settled. I'll approve the transfer. You'll start working there on the first of October.

W 안녕하세요, Cutler 씨. 당신이 요청한 바에 따르면, 당신은 다른 지사로의 전근에 관심이 있으시군요. 특별히 세인트루이스를 언급했고요. 이유를 물어봐도 될까요?
M 그곳은 제 부모님들이 살고 계신 곳이에요.
W 그분들과 함께 사실 생각인가요?
M 아니요, 하지만 두 분 모두 연로하셔서, 그분들께 도움이 필요하신 경우를 대비하여 제가 그 근처에 살고 싶어요. 하지만 제 아내와 제가 그분들과 함께 살지는 않을 거예요.
W 좋아요. 음, 세인트루이스 지사에 자리가 있기는 하지만, 마케팅부에 있어요.
M 제가 담당할 수 있어요. 이곳에 고용되기 전, 전에 일했던 회사에서는 제가 마케팅 업무를 맡았거든요.
W 그렇다면 해결되었군요. 전근을 승인할게요. 10월 1일에 그곳에서 업무를 시작하게 될 거예요.

file a request 요청하다, 청원하다 | **specifically** 특별히 | **elderly** 나이가 많은, 연로한 | **in case** ~하는 경우를 대비하여 | **handle** 다루다, 처리하다 | **previously** 이전에 | **settle** 해결하다 | **approve** 승인하다

56 화자들은 주로 무엇을 논의하는가?
 (A) 다른 회사로의 이동 가능성
 (B) 전근에 대한 남자의 바람
 (C) 마케팅부의 상황
 (D) 남자의 퇴사 의도

possibility 가능성 | **desire** 바람 | **intention** 의도, 의향

| 해설 | 남자의 전근 요청을 처리하기 위해 여자가 몇 가지 질문을 하고 있는 상황이다. 따라서 정답은 (B)이다.

57 남자는 왜 세인트루이스에 살고 싶어하는가?
 (A) 가족과 가까이 있기 위해
 (B) 그곳 학교에 다니기 위해
 (C) 예전 상사와 함께 일하기 위해
 (D) 그곳에서 새로운 지점을 개설하는 일을 돕기 위해

| 해설 | 전근 이유를 묻는 여자의 질문에 남자는 '부모님에게 도움이 필요한 경우를 대비하기 위해 부모님과 가까운 곳에 살고 싶다'(I would like to be near them in case they require assistance)고 답한다. 따라서 그가 세인트루이스에서 살고 싶어하는 이유는 (A)이다.

58 남자는 왜 "I can handle that"이라고 말하는가?
 (A) 자신이 출장을 갈 수 있다는 점을 입증하기 위해
 (B) 자신이 기꺼이 낮은 급여를 수락하겠다는 점을 나타내기 위해
 (C) 자신이 마케팅부에서 일을 할 수 있음을 주장하기 위해
 (D) 기꺼이 승진을 하겠다는 마음을 보이기 위해

be capable of ~을 할 수 있다 | **be willing to** 기꺼이 ~하다 | **willingness** 기꺼이 함

| 해설 | 세인트루이스 지사에 자리가 있기는 하지만, 그 자리는 마케팅부에 있다는 이야기를 듣고 남자가 한 말이다. 따라서 정답은 '그 자리에 자신이 적합하다'는 의미와 상통하는 (C)이다.

[59-61]

W Mr. Tanaka, I know we're planning to meet tomorrow at 9:30, but would it be acceptable to postpone our meeting until the day after tomorrow?
M How come you need to delay the meeting?
W There's a problem in one of the laboratories, so I need to spend the entire day at the Brighton facility tomorrow.
M Ah, I see. Well, Thursday doesn't work for me because I'm attending a sales conference in Framingham. How does Friday sound?
W Morning or afternoon?
M Either. I'm free all day.
W Let's get together in the morning then since I'm not sure how long we need to talk for. How about at 9:00 in my office?
M That works for me. I'll be sure I don't have any meetings the entire morning just in case.

W Tanaka 씨, 우리가 내일 9시 30분에 회의를 할 계획이라는 것은 저도 알고 있지만, 회의를 모레 이후로 미루는 것은 어떠신가요?
M 왜 회의를 미뤄야 하나요?
W 실험실 중 한 곳에 문제가 생겨서, 제가 내일은 하루 종일 Brighton 시설에 있어야 하거든요.
M 아, 알겠어요. 음, 목요일은 제가 프레이밍햄에서의 세일즈 컨퍼런스에 참석할 것이라서 시간이 안 되어요. 금요일은 어떠신가요?
W 오전이요, 아니면 오후요?

112

M 둘 중 아무 때나요. 저는 하루 종일 시간이 비어 있어요.
W 그러면, 우리가 얼마나 오래 이야기를 하게 될 것인지 확실하지 않기 때문에, 오전에 만나기로 하시죠. 9시에 제 사무실이 어떠신가요?
M 저는 좋아요. 만약의 경우를 대비해서 오전 중에 회의가 잡히지 않도록 확실히 해 둘게요.

acceptable 받아들일 수 있는 | **postpone** 미루다, 연기하다 | **the day after tomorrow** 모레 | **laboratory** 실험실 | **facility** 시설 | **all day** 하루 종일 | **get together** 모이다, 만나다 | **just in case** 만약의 경우를 대비하여

59 여자는 내일 무엇을 할 계획인가?
 (A) 콘퍼런스에 간다
 (B) 실험실을 방문한다
 (C) 프레이밍햄으로 여행을 간다
 (D) 컨설턴트를 만난다

consultant 상담가, 컨설턴트

| 해설 | 남자가 회의를 미루자는 이유가 무엇인지 묻자, 여자는 '실험실'에서 문제가 생겼다고 답한 후, I need to spend the entire day at the Brighton facility tomorrow라고 그 이유를 밝히고 있다. 따라서 여자가 내일 할 일은 (B)의 '실험실 방문'이다.

60 화자들은 언제 회의를 할 것인가?
 (A) 화요일에
 (B) 수요일에
 (C) 목요일에
 (D) 금요일에

| 해설 | 회의를 미루자는 제안에 남자는 목요일은 시간이 안 되고 금요일은 괜찮다고 말한다. 여자도 이에 대해 긍정적인 반응을 보이고 있으므로 화자들이 회의를 하게 될 요일은 (D)의 '금요일'이다.

61 남자는 왜 "That works for me"라고 말하는가?
 (A) 여자에게 그녀가 한 말을 다시 한 번 말해달라고 요청하기 위해
 (B) 여자에게 그 문제에 대해 더욱 힘써달라고 요청하기 위해
 (C) 여자의 제안을 승낙하기 위해
 (D) 여자와 만날 또 다른 시간을 제안하기 위해

repeat 반복하다 | **agreement** 동의, 승인 | **alternative** 대안의

| 해설 | 'That works for me'는 '나로서는 좋다'라는 승낙의 뜻으로, 여자의 말이 'How about at 9:00 in my office?'라는 제안에 대한 답이다. 따라서 (C)가 정답이다.

[62-64]

Man Before we conclude our weekly staff meeting, is there anything else we ought to cover? Maya, do you have something to add?
Woman A Yes, I do. The computers we're using are getting rather old, so we should strongly consider upgrading them.
Man There isn't enough money in the budget for that.
Woman A I understand, but we can't run a lot of new programs on our computers.
Woman B That's a big problem, Jason. I tried to put the latest accounting software on my computer yesterday, but I couldn't do it.
Woman A You had problems with that program as well?
Woman B Yeah. If I can't upgrade to the new software, I'm going to be a lot less efficient at my job.

Man Okay. I'll speak with Mr. Prokofiev and see if we can get some additional funding.

Man 이번 주 직원 회의를 마치기 전에, 우리가 다루어야 할 문제가 또 있나요? Maya, 추가해야 할 사항이 있나요?
Woman A 네, 그래요. 우리가 사용하고 있는 컴퓨터가 다소 오래 되어서, 컴퓨터 업그레이드를 강력히 고려해 보아야 해요.
Man 예산상 그에 대한 자금은 충분치가 않아요.
Woman A 이해는 하지만, 우리 컴퓨터로는 다수의 새로운 프로그램들을 작동시킬 수가 없어요.
Woman B 그건 큰 문제예요, Jason. 저는 어제 제 컴퓨터로 최신 회계 소프트웨어를 설치하려고 했지만, 그럴 수가 없었죠.
Woman A 그 프로그램과도 문제가 있었죠?
Woman B 예. 새 소프트웨어로 업그레이드를 할 수 없다면, 업무가 상당히 비효율적이 될 거예요.
Man 알겠어요. 제가 Prokofiev 씨와 이야기를 해서 추가적인 자금을 지원받을 수 있는지 알아볼게요.

conclude 결론짓다, 마무리하다 | **cover** 덮다; 다루다 | **add** 추가하다, 더하다 | **latest** 최신의 | **efficient** 효율적인, 효과적인 | **funding** 자금 지원

62 남자가 "There isn't enough money in the budget for that"이라고 말할 때 남자는 무엇을 의미하는가?
 (A) 회사가 새 컴퓨터를 구입하지 않을 것이다.
 (B) 올해에는 어떤 직원의 급여도 인상되지 않을 것이다.
 (C) 새 사무용품에 관한 주문이 모두 취소될 것이다.
 (D) 직원들은 더 이상 콘퍼런스에 참석할 수 없다.

pay raise 임금 인상

| 해설 | 컴퓨터를 업그레이드해야 한다는 여자의 제안에 대한 남자의 답변이다. '예산상 돈이 충분하지 않다'는 말은 회사에 구입할 여력이 없다는 뜻을 나타내기 때문에 (A)가 정답이다.

63 여자들은 무엇에 관한 문제를 겪었는가?
 (A) 사장과 만날 시간을 정하는 것
 (B) 컴퓨터 프로그램을 설치하는 것
 (C) 프로젝트에 관한 자금 지원을 받는 것
 (D) 직원 회의에 참석하는 것

install 설치하다

| 해설 | 여자A는 '새로운 프로그램을 작동시킬 수 없다'(we can't run a lot of new programs)는 점을, 여자B는 '회계 프로그램을 설치할 수가 없다'(I tried to put the latest accounting software on my computer yesterday, but I couldn't do it)는 점을 각각 문제로 삼고 있다. 따라서 여자들이 겪은 문제는 (B)이다.

64 남자는 자신이 무엇을 할 것이라고 말하는가?
 (A) 기존 기기를 교체한다
 (B) 프로그램을 다운로드한다
 (C) 전문가와 이야기한다
 (D) 자금을 요청한다

expert 전문가

| 해설 | 대화의 마지막 부분에서 남자는 '추가적인 자금을 지원받을 수 있는지'(if we can get some additional funding) 물어보겠다고 말한다. 따라서 남자가 하게 될 일은 (D)이다.

[65-67]

W Hello. This is Wilma Peterson calling from Waterman Electronics.

Electronics.
M Good afternoon, Ms. Peterson. Is there something I can help you with?
W Yes, there is. I ordered a large number of T-shirts for my company's annual summer picnic. But I realized that I miscounted the number of employees we have.
M Sure. Do you need to purchase some more shirts?
W Yes. I forgot we recently hired a couple of new workers, so they need shirts, too.
M No problem. How big are they?
W They're both around average size, so could you add two more shirts to the size I ordered the most of, please?
M No problem. And just to inform you, we'll send the T-shirts out on Wednesday, so they should arrive by Friday.
W Thanks so much.

W 안녕하세요. 저는 Waterman 전자의 Wilma Peterson이에요.
M 안녕하세요, Peterson 씨. 제가 도와 드릴 일이 있을까요?
W 네, 있어요. 저는 올해 회사의 여름 야유회를 위해 다량의 티셔츠를 주문했죠. 하지만 제가 저희 직원들의 숫자를 잘못 계산했다는 점을 깨달았어요.
M 그러시군요. 셔츠를 더 구입하셔야 하나요?
W 네. 얼마 전에 신입 직원을 두어 명 고용했다는 점을 제가 잊고 있었는데, 그들에게도 셔츠가 필요해죠.
M 문제 없습니다. 크기가 어떻게 되나요?
W 두 사람 모두 평균 사이즈 근처이기 때문에, 제가 주문한 대다수의 셔츠 크기로 두 장 더 추가해 주실 수 있으신가요?
M 문제 없어요. 그리고 참고로 말씀을 드리면, 저희는 티셔츠를 수요일에 보내 드릴 것이어서, 금요일까지는 도착을 할 거예요.
W 정말 고마워요.

a large number of 다수의, 많은 | realize 깨닫다 | miscount 잘못 세다 | inform 알리다, 통지하다

65 여자는 왜 티셔츠를 필요로 하는가?
 (A) 회사 야유회를 위해
 (B) 콘퍼런스를 위해
 (C) 현장 학습을 위해
 (D) 스포츠 행사를 위해

field trip 현장 학습

| 해설 | 대화 초반부에서 여자는 '회사의 야유회를 위해'(for my company's annual summer picnic) 티셔츠를 주문했다고 말하고 있으므로 정답은 (A)이다.

66 도표를 보아라. 여자는 어떤 사이즈의 셔츠를 더 주문하는가?
 (A) 스몰
 (B) 미디움
 (C) 라지
 (D) 엑스 라지

| 해설 | 여자는 so could you add two more shirts to the size I ordered the most of, please라고 말하면서 주문한 대다수의 셔츠 크기로 두 장을 추가해 줄 것을 요청하고 있다. 도표에서 가장 많은 장수를 차지하고 있는 크기는 M이므로(26장) 정답은 (B)이다.

67 회사는 언제 셔츠를 발송할 것인가?
 (A) 화요일에
 (B) 수요일에
 (C) 목요일에
 (D) 금요일에

| 해설 | 대화 후반부의 we'll send the T-shirts out on Wednesday라는 말에서 셔츠는 (B)의 '수요일'에 발송될 예정임을 알 수 있다. 참고로 (D)의 '금요일'은 셔츠가 도착하는 요일이다.

[68-70]
W Here are your credit card and receipt, sir.
M Thank you very much. Oh, by the way, could you give me a bit of assistance, please?
W I'll do my best. What do you need?
M I'm looking for a store that sells kitchenware. My colleagues told me there is one in the mall here, but I can't find it anywhere on the map.
W Ah, you're looking for Taylor's. It opened a few days ago, so that's why you can't find it listed. All you need to do is go to the floor above us. Take the escalator up and then turn to the right.
M That's easy. Thanks for your assistance.
W You're welcome. And thank you for shopping at Wilson's. Please come again soon.
M I will. Thanks.

W 신용 카드와 영수증이 여기에 있습니다, 고객님.
M 정말 고마워요. 오, 그건 그렇고, 제게 약간의 도움을 주실 수 있으신가요?
W 최선을 다할게요. 무엇이 필요하신가요?
M 저는 주방용품을 판매하는 매장을 찾고 있어요. 제 동료가 이곳 쇼핑몰 안에 하나가 있다고 말해 주었는데, 지도상 어느 곳에서도 찾을 수가 없군요.
W 아, Taylor's를 찾고 계시는군요. 이틀 전에 오픈을 했기 때문에, 목록에서는 찾으실 수 없을 거예요. 우리가 있는 곳에서 한 층 위로 올라만 가시면 되어요. 에스컬레이터를 타고 올라가신 후, 우회전 하세요.
M 간단하군요. 도와 주셔서 고마워요.
W 천만에요. 그리고 Wilson's에서 쇼핑해 주셔서 고맙습니다. 또 오세요.
M 그럴게요. 고마워요.

by the way 그런데, 그건 그렇고 | kitchenware 주방용품 | mall 쇼핑몰

68 남자는 무엇을 구입하고 싶어하는가?
 (A) 서적
 (B) 전자 제품
 (C) 의류
 (D) 주방용품

| 해설 | 'I'm looking for a store that sells kitchenware.'라는 남자의 말을 통해 남자가 구입하고 싶어하는 것은 (D)의 '주방용품'임을 알 수 있다.

69 남자는 왜 도움을 요청하는가?
 (A) 그는 전에 쇼핑몰을 방문해 본 적이 없다.
 (B) 예상했던 것보다 매장이 문을 일찍 닫았다.
 (C) 매장이 지도에 나타나 있지 않다.
 (D) 그는 매장의 상호명을 잊었다.

| 해설 | 남자는 자신이 주방용품점을 찾고 있는데, '지도에서 찾을 수 없다'(I can't find it anywhere on the map)며 여자에게 매장의 위치를 묻고 있다. 따라서 남자가 도움을 청하는 이유는 (C)이다.

70 도표를 보아라. 남자는 어느 층으로 가야 하는가?
   (A) 2
   (B) 3
   (C) 4
   (D) 5

| 해설 | 남자가 찾는 주방용품점에 가기 위해 여자는 '한 층 더 위로 가야 한다'(go to the floor above us)고 안내한다. 한편 대화의 후반부에서는 화자들이 Wilson's라는 매장에 있다는 것을 알 수 있다. 이 두 가지 사항을 종합하면 남자가 찾는 주방용품점은 Wilson's 서적이 있는 3층의 위층, 즉 (C)의 4층에 있다는 점을 알 수 있다.

PART 4   p.183

[71-73]

W Good afternoon, Craig. It's Julie. I'm afraid I'm going to miss our meeting thirty minutes from now. I was on my way to your office when I received a call from my son's school. Apparently, he broke his leg while playing soccer during recess, so he has been taken to the hospital. I've got to get there as soon as I can, so that's where I'm heading now. Would you mind meeting me tomorrow in the afternoon? I'm available any time after lunch. How about sending me a text message since I won't be able to answer my phone at the hospital? I hope you understand.

W 안녕하세요, Craig. Julie예요. 안타깝지만 지금부터 30분 후에 있을 회의에 제가 참석하지 못할 것 같아요. 당신 사무실로 가던 중에 저는 아들의 학교로부터 온 전화를 받았어요. 듣자 하니, 아들이 쉬는 시간에 축구를 하다가 다리가 부러져서, 병원으로 옮겨졌다고 하더군요. 가능한 빨리 그곳에 도착해야 하기 때문에, 저는 지금 그곳으로 가고 있어요. 저와의 회의를 내일 오후에 해도 괜찮을까요? 점심 시간 이후로는 아무 때나 만날 수 있어요. 병원에서는 전화를 받을 수가 없을 수도 있기 때문에 제게 문자 메시지를 남기는 것이 어떨까요? 당신이 이해해 주기를 바라요.

on one's way to ~으로 가는 도중에 | **recess** 휴회, 휴식 | **take A to B** A를 B로 데리고 가다 | **head** 향하다 | **available** 이용할 수 있는; 만날 수 있는

71 무엇이 문제인가?
   (A) 화자는 약속에 대해 잊고 있었다.
   (B) 화자의 아들이 부상을 당했다.
   (C) 화자는 학교에 늦을 것이다.
   (D) 화자의 상사로 인해 그녀가 회의에 가지 못하게 되었다.

| 해설 | 화자는 약속을 지키지 못하는 이유를 '아들이 쉬는 시간에 축구를 하다가 다리가 골절되어'(he broke his leg while playing soccer during recess) 학교로 가야 하기 때문이라고 밝히고 있다. 따라서 문제로 볼 수 있는 것은 (B)이다.

72 화자는 언제 Craig와 만나고 싶어하는가?
   (A) 오늘 오후
   (B) 오늘 저녁
   (C) 내일 오전
   (D) 내일 저녁

| 해설 | 대화의 후반부에 화자는 'Would you mind meeting me tomorrow in the afternoon?'이라고 말하면서 상대방에 내일 오후에 만나자는 제안을 하고 있다. 보기 중에서 '내일 오후'에 해당되는 시간대는 (D)의

'내일 저녁'뿐이므로 (D)가 정답이다.

73 화자는 Craig에게 무엇을 할 것을 요청하는가?
   (A) 회의에 다른 사람을 초청한다
   (B) 회의가 가능한 시간에 관해 그녀에게 연락을 한다
   (C) 그녀에게 문자로 연락처를 남긴다
   (D) 그녀가 요청한 보고서를 팩스로 보낸다

availability 유효성; 가능성 | **contact number** 연락처 | **fax** 팩스를 보내다

| 해설 | 대화의 후반부에서 화자는 회의를 미루자는 제안을 한 후, 상대방에게 이에 관한 의견을 문자 메시지로 알려 줄 것을 부탁하고 있다. 따라서 정답은 (B)이다.

[74-76]

M It appears as though the unseasonably warm weather we've been getting in December is about to come to an end. Expect temperatures to plummet from today's high of 15 degrees to 3 degrees by tomorrow afternoon. And that's not the worst part. Tomorrow night, the temperature is going to drop below freezing, and it's highly likely that we'll see some snow flurries around midnight. By the day after tomorrow, you can expect up to 5 centimeters of snow along with temperatures as low as minus 5 degrees Celsius. So be sure to dress warmly when you go out tomorrow and be prepared for snowy conditions.

M 12월에 누려 왔던 계절에 맞지 않는 따뜻한 날씨가 곧 끝날 것으로 보입니다. 오늘 15도였던 최고 기온은 내일 오후 3도로 급격히 떨어질 것으로 예상됩니다. 그리고 가장 좋지 않은 소식은 그것이 아닙니다. 내일 밤, 기온이 영하로 떨어질 것이며, 자정 무렵에는 눈발이 날릴 가능성이 높습니다. 모레에는, 섭씨 영하 5도의 낮은 기온과 함께 최대 5센티미터의 눈이 내릴 것으로 예상됩니다. 그러니 내일 외출을 하실 때에는 반드시 옷을 따뜻하게 입으시고 눈이 올 경우를 대비하십시오.

appear as though ~처럼 보이다, ~인 것 같다 | **unseasonably** 계절에 맞지 않게 | **be about to** 막 ~하려고 하다 | **plummet** 곤두박질치다 | **drop** 떨어지다 | **below freezing** 영하로 | **it is highly likely that** ~할 가능성이 높다 | **snow flurry** 눈발

74 12월 날씨는 어떠했는가?
   (A) 정상이었다
   (B) 평년보다 따뜻했다
   (C) 추웠다
   (D) 매우 추웠다

| 해설 | 담화의 첫 문장에서 화자는 12월의 날씨를 unseasonably warm weather we've been getting이라고 소개하고 있다. 따라서 현재까지 12월의 날씨는 (B)의 '평년보다 따뜻했다'라고 설명할 수 있다.

75 화자가 "And that's not the worst part"라고 말할 때 화자는 무엇을 의미하는가?
   (A) 날씨가 나빠질 것이다.
   (B) 그는 조금 전에 좋지 않은 소식을 들었다.
   (C) 며칠 동안은 비가 그치지 않을 것이다.
   (D) 추운 날씨가 계속될 것이다.

| 해설 | 주어진 문장을 통해 화자는 '(앞서 말한) 이것이 가장 나쁜 점은 아니다'라고 말한 후, 이후 기온이 내려가고 눈이 내릴 것이라고 예보한다. 따라서 주어진 문장에서 화자는 (A)의 '날씨가 악화될 것'이라는 사실을 우회적으로

115

나타내고 있다.

> **700점 넘기 포인트** 주어진 문장에서 화자가 의도한 바를 묻는 문제의 경우, 지시어가 무엇을 가리키는지에 주의해야 한다. 위 문제에서 주어진 문장 속의 that은 앞서 언급한 날씨, 즉 '날씨가 추워져 기온이 3도까지 내려간다'는 것이다. 따라서 '그것이 가장 나쁜 점이 아니다'라는 언급은 앞으로 그보다 더 좋지 않은 날씨가 예상된다는 의미를 내포하고 있다.

76 모레 날씨는 어떨 것인가?
 (A) 따뜻하고 흐리다
 (B) 춥고 바람이 분다
 (C) 춥고 눈이 내린다
 (D) 춥고 비가 온다

| 해설 | 문제에서 the day after tomorrow(모레)가 핵심어구이므로 이와 관련된 부분을 집중해서 듣는다. '모레'의 날씨는 'By the day after tomorrow, you can expect up to 5 centimeters of snow along with temperatures as low as minus 5 degrees Celsius.'에서 찾아볼 수 있으므로 정답은 (C)가 된다.

[77-79]

W I've got some great news for all full-time and part-time employees here at the Western Department Store. You are now eligible for membership at the Coldwater Swimming Pool, which has just opened for the summer. Full-time employees can receive 50% off an individual or family membership while part-timers are eligible for 30% discounts on either type of membership. Both types of employees qualify for 60% discounts on swimming lessons. If you're interested in this great deal, speak with Juliet Foreman in the personnel office on the second floor. She can provide you with all of the details.

> W 이곳 Western 백화점의 정규직 및 계약직 직원분들께 좋은 소식이 있습니다. 이제 여러분들께서는 Coldwater 수영장의 회원 자격을 얻으실 수 있는데, 이곳은 여름을 맞이하여 얼마 전에 문을 연 수영장입니다. 정규직 직원분들께서는 개인 회원 혹은 가족 회원으로 가입하실 때 50%의 할인 혜택을 받으실 수 있고, 계약직 직원분들께서는 두 경우 중 한 경우에 30%의 할인을 받으실 수 있습니다. 두 유형의 직원 모두 수영 강습에 대해서는 60%의 할인을 받으실 수 있습니다. 이처럼 좋은 조건에 관심이 있으시면, 2층 인사부의 Juliet Foreman에게 말씀해 주십시오. 그녀가 모든 세부 정보들을 알려 드릴 수 있습니다.

full-time 정규직의 | **part-time** 파트타임의, 비정규직의 | **be eligible for** ~에 대한 자격이 있다 | **individual** 개인 | **deal** 거래 | **personnel office** 인사과 | **detail** 세부 사항

77 안내 방송의 목적은 무엇인가?
 (A) 환불을 받는 법을 설명하기 위해
 (B) 행사의 마감 날짜를 언급하기 위해
 (C) 청자들에게 세일에 관해 상기시키기 위해
 (D) 특별 행사를 설명하기 위해

rebate 환불 | **deadline** 마감 시간 | **remind** 상기시키다, 기억나게 하다 | **special offer** 특가 상품

| 해설 | 'Coldwater 수영장'에서 회원 등록 시 받게 될 직원 할인 혜택에 대해 안내하고 있으므로 안내 방송의 목적은 (D)로 볼 수 있다.

78 수영 강습의 할인 혜택은 누가 받을 수 있는가?

 (A) 직원 자녀
 (B) 정규직 직원만
 (C) 계약직 직원만
 (D) 모든 직원

| 해설 | 수영 강습에 대한 60% 할인 혜택은 '두 유형의 직원들 모두'(both types of employees)에게 적용된다고 했으므로 정답은 (D)이다.

79 화자들은 더 많은 정보를 얻기 위해 무엇을 해야 하는가?
 (A) 이메일을 보낸다
 (B) 수영장에 연락한다
 (C) 다른 직원에게 이야기한다
 (D) 팜플렛을 읽는다

| 해설 | 담화의 마지막 부분에서 정보를 더 얻고자 하는 사람은 '인사부의 Juliet Foreman이라는 직원에게 이야기하라'(speak with Juliet Foreman in the personnel office)고 안내한다. 따라서 화자들이 해야 할 일은 (C)가 된다.

[80-82]

W The Lexington Orchestra is holding open auditions this Saturday, April 2. The auditions will be held in the Cogswell Concert Hall from 9 A.M. until 8 P.M. No reservations are necessary. Simply show up with your instrument. You'll be asked to play two classical pieces and one modern piece of the conductor's choice. We welcome individuals who can play any instrument, but we're particularly interested in having more violins in the orchestra this year. Please note that members of the orchestra won't receive any financial compensation but will be given four complimentary tickets to each of the six summer performances.

> W Lexington 오케스트라가 이번 주 토요일인 4월 2일에 공개 오디션을 실시할 예정입니다. 오디션은 Cogswell 콘서트 홀에서 오전 9시부터 오후 8시까지 진행될 것입니다. 사전 등록은 필요하지 않습니다. 악기만 가지고 오십시오. 여러분들께서는 클래식 음악 두 곡과 지휘자가 선택한 현대 음악 한 곡을 연주하라는 요청을 받게 되실 것입니다. 저희는 어떤 악기든 연주할 수 있는 분들을 환영하지만, 올해에는 특히 오케스트라의 바이올린 연주자들을 더 모집하는데 관심이 있습니다. 오케스트라의 단원들은 금전적인 보상은 받지 못하게 될 것이나, 여섯 번의 여름 공연에 대한 각각 4장의 티켓을 무료로 받게 될 것이라는 점을 유념해 주십시오.

open audition 공개 오디션 | **reservation** 예약, 사전 등록 | **show up** 모습을 나타내다 | **instrument** 악기 | **piece** 곡 | **conductor** 지휘자 | **note** 주목하다 | **financial** 금전적인, 재정적인 | **compensation** 보상 | **complimentary** 무료의

80 안내 방송은 누구를 위한 것 같은가?
 (A) 연주자
 (B) 관객
 (C) 지휘자
 (D) 음악 교사

instructor 강사, 교사

| 해설 | 오케스트라의 '공개 오디션'(open auditions)에 대한 안내를 하고 있으므로 안내 방송의 대상은 오디션에 참가할 사람, 즉 (A)의 '연주자'가 될 것이다.

81 행사에 대해 언급된 것은 무엇인가?

116

(A) 이틀 동안 계속될 것이다.
(B) 개인들은 세 곡의 음악을 연주해야 한다.
(C) 참석자들은 두 개의 악기를 연주할 수 있어야 한다.
(D) 바이올리니스트만이 오디션 참가가 독려된다

encourage 격려하다, 고무시키다 | **try out** 선발 시험을 치르다

| 해설 | 'You'll be asked to play two classical pieces and one modern piece of the conductor's choice.'에서 참가자들은 클래식 두 곡과 현대 음악 한 곡을 연주해야 한다는 점을 알 수 있으므로 정답은 (B)가 된다. 오디션은 '4월 2일' 하루에 진행될 것이므로 (A)는 잘못된 내용이고, (B)의 '참가자들이 두 개의 악기를 연주해야 한다'는 언급은 담화에서 찾아볼 수 없다. 또한 바이올리니스트 모집에 보다 관심이 있다는 내용은 있지만, (D)와 같이 '바이올리니스트만 오디션 참가가 장려된다'는 것은 일종의 비약이다.

82 오케스트라 단원들은 무엇을 받는가?
(A) 급여
(B) 공연 CD
(C) 악기
(D) 콘서트 티켓

| 해설 | 대화의 마지막 부분에서 오케스트라 단원의 혜택에 대해 내용을 찾을 수 있다. 화자는 '금전적인 보상'(financial compensation)은 받을 수 없지만 여름 공연에 대해 각각 '4장의 무료 티켓'(four complimentary tickets)을 받을 수 있다고 했으므로 정답은 (D)가 된다.

[83-85]

M I know that each and every one of you works hard and that you have numerous deliveries to make on your routes. However, I've been getting some complaints from our customers regarding mistakes you've been making. We got a call this morning from a customer who claimed that the items in the package he received were shattered. They were antiques, so he's requesting $1,200 in compensation. Another customer remarked she was given a package belonging to someone else. We need to cut down on these and other mistakes. So please be more careful, or I'm going to have to let some of you go if you can't improve your performance.

M 여러분 각자가 그리고 여러분 모두가 열심히 일을 하고 있다는 점, 그리고 여러분들이 맡고 있는 배달 업무가 많다는 점도 저는 알고 있습니다. 하지만, 저는 여러분들이 저지르는 실수에 관해 고객들로부터 몇몇 불만 사항을 받고 있습니다. 오늘 아침 자신이 받았던 상자 안의 제품이 부서져 있었다고 주장하는 고객으로부터 한 통의 전화를 받았습니다. 그것은 골동품이었고, 그래서 그는 배상액으로 1,200달러를 요구하고 있습니다. 또 다른 고객은 자신에게 다른 사람의 소포가 왔다고 언급했습니다. 우리는 이러한, 그리고 그 밖의 실수들을 줄여야 합니다. 그러니 보다 신경을 써 주시기를 바라며, 그렇지 못하는 경우, 성과가 나타나지 않으면 여러분 중 일부는 이곳을 떠나야 할 것입니다.

numerous 많은 | **route** 노선, 루트 | **shatter** 산산조각이 나다 | **antique** 골동품 | **compensation** 보상 | **remark** 언급하다 | **belong to** ~에 속하다 | **cut down** 줄이다, 삭감하다

83 화자는 누구에게 이야기를 하고 있는가?
(A) 전화 교환원
(B) 선적부 직원
(C) 배달 직원
(D) 사무실 접수 담당자

telephone operator 전화 교환원 | **personnel** 직원 | **receptionist** 접수 담당자

| 해설 | 화자는 청자들의 업무를 deliveries라고 지칭하고 있으며 청자들에게 택배를 받은 고객들의 불만 사항을 알리고 있다. 따라서 청자의 신원은 (C)의 '배달 직원' 혹은 '배달 기사'로 볼 수 있다.

84 화자는 어떤 문제를 언급하는가?
(A) 돈을 도둑맞았다
(B) 일부 상자가 분실되었다
(C) 일부 물품이 파손되었다
(D) 일부 주문품이 도착하지 않았다

| 해설 | 화자는 불만 사항의 예로서 '택배를 받은 물품이 파손되었다'(the items in the package he received were shattered)는 점과 '다른 사람의 택배를 받았다'(she was given a package belonging to someone else)는 점을 들고 있다. 따라서 이 중 전자를 언급하고 있는 (C)가 정답이다.

85 화자는 어떤 일이 일어날 수도 있다고 암시하는가?
(A) 사람들이 일자리를 잃을 수도 있다.
(B) 사람들이 정직을 당할 수도 있다.
(C) 사람들이 교육을 더 받게 될 수도 있다.
(D) 사람들이 전근을 갈 수도 있다.

suspend 매달다; 정직시키다, 정학시키다

| 해설 | 담화의 마지막 문장에서 화자는 상황이 개선되지 않는 경우에는 '일부 사람들을 내보낼 것'(I'm going to have to let some of you go)이라고 경고하고 있다. 따라서 화자가 암시한 점은 (A)이다.

[86-88]

W We've narrowed the job search down to the following three candidates: Vladimir Sobieski, Wilma Howard, and Maya Freeman. Each applicant has outstanding credentials and comes highly recommended. They all spent time here interviewing as well. Now, we need to arrive at a consensus regarding whom we should offer the open position to. I have my own personal favorite, but I'd like to hear from every one of you regarding yours. So let me give you all a chance to speak in support the person you'd like to become your new colleague. Jeff, let's start with you.

W 채용 공고를 통해 다음 세 명의 후보로 범위를 좁혔습니다: Vladimir Sobieski, Wilma Howard, 그리고 Maya Freeman입니다. 각 지원자들은 특별한 자격증을 보유하고 있고 많은 추천을 받았습니다. 또한 그들 모두가 이곳에서 면접을 보았습니다. 이제, 누구에게 공석인 자리를 제안해야 할 것인지에 관해 우리는 합의에 도달해야 합니다. 저도 개인적으로 선호하는 사람이 있기는 하지만, 여러분들의 선호도에 관해 여러분 모두의 이야기를 듣고 싶습니다. 그러니 여러분의 동료가 되었으면 하는 사람을 지지할 수 있는 발언 기회를 여러분 모두에게 드리도록 하겠습니다. Jeff, 당신부터 시작하죠.

job search 구인[구직] 활동 | **narrow down** (범위 등을) 좁히다 | **candidate** 후보 | **outstanding** 눈에 띄는, 탁월한 | **credential** 자격증 | **spend time -ing** ~하느라 시간을 보내다 | **consensus** 합의 | **open position** 공석 | **chance** 기회

86 무엇이 주로 논의되고 있는가?
(A) 몇몇 입사 지원자들의 자질
(B) 실시될 면접

(C) 현재 진행 중인 구인 과정
(D) 곧 충원이 되어야 할 직위

qualification 자격, 자질 | **currently** 현재

| 해설 | 화자는 담화의 시작 부분에서 채용 가능성이 높은 세 명의 입사 지원자들 소개한 후, 누구를 선택해야 할 것인지에 관해 청자들의 의견을 묻고 있다. 따라서 담화의 주제는 (C)로 볼 수 있다.

87 화자는 자기 자신에 대해 무엇을 언급하는가?
(A) 그녀는 채용에 관해 선호하는 사람이 있다.
(B) 그녀는 이미 최종 결정을 내렸다.
(C) 그녀는 Vladimir Sobieski와 두 차례 만난 적이 있다.
(D) 그녀는 면접을 더 실시하고 싶어한다.

| 해설 | 담화 후반부의 'I have my own personal favorite, but I'd like to hear from every one of you regarding yours.'라는 문장에서 화자는 자신이 선호하는 사람이 있다는 점을 언급한다. 따라서 정답은 (A)이다. 최종 결정을 내리기 전에 청자들의 의견을 구하고 있으므로 (B)는 사실과 다른 내용이며, (C)와 (D)는 언급된 바 없는 사항이다.

88 화자는 왜 "Jeff, let's start with you"라고 말하는가?
(A) 그가 후보 중 한 명에게 이야기를 해야 한다는 점을 말하기 위해
(B) 그에게 자신이 지지하는 사람을 말하도록 요청하기 위해
(C) 그가 지금 발표를 해야 한다는 점을 말하기 위해
(D) 그에게 면접 결과를 알려 달라고 요청하기 위해

| 해설 | 바로 앞 문장에서 화자는 '각자가 지지하는 사람들에 대해 발언할 기회를 주겠다'고 했다. 따라서 주어진 문장을 통해 화자가 말하려고 하는 바는 Jeff라는 사람을 시작으로 청자들의 의견을 듣겠다는 것이므로 정답은 (B)이다.

[89-91]

W As you know, we offered managerial positions to three applicants last week. We received positive responses from two of them. Both Jay Carpenter and Katy McDaniel accepted our offers and will begin working here two weeks from today. As for Delilah Cohen, she demanded more money than we're willing to offer, so we've retracted our offer of employment to her. We contacted Lucy van Horton this morning, and she requested one day to consider our offer. I think she's concerned about having to come here from across country, but I've been authorized by HR to cover her moving expenses if she requests that.

W 아시다시피, 우리는 지난 주에 세 명의 지원자에게 관리직을 제안했습니다. 그들 중 두 명으로부터는 긍정적인 대답을 받았습니다. Jay Carpenter와 Katy McDaniel은 우리 제안을 받아들였고 오늘부터 2주 후에 이곳에서 업무를 시작하게 될 것입니다. Delilah Cohen에 대해 말하자면, 그녀는 우리가 제공하려고 했던 것보다 더 많은 급여를 요구했기 때문에, 우리는 채용 제안을 철회했습니다. 우리는 오늘 아침 Lucy van Horton과 연락을 취했는데, 그녀는 우리의 제안을 생각해 볼 수 있도록 하루를 달라고 요청했습니다. 그녀가 전국을 가로질러 이곳으로 와야 한다는 점에 대해서 걱정하고 있는 것 같지만, 저는 그녀가 요청하는 경우 그녀의 이사 비용을 지원할 수 있는 권한을 인사부로부터 위임받았습니다.

managerial 관리직의 | **as for** ~에 대해 말하자면 | **demand** 요구하다 | **be willing to** 기꺼이 ~하다 | **retract** 취소하다, 철회하다 | **contact** 연락하다 | **ask for** ~을 요청하다 | **be concerned about** ~에 대해 우려하다 | **authorize** 권한을 주다 | **expense** 지출, 경비

89 Jay Carpenter는 어떤 일자리를 수락했는가?
(A) 인사부 직원
(B) 컴퓨터 프로그래머
(C) 관리자
(D) 소프트웨어 디자이너

| 해설 | 담화의 시작 부분에서 세 명의 후보에게 제안된 자리는 managerial positions(관리직)라는 사실을 알 수 있으므로 정답은 (C)가 된다.

90 Delilah Cohen에게 이루어진 제안은 왜 철회되었는가?
(A) 그녀는 더 높은 급여를 원했다.
(B) 그녀는 보다 많은 수당을 요구했다.
(C) 그녀는 2주 후에 업무를 시작하는 것을 원하지 않았다.
(D) 그녀는 보너스를 주장했다.

benefit 혜택; 수당 | **bonus** 보너스, 상여금

| 해설 | 채용 제안을 철회된 이유는 she demanded more money than we're willing to offer라는 어구에서 찾을 수 있다. 급여를 더 많이 요구한 것이 철회의 이유이므로 (A)가 정답이다.

91 여자는 Lucy van Horton을 위해 무엇을 할 수 있는가?
(A) 그녀에게 건강 보험을 제안한다
(B) 그녀에게 이사 비용을 지원한다
(C) 그녀가 집을 찾는 것을 돕는다
(D) 그녀의 초봉을 인상시킨다

health insurance 건강 보험

| 해설 | 담화의 마지막 문장에서 화자는 Lucy van Horton이 이사에 관한 걱정을 하고 있다고 말한 후, '나는 그녀의 이사 비용을 지원할 수 있는 권한을 인사부로부터 위임받았다'(I've been authorized by HR to cover her moving expenses)고 언급한다. 따라서 보기 중 화자가 할 수 있는 일은 (B)이다.

[92-94]

W Hello, Ms. Richardson. This is Emily Jenkins from JW Consulting. I sent you a schedule of the activities for next week's workshop by e-mail, but I haven't received a response yet. I'd like you to know I've decided that you're not going to give the lecture on foreign currency exchange this year. Instead, I'd like you to speak about solving workplace problems. The reason is that Brian Andropov just informed me he can't participate in this year's workshop, so you'll be taking his place. Thus you'll be speaking on a different day than you were previously scheduled. Let me know if this is going to be a problem.

W 안녕하세요, Richardson 씨. 저는 JW 컨설팅의 Emily Jenkins입니다. 저는 당신에게 이메일로 다음 주 워크숍의 행사 일정을 보냈지만, 아직 답장을 받지 못했습니다. 올해에는 당신이 외화 환전에 관한 강연을 하지 않아도 된다는 결정이 내려졌다는 점을 알려 드리고자 합니다. 대신, 당신이 직장 내의 문제 해결에 관한 강연을 맡아 주었으면 합니다. 그 이유는 Brian Andropov가 제게 올해 워크숍에 참가하지 못할 것이라고 조금 전에 알려 줘서, 당신이 그를 대신하게 될 것이기 때문입니다. 따라서 당신은 기존에 예정되어 있던 날과 다른 날짜에 강연을 하게 될 것입니다. 이러한 점이 문제가 될 것인지 제게 알려 주십시오.

response 대답, 응답 | **foreign currency** 외화 | **workplace** 직장, 일터 |

participate in ~에 참가하다 | take one's place ~을 대신하다 | thus 따라서

92 Jenkins 씨는 누구인가?
(A) 강사
(B) 컨설팅 회사 직원
(C) 콘퍼런스 참가자
(D) 은행원

lecturer 강사, 연사 | consultant 상담사, 컨설턴트 | banker 은행가, 은행원

| 해설 | 담화의 첫 문장에서 화자는 자신을 'JW 컨설팅' 소속이라고 밝히고 있다. 따라서 정답은 (B)이다.

> ✅ **700점 넘기 포인트** 회사나 부서를 가리키는 표현으로 화자의 신원을 확인하도록 하자. 예컨대 부동산 업체는 real estate agency로 나타내는데, real estate agent는 '부동산 중개인'을 뜻할 수도 있지만 '부동산 직원'을 가리킬 수도 있다. 한편 회계부는 Accounting Department로 나타내며, 이와 관련해서 accountant라는 단어가 사용되는 경우에는 '회계사' 보다 '회계부 직원'이라는 의미가 드러난다. 이 문제에서도 consultant는 '전문 상담사'라는 의미보다는 '컨설팅 회사 직원'이라는 의미로 받아들여야 한다.

93 도표를 보아라. Richardson 씨는 언제 강연을 하게 될 것인가?
(A) 월요일에
(B) 화요일에
(C) 수요일에
(D) 목요일에

| 해설 | Richardson 씨는 원래 foreign currency exchange(외화 환전)에 관한 강연을 할 계획이었으나, 화자는 그녀에게 Brian Andropov를 대신하여 solving workplace problems(직장 내의 문제 해결)에 관한 강연을 해 달라고 요청하고 있다. 따라서 solving workplace problems를 주제로 한 강연이 이루어질 날을 도표에서 찾으면 (A)의 '월요일'이 정답이다.

94 Brian Andropov는 무엇을 했는가?
(A) 콘퍼런스 참석을 위한 비용을 지불했다
(B) 콘퍼런스를 기획했다
(C) 콘퍼런스에서 연설을 하기로 동의했다
(D) 콘퍼런스에서 자신의 역할이 끝났다

organize 기획하다, 조직하다 | role 역할

| 해설 | 화자는 Richardson 씨가 강연 일정을 변경해야 하는 이유로 Brian Andropov just told me he can't participate in this year's workshop이라고 말하고 있다. 이를 통해 Brian Andropov라는 사람은 올해 워크숍 참석이 불가능하다는 점을 알 수 있으므로 정답은 (D)이다.

[95-97]

M Welcome to McMaster's Farm. We have one of the largest farms in the area. We grow crops and raise animals here on the farm. As you can see in the fields directly behind me, the corn is growing high and is almost ready to be harvested. The fields in the east are full of grass. We're going to go horseback riding in them a few minutes from now. To the east are where the sheep graze during the day. And right behind you is the barn, which you can see clearly. The field in back of it currently has some tomatoes and potatoes growing in it.

M McMaster's 농장에 오신 것을 환영합니다. 저희는 이 지역에서 가장 큰 농장 중 하나를 소유하고 있습니다. 저희는 이곳 농장에서 작물을 재배하고 동물을 기릅니다. 제 바로 뒤쪽에 있는 들판에서 보실 수 있듯이, 옥수수가 높이 자라고 있고 수확할 준비가 거의 다 되었습니다. 동쪽의 들판은 풀로 가득합니다. 저희는 지금부터 몇 분 후에 그곳에서 말을 타게 될 것입니다. 동쪽에는 낮 동안에 양들이 풀을 뜯어 먹는 장소가 있습니다. 그리고 여러분 바로 뒤쪽에는 외양간이 있는데, 이곳은 명확하게 보일 것입니다. 그곳 뒤쪽의 들판에는 현재 토마토와 감자가 자라고 있습니다.

farm 농장 | grow 자라다, 재배하다 | raise 기르다, 양육하다 | directly 곧장; 바로 | be about ready to ~할 준비가 되다 | harvest 수확하다 | be full of ~으로 가득하다 | go horseback riding 말을 타러 가다 | graze 풀을 뜯어 먹다 | barn 외양간, 헛간

95 화자는 누구인가?
(A) 여행 가이드
(B) 교사
(C) 농부
(D) 말 조련사

| 해설 | 담화의 시작 부분에서 들을 수 있는 we have one of the largest farms, 그리고 we grow crops and raise animals와 같은 어구들을 통해 화자는 농장을 소유하고 있고 곡식과 가축을 기르는 사람이라는 점을 알 수 있다. 따라서 화자의 직업은 (C)의 '농부'이다.

96 화자는 옥수수에 대해 무엇을 언급하는가?
(A) 잘 자라지 못하고 있다.
(B) 곧 뽑힐 것이다.
(C) 수확되었다.
(D) 최근에 심어졌다.

| 해설 | 화자는 옥수수를 소개한 후, '곧 수확이 될 것이다'(is almost ready to be harvested)라고 말한다. 따라서 정답은 (B)이다.

97 도표를 보아라. 어느 들판에서 말을 탈 수 있는가?
(A) 1번
(B) 2번
(C) 3번
(D) 4번

| 해설 | 화자는 'The fields in the east are full of grass.'라고 말한 다음, 그곳에서 말을 탈 것이라고 안내한다. 따라서 동쪽에 있는 들판인 (D)의 '4번'이 정답이다.

[98-100]

M Hello. This is Mark Kelly. I'm calling because I was overcharged on my phone bill one month. This summer, I visited Europe for two and a half months and didn't take my phone. Before leaving in June, I used my phone a few times, but I didn't use it in either July or August. I expected only to pay the basic rate 50 dollars each month, but I somehow got charged extra money. I don't believe I should pay that since I didn't start using my phone again until September. Would you please call me back at 504-5495 to let me know what's going on?

M 안녕하세요. 저는 Mark Kelly입니다. 저는 한 달간의 전화 요금이 과도하게 부과되었기 때문에 전화를 드리고 있습니다. 이번 여름, 저는 2개월 반 동안 유럽을 방문했으며 전화를 가지고 가지 않았습니다. 6월에 출발하기 전에, 저는 전화를 몇 차례 사용하기는 했지만, 7월이나 8월에는 사용을 하지 않았습니다. 저는 매달 기본 요

금인 50달러만 납부하면 될 것으로 기대했지만, 이상하게도 추가적인 요금이 부과되었습니다. 제가 9월까지는 전화를 다시 사용하지 않았기 때문에, 제가 그러한 요금을 납부해야 한다는 점은 믿을 수가 없습니다. 504-5495로 제게 다시 전화를 주셔서 일이 어떻게 진행되고 있는지 알려 주시겠습니까?

overcharge 과도한 요금을 부과하다 | **basic rate** 기본 요금 | **somehow** 왜 그런지 모르겠지만

98 화자가 전화를 한 목적은 무엇인가?
(A) 서비스를 취소하기 위해
(B) 불만을 제기하기 위해
(C) 전화 요금을 납부하기 위해
(D) 새로운 서비스를 요청하기 위해

| 해설 | 전화를 사용하지 않은 기간에 전화 요금이 과도하게 납부되었다는 사실을 알리고 있다. 따라서 화자가 전화를 한 목적은 (B)로 볼 수 있다.

99 화자는 자신이 무엇을 했다고 말하는가?
(A) 전화기를 가지고 휴가를 떠났다
(B) 몇 달 전에 서비스를 취소했다
(C) 두어 달 동안 해외 여행을 했다
(D) 전화기로 해외에 전화를 걸었다

| 해설 | 화자는 '2개월 반 동안 전화기 없이 유럽에 있었다'(I visited Europe for two and a half months and didn't take my phone)고 주장한다. 따라서 그가 한 일은 (C)이다.

100 도표를 보아라. 화자는 어떤 달에 과도한 요금이 부과되었다고 생각하는가?
(A) 5월
(B) 6월
(C) 7월
(D) 8월

| 해설 | 화자는 6월에 해외로 출발하여 7월과 8월을 해외에서 보냈다고 말한다. 한편 기본료가 50달러라고 했으므로 도표를 통해 과도한 요금이 부과된 달은 (D)의 '8월'임을 알 수 있다. 참고로 이때 과도하게 부과된 요금은 20달러일 것이다.

PART 5   p.188

101 정비사가 결함이 있는 부품을 교체할 것인데 엔진을 수리하기까지 약 한 시간 정도가 필요할 것이다.
(A) 이반
(B) 버리는
(C) 결함이 있는
(D) 결함

replace 교체하다 | **defection** 이반, 저버림, 변절 | **defect** 결함; 버리다, 배반하다 | **defective** 결함이 있는

| 해설 | 빈칸에는 '결함이 있는'이라는 의미의 단어가 들어가야 가장 자연스러운 문장이 완성된다. 따라서 정답은 (C)의 defective이다. 참고로 defect는 명사로 '결함'이라는 의미를, 동사로는 '버리다', '배반하다'라는 의미를 갖는다.

102 회사와 관련이 있는 모든 사람들에게 매년 열리는 사내 무도회의 초청장이 모두 발송되었다.
(A) 모든 사람
(B) 각각
(C) 누군가
(D) 누구

invitation 초대, 초대장 | **ball** 공; 무도회 | **associated with** ~와 관련이 있는 | **firm** 회사

| 해설 | all the invitations라는 어구에 주의하면 초대장이 관련자들 '모두'에게 보내졌다는 의미가 완성되어야 함을 알 수 있다. 따라서 정답은 '모든 사람'이라는 의미를 지닌 (A)가 된다.

103 Kenmore Technology에 Davenport 시설을 매각하려는 결정을 Durant 씨가 승인할 가능성이 높다고 예상된다.
(A) 승인하다
(B) 재촉하다
(C) 움츠리다
(D) 묘사하다

widely 널리 | **facility** 시설 | **prompt** 신속한; 재촉하다 | **withdraw** 움츠리다; 철수하다; 인출하다 | **portray** 묘사하다

| 해설 | decision을 목적어로 취할 수 있는 동사를 고르도록 한다. 보기 중에서는 (A)의 approve(승인하다)가 가장 자연스러운 의미를 완성시키므로 정답은 (A)이다.

104 McDaniel 씨는 모든 지역 신문과 잡지에 그의 스튜디오에 관한 광고를 게재할 계획을 갖고 있다.
(A) 두는
(B) 둘 것이다
(C) 둘 계획이다
(D) 두는

plant to ~할 계획이다 | **local** 인근의, 지역의

| 해설 | place의 알맞은 형태를 묻는 질문이다. plan이 to부정사와 함께 쓰인다는 점을 알고 있으면 정답은 (C)의 to place라는 점을 쉽게 알 수 있다.

105 모든 선적물은 48시간 이내에 도착할 것이라는 점이 보장되며, 그렇지 않은 경우에는 발송자가 지불한 금액을 Gateway 택배가 환불해 드릴 것입니다.
(A) 약속하다
(B) 가정하다
(C) 길들이다
(D) 보장하다

shipment 선적, 선적물 | **assume** 가정하다, 추측하다 | **condition** 조건; 길들이다, 영향을 미치다 | **guarantee** 보장하다, 보증하다

| 해설 | 내용상 문장의 전반부는 '택배 배송이 48시간 이내에 확실히 보장될 것이다'라는 의미를 나타내어야 한다. 따라서 정답은 (D)의 guaranteed이다. (A)의 promise가 비공식적이고 상대적으로 가능성이 낮은 약속을 의미하는 반면, guarantee는 공식적이고 가능성이 높은 보장 내용을 나타낸다.

106 경비를 줄임으로써 Wilson 전자는 올해 2/4분기에 수익을 낼 수 있었다.
(A) 폐지하다
(B) 감소하다
(C) 줄이다
(D) 지지하다

reduce 줄이다, 삭감하다 | **expense** 경비, 지출 | **enable A to B** A가 B를 할 수 있게 하다 | **profitable** 수익성이 있는 | **abandon** 폐지하다 | **decline** 쇠퇴하다, 감소하다

| 해설 | 문장의 의미상 빈칸에는 '줄이다'라는 의미를 갖는 단어가 들어가야 한다. 보기 중 (B)와 (C)가 그러한 의미를 갖는데, decline은 자동사로 쓰이기 때문에 expenses를 목적어로 취할 수가 없다. 따라서 정답은 '줄이다'라는 의미를 가진 타동사, (C)의 Reducing이다.

107 소비자들은 송장을 메일이나 팩스로 받겠다는 선택을 할 수 있다.
 (A) ~ 안에
 (B) ~에
 (C) ~을 통해
 (D) ~ 주변에

invoice 송장, 청구서 | through the mail 우편으로

| 해설 | '우편으로'라는 의미는 through the mail이나 by mail로 나타낸다. 따라서 정답은 (C)이다.

108 기기들이 지속적으로 사용되고 있기 때문에, 다음 주 중에 점검을 받아야 한다.
 (A) 지속하다
 (B) 끊임없는
 (C) 지속성
 (D) 지속적인

machinery 기계(류) | continual 끊임없는, 반복되는 | inspect 점검하다, 조사하다 | continuity 지속성

| 해설 | 빈칸에는 명사 use를 수식할 수 있는 형용사가 들어가야 한다. 따라서 정답은 (B)와 (D) 중 하나인데, 주절의 의미가 '점검을 받아야 한다'는 의미이므로 그 이유가 되기 위해서는 (D)의 continuing(현재 계속되고 있는)보다는 (B)의 continual(반복적인, 끊임없는)이 정답으로 보다 적절하다.

109 수확량이 좋지 못했기 때문에, 농업에 종사하는 많은 사람들이 파산을 선언해야 했다.
 (A) 파산시키다
 (B) 파산된
 (C) 파산
 (D) 파산하는

on account of ~ 때문에 | harvest 수확, 수확량 | sector 분야 | declare 선언하다 | bankruptcy 파산

| 해설 | 빈칸에는 declare의 목적어 역할을 할 수 있는 명사가 들어가야 한다. 따라서 정답은 '파산'이라는 의미를 지닌 (C)의 bankruptcy이다. 참고로 bankrupt는 형용사로 쓰일 경우 '파산한'이라는 의미를, 동사로 쓰일 경우 '파산시키다'라는 의미를 갖는다.

110 Beale 박사는 로봇 공학과 의학 분야의 업적으로 인해 전 세계적으로 유명하다.
 (A) 유명하다
 (B) 승인하다
 (C) 드러내다
 (D) 참가하다

be renowned for ~으로 유명하다 | internationally 국제적으로 | field 뜰, 들판; 분야 | robotics 로봇 공학

| 해설 | be renowned for(~으로 유명하다)라는 표현을 알고 있으면 정답이 (A)라는 점을 쉽게 알 수 있다. be known for, be famous for 등도 같은 의미를 나타낸다.

111 모든 회원에게 제공되는 특별 할인은 1,000달러 이상의 구매 물품에 대해서는 적용되지 않는다.
 (A) 제공되었다
 (B) 제공되다
 (C) 제공될 것이다
 (D) 제공되는

| 해설 | 문장 전체의 동사가 does not apply이므로 빈칸에는 주어인 the special discount를 수식할 수 있는 수식어가 들어가야 한다. 보기 중에서 수식어 기능을 할 수 있는 것은 현재분사 형태인 (D)의 being뿐이므로 (D)가 정답이다.

112 Robin 전자의 최신 버전의 노트북 컴퓨터는 이전 버전의 모델보다 속도가 두 배 더 빠르다.
 (A) 빠른
 (B) ~만큼 빠른
 (C) 가장 빠른
 (D) ~보다 빠른

| 해설 | twice라는 배수 표현에 유의하여 정답을 찾도록 한다. 배수 표현을 이용한 비교 구문은 「배수사 + as + 원급 + as」 혹은 「배수사 + 비교급 + than」으로 나타낼 수 있다. 정답은 (B)의 as fast as이다. 참고로 (D)가 정답이 되기 위해서는 문제의 twice가 two times로 바뀌어야 한다.

113 주말 동안 돈벌이가 되는 일자리를 구하려는 수천 명의 사람들이 피오리아의 취업 박람회에 모습을 나타냈다.
 (A) 피고용인
 (B) 고용인
 (C) 일자리
 (D) 고용 자격을 갖춘

in search of ~을 찾아서 | gainful 돈벌이가 되는 | job fair 취업 박람회 | employment 고용, 채용, 직장 | employable 고용 자격을 갖춘

| 해설 | '취업 박람회'(job fair)에 무엇을 찾기 위해 사람들이 모였을지 생각해 보면 정답을 가늠하기 쉽다. 정답은 (C)의 employment(고용, 일자리)이다.

> ☑ 700점 넘기 포인트 참고로 employer와 employee는 각각 '고용인', '피고용인'이라는 의미이다. 만약 이들의 의미가 헷갈린다면 employ의 원래의 뜻을 생각해 보도록 하자. employ는 '고용하다'라는 의미이므로 employer가 고용을 하는 사람, 즉 '고용주'라는 의미를 나타낸다.

114 여행 가방의 무게가 허용량보다 3킬로그램이 더 나갔기 때문에 Rogers 씨는 추가 비용을 지불해야 했다.
 (A) 무게가 나가다
 (B) 나타나다
 (C) 측정하다
 (D) 평가하다

extra fee 추가 요금 | suitcase 여행 가방 | weigh 무게가 나가다 | measure 측정하다 | evaluate 평가하다

| 해설 | her suitcase를 주어로 삼을 수 있고 빈칸 이후의 more than 3 kilograms와 어울려 사용될 수 있는 동사는 (A)의 weighed(무게가 나가다)뿐이다. 참고로 (C)의 measured(측정하다)와 (D)의 evaluated(평가하다)는 주로 주어가 사람일 때 쓰일 수 있는 동사이다.

115 웹사이트에 채용 공고가 게시된 지 이틀 후, 200통 이상의 지원서가 회사의 우편함에 도착했다.
 (A) 게시했다
 (B) 게시될 것이다
 (C) 게시하고 있다
 (D) 게시되다

| 해설 | 동사 post의 알맞은 형태를 묻는 문제이다. 먼저 부사절 내의 주어가 the jobs이므로 post가 동사로 사용되기 위해서는 수동태 형식이 되어야 한다. 또한 주절의 시제가 과거이므로 부사절의 시제도 과거나 과거완료가 되어야 한다. 보기 중에서 이러한 조건을 만족시키는 것은 (D)의 were posted 뿐이다.

116 Poko 주식회사의 새로운 소프트웨어는 저렴할 뿐만 아니라 시중에 나와 있는 다른 어떤 것보다 효율적이다.
 (A) 다른
 (B) 그때

(C) 그 밖의
(D) ~인 것

not just A but also B A뿐만 아니라 B도 | **efficient** 효율적인, 효과적인 | **on the market** 시장에 있는, 시중에 나와 있는

| 해설 | 비교급을 이용하여 최상급의 의미를 나타내고 있다. 따라서 빈칸에는 anything과 어울려 쓰일 수 있는 (C)의 else가 들어가야 한다.

117 직원들은 경영진이 제시한 상여금과 급여 인상분을 만장일치로 받아들였다.
(A) 올랐다
(B) 인상
(C) 올리는
(D) 올라간

unanimously 만장일치로 | **bonus** 보너스, 상여금 | **pay raise** 급여 인상 | **management** 경영, 경영진

| 해설 | raise는 타동사로 '올리다'라는 의미로 쓰이거나 명사로 '(급여) 인상'이라는 의미로 사용된다. 따라서 정답은 bonus와 가장 자연스럽게 and로 연결될 수 있는 (B)의 raise이다.

118 지역 업계에서 Jefferson Lee는 믿을만하고 정직한 사람이라는 명성을 가지고 있다.
(A) 기준
(B) 지위
(C) 조건
(D) 명성

reputation 명성 | **business community** 업계, 재계 | **dependable** 믿을 수 있는 | **status** 지위

| 해설 | for being a dependable and honest man이라는 어구와 가장 잘 어울릴 수 있는 명사는 (D)의 reputation(명성)이다.

119 대학에서 공학 학위를 취득하고 자격을 갖춘 지원자만이 World Tech 주식회사의 채용에 고려될 것이다.
(A) 자격을 갖추다
(B) 자격을 갖춘
(C) 자격
(D) 품질이 뛰어난

qualified 자격을 갖춘 | **graduate** 졸업하다 | **degree** 학위 | **engineering** 공학 | **qualitied** 품질이 뛰어난

| 해설 | 빈칸에는 applicants를 수식할 수 있는 형용사가 들어가야 하기 때문에 정답은 (B)와 (D) 중 하나이다. 하지만 (D)의 qualitied는 '품질이 뛰어난'이라는 뜻으로 applicants를 자연스럽게 수식할 수 없다. 따라서 정답은 (B)의 qualified(자격을 갖춘)이다.

120 원치 않는 겨울 의류를 처리하려는 노력의 일환으로, New Style Fashions는 최대 70%의 할인을 제공하는 세일을 실시했다.
(A) ~한 것
(B) ~한 때
(C) ~한 곳
(D) ~한 것

in an effort to ~하려는 노력으로 | **get rid of** ~을 제거하다

| 해설 | 빈칸에 들어갈 알맞은 관계사를 묻는 문제이다. 빈칸에는 sale을 가리킬 수 있는 that이나 which가 들어갈 수 있는데, 빈칸 앞에 전치사 in이 있으므로 정답은 (D)의 which가 된다. 만약 in이 없다면 (C)의 where가 정답이 될 것이다.

> **✓ 700점 넘기 포인트** 관계사를 묻는 문제가 어렵다고 생각하면 관계사가 있는 절을 완전한 문장으로 바꾸는 연습을 해 보자. 위 문장의 경우 관계사절을 완전한 문장으로 바꾸면 'It offered discounts of up to 70% in the sale.'이 된다. 따라서 관계사 자리에는 in which나 where가 올 수 있으며, in을 문장 맨 뒤로 이동시키는 경우에는 that도 정답이 될 수 있다.

121 탑승 구역으로의 입장이 허가되는 유일한 사람은 유효한 티켓을 가지고 있는 사람들이다.
(A) 품위가 있는
(B) 유효한
(C) 말의
(D) 법적인

boarding area 탑승 구역 | **valid** 유효한 | **dignified** 품위가 있는, 위엄이 있는 | **verbal** 말의, 언어의 | **legal** 법적인

| 해설 | 보기 중에서 tickets을 자연스럽게 수식할 수 있는 형용사는 (B)의 valid뿐이므로 (B)가 정답이다.

122 설문 조사가 끝나면, 적절하게 분석될 수 있는 형태로 데이터가 집계되어야 한다.
(A) 끝나다
(B) 끝내다
(C) 끝낼 것이다
(D) 끝나고 있다

survey 설문 조사 | **compile** 종합하다, 집계하다 | **properly** 적절히 | **analyze** 분석하다

| 해설 | 동사 complete의 알맞은 형태를 묻는 문제이다. complete(끝나다, 완료하다)의 주어가 the survey이므로 수동태 형식이 사용되어야 하며, 시제 일치의 원칙에 따라 현재시제가 사용되는 것이 자연스럽다. 따라서 이 두 가지 조건을 만족시키는 (A)의 is completed가 정답이다.

123 계약 조건에 따르면, 다음 2년 동안 늦어도 매달 5일까지 금액이 지급되어야 한다.
(A) 각각의
(B) 어떤
(C) 어떤
(D) 어떤

term 조건, 조항 | **agreement** 합의, 계약 | **payment** 지급, 지불

| 해설 | 내용상 '매달 5일 이전에 지급이 이루어져야 한다'는 의미가 완성되어야 한다. 따라서 정답은 (A)의 each이다.

124 지역 라디오 방송국인 WTRT는 주요 광고주들에게 광고료를 할인해 주고 있다.
(A) 후원
(B) 후원을 하는
(C) 광고주
(D) 후원을 받는

rate 요금 | **advertisement** 광고 | **primary** 주요한 | **sponsor** 후원자; 광고주

| 해설 | 주어가 the local radio station(지역 라디오 방송국)이라는 점, 그리고 rates on advertisements(광고료)에 할인이 이루어진다는 내용을 고려하면 빈칸에는 '광고주'라는 의미인 (C)의 sponsors가 들어가는 것이 가장 자연스럽다.

125 David's의 매장 매니저는 고객들이 서비스에 대해 불만을 제기하는 경우, 항상 고객들에게 전화를 걸어 후속 조치를 취한다.
(A) 수소문하다
(B) 후속 조치를 취하다

(C) 충고하다
(D) 피드백

follow up 후속 조치를 취하다 | **ask around** 여기저기 물어보다, 수소문하다

| 해설 | 고객들이 불만을 제기하는 경우 '매장 매니저'(store manager)가 어떤 행동을 할지 생각해 보면서 정답을 찾도록 한다. 정답은 '후속 조치를 취하다'라는 의미인 (B)의 follow up이다.

126 성장하고 있는 체인점 식당인 Henry's Fish and Chips는 내년 이맘때쯤까지 25개국 이상으로 확장될 것이다.
(A) 성장
(B) 성장하는
(C) 성장하다
(D) 재배자

| 해설 | 빈칸에는 chain restaurant을 수식할 수 있는 형용사가 들어가야 하므로 (B)의 growing이 정답이다. 참고로 Henry's Fish and Chips와 a growing chain restaurant은 동격이다.

127 어젯밤 Chandler 씨의 변호인인 Scott 씨는 그녀의 직원 파일 중 어떤 것에 대해서도 공개를 거부했다.
(A) 거부하다
(B) 거부하고 있다
(C) 거부했다
(D) 거부했다

refuse 거부하다, 거절하다 | **release** 공개, 공표 | **personnel** 직원

| 해설 | last night이라는 명백한 과거를 나타내는 부사구가 있으므로 빈칸에는 과거시제의 동사가 사용되어야 한다. 따라서 정답은 (D)이다.

128 의제상의 몇몇 사항들은 휴회가 될 때까지 회의에서 다루어지지 못했다.
(A) 정도
(B) 의제
(C) 원고
(D) 직원

agenda 의제, 안건 | **by the time** ~할 때까지 | **adjourn** 휴회하다 | **transcript** 원고

| 해설 | meeting(회의)에서 다루어질 수 있는 것이 무엇인지 생각해 보면 정답은 (B)의 agenda(의제, 안건)임을 쉽게 알 수 있다.

129 추가적인 제품 정보에 대해서는, 회사의 웹사이트를 방문하여 팜플렛을 다운로드받을 수 있다.
(A) ~을 위해
(B) ~와 함께
(C) ~에 의해
(D) ~을 통해

additional 추가적인 | **pamphlet** 팜플렛

| 해설 | 알맞은 전치사를 묻는 문제이다. 내용상 '목적'의 의미를 갖는 전치사가 들어가야 하므로 정답은 (A)의 For가 된다.

130 Nelson 사의 실험실에서 잠재적으로 유익한 의약품에 관한 연구가 실시되고 있다.
(A) 정력적으로
(B) 잠재적으로
(C) 조심스럽게
(D) 참을성 있게

potentially 잠재적으로 | **beneficial** 이로운, 유익한 | **pharmaceutical** 의약품, 약 | **laboratory** 실험실 | **energetically** 정력적으로, 활기차게 | **patiently** 참을성 있게, 끈기 있게

| 해설 | 빈칸에는 형용사인 beneficial(잠재적으로)을 가장 자연스럽게 수식할 수 있는 부사가 들어가야 한다. 보기 중에서는 (B)의 potentially(잠재적으로)가 의미상으로 가장 적합한 부사이다.

● PART 6   p.192

[131-134]

받는 사람: Samantha Wallace, Edward Kershaw
보낸 사람: Ted Winters
제목: 변화
날짜: 6월 10일

저는 한 가지 아이디어에 대해 생각을 하고 있는 중인데, 당신 둘이 그에 대해 어떻게 생각하는지 알고 싶어요. 영업부와 마케팅부가 함께 일을 하는 경우가 많기 때문에, 저는 두 부서를 같은 공간에 두는 것을 고려 중이에요. 그래서 영업부는 더 이상 1층에 있지 않고, 마케팅부도 3층에 있지 않게 될 거예요. 대신, 그들은 넓고 트여 있는 2층에 있게 될 것이죠. 각 부서의 부장과 차장의 사무실을 제외하고는 개인 사무실이 없을 거예요.
저는 이로써 두 부서의 직원들 간의 팀워크가 강화될 것이라고 믿어요. 영업부 사람들이 무엇을 하는지 알게 됨으로써, 마케팅부 사람들은 더 나은 광고를 제작할 수 있을 것이고 쇼핑객들에게 제품 구입을 유도할 수 있는 더 많은 방안을 마련할 수 있을 거예요. 그리고 마케팅부 사람들이 어떻게 생각하는지를 파악함으로써, 영업부 직원들은 제품을 판매할 수 있는 보다 효율적인 방법을 떠올릴 수 있을 거예요. 이러한 제안에 대해 당신 둘은 어떻게 생각하나요? 시간이 있을 때 이 아이디어에 관한 피드백을 알려 주는 것이 어떨까요?

collaborate 협력하다, 협동하다 | **no longer** 더 이상 ~하지 않는 | **except for** ~을 제외하고 | **assistant director** 차장 | **foster** 기르다, 양육하다; 발전시키다 | **sense of teamwork** 팀워크 | **create** 창조하다, 제작하다 | **devise** 고안하다 | **induce** 유인하다, 꾀다 | **come up with** (생각 등을) 떠올리다 | **pitch** 홍보하다, 판매하다 | **proposal** 제안

131 (A) 각각의
(B) 몇몇의
(C) 둘 중 하나의
(D) 양쪽 모두의

| 해설 | Ted Winters라는 발신인이 Samantha Wallace와 Edward Kershaw라는 두 명의 사람에게 사무실 재배치에 관한 의견을 묻고 있다. 따라서 정답은 (D)의 Both이다.

132 (A) 그리고
(B) ~ 또한 아닌
(C) 따라서
(D) 어떤

| 해설 | 내용상 빈칸에는 부정의 의미를 포함하고 있는 단어가 들어가야 한다. 보기 중에서 그러한 단어는 (B)의 nor뿐이다. 참고로 nor는 and와 not의 의미를 동시에 나타내는 단어로, 통상 nor가 문두에 쓰이면 문장 내의 주어와 동사의 위치가 바뀐다.

133 (A) 지식
(B) 앎
(C) 알 수 있는
(D) 알게 될 것이다

| 해설 | 빈칸 앞에 전치사 by가 있고 빈칸 뒤에는 목적어 역할을 하는 절이 뒤따르고 있다. 따라서 빈칸에 들어갈 말은 동명사 형태를 갖추고 있는 (B)의 knowing이다.

134 (A) 제가 한 모든 일이 잘 될 것이라는데 동의하지 않나요?
  (B) 모든 사람들이 저희가 마련한 변화를 승인해 줄 것이라고 생각하지 않나요?
  (C) 시간이 있을 때 이 아이디어에 관한 피드백을 알려 주는 것이 어떨까요?
  (D) 당신 둘이 책상을 옮기기 시작할 수 있는 때는 언제가 될까요?

| 해설 | (A)의 경우, 이 글이 아직 실행에 옮기지 않은 아이디어에 관한 내용이므로 이를 '자신이 한 것'(everything I did)이라고 지칭할 수는 없다. 발신인이 자신의 아이디어를 밝히고 있으므로 '우리가 마련한 변화'(the changes we made)에 대해 언급한 (B) 역시 정답이 아니다. (D)는 글의 내용과 전혀 관계가 없으므로 정답은 자신의 아이디어에 대해 상대방의 피드백을 요청한 (C)이다.

[135-138]

전기가 끊깁니다

9월 14일 목요일, 시 일부 지역에 전기가 들어오지 않을 것입니다. 정전 예정인 지역은 Eastern 가와 Kenmore 로의 사이에 있는 Carter 가가 될 것입니다. Alameda 전력 직원들이 Carter 가에서 고압선 작업을 할 것이기 때문에, 안전하게 작업이 이루어지도록 그곳 전기가 차단되어야 합니다. 전기는 오전 9시에 끊겨서 오전 11시 30분경에 다시 들어올 것입니다. 영향을 받게 되는 주민분들께서는 주의하셔서 이 시간에 대한 대비를 하셔야 할 것입니다. 작업이 11시 30분에 완료되지 않는 경우, 전기는 계속해서 차단될 것입니다. 주민들께서 인부들의 작업 과정에 대한 정보를 얻으실 수 있도록 시 공무원들이 해당 지역에서 확성기를 통해 안내를 할 것입니다. Alameda 전력의 웹사이트인 www.alamedapower.com/carterstreet를 방문하셔서 어떤 곳이 정전 대상 지역인지 확인하시길 바랍니다. 질문이나 불만 사항은 info@alamedapower.com으로 이메일을 보내시면 수신 4시간 이내에 답변이 이루어질 것입니다.

electricity 전기 | **blackout** 정전 | **high-powered line** 고압선 | **precaution** 주의 | **prepare** 준비하다, 대비하다 | **loudspeaker** 확성기 | **update** 최신 정보를 주다; 업데이트하다

135 (A) 공사 인부들은 이번 주 금요일인 10월 10일에 도로를 보수할 것입니다.
  (B) 7월 25일 목요일, Carter 가에서 수도관이 수리될 것입니다.
  (C) 9월 14일 목요일, 시 일부 지역에 전기가 들어오지 않을 것입니다.
  (D) 이번 주 토요일인 8월 11일에 Freemont 지역에서 가스가 차단될 것입니다.

neighborhood 근처, 인근

| 해설 | 제목 및 전체적인 내용에서 알 수 있듯이, 이 글은 정전에 관한 안내문이다. 따라서 정답은 정전 소식을 전하고 있는 (C)이다.

136 (A) 더 안전한
  (B) 가장 안전한
  (C) 안전하게
  (D) 안전

| 해설 | to부정사구 안에 들어갈 safe의 알맞은 형태를 묻는 문제이다. to부정사구 안에 생략되어 있는 품사가 없기 때문에 정답은 수식어, 즉 부사 형태인 (C)의 safely이다.

137 (A) 영향을 받은
  (B) 기분이 상한
  (C) 결석한
  (D) 보도된

upset 기분이 상한 | **absent** 결석한

| 해설 | 주의해서 대비를 해야 할 사람은 정전으로 '영향을 받게 될' 사람들이다. 보기 중에서 이러한 의미에 가장 부합되는 단어는 (A)의 affected이다.

138 (A) 결정
  (B) 발표
  (C) 수리
  (D) 업그레이드

| 해설 | by loudspeaker(확성기를 통해)와 가장 잘 어울릴 수 있는 단어를 고르도록 한다. 정답은 (B)인데, make an announcement는 '발표하다' 혹은 '통지하다'라는 의미로 자주 사용되는 표현이다.

[139-142]

받는 사람: Mary Lewis <m_lewis@dmmt.com>
보낸 사람: Eloise Purcell <eloisep@dmmt.com>
제목: 회의
날짜: 10월 3일

Mary,

우리가 오늘 점심 시간 직후에 만나기로 한 것은 저도 알고 있지만, 안타깝게도 제가 그때 당신과 만나지 못할 것 같아요. 제 상사인 Colter 씨께서 어젯밤에 도착한 스페인 고객들을 위해 제가 발표를 해야 한다고 요청하셨어요. 저는 오늘 오후 2시 30분에 그들과 최신 소프트웨어 제품의 이점에 대해 이야기를 해야 해요. 하지만, 저는 아직 어떤 발언도 준비해 놓지를 못했어요. 따라서 저는 그때까지 제가 말하고자 하는 것을 준비하기 위해 모든 시간을 써야 해요.

당신 일정상 내일 오전은 어떤가요? 저는 9시부터 12시까지는 시간이 많기 때문에, 그때 당신을 만날 수 있어요. 당신이 그때 안 되는 경우, 저는 4시와 6시 사이에도 시간을 낼 수 있어요. 당신에게 회의를 하기에 가장 좋은 시간이 언제인지 제게 알려 주는 것이 어떨까요? 이처럼 촉박한 통보로 회의를 취소시켜서 미안하지만, 이번 일은 제가 어떻게 할 수 없는 문제잖아요. 당신이 이해해 주기를 바라요.

그럼 이만,
Eloise

supervisor 감독관, 관리자 | **request** 요청하다, 요구하다 | **give a presentation** 발표하다 | **delegation** 대표단 | **benefit** 혜택, 이익 | **notice** 통보 | **out of one's control** 어쩔 수 없는

139 (A) ~인 것
  (B) ~한 때에
  (C) ~한 곳에서
  (D) ~인 것

| 해설 | 알맞은 관계사를 묻는 문제이다. that절 안을 중심으로 살펴보면 빈칸에는 delegation을 선행사로 삼을 수 있는 주격 관계대명사가 들어가야 하기 때문에 보기 중 정답은 (D)의 that이다.

140 (A) 하지만, 저는 아직 어떤 발언도 준비해 놓지를 못했어요.
  (B) 당신이 모르는 경우를 위해 이야기를 하면, 저는 그 소프트웨어의 책임 디자이너였어요.
  (C) 안타깝게도, 그 소프트웨어는 아직 커다란 문제점을 가지고 있어요.
  (D) 따라서, 저는 가능한 빨리 스페인으로 떠날 거예요.

in case ~하는 경우에, ~하는 경우를 대비하여 | **consequently** 그 결과로, 따라서

| **해설** | 빈칸 이후의 문장에서 발신자인 Eloise Purcell은 '남은 시간을 발언 준비에 모두 써야 한다'고 말한다. 따라서 빈칸에는 그 근거가 될 수 있는 (A)가 들어가야 가장 자연스러운 문맥이 완성된다.

141 (A) 다양한
 (B) 거의 없는
 (C) ~가 아닌
 (D) 많은

a variety of 다양한

| **해설** | 문맥상 빈칸에는 time을 수식하여 '많은 시간'이라는 뜻을 완성시킬 수 있는 표현이 들어가야 한다. 따라서 정답은 셀 수 없는 명사를 수식할 때 사용되는 (D)의 plenty of(많은)이다.

142 (A) 분명한
 (B) 짧은
 (C) 놀라운
 (D) 꽉 끼는

apparent 분명한 | **tight** 꽉 끼는; 단단한

| **해설** | 여유를 두지 않고 촉박하게 이루어진 통보는 보통 short notice로 나타낸다. 따라서 정답은 (B)이다. 참고로 on short notice는 '갑자기' 혹은 '예고를 충분히 하지 않고'라는 뜻의 관용 표현이다.

[143-146]

Bixby 은행이 시내 중심가에 신규 지점을 개설할 것이다

햄프턴 시 (1월 17일) – 어제, Bixby 은행이 햄프턴 시의 중심가에 신규 지점을 개설할 것이라고 Bixby 은행의 대변인이 발표했다. 이 지점은 Silverwood 쇼핑 센터의 2층에 위치하게 될 것이다. Bixby 은행은 주에서 가장 빠르게 성장하고 있는 은행이다. 몽고메리에 본사를 둔 이 은행은 지난 2년 동안 빠른 속도로 지점을 개설해 왔다. 올해에는, 주 전역에 30개 이상의 지점을 개설할 계획이다. 쇼핑몰 내 지점은 햄프턴 시에서 4번째 Bixby 은행 지점이 될 것이다. 고객 관리와 우수한 서비스를 강조한 덕분에, 이 은행은 크게 성장하고 있다. 최근 설문 조사에서, 고객을 얼마나 잘 대우하는지와 그들에게 어떤 서비스를 제공하는지에 관해 Bixby 은행이 다른 모든 경쟁업체보다 훨씬 높은 순위에 올랐다. 작년 Bixby 은행은 2천5백만 달러 이상의 수익을 기록했으며, 애널리스트들은 올해 수익이 두 배 이상 오를 것으로 믿고 있다.

spokeswoman 대변인 | **headquarter** 본사를 두다 | **swift** 빠른 | **pace** 보폭; 속도 | **thanks to** ~ 덕분에 | **relation** 관계 | **rank** 등급을 매기다. 순위를 차지하다 | **competitor** 경쟁자 | **profit** 이윤, 수익 | **analyst** 분석가, (증권사의) 애널리스트

143 (A) 열었다
 (B) 열었다
 (C) 열 것이다
 (D) 열기 위해

| **해설** | 알맞은 시제를 묻는 문제이다. 앞으로 나타낼 일을 나타내기 위해서는 미래시제를 사용해야 하는데, 현재진행형으로도 가깝거나 확실한 미래를 나타낼 수 있기 때문에 정답은 (C)의 is opening이 된다. 참고로 주절의 동사가 과거일 때도 미래의 일은 미래시제로 나타내는 것이 현대 영어의 특징 중 하나이다.

144 (A) 쇼핑 센터는 매출이 악화되어 최근에 문을 닫았다.
 (B) 전문가들은 Bixby 은행이 서비스를 개선시켜야 한다고 생각한다.
 (C) Bixby 은행은 주에서 가장 빠르게 성장하고 있는 은행이다.
 (D) 이는 은행이 개설할 첫 번째 지점이 될 것이다.

| **해설** | (A)는 Bixby 은행과 직접적으로 관련이 없는 '쇼핑 센터'에 대해 이야기하고 있기 때문에, (B)는 신규 지점 개설 소식에 어울리지 않는 은행의 서비스를 지적하고 있기 때문에 모두 정답이 될 수 없다. 정답은 Bixby 은행이 어떤 은행인지를 소개하고 있는 (C)이다. 햄프턴 지점이 Bixby 은행의 첫 번째 지점이라는 정보는 찾아볼 수 없으므로 (D)도 오답이다.

145 (A) 강조
 (B) 인상
 (C) 고려
 (D) 헌신

impression 인상 | **consideration** 고려 | **dedication** 헌신

| **해설** | '고객 관리'와 '우수한 서비스'를 어떻게 하면 은행이 성장할 수 있는지 생각해 보자. 정답은 (A)의 emphasis(강조)로, emphasis는 주로 전치사 on과 함께 사용된다.

146 (A) 고려하다
 (B) 대우하다
 (C) 지명하다
 (D) 행동하다

behave 행동하다, 처신하다

| **해설** | 문맥상 보기 중에서 자연스럽게 its customers(고객)를 목적어로 삼을 수 있는 동사는 (B)의 treats(다루다, 대우하다)뿐이다.

PART 7
p.196

[147-148]

Petunia 문구점
귀하의 사무실에 필요할 수도 있는 모든 것을 갖추고 있습니다.

Main 로 999번지, 디모인, 아이오아
Tel: 293-2394   Fax: 293-2395

고객: Harold Marley
주소: Brighton 가 41번지, 디모인, 아이오아
전화번호: 954-4502

주문일: 3월 23일 화요일
발송일: 3월 23일 화요일

주문 번호: 454-5055

제품 설명	제품 번호	주문 수량	단위당 가격	총 비용
스테이플 (박스당 1,000개입)	565595	3	$2.00	$6.00
복사 용지 (박스당 5,000장)	965686	2	$22.00	$44.00
2번 연필 (박스당 10개입)	103434	10	$5.50	$55.00
검정색 볼펜 (박스당 20개입)	249558	4	$9.00	$36.00
파란색 볼펜 (박스당 20개입)	249560	3	$9.00	$27.00

소계: $168.00
배송비: $12.00
총계: $180.00

주문에 감사드립니다. 귀하의 주문은 5205로 끝나는 신용카드로 청구되었습니다. 배송과 관련된 질문은 matt@petuniastationery.com으로 Matt Stone에게 연락하시기 바랍니다.

bill 청구서; 청구서를 보내다

147 얼마나 많은 연필이 주문되었는가?
(A) 10개
(B) 60개
(C) 80개
(D) 100개

| 해설 | 주문 내역을 살펴보면 연필은 10개입 박스로 10개가 주문되었다. 따라서 주문된 총 개수는 (D)의 '100개'이다.

148 가장 비싸지 않은 제품의 제품 번호는 무엇인가?
(A) 103434
(B) 249558
(C) 565595
(D) 249560

| 해설 | '단위당 가격' 항목을 살펴보면 각 제품의 개당 가격을 파악할 수 있다. 가장 비싸지 않은 제품은 단위 가격이 2달러인 스테이플로, 스테이플의 제품 번호는 (C)의 '565595'이다.

[149-150]

Walker, Harriet　　　　　　　　　　　　　　　9:12 A.M.
안녕하세요, Davis 씨. 제 이름은 Harriet Walker예요. Sandpiper 택배 직원이죠. 오늘 당신에게 배송하고자 하는 택배가 하나 있어요.

Davis, Sam　　　　　　　　　　　　　　　　　9:15 A.M.
잘 되었군요. 언제 이곳으로 오실 계획인가요?

Walker, Harriet　　　　　　　　　　　　　　　9:17 A.M.
택배 기사님이 10시에서 10시 30분 사이에 댁에 도착하는 것으로 예정되어 있어요. 그때 집에 계실 건가요?

Davis, Sam　　　　　　　　　　　　　　　　　9:18 A.M.
없을 것 같아요. 12시는 어떤가요?

Walker, Harriet　　　　　　　　　　　　　　　9:21 A.M.
저희 택배 직원들은 12시와 1시에 의무적으로 점심 시간을 가지고 있죠. 오후에 댁에 계시는 시간이 있으신가요?

Davis, Sam　　　　　　　　　　　　　　　　　9:22 A.M.
저로서는 2시 30분이 좋을 것 같아요. 택배 기사님께서 도착하시기 전에 제게 전화를 달라고 해 주세요.

Walker, Harriet　　　　　　　　　　　　　　　9:25 A.M.
그 시간에 그곳으로 가실 수 있을 거예요. 댁을 방문하시기 10분 전에 전화를 드리라고 말씀드려 놓을게요. 고맙습니다.

deliveryman 배달원, 택배 기사 | **personnel** 직원 | **mandatory** 강제적인, 의무적인 | **residence** 주거

149 오전 9시 18분에, Davis 씨가 "I'm afraid not"이라고 썼을 때 그는 무엇을 의미하는가?
(A) 그는 특정 시간에 집에 없을 것이다.
(B) 그는 택배를 받았다는 것을 기억하지 못한다.
(C) 그는 택배 기사가 도착하는 것을 기다릴 수 없다.
(D) 그는 Sandpiper 택배를 방문할 수 없다.

| 해설 | 'I'm afraid not.'이라는 문장에서 생략되어 있는 부분을 써서 완전한 문장으로 다시 만들면 'I'm afraid that I will not be home then.'이라는 문장이 완성된다. 따라서 주어진 문장의 의미는 (A)로 볼 수 있다.

150 택배 기사는 몇 시에 Davis 씨에게 전화를 걸 것인가?
(A) 오후 2시에
(B) 오후 2시 10분에
(C) 오후 2시 20분에
(D) 오후 2시 30분에

| 해설 | Davis 씨는 '2시 30분'에 택배가 오면 좋겠다고 적었고, Walker 씨는 택배 기사에게 이야기해서 '도착 10분전'(10 minutes before he visits your house)에 미리 전화를 하라고 이야기하겠다고 적었다. 따라서 택배 기사가 전화를 하게 될 시점은 (C)의 '2시 20분'이 된다.

[151-152]

받는 사람: 데이턴 시 공무원
보낸 사람: 시청 Frieda Thompson
날짜: 5월 26일
제목: 자원봉사

곧 여름이 다가올 것인데, 여름은 시내 공원과 레크레이션 시설에 있어서 연중 가장 바쁜 시기입니다. 예산 삭감 때문에, 우리는 몇 명의 공원 관리인들을 해고해야만 했습니다. 7곳의 시 공원에서 정규직으로 일을 하고 있는 직원은 불과 6명뿐이며, 공원 중 일부는 상당히 넓습니다. (따라서 우리에게는 가능한 많은 사람들의 도움이 필요합니다.)
그런 이유로 우리는 이번 주 토요일인 5월 29일에 대청소의 날을 가지려고 합니다. 이는 순수한 자원봉사 활동이지만, 여러분 중 가능한 많은 분들이 그러한 노력에 동참하기를 바랍니다. 우리는 공원에서, 페인트 칠하기, 쓰레기 수거, 잔디 깎기, 그리고 간단한 수리 작업을 포함하여, 온갖 종류의 정리 작업을 하게 될 것입니다. 보수는 지급되지 않지만, 하루 종일 일을 하시는 분들은 누구라도 6월이나 7월 중 하루 동안의 유급 휴가를 받게 될 것입니다.
일을 돕는데 관심이 있으시면, 내선 번호 4032로 Debby Reynolds에게 연락을 주십시오. 우리는 5월 29일 8시 30분에 시청 주차장에서 모일 것입니다. 그런 다음, 차를 타고 배정된 작업을 하러 가게 될 것입니다. 자원봉사에 참여한 모든 분들에게는 무료 티셔츠와 점심 식사가 제공될 것입니다.

around the corner 목전에 와 있는 | **recreation** 레크레이션 | **budget cut** 예산 삭감 | **lay off** 해고하다 | **groundskeeper** 공원 관리인 | **extensive** 광활한, 넓은 | **purely** 순전히 | **parking lot** 주차장 | **work assignment** 업무 배당, 업무 할당

151 회람에 따르면, 자원봉사자들이 왜 필요한가?
(A) 시 공원의 상태가 좋지 못하다.
(B) 겨울 날씨로 큰 피해가 발생했다.
(C) 모든 일을 처리할 수 있는 직원들이 충분하지 않다.
(D) 시는 비용을 절약하여 다른 프로젝트에 사용하고자 한다.

| 해설 | 회람의 첫 번째 단락에서 예산 삭감으로 공원 관리인들이 해고되었고 지금은 '7군데의 공원에 6명의 직원만이 있다'(only 6 full-time employees to work at the city's 7 parks)는 점을 알리고 있다. 따라서 자원봉사자가 필요한 이유는 일손이 부족하기 때문이므로 (C)가 정답이다.

152 [1], [2], [3], 그리고 [4]로 표시된 위치 중에 다음 문장이 들어가기에 가장 알맞은 곳은 어디인가?
"따라서 우리에게는 가능한 많은 사람들의 도움이 필요합니다."
(A) [1]
(B) [2]
(C) [3]
(D) [4]

| 해설 | [1]의 바로 앞 문장에서 '일손이 부족하다'는 점을 언급하고 있으므로 주어진 문장은 (A)의 [1]에 들어가는 것이 바람직하다.

> **700점 넘기 포인트** 인과 관계를 파악하면 문장 삽입 문제를 쉽게 풀 수 있다. 원인이 주어지면 그 다음에는 결과가 이어지는 것이 원칙이므로, so, therefore, thus 등의 단어가 등장하면 무엇이 원인이고 무엇이 결과인지를 파악한 후에 문제를 풀도록 하자.

[153-155]

9월 18일

친애하는 Hansen씨께,

이 편지는 귀하의 케이블 텔레비전 청구서와 관련해서 작성된 것으로, 현재 귀하의 청구 기한은 2개월 정도 지났습니다. 현 시점에서, 귀하가 지불하셔야 할 금액은 134.65달러입니다. 이는 늦어도 9월 29일까지 전액 지불되어야 합니다. 인근 은행 어느 곳에서나 현금으로 지불하실 수도 있고 수표를 작성하셔서 Ace Cable Systems로 보내 주셔도 좋습니다. 수표로 지불하시는 경우에는, 만기일까지 저희 사무실에 도착할 수 있도록 반드시 미리 부치셔야 합니다. 요구한 기한까지 요금을 전액 지불하지 않으시면 그 결과로 케이블 텔레비전 서비스가 즉시 종료될 것입니다. 귀하의 서비스는 요금을 전액 납부하셔야 다시 제공될 수 있습니다. 또한 서비스를 다시 받기 위해서는 50달러의 추가 요금을 내셔야 합니다. 이번 달 요금을 납부하지 않으시면, 귀하의 청구서는 미수금 처리업체로 넘겨질 것이며, 이는 귀하의 신용 등급에 부정적인 영향을 미칠 수 있습니다.

Silvia Patterson 드림
Ace Cable Systems

with regard to ~에 대하여 | **overdue** 기한이 지난 | **in cash** 현금으로 | **make out a check to** ~에게 수표를 발행하다 | **by check** 수표로 | **post** (우편으로) 부치다 | **due date** 마감일, 기한 날짜 | **failure** 실패 | **termination** 소멸 | **reestablish** 재건하다; 복직시키다 | **reconnect** 다시 연결하다 | **collection agency** 미수금 처리업체 | **credit rating** 신용 등급

153 9월 29일에 어떤 일이 일어날 것인가?
 (A) 서비스가 종료될 수도 있다.
 (B) 수표가 현금화될 것이다.
 (C) 청구서가 우편으로 보내질 것이다.
 (D) 고객에게 연락이 갈 수도 있다.

| **해설** | 문제의 September 29가 핵심 어구이므로 이 날짜가 언급되고 있는 부분을 찾아보도록 한다. 편지의 내용을 통해 '9월 29일'은 연체료 납부 기한임을 알 수 있는데, 이때까지 납부를 하지 않으면 '케이블 텔레비전 서비스가 중단될 것'(will result in the immediate termination of your cable television service)이라고 적혀져 있다. 따라서 9월 29일에 일어날 수 있는 일은 (A)이다.

154 Hansen 씨는 무엇을 하라는 지시를 받는가?
 (A) 은행에서 계좌를 신설한다
 (B) 9월 29일 이후에 수표를 보낸다
 (C) 즉시 결제를 한다
 (D) 미수금 처리업체에 연락한다

| **해설** | Patterson 씨는 편지에서 연체료에 대해 안내한 후, 'This must be paid in full no later than September 29.'라고 말한다. 따라서 이 글은 연체료 납부 독촉 편지로, Hansen 씨가 요청받고 있는 사항은 (C)로 볼 수 있다.

155 Ace Cable Systems에 대해 암시되어 있는 것은 무엇인가?
 (A) 9월 29일 이후에는 Hansen 씨와 연락을 중단할 것이다.
 (B) 곧 Hansen 씨의 집으로 사람을 보낼 것이다.
 (C) Hansen 씨에게 50달러의 비용으로 상품을 업그레이드해 줄 것이다.
 (D) 현재 미납하고 있는 요금에 대해 Hansen 씨를 고소할 것이다.

communicate with ~와 의사 소통하다 | **sue** 고소하다

| **해설** | 편지의 마지막 부분에서 Ace Cable Systems의 직원인 Patterson 씨는 요금이 납부되지 않으면 '청구서가 미수금 처리업체로 보내질 것'(your bill will be turned over to a collection agency)이라고 경고한다. 그렇게 되면 미납 요금의 문제는 미수금 처리업체가 담당하게 될 것이므로 (A)가 타당한 내용이다.

[156-158]

Sunrise 캠핑장에 오신 것을 환영합니다

Rainier 산의 Sunrise 캠핑장을 이용해 주셔서 감사합니다. 반드시 다른 야영객들을 정중하게 대하시고 그들을 방해하지 않도록 최선을 다해 주십시오. 이곳에 머무시는 동안, 아래 세 가지 규칙들을 반드시 준수하셔야 합니다:

1) 샤워실의 물을 낭비해서는 안 되는데, 샤워실은 캠핑장의 북동쪽과 남동쪽 코너에 있습니다. 샤워를 짧게 하시고 수도꼭지의 물이 계속 흐르도록 놔두지 마십시오.
2) 불이 모두 꺼졌는지 그리고 타고 있는 불이 방치되고 있지는 않은지 확인하십시오. 물을 붓고, 휘젓고, 물을 부어야 한다는 점을 기억하십시오. 먼저, 불에 물을 붓고, 그 다음에 석탄과 재를 휘저으십시오. 그런 다음에는, 불이 탔던 곳에 물을 더 부으십시오. 장작은 저렴한 금액으로 1번 구역에서 구입하실 수 있습니다.
3) 캠핑장에 쓰레기를 버리지 마십시오. 오염을 예방하고 야생 동물이 이곳으로 오는 것을 막기 위해 장소를 깨끗이 사용해 주십시오. 쓰레기 투기로 적발된 사람은 그가 누구라도 100달러의 벌금을 물게 될 것입니다.

캠핑의 기본 원칙을 기억하십시오: 캠핑장에서 여러분이 남겨야 할 것은 발자국뿐입니다.

캠핑장 관리자와 이야기를 하시려면 805-4395로 전화를 주시고, 공원 경비원에게 연락을 하시려면 595-4943으로 연락을 주십시오.

courteous 공손한 | **fellow** 동료 | **disturb** 방해하다 | **obey** 복종하다 | **waste** 낭비하다, 버리다 | **faucet** 수도꼭지 | **extinguish** (불을) 끄다 | **pour** (액체를) 붓다, 따르다 | **stir** 휘젓다 | **ash** 재 | **firewood** 장작 | **garbage** 쓰레기 | **pollution** 오염 | **litter** 어지르다, 쓰레기를 버리다 | **Golden Rule** 기본 원칙 | **ranger** (공원 등에서의) 경비원

156 지시 사항은 누구를 위한 것인가?
 (A) 공원 경비원들
 (B) 당일치기 방문객들
 (C) 등산객들
 (D) 숙박을 하는 사람들

| **해설** | 캠핑장의 주의 사항에 대한 글이므로 이 글은 야영객들을 대상으로 작성된 것임을 알 수 있다. 따라서 (B)와 (D) 중에 하나가 정답인데, '샤워 시설'과 '모닥불' 등에 관한 주의 사항이 적혀져 있으므로 (B)보다는 (D)가 정답으로서 더욱 적절하다.

157 캠핑장에서 무엇을 구매할 수 있는가?
 (A) 병에 든 물
 (B) 나무
 (C) 간식
 (D) 텐트

| **해설** | 두 번째 주의 사항 중 'Firewood can be acquired in lot #1 for a minimal fee.'라는 문장을 통해 캠핑장에서 장작을 구입할 수 있다는 점을 알 수 있다. 정답은 (B)이다.

158 어떤 행동이 벌금을 부과하게 만들 수 있는가?
   (A) 쓰레기 투기
   (B) 소음 유발
   (C) 야생 동물에게 먹이 주기
   (D) 물 낭비

| 해설 | 벌금과 관련된 내용은 세 번째 주의 사항 중 'Anyone who is caught littering will be fined $100.'라는 문장에서 확인할 수 있다. 정답은 (A)의 '쓰레기 투기'이다.

[159-161]

시내에 새로운 상점이 생기다

뉴헤이븐 (6월 15일) – 시내 방문객들은 넘쳐나는 상점과 그들이 만들어 내는 활기찬 분위기 때문에 쉽게 길을 잃을 수 있다. 자신이 Third 로와 Eli 길의 코너에 있다는 사실을 알게 된 이들은 반드시 Watson's Arts and Crafts 안을 들여다 보아야 한다. 새로 생긴 상점이지만, 이곳은 뉴헤이븐에서 작은 역사와 열정이 담겨 있는 곳이기도 하다.

상점 주인인 Rachel Watson은 올해 5월에 매장 문을 열었다. "저희 아버지께서는 예술을 사랑하셨고 예술이 모든 사회의 심장이라고 믿으셨어요. 저는 매장 전체에 그분이 만드셨던 예술 작품 중 일부를 전시하는 동시에, 예술가들을 위한 물품을 제공하는 상점을 열어 그분을 기리기로 결심했죠."라고 그녀는 말했다. 상점 벽을 장식하고 있는 수많은 그림과 드로잉 작품은 모두 돌아가신 그녀의 아버지인 Marcus Watson이 그린 것이다. Watson 씨는 지역 사회에서 유명했던 화가였지만, 작년에 세상을 떠났다.

Watson's Arts and Crafts의 고객들은 멋진 서비스를 받을 수 있을 뿐만 아니라 뛰어난 예술 작품을 감상할 수 있는 기회도 가질 수 있다. 상점의 단골 고객인 Tony Brown은 "Watson 씨는 예술을 이해하고 낮은 가격으로 제품들을 판매하지만, 본질적으로 미술관인 곳을 오픈함으로써 지역 사회에 도움을 주고 있어요. 저는 무언가를 구입하는 대신, 때때로 작품들을 감상하러 여기에 오곤 하죠."라고 말했다. 고객들은 예술 작품이 곧 사라질 것이라는 걱정을 할 필요가 없다. 거액의 제안에도 불구하고, Watson 씨는 지금까지 아버지의 작품 중 어느 것에 대해서도 판매 요구를 거절하고 있다.

on account of ~ 때문에 | **plethora** 과다, 과잉 | **vibrant** 활기찬 | **passion** 열정 | **honor** 기리다 | **simultaneously** 동시에 | **adorn** 장식하다 | **pass away** 죽다 | **opportunity** 기회 | **admire** 존경하다; 감상하다 | **ware** 제품, 물품 | **do ~ a service** ~에게 봉사하다, ~에게 도움을 주다 | **essentially** 본질적으로 | **hefty** 크고 무거운; (돈이) 두둑한 | **thus far** 지금까지

159 Watson 씨의 작품은 어디에 전시되어 있는가?
   (A) Watson's 씨의 집에
   (B) 인근 미술관에
   (C) Watson's Arts and Crafts에
   (D) Eli 길을 따라

| 해설 | 기사 두 번째 단락의 displaying some of the artwork he created throughout the store라는 어구와 all of the numerous paintings and drawings adorning the walls of the store라는 어구를 통해 그의 작품들은 상점 안에 전시되어 있다는 점을 알 수 있다. 따라서 (C)가 정답이다.

160 Brown 씨에 대해 무엇이 암시되어 있는가?
   (A) 그는 미술 작품을 만든다.
   (B) 그는 Watson 씨를 안다.
   (C) 그는 Watson 씨와 친구이다.
   (D) 그는 Watson's Arts and Crafts에서 일한다.

| 해설 | Brown 씨가 한 말 중 마지막 문장인 'There are times that I come here just to admire the works instead of to buy something.'이 정답의 단서이다. 기사의 내용을 통해 Watson's Arts and Crafts는 '미술 재료들을 판매한다'는 점을 알 수 있는데, Brown 씨는 '무언가를 사지 않을 때에도 작품을 보러 온다'고 말했다. 따라서 이를 역으로 해석하면 '그가 무언가를 사러 올 때도 있을 것'이므로 그는 예술 활동을 하는 사람일 것이다. 그러므로 (A)가 정답이다.

161 3단락 14줄의 "hefty"라는 단어의 의미와 가장 가까운 것은?
   (A) 지속되는
   (B) 무거운
   (C) 상당한
   (D) 독특한

persistent 지속되는 | **considerable** 상당한, 많은 | **unique** 독특한; 유일한

| 해설 | hefty는 '크고 무거운' 혹은 '금액이 두둑한'이라는 뜻을 지닌다. (B)의 heavy와 같은 의미로 쓰일 수도 있지만, 여기에서는 (C)의 considerable(상당한, 많은)과 같은 뜻으로 사용되었다.

[162-164]

Denton 상인 협회에서 연례 회의를 개최합니다

Denton 상인 협회에서 지금부터 석 달 후인 6월 20일 금요일부터 6월 22일 일요일까지 연례 회의를 개최할 예정입니다. 이번 행사는 Carlyle 컨벤션 센터에서 열릴 것입니다. 협회의 모든 회원들은 행사에 참여하실 자격이 있으며, 게스트 또한 입장이 허용됩니다. 현재 회의를 위한 등록을 받고 있습니다. 온라인 지원서는 www.dentonmerchants.org/annualmeeting으로 제출하실 수 있으며, 혹은 509-2395로 전화를 하셔서 좌석을 예약하실 수도 있습니다. 6월 10일 이후에는 등록이 마감되고, 정문에서도 티켓을 구입하실 수가 없습니다. 3일간 회의의 참가비는 회원의 경우 75달러이며 게스트는 100달러입니다. 이 참가비로, 모임의 마지막 날 밤에 있을 연회를 제외하고, 모든 행사에 참여하실 수 있습니다. 연회의 참가비는 회원이나 비회원 모두 똑같이 50달러입니다. 회의의 활동 및 연사에 관한 리스트는 협회의 웹사이트에서 얻으실 수 있습니다. 초청 연사들의 강연이 여러 차례 있을 예정인데, 여기에는 상인들이 직면하게 되는 법적 문제, 세법에서 최근 변경된 사항, 그리고 인터넷으로 효과적인 광고를 하는 법에 관한 강연이 포함됩니다.

be eligible to ~할 자격이 있다 | **permit** 허락하다, 허가하다 | **fee** 요금 | **access** 접근, 입장; 접근하다, 입장하다 | **banquet** 연회 | **legal** 법적인 | **face** 마주하다 | **effectively** 효과적으로

162 공지는 누구를 위해 작성되었을 것 같은가?
   (A) 상점 주인
   (B) 세무사
   (C) 지역 주민
   (D) 음식 공급업자

tax attorney 세무사

| 해설 | 공지의 제목에서 merchant(상인)라는 단어의 뜻을 알면 쉽게 문제를 풀 수 있다. 정답은 (A)의 '상점 주인'이다.

163 공지에 따르면, 사실이 아닌 것은 무엇인가?
   (A) 회원들은 초대 손님보다 행사 참가비를 더 적게 낸다.
   (B) 회의는 3일간 지속될 것으로 예정되어 있다.
   (C) 회의 등록은 온라인으로만 가능하다.
   (D) 회의가 열리는 날에는 티켓이 판매되지 않을 것이다.

| 해설 | 회원의 참가비는 75달러이고 비회원의 참가비는 100달러이기 때문에 (A)는 사실이고, 행사 기간은 6월 20일부터 22일까지라고 적혀 있으므로 (B) 또한 맞는 내용이다. 등록은 6월 10일 까지이며 '현장에서의 티켓 구매는 불가능하다'(tickets may not be purchased at the door either)고 안내되

어 있으므로 (D) 역시 사실이다. 따라서 정답은 (C)인데, 회의 등록은 온라인이나 유선으로 가능하다고 안내되어 있다.

164 비회원이 회의와 연회에 참석하기 위해서는 얼마를 지불해야 하는가?
(A) 75달러
(B) 100달러
(C) 125달러
(D) 150달러

| 해설 | 비회원의 경우 회의 참가비가 100달러이고 연회 참가비는 50달러이므로 정답은 이 둘을 합한 (D)의 '150달러'이다.

[165-167]

받는 사람: 전 직원
보낸 사람: 기술지원부 Ernest Jenson
제목: 이번 주 금요일
날짜: 4월 9일 화요일

회사의 메인 컴퓨터 서버가 금요일인 4월 12일 오후 3시부터 오후 9시까지 작동을 멈출 것이라는 점을 전 직원들에게 공지합니다. 이러한 중단 조치는 시스템 업그레이드 때문에 필요한데, 업그레이드를 통해 컴퓨터 시스템이 보다 빠른 속도로 그리고 훨씬 더 효율적으로 작동하게 될 것입니다. 동시에, 직원들의 전체적인 생산성을 향상시켜 줄 시간 절약 프로그램이 몇 개 설치될 것입니다. 이 새로운 프로그램은, 4월 15일 월요일 오전 8시에 회사 웹사이트에 업로드될 예정인, 사내동영상에서 기술지원부에 의해 상세히 설명될 것입니다.

3시를 시작으로 6시간 동안, 직원들은 컴퓨터 시스템을 이용할 수 없습니다. 따라서, 중단 조치가 시작되기 전에, 직원들은 현재 하고 있는 일은 어떤 것이든 저장을 해야 합니다. 회사 컴퓨터 시스템과 개인용 플래시 드라이브 모두에 작업물을 저장하실 것을 강력히 추천합니다. 또한, 업그레이드 기간 중에 손실된 파일에 대해서는 기술지원부가 책임을 지지 않을 것입니다. 그러니 민감하거나 중요한 파일을 지닌 개인들은 이를 외장 저장 매체에 복사를 해 둘 것이 요망됩니다. 협조에 감사를 드리며 중단 조치로 인해 큰 불편이 초래되지 않기를 바랍니다.

hereby 이로써 | **notify** 알리다, 통지하다 | **shut down** 작동을 중지시키다, 폐쇄하다 | **effectiveness** 효율성 | **at the same time** 동시에 | **timesaving** 시간을 절약하는 | **output** 산출량 | **interoffice** 부서간의 | **upload** 업로드하다 | **flash drive** 플래시 드라이브 | **advisable** 권할 만한 | **sensitive** 민감한 | **valuable** 소중한 | **external** 외부의

165 컴퓨터 시스템은 왜 작동이 중단될 것인가?
(A) 회사의 회계용 소프트웨어를 업그레이드하기 위해
(B) 시스템의 바이러스를 제거하기 위해
(C) 새로 구입한 컴퓨터를 설치하기 위해
(D) 컴퓨터를 보다 효율적으로 만들기 위해

| 해설 | 컴퓨터 시스템의 작동 중단은 '업그레이드'를 위한 것으로, 업그레이드의 효과는 '속도와 효율성의 증가'(at a higher speed and with greater effectiveness)로 적혀 있다. 따라서 정답은 (D)로 보아야 한다. 단순히 작동 중단의 목적이 '업그레이드' 때문이라고 생각해서 섣불리 (A)를 정답으로 고르는 실수는 하지 말아야 한다.

166 4월 15일에 어떤 일이 일어날 것인가?
(A) 업그레이드가 완료된다.
(B) 동영상 시청이 가능할 것이다.
(C) 손실된 파일들이 복구될 것이다.
(D) 컴퓨터 시스템의 작동이 중단될 것이다.

| 해설 | April 15라는 날짜는 첫 번째 단락 마지막 문장에서 찾을 수 있는데, 여기에서는 4월 15일에 '프로그램 설명 동영상이 회사의 웹사이트에 업로드될 것'(an interoffice video that will be uploaded onto the company's Web site)이라고 언급되어 있다. 따라서 (B)가 정답이다.

167 직원들은 무엇을 하라는 조언을 받는가?
(A) 중단 조치 전에 컴퓨터를 끈다
(B) 금요일에는 집에서 노트북 컴퓨터를 가지고 온다
(C) 안전한 보관을 위해 중요한 파일을 이동시킨다
(D) 질문이 있으면 기술지원부에 연락한다

| 해설 | 권고 사항은 두 번째 단락에 나타나 있다. '작업한 것을 회사 컴퓨터 시스템과 플래시 드라이브에 저장하라는 것'(saving the work both on the company's computer system and on a personal flash drive)과 '중요 파일은 외장 저장 매체에 복사해 둘 것'(copy them to an external source)이 그것이다. 따라서 이와 관련된 내용은 (C)이다.

[168-171]

Wright, Bruce 3:34 P.M.
방금 전 인사부에서 공석인 자리를 위해 우리가 면접을 봤으면 하는 사람들의 리스트를 받았어요.

Bannister, William 3:35 P.M.
그들이 누구인가요?

Wright, Bruce 3:36 P.M.
리스트에는 4명이 있어요: Melissa Abercrombie, Shen Wu, Patrick Kennedy, 그리고 Molly Toole예요.

Houston, Jennifer 3:38 P.M.
제 기억이 맞는다면, 리스트의 두 번째 사람이 가장 적격이었어요. 하지만 다른 세 명에 대해서는 기억이 잘 나지 않는군요.

Bannister, William 3:40 P.M.
저는 6년 전에 Patrick Kennedy와 함께 학교를 다녔어요. 그가 근면한 사람이라고 기억하는데, 그와 연락을 해 본 적은 없어요.

Wright, Bruce 3:43 P.M.
음, 우리는 오늘 모든 사람에게 연락을 해서 면접을 봐야 한다고 알려야 해요. 어, 물론, 그들이 아직도 관심이 있는 경우에요.

Houston, Jennifer 3:45 P.M.
원한다면 제가 할게요. 저는 조금 전에 보고서 작성을 끝내서 얼마간의 시간이 있어요. 면접 날짜에 문제가 있는 경우에는 제가 그들에게 어떻게 말할까요?

Wright, Bruce 3:47 P.M.
좋은 질문이군요. 면접은 1월 10일이나 11일 중 하루에 이루어질 예정이에요. 제가 인사부에 연락해서 다른 날짜가 가능한지 물어 볼게요.

Houston, Jennifer 3:50 P.M.
그렇게 하면서, 그들이 시외에서 오는 경우, 우리가 여행 경비를 지원할 수 있는지도 알아봐 주세요.

Wright, Bruce 3:52 P.M.
물론이죠. 잠시 후에 돌아올게요. 하지만 지금 이메일을 확인해보세요. 각 인물들에 대한 연락처를 제가 방금 전에 보냈어요.

open position 공석 | **qualified** 자격이 있는 | **recall** 회상하다, 기억하다 | **hardworking** 근면한, 부지런한 | **keep up with** ~와 연락하고 지내다 | **acceptable** 받아들일 수 있는 | **travel expense** 여행 경비 | **contact information** 연락처

168 무엇이 주로 논의되고 있는가?
(A) 즉시 지원자들을 면접해야 할 필요성

(B) 채워지게 될 일자리
(C) 인사부에 문의할 질문
(D) 면접을 볼 지원자들

| 해설 | '공석에 대해 인사부에서 면접을 보았으면 하는 지원자들'(people HR wants us to interview for the open position)에 대해 이야기하고 있다. 따라서 논의의 주제는 (D)이다.

169 Houston 씨는 지원자들에 대해 무엇을 언급하는가?
(A) 그들 모두 훌륭한 이력서를 제출했다.
(B) 그녀는 이미 두어 명을 면접했다.
(C) 그들 중 누구도 적임이지가 않다.
(D) 한 사람이 다른 사람들보다 뛰어난 자질을 갖추고 있다.

credential 자격, 자격증

| 해설 | Houston 씨는 '명단에 있는 두 번째 지원자가 가장 적격이다'(the second one on the list is the most qualified)라고 말한 후, 나머지 사람들에 대해서는 기억이 잘 나지 않는다고 언급한다. 따라서 (D)가 언급된 내용이다.

170 오후 3시 40분에, Bannister 씨가 "I haven't kept up with him at all"이라고 썼을 때 그는 무엇을 의미하는가?
(A) 그는 Kennedy 씨를 잘 기억하지 못한다.
(B) 그는 Kennedy 씨가 적합하지 않다고 생각한다.
(C) 그는 학창 시절 이후로 Kennedy 씨와 이야기를 해 보지 못했다.
(D) 그는 Kennedy 씨와 일을 잘 해 본 적이 없다.

| 해설 | keep up with는 '~와 연락하고 지내다'라는 의미이므로 그가 주어진 문장을 통해 표현하려는 바는 (C)로 볼 수 있다.

171 Wright 씨는 Houston 씨에게 무엇을 하라고 말하는가?
(A) 인사부에 연락한다
(B) 이메일을 읽는다
(C) 전화를 한다
(D) 이력서를 본다

| 해설 | 메시지 창의 마지막 부분에서 Wright 씨는 'But check your e-mail now.'라고 말한 후, 이메일에 면접 대상자의 연락처가 들어 있다고 말한다. 따라서 Wright 씨가 요청한 사항은 (B)이다. 참고로 (A)는 Wright 씨가 할 일이다.

[172-175]

보낸 사람: Fred Stallings ⟨fred_stallings@wprinters.com⟩
받는 사람: Wanda Lancaster ⟨wandal@familymail.com⟩
제목: 주문 번호 5AR-5594
날짜: 11월 12일

친애하는 Lancaster 씨께,

저희는 오늘 아침 Wellington All-in-One 460 프린터에 관한 귀하의 주문 요청을 받았습니다. 안타깝게도, 그 프린터는 더 이상 재고가 없으며, 저희 회사는 그 제품의 생산을 중단했습니다. 이러한 불편을 드리게 되어 죄송합니다.
주문을 취소하고 싶으신 경우, 제게 알려 주시면, 제가 귀하의 신용 카드로 환불 절차를 밟도록 하겠습니다. 하지만 저희 회사의 프린터를 계속해서 구매하고 싶으시면, 저는 Wellington All-in-One 470 프린터를 추천해 드리겠습니다. 이는 귀하께서 주문하려고 하셨던 프린터와 같은 제품군에 속해 있습니다. 실제로, 몇 가지 추가 기능이 포함되어 있다는 사실을 제외하면 460과 동일한 제품입니다. 460과 똑같이 프린터이자, 스캐너이며, 팩스 기기인 동시에 복사기입니다. 하지만 스캔한 문서를 프린터에서 곧바로 이메일 첨부 파일로 전송할 수 있습니다. 그 외에도,

460에서 사용되는 것보다 잉크 카트리지가 약간 더 크기 때문에, 여기에 사용되는 잉크 카트리지가 더 오래 갑니다.
이 이메일에 파일 하나를 첨부해 두었습니다. 거기에는 470 모델의 상세 사항을 설명하는 브로셔가 포함되어 있습니다. 470이 460보다 가격이 약간 더 높기는 하지만, 460에 지불하셨던 가격과 동일한 가격으로 귀하에게 470을 판매할 수 있는 권한이 제게 있습니다. 따라서 470을 원하신다고 제게 답장을 주시면, 제가 그것을 즉시 보내도록 하겠습니다.

Fred Stallings 드림
고객 서비스 담당
Wellington Printers

place an order 주문을 하다 | **in stock** 재고가 있는 | **cease** 중단하다 | **manufacture** 제조, 생산 | **recommend** 추천하다 | **belong to** ~에 속하다 | **extra** 추가 | **attachment** 첨부, 첨부 파일 | **contain** 포함하다 | **specification** 상세 사항, 사양 | **authorize** 권한을 위임하다 | **at once** 즉시

172 이메일은 왜 작성되었는가?
(A) 대체할 수 있는 제품을 제안하기 위해
(B) 실수를 사과하기 위해
(C) 회사의 신제품을 홍보하기 위해
(D) 고객의 불만을 처리하기 위해

| 해설 | 주문한 프린터의 재고가 없기 때문에 그에 대한 환불을 해 주거나 다른 상품으로 대체해 주겠다고 안내하고 있다. 따라서 이메일이 작성된 이유는 (A)로 볼 수 있다.

173 이메일에 따르면, 470 모델은 460 모델과 어떻게 다른가?
(A) 전기를 덜 사용한다.
(B) 문서를 직접 이메일로 보낼 수 있다.
(C) 고속으로 사진을 출력할 수 있다.
(D) 팩스 기기를 포함하고 있다.

| 해설 | 460과 470 프린터의 차이는 '스캔한 문서를 바로 이메일로 보낼 수 있는 기능'(the ability to send scanned documents as e-mail attachments straight from the printer)의 여부와 '카트리지의 수명'에 있다. 따라서 이 중 첫 번째 특성을 언급하고 있는 (B)가 정답이다.

174 Stallings 씨는 Lancaster에게 이메일과 함께 무엇을 보냈는가?
(A) 정보
(B) 송장
(C) 주문서
(D) 사진

| 해설 | 마지막 단락에서 Stallings 씨가 파일에 첨부한 것은 a brochure describing the specifications of the 470 model(470 모델의 사양이 설명되어 있는 브로셔)임을 알 수 있다. 따라서 정답은 이를 '정보'로 바꾸어 표현한 (A)이다.

175 Lancaster 씨가 470 모델을 받기 위해서는 무엇을 해야 하는가?
(A) 돈을 더 지불한다
(B) 주문서를 작성한다
(C) 대기자 명단에 이름을 올려 놓는다
(D) 이메일로 답장을 보낸다

waiting list 대기자 명단

| 해설 | 이메일의 마지막 문장에서 Stallings 씨는 '470을 원한다고 답장만 하면'(simply respond to me that you would like the 470) 제품을 보내 주겠다고 적고 있다. 따라서 정답은 (D)이다.

[176-180]

Carney 조선에서 새로운 영업 이사를 영입하다

노포크 (6월 16일) 국내에서 가장 큰 조선업체 중 하나인 Carney 조선이 회사의 영업부 이사로 활약할 Jerod Morris를 영입했다고 발표했다. Morris 씨는 7월 1일에 새로운 직위를 맡게 될 것이다. 이러한 움직임은 여러 업계 전문가들에 의해 높이 평가되었고, 전문가들은 그가 이전에 일을 했던 세 곳에서의 성공 기록을 언급하고 있다. 그의 가장 최근의 직위는, Gregory Manufacturing에서였는데, Morris 씨는 수백만 달러의 손실을 보던 회사를 단 3년 만에 5천만 달러 이상의 수익을 거두는 곳으로 바꾸어 놓는데 일조했다. 그는 최근에 수익 감소가 목격되고 있는 Carney에서도 같은 일을 해낼 것으로 예상된다.

Carney 조선의 대표 이사인 Darren Jackson은 "Morris 씨를 이사로 맞게 되어 정말로 기쁩니다. 저희는 업계에서의 그의 인맥과 뛰어난 경영 마인드를 바탕으로 매출을 증대시켜서 다시 한 번 국내 1위의 조선업체가 될 수 있을 것으로 확신합니다."라고 논평했다. Carney는 작년에 7억 7천 5백만 달러의 수익을 거두었으며 내년에는 수익이 소폭 증가할 것으로 예상하고 있다.

shipbuilding 조선 | serve as ~으로 기능하다, ~으로 활동하다 | assume 떠맡다 | cite 인용하다 | transform 바꾸다, 변형시키다 | mere 단순한 | revenue 수입 | decline 감소, 쇠퇴 | comment 논평하다 | confident 확신하는 | contact 접촉; 인맥 | project 투영하다; 예상하다

받는 사람: Jerod Morris 〈jmorris@carneyships.com〉
보낸 사람: Cindy Roman 〈cindyr@carneyships.com〉
제목: 회의
날짜: 7월 1일

친애하는 Morris 씨께,

인사부와 Jackson 대표 이사님과의 만남이 끝났기를 바랍니다. 저희 모든 영업부 직원들은 당신을 만나 당신과 함께 일을 하기를 고대하고 있습니다. 오늘 바쁜 하루가 예정되어 있다는 점을 당신께서 아셨으면 합니다. 점심 시간이 끝나는 대로, 당신은 Rajiv Merhra와 Scott Pulaski와 만나기로 되어 있는데, 두 사람은 모두 이곳에서 직위가 높은 영업부 직원입니다. 그들은 당신이 얼마 전 떠난 회사와의 잠재적 계약에 대해 당신과 이야기를 해야 합니다. 당신이 그곳에 5년 간 있었기 때문에, 그들은 어떻게 협상에 대처해야 하는지에 대해 당신이 소중한 의견을 제공해 줄 수 있을 것으로 기대하고 있습니다.

그 후, 2시에는, Wellman 사와 CGR 주식회사가 체결한 거래에 관한 회의가 예정되어 있습니다. 회의를 마치기까지 한 시간 반이 걸릴 것입니다. 4시에는, 오늘 마지막 미팅에 참석하셔야 합니다. Karen Chu와 Dansby Burgess와의 회의입니다. 이 회의는 주로 그들이 당신을 만나서 당신의 경영 스타일을 알기 위한 자리입니다. 하지만, 그들은 Sybax 사의 이야기를 꺼낼 것입니다. 당신 책상에 그와 관련된 정보가 들어 있는 폴더가 있습니다.

필요한 것이 있으시면, 이 이메일에 답장을 주시거나 내선 번호 21번으로 제게 전화를 주십시오.

그럼 이만 줄이겠습니다.

Cindy Roman

as soon as ~하자마자 | senior 직위가 높은 | potential 잠재적인 | depart 떠나다 | invaluable 매우 소중한 | insight 통찰력, 식견 | as to ~에 관해 | approach 접근하다, 다가가다 | bring up (화제 등을) 꺼내다 | relevant 관련이 있는

176 기사는 어디에서 찾아볼 수 있을 것 같은가?

(A) 분기별 보고서에서
(B) 레저 잡지에서
(C) 경제 잡지에서
(D) 여행 웹사이트에서

quarterly 분기별

| 해설 | 'Carney 조선'이라는 회사가 신임 영업 이사를 영입했다는 소식을 전하고 있다. 따라서 보기 중 이와 관련된 내용을 전할 수 있는 매체로 가장 적합한 것은 (C)의 '경제 잡지'이다.

177 Carney 조선에 관해 언급된 것은 무엇인가?

(A) 작년에 5천만 달러의 수익을 거두었다.
(B) 최근에 대표 이사로 Darren Jackson을 영입했다.
(C) 작년보다 많은 수익을 낼 것으로 예상된다.
(D) 지난 달에 수백만 달러의 거래를 성사시켰다.

| 해설 | 기사의 마지막 문장에서 '내년에는 수익이 약간 인상될 것으로 예상된다'(is projecting a slight increase in the coming year)고 말하고 있으므로 Carney 조선에 관해 언급된 사항은 (C)이다.

178 Roman 씨는 왜 이메일을 작성했는가?

(A) 미팅에 관한 정보를 제공하기 위해
(B) Sybax 사에 대해 묻기 위해
(C) 채용을 축하하기 위해
(D) Morris 씨에게 자신과 직접 만날 것을 요청하기 위해

| 해설 | 이메일 전반에 걸쳐 Morris 씨가 오늘 하게 될 일을 알려 주고 있다. 따라서 이메일의 주제는 '일정에 관한 정보를 제공하기 위한 것'이므로 정답은 (A)가 된다.

179 Roman 씨는 어디에서 일을 하는가?

(A) Sybax 사에서
(B) Gregory Manufacturing에서
(C) Carney 조선에서
(D) CGR 주식회사에서

| 해설 | 이메일 첫 번째 단락의 두 번째 문장, 'All of us in the Sales Department are looking forward to meeting you and to working with you.'를 통해, Roman 씨는 Morris 씨와 같은 회사의 영업부 직원임을 알 수 있다. 따라서 그녀가 일하는 곳은 (C)이다.

180 Morris 씨는 점심 식사 후에 무엇을 할 것인가?

(A) Sybax 사와 계약을 체결한다
(B) Wellman 사에 관해 이야기한다
(C) Gregory Manufacturing에 관해 논의한다
(D) CGR 주식회사의 직원들과 만난다

representative 대표, 대리인

| 해설 | 두 번째 지문인 이메일의 첫 번째 단락에서 Roman 씨는 Morris 씨가 점심 식사 후에 영업부 직원을 만나게 될 텐데, 그들은 Morris 씨가 직전에 일했던 회사와의 계약에 관해 조언을 듣고자 한다고 적고 있다. 한편 첫 번째 지문인 기사에서 Morris 씨의 '최근 직위'(his most recent position)가 Gregory Manufacturing에서였다고 나와 있으므로 결국 Morris 씨가 하게 될 일은 (C)가 된다.

[181-185]

8월 3일

친애하는 Jacoby 씨께,

저희 Fifth Avenue 패션은 저희가 지면 및 방송 광고를 진행하기 위해 귀하의 마케팅 업체를 선정한 점을 알려 드리게 되어 기쁘게 생각합니다. 몇몇 자격이 충족되는 업체와의 계약도 고려해 보았지만, 귀사가 나

머지 업체들보다 월등히 뛰어났습니다.
남성용 캐주얼 의류의 신상품 라인이 10월 말에 출시될 것이기 때문에, 저희는 그에 대한 프로모션이 시작되기를 갈망하고 있습니다. 또한, 올해 남성 및 여성 정장에 대한 판매가 예상했던 것보다 저조합니다. 올해 마지막 분기에는 그러한 의류들이 고객에게 더욱 매력적인 것이 될 수 있도록 Freeman 사가 몇 가지 방안들을 떠올려 주시기 바랍니다. 마지막으로, 저희는 저희 의류를 해외 시장, 특히 러시아, 일본, 그리고 스웨덴에 수출하는 것을 고려하고 있습니다. 저희는 귀사에게 그러한 나라들을 위한 광고 캠페인을 제작해 주실 것을 요청드리게 될 것입니다.

다음 주 월요일인 8월 11일에 귀하의 직원들과 만나는 것이 가능할까요? 우리의 관계를 확정시키기 위해 귀사와 계약을 체결하고 싶습니다. 그리고 귀사에게 바라는 지면 및 방송 광고 활동에 대한 접근법에 대해서도 논의를 하고 싶습니다. 가장 이른 편한 시간에 852-5743으로 제게 연락을 주시기 바랍니다.

Kendrick Carpenter 드림
마케팅 부사장
Fifth Avenue 패션

opt 선택하다 | **stand head and shoulders** 월등히 뛰어나다 | **be eager to** ~하기를 열망하다 | **come up with** (아이디어 등을) 떠올리다 | **appeal** 호소하다 | **particularly** 특히 | **relationship** 관계 | **additionally** 추가적으로, 또한 | **approach** 접근법

Fifth Avenue 패션
연간 매출액

다음은 남성 및 여성 의류의 분기별 매출액입니다.

	1분기	2분기	3분기	4분기
남성용 캐주얼 의류	16,494달러	18,549달러	21,392달러	19,594달러
남성용 정장	11,899달러	9,856달러	8,435달러	14,770달러
여성용 캐주얼 의류	26,667달러	30,321달러	33,568달러	37,948달러
여성용 정장	15,695달러	14,890달러	14,857달러	14,098달러

181 Jacoby 씨는 어떤 직종과 관련이 있는 것 같은가?
(A) 영업
(B) 마케팅
(C) 회계
(D) 선적

| 해설 | Jacoby 씨는 첫 번째 지문인 편지의 수신인으로, 발신자인 Carpenter 씨에 의해 광고 의뢰를 받고 있다. 따라서 그는 (B)의 '마케팅' 업무를 담당하는 사람으로 볼 수 있다.

182 편지에서, 2단락 4줄의 "appealing"이라는 단어와 그 의미가 가장 유사한 것은?
(A) 매력적인
(B) 명백한
(C) 감당할 수 있는
(D) 접근할 수 있는

apparent 명백한, 분명한 | **affordable** 감당할 수 있는, 입수할 수 있는 | **accessible** 접근할 수 있는, 이용할 수 있는

| 해설 | appealing은 '호소력이 있는', 혹은 '매력적인'이라는 뜻으로, 보기 중에서는 (A)의 attractive(매력적인)와 가장 유사한 의미를 나타낸다.

183 편지에 의하면, Fifth Avenue 패션에 관해 언급되지 않은 것은 무엇인가?
(A) 다른 나라에 의류를 팔고 싶어한다.
(B) 자신을 위해 일을 해 줄 Freeman 주식회사를 고용했다.
(C) 10월에 신제품을 판매할 예정이다.
(D) 2분기에 경미한 손실을 기록했다.

| 해설 | 편지의 두 번째 단락에서 (A)와 (C)의 내용을, 첫 번째 단락에서 (B)의 내용을 확인할 수 있다. 두 번째 단락에서 매출이 예상보다 저조하다는 내용은 언급되어 있지만, 이것이 '손실을 보았다'는 의미와 직결되는 것은 아니므로 (D)는 언급된 바 없는 사항이다.

184 2분기에 어떤 종류의 의류가 가장 낮은 판매량을 보였는가?
(A) 여성용 캐주얼 의류
(B) 여성용 정장
(C) 남성용 캐주얼 의류
(D) 남성용 정장

| 해설 | 두 번째 지문의 표를 보면 2분기에 가장 낮은 판매량을 보인 것은 9,856달러를 기록한 (D)의 '남성용 정장'이다.

185 Freeman 주식회사에 관해 무엇이 암시되어 있는가?
(A) 수년간 Fifth Avenue 패션과 함께 긴밀히 협조했다.
(B) 여성용 캐주얼 의류의 매출 증가에 도움을 주었다.
(C) 남성용 정장을 위한 성공적인 광고 캠페인을 제작했다.
(D) 의류 판매로 증가된 수익 중 일정 퍼센트를 받게 될 것이다.

be responsible for ~에 대한 책임이 있다

| 해설 | 첫 번째 지문인 편지의 내용을 통해 Freeman 주식회사는 8월에 계약을 체결한 것으로 추측할 수 있으며, 따라서 Freeman 주식회사가 제작한 광고는 Fifth Avenue 패션의 4분기 매출에 영향을 주었을 것이라고 생각해 볼 수 있다. 두 번째 지문의 표에서는 4분기 남성용 정장 매출이 상대적으로 크게 증가했음을 알 수 있으므로 (C)가 정답으로서 가장 적절하다.

[186-190]

Portland 취업 박람회

제11회 Portland 취업 박람회가 4월 10일 금요일과 4월 11일 토요일에 열릴 예정입니다. 올해 박람회는 그 어떤 때보다도 크고 활발할 것으로 보입니다. 행사는 Portland 시민 회관에서 열릴 것이며 매일 오전 8시에 시작하여 저녁 7시에 종료될 것입니다. 450개의 지역 기업, 국내 기업, 그리고 외국 기업의 대표들이 참가를 약속하고 있습니다. 이러한 기업들은 항공우주 산업, 금융업, 제조업, 로봇 공학, 그리고 조선업 분야에서 가장 큰 명성을 지니고 있습니다. 또한, 지역 항공기 제조업체인 Plautus도 참가를 할 예정인데, 이곳은 박람회에서 100명을 채용하기를 희망하고 있습니다. 참가자 중 일부는 즉석에서 면접을 보게 될 것이므로 참가자분들께는 정장을 입고 오실 것을 권해 드립니다. 또한 이력서, 포트폴리오, 그리고 기타 서류들도 가지고 오셔야 합니다. 입장은 무료이며, 예약을 하실 필요는 없습니다.

promise 약속하다; ~처럼 보이다 | **conclude** 결론을 짓다; 끝나다 | **representative** 대표 | **international** 국제적인 | **pledge** 맹세하다, 약속하다 | **aerospace** 항공우주 산업 | **robotics** 로봇 공학 | **formal clothes** 정장 | **on the spot** 그 자리에서, 즉석에서

Portland 취업 박람회가 성황리에 끝나다

포틀랜드 (4월 12일) – Portland 취업 박람회가 어제 끝났는데, 조직 위원들은 이를 박람회 역사상 가장 성공적인 것으로 평가하고 있다. 15,000명 이상의 구직자들이 일자리를 얻기 위해 Portland 시민 회관을 방문한 것으로 추정된다. 지금까지 가장 인기가 높았던 부스는

Plautus의 부스로, 이 회사는 박람회 참가자들을 채용하겠다는 의사를 공개적으로 발표한 바 있다. Plautus는 실망하지 않았다. 회사 대변인인 Rod Merchant는 "우수한 자질을 갖춘 참가자들 덕분에 저희는 애초에 계획했던 것보다 두 배가 많은 사람들을 채용하게 되었습니다. 저희는 올해 박람회의 결과에 대해 매우 만족하고 있습니다."라고 말했다. 기타 다국적 기업들, 예컨대 Orion, Walker Research, 그리고 PT Systems 역시 박람회에서 몇몇 사람들을 채용했다고 발표했다. Orion 대표인 Wilma O'Neil은 "이는 전국 최고의 취업 박람회 중 하나입니다. 저희는 이곳에 왔을 때 교육을 많이 받고 의욕이 넘치는 참가자들을 구하게 될 것이라는 점을 알고 있었습니다."라고 말했다.

organizer 조직자, 기획자 | **jobseeker** 구직자 | **estimate** 추산하다, 추정하다 | **attempt** 시도 | **land a job** 일자리를 구하다 | **by far** 지금까지 | **publicly** 공개적으로 | **intention** 의도, 의향 | **convince** 설득시키다 | **initially** 처음에 | **ambitious** 야망이 있는

받는 사람: 연구개발부 전 직원
보낸 사람: 인사부 David Murphy
제목: 신입 사원
날짜: 4월 21일

이곳 Plautus의 연구개발부에 38명의 신입 사원들이 근무를 시작하게 될 것이라는 점을 알려 드립니다. 이 사원들은 모두 5월 1일 월요일에 일을 시작하게 될 것입니다. 그들 모두가 Portland 취업 박람회에서 채용되었는데, 여러분 중 많은 분들께서도 이곳 일자리를 박람회에서 찾으셨습니다. 이처럼 많은 수의 직원을 동시에 채용해 본 적이 없기 때문에, 우리는 오리엔테이션이 반드시 원활하게 진행되도록 만들어야 합니다. 여러분 부서의 장이신 Samir Punjab과의 면담 후, 저는 멘토링 프로그램을 실시하기로 결심했습니다. 여러분 중 일부는 신입 사원의 멘토로서 활동하는 일을 담당하게 될 것입니다. 새로운 업무에 대해 멘티들이 알아야 하는 모든 사항들을 가르쳐야 할 책임을 맡게 될 것입니다. 저는 여기에 관련된 모든 분들이 자발적으로 참여하기를 바랍니다. 따라서 자신이 좋은 멘토가 될 것이라고 생각하면, 저에게(내선 번호 549) 혹은 Punjab 씨에게 4월 25일까지 연락을 주시기 바랍니다.

smoothly 매끄럽게 | **consult** 상담하다 | **assign** 할당하다, 위임하다 | **mentor** 멘토 | **mentee** 멘티 | **involved** 관련된, 개입된

186 Portland 취업 박람회에 관해 언급되지 않은 것은 무엇인가?
 (A) 약 450개의 기업들이 그곳에 대표를 보냈다.
 (B) 여러 차례 열렸다.
 (C) 그곳에서 기업들은 면접을 실시한다.
 (D) 부스를 설치하기 위해서는 기업이 비용을 지불해야 한다.

represent 대표하다 | **multiple** 다수의, 복수의 | **occasion** 경우

| 해설 | 첫 번째 지문인 안내를 통해 취업 박람회에 관한 내용을 확인할 수 있다. 부스 설치 비용에 대해서는 언급된 바 없으므로 (D)가 정답이다.

187 안내에서, 5줄의 "pledged"라는 단어와 그 의미가 가장 비슷한 것은?
 (A) 약속하다
 (B) 결심하다
 (C) 등록하다
 (D) 지불하다

| 해설 | pledge는 '맹세하다', '서약하다', '약속하다'라는 뜻이다. 따라서 보기 중 이와 가장 의미가 비슷한 것은 (A)의 promised(약속하다)이다.

188 Plautus에 대해 무엇이 암시되어 있는가?
 (A) Portland 취업 박람회에서 200명을 고용했다.
 (B) 국내에서 가장 큰 항공기 제조업체이다.
 (C) 최근에 Walker Research와 합병했다.
 (D) Portland 취업 박람회를 설립한 곳 중 하나이다.

| 해설 | 두 번째 지문인 기사에서 Plautus의 대변인은 참가자 자질이 우수하여 '원래 계획했던 것보다 두 배의 직원을 채용했다'(hire double the number of individuals that we had initially planned)고 밝혔다. 한편 원래 채용하려고 했던 인원은 첫 번째 지문인 안내에서 100명으로 소개되어 있으므로, Plautus가 최종적으로 고용한 인원은 200명임을 짐작할 수 있다. 따라서 정답은 (A)이다.

189 Murphy 씨는 왜 회람을 작성했는가?
 (A) 사람들로 하여금 새로운 일자리에 지원하도록 하기 위해
 (B) 자발적인 프로그램 참여를 요청하기 위해
 (C) 신입 직원들을 소개하기 위해
 (D) 새로운 오리엔테이션에 대해 알리기 위해

| 해설 | 회람의 후반부에서 Murphy 씨는 'I'd prefer that everyone involved be a volunteer.'라고 말한 후, 자신이나 Punjab 씨에게 멘토 프로그램에 대한 참여 여부를 알려 달라고 당부하고 있다. 따라서 회람을 작성한 이유는 (B)로 볼 수 있다.

190 Punjab 씨는 어디에서 일을 하는가?
 (A) 인사부에서
 (B) 제작부에서
 (C) 연구개발부에서
 (D) 회계부에서

| 해설 | 회람에서 Samir Punjab은 head of your department로 소개되어 있는데, 회람의 대상은 '연구개발 전 직원'이다. 따라서 그가 근무하는 부서는 (C)의 '연구개발부'가 될 것이다.

[191-195]

Winston Academy
시내 최고의 글쓰기 수업을 제공합니다

Winston Academy에서 수업을 듣는 것이 어떨까요? 여름 학기가 곧 시작될 예정이며, 저희는 흥미로운 수업들을 마련해 놓았습니다. 정규 수업 이외에도, 처음으로 개설된 4개의 수업에 대해 알려 드립니다:

수업	수강 번호	강사	시간
소설 쓰기	11	May Carpenter	월, 화 - 오전 9시 - 오전 11시
시	42	Josh Herald	수 - 오후 1시 - 오후 4시
에세이 쓰기	38	Stan Morris	월, 금 - 오후 1시 - 오후 3시
논픽션 쓰기	23	Alicia Woodruff	목, 금 - 오전 10시 - 오후 12시

학기는 6월 1일 시작되며 8월 20일에 종료됩니다. 모든 강사들은 국내 대학의 교수들로, 이들은 책을 출판한 작가이기도 합니다. 수업을 수강했던 많은 학생들이 책을 출판한 작가가 되었습니다. 이번 학기의 모든 과목에 대한 수강료는 800달러입니다. 더 많은 정보를 원하시면 485-5837로 전화를 주십시오.

semester 학기 | **be about to** 막 ~하려고 하다 | **in addition to** ~이외에도 | **for the first time** 처음으로, 최초로 | **go on to** ~으로 나아가다

5월 16일

친애하는 Lincoln 씨께,

제가 이번 여름 Winston Academy에서 강사로서의 일을 수행하지 못하게 될 것 같다는 점을 알려 드리게 되어 유감입니다. 저는 수업을 진행하고 책을 마무리하기 위해 여름 내내 이곳 녹스빌에 있을 계획이었지만, 저희 대학의 학과장님께서 제 수업이 대학에 필요하다는 지시를 내리셨습니다. 듣자 하니, 저희 대학의 여름 계절 학기 강사 중 한 분이 아프셔서 석 달 정도 입원하셔야 한다고 하더군요. 그분은 두 개의 여름 학기 수업을 맡기로 예정되어 있었습니다. 영문학과에서는 인근 지역에서 대체 강사를 찾을 수가 없었고, 그래서 학장님께서는 제가 그를 대신하여 수업을 맡기 위해 제가 샬럿으로 돌아와야 한다고 말씀하셨습니다. Winston Academy에서 저의 첫 수업을 하게 되기를 고대하고 있었기 때문에, 저는 크게 상심하고 있습니다. 불편을 끼쳐 드려서 죄송하며, 적합한 대체 강사를 찾으실 시간이 충분하기를 바랍니다.

Stan Morris 드림

fulfill 이행하다 | **duty** 임무, 업무 | **instruct** 지시하다 | **dean** 학과장 | **hospitalize** 입원시키다 | **replacement** 대체, 교체 | **insist** 주장하다 | **in one's place** ~을 대신하여 | **suitable** 적합한, 적절한

받는 사람: Christine Solo <csolo@personalmail.com>
보낸 사람: Susan Lincoln <slincoln@winstonacademy.com>
제목: 여름 시간표
날짜: 5월 20일

친애하는 Solo 씨께,

최근에 귀하께서는 올해 David Powell이 아카데미의 강사가 될 것인지를 물으셨고, 저는 그렇지 않을 것이라는 답변을 드렸습니다. 하지만, 시간표에 갑작스러운 변경 사항이 생겨서 강사 중 한 분이 이번 여름에 수업을 진행하지 못하게 되었습니다. 그 결과, Powell 씨께서 이번 여름 Winston Academy의 강사가 되실 것입니다. 그분은 적절한 에세이 쓰는 법에 관한 수업을 맡으실 예정입니다. 저는 귀하께서 그에 관해 배우는 것에 관심을 표현해 주셨다고 알고 있기 때문에, 이번 기회는 그러실 수 있는 완벽한 기회가 될 것입니다. 현재 이 수업에 남아 있는 자리는 5석이며, Powell 씨가 이곳의 많은 학생들에게 인기가 많으므로 서둘러 등록하시기를 당부드립니다. 그분께서 수업을 하신다는 점을 알게 되면 많은 학생들이 등록을 하러 몰려들 것입니다.

Susan Lincoln 드림
Winston Academy

as a result 그 결과, 따라서 | **proper** 적절한 | **express** 표현하다 | **enroll** 등록하다 | **rush** 서두르다, 돌진하다

191 Herald 씨에 대해 무엇이 암시되어 있는가?
(A) 그는 전에 Winston Academy에서 일을 한 적이 있다.
(B) 그는 많은 학생들에게 인기가 높다.
(C) 그는 Winston Academy에서 공부를 했다.
(D) 그는 대학생들에게 시를 가르친다.

| 해설 | Mr. Herald라는 이름은 첫 번째 지문의 시간표에서 찾을 수 있는데, 여기에서 그는 Poetry(시) 수업을 담당할 것이라는 점을 알 수 있다. 따라서 정답은 (D)이다.

192 Winston Academy는 어떤 수업의 강사를 새로 구해야 하는가?
(A) 에세이 쓰기
(B) 시
(C) 소설 쓰기
(D) 논픽션 쓰기

| 해설 | 두 번째 지문인 이메일을 통해 Morris 씨가 수업을 할 수 없게 되었다는 사실을 알 수 있고, Morris 씨의 수업은 첫 번째 지문에서 '에세이 쓰기'로 나와 있다. 따라서 Winston Academy가 새로 구해야할 강사는 (A)의 '에세이 쓰기' 강사이다.

193 Morris 씨는 왜 Winston Academy에서 일을 할 수 없는가?
(A) 보상이 충분하지 않다.
(B) 그는 여름 동안 다른 도시에 있어야 한다.
(C) 그는 아파서 입원 중이다.
(D) 그는 8월말까지 자신의 책을 완성시켜야 한다.

compensation 보상 | **sufficient** 충분한

| 해설 | 두 번째 지문인 편지에서 Morris 씨는 Winston Academy의 수업을 할 수 없게 되었다는 소식을 전한 후, 그 이유로 학과장이 자신에게 '대학에서의 수업을 요청했다'(my services are required on campus)고 말한다. 즉, 그는 '녹스빌'이 아닌 '샬럿'에 있는 대학에서 수업을 해야 하므로 정답은 (B)가 된다.

194 Powell 씨는 언제 수업을 하기로 예정되어 있는가?
(A) 월요일과 화요일에
(B) 월요일과 금요일에
(C) 수요일에
(D) 목요일과 금요일에

| 해설 | 세 번째 지문인 이메일에서 Powell 씨는 '에세이 수업'을 맡게 될 것임을 알 수 있다. 따라서 에세이 수업을 첫 번째 지문의 시간표에서 찾으면 이 수업은 (B)의 '월요일과 금요일' 오후 1시에서 3시까지 진행되는 것으로 나와 있다.

195 Lincoln 씨는 Solo 씨에게 무엇을 하라고 권하는가?
(A) 빨리 수강료를 지불한다
(B) 수업에 등록한다
(C) Powell 씨와 이야기한다
(D) 시에 대해 배운다

| 해설 | 세 번째 지문의 후반부에서 Lincoln 씨는 Solo 씨에게 Powell 씨의 수업이 인기가 많으니 '서둘러 등록할 것을 권한다'(I suggest that you hurry to enroll)고 말하고 있다. 따라서 그녀가 제안한 사항은 (B)이다.

[196-200]

Silver Lake 아파트가 공개됩니다

이번 주 토요일과 일요일인 8월 1일에서 2일까지, Silver Lake 아파트가 공개 행사를 갖습니다. 2년 간의 공사 끝에, Silver Lake 아파트가 거의 완공되었습니다. 따라서 10월 초에 입주가 가능합니다. 매매 혹은 임대가 가능한 아파트가 아직도 250채 이상 남아 있습니다. 여기에는 침실 2개, 침실 3개, 그리고 침실 4개가 구비된 아파트도 포함됩니다. 가구가 비치된 것과 가구가 비치되지 않은 것 모두를 선택하실 수 있습니다. 하지만 가구가 비치된 아파트는 모두 임대만 가능합니다. Silver Lake 아파트의 시설은 최상급이며, 단지는 녹스빌의 우수한 학교들과 주요 상점가 근처에 위치해 있습니다. 이번 공개 행사에 오시는 모든 분들을 환영합니다. 구입이 가능한 아파트들을 둘러 보실 수도 있으며, 또한 방문객들께서는 단지 전체를 구경하시게 될 것입니다. 보다 많은 정보나 단지로 오는 길을 안내받기 위해서는 984-5859로 전화를 주십시오.

open house (신축 주택이나 아파트를 볼 수 있게 하는) 공개 행사 | **unit** 단위; (아파트 등의) 한 채 | **furnish** 가구를 비치하다 | **top notch** 최고의 | **complex** 복합한; 단지

받는 사람: inquiries@desmondrealty.com
보낸 사람: patsanders@homemail.com
제목: Silver Lake 아파트
날짜: 8월 6일

관계자분께,

지난 여름, 제 아내와 저는 Silver Lake 아파트에서 열린 공개 행사에 참석했습니다. 저희는 그곳에서 본 것에 매우 깊은 감명을 받았고, 그곳에서 살아야겠다는 결심을 했습니다. 저희는 11월에 녹스빌로 이사할 계획이며, 앞으로 3년 동안 그 도시에서 살 의향이 있습니다. 그 후에는, 덴버에 있는 저희 회사의 본사로 제가 전근하게 될 것 같습니다. 따라서, 저희는 아파트 매매에 관심이 있는 것이 아니라 한 채를 임대하고자 합니다. 제 아들들 모두가 자신의 방을 가질 수 있도록 저희는 침실 3개짜리 아파트를 구하고 싶습니다. 저는 현재 마이애미에 있지만 계약서에 서명을 해야 하는 경우에는 언제라도 비행기를 타고 녹스빌로 갈 준비가 되어 있습니다. 제가 원하는 아파트의 월세는 여전히 2,200달러인지요?

Patrick Sanders 드림

extremely 극도로, 매우 | **headquarters** 본사 | **arrange** 준비하다, 마련하다 | **monthly rent** 월세

받는 사람: patsanders@homemail.com
보낸 사람: rdesmond@desmondrealty.com
제목: Silver Lake 아파트
날짜: 8월 8일

친애하는 Sanders 씨께,

Silver Lake 아파트에 관해 문의해 주셔서 고맙습니다. 귀하와 마찬가지로, 많은 분들께서 아파트의 상태에 크게 만족하셔서, 이곳은 시 전체에서 가장 인기가 높은 부동산 중 한 곳이 되었습니다. 그러한 사실 때문에, 침실 3개짜리 아파트는 더 이상 구하실 수가 없습니다. 또한, 침실 2개짜리 마지막 아파트가 오늘 아침에 매매되었습니다. 현재 남아 있고 임대가 가능한 아파트는 침실 4개짜리만 몇 채 있을 뿐입니다. 물론, 이 아파트들의 임대료는 약간 높습니다. 침실 3개짜리 아파트를 임대하는 대신 침실 4개짜리 아파트를 임대하시면 월 600달러의 비용이 더 듭니다. 귀하께서 여전히 관심이 있으신 경우, 제게 즉시 알려 주시면, 제가 환불 불가의 조건으로 2,500달러를 받은 후, 귀하께서 계약서에 서명을 하시기 위해 여기로 오실 때까지 제가 귀하를 위해 아파트 한 채를 확보해 둘 수 있습니다. Silver Lake 아파트에 더 이상 관심이 없으시다면, 귀하께서 분명 마음에 들어 하실, 인근 지역의 다른 부동산들을 제가 몇 건 소개해 드릴 수 있습니다.

그럼 이만 줄이겠습니다,

Richard Desmond
Desmond 부동산

property 재산 | **nonrefundable** 환불이 되지 않는 | **reserve** 따로 남겨 두다, 유보하다; 예약하다 | **introduce** 소개하다 | **approve of** ~을 승인하다, ~을 좋다고 생각하다

196 Silver Lake 아파트에 대해 언급된 것은 무엇인가?
 (A) 녹스빌 교외에 있다.
 (B) 학교 맞은 편에 있다.
 (C) 여전히 건설 중이다.
 (D) 20층 높이이다.

suburb 교외

| 해설 | 첫 번째 지문인 광고의 내용에서 정답을 확인할 수 있다. 아파트 위치에 대해서는 주변에 학교와 주요 상가가 있다는 점만 언급되어 있으므로 (A)와 (B)는 확인이 불가능한 사항이고, 아파트 층수나 높이에 대한 언급은 전혀 찾아볼 수 없으므로 (D) 또한 오답이다. 따라서 정답은 (C)인데, 이는 아파트가 '거의 완공되었다'(is almost complete)는 표현에서 확인할 수 있다.

197 공개 행사에서 어떤 일이 일어날 것인가?
 (A) 공사가 중단될 것이다.
 (B) 계약이 체결될 것이다.
 (C) 방문객들이 견학을 하게 될 것이다.
 (D) 발표가 이루어질 것이다.

| 해설 | 첫 번째 지문에서 공개 행사에서 예정된 일은 'Tours of the available apartments will be given, and visitors will be shown around the entire complex as well.'로 나타나 있다. 따라서 (C)가 정답이다.

198 Sanders 씨는 언제 Silver Lake 아파트를 방문했는가?
 (A) 8월 1일에
 (B) 8월 2일에
 (C) 8월 6일에
 (D) 8월 8일에

| 해설 | 두 번째 지문인 이메일에서 Sanders 씨는 '지난 일요일'(last Sunday) 공개 행사에 참석했다고 밝혔는데, 첫 번째 지문에서 공개 행사는 토요일과 일요일, 즉 '8월 1일'과 '2일'에 개최할 것이라고 안내되어 있다. 따라서 이 두 가지 사실을 종합하면 그가 아파트를 방문한 날은 (B)의 '8월 2일' 이다.

199 Silver Lake 아파트의 침실 4개짜리 아파트는 가격이 얼마인가?
 (A) 월 2,000달러
 (B) 월 2,200달러
 (C) 월 2,500달러
 (D) 월 2,800달러

| 해설 | 두 번째 지문인 이메일에서 Sanders 씨가 원하는 침실 3개짜리 아파트는 월세가 2,200달러임을 알 수 있고, 세 번째 지문인 이메일을 통해서는 침실 4개짜리 아파트의 월세가 침실 3개짜리 아파트 월세보다 600달러 더 높다는 점을 알 수 있다. 따라서 침실 4개짜리 아파트의 월세는 (D)의 '2,800달러'일 것이다.

200 Desmond 씨는 Sanders 씨에게 무엇을 하라고 제안하는가?
 (A) 아파트를 임대할 것이라는 점을 보증하기 위해 비용을 지불한다
 (B) 다가 오는 이번 주말에 녹스빌로 온다
 (C) 임대 대신 아파트 매매를 고려한다
 (D) 더 낮은 가격으로 더 작은 아파트를 구한다

| 해설 | 세 번째 지문인 이메일의 후반부에서 Desmond 씨는 Sanders 씨에게 '2,500달러를 내면 Sanders 씨가 계약을 하러 오기 전까지 아파트 한 채를 확보해 두겠다'(once I receive a nonrefundable payment of $2,500, I can reserve a unit for you until you are able to fly here to sign a contract) 고 말한다. 따라서 그가 제안한 사항은 (A)로 볼 수 있다.